The Story of Scotland

The Five Sisters of Kintail, seen from Mam Rattigan.

Photo. Douglas Scott 1956

The Story of Scotland

by

JANET R. GLOVER

FABER AND FABER
24 Russell Square
London

First published in mcmlx
by Faber and Faber Limited
24 Russell Square London W.C. 1
Printed in Great Britain by
R. MacLehose and Company Limited
The University Press Glasgow
All rights reserved

In memory of
ALICE AND REAVELEY GLOVER

Contents

Contents

Illustrations

11

Maps

Foreword and Acknowledgements

There is much more interest nowadays than formerly in the traditions of the past, perhaps because they are becoming so rapidly overlaid, and there is also more speculation as to why Scottish people think and react as they do in the contemporary situation. At the same time, people are able to enjoy the Scottish countryside more readily than their parents and grandparents could, and this enjoyment is enhanced by some knowledge of what went on there in earlier times. While therefore the publications of specialists who have pursued close research are of the greatest value, there remains still a real need for general histories of a more popular nature. This book has been written specially for the general reader in an effort to meet that need.

I am grateful for the advice so generously given me on certain points by the Rev. Stewart Mechie, M.A., B.D., of Glasgow: and by Professor G. O. Sayles, M.A., D.Litt., M.R.I.A., Mr. W. R. Humphries, M.A. and Mr. J. M. Henderson, T.D., M.A., of Aberdeen University.

Mrs. Arnold Gomme has devoted her scholarship and skill to the construction of the maps which make the relevant narrative much easier to follow.

My friends Mrs. M. O. Clarke and Miss R. I. M. Murdoch, Mr. and Mrs. A. D. Cuthbert and Mr. John Rannie have all encouraged me by patiently reading a number of the chapters and discussing them with me. My sisters, Mary and Elizabeth Glover, have gone through the whole book in manuscript; indeed without their help I would have had the utmost difficulty in completing it.

Mrs. Winifred Shaw has shown great consideration in typing and retyping almost every chapter, often completing sections at short notice.

I owe much to all these people and of course to many more. In particular, I must refer to the members of Laurel Bank School, Glasgow, who have given me such courteous attention in Scottish History classes, but who have never let me off without vigorous and critical scrutiny of the conclusions we have arrived at together.

JANET R. GLOVER

GLASGOW
December, 1958

PART ONE

Early and Medieval Scotland

CHAPTER 1

Pioneers

Not far from Oban, there stand cliffs which thousands of years ago were battered by powerful seas. The breakers hollowed out caves in these sea-walls and gradually smooth beaches were formed in front of them; later on the seas retreated and the line of cliffs now stands far back from the shore. The caves became the homes of the earliest inhabitants of Scotland about whom we have any knowledge.

These people came from Europe. They crossed to Britain from the Baltic shores, and they settled in the Oban caves and in some of the Hebridean islands, especially Tiree. This was probably some 3,000 years before the birth of Christ. They were followed by other immigrants from Europe, who worked their way to Scotland by sea from Mediterranean regions. Some of their sites have been detected near Stirling, which was at the head of a huge estuary sweeping right inland: there is evidence that whales were stranded by ebbing tides on mudflats in parts of the Forth valley now far from the coast. Stone Age culture has also been traced in Galloway, Argyll, the Hebrides, Caithness, Sutherland and the Orkneys.

While there are naturally no written records of these early immigrants, the land is rich in remains of prehistoric building sites, often unfortunately concealed by later dwellings super-imposed upon them. Primitive people left garbage lying around in such quantity that archaeologists can sort out the contents of their middens or rubbish dumps and form some impression of how they lived. Geologists can tell us something about their agriculture by analysing soil, and air photography reveals evidence of ancient tillage.

These people brought seed-corn and domesticated animals with them. They hacked at the soil with clumsy bone and stone implements, choosing places where virgin forest was not too dense, and they produced patches of bere, a primitive form of barley. For lack of winter fodder, they slaughtered many animals young. They made stone bobbins and whorls and wore rough textiles, fixing their garments with bone pins and brooches. Their women liked beads and painted their faces with home-made beauty preparations. They all ate quantities of shell-fish. Professor Piggott has described in *Scotland Before History* the constant need these people had for durable flint axe heads: he suggests that Stone Age men in Scotland imported them from the English Lake District and from Antrim. For all their primitive ways, Stone Age people could organize barter from far afield and they travelled great distances for the purpose. One advantage they enjoyed was kinder weather than we now know in Scotland. The prevailing winds were easterly, harsh storms less frequent, hours of sunshine longer. The mainland and some of the islands were clothed by splendid pine forests, which farmers found very difficult to clear, but as yet the peat blanket had not yet appeared and so the soil was easier to till.

In the Bay of Skaill, on the West Mainland of Orkney, there lies a settlement now known as Skara Brae, constructed probably rather later than 2,000 B.C. Its inhabitants made their way to that windswept site across the Pentland Firth, bringing with them sheep, goats and cattle. Even in those days, Orkney yielded no timber suitable for building, so most ingenious use had to be made of the local flagstone. How long they lived there we do not know, but they abandoned Skara Brae suddenly and in panic, because of a dreadful storm. The village was completely engulfed in sand, which preserved the fabric for many centuries, and in the 1930s it was excavated under the direction of Professor Childe. Today it is roofless, but you can walk through its passages, stand in tiny houses, and handle the shelves, the neat little stone dressers, the hearths, the box-bed frames, and the stone limpet boxes where the shell-fish were stored in seawater. The Skara Brae people knew nothing of sanitation and lived in appalling filth, munching their mutton bones in bed and pitching remains of their meals and other refuse onto rubbish dumps over the wall. They had neither textiles nor grain, unlike their contemporaries in Scotland and the Hebrides; in fact, they maintained a way of life characteristic of a much earlier age. The designs they scratched on their stones were derived from a Mediterranean culture and their pottery was of a type used in southern England.

Some of the Stone Age settlers in Scotland were of the culture known as Megalithic. This name is derived from two Greek words meaning 'big stones' and it was their ability to handle enormous blocks of stone which caused this distinctive title to be given them. They erected burial vaults for their dead, some quite small and some imposingly large. Most of these vaults are approached by narrow passages tunnelled through the earth, many are now covered by conical mounds of grass-grown turf, but some were entirely underground. Some have several compartments or stalls, some only a single chamber. Their erection implies a large labour force, considerable engineering skill and strong views about the after-life, derived from a Mediterranean civilization. Even if you are unaccustomed to archaeological study and unattracted to prehistory, you cannot fail to be awed by the magnificent examples of Megalithic work, nearly 4,000 years old, still standing in the Orkneys. Maes Howe in Stenness is the best known. Its mound is 24 feet high and it is 115 feet in basic diameter. In it are slabs of dressed stone 8 to 10 feet in length. How stones of such weight were transported, tooled, erected, nobody exactly knows.

Some time between 1800 and 1500 B.C., there came a fresh incursion into Scotland by people known as Beaker Men. Some archaeologists suggest that they had originally lived on lands now drowned by the North Sea. Others say that they came from the North European plain. They settled at points along the east coast of Scotland and gradually moved inland. They merged well enough with the Megalithic settlers and their sites are identified by remains of their more refined pottery. They buried their dead in individual, not in communal, graves, and beside the corpses they put personal possessions, such as flint knives, flint-tipped arrows and sometimes bows. These people used bronze for some of their implements, and they were the first in Scotland who did so.

Later on other bronze-users came to Scotland from Europe, some time after 1500 B.C. These were the people who set up the huge circles of carefully spaced upright blocks of stone, which

19

MAP 1.
DISTRIBUTION OF
THE BROCHS AND
VITRIFIED FORTS

Broch areas
Vitrified fort
        areas

0 10 20   40   60   80   100 Miles
0 20 40 60 80 100 120 140 160 Kms.

SHETLAND
Is.

Sumburgh
Hd.

ORKNEY
Is.

Pentland Firth

CAITH-
NESS

Callern

Stornoway

SUTHERLAND

HEBRIDES Is.

ROSS

Oban

ARGYLL

Pentland
Hills

GALLOWAY

Φ. Γ.

still survive in considerable numbers, often much damaged, some-times almost obliterated. You can see such circles in many parts of Scotland, but especially in the outer Hebrides. One of the finest stands a hundred feet above the seashore near Callernish, approached by a splendid avenue of monoliths, and embracing in its midst a chambered cairn. At Stenness in Orkney, there is an even larger and more magnificent circle called the Ring of Brodgar, as solitary and imposing as any man-made monument could be. We do not know the philosophy which inspired the builders, but these structures had religious significance, probably connected with worship of the sun. The Avebury Circles in Wiltshire are of the same era.

Bronze Age men liked gold, which they got from Ireland, and which they made into personal ornaments. They seem to have been tireless seamen, undertaking journeys to Ireland, the Outer Hebrides, Scandinavia and Europe. They took to cremating their dead, and they left little in the way of refuse dumps—two serious disadvantages for the archaeologist.

It was not until about the 10th century B.C. that people of Celtic stock, speaking a Celtic language, appeared in Scotland. They too were bronze-users and their ancestral home lay some-where between the head waters of the Danube and the Rhine. They are known to historians as Goidelic Celts and they made their first settlements in Western Scotland and Ireland. Their very ancient Indo-European language influenced many parts of Europe and formed the basis of Irish, Manx and Gaelic. Much later, about the 4th century B.C., they were joined by another influx of people originating from the same stock, known as Brythonic Celts, from whose language Breton, Welsh and Cornish derived.

One branch of the Brythonic Celts was formed by the Picts. They are perhaps the most elusive of the peoples whose journeys brought them to Scotland in prehistoric times. They probably settled first in Ireland and thence crossed to the West of Scotland, though when they did so is uncertain. They established a hold on almost the whole area north of the Forth, and traces of their hill forts have been found from the Pentland Hills to the Pentland Firth—indeed the name Pentland is believed to derive from an early form of the name Pict. They made settlements in Orkney and Galloway too. While they preferred hill-tops, they sometimes drove stakes into bogs or marshes and erected platforms on them to form buildings now known as crannogs. Although they apparently had a written literature, it has not survived and little is known about their language, but they were skilled and fearless seamen and like other Celtic invaders they could handle iron with artistry and dexterity.

The strangest relics of the three centuries before Christ in our country are the stone towers known as brochs. These are believed to have been built by the Picts, or by one branch of them. Several hundred were built in the north and west of Scotland, in the Shetlands, Orkneys and Hebrides, but very few elsewhere. The towers were all planned to type, probably within a short period of time. They are almost all placed so as to command a wide view of some estuary or sea inlet, though by no means always near a good harbour. The sea entries they overlooked in the Orkneys were of such significance that in the Second World War the British had defensive posts near most of them.

Whoever designed the master plan was an architect of genius. The broch is a circular tower, with a slight inward slope like a lighthouse. The walls of the tower are double, with a space between the outer and the inner face, spanned by stone landings and by a winding staircase. As you climb this staircase, you can see into the circular court within the tower, because there are windows cut in the inner wall. No lime or mortar was used in making the brochs, each one of which required about 4,500 tons of stone. There was only one entry into each of the towers, defended by a great inner door and by guardrooms cut in the thickness of the wall. Outside the entrance were clusters of huts and hovels, whose owners could retreat for safety into the tower when necessary. The people who lived there were fishermen and farmers, they wore woven textiles, kept domestic animals, and used iron tools, though not many such tools and no weapons of war have been unearthed on the sites.

Who designed the brochs and why? Who could command the labour force required? We do not know. No other country has similar buildings. The brochs must have been almost impregnable shelters when they were built, but useless as bases for aggressive warfare. As you pick your way through the huddled ruins round the broch of Gurness, or look out from the summit of the almost perfect broch of Mousa, you sense the unanswerable problems of a forgotten people. The problems are made more complex because, well into medieval times, families squatted in these lonely and insanitary strongholds, so that enormous middens of broken and squalid refuse collected around them.

It is no easier to discover the truth about the other architectural triumph of this period, the vitrified forts, so called because their stone walls have been fused by heat. These castles were probably built earlier than the brochs, not by northern people but by invaders from Gaul. These Gallic builders often chose hill-top sites for their castles, which are comparable to a type common in western Europe. Some were oblong, some rounded, but all had double walls of solid masonry, with wooden tiebeams built across the intervening space. By means and for reasons not fully understood, these beams were burnt out in almost all the Scottish forts of this type, and the fierce heat fused the stones in the walls.

The vitrified forts were built by people who made their way up the east coast and crossed to the west by the Great Glen. Remains are found in Argyllshire, along the estuaries of the Forth and the Clyde and in Galloway, and often they were placed with obvious regard to the strategy of coastal defence. It appears that the forts fell into disuse some time in the 2nd century B.C., though descendants of the original Gallic inhabitants lived on in southern Scotland until Roman times.

Little as we know about Scotland in the decades preceding the Christian era, historians agree that the people north of the Border hills developed a political organization, with a central authority capable of exacting obedience, that they were skilled in metallurgy and that more travelling was done by sea and by land than one might suppose. It is clear, too, that there was a strong sense of the presence of supernatural powers, an expectation of life after death and an urge to make provision for it.

That all the various groups of settlers owed much to Europe is obvious, for it was from Spain, France, the Low Countries,

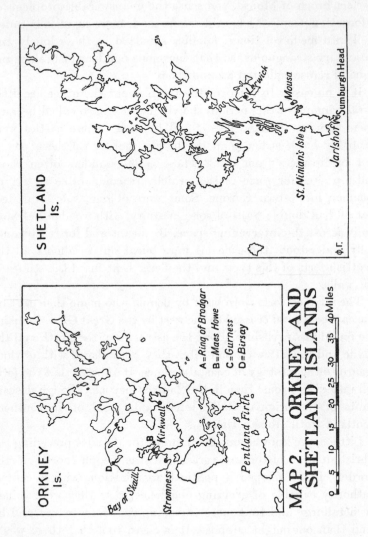

ORKNEY
Is.

Bay of Skaill

D

C

Stromness

B

Kirkwall

Pentland Firth

A = Ring of Brodgar
B = Maes Howe
C = Gurness
D = Birsay

0   5   10   15   20   25   30   35   40 Miles

MAP 2. ORKNEY AND
SHETLAND ISLANDS

SHETLAND
Is.

Lerwick

Mousa

St. Ninian's Isle

Jarlshof

Sumburgh Head

Φ.Γ.

Germany and the Baltic regions that they came. No race settled north of the Border which did not also settle south of it. The centuries before the Christian era will become better known to us as the evidence of hidden hut-foundations, burial places, ploughed sites and middens is interpreted, if only the work involved can be carried through before our own contemporary building projects have destroyed too many ancient monuments. Such study will reveal much that is common to the origins of both Scotland and England.

CHAPTER 2

Legions

The earliest written records of Scotland were the work of a foreigner and they make sad reading. In the 1st century, A.D., the historian Tacitus married the daughter of Agricola, a Roman general who invaded Scotland. Most areas reached by the legions suffered the miseries of Roman invasion without enjoying the benefits of Roman civilization. In three and a half centuries the Romans succeeded in imposing military control here and there in Scotland, but only in the south-east did they establish law and order. Tacitus makes this clear in his record of Agricola's work and no subsequent commander was able to alter the picture.

In 81 A.D., Agricola advanced to the Forth-Clyde line, which he planned to hold by a chain of forts. During the next fourteen months he established a headquarters at Stirling, already recognized as a point of supreme strategic advantage, and he intended to push north, camping beside navigable rivers, building forts as he went, and always keeping in touch with his fleet.

In the late summer of 83, the northern Pictish tribes, described by Tacitus as Caledonians, made a massed resistance, and there took place the first in the agelong series of battles in which Highland dwellers pitted ferocious courage and outdated weapons against metal armour and disciplined experience. The Picts were led by the first military chieftain whose name has been recorded in Scottish history, Calgacus. They suffered a crushing defeat at the hands of Agricola's 9th Legion at Mons Graupius, a battle-site not yet exactly identified, though it is known to have been near the Roman fort called Raedykes, not far from Stonehaven. After the battle, Agricola fell back to winter-quarters at Inchtuthill, but he ordered his fleet to survey the coast as far north as possible. Inchtuthill is ten miles north of Perth on the north bank of the Tay. The camp covered fifty-five acres of ground and had accommodation for seven to ten thousand officers and men, a hospital, an administrative block and well-surfaced roads for transport.

Agricola was disgusted early in 84 to receive orders recalling him from the north, and his departure meant the end of the Roman advance in strength towards the Moray Firth. Thus the Picts discovered, as other people in Scotland were to do, that defeat in pitched battle need not spell political subjection. What happened to the 9th Legion is unknown, but disaster obliterated it early in the 2nd century. It disappeared, as the legions of Varus had done in the German forests about a century earlier.

Hadrian, a most dynamic Roman, made a tremendous effort to stabilize the frontier against the Caledonians in 121 A.D. He built the wall which bears his name and which can still be seen at certain points in Northumberland. It stretched for 73 miles from South Shields to Carlisle and was flanked by defensive posts on the Cumberland coast. Some 14,000 men were employed in the building, which must have absorbed two million cubic yards of material. The eastern sections of the rampart were faced with dressed stone and measured eight to ten feet wide at the base, six feet at the top: towards the west, turf and clay were substituted for stone.

In 140 A.D., Lollius Urbicus became Governor of Britain. He pushed north again to the Forth-Clyde isthmus to build the wall named after the Emperor Antonine. This was 37 miles in length, and defended by 19 forts. It was more economically constructed than Hadrian's because it was made of turf on the western stretches, clay on the eastern, without stone, and the barracks for the men were cheaply assembled wooden hutments. Lollius Urbicus used some sites originally developed by Agricola and he advanced north as far as Inchtuthill, while the garrisons on Hadrian's Wall were still maintained. It looks as if the Romans meant to establish control over the areas between the walls and even to extend their rule into Perthshire.

The legions employed in these enormous undertakings included men from Germany, Gaul, Spain, Egypt and the Middle East, and the medley of camp-followers and merchants which followed them was also drawn from many countries. Rome believed in transporting subject tribes almost wholesale, and while continentals were serving on the Borders, British conscripts were at work in the Württemberg forests. The foreign legionaries in Scotland married local girls and founded families, whom they nurtured in the faith of their childhood. Altars to Mithras, Mars, Isis and other gods have been found on the walls.

There had been Christians in the Roman army since the days when St. Paul converted the guards to whom he was chained. Christian legionaries brought their faith to Britain and tiny communities began to practise the new rites and to attract other worshippers as well. As early as 208, Tertullian wrote that 'places among the Britons unpenetrated by the Romans have come under the rule of Christ'. Christian worship was practised among some of the soldiers on the walls and it was carried thence into regions more remote than Tertullian guessed.

Little is known of how ordinary people lived at this time. The Picts were the dominant race in Scotland, with thriving communities in the valleys of the Tay and the Earn, and a centre of considerable importance at Dunkeld. Their buildings varied from district to district, but one type has recently become better known to archaeologists. This is the 'wheelhouse', a roughly circular building, about 35 feet across, divided into ten or twelve separate dwellings by stone piers, set in radial fashion from the outer walls to the middle of the enclosure. In 1957, excavation for a rocket site on South Uist laid bare several wheelhouses, and others have been discovered on the mainland.

The Picts exploited their natural advantages against the Romans. The mountain barrier of the Grampians and the thick forest enabled them to wage guerrilla warfare, and the legions found their task most unpalatable. By the end of the 2nd century and the beginning of the 3rd, it was clear that the ambitions of Lollius Urbicus could not be realized, especially in view of the troubles south of the Border. Severus made a naval base at Cramond on the Forth in 208, but soon afterwards Antonine's Wall was abandoned and the northerly stations evacuated.

In the middle of the 3rd century however the Picts were faced with new dangers from another quarter. Now began the pressure of those Scots, who later bestowed their name upon the country they invaded, but who at this time came from Ireland. Like the Picts, they were of Celtic origin, though their speech had developed differently and they were to all intents and purposes foreigners. They settled between Oban and Lochgilphead, pushed into Kintyre, Arran, Islay and other western islands, also along the shores of Loch Fyne and Loch Long and elsewhere on the western coast. Their territory became known as Dalriada, after their Irish homeland.

The Scots from Ireland were in constant conflict with the Picts, but in the middle of the 4th century the two hostile peoples joined together in a violent attack upon the Romans, with a third and ominous ally—the Saxons, now beginning to penetrate the eastern approaches to the heart of Scotland. This onslaught was stimulated partly by hatred of the common enemy, partly by the weather. During the 4th century, a period of heart-breaking rains began, which made agriculture more difficult than ever before. Driven by a land-hunger which affected all western Europe too, and by savage dislike of the Romans, the Picts attacked Hadrian's Wall. From 367 onwards, they battered it, overwhelmed its garrisons, then stormed across the Border hills, while the Scots and the Saxons came in by sea from the west and the east. There followed a barbarous adventure across Britain, in which many villas were destroyed, though some of the towns survived, because of their stalwart defences.

From this disaster Roman authority in Britain would certainly have recovered, but for the multiplication of troubles within the Empire, in the face of which all armed manpower had to be recalled from the fringes and frontiers. By the end of the 4th century the Roman stations in Scotland had been stripped of soldiers.

What did Roman influence in Scotland amount to? The Ordnance Survey Map of Roman Britain, published in 1956, shows that military roads ran further north and Roman sites were more numerous than earlier maps suggested. In the Lowlands, in Perthshire and up the east coast, Pictish tribesmen must have become all too familiar with Roman military authority. As far away as Shetland, Roman coins have been unearthed on

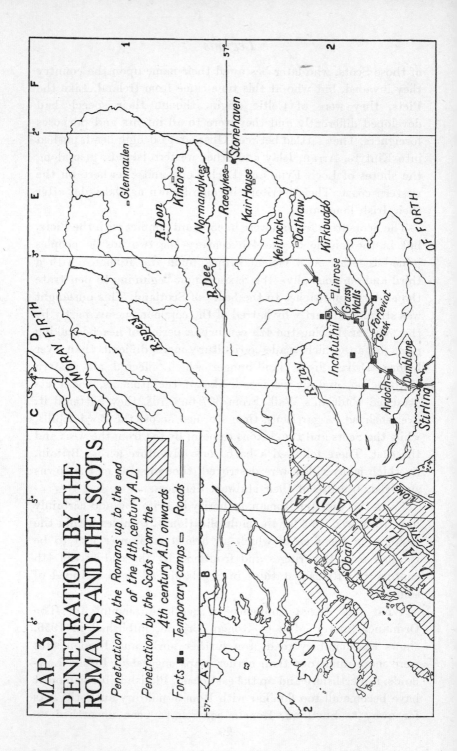

MAP 3.
PENETRATION BY THE
ROMANS AND THE SCOTS

Penetration by the Romans up to the end
of the 4th. century A.D.

Penetration by the Scots from the
4th century A.D. onwards

Forts ■ Temporary camps □ Roads ═══

Glenmailen

R.Don

Kintore

Normandykes

R.Dee

Raedykes

Stonehaven

Kair House

Keithock

Oathlaw

R.Spey

Kirkbuddo

Linrose

Grassy Walls

Inchtuthil

Fonteviot

Gask

Dunblane

Ardoch

Stirling

MORAY FIRTH

R.Tay

OF FORTH

DALRIADA

Oban

LYNE OF LORN

ANTONINE WALL

HADRIAN'S WALL

Housesteads
Great Chesters
Birdoswald
Castlesteads
Carlisle
Corbridge Chesters
Newcastle
South Shields
Catterick

Cramond
Carriden
Mumrills
Falkirk
Castlecary
Bar Hill
Kirkintilloch
Cadder
New Kilpatrick
Duntocher
Old Kilpatrick
Whitemoss
Lurg Moor
Rough Castle
Inveresk

FIRTH

FIRTH OF CLYDE

ARRAN
KINTYRE
ISLAY
JURA

50 Miles
80 Kms.

broch sites. But Scotland was never absorbed into the Empire. Town life, ordered civic prosperity, easy transport by well-metalled trunk roads, regular commerce and business and social life—none of these great benefits was established in Scotland, where Rome was known only as an alien power seeking to establish military occupation by ruthless force of arms.

CHAPTER 3

Evangelists

At the end of the 4th century, the Picts were supreme from Caithness to the Forth. Their internal communications were somewhat impeded by the bony shoulders of the Grampians, whose diagonal slant across Perthshire was known to early historians as the Mounth, but there were well-known passes over these great hills, and the Picts made ample use of their fleet along the east coast. Because they were skilled seamen, they kept in reasonably close touch with their outposts in the Orkneys, despite the dangers of the Pentland Firth. Here and there they penetrated by the Great Glen towards the Hebrides and they had settlements on Skye, Raasay, Bute and the Mull of Kintyre.

The long mountain barrier from Loch Lomond to Cape Wrath formed a more difficult obstacle than the Mounth, and it defied travellers except at a few crossing places such as Glengarry. It was known as Drumalban and west of it lay Dalriada, the area colonized by Scots from Ireland in the late 4th century and greatly developed by them afterwards. Around the southern shores of the Clyde estuary lived the Britons, people who had come from Cumbria during the Roman conquest, while across on the east, the Angles were beginning to make settlements in Lothian. The country as a whole was known to early chroniclers as Alban, a name coined perhaps because of the snow-capped mountains.

Between the 4th and the 7th centuries, Picts, Scots, Britons and Angles were all converted to Christianity. The Christian missionaries who did this tremendous work faced not only traditions of paganism but also political divisions and barriers of language and geography. The missionary movement of these centuries produced many strong characters who deeply impressed

MAP 4.

Land of 1000 feet and over

Boundary of Dalriada

DRUMALBAN AND THE MOUNTH

0 10 20   40   60   80 Miles

CAITHNESS

SUTHERLAND

ROSS

MORAY FIRTH

Raasay

Skye

Applecross

Glenshiel

The Great Glen

INVERNESS

NORTHERN PICTS

MORAY

R.Spey

Deer
New Old

R.Don

R.Dee

Arisaig

Tiree

Iona

Lorn

Mull

Dunadd

Drumalban

The Mounth

SOUTHERN PICTS

Dunkeld

R.Tay

Dunsinane

Dunnichen

FIRTH OF TAY

St.Andrews

Forteviot

Dunfermline

Tarbert

Tarbet

R.Forth

FIRTH OF FORTH

DALRIADA

Kintyre

Queensferry

ANGLES Edinburgh

Glasgow

BRITONS

R.Clyde

R Tweed

Holy
I.

Carham

Alnwick

Dumfries

Whithorn

Φ.Γ.

their contemporaries, but among them all there were four of special distinction. These were St. Ninian, St. Columba, St. Moluag and St. Maelrubha.

How St. Ninian first learned his faith is unknown, but it seems that his parents were Christian, influenced perhaps by Roman legionaries or camp-followers. During his youth Ninian went to Rome. What he thought about the corruption flourishing there, even among religious leaders, we do not know. On his way back to Scotland, Ninian stayed at Tours, the monastic centre of St. Martin, an experience which was for him a spiritual climax. There he found men dedicated to poverty, living in solitude, devoted to meditation and worship.

When he returned to Strathclyde in 397 or 398, Ninian founded a monastery, known as Candida Casa, at Whithorn near the Solway. A little west of it, he established a group of cells on a lonely promontory, the Isle of Whithorn. At an even less accessible spot, for uninterrupted meditation, he selected a cave in the cliffs. In this way he gave Scotland its first monastic institution, following the example of St. Martin. It is difficult for us to realize what an immense instrument for good the monastic system was in its early days. It gave dedicated men time for regular prayer and recollection, it showed secular people the love and humility of Christ in action, and it gave the early missionaries the support of an organized spiritual community.

Candida Casa became a centre for training missionary monks and a starting-place for evangelists. The men whom Ninian trained learned from him the liturgy of St. Ambrose, the order of service used in Rome when Ninian made his pilgrimage there. For lack of stately buildings and trained choirs, they could not have followed it exactly, but the beautiful Latin prayers, responses and hymns gave them a matchless vehicle for worship, which sustained them wherever they went. Through this order of service Christians living in pagan surroundings emphasized the heavenly realities so easily missed by people untrained in the discipline of worship.

Variations of ceremony and custom were inevitable in a country so remote from the rest of Christendom. The churches founded by Ninian and his successors adopted the calendar and the date of

35

Easter approved by the Council of Arles in 314. Twice in the 5th and once in the 6th century, Rome altered this calendar, and the final dating of the Christian year was different from that observed in Scotland. The Celtic monks also adopted a different style of tonsure. These and other ritual matters were to cause controversy later on.

St. Ninian began his work in his own Strathclyde amongst the Britons, then went to eastern and central Scotland among the Picts, who would have no difficulty in understanding him. His mission extended through the passes in the Mounth, towards Sutherland and Caithness, and down the Great Glen. The men who made these journeys had to endure wild weather and unsatisfied hunger, to make steep climbs and to pass cold nights in the open. The traveller in Scotland's forests and hills might encounter bears and wolves, boars and wild cats. He could have a shot at red deer and, in northern parts, probably reindeer too—and what he did not use for his own meal the eagles would finish for him. The earliest missionaries must have been men of strong physique and nerve. The spiritual vitality of Ninian and his colleagues is revealed in the fact that remote communities of Picts were indeed converted and did learn to worship in tiny churches which were established all along these routes. It seems that it was the humbler people who were influenced, as in New Testament times, and that the royal house continued in its pagan beliefs.

Ninian's monks went as far as the Orkneys and Shetlands, where churches were established on some of the smaller islands and on lonely promontories rather like Whithorn itself. It seems that the Scots of Dalriada had little share in this mission, partly because of their strange language, partly because of Drumalban's barrier.

But Christians and others suffered from the marauding habits of the men in Irish Dalriada. One Irish king, Niall of the Nine Hostages, has various claims to notoriety. Tradition has it that in his last raid on Strathclyde he captured a Christian boy called Patrick. For six years Patrick slaved in Ireland as a swineherd, until he escaped to France, where he nearly died of exposure. When at last he returned to his home in Strathclyde, this extraordinary saint found himself compelled by spiritual guidance to return to Ireland, the land of his misery, as an evangelist, drawn in part no doubt by recollection of the close communion with God which he had experienced there in his lonely boyhood. He went back about 432, the year when St. Ninian is believed to have died. St. Patrick was successful in this venture, in spite of opposition, and he attracted a number of followers from Candida Casa, whose influence was thus strengthened among the Irish Picts.

The Scots of Ireland, meantime, had been consolidating their gains in Scotland. Fergus MacErc with his two brothers, Angus and Loarn, led a fresh invasion in 498. Parts of Argyllshire were occupied by Loarn, whose name survives in Lorne, and his head-quarters were at Dunnolly Castle, near Oban. Fergus founded a royal line, whose capital was fixed at Dunadd, near Crinan, where a large castle became the residence of the kings of Dalriada. They were still to some extent controlled from Ireland and they were obliged to pay taxes to the rulers there.

The Scots of Ireland developed a Christian Church of their own, and they sent missionaries to their colonists in Dalriada. One of these was St. Oran, who established holy places in Iona, Mull and Tiree, though it seems unlikely that he touched the mainland. He died of plague in 548. That Dalriada was beginning to experience Christian influences made the growing menace of its strength no more pleasing to the Picts, who deeply resented their unwelcome neighbours. In 560, the Pictish King Brude MacMailchon inflicted a crushing defeat on the Scots, in which their king was killed. His successor Conall was deprived by Brude of the right to call himself king. This reverse greatly dispirited the men of Dalriada, whose future now seemed much less assured.

In these circumstances, Columba's arrival in Dalriada in 563 was an event of major importance, politically, as well as in religious matters.

Columba's was a strange and complex character. His royal descent from Niall of the Nine Hostages may account for his ambition, his pride, and his explosive spirit. He had unlimited energy of mind and tireless physique, so that he was able to give full rein to his numerous gifts—seamanship, statecraft, evangelism, administration. The other side of his character is shown

in his feeling for poetry, his delight in the subtle loveliness of the
Hebridean islands, his joy in the changing colours of sky and sea
and mountain, in the delicacy of wild flowers, in the flight and
song of birds. As he grew older, he became gentler and more
loving towards the plain folk around him, over whom he came to
exercise an influence at once magnetic and charitable. Throughout
his eventful life, Columba was possessed by a passion for worship,
which gripped him no less when he was involved in one of his
bitter quarrels or deep-laid political schemes than when he was
lost in mystic contemplation of God's goodness, in the exquisite
solitude of Iona.

Columba was renowned in Ireland as a founder of many
churches—Derry, Durrow and Kells for example—and he was
probably well known to Oran's successors in the Hebrides. He
embarked for Iona because of a tragedy, so familiar that it is
easy to overlook the extraordinary way in which he lived it down.
Always an ardent collector and copyist of manuscripts, he had
secretly transcribed a rare Gospel belonging to one of his teachers
at Moville in Ireland, a man named Finbar, who had originally
come from Candida Casa. The document may have been brought
from Rome or Tours by Ninian himself. When Finbar discovered
that Columba had copied it, he claimed the new manuscript as
his own. Columba appealed against the decision in hot anger,
and lost the appeal. The case became a public scandal and furious
partisanship on each side led to civil war. Columba was excommunicated, and though the excommunication was later annulled,
he was advised to leave Ireland.

Columba departed in a mood of intolerable grief, caused more
by nostalgia for the land of his birth than regret for the outrage.
His penance gave him new purpose in life however. He intended
to build up the church in Dalriada and to re-establish the broken
political fortunes of his countrymen there.

In fulfilment of his first aim, Columba set up his headquarters
in 563 on Iona, which became a centre for many journeys among
the islands and on the mainland, the inspiration of the second
main stream of Celtic evangelism, one which influenced the Scots
as profoundly as St. Ninian's had affected the Britons and the
Picts. He has been described as a 'golden-mouthed preacher of

Christ'. He and his companions worked ceaselessly among the Scots west of Drumalban and established many churches along the estuaries and in the glens. Columba visited Skye, an outpost of Pictish territory, and in old age he went to the mainland and met Kentigern, the much-revered saint whose centre was Glasgow. These however were incidental journeys, as his special sphere was always Dalriada. Perhaps his most famous departure from it was when he paid a state call on King Brude at Inverness, along with the two Irish Picts named Kenneth and Comgall, who probably carried through the negotiations for Columba, because he was never fluent in the Pictish language. Their business was to secure Brude's sanction for a mission to the Orkneys, and the extent of his authority is revealed in the chroniclers' assurance that Cormac, the leader of the Orkney venture, was saved from martyrdom by Brude's safe-conduct.

Columba was determined to redress the political disasters of 560 and to re-establish the monarchy. He persuaded the Scots to pass over the rightful successor of the demoted king and to appoint instead a man named Aidan. This king earned an uncomfortable title—Aidan the False—but he turned the tide of misfortunes for the Scots, who once again began to outrival the Picts in strength and influence. Columba also negotiated a relief from tax payments by Dalriada to Ireland.

Columba's biography was written within a century of his death by Adamnan, an abbot of Iona. Like many medieval works, it is full of highly exaggerated stories designed to magnify the piety of its subject, but it gives interesting information. We learn of Columba sharing in the field-work, of corn being ground in the mill, of a horse drawing a wheeled cart—so there was a well-organized system of agriculture, and people could make roads with reliable surfaces. There is an irresistible ring of truth in an anecdote about a monk called Baithene. So holy was he, that while carrying a sheaf of corn in one arm, he extended the other in grateful prayer, and 'in his devotion did not even remove the midges which settled on his face'. When the monks needed to repair their buildings, timber was in such short supply that they went to Glenshiel for logs, lashed them on behind their coracles, and towed them all the way back to Iona, grousing, as sailors will, when they had to wait for a suitable following wind. So many sea journeys in all weathers are recorded that one is lost in admiration of the men who built and navigated those tough little coracles.

One reads too of much hospitality, of friendship offered to undistinguished sufferers, of affectionate personal relationships between Columba and his companions, of passionate and deeply sincere prayer. From Adamnan one can catch something of Columba's spirit, for the snatches of conversation recorded show his awareness of beauty, his poet's flair for descriptive phrase, also a certain astringency which reveals the saint's sterner side. Adamnan wrote most beautifully about Columba's death and then addressed himself to future copyists: 'I beseech all those that may wish to copy these books, nay rather I conjure them through Christ, the judge of the ages, after carefully copying them to compare them with the exemplar from which they have written and also to append this conjuration in this place.'

Iona, like Whithorn, became a training centre for missionaries, the inspiration of St. Cuthbert, who worked in Lothian, St. Aidan of Northumbria and very many more, whose names are recorded and whose foundations are known. But it was not the only focus of Christian work. There is no space here to give a full account of the different missionary influences at work in the land, but two especially interesting saints, both trained at Bangor in Ireland, must be mentioned. St. Moluag was an Irish Pict who came to Scotland in 562 and made Lismore his centre. This island lies in the mouth of the Great Glen, a point from which one can travel to the islands or journey across the great rift of Scotland to the east coast. From Lismore, Moluag developed a mission among the Picts. He went to the Moray Firth and worked in the Spey Valley, on the Aberdeenshire coast, on Skye and Raasay and for awhile on the Campsie Hills near Glasgow. He seems to have been a gentler person than St. Columba, but he won the title 'Moluag of the Hundred Monasteries.'

The other missionary giant of the period lived later and his foundation was the most remote of all. He was called Maelrubha and like Columba he was descended from the royal Niall. He trained at Bangor and became Abbot there, but in 671 he resigned his post and set off for Scotland. He worked in Kintyre, on Loch Fyneside, at Arisaig and afterwards in Skye, which he came to know well. He founded his monastery at Applecross in 671. It is a delectable spot, readily reached by boat from Skye, but blocked off from neighbouring glens by miles of gaunt, rock-strewn mountain, still a handicap to travellers by road, impassable during winter months. None the less, Maelrubha travelled even further than Columba or Moluag, to and fro in Dalriada and right into the heart of Pictish territory.

The attraction of island and peninsula sites for these early missionaries is very noticeable. You see this at Birsay on the north-west edge of the Mainland of Orkney, where a tiny church was built in the late 7th century, a place you can approach only at low tide over a ridgeway of stones. A similar site is the one on St. Ninian's Isle in Shetland, where excavations in July 1958 led to the discovery of a 12th century church, superimposed on the much earlier one: a hoard of beautiful metal ornaments made with Celtic designs was found there, with many sculptured stones. On Holy Island, near Bamburgh, there was another missionary centre isolated at high tide, from which in the 7th century St. Aidan of Iona began the Christian penetration of Northumbria, the centre of the Angles.

These men who clearly thrived on solitude and loved natural beauty showed their aesthetic quality in sculpture. The splendid crosses of the Celtic church reveal a craftsmanship unrivalled by any other product of the period. Intricate but freely flowing lines, geometrically interwoven, form the basis of the designs carved upon the shafts, some of which were six to eight feet in height. Birds, beasts, leaves, flowers and human figures were worked into the pattern too. The Ruthwell Cross near Dumfries is the best known, but up and down the country there are cross shafts and stone slabs bearing fragments of this lovely sculpture, Scotland's finest tangible relic of the Celtic Church.

Of the buildings in which the new congregations worshipped, virtually nothing remains, because of the destruction wrought by Vikings later on. It seems that they were nearly all tiny, designed to shelter the altar where mass was celebrated, not the wor-shippers, who heard the preaching of the saints in the open air.

It is by place-names, by the dedication of later churches, by fragments of sculpture that Celtic foundations are traced.

The Celtic Church was monastic. It demanded poverty and obedience from its clergy, who were all monks. There were no secular priests, no organized parishes, no diocesan administration and no supreme authority at the top. Bishops were consecrated to ordain monks, but they were under the obedience of the Abbots to whose houses they belonged. Riches this Church never accumulated, uniformity it never demanded. Marriage took place among some of its monks and this was not considered wrong. Some of its buildings were so placed that the sanctuary faced east, some were not. Celebration of mass and of baptism varied in detail from place to place.

This lack of organized administration was both the strength and the weakness of the Celtic mission. Founded by men who had a passion for preaching and a natural gift for worship, sustained by the practice of prayer, hymn-singing, and study of the scriptures, it appealed to the Celtic people who responded to a personal approach. Some of the sordid by-products of wealth, orthodoxy and power, so marked in Rome and other influential centres, never developed in the Church of St. Ninian and St. Columba. But when it met with opposition from a much more highly organized body, with international affiliations, this smaller and weaker Church had no resources with which to fight back.

In the 7th century there appeared from the south men who owed their allegiance to Rome and who were briefed by the Pope and by St. Augustine of Kent to carry out the conversion of Britain. When their representatives met Christian communities in Northumbria they were horrified to discover unorthodox practices. And so bitter controversy broke out over the tonsure and the date of Easter, and an unedifying story it makes. Now was illustrated perhaps for the first time in British history, the ungodly capacity of Christians for mutual hatred. Bede, the historian of the Anglo-Saxons, admits in one passage that the Celtic Christian 'held in his heart and venerated and preached nothing other than do we: that is the redemption of the human race through the passion, the resurrection and ascension to the skies of the Mediator between God and men'. This should have been the healing bond between two active and devoted branches of the one Church. But to the Anglo-Saxon priests the calendar which permitted Easter to fall on a date other than their own seemed a barbarous contravention of the 6th century Roman decree: as Bede, inaccurately and censoriously, declared—'The Britons . . . wrongfully and from wicked lewdness set themselves against the appointed Easter of the whole Catholic Church.'

In the year 664, when Britain was afflicted by an earthquake, an eclipse of the sun and a violent epidemic of yellow plague, the Synod of Whitby was called to discuss the problem of Easter's date, by Oswy, King of Northumbria. He was a devout man who owed his faith to Iona. His wife, Eanflaed, was a Mercian princess, who followed the teaching of the Anglo-Saxon Church. Thus the court witnessed the celebration of two Easters each year. As Bede put it, 'when the King, having ended his fasting, was keeping the Paschal Feast, the Queen and her retainers would still be fasting and celebrating Palm Sunday'—certainly a confusing situation. So Oswy called a conference and the Queen's protagonists won the day. In humiliation the Celtic representatives retreated to Iona to talk the distasteful situation over at their headquarters.

The monks of Iona disagreed about it. In 688, Adamnan, their Abbot and the biographer of Columba, accepted the new ruling but failed to persuade the others. From 704 till 722, there were rival abbots in Iona, upholding the two opposite systems, but such dissension could not last and complete capitulation followed very soon. Celtic customs however died slowly in northern England and still more slowly in Scotland. It was not until the 12th or 13th century that the last resistance to the Roman ways disappeared.

The achievement of the Celtic missionaries illustrates the power of a living faith in the living Christ. These men were the first to offer the satisfactions of a real religion to a pagan people who were sensitive to spiritual forces. The collapse of their Church is one of the many sad developments in Scottish history. Roman organization was too strong for Celtic Christians and in the 8th century they were subjected to new and uglier attacks from quite a different quarter.

CHAPTER 4

Vikings and Normans

The Vikings began to attack Scotland towards the end of the 8th century. The resistance they met was weakened by the hostility between the Picts and the Scots, who had not yet merged into one Celtic block, while the Strathclyde Britons and the Lothian Angles were still separate communities and offered no concerted defence.

For a time the Norsemen swung between Norway where they wintered and the Orkneys where they spent their summers. Gradually they made permanent settlements in these islands and in the Shetlands. Their long houses were often built over the sites of Stone Age dwellings as at Sumburgh or of Celtic monasteries as at Birsay. In the 790s, they began to turn their magnificent ships towards the islands and coasts of Scotland.

Applecross, the most northerly Christian centre, took the first onslaught in 793 or 794; Lindisfarne on Holy Island was attacked immediately after. The Vikings at this stage were sea-raiders using their ships as their base, and because the Celtic Church had favoured islands and coastal sites, it suffered grievously. Iona was attacked in 795, 802, 806, 825 and at frequent intervals throughout the 9th and 10th centuries. The chroniclers throughout Britain were prolific in their lamentations. As one of them sadly wrote: 'There always were and there always will re-appear those that are spurred on by evil rage against the servants of the Lord.'

Christian communities were ravaged, monastic buildings sacked, valuable Church plate and illuminated manuscripts, often in pieces and shreds, taken back to Norway as keepsakes for womenfolk. The Celtic Church, already undermined by its controversy with the Anglo-Saxons, never regained its former vitality.

44

Vikings and Normans

As time went by, the Vikings settled in the islands and also on the seaboard fringes of the mainland. Tangible evidence of their way of life is now much less than it should be, on account of the comparatively modern destruction of it, but records through the centuries give tantalizing hints. A late 17th century writer, for example, describes a ship-burial unearthed at Stranraer in 1681. It lay 'a considerable distance from the shore, unto which the sea, at the highest spring-tide, never comes. It was transversely under a little bourne and wholly covered with earth to a considerable depth, for there was a good yard with kale growing in it upon the one end of it. By the part of it which was gotten out, my informers who saw it conjecture that it was pretty large.'

We know most about the Norsemen who lived in the jarldom of the Orkneys, which for a long time included Sutherland and Caithness, and whose recorded history goes back to 880. The Orkney Earls were versatile, interesting and violent. One of them, Earl Rognvald, was the father of Rollo, the conqueror of Normandy and the ancestor of Duke William. Rognvald's brother succeeded him as Earl and in 995 forced a mass conversion to Christianity upon Orcadian chieftains. During the 11th century, the ideas of this religion were gradually absorbed and the persecution of Christian communities abated.

The Orkneyinga Saga of the 11th and 12th centuries suggests that the Orkneys enjoyed considerable if rather rugged prosperity, especially in the 12th century, when large farms were worked and much grain produced. A good deal of building was done on a grand scale for the times, since castles were made of stone and furnished with large drinking-halls for lavish entertainment. Vikings were good at enjoying themselves. Unlike the Icelanders, Norsemen in Orkney seem to have had little interest in prolonged lawsuits and did not indulge in family vendettas. Their poetry concentrated upon love-themes and seafaring ventures, with much less emphasis upon murder than appears in the Icelandic sagas.

We have little knowledge of how the Shetlands fared, though their rulers owed allegiance to the Earls of Orkney. Then, as now, less grain could be harvested in these windswept islands and they were always proportionately poorer. We know hardly any more

about the Hebrides in early medieval times, except that here the
Norse weakness for family feuds did much more harm than in
the Orkneys. It seems, indeed, as if the best Viking adventurers
were attracted to the Orkneys and that for a number of generations they made the most of their opportunities there. The racial
background, the language, the customs, even the household gear
and other implements in use on these islands, became Norse in
character and remained so for many centuries.

In the 9th century, when the full onslaught of Norse attack
was being experienced, a more unified authority began to emerge
in Scotland. In 841, Kenneth McAlpin became King of Dalriada.
This King, we are told by the chroniclers, 'led the Scots from
Argyle into the land of the Picts, with marvellous astuteness',
and 'reigned over the Scots for sixteen years, after destroying
the Picts'. The Chronicle of Huntingdon tells us that after
'Danish pirates had occupied the shores and with the greatest
slaughter had destroyed the Picts who defended the land,
Kenneth passed over into and turned his arms against the
remaining territory of the Picts and after slaying many, drove
the rest to flight. And so he was the first of the Scots to obtain
the monarchy of the whole of Albania, which is now called
Scotia.'

It seems therefore that Kenneth's astuteness lay in descending
upon a people already exhausted by other terrible enemies. He
fixed his capital at Forteviot, the centre of Pictish territory. He
transferred the relics of Columba to Dunkeld, which became a
focal point of religious organization. He began the evil practice
of Border-raiding, with a view to securing Lothian too. Kenneth
died of a tumour in 858 and was buried in Iona, the traditional
resting-place of Scottish kings.

How far Kenneth McAlpin really united his two peoples
is uncertain, for though the Picts and the Scots were hence-
forth ruled by one King, and their land became known as Scotland, the differences between the two were not ironed out for
many a long day. The mysterious thing is that recorded history
has so little to tell us about the Picts, although these
people had dominated most of Scotland for over a thousand
years.

Kenneth's successors in the 9th and 10th century were unable to extend their frontiers because of the Vikings. During these years of insecurity, a strange sect called the Culdees developed among Pictish Christians and persisted for some two centuries at a number of centres—Monymusk, Abernethy, Scone, Dunkeld, Muthill, St. Andrews and Lochleven, for example. The name seems to have been derived from Célé De, Companion of God. Still less than the Celtic missionaries did the Culdees follow the orthodox rites of the Roman Church. The movement was spontaneous and it stimulated different rules of life in different places. Some of the Culdees were hermits, some lived in community, some were married, others celibate.

In 1005, Malcolm II became King of the Picts and Scots. He defeated the Angles at Carham in 1018 and made Lothian permanently part of Scotland, an event lamented by the English chroniclers. He was succeeded by a grandson, Duncan, who had already inherited the kingdom of Strathclyde through connections on the distaff side, and who therefore extended his rule south of the Borders into Cumberland, a larger sphere of influence than any earlier king in Scotland could claim. This was the Duncan slain by Macbeth in 1040, after six rather unhappy years on the throne. Macbeth's character has suffered unjustly at the hands of Shakespeare, as he ruled Scotland well for some seventeen years, and there is evidence that the country enjoyed some prosperity during his reign.

One result of Duncan's untimely death was the effect it had on his two young sons. Malcolm, known as Canmore or Bighead, was sent as a nine-year-old to England, to be brought up by his maternal uncle, Siward, Earl of Northumbria. This Siward was a man of influence with Edward the Confessor, King of England, was influenced by men familiar with French culture. The younger and he took his young nephew to Edward's court, where the boy brother, Donald Bane, was sent to the Hebrides, where his sympathies became identified with Norse chieftains and Gaelic islanders who were out of touch with European thought. The separate treatment of these two brothers was to cause trouble later.

Siward, Earl of Northumbria, fought against Macbeth on behalf of Malcolm Canmore, who was recognized as king in 1058.

Soon after this, Malcolm married Ingibiorg, daughter of Thorfinn the Mighty, Earl of the Orkneys, a man notorious for his annual expeditions each summer to plunder Scotland, Wales and Ireland. Thorfinn was described as the 'biggest of men in stature and the strongest; ugly in appearance; black-haired; sharp-featured; and large-nosed; and somewhat beetle-browed; and most soldierly . . . a great man of vigour and greedy, both of wealth and of honour'. Like many another Viking, Thorfinn visited Rome, where the Pope gave him an audience and also absolution for all his sins. In his old age he became milder and founded a splendid church at Birsay, where he was buried in 1065, after being Earl of the Orkneys for sixty years.

Perhaps Ingibiorg lacked the tough constitution of her father, for she died soon after he did, leaving her husband with three little sons. Malcolm then looked for another helpmeet, and found one, as a result, so the chroniclers say, of a violent storm in the Forth. The wind blew upon the Scottish shore a ship with distinguished passengers on board—Edgar Atheling and his sisters Margaret and Christina.

The background of this storm-driven family needs some explanation. Their father was Edward the Confessor's nephew and they had all been brought up in Hungary. They had arrived in England in 1057 when Margaret, the eldest, was only twelve and they then experienced life at the court of Edward the Confessor. Margaret was specially susceptible to that pious King's influence as she had been devoted to religious practices from childhood.

When Edward the Confessor died in January 1066, Margaret's brother, Edgar, had quite a convincing claim to the English throne, but he never seemed to regret his failure to secure it. 'Handsome, well-spoken and unmartial', a genial talker, a charming light-weight, Edgar lacked the moral fervour so characteristic of his sisters. They all found the atmosphere in England less congenial after William the Conqueror arrived, so they embarked in 1069 for the continent, and according to tradition were blown by contrary winds into the Forth. Malcolm IV offered them hospitality and lost his heart to Margaret. He married her in 1069. Perhaps they found a bond in their sympathy for French people, their interest in French ideas, which they had both learned in childhood at the English court.

From 1069, the year of Malcolm's marriage to Margaret, until 1124 when David I became king, Norman influences began to affect Scottish society in the southern parts of the country. There was no military conquest, as in England, but a steady inflow of people and ideas, encouraged by Malcolm and Margaret and their sons.

When Margaret married Malcolm she was about twenty-four, little more than half her husband's age. She was determined to improve him, his friends and his country. With supreme assurance of her own rectitude, she devoted her considerable intelligence to this task. She had a continental love of splendour, so Malcolm and his courtiers had to fit themselves out with fur and velvet and jewellery; gold and silver dishes appeared on the royal tables; ornamental hangings were pegged up on the walls of the king's residences, serving the double purpose of decoration and draught exclusion. Manners and ceremonial were made more stately, and the King began to appear on special occasions with an official bodyguard. Margaret herself appreciated luxuries and encouraged her courtiers to do likewise, so that foreign merchants began coming to Scotland. These interests of the new Queen were not without economic significance, and they were fostered by the refugees from the south who came to Scotland when the Conqueror's policy became too oppressive for them.

It was in religious matters that Margaret's energies found the greatest scope. She was astonished to discover that in Scotland services were not conducted as they were in the south, that Sunday was not kept free from normal labour, that Mass was infrequently and variously celebrated. She could not approve of the way Lent was observed, she was dismayed that people did not communicate on Easter Sunday, and that the sacred rituals were sometimes conducted in the vernacular. With fortitude and singleness of mind the Queen laboured to bring the worship of her adopted country into conformity with Roman practice. She was lavish in her gifts to the churches where she worshipped, as she was in her charities to the poor, indeed there is a suggestion of exhibitionism in some of her almsgivings. She encouraged pilgrimages as means of promoting personal devotion, and established foundations at North and South Queensferry, on either side of the Forth, for the benefit of pilgrims to St. Andrews.

Queen Margaret made an impression on her contemporaries in south-east Scotland, because of her devoutly religious life. Her biography was written soon after her death by Turgot, who became Bishop of St. Andrews, and its records of her good works reflect the public opinion of the day.

Meantime, political relations between Malcolm III and William the Conqueror varied. Malcolm was not much involved in William's affairs, but was prepared to offer hospitality to his brother-in-law Edgar, and to anybody else from the south who cared to visit him. He was mainly interested in retaining a hold on the large, indeterminate Border country which sprawled across the hills of Cumberland and Northumberland. Raiding in the vicinity of this unfortunate area was already frequent: both cattle and slaves were regularly rounded up and driven off by marauders from both sides, and the Scots did not lose on these illegal projects.

William for his part early realized that to conquer Scotland thoroughly would be impossible. He satisfied himself with a demonstration of strength. Like the Romans almost exactly a thousand years earlier, he organized in 1072 an immensely complicated movement of his army and his navy to the Firth of Tay and there Malcolm became 'his man'. Exactly what this involved in general is hard to say, but Duncan, Malcolm's eldest son by Ingibiorg, discovered that for him in particular it involved a long journey. He was sent to England as a hostage, and there remained for some fifteen years.

In 1080, William's eldest son, Robert, arrived in Scotland with an army, soon after the harrying of northern England by his father's troops. Although his business was to punish the Scots for raiding over the Border, there was no fighting. Amicable conversations were followed by the surrender of more hostages and a christening service in which Robert became the godfather of Malcolm's infant daughter Maud. On his way home Robert established a New Castle on the Tyne, perhaps to mark the northern limit of his father's kingdom.

Things changed for the worse when the Conqueror died and his second son, Rufus, became King of England. Malcolm refused to pay homage to him, on the grounds that allegiance was owed only to the eldest brother, Robert. William Rufus therefore launched an attack upon southern Cumbria, planted the district with 'a great multitude of churlish folk', and built a castle at Carlisle. Later he invited Malcolm III to journey into England and discuss things with him, and on receipt of a safe-conduct, Malcolm set out. On his way south, he assisted in a foundation ceremony at Durham Cathedral. But when he arrived at Gloucester, Rufus refused to see him, an insupportable insult to Malcolm's dignity.

Hitherto any incursions into English territory made under Malcolm III had been in the nature of Border raids. Ordericus Vitalis, a 12th century English chronicler, gave an account of Scottish character not endorsed by later historians. 'Though they are fierce in battle,' he wrote, 'yet they love ease and quiet, decline to let themselves be troubled by neighbouring kingdoms and are given to the practice of the Christian religion rather than of arms.' In 1093, bruised in spirit from the shock of insult, Malcolm III gathered up his forces for an attack upon England which hardly justified the words of Ordericus Vitalis. It was to prove his last undertaking, for at Alnwick Malcolm was killed in ambush, by a Norman called Morel, with whom he was on close terms of intimacy. The news of the disaster shocked the English court, where Malcolm was a popular figure.

The Queen heard of his death, and that of her eldest son Edward, when she herself was ill in bed. Characteristically, she composed herself to die also, having no desire to survive him, and within three days she had passed away, firm to the last in religious faith and in wifely affection.

When Turgot wrote Margaret's biography in the early 12th century, he obviously thought of her as a saint, though her canonization did not take place till 1249. The force of her character is strikingly shown because almost all of her eight children held the same view, and most of them shared her religious convictions. Between them all, these eight won considerable worldly success, which was in keeping too with their parents' example. The two eldest were the least distinguished. Edward died with his father at Alnwick, Edmund by political intrigue became the black sheep of the family; Ethelred was an Abbot, Edgar, Alexander and David all Kings of Scotland. The two sisters, Maud and Mary, after rather a stormy childhood, both achieved distinction, for the former married Henry I of England and became Queen of England, while the latter married Eustace of Boulogne.

On Malcolm's III's death, his brother Donald Bane was elected King, in accordance with an ancient Celtic tradition called tanistry, by which a brother's claim was stronger than a son's. Donald Bane, now sixty, had always been doggedly resistant to his brother's ideas and he instituted a complete change of policy. There followed a reaction against French, English and Norman ideas.

Four of Malcolm III's sons were despatched to England forthwith and there experienced a Norman upbringing, directed by their uncle, Edgar Atheling. Their sisters were already being educated at Romsey Abbey in Wiltshire, a foundation for nuns where many Norman ladies spent their childhood. The stern Christina, Margaret's sister, was one of the senior members of the community and *in loco parentis* she beat her little nieces and cowed them with rebukes. Meantime Duncan, son of Malcolm and Ingibjorg, had spent some fifteen years at the Norman Court as a hostage. Medieval parents of royal status sent their children away to alien and even enemy courts with strangely little compunction. In the case of Malcolm's family, the results were very satisfactory, odd though the whole régime may seem to us.

William Rufus did not approve of Donald Bane and sent Duncan, Ingibiorg's son, now in his early thirties, to dethrone him by force. This Duncan did, but he was murdered almost immediately; not long after this, in 1097, Malcolm III's son Edgar was made King. Edgar's success was achieved with Anglo-Norman assistance, and he rewarded those who had helped him: so more Normans than ever passed over the Border to settle in Scotland.

Edgar recognized the loss of the Hebrides by formally ceding them to Magnus Barelegs, King of Norway. The terms stated that Magnus could claim all land west of a line that a galley could pass over, so the Norse King seated himself at the helm of his ship, while his sweating henchmen hauled it from Tarbert, at the north-east end of the Kintyre peninsula, across to the sea on the west. This haulage of sea-going ships was fairly common, in fact the name Tarbert is believed to be derived from a word meaning 'Draw-Boat', and it is to be found at various narrow necks of land in Scotland. By this device, Magnus secured a good slice of the mainland in addition to the islands. Iona became Norse territory, and the degraded Donald Bane was the last king to be buried there.

Edgar, who never married, was succeeded by Alexander, perhaps the least attractive member of this gifted family. Chroniclers describe him as 'generous beyond his means to newcomers', a man 'who wishes to do everything in his kingdom alone, by himself, and will not suffer any interference from any authority whatever', 'devoted to clerks', 'severe towards men of his own land'. Like most of his family, he was generous to the Church. He set up foundations for Canons Regular at Scone, at Dunkeld and on an island in Loch Tay, and also on Inchcolm in the Forth. He appointed Turgot, prior of Durham, as Bishop of St. Andrews, after rather a long vacancy; he restored the bishopric of Dunkeld and founded a third in Moray.

Alexander, Edgar's brother, probably exercised royal control only over the land between the Forth and the Spey. Argyll, Ross, and even Moray, were too remote to administer effectively, and they were almost independent of his authority. Cumbria was ruled by Alexander's brother, Earl David, according to the terms of Edgar's will, and Ayrshire and Galloway were included in his sphere also.

Alexander assisted Henry I of England in a brutal invasion of Wales. Did he ponder the question why his own land was spared such treatment? It was of course because his sister Maud, emancipated from her Aunt Christina's discipline, had married Henry I, the only Scottish princess who ever became Queen of England and one who was dearly loved. Henry was father-in-law as well as brother-in-law to Alexander, by the latter's marriage to one of Henry's numerous illegitimate daughters, Sibylla. She was a lady of royal tastes, who liked splendour and stateliness.

She enlarged Alexander's corps of personal attendants, and court life in Scotland continued to grow more like that in England.

When Alexander died, without a legitimate heir, he was succeeded by David, the most vigorous and original of the brothers. He was Earl of Cumbria in his own right, Earl of Northampton and Huntingdon by his marriage to a rich Norman heiress. In fact this Scottish prince, Henry I's brother-in-law, was one of the most prominent barons in England, holding a place of honour in Henry I's court. He was gifted and popular, capable of holding men's loyalty, well equipped for kingship, and like his mother devoted to organized religion and stately services. Because he was a good Norman, hunting was his favourite sport, litigation his hobby, rule by charter an accepted habit. His friends in England were mainly Norman or Breton in origin. Of these Robert de Brus was one, son of a man of the same name from Cotentin, who had fought at Hastings. Bernard, Lord of Bailleul in Picardy, was another—he built Barnard Castle in Teesdale and became known as Baliol or Balliol.

David came to a land where people still lived and worshipped in buildings made of wattle and woodwork, where towns hardly existed, where industry was primitive, where men bartered goods and services because they had no metal currency. The feudal system was hardly known in Scotland as yet, allegiance was given to local chieftains who were reluctant to recognize the claims of higher authority. Different parts of Scotland were separated from each other by uninhabited hills and moors, the elk was still found in the north, wolves, bears and lynxes were common enough in most places. There were dialects which were incomprehensible to travellers who went too far afield from home. The influence of the Church was superficial because the organization of parishes, each with its church and its priest, had not yet taken place, there were only three bishoprics for the whole country, and monasteries were few and far between.

David ruled from 1124 to 1153. In these three decades, permanent changes were effected, so that by the end of the 12th century, Scotland south and east of Norse territory was completely different from the kingdom won by force of arms for Malcolm III in 1058.

CHAPTER 5

David I

A Cistercian historian, Ailred of Rievaulx, knew David I and his court well because he had been brought up with David's son Henry, whom he dearly loved. Ailred could have become the King's trusted counsellor, but in 1135 he underwent an experience akin to conversion which led him to join the abbey of Rievaulx in Yorkshire. When Prince Henry died years later, still a young man, Ailred unburdened himself about his long separation from his royal friends. 'In the body but never in mind or affection, in order to serve Christ, I left him in the full bloom of his prime, as also his father, now flourishing in hale old age, whom I have loved beyond all mortals.'

Ailred had more to say in 1153 when David I also died. 'O desolate Scotia, who shall console thee now? He is no more who made an untilled and barren land a land that is pleasant and plenteous, who adorned thee with castles and cities and lofty towers, enriched thy ports with foreign wares, gathered the wealth of other kingdoms for thine enjoyment, changed thy shaggy cloaks for precious raiment, clothed thine ancient nudity with purple and fine linen, ordered thy barbarous ways with Christian religion.' Graeme Ritchie, author of *The Normans in Scotland*, says of this passage that 'for all its rhetoric, it is a singularly exact epitome of David's achievements.'

During his long residence in England, David had seen much that he admired, and when he became King he introduced into Scotland many features of Norman society and government. The Norman state was feudal and its principles required that land should be managed by people responsible to the King, with recognized obligations; that the royal revenues should be efficiently administered, and accounts inspected; that justice should be enforced by royal officials, themselves under supervision; that defence should be organized from castles under the King's direct control. David shared the Norman respect for the Church too, because he was personally devout, but also because religion, properly organized, gives society stability.

When he arrived back in Scotland, David awarded large areas of land to his Anglo-Norman friends, and to tenants from his English estates, and in doing so introduced a much more strictly feudal system of ownership. For the first time in Scottish history, land grants were now generally confirmed by Charters, set out in Latin and signed by witnesses. The earliest of David's charters still extant, a document measuring $6\frac{1}{2}$ by $3\frac{3}{4}$ inches, confirmed the grant of about 200,000 acres in Annandale to Robert de Brus, who already owned 80 manors in Yorkshire. De Bourneville, de Morville, de Graham, de Sommerville, Oliphant, Fitzalan, de Bailleul, Comyn—these are some of the names among the new Norman tenants-in-chief. David gave them lands, because they understood administration and were used to the responsibility involved in running big estates. By education and upbringing, David was at one with these Anglo-Normans, whose traditions were his and whose reactions he could predict and understand. Their obligations to him were sacred because of the vows they took as his liegemen. Such people he felt he could trust.

The former landowners in Scotland seem to have objected little to David's arrangements because they lost little by them. They continued on their accustomed holdings as tenants of the new Norman overlords rather than directly of the King. The lower social orders included various ranks of free landholders and also serfs. These serfs were considered part of the property and they were not allowed to go elsewhere. They probably detected little change in their lives, except that they had to work harder, since the new nobility were quick to begin building castles, to intensify agriculture and to develop home farms and gardens.

David's land policy caused far-reaching changes which later created difficulties. The ordinary folk of Scotland still spoke Gaelic, the new nobility French, the literate classes, which were largely ecclesiastical, Latin. Thus Gaelic hardly made its way into written literature at all. This meant that a language barrier developed which emphasized class barriers, always a harmful situation.

David I

Another ominous feature was that powerful men in Scotland owned land on two sides of the Border and paid homage to two Kings. David himself owed allegiance for his English territories to the English King. So later on, when war broke out between the two countries, the leading men in Scotland hardly knew where their first loyalties lay. Worst of all was the radical defect which bedevilled all feudal countries. The overlords became too powerful for any monarch to hold them. The purpose of government on a national scale is to eliminate private wars: the effect of a feudal organization is to stimulate private wars between the great family factions of which feudal society is composed. National and feudal systems are incompatible, as medieval Kings in France and England discovered, as well as those in Scotland.

In the twentieth century it is easy to look back and to criticize David I. This is mistaken. National feeling as we understand it was unknown then in Europe. David had to handle a country in which tribal and local disorder was chronic and in which the King's writ ran only within a limited sphere. The land organization he worked out met the difficulties as he knew them and gave Scotland a chance to build up a better way of life.

Anglo-Norman overlords were quick to build castles. Castles were at once the means of maintaining feudal authority and the symbols of feudal power. Dark, dirty and damp little erections they were, constructed of wood, with outside staircases and few amenities, perched on the top of artificially raised earthern mounds and surrounded by water-filled, stagnant ditches. Below the mound, each castle had an enclosed area, also entrenched and palisaded, for stables, smithy and garrison quarters. Beyond this again were enclosed fields, and, generally, gardens. The men who did the work were local peasants such as Gillepatrick, Ragewin and Ulchil, whose names we know because they were the personal property of David himself and presented by him to the Church of the Holy Trinity at Dunfermline.

A multitude of minor officials was required for the maintenance even of small castles and domains. In *The Normans in Scotland*, Graeme Ritchie lists clerks, bailies, falconers, fletchers, foresters, lorimers, porters, sergeants, tailors, taverners and others. As with the more stately officials of David's court, many of these

57

were Norman by origin, though they identified themselves with the country of their adoption. Their designations gradually became surnames.

Administration had been developed on Norman lines to a certain extent by Alexander, David's brother. He had appointed such officials as Chancellor, Constable, Chamberlain, Marshal and Steward to supervise the various departments of the royal household. David continued all these offices and added others, again giving them to Anglo-Normans. From these officials, he selected some, along with certain bishops, to form a central governing body, which was always at hand to give him advice and to receive his instructions. It could handle at high level the awkward and difficult problems of administration and justice. It was particularly concerned with financial matters, now of increasing importance, though later these came to be dealt with separately in the Court of the Exchequer. To central headquarters also came justiciars, those barons whom David appointed to travel on circuit, hearing judicial cases and settling other problems too. The justiciars carried the King's authority further afield than he could go himself, and they heard appeals from the Sheriff Courts.

David appointed Sheriffs, although there were as yet no shires. These officials administered the King's personal domains from the royal castles, summoned juries to give evidence in civil and criminal cases, collected feudal dues and supervised defence. Their judicial work was scrutinized by the travelling judges, their financial records by the Exchequer Court, their military arrangements by the Constable.

David therefore established the beginnings of a rule of law, not only in central and southern Scotland but also as far away as Moray. Unfortunately, this did not develop in the turbulent centuries which followed. In medieval Scotland local law-courts under feudal barons and sheriffs pursued their own way, with little reference to central authority and small interference from it. In England the King's judges gradually established control over civil and criminal procedures and the mighty authority of the common law was there based on the precedents accumulated by these judges. In Scotland on the other hand, decisions made in the local courts affected only the people involved in each separate case, and no common law was evolved. This meant that ordinary people had much less chance of securing reasonable justice than in England, especially as the powers over both baronial and sheriff courts often became hereditary, vested in one family of great local prestige, while rights of appeal were scanty and very hard to put into effective action.

David I was aiming at a national system of justice and administration, in which the King should be no mere figurehead. He and his advisers and officials were constantly on the move from one royal castle to another, because he wanted to keep in touch with his people everywhere. There was also the economic factor: feudal dues were paid in kind, so the court had to move away from any one centre when the perishable goods there stored up for the King had been consumed.

David was a devout man. He realized that the Celtic Church had been under-organized, particularly in its lack of parishes, and also in its lack of dioceses which could be supervised by bishops. The origin of the Scottish bishoprics is obscure. All that can be said for certain is that, by the end of David's reign, the country had been divided into nine dioceses—St. Andrews, Dunkeld, Moray, Glasgow, Ross, Caithness, Aberdeen, Dunblane and Brechin. The bishops he appointed were Anglo-Normans, who were valuable to him as members of his court and participants in his work of government.

During David's reign some parishes were established, but this work was of slow growth and a long time passed before there were enough to serve the needs of the country. There must have been many people living far away from the nearest church, untended by any priest and therefore ignorant of the Christian religion.

The 12th century was a time of renaissance in Europe. One manifestation of revitalized thinking was the Cistercian movement which reformed monasticism. This was started at Cîteaux and much influenced by St. Bernard of Clairvaux. His understanding of the gentleness of Christ brought fresh religious insight and new ways of expressing it. Though he may not have been the author, his characteristic piety finds expression in 'Jesus, the

MAP 5.
XII CENTURY RELIGIOUS FOUNDATIONS

Urquhart
Kinloss
R.Spey
R.Don
Monymusk
R.Dee
N.Esk
S.Esk
Restennet
Coupar Angus
Arbroath
Scone
R.Tay
Lindores
St.Andrews
Lochleven
Isle of May
Cambus-
kenneth
Dunfermline
Inchcolm
Holyrood
New Battle
Paisley
R.Clyde
Kilwinning
Melrose
R.Tweed
Kelso
Lesmahagow
Selkirk
Dryburgh
Jedburgh
Glenluce
Soulseat
Dundrennan
Whithorn

Φ.Γ.

0 10 20   40   60   80   100 Miles
0 10 20 40 60 80 100   160 Kilometres

very thought of Thee with sweetness fills my breast', and other hymns written originally in beautiful Latin, sung by Christians to this day in many other languages. St. Bernard also preached the poverty of Christ. One historian has described the Cistercian movement as 'an outcome of the mighty but ever-changing influence of the idea of renunciation'.

Cistercian abbeys were built on sites far from human habitation and the buildings were austere. All physical comfort was forbidden so that men might discipline the flesh and dedicate the spirit, garments were made of undyed wool and designed without ample folds, monks were not allowed to wear shirts under their habits, food was of the simplest. The daily routine was divided between prayer, meditation, reading, corporate worship and manual labour. The services were stripped of all aesthetic appeal. Ailred of Rievaulx expressed the Cistercian views when he denounced sculpture, wall-paintings, engravings, choral and organ music. The latter he described as 'that terrible blast of bellows, simulating rather the roar of thunder than the sweetness of the human voice' and he also condemned in one sweeping sentence 'the tinkling of cymbals, warblings, superfluous beauty, pleasure of the ear and lust of the eye'.

Self-abnegation always makes an appeal to idealistic people and the Cistercian movement attracted some of the finest and most thoughtful men. The abbeys became centres of religious inspiration, and also of enlightened agriculture, for manual labour was done in the fields and on the pastures. The Cistercian foundations, designed to divorce the monastic movement from wealth, ironically enough, created yet more wealth by their excellent farming methods. They also promoted scholarship in their libraries. It has been said that the one luxury permitted was the enjoyment of perfect Latin prose.

During the 12th century, many Cistercian foundations were established in Scotland, where valleys remote from human habitation were plentiful. Fergus of Galloway, his successor Roland, Reginald of the Isles, Hugh de Morville, Walter Fitzalan, the Earls of Mar and of Buchan were among the many landowners who endowed abbeys. Often they handed over parishes recently formed on their estates to some monastery as an endowment combined with responsibility. The Order of Tyron and various Orders of Regular Canons were popular as well as that of Cîteaux.

David I naturally supported this trend. Of all Scottish Kings, he did most to enlarge the influence of the monasteries. In some cases he introduced Cistercians to places where there had been earlier foundations, as at Melrose and Newbattle, elsewhere he gave them new sites. To Dunfermline, where his parents were buried, he made generous gifts; he granted Lesmahagow and Kelso to the Tironensians, Holyrood and Lochleven to the Augustinian Canons. All these he endowed with land and to many of them Anglo-Norman abbots were appointed. The old Culdee foundations David uprooted. He brought them to an end because to him they represented an unorthodox element of dissent.

The enrichment of the Church helped Scotland at the time, when Scotland was, as Ailred said, 'barbarous' for lack of Christian organization, 'untilled and barren' for lack of agriculture. Later generations suffered however. The King's domains were reduced by David I's generosity to the Church, and because of their diminished capital, his successors had to impose unpopular taxation. The parish churches were not always faithfully administered by those monasteries to whose care they had been entrusted, and as time passed, Church lands became more and more valuable. The temptation to misuse accumulated wealth later proved too much for both bishops and abbots.

The 12th century was a period when many little parish churches were built. They had solid stone walls, massive round pillars, tiny round-headed windows and arched doorways. They usually had no aisles, but consisted simply of a small nave and a smaller chancel, sometimes with a rounded eastern apse, sometimes with a western tower. At Leuchars and Dalmeny near Edinburgh are almost unspoiled examples of these smaller churches, at Muthill and Dunning in Perthshire fine western towers, and the little chapel in Edinburgh Castle attributed to Queen Margaret is also 12th century in origin. You can see fragments of Norman work still in a number of churches, for example Monymusk and Tyninghame, and in quite deserted places such as the Craignish peninsula you come across ruined remains showing the characteristics

David I

of this time, when stone was reserved for religious purposes and handled with loving care. Kirkwall and Dunfermline, larger and more splendid in design, show how Scottish craftsmen made this beautiful and dignified style of building their own. Perhaps the richest example of their ingenuity in decoration is the archway at Whithorn Priory, which is enfolded in layer upon layer of sculpture.

The renewed vitality of the Church in Europe at this time was shown in the enthusiasm for Crusading. Not so many people went from Scotland as from England because the population was limited, poverty-stricken and remote, but enough did for William of Malmesbury to note laconically: 'Then the Welshman gave up poaching and the Scot fraternising with fleas.'

Some of the most enthusiastic of the northern Crusaders were Orcadians. Earl Hakon went early in the 12th century and on his return built a round church at Orphir, of which unfortunately only the apse remains. Only five similar churches were built in the British Isles; a perfect example is still used for public worship in Cambridge.

Another famous Orcadian Crusader was Earl Rognvald. He set out in 1150, and was delayed by a snowstorm, from which he sheltered with his men in the sombre Megalithic tomb-chamber called Maes Howe, then some 3,000 years old. They rifled its contents and made doodles and drawings on its interior walls. To this day you can see their runes and their delicately executed emblems. Rognvald and his friends underwent acute strain in Maes Howe, as one of their number went mad there. They enjoyed the rest of their adventures however, espedially in France and Spain, where they made love and wrote love poems. They called at Crete, survived 'the tempestuous wind called Euroclydon', reached Acre, visited Jerusalem and bathed in the Jordan. They had little fighting to do as most of the Holy Places were now in the hands of Christian rulers. They came home by Constantinople and sailed up the Danube with all their sails spread before a beam-wind, to impress the local inhabitants on both sides of the river. When he got home, Rognvald built St. Magnus Cathedral in Kirkwall. It still stands, solid and dignified and beautiful, very much as his architects designed it. In the end Rognvald himself was canonized.

63

Interest in the Crusades lasted well into the 13th century. Walter Fitzalan went, and so did his brother John, who was killed at Damietta in 1249. Among others were the Earls of Atholl and Carrick, both of whom died abroad.

The 12th century renaissance in Europe found expression partly through the stimulus given to town life at this time. Kings and nobles in France, Germany and England favoured the growth of towns where men with goods for sale could gather and do their business.

Hitherto there had been little buying or selling in Scotland except through primitive forms of barter. David I tried to make a standard system of weights and measures for the encouragement of internal trading, and it is amusing to find that the inch was to be reckoned by setting three grains of bere end to end, or by measuring the width of the masculine thumb. Three men, it was said, were needed to get an average result—'a mekill man, and a man of measurable stater' and 'a lytil man'. The king also established two royal mints, one at Berwick, one at Roxburgh, to issue silver pennies, the first metal currency officially sanctioned in Scotland.

At least fourteen towns claim that they were originally granted burgh status by David, who enjoyed referring to 'my burghs' and stayed frequently in them on his journeys. Among the more important were Stirling, Perth, Dunfermline and Edinburgh.

A burgh enjoyed valuable rights, for its burgesses were granted freedom from tolls throughout the kingdom, they could hold markets and fairs at regular intervals, they had monopolies in the making of certain goods for sale, such as bread, beer, cloth, and they also had exclusive rights in the export of local products.

The opportunities thus opened up appealed to foreigners. Flemish wool merchants settled in burghs on or near the east coast, particularly in Berwick and Aberdeen, Anglo-Norman and French craftsmen made homes in various other burghs and the business they promoted improved prosperity. Commercial travellers also toured the fairs. Such was a Lincolnshire trader called Godric, who journeyed in England, France and Denmark, buying local products cheap and selling them elsewhere at higher prices. He came often to Scotland. His business career had an unusual climax, for he was so impressed with the traditions of the Northumbrian St. Cuthbert that he entered the religious life and was afterwards canonized.

In later years, the burghs became a hindrance to the nation's economic progress, because of their monopolies and restrictive practices, but in the 12th century they stimulated the accumulation of wealth. Although they were always defended by ramparts or palisades, they must have looked rural enough, as they had gardens and orchards within these walls, and their burgesses farmed the burgh fields outside. Unfortunately, being built of wood, the little towns were susceptible to people's carelessness and dreadful fires were frequent. In 1244, eight burghs were burned to ashes.

David's rule of nearly thirty years was on the whole peaceful. Three major controversies arose, all in connection with problems that remained unsolved for a long time.

The Archbishop of York wanted to control the new Scottish bishoprics and this provoked a long wrangle which lasted till 1192, when Pope Celestine III declared that the Scottish Church was to be directly subject to Rome. Even this ruling did not prevent later English archbishops from trying to interfere in Scotland.

Another perennial source of discord concerned Northumbria. This controversy became involved in a third and bigger cause of friction in 1135, when Henry I of England died. His son had been drowned in the English Channel, and the English throne was now claimed by his daughter Matilda, who had to contend with the rival claim of her cousin Stephen, son of William the Conqueror's daughter Adèle.

For David the affair was very awkward. Henry I had married his sister, Maud, and Henry's heiress was his niece. Stephen had married another niece also called Maud, daughter of David's sister Mary. Thus family relationships were much disturbed, and it was difficult to know which side to support.

In the event, David invaded England on behalf of Matilda, Henry's daughter. His forces captured a number of valuable castles, including Alnwick and Newcastle, but while this was going on, David's son was negotiating with Stephen under his father's instructions, so that the Scottish King had his foot in both camps. What did he really want? Undoubtedly Northumbria.

In 1138, David assembled a great army and prepared for an engagement at Cowton Moor in Yorkshire. The chroniclers set out the tradition that Robert de Brus and Bernard de Bailleul, both arrayed on the English side, came out to parley with David for the sake of peace. Moving speeches are recorded, in which the aged Brus pointed out that there were old friends on both sides and that David owed everything to the support of men he now proposed to slaughter. It was the first major occasion when the clash of loyalties became intolerable for men whose associations were strong on each side of the Border. It is said that David wept when he heard Brus speak. But he went on with the fight.

It is known in history as the Battle of the Standard, because the Archbishop of York lashed to a wagon a tall ship's mast, on which was elevated the Sacred Host and the banners of the patron saints. In David's army, the men of Galloway caused confusion at the eleventh hour because they insisted on their ancient right to lead the first attack, although they were unmailed. David had ample numbers of feudal knights and men-at-arms properly protected, but he gave in to the Galwegians. The result was described by Ailred: 'The southern flies swarmed forth from the caves of their quivers and flew like closest rain; and irksomely attacking the opponents' breasts, faces and eyes, very greatly impeded the attack.' An English historian put it differently: 'The Scots were preceded by actors, dancers and dancing girls, and we by the Cross of Christ and the relics of the saints.' The Galwegians wore the kilt—though not the tartan kilt we know—and it proved an inadequate battle-dress, despite the wild war-cries and leaping movements of its wearers.

Though David was defeated in this battle, he got what he wanted. His son's negotiations with Stephen were so successful that Northumbria was ceded as a fief and the Scottish frontier extended south to the Tees. When David died in 1153, Scotland was in a stronger position with regard to the state of the Border than ever again.

Critics analysing David's work from a modern point of view find fault with him, because of his Norman interests and his

David I

neglect of the Celtic and Gaelic background of his country. It is worth asking what Scotland needed in the 12th century and whether the tribal organization of the Celtic peoples could meet that need. There is no evidence that the Celtic way of life could promote law and order, business, peace, security or worship. These benefits were stimulated by David's feudal policies and they produced immediate results. Judged by the standards of European civilization in his day, David was a very great ruler, who vastly improved conditions of life for ordinary folk. Ailred's admiration for him was well-founded.

CHAPTER 6

A Time of Hope : The Thirteenth Century

David I lost his only son, Henry, the prince whom Ailred had missed so much. The crown therefore passed in 1153 to Henry's eldest boy, Malcolm, a child of eleven, but he survived only until 1165. He has followed by his brother, William, who reigned until 1214, and who was known as William the Lion.

During the sixty years of these two brothers, the controversy about Northumbria moved into a new stage; the Celtic lords of Galloway and Argyll tried to break free from the Scottish Kings; the burghs flourished and so did the Church. In the main, it was a time of peace and promise.

The year after Malcolm IV's accession, Henry II became King of England. He was powerful enough to insist that Northumbria should be restored to him, a loss which William the Lion deeply resented. William organized a grand invasion of England in 1174, a well-chosen moment when Henry was facing the consequences of Becket's murder and when the disloyalty of his sons was a dreadful humiliation for him. Henry must always have recollected William's invasion with pleasure however, for only a few hours after he had completed his humiliating penance at Canterbury, the Scottish King was captured at Alnwick. The thick east coast mist which helped the English on this occasion was regarded by them, and also by William himself, as evidence that God had forgiven the penitent Henry.

William was taken to Normandy, and there forced to accept the Treaty of Falaise. Scotland was laid under feudal subjection to England, the Scottish Church under the English Primate, Northumbria was confirmed as English territory, castles in southern Scotland were invested with English troops.

68

William was released after some months. He had to wait nearly fourteen years before events took a more promising turn for Scotland.

In 1192, Pope Celestine III made his pronouncement that the Scottish Church was to be directly under the jurisdiction of Rome, not under that of English archbishops. In 1189, Richard Cœur-de-Lion, desperate for money to finance his Crusade, ceded to William the castles surrendered in 1174 and renounced his feudal superiority in Scotland. In return William was to pay 10,000 marks. The fact that this sum could be raised shows that Scotland was growing wealthier, and aware of the value of freedom.

From 1174 until 1292, no warfare interrupted the peaceful relations between England and Scotland.

Meanwhile the Celtic chieftains took advantage of the setbacks suffered by the Scottish royal house. Three times Fergus, Lord of Galloway, rebelled against Malcolm, whose forces finally defeated him; royal officials then built castles in his territory and colonized the districts round them. Fergus, a great founder of monasteries, at last retired to Holyrood Abbey, and there died in 1161. His sons rebelled again, when William the Lion was Henry II's captive, and slaughtered the Anglo-Norman garrisons and colonists. When William the Lion returned to Scotland, he built, and fortified with castles, burghs at Ayr, Lanark and Dumfries upon which to base his defence against Galloway. It was a long time before this inaccessible and entirely Celtic province was pacified. The last of the old Celtic Lords was Alan of Galloway who died in 1234; he was succeeded by three daughters, all of whom became the wives of distinguished Anglo-Norman lords—Roger, Earl of Winchester, John Balliol of Barnard Castle and William, Earl of Aumale.

Argyll was the other centre of Celtic resistance. During Malcolm IV's reign, Somerled was its Lord, and he had Norse blood in his veins. He was never induced to accept the King's rule. In his last outbreak, he sailed up the Clyde in an effort to destroy Malcolm's power, but he was defeated and killed by the men of Walter Fitzalan, the Steward of Scotland and Lord of Renfrew. Norse influence always encouraged the native lords of Argyll to resist Scottish Kings, who had trouble to face from this quarter until the Norse rule was ended in 1263.

In spite of these conflicts with English kings and western chieftains, Scotland's prosperity developed while David's sons were on the throne. The well-trodden routes leading north over the Border still attracted southerners and foreigners who wanted to make good, and while some were ne'er-do-weels escaping from debt or disgrace, others were sound men. There was a considerable colony of Flemings, for example, who settled in upper Clydesdale; their names may be traced in the villages of Lamington, Symington, Thankerton, Wiston and others, all situated on rich farming land where their flocks of sheep contributed to the wool trade briskly pursued in the royal burghs. The monasteries already founded did not suffer from the barbarous warfare which afflicted them later on and their numbers increased throughout the final years of the 12th century.

Scotland enjoyed a stability in the 13th century which contrasted sharply with what was to happen later on. After William the Lion's death in 1214, his son and grandson, Alexander II and Alexander III, covered between them seventy-two years. Both were capable men, and the administration they inherited from David I was a good one.

Alexander II's reign was disturbed by rebellion in Galloway, Argyll, Moray and Caithness, but these outbreaks were crushed and they were the last major attempts by the remote regions to divorce themselves from the rest of Scotland. Alexander II wanted to regain Northumbria, but fortunately accepted a settlement of the controversy which proved permanent and which gave him five estates in northern England in compensation. This closed one source of war danger.

The kingdom Alexander II left to his son, the third Alexander, was full of promise. Although he died in mid-life when his heir was a child, there was no setback because the system of government was sound enough to survive a ruler's boyhood.

The second part of the 13th century was a brief but long-remembered golden age for Scotland. Medieval kingdoms needed above all else strong personalities to rule over them. Given long periods of continuous leadership by Kings of integrity, law and order could be maintained and normal life for ordinary people could be tolerable. In the mid-13th century, these conditions did obtain in Scotland and but for a few sharp and localized interruptions there was no warfare to wreck the nation's economy. Never again was Scotland independently to enjoy a similar stretch of years in which to build up prosperous and civilized ways of life.

Alexander III experienced only one threat to his kingdom, in 1263. In this year, the aged King Hakon of Norway brought a great Viking fleet south to punish Scotland for its encroachments into the Norse domains on the Hebrides. He delayed too long in the Orkneys and in Skye however, and Alexander III put off engaging battle until the October storms broke and did most of the work for him. Hakon's fleet, the largest host ever to have left Norway, was destroyed off Largs, with little loss on the Scottish side. Hakon died at Kirkwall on his way home. The Hebrides submitted to Scottish rule and Alexander III's daughter, Margaret, went to Norway as the bride of the new King, Eric.

Meantime Alexander was enjoying friendly relations with England. Henry III's daughter Margaret was his wife, and the two royal families respected each other and corresponded as amicably as any relatives could wish to do.

Statisticians judge from the meagre records available that the total population of the Scottish mainland at this time numbered only about 400,000, of whom far the majority lived south of the Highland line. Alexander's authority over this scattered and thinly spread population was exercised through sheriffs and justiciars, operating from the royal castles which were the centres of administration even in distant places like Cromarty, Dingwall, Inverness and Nairn. In 1264, the King's revenue from feudal dues and customs reached over £5,000, a sum five times larger than the same sources could produce forty years later.

Prosperity developed most of all in the burghs of the east. Berwick was described in 1266 by the chronicler of Lanercost as 'a city so populous and of such trade that it might justly be called another Alexandria, whose riches were the sea and the water its walls. In those days, its citizens being most wealthy and devout gave noble alms.' Norse writers confirm that Berwick was the richest Scottish town at this time, commanding control over much of the Baltic and north-European trade. Exports consisted mainly of wool, but included also furs, skins and salted fish: imports were wines, woven materials, spices and corn.

Burgh life was only one manifestation of increasing wealth. Much building was done in the 13th century. Between 1240 and 1249, the Bishop of St. Andrews consecrated 140 churches in various parts of the kingdom. This was a time when men wanted to create beauty to the glory of God and the symbolism of tall pillars and vaulted roofs was used to draw people's thoughts away from themselves and upwards to God. Even the ruins of Elgin Cathedral, now a wrecked skeleton, show that its proportions were as splendid in balance and scale as those of many continental buildings of the same period. At the cathedrals of Dunblane and Glasgow, you can see 13th century Scottish work at its best and almost unspoiled. The massive lines of these buildings do not show the slender grace of the contemporary Early English style, but their strength is expressed with reverence, their dignity is vigorous rather than solid; and there are subtle varieties in the structural design and in the sculpture which give light and fluency without the disturbance of over-decoration. Dornoch Cathedral is another 13th century work and there were many monasteries built at this time too—Pluscardine, Deer, Culross, Beauly, Sweetheart are among them.

Architects and craftsmen were employed in castle-building too, since barons wanted more durability in their strongholds than the wooden structures of David's day could provide. Instead of the old earthworks, stone walls were built round a new castle with towers to defend the entrances. The great keep within had immensely thick walls, with slits of windows which were shuttered but not glazed. The main hall on the first floor was larger than formerly, the staircases were indoors, the defence works more imposing, but living conditions must have been as damp and squalid as ever.

Personal calamities ultimately wrecked the happiness of Alexander III and brought disaster to his country. In 1275, his wife Margaret died; he lost a little boy in 1281; not long after, his daughter, the Queen of Norway died, and so did his eldest son. In an effort to stabilize the succession, he married again in 1285. The following year, when his young wife was staying at Kinghorn,

A Time of Hope: the Thirteenth Century

Alexander made a night journey from south of the Forth to see her. His horse slipped in the darkness. The great King was thrown over the cliffs and killed.

CHAPTER 7

A Time of Desolation

Alexander's death at the age of forty-five was a national disaster. Had he lived another twenty years, he could have guided his country through a time of acute danger from England. Had he been spared a prince to succeed him, that young man would have inherited not only the kingdom but probably also the fine qualities of an admirable family.

Six Guardians of the realm were appointed to carry on the government for Alexander's heiress, the three-year-old daughter of the Norwegian King. Almost immediately, Edward I of England suggested the little girl's betrothal to his own young son, and in 1290 a marriage treaty was signed at Brigham. Its carefully drawn terms show that Scottish barons understood the risks involved. Scotland was to remain a separate and independent kingdom, with its own Parliament and laws, Scots were not to do homage to an English King and if the Queen died childless a Scottish heir was to succeed her North of the Border.

Responsible Scotsmen respected Edward I, but they saw the iron hand slip out of the velvet glove for a moment when he suggested that castles in southern Scotland should be garrisoned by English troops. This they hotly refused. It was agreed, however, that the Queen should be brought up in Scotland; a ship was sent to fetch her and Edward offered a consignment of sweetmeats and raisins. Everybody felt satisfied except one old man, Robert de Brus, the sixth of the name, a descendant of William the Conqueror's knight.

This Brus, or Bruce, had been heir-presumptive in 1238, when it seemed that Alexander II's Queen would bear no children. The birth of Alexander III had been a personal disappointment for Bruce, the death of the great King had raised his hopes. But he had to content himself with being one of the Guardians and he reluctantly agreed to the Treaty of Brigham.

And then came the shattering news that the Queen had died on the journey from Norway.

Thirteen lords forthwith put forward claims to the Scottish throne. The two strongest were those of John Balliol and Robert Bruce, both descendants of David I's youngest son, of whom Balliol was great-grandson, and Bruce grandson. Balliol's grandmother had been the elder daughter, Bruce's mother the younger. By modern law, Balliol's was the better case, but medieval Scotland gave some weight to Bruce's closer proximity to David.

Both were powerful men. Balliol's father had owned half Galloway by his marriage to Devorguilla, daughter of Alan of Galloway, and by inheritance he had Border lands, thirty English manors and rich French properties. He had founded Balliol College in Oxford as an act of penance for assaulting the Bishop of Durham; his widow, Devorguilla, was the devoted and loving woman who founded Sweetheart Abbey in memory of her husband and who took more care than he to give his College a sound endowment. Their son John was a man to be reckoned with, especially after his sister married John Comyn, Lord of Badenoch and Guardian of the realm. The powerful Comyn interest always supported Balliol in the troubles that followed.

Robert Bruce, the former heir-presumptive, was Lord of Annandale. He too owned land in England, and he had married the daughter of the Earl of Gloucester. He had been Sheriff of Cumberland and governor of Carlisle and had often served on the English King's Bench. His son, the seventh Robert Bruce, married the widowed Countess of Carrick and so acquired her title and inheritance.

Balliol, Comyn and Bruce knew each other well and were all well-known to Edward I, because they frequently visited their English estates and because all three had fought for Edward and his father during de Montfort's civil war.

When the quarrel between Balliol and Bruce over the inheritance began, the Bishop of St. Andrews wrote to Edward I and begged him to come north at once and assist the Scottish barons to settle the matter. All the claimants seemed willing to let Edward decide for them, nor apparently did it occur to them that he might abuse his powers.

So Edward came and presided over the convention at Norham-on-Tweed in May 1291, a gathering attended by bishops and barons, and conducted with scrupulously judicial procedure. Twenty-four English and eighty Scottish auditors were appointed to scrutinize the claims. On November 17th, 1291, in the great hall of Berwick Castle, Edward announced the award to Balliol. Old Robert Bruce therefore laid upon his son, the seventh Robert, now Earl of Carrick, the duty of pursuing the family rights.

Edward began at this point to claim feudal superiority over Scotland. He insisted that Balliol should pay homage, proclaimed his right to hear appeals from Scotland, summoned Balliol to London to answer charges brought against him by his own subjects, demanded money contributions for English military projects and in 1294 ordered Balliol to join him with feudal vassals and hosts in an invasion of France.

What is the explanation of Edward's hardened attitude, his deliberate goading, his legal fictions invented to justify aggression? Edward concentrated the whole weight of his administrative and military machine upon the task of reducing Scotland to the condition of an English shire and an evil fever of hatred seemed to possess him. Perhaps he was corrupted by power, for he exercised enormous authority in England: possibly his bloody conquest of Wales had given him a lust for further military glory. Whatever the reason, from 1292 onwards his attitude towards Scotland was that of a dictator, insatiably hungry for domination. It was infinitely sad. For almost a hundred and thirty years no serious controversy had broken the peace between England and Scotland, but now future relationships were poisoned.

Balliol, exasperated beyond endurance, renounced his allegiance to Edward and in 1295 negotiated an alliance with France and prepared an invasion of north England. Balliol has been vilified by historians, and nicknamed Toom Tabard, Empty Coat, a man with the trappings but not the reality of kingship. Nonetheless, it was he who took this desperate initiative and launched the alliance with England's fiercest enemy, an alliance renewed by subsequent Scottish monarchs over a period of three hundred years.

Edward's agents always gave him prompt information about Balliol's activities. In good weather a mounted knight, travelling at speed, required about a fortnight to reach London from Berwick. Yet Edward almost always knew his enemy's movements ahead, in spite of the difficulties created by Scotland's forests, rivers, estuaries, bogs and horrible storms. Only two days after Balliol's army crossed the Border, Edward's entered Scotland, bent upon punitive revenge. This was in the spring of 1296.

The feudal barons in Scotland were now faced by an insoluble conflict of loyalties. Many were Edward's vassals because of large estates owned in England; they had no respect for Balliol; they had no experience of political controversy or what happens to countries in time of invasion: as yet, national feeling in western Europe was almost non-existent. Taken by surprise and confused, more than eighty met Edward at Wark Castle and gave him their homage as if he were the King of Scotland: amongst these were the seventh Robert Bruce, and his son the eighth Robert Bruce, who later became King. When Balliol heard this, he confiscated all the Bruce properties in Scotland and conferred them upon his brother-in-law, John Comyn.

From this moment onwards, the struggle in Scotland became a three-cornered one. Edward was fighting to bring Scotland under his direct control. The Balliol-Comyn interest was contested by the Bruces, and both of these powerful family groups believed that the downfall of the other would secure the throne for their own representative. Each therefore sought the policy best calculated to further personal advantage. Ordinary people did not understand the issue at all, but they soon learned to dread English authority. As for the Church, whose leaders were some of the most experienced and best-educated men in the country, its influence was at first paralysed because it was sharply divided. The Bishop of St. Andrews stood by Balliol, the Bishop of Glasgow by Bruce.

After he had received the homage of the nation's leaders at Wark, Edward moved with his great host to Berwick. This town's inhabitants, long accustomed to peaceful commerce and civilized business, simply did not believe that war was coming to them, and no preparations were made for defence until long past the last moment. The destruction of Berwick, carried out under Edward's instructions, was one of the most outrageous affairs he was ever responsible for. Many hundreds of people were slaughtered, including almost the entire Flemish colony, buildings were sacked, for days the licence of soldiers was unchecked. The horror of the whole affair made the deepest impression on Scotland. By this one preliminary action, Edward implanted that bitter hatred for all things English which was to be nourished so consistently by English policy during the next three hundred years.

Edward intended to rebuild Berwick as an English base and asked the citizens of London to select four skilful men who knew how to 'plan, order and lay out a new town'. Its commercial status was never recovered and Edinburgh became the principal trading centre for Scotland. The customs of Berwick, which, according to some historians, had totalled £2,000 in Alexander's day, yielded £120 by 1305.

The bloody affair at Berwick was followed by a military engagement at Dunbar, in which Edward's forces, considerably strengthened by contingents from Bruce and other Scottish lords, inflicted immense slaughter on Balliol's. John Balliol gave up his crown, and after three years in the Tower of London, retired to the family estates in France and died in 1313, a broken, forgotten failure.

From Dunbar, Edward proceeded on a triumphal tour through Scotland, taking possession of castles all the way from Roxburgh to Elgin and even further north. In August 1296, he returned to Berwick, where a massed act of allegiance was staged in which great numbers of Scots swore fealty to him. Many of their names are recorded in documents which still exist and are known as the Ragman Rolls. Some key nobles were taken south with Edward to serve in his French wars, but apart from these, it was proclaimed that no Scot was to leave the country. Quantities of charters and official records were confiscated and either destroyed or taken to London, along with what was believed to be the Stone of Destiny, upon which Scottish Kings had always been invested with their royal authority. The stone which Edward took was placed in Westminster Abbey, but some people think that he was duped and knew it. If so, the whereabouts of the real stone is still a matter of conjecture.

English officials were left to govern Scotland in Edward's name. English garrisons held every castle of importance. Edward was well satisfied and considered that the conquest of Scotland was complete.

In reality, it had not yet begun. So far the Scottish people had had no chance to organize themselves against the English incursion, nor indeed any special motive for doing so. The slaughters they experienced in 1296, the iron dictatorship established thereafter, the barbarity of the English garrisons, all these hardened Scottish national feeling. This change in the situation was masked by the jealousy between the Balliols and the Bruces, which delayed the nation's awakening, though the Comyn family was consistent throughout the worst years in its determination to drive the English out.

The first warning Edward had that all was not as he thought came with the news of William Wallace's sudden action at Stirling Bridge in 1297, when by excellent strategy perfectly carried out, the Scots annihilated a great English force. This isolated action led to little practical result, except a terrible renewal of Edward's punitive measures. Its significance was incalculable however. Wallace's army had included men from every part of the country, Galwegians, Highlanders, contingents from the north-east, and from central Scotland. It was an expression of national fury and its dramatic success proved to the Scots that the dreaded English were not insuperable. The importance of the affair may be gauged by the treatment given to Wallace when at last he was captured by Edward's agents in 1305. He was one of the first people to be tried as a traitor in the great hall at Westminster. All the medieval love of colour, drama and climax must have been gathered up in the setting of that scene, when Wallace was condemned to death by some of the most revolting barbarities known to medieval people.

The years 1298 to 1305 were some of the most miserable in Scottish history. While Edward's officials, agents and soldiers were in command everywhere, the Comyns did what they could to turn the tide, but resistance was always followed by fresh ravaging. In 1298, 1300, 1301 and 1302 and 1303, Edward sent his armies north for this purpose. Here and there, a well-provisioned castle held out for some months, as at Bothwell, which lasted for a year and nine weeks, and at Stirling, which was defended for three months. Always however it seemed that Edward's immense resources, and the thorough way in which he used them, must inevitably overcome Scottish endurance. His campaign in Galloway, for instance, was supplied from a fleet of sixty vessels, manned by 1500 men, based on Kirkcudbright. In 1303, he had two elaborate, fortified bridges constructed at King's Lynn, at a cost of over £1,000. Thirty ships carried them north, and they were assembled below Stirling, to enable the English forces to get across the Forth. For the siege of Roxburgh in 1303, between ten and twelve thousand men were mustered, including contingents from Ireland. Scotland's limited resources could not stand up to such large-scale organization, amply financed and administered by a nation five times her strength in population.

Much courageous resistance was organized by John, the Red Comyn, nephew of John Balliol and the accepted leader of the Balliol-Comyn faction. He considered himself the rightful heir to the throne and, with this in mind, he struggled on until 1304. But then he seemed to give up hope: he made his peace with Edward and became his liegeman.

Many others had done this during the bad years and Edward was diplomat enough to treat these high-ranking nobles with some generosity, and also to use them. The eighth Robert Bruce served him both as Governor of Carlisle and as Sheriff of Lanark, and his men were often conscripted to fight beside English soldiers. Edward's motive was to make it worth these men's while to yield. By 1305 it seemed as if Scottish resistance were spent.

The eighth Robert Bruce, now the head of his house, was restive however, despite his long record of service to Edward I. There are no records which reveal his thoughts and one can only guess at his motives, but it is known that from 1304 onwards he was in secret league with the Bishop of St. Andrews and others, waiting for the time when he could at last and finally renounce his feudal obligations to Edward I, assert himself against the Comyns and assume the crown which he believed should be his.

He asserted himself sooner than he intended and in a quite unpremeditated fashion. In February 1306, he and the Red Comyn and other nobles were in conference at Dumfries. An acute altercation arose, nobody can tell exactly how or why. In the physical violence that followed, Bruce killed the Red Comyn, in the sanctuary of the church at Dumfries.

Though Bruce almost certainly had no intention of such a shocking outcome to the old family feud, he instantly took what advantage he could of the situation. He went to Scone and there arranged the strangest coronation ceremony in recorded Scottish history. He was supported by four loyal younger brothers, by his very able nephew Thomas Randolph, by the Bishops of Glasgow, St. Andrews and Moray, and by a limited number of powerful nobles. In his favour were the facts that the Comyn family was practically ruined already, that Edward I was old and failing, that the young Edward of England was a foppish weakling.

His position was most unenviable. All Scotland was horrified by the sacrilegious nature of his crime. As soon as the news of it became known, Bruce and all connected with it were excommunicated. In a savage burst of fury, Edward I again gathered his forces to punish Scotland, with devastating success. Bruce was defeated at Methven and he became a hunted refugee. For months he was in hiding, in Kintail, in Kintyre, in an island off the Irish coast, possibly also in Orkney or even Norway. During these terrible months, three of his brothers were captured and executed, his wife, his young daughter and his two sisters taken prisoner, and some twenty of his principal supporters hanged.

Early in 1307, the tide turned. In the spring of that year a great band of Yorkshiremen and Borderers were slaughtered by Bruce's men in Glentrool. In May, Bruce won a bigger engagement at Loudon Hill. On July 7th, Edward I died.

CHAPTER 8

Robert Bruce

The new English King, Edward II, had no stomach for war. Perhaps he had sublimated his martial instincts by making a pet of a tame lion, which he took about with him on a collar and chain. He found the Scottish project dreary, and soon called it off, leaving the English garrisons to manage as best they might, seriously short of provisions.

From 1307 onwards, therefore, Bruce had a better chance. He first planned a campaign north of the Forth and Clyde, which took some time to complete. By summer 1309, only Dundee and Banff remained in English hands north of the Tay, only Perth, Stirling and Kirkintilloch between the Tay and the Forth-Clyde line. It took him rather longer to dislodge English influence from Galloway and Lothian, but by 1311 he was strong enough to invade England. The richest farmlands in Scotland had been disastrously harried by the English, Scottish monasteries and churches often desecrated, but from now on people living as far south as Appleby in Westmorland and Richmond in Yorkshire learned to dread the Scots as if they were agents of the Devil himself. This perpetual harrying of people who lived within striking distance of either side of the Borders was a *damnosa haereditas* for almost three centuries.

Bruce made a special point of destroying castles in his own country, for it was by means of these administrative strong points that the English power had been consolidated, and he wanted them permanently levelled to the ground.

His progress was hindered by the family feuds which had been nurtured by English interference. All Comyn's supporters, such as the Earl of Buchan, the Ross interest in northern Scotland, the men of Argyll and Lorne, the McDowalls of Galloway—these and many more hated Bruce worse than they hated Englishmen.

By slow stages, with pitiless disregard for the life and property of plain folk, Bruce beat these family factions down.

In 1313 Bruce captured Perth, Roxburgh and Edinburgh. In central Scotland, there remained only Stirling, which was still held by the English, though its defenders were now in desperate straits. Edward II at last bestirred himself for the relief of his troops within this almost impregnable fortress. Enormous supply trains and large engines of war were assembled on the old scale, far beyond anything that Bruce could rival. In 1314 the two armies met in an engagement which is probably better remembered in Scotland than any other in her history.

The success won by the Scots at Bannockburn, below Stirling, in 1314, was due to Bruce's superior generalship. His army was on higher ground than the English, who tried to advance over the almost water-logged stretches of land through which the Bannock-burn flowed. The heavily mailed, mounted knights found their horses collapsing under them because of the spiked pot-holes prepared by the Scots. Worse still, the English archers had no room for deployment. All battles between medieval English and Scottish armies were conditioned by the freedom with which the English could use their dreaded archery. The Scots never produced anything comparable to the English or Welsh bowman, against whom they had no adequate defence. But archers did need room to move freely. Bruce knew this, and chose his battle site in such a way that the English bowmen were virtually useless. Bannockburn was such an overwhelming triumph for the Scots that the English gave up all pretence of maintaining any hold in Scotland, and many Scotsmen hitherto disaffected from Bruce came over to his side.

The next objectives were Berwick and Carlisle, the two gateways for armies crossing the Border. Bruce organized large-scale attacks upon both, meeting with success at Berwick and complete failure at Carlisle. The two campaigns spread over several years and were supported by great invasions into Yorkshire and Westmorland. In 1320, Edward II tried another invasion of Scotland, but had to retreat, pursued by Bruce to Rievaulx. Edward's personal baggage and a number of distinguished people were captured and then, as Bain puts it, 'Bruce roamed

MAP 6.
THE WARS OF INDEPENDENCE

Elgin
Banff
R. Spey
R. Don
R. Dee
N. Esk
S. Esk
R. Tay
Scone
Dundee
Methven
Dupplin Moor
Perth
R. Forth
Stirling
Kinghorn
Dunbar
Bannockburn
Kirkintilloch
Linlithgow
Edinburgh
R. Clyde
Bothwell
Halidon Hill
Berwick
Norham-on-Tweed
Loudoun Hill
R. Tweed
Roxburgh
R. Nith
Otterburn
Glen Trool
Wark
Kirkcudbright
Dumfries
R. Tyne
Carlisle

Sites of battles other than those of towns......✗

0 10 20 40 60 80 100 Miles

0 10 20 40 60 80 100 160 Kilometres

freely about Yorkshire, taking ransoms from Ripon, Beverley and other places, and retired to his own country unmolested.'

At last, in 1327, the English were ready to negotiate. Edward II was deposed in that year by the evil partnership of his wife, Isabella, and a group of barons under Mortimer. Isabella and Mortimer agreed to a treaty signed in 1328 at Northampton. This document is still preserved in Edinburgh. It stated the English recognition of Scotland as an independent country and of Bruce as its King, with the provision that Scots who had supported the English interest during the wars were to be given back the lands Bruce had confiscated. As a guarantee of permanence, the treaty was supported by a device frequently used in the Middle Ages. The young Joanna, Edward II's daughter, was married to the five-year-old David, Robert Bruce's son and heir. Thus after thirty-six years of unprincipled scheming for each other's ruin, the royal families were to be united by the matrimony of two children.

During the years following 1306, and while he was battling through arduous military engagements and political negotiations, Bruce himself became a different person. Brought up as an Anglo-Norman baron, he had passed his earlier years like others of his social class, fulfilling as best he might both personal ambition and feudal obligation. In his younger days he apparently had no conception of Scotland as a national entity or of any responsibility towards his country and people. The extraordinary thing is that, from the day when he committed murder with sacrilege, Bruce began to see that he must create in Scotland a people united by loyalties greater than feudal bonds could promote. His idea of kingship steadily deepened as the years went by and as his experience of private grief and physical endurance became harsher.

The murder of Comyn which started Bruce on this most significant phase was a crime which Christendom could not forgive. Bruce's excommunication was continued and renewed. Nonetheless, he had the support of many Church leaders from the day of his coronation onwards. They called a gathering together in 1310, when by formal oath they bound themselves to his support, in defiance of Christendom's laws. The most remarkable evidence of the stiffening of public opinion in his favour however, was the meeting which took place at Arbroath in 1320. It was a gathering of barons and clergy, who produced a Declaration, or a formal letter, which they sent to the Pope, in the name of the nobles and of the Community of Scotland.

The Declaration explained that the people of Scotland were devoted to Robert, their King, that they would continue to resist Edward while even a hundred of them were alive, that freedom meant everything to them. 'We fight not for glory nor riches nor honour, but only for that liberty which no true man relinquishes but with his life'—'libertatem solummodo quam nemo bonus nisi simul cum vita amittet'. Of Robert they wrote: 'By the Providence of God, the right of succession, those laws and customs which we are resolved to defend even with our lives, and by our own just consent, he is our King.' The extraordinary statement continued with words of great interest, words designed perhaps to carry a hint of warning to Bruce's successors. 'Yet Robert himself, should he turn aside from the task he has begun, and yield Scotland or us to the English King or his people, we should cast out as the enemy of us all, as the subverter of our rights and of his own, and we should choose another King to defend our freedom.'

The forthright statement of Scottish devotion to freedom and the uncompromising assertion of the will of the community require some explanation. Whose was the initiative in calling such a meeting and in drafting such a document? It is clear that the author of the ringing words must have been a man of intellectual distinction. Probably it was Bernard, Abbot of Arbroath. At any rate the man who reduced a profound political philosophy to such splendidly rhythmic phrases knew his Sallust, because there are interesting parallels between some of the sentences in the Declaration and some in the *Catilene*.

The Declaration proves that Scottish national feeling, at least among some of the barons, was now aroused, and had been captured by Bruce. He had taken years to see what course to adopt in the complex circumstances of the times, but once he made the cause of Scottish national freedom his own, he evoked from certain of his people a loyalty and initiative of which this letter to the Pope is plain evidence.

86

There is so much to be guessed at in medieval history. Why is the original Declaration of Arbroath, with its many seals, still to this day in Scotland? Was it because of this document that the Pope annulled Robert's excommunication soon after 1320? Nobody knows.

One other gathering of Robert's reign must be described, the Parliament he held at Cambuskenneth in 1326. This is the first recorded occasion on which a Scottish King summoned clergy, barons and also representatives of the burghs to a Parliament. Two important matters were dealt with, one financial, the other political. A contribution of one-tenth on all rents was decided upon for Robert, to defray the expenses of government. To safeguard the succession, oaths of allegiance were paid to Robert's little son, David, with an additional vow of loyalty, in the event of his death without heirs, to the son of Margery Bruce. This Margery, a much-loved daughter of Robert, had married Walter Fitzalan, the Hereditary Steward of Scotland. He was known more briefly as Walter the Steward, or simply Walter Steward. The surname became Stewart, and Walter and Margery the founders of the future Scottish royal family.

Why was Robert concerning himself about the succession in 1326? Again we do not know—but by 1327 he was ill. The extreme hardships he had endured for so long, especially those of 1306, had probably taken their toll and Bruce was exposed like everybody else to diseases which 20th century Scotland never sees. He died in 1329—a leper, according to tradition. And his son was only six.

CHAPTER 9

Medieval Confusion

The strength of medieval kingdoms depended upon the strength of their rulers, for when the monarchy was weak, the barons could wage the private wars which were the curse of feudal societies. The Scottish barons degenerated into unprincipled opportunists once Bruce's strong hand was removed and they made full use of the English King's equally unprincipled opportunism. The result was decades of misery for ordinary people.

When Robert I died, Thomas Randolph, Earl of Moray, was made regent for David II. He was Bruce's nephew, a strong personality and a fine leader, steeped in the traditions built up by his King, but he flatly refused to carry out one part of Bruce's treaty with the English. It was more than he could stomach to restore large properties to Scotsmen who had collaborated with the Edwards, doing their utmost to bring ruin to Bruce. So the Disinherited, as they came to be called, angrily turned to Edward III for help.

Edward III resurrected the Balliol interest in the person of Edward, the son of Toom Tabard. After his coronation at Scone, this man paid homage for Scotland, as his father had done, and surrendered Edinburgh, Berwick and all the land between Linlithgow and the Solway; he even offered to marry Edward's sister Joanna, and 'to provide otherwise for her husband, David', a gallantry which was never carried out.

Moray, the only man who could have held Scotland together, died just when these troubles were beginning. There was now a dearth of able, vigorous patriots, partly because so many had been wiped out in earlier fighting. Resistance was made by Scottish armies, but under new and inferior generalship, by men who had neither the training nor the military scholarship needed.

88

They had not studied Bruce's principles of strategy. The English were supremely successful at the battles of Dupplin Moor and Halidon Hill, in 1332 and 1333, because their archery was allowed full scope for its destructive work.

The ugliest part of the whole business was that prominent Scottish barons and prelates changed sides without scruple, so that the English armies were assisted by men who had been the sworn vassals and trusted supporters of Robert I. The fine phrases of the Arbroath Declaration were forgotten and its lofty ideals passed out of men's minds. As for the young David and his adolescent wife, Joanna, they were sent to France for safe-keeping. The Bruce interests and the government of Scotland passed under the guardianship of another Robert, son of Walter the Steward and Margery, the old King's daughter.

Soon however, Edward III became absorbed in his prolonged adventures in France. This gave the more resentful Scottish nobles their opportunity, and from 1340 onwards many went to France and spent their lives and fortunes fighting against England in these opening phases of the Hundred Years' War. The alliance between France and Scotland drew some of the best Scots into this profitless way of life for nearly three centuries.

During the 1340s, however, there were Scots who bestirred themselves in their own country to regain some of the lost strongholds and displayed something of the old spirit. Perth, Stirling, and Edinburgh were recovered; at Dunbar, Black Agnes, the Earl of Moray's stalwart daughter, conducted a defence which has become one of Scotland's sagas of courage. In 1346, David II himself made an effort to wear the mantle of his father. He invaded England and carried out horrible acts of cruelty in defenceless villages, only to be defeated at Neville's Cross and captured by the English.

Scotland was now left in a state of anarchy. Edward Balliol's friends seized what they could get. Scots allied to English interests were stronger than anybody else. Once again, Robert the Steward, David's nephew, was faced with the task of administration, but he could not restore order.

David II remained in England for twelve years and greatly enjoyed his captivity. The court life of Edward III was more palatable to him than the work of kingship, and even when his release had been bought by an enormous ransom, he and Joanna liked to go back to England. No more of a patriot than Edward Balliol, he did not mind the fact that much of Scotland lay in English hands. Robert, the nephew upon whom so much of his own responsibility had fallen, he cordially hated.

David II's inglorious reign ended in 1371. He was followed by Robert the Steward, whom he disliked so much. This King, Robert II, was little more than a crowned noble and could not check the baron's lawlessness. Of this period, a contemporary wrote: 'In those days there was no law in Scotland; but the great man oppressed the poor man and the whole kingdom was one den of thieves. Slaughters, robberies, fire-raisings and other crimes went unpunished, and justice was sent into banishment, beyond the kingdom's bounds.'

Once, indeed, decisive action was taken by feudal leaders against the national enemy instead of against their own country-men, in 1388, when the Border Douglases invaded Northumber-land and defeated their opposite neighbours, the Percys, at Otterburn or Chevy Chase. The miseries inflicted during this campaign were long remembered in England, especially at Appleby which never recovered its former prosperity; even in 16th century records, references were made to the losses sustained by this little town in 1388.

Robert II had to face the task of producing David II's ransom, which was never fully paid and which caused endless wrangles with the English. In his efforts to raise it, Robert was obliged to increase customs duties and to levy taxes. The sanction he needed for such unpopular decisions he sought and gained from Parliament. His handling of this political institution was to have long-term results and needs some explanation.

Parliament was one of the great developments in medieval Western Europe. Meetings of responsible people were summoned in one form or another in most countries from Bohemia to Iceland, during the Middle Ages, to discuss and to settle public problems. The chief landowners and higher clergy were normally the only people summoned and medieval Parliaments were quite unlike any modern gathering of the same name.

Medieval Confusion

In England, Parliament became as nowhere else a political institution. Under Henry III, and still more under Edward I, it was made an integral part of the administrative system, meeting regularly to solve the problems of government and to supervise the dispensation of justice. Occasionally the lesser gentry and the wealthy burgesses were required to attend Parliament, mainly in order to discuss proposed taxation. By Edward III's reign, these knights and burgesses were invariably summoned and Parliament became a means whereby royal funds, and therefore royal policy, could in some measure be controlled by those who represented the richer classes of society. The process took many centuries to reach its culmination, but the English Parliament eventually assumed at least the forms of democratic government and could no longer be used as an instrument of royal or aristocratic authority. The share in its deliberations taken by wealthy commoners was a most important feature of this development.

The Scottish Parliament also grew out of the advisory Council which met under early medieval Kings for administrative and for judicial business and, as in England, it was attended by the chief lords and higher clergy. Robert I had summoned lesser gentry and burgesses to it in 1326, and Robert II continued this practice, because he was in desperate need of financial assistance. This the gentry and burgesses greatly resented, because a country with so small a population could not afford the loss of such people for weeks at a time from their normal work. Parliamentary authority was therefore delegated to committees, so that citizens might be spared the irritation of attending throughout the sessions. In this way, the Scottish Parliament was strangled, for legislation passed under the control of a small group of senior clerics and barons. In the 15th century, the delegation of powers was so carefully worked out that Scottish commoners never exerted any real influence in their Parliament, which was therefore dominated by feudal overlords.

When Robert II died in 1390, he was succeeded by his son John, Earl of Carrick, who disliked the unfortunate association connected with Kings called John, and therefore adopted the name Robert III. This Robert was lamed by a horse's kick in 1385 and never became physically fit again, so he depended much, as his father the second Robert had done, upon the help of his brother, the Duke of Albany.

Robert III decided that his heir, Prince James, should be sent to France for safety against English interference and a ship from Danzig was chartered in 1406 to fetch the little boy from Bass Rock. The captain was set upon by pirates from the Norfolk coast, who seized the prince and sent him to the English court: and, only a month later, Robert III died. Eighteen years, all his boyhood and youth, James spent in England, while the Duke of Albany and his son, Murdoch, acted as Regents. All his life James believed that from personal ambition these two neglected negotiations for his release and he never forgave them.

The latter part of the 14th century was a time when ordinary people in Scotland had to face a bitter daily struggle for existence. Their troubles were due partly to the social organization of the country, partly to economic conditions, partly to the degeneracy of the Church. The lack of effective political leadership naturally enabled rogues of many varieties to ride roughshod over other people.

There were great families which managed to consolidate their estates and to build up kingdoms within the kingdom. Such were the Douglases, descended from Robert I's fine supporter, the good Sir James, but later tainted by their preference for the Balliol interest. The head of the family became Warden of the Marshes and Lord of Galloway, appointments of immense importance, awarded by David II, with cynical disregard of Douglas disloyalty. In 1358, the family's Earldom was created. By a series of well-planned marriages, the Earls of Douglas acquired the lands of other great lords, and two of them married into the royal family. At the end of the 14th century, the fourth Earl, Robert III's son-in-law, was a dangerous rival to the King, with an accumulation of properties sprawling over Galloway, Douglasdale, Annandale, Clydesdale, Lothian, Stirlingshire and Moray.

Meantime, an almost autonomous kingdom was developing in the Isles, whose people had always followed a separate way of life. In this, they were supported by West Highland interests. The Lords of Argyll and Lorne had been Bruce's deadly enemies and although Highlanders and Islesmen had fought for the King at Bannockburn, no tradition of loyalty was built up. The Lord of the Isles had supported Edward Balliol and had refused outright to contribute to David II's ransom.

This was the period when the clan system became more clearly defined. Its origins of course were very much earlier and are not to be found in written records, which date only from about the end of the 14th century. The clan was composed of closely interrelated family groups, all owing loyalty to a chieftain whose authority was unassailable. During the Middle Ages, chieftains established judicial procedures in their own courts by traditional rights which passed from father to son. They dealt summarily with criminal and civil cases, without reference to Sheriffs or other royal officials; their decisions were anything but impartial, since it was considered a matter of honour to avenge all injuries to the life or property of the family in no matter what circumstances. Vicious punishments were carried out, including death by execution and by drowning.

The chieftains identified themselves with their people and knew many of them individually and the clans held together as social units, giving their members a certain sense of community. But the chieftains maintained interminable vendettas against each other, in the interests of which they called out their clans for prolonged and bloody wars, Organized cattle-raiding and wife-stealing were accompanied by murder, betrayal and cruelty, so that for centuries tragedy was inseparable from the daily lives of people who inhabited one of the most exquisitely beautiful regions of Europe.

The clansmen lived in miserable conditions even during the uncertain spells of peacetime. Autumn gales destroyed on average every fourth harvest, the soil was either sour and thin, or else water-logged. The patches of primitive bere and oats which were cultivated could be ruined by raiders from other glens, and the scraggy cattle were always in danger of being stolen, especially in summer when they were pastured high up in the hills. Families lived in long, low-built huts, made on the Scandinavian model. The walls were piled up with stones and pebbles held together by mud, the roofs were heather thatch, there were neither windows nor chimneys, so the peat-smoke hung about day and night. Draught was excluded better than one might think by five-foot-thick walls; but damp and filth were unavoidable, especially in winter, when animals shared the dwellings with their owners. To all other smells was added the acrid odour of stale manure which was saved up to be spread over the little fields. The limited gear and equipment needed for such a way of life were home-made, even to the plough, an instrument of ancient design, known to historians as the caschrom. Caschrom means crooked foot, and the instrument had a single curved metal blade at the end of a long wooden shaft. It was really a glorified spade and the ploughman himself dug into the soil with it by pressing his foot on a small pedal above the blade: he moved backwards as he drove his furrow, a slow laborious progress which made for limited husbandry.

South of the Highland line, agriculture was still based on the ancient run-rig system. The land round a group of dwellings was divided into two parts, the infield close at hand on the more fertile ground of the valley or the lower hill slopes, the outfield further off and higher up. The infield was divided into rigs, or strips, which ran up and down the hillsides across the contours, separated by unploughed lines known as balks. On the infield was bestowed all the manure collected during the winter months and it was ploughed by an enormous, locally made contraption of unwieldy bulk, which needed several oxen to work it in relays. The rigs were shared out among the people, re-allotted at short intervals, sometimes every second year, and they were planted with bere or oats, season after season. It was a case of perpetual tillage under communal ownership, a state of affairs unlikely to stimulate initiative or farming skill. The outfield was used for pasture, except once in a decade or so when a portion of it would be put under cultivation for a couple of seasons; and it too was communally held.

There was nothing in Scotland comparable to the English manorial system, which enabled a class of copyholders to emerge, men who had recognized rights in the land which could be defended in the law courts. Scottish tenants could be ejected at short notice by their feudal superiors and often were. Their insecurity was the worse because they had no recognized rights to common land; so that whereas English villagers enjoyed the use of a common on which to pasture their beasts, Scottish peasants had to drive them to the more remote outfield or the mountain glens.

In a country whose people lived at such a low level of prosperity, disease ran a terrible course. Leprosy, plague, agues and bowel complaints, illnesses of a loathsome nature unknown nowadays in western Europe, took toll of life in a way we can hardly imagine. Plague found its way north of the Border amongst the booty and prisoners captured on more than one Scottish invasion of England; it is believed to have killed a third of Scotland's people in the 14th century; it ruthlessly penetrated the dirt-infested houses all through the 15th and 16th centuries, often coinciding with famine. The last recorded outbreak in Aberdeen was in 1648.

From the infection of leprosy, plague and the rest, wealthier people were by no means free. The more spacious castles with open court-yards of the 13th century had been destroyed under Bruce's instructions, and 14th century lords lived in squat, solid keeps which were square-built, almost innocent of drainage, and so congested that there was personal privacy for nobody. Physical well-being as we know it could not be maintained in any rank of society.

The 14th century was of course a period when all western Europe was afflicted by civil wars, plague, poverty, hardship. That conditions in general were worse in Scotland than elsewhere seems however apparent. The French historian of the day, Froissart, puts revealing words into the mouth of French knights sent to Scotland in 1385: 'What could have brought us hither? We have never known till now what was meant by poverty and hard living.'

The influence of the Church counted for little. Statutes passed by a reforming synod of St. Andrews towards the end of the period show why. Excommunication was threatened against people who practised any out of a comprehensive list of sins—coin-clipping, perjury, sacrilege, witchcraft, laying unwanted babies at church doors, violence against parents or ecclesiastical persons. The laymen thus warned were set a poor example by their priests. The same synod decreed that rectors were to stop living with women, they were to reside in their benefices and neither to engage in secular business nor to accept fees for saying masses.

Clergy were degenerate and they had little chance of being different. It was almost impossible to secure an education beyond the most perfunctory teaching by rote of liturgical routine. Some young men found their way to Oxford, others to France, where there was an endowment instituted by the Bishop of Moray to keep four poor scholars from his diocese at Paris University. On the whole, however, the clergy were an ignorant and depraved lot, and they were given no encouragement by their leaders to be otherwise. Bishops and abbots were often soldiers by choice and by habit, as indeed they had to be when armed attack was so common. Many fine buildings were wrecked in warfare and not always by alien hands. In 1390, for example, Elgin Cathedral was burnt out by 'wyld, wykkyd, Heland men' under the Earl of Buchan, a lord known to contemporaries as the Wolf of Badenoch. Private wars between barons caused much damage to church buildings and English armies on the Borders constantly desecrated such monasteries as Melrose, Jedburgh, Kelso and others that lay on their route. It was impossible for religion to flourish in such conditions.

In England, Wyclif's influence by this time had set men thinking and the Lollard movement he founded anticipated the Reformation in some ways. The Lollards reached Scotland too, though not in any great number; the first of their martyrs, an Englishman named Resby, was burned, by order of the Scottish government in 1407, an ugly omen of much that was to follow.

The high promise of the 12th and 13th centuries came to no fulfilment because of the disasters following Alexander III's death. Scotland desperately needed the chance to revive and rebuild and only a strong King could provide it. The chance came when at long last, in 1424, James I rode north, a free man.

CHAPTER 10

The Fifteenth Century

This chapter and the following one describe changes which influenced the lives of ordinary Scottish people for some three hundred years.

The 15th century opened in unpromising circumstances, for during the absence of James I in England, the great lords made unprincipled use of their opportunities to consolidate their own strength. There were other setbacks in the middle years of the century because James I, James II, and James III all died prematurely, but important traditions in local and parliamentary government were established: later on, James IV's vigorous leadership stimulated a new resilience among his people. A most unfortunate feature of the period, the last phase of unchallenged Catholicism, was the prolonged stagnation in religious affairs, at the very time when the leaders of the old Church could have done much to safeguard their principles and build up their spiritual resources.

James I spent a restless youth, fretting over his captivity, hating his lack of means to keep a decent wardrobe, fuming over the Albanys' reluctance to arrange his return; but Henry IV saw to it that he was educated, both in literary and knightly pursuits. The prince's lively mind and flair for poetry gave him a means of escape from his cramping circumstances and he was probably more widely read than any previous Scottish King. He took part in most of the great court occasions and accumulated much information about English institutions. He also kept in touch with Scottish developments, of which three must have especially excited him.

The first was a rebellion organized by Donald, Lord of the Isles. He wanted to seize the Earldom of Ross, and thus extend his authority over most of the northern mainland. Henry IV, who nurtured every dissension in Scotland, gave Donald promise of support, though being a cautious man, he offered him little else. The Earl's forces swept across towards Aberdeen, and were defeated at Harlaw in 1411 by the Earl of Mar, the Provost of Aberdeen and the Frasers. The battle was an incident in a mighty clan conflict, but its significance was national. Had Donald succeeded, Scotland would have been divided into two kingdoms.

The year 1411 was marked by a second event of national importance. Bishop Wardlaw founded St. Andrews University. It was a tiny institution and it passed through difficult times but it gave Scottish boys the chance of having some education in Canon Law and Theology before going abroad to French or Italian Universities.

James experienced personally the effects of a third development. In 1419, when Rouen was captured by Henry V, the French appealed to Scotland for armed assistance, and some six or seven thousand men were accordingly sent over. Henry decided that James had better come to France in person, hoping that the Scots might be persuaded by their prisoner-King's presence in the English army to go home. James did not take the nature of his mission very seriously, but he found the experience of English army life abroad exhilarating. He was impressed by the handling of siege engines and the use of archery, which he could now observe from an angle unusual to Scotsmen. He fretted more than ever when he returned to England. Some grim satisfaction he must have derived from the news of Scots' activities in France, for they fought along with the armies of Joan of Arc on behalf of the French King, and at Beaugé, in 1421, Scottish arms turned the tide. During the 15th century, the Scots Guards became famous for their services in France and drew many useful young men away from their own country. French soldiers and peasants, who did not much like their protagonists, termed them 'sacs à vin' and 'mangeurs de mouton'.

After Henry V's death in 1422, serious negotiations were set afoot for the release of James. Again, a crippling ransom was demanded, and a truce was agreed, which should have stemmed the tide of Scottish reinforcements to France. James returned to

The Fifteenth Century

Scotland in the highest spirits in 1424, the happier at this happiest moment of his life because he had with him Lady Joan Beaufort, whom he married for love, an unusual experience for a medieval King. He expressed his feelings about this in a poem called *The Kingis Quair*. He was unlike other monarchs too in his idealism, which he summed in words now famous: 'If God give me but the life of a dog, I will make the key keep the castle and the bracken-bush the cow.'

It was not easy for him. For almost a century, the Scots Lords had known no strong monarch: and they had been most ill-advisedly bribed by the weak Stewart Kings with enormous grants from royal properties, so that by 1424 crown lands had been reduced to relatively small proportions.

James I lost no time. He had hardly returned before the Duke of Albany was arrested to stand trial before Parliament, for treasonable neglect during the regency. On the eve of this trial, Albany's son instigated an unfortunate revolt which was soon crushed, but which hardened opinion against his father. Albany, his father-in-law and his two sons were all executed and the family properties annexed to the crown.

James followed up his ferocious beginning by enforcement of the rule of law. Even his most important subjects were punished for resisting it, and the powerful Earl of Douglas was imprisoned in 1428. James penetrated the north and west as no earlier King had dared and he recovered some of the lost crown lands. He also confiscated a number of wealth-bearing properties, especially in the Lowlands.

In order to raise his ransom, James instituted some unfamiliar financial measures. The whole kingdom was assessed for taxation with an efficiency which omitted no moneyed class, customs duties were increased, the export of gold and silver stopped. Everybody groused about it and James himself grudged sending instalments of his hard-earned resources to England, theoretically in payment of expenses incurred during his imprisonment, though he had been kept so short of necessities. The taxation lapsed and so did the payments, but James continued to extract money by every other means he could think of and he also borrowed it from his richer subjects.

Within his first year, James summoned Parliament and presented it with a legislative programme designed to improve economic conditions and defence measures. No detail was too small for his attention. Salmon-fishing in the close season was prohibited, rooks and wolves were to be destroyed, peas and beans cultivated, corn marigolds weeded out of the fields. Football and poaching were forbidden, hostelries were to be built in the burghs, prices were fixed, even clothing was regulated to prevent extravagance by the citizens. Scotsmen have always resented this kind of interference with private affairs, and although all these measures would have improved the general standard of living, they were neglected and James had not sufficient executive power to insist that they should be carried out. His instructions that sheriffs should inspect people's arms and enforce regular practice, especially in archery, would also have been good for the country had they been effective.

It was offensive to James to discover that Parliament was overloaded with judicial work which should long since have been disposed of. The sheriff courts and the courts of the travelling justices were giving no satisfaction; because Parliament was the highest court of appeal, all sorts of complaints were being laid before it and left unsettled from one session to another. It took the King no time at all to decide that the traditional methods of securing justice in civil disputes were inadequate and early in his reign he made Parliament legislate about the matter. 'Certane discret personis of the thre estatis' were to be chosen, nine in all, to sit under a Chancellor three times a year and 'know, examyn, conclude and finally determyne all and sundry complayntis'. This was the origin of the Court of Session. Of course it did not meet regularly as James had hoped. It was another of his excellent ideas, one which ultimately materialized, but not during his lifetime. Much later, in the 16th century, the College of Justice evolved from his Court.

Unlike some of his contemporaries, James was moved to discover that some people were too poor to pay for actions at law; he had a statute passed that for the love of God, any 'pur creatur' so placed was to be given the help of 'a lele and a wys advocate', a poor man's lawyer in fact.

The Fifteenth Century

Religious matters were also much in James I's thoughts. Benedictine and Augustinian foundations in Scotland were ordered to reform their ways and to carry out the regulations of monastic life. To reduce the interference of Rome he tried to make it illegal to purchase benefices from the Pope, and it would have been well if this had succeeded, because the Pope's traffic in ecclesiastical appointments did much harm to the Scottish Church during the one century now left before the crisis of the Reformation. Already signs of restlessness were appearing which contemporaries could not interpret but which are significant to the historian. Heresy was shocking to James, whose legislation sanctioned its punishment by burning, and a Bohemian called Paul Crawar suffered this torture in 1433 at St. Andrews, later the scene of many similar executions.

Altogether, James worked Parliament hard. He would have liked to create a House of Commons, such as he had seen in action in England, as this would have helped him in standing up to the barons. It would also have enabled the Scottish Parliament to become gradually more representative of national feeling and to give the country a more democratic constitution.

Already, however, tradition had hardened against any such development and James was dismayed by the reluctance of any but feudal overlords and high-ranking clerics to attend. He tried to encourage as many free landowners as possible to come, but the feudal background was too strong for him. In 1248, therefore, it was arranged that tenants-in-chief were to be personally summoned by writ, and were to come, but lesser freeholders were to be excused if they appointed two commissioners from each shire to represent them: and only the royal burghs were entitled to choose members to speak for townsfolk. Even this was not fully implemented and later a Committee was formed, whose members became known as Lords of the Articles. This committee did all the real work of initiating and drafting legislation, so that Parliament itself became an institution which merely ratified the decisions of an executive council, and its members often had only the haziest idea of what they were sanctioning. As it continued to meet in one assembly, the few burgesses and commoners who

101

were there had little chance of expressing opinions contrary to those of the great lords. So Parliament excited little interest in Scotland, until the end of the 17th century when reforms made it much more effective.

For thirteen years, James worked to achieve his ideals, with superb confidence and small concern for the many people he offended. In this comparatively short time, he went a long way towards making the key and the bracken-bush more reliable custodians of property.

He also built up the prestige of royal authority, at the expense of much else, for James exasperated many whom he had also humiliated and people were angered by his personal extravagance. When Linlithgow Palace was burnt out in 1424, the King spent over £2,000 rebuilding it on a splendid scale although at that very time he was legislating for heavy taxation. He dressed magnificently, spent freely on himself and his family, apparently with no idea that he could be in any personal danger. Horrible vengeance came in 1437, when Sir Robert Graham burst into the presence of James and his Queen, and murdered him. By this crime, Scotland lost the strong leadership the country had needed so long and once more the wrangles of unscrupulous family groups bedevilled the country's affairs.

The Earl of Douglas was made regent for James II, who was only seven. In addition to the French lordships of Touraine and Longueville, Douglas owned more estates in Scotland than anybody and it seemed possible that he might establish supreme control, but he died in 1439, leaving two young sons. Their implacable enemy was the Earl of Crichton. It was Crichton who became the King's guardian and he rejoiced in his chance to break the hated Douglas power. By a thoughtfully planned and brutally exercised plot he had the young Earl and his brother murdered at a dinner-party: the little King saw how it was done, and remembered. The great Douglas estates were divided up, but the eighth Earl, a cousin of the murdered boys, set himself to consolidate them again. In 1452, James II, now nearly twenty-three, himself stabbed and killed this rival to his own power and the house of Douglas never recovered its influence. The violent way in which it was humbled reveals 15th century morality at its worst, but for James II it meant increased security, since no comparable family group could threaten his position.

During the mid-15th century, England was suffering from the baronial feuds which flared up into the Wars of the Roses, so English invasions abated, and in Scotland town life had a chance to revive. New burghs were founded, known as burghs of barony. They were not entitled to send representatives to Parliament, and they were never given any trade monopoly nor were they allowed to share in export and import trade. They could however hold markets and fairs and their burgesses began to make money.

Within the burghs, a new class of society began to emerge, the craftsmen. Their Incorporated Associations gradually became powerful enough to rival the older Merchant Gilds. The craftsman was a specialist, skilled in making shoes, saddles, garments, household gear or implements of various kinds. The merchant did international business, selling raw materials and buying foreign wares wholesale at such centres as Bruges and Middelburg. The craftsmen, who lived by manual skill, were regarded by the merchants as socially inferior, nouveaux riches, and every effort was made by the merchants to exclude them from office on the burgh councils. In 1469 an act was passed to prevent the 'gret truble and contentione', the 'clamour' of 'sympil persons', which occurred in open elections. Retiring councillors were now to choose the new ones, so that local government fell into the hands of small but powerful family groups. Burgh representatives to Parliament were chosen exclusively from the councils and these families therefore exercised a most undemocratic influence on national as well as municipal affairs. The effect of this unfortunate act was the more damaging because the only burghs which enjoyed even this restricted franchise were those holding royal charters. One of the strangest features in Scottish constitutional history is that this defect was not dealt with until the 19th century, so that for nearly four hundred years townsmen were inadequately represented in Parliament.

The burghs were very small. In the mid-15th century Glasgow had about 1,500 inhabitants; in the early 16th Aberdeen had less than 3,000. Most houses were still made of timber, and the narrow streets were always dirty because of the middens which people piled up at their doors. Tiny as the communities were, they jealously guarded all their rights and so villages were prevented from holding markets and fairs, and village crafts and industries were discouraged, to the great disadvantage of the country as a whole. Not until the 17th century did people realize that trade and industry were a national concern which should be liberated from medieval privilege and parochialism, and even then this idea was strenuously opposed by the burghs.

Landowners in the 15th century interested themselves in making their homes more comfortable. Experience in the French wars had given many of them new ideas about architecture and they began to enlarge their castles. Courtyards were added, with defensive towers at the corners and additional sets of buildings surrounded these courtyards, which therefore formed quadrangles. So more domestic apartments were provided, kitchen quarters became more spacious, banqueting halls larger: and as windows were at last designed to admit light, family life must have become more comfortable. James III employed an unpopular Scottish friend of his to build him a magnificent hall in Stirling Castle, which you can still see. French masons designed the royal apartments there and they were among the first to bring Renaissance ideas of architecture into Scotland. But defence against enemies was still the main purpose of castle-building, even though artillery had by now made large stone-built establishments less secure than in earlier days.

While richer men's homes were more spacious, fittings and furniture were still of the simplest. In the hall, the dining-table was a trestle, removed at night, so that servants could sleep on the floor. Only the service-table by the wall would be a fixture. There were no carpets or cupboards; one oak chair would be placed at the head of the table for the lord, everybody else sat on backless benches or stools. People ate off wooden trenchers or pewter, men carried their own knives, forks were hardly known; good manners demanded that food should be carried to the mouth with two fingers and a thumb only, and not in fistfuls.

In Scotland, neither burgesses nor landowners accumulated riches on the scale of the English wool merchants, in fact wealth was concentrated in the great monastic estates. Many of these, and especially the Cistercian ones, were managed better than those of any lay landlord in the period. Records of Cupar Abbey, for example, show that its great properties were drained, fertilized and cropped by methods which ensured excellent harvest, and the Cupar monks also developed something akin to ley-farming, a six-year rotation of crops designed to produce first-class grassland. Many monasteries planted orchards and herb gardens too.

It seemed as if the monasteries possessed almost unlimited means, but 15th century developments made this wealth largely illusory. The ecclesiastical dues extracted from Scotland by Rome became steadily heavier. In 1483, Arbroath had to pay 3,000 gold crowns to buy the Pope's confirmation of their newly elected Abbot, and this kind of thing reduced the Church to desperate straits at a time when Scottish Kings were learning fresh ways of extracting cash grants from religious foundations. By the end of the 15th century Abbots, and Bishops too, were beginning to feu large properties in an effort to balance their accounts. Feuing was a form of heritable land tenure based on a fixed rent, but though the feus brought the Church an immediate income, the cost of living was rising steeply and so the value of the fixed rents soon became nominal. Historians living in the 16th century all agreed that the Church was alienated from the people by its riches, and this was the common opinion, but the fact was that its capital assets were steadily dwindling.

That there were enlightened religious leaders at this time is proved by the history of Scotland's universities. Bishop Turnbull founded Glasgow University in 1451, and his Cathedral was closely involved in its progress for many years. The previous year St. Salvator's College in St. Andrews was set up, a residential centre of corporate life which afforded its students many advantages. Its founder was Bishop Kennedy of St. Andrews, a man of ability and patriotism who gave the Church excellent leadership. In 1495, Aberdeen University was established by another great churchman, Bishop Elphinstone. These three fine men were however exceptional and on the whole the leading ecclesiastics did nothing to stem the abuses which were becoming flagrant in church life.

When James II took over the direction of affairs in the 1450s, he proved to be a man of some energy. Ambitious to drive the English out of Roxburgh and Berwick, their last two strongholds in Scotland, he took a personal interest in the military preparations, particularly in a new type of cannon which was to be used at Roxburgh. The ill-luck which dogged the Stewart family now appeared again in a ghastly accident. The machine exploded while James was examining it and he was killed on the spot, in 1460, his thirtieth year. Roxburgh was taken by the Scots a few days later and destroyed to the point of obliteration. Berwick was also regained by the Scots, but in 1482 the English captured it again and it has remained English territory ever since.

Bishop Kennedy of St. Andrews, a real statesmen and a strong personality, became regent for the nine-year-old James III, but he died in 1465. During his few years in office, Kennedy negotiated successfully with the English who had now reached a critical stage in the Wars of the Roses, so that both sides wanted peace on the Border.

James III grew into a man whom 15th century people could not understand. He was a poor horseman, he was bored by athletic pursuits, disgusted by warfare, unsuccessful in knightly skills. He preferred his own company to that of other people, avoided men of noble birth, made friends with musicians and interested himself in architecture and necromancy. One interesting political achievement he did carry through in 1470, when he exchanged royal estates in Fife for the islands of Orkney and Shetland and thus became Earl of Orkney. This was confirmed by the Scottish Parliament in 1472, and these remote places became legally part of Scotland. The year 1472 saw the fulfilment of another semi-political success when the Pope made St. Andrews a metropolitan see, which freed Scotland at last from the interference of English Archbishops.

James III's nobles became alienated by his morose, suspicious nature and his tactless ways. They unscrupulously captured the sympathy of his young heir, who was about fifteen, and organized a revolt in 1488. During the rout of his troops from Sauchieburn, James III's horse bolted. The King was thrown to the ground. An unknown, but possibly priestly hand stabbed him as he lay helpless in the kitchen of a local miller's wife.

CHAPTER 11

James IV

People who knew James IV personally, even those who did business with him by correspondence, were always impressed by him. He had phenomenal energy of mind and body, an infectious zest for the enjoyments of life, an invigorating approach to everything. The great scholar Erasmus, who tutored one of his many illegitimate sons, mustered an imposing sequence of superlatives. 'He had a wonderful force of intellect, an incredible knowledge of all things, an invincible magnanimity, the sublimity of a royal heart, the largest charity and the most profuse liberality. There was no virtue which became a prince, in which he did not so excel as to gain the praise even of his enemies.' Pedro De Ayala, for several years Spanish Ambassador in Scotland, knew the King better than Erasmus and understood his faults, partly no doubt because they spent many long dark evenings playing cards together. But De Ayala had good things to say about him too. He admired the physical courage of the King, his self-confidence, his willingness to hear what his Council had to advise and then to make his own decisions. De Ayala was amazed at James IV's regularity in worship, his habit of fasting twice or three times a week; he was impressed also by his consistently moderate appetite for food and drink in the midst of a gluttonous society, and by his facility in picking up foreign languages.

James IV was certainly the most popular King Scotland had had for a long time and also the best known to his subjects. His extraordinary restlessness has been recorded by many writers. There seemed no limit to his energy. A fortnight here, two or three days there, a weekend somewhere else and then a prolonged journey to the far North and back to where he originally started from—this kind of programme constituted his normal way of life.

Everywhere he went, he had time and interest for ordinary people, he talked to everybody and was easy to approach, he enormously enjoyed all forms of sport, he loved horses and dogs, and he spent freely. His habitual extravagance and personal ostentation appealed to the people of his day, who liked him for his love of fine clothes and jewels and gear, as well as for the generosity he showed to such an unusual degree. The kitchen boy who broke his leg, the beggar woman on the roadside, the blind man 'be the gait', the man whose corn was trampled down by the royal horses, the sailor who fell from the rigging—these and many more received money gifts from him and all appear in the records of his personal expenses. His pleasure in dancing, in dicing, in playing cards, in watching guisers and taking part in all kinds of recreation endeared him to people too. That he founded a large family of illegitimate children and constantly sought and enjoyed the company of his mistresses seems to have been taken as understandable and perhaps even as another point in his favour.

For all his enjoyment, sensual, aesthetic and personal, the King could never rid himself of a devastating sense of guilt for his father's death. Though James IV had not actually killed him, James III's tragedy had been due in part to his son's collaboration with traitors. The prayers and pilgrimages and penances which impressed people so much were probably all carried out because of this sense of guilt, and the King's almost abnormal search for diversions and his distaste for relaxation may have stemmed from the same thing. All his life he wore a metal belt under his clothing to remind him of his shame.

The celebrations which took place at James IV's wedding in 1503 show what he could do when he really meant to stage a splendid show and they made an enormous impression at the time. The bride was Margaret Tudor, daughter of England's King, Henry VII. The marriage of course had its political significance, as the long preliminaries in negotiation and the carefully worded treaty show. It was to ensure for Scotland and England 'a good, real, sincere, true, entire and firm peace, bond, league and confederation on land and sea, to endure for ever'. Special clauses made new safeguards for the peaceful control of the

Borders. The Pope's sanction was invoked and whichever King broke his vows was to be excommunicated.

James rode out to meet his bride in splendid state and showed her dramatic gallantry. He accompanied her on the last leg of the journey into Edinburgh where money had flowed unceasingly in the preparation of pageantry, music, decoration, feasting and general jollification. Hundreds of pounds had gone to the King's own wedding garments and to those of his pages, thousands more to purveyors of food and wine, masons, builders, armourers, jewellers, joiners, minstrels, players and many more. Cloth of gold seemed to be in plentiful supply in Scotland that year, and at one of the royal feasts the menu included some sixty dishes, of which roast swan was one.

At the wedding itself, the King wore a white damask gown, crimson sleeves in his jacket, a cloth of gold doublet, scarlet hose. The crimson was taken up in the velvet border and lining of the Queen's robe, her train was carried by the Countess of Surrey, she wore her long hair loose under a rich coif and a little gold crown, specially made for her in Edinburgh by John Currour from eighty-three Treasury coins.

The modern reader cannot help feeling some sympathy for Margaret Tudor, then only thirteen years old, facing life in a strange country fully fifteen days' uncomfortable travel from home, with a man seventeen years her senior, already experienced in sexual relations, and reluctant to part with his mistresses. As time went by, however, she proved herself a true sister of Henry VIII, a virago of a woman, well able to impose her wishes on the people with whom she had to do.

The King perhaps understood that Margaret was bound to be frightened and homesick. He let her sit on the arm of his chair because she found her allotted stool too low, he had the walls plastered in the palaces at Stirling and Holyrood, he was patient about her luggage—twenty-four carts were required to carry her dresses on one occasion from Linlithgow to Edinburgh. Quite soon however, thirteen-year-old Margaret was writing to her father to complain that she was not being sufficiently considered, because her husband and his advisers were overriding her wishes.

The Queen generally stayed in or near Edinburgh, which now became the accepted capital, and James often made it the headquarters from which he set out on his interminable journeys to and fro in his kingdom. Margaret's share in these journeys was necessarily hindered after a while by her child-bearing. Between 1507 and 1514, she gave birth to six children, of whom only the future James V survived infancy. How lonely and disillusioned did these experiences make her feel? We do not know.

Music was a necessity to James. When he travelled, he sometimes sent Currie the Court Fool ahead, but journeying with him, he invariably had an odd collection of guisers, bards and Italian musicians. These accompanied him even when he was on pilgrimage to St. Ninian's shrine at Whithorn or to St. Duthac's at Tain. He played the lute himself, and the court baggage always included lyres, pipes, stringed instruments, and sometimes even a collapsible organ, which was actually hauled over the Mounth and re-assembled at the King's destination. One can safely guess that James enjoyed the songs which people sang in the fields and steadings. R. L. Mackie quotes some of their titles in *James IV of Scotland* (1958)—'Broom, broom on hill', 'The Frog cam to the Mill Door', 'Be yon woodside' and 'Late, late on evenings'.

James took an interest in religious music too. He endowed his Chapel Royal with sixteen canons and 'as many prebends skilled in song, with six boy clerics . . . trained in song or fit to be instructed therein'. The Royal Musical Association published in 1957 *Music of Scotland* 1500-1700. In this, a collection of 16th century choral and instrumental works has been assembled. It includes religious music, composed by Robert Carver of Scone in 1508, in a style described as 'massive yet vigorous'. James must have known Carver and listened to his works.

The King enjoyed poetry as well as music and this was a pleasure shared by many of his subjects. It was stimulated by local minor poets, of whose work little now remains in identifiable form, and also by some who have become famous. The best known are Robert Henryson, Gavin Douglas and William Dunbar.

Robert Henryson lived in the last part of the 15th century and died when James IV was still a young man. He wrote poems, ballads, metrical forms of Aesop's Fables, and a longer work

110

called *The Testament of Cresseid*, designed as a sequel to Chaucer's *Troilus and Criseyde*. People liked his work for its vivid, rhythmic lines, its good, earthy vernacular and its undertones of melancholy. Henryson's narrative poems were full of chivalry and drama and they appealed to men and women whose lives offered little that was romantic. Like many Scots, he was fond of pointing the moral and some of his versified fables had a topical reference. His best gift was perhaps descriptive. Country scenes familiar to rural people, country folk, animals, birds, stand out in lyrical but pointed phrases, touched both with humour and with pity. His understanding, his capacity indeed for identifying himself with other people, sometimes stirred him to write poetry of the highest quality. R. L. Mackie says of his *Testament* that there are passages in it 'that Chaucer would have been proud to call his own', which in fact Chaucer could not have bettered. But though Henryson's work may have something of Chaucer's quality, it is necessarily different in character, for Henryson was born and nurtured in Scotland: and so his poetry reflects the mind and emotions of a people Chaucer never knew.

Gavin Douglas was a son of the Earl of Angus and he became Bishop of Dunkeld. He was more of a scholar than Henryson. He too wrote allegories, but they were long and involved and too heavily moral in tone to appeal to most readers; they are redeemed by his gift of description, especially of natural scenery, though even this was often devoted to wintry, shadowed beauty. Douglas undertook the astonishing task of translating Vergil's *Aeneid* into Scots verse, and here he was breaking new ground, for no Scottish writer had attempted such a thing before.

The most prolific writer in James IV's day was William Dunbar, known in contemporary English society as 'The Rhymer of Scotland', a sort of Poet Laureate really, for he had an annual pension from the King, which he himself considered very niggardly. In his poems, Dunbar described many of the great occasions of the day, tournaments, city functions, the royal wedding, the Queen's visit to Aberdeen. He also wrote about the King's illicit love affairs, about the merchants of Edinburgh, about James Dog, the Keeper of the Queen's Wardrobe and Currie the Court

Fool. Like the others, Dunbar loved allegory and, in the elaborate poem called *The Golden Targe*, he described a dream, in which he witnessed the triumph of Love in a conflict with Reason. *The Lament for the Makars*, an elegy, pays tribute to poets such as Blind Harry, Shaw, Kennedy and some forgotten authors whose works have been lost. 'Timor mortis conturbat me' was the sobering refrain of this lament, which invited its readers to grieve over the shadows closing round us all. There is a strange undercurrent of religion in some of Dunbar's work, a religion relieved by little hope, rather perhaps an obsession with death than a confidence in redemption. He wrote humorous and satirical verse too however and at times descended with lusty enjoyment to the bawdy. He had none of Henryson's gift of pity, except for himself and his own grievances.

Modern readers are bound to have difficulty in understanding the poetry of this time, written in archaic language and expressing the contemporary mood. You get the impression that people lived under a cloud, of which they were not always consciously aware. Storm, rain, cold evening shadows, the flight of bats, sombre though often majestic manifestations of natural beauty, seemed to focus men's attention more than the sunlit uplands. Were they afraid? If so, what did they fear? Of joyous gaiety, of contemplative poetry there was apparently little. Nonetheless, these writers opened a new world to their contemporaries and secular literature began to count for something at last.

De Ayala was impressed by the King's love of reading and by his knowledge of Latin, French, German, Flemish, Italian and Spanish. R. L. Mackie suggests that James had a nodding acquaintance rather than real knowledge of these languages, and that, while he bought books from time to time, there is not much evidence of his reading them frequently. Nonetheless, James was interested in literature and he could not fail to be attracted to the new printing technique, known in London since 1476. Two burgesses of Edinburgh, Walter Chapman and Andrew Myllar, were granted a patent by James IV in 1507, to establish a printing press operated with movable metal types, the first of its kind in Scotland. The King thought it would be useful for the printing of statutes, mass-books and chronicles. So indeed it was. The Church and the Universities were almost immediately able to secure better supplies of professional literature.

But the introduction of printing was far more important than the King could guess. Now, for the first time, relatively cheap books could be produced quickly. The printers at once realized that they could command a market far exceeding clerical or academic limits if they catered for other interests as well. Printing made a more significant and immediate effect on popular thought than any modern invention prior to radio. It brought to Scotland ideas profoundly exciting and disturbing. Ten years after Chapman and Myllar began printing Dunbar's poems, Luther made his explosive protest against Indulgences, and the Reformation began. Its work was done in the printers' establishments quite as much as in the pulpits, for books were now produced so that they could be read by the many rather than looked at by the few.

Under different circumstances James IV would have enjoyed the new vitality of Renaissance writers and he was enthusiastic about Bishop Elphinstone's university at Aberdeen. As he pointed out to Pope Alexander VI, people in northern Scotland lived too far away from St. Andrews and Glasgow to make proper use of them for their sons' education. He was delighted when King's College, named in honour of himself, was built in Aberdeen: its first principal, Hector Boece, knew Erasmus and was in sympathy with the new Greek studies of the day, though he did not succeed in revitalizing Scottish students or their teachers.

In the early 16th century, European and English Universities were much influenced by the humanism of the Renaissance scholars, such as Erasmus, Colet, Melancthon. 'Literae humaniores' constituted a study of the best Greek and Roman classics in the original text and not in bad translations. The new humanists tested long-accepted ideas by examining afresh all the available evidence, and they thought of the old-fashioned schoolmen with much the same impatience that certain schools of scientists have recently adopted towards defenders of a classical education.

This enjoyment of classical literature, with its stimulus to bold thinking, informed criticism and fluent, beautiful writing, unfortunately hardly touched the Scottish Universities. Here the traditional disciplines of the Middle Ages were carried on, although their vitality was now outworn. Medieval scholasticism, based on logic, had afforded genuine intellectual life to the best minds of the 13th and even 14th centuries, but it had degenerated into a pointless and sterile system by this time.

The most renowned Scottish scholar in the early decades of the 16th century was probably John Major, a man of massive learning, who wrote the old, pedantic Latin and enjoyed the fruitless logical disputations of former years. Of him, Melancthon wrote with a venomous exasperation which still rings across the centuries: 'He is now, I am told, the Prince of Paris divines. Good Heavens! What wagonloads of trifling! What pages he fills with disputes whether there can be any horsemanship without a horse, whether the sea was salt when God made it.'

For seventeen years in the mid-16th century, Major was Provost of St. Salvator's College in St. Andrews, upholding the outworn ideals of the past and resisting ideas of his age both in religion and in learning. *The History of Scotland* which he wrote is a work of great interest as it reflects so clearly the attitude of its author and the climate of thought in which he lived. It can be read in an English translation published by the Scottish Historical Society. Not all his statements may be taken at their face value, emphatic and vivid as many of them are.

James was determined that the three Scottish Universities should serve the country in a practical way, rather than continue as training centres exclusively for professional ecclesiastics, because he believed that if the sons of the nobility were properly educated, responsible secular officials would do their work more effectively. As early as 1496, he had a statute passed by which the eldest sons of all freeholders were to be sent to grammar schools and thereafter to a university, a most original measure, unprecedented in a country where literacy had been almost confined to the church. Perhaps because so many boys arrived on their doorsteps at the early age of thirteen or fourteen, the universities developed the unfortunate system called regenting.

James IV

By this, one master or regent saw a whole generation of students through the entire academic course of several years. This had the advantage of giving wild adolescents continuous handling by one man who knew them well, but it prevented specialization, limited original research and made for uninspired teaching. It continued in the Scottish Universities until the 18th century.

During James IV's reign, life became easier and conditions better. The ledgers of Andrew Halyburton, a prosperous Scottish merchant, illustrate this. At Middelburg and other European centres, Halyburton bought damasks, silks, velvets, writing-paper, feather beds and pillows, jewels, tombstones, carts, wheelbarrows, groceries, especially spice, olives, figs, almonds and raisins. In return, he exported the traditional products, namely hides, wool, furs, and salted fish. Europe was still Roman Catholic and consumed quantities of red herrings and similar fare during the frequent fasts, and people were still so exposed to furious winter winds that much clothing was made of leather and fur.

Halyburton's books reveal important facts. Scotland was unable to make at home goods which a well-developed country should have produced: she had no skills with which to manu facture articles for export: her balance of trade depended on raw materials of a primitive kind which foreigners could make into saleable articles. It is significant too that most of his imported luxuries were bought by ecclesiastical dignitaries and not by Scottish nobles or burgesses.

What these 15th century ledgers do not reveal is probably more significant than anything else. Where trade moves, ideas move. Not only the men of business themselves, but also their servants must have observed strange ways and talked of this and that in the cities of Europe. A new vitality of thought began to develop in Scotland among people who had had little formal education.

There were however no wealthy cities with capital to spare, no citizens rich enough to patronize the arts. This is one reason why the Renaissance did not influence Scotland so much as other European countries. There seems little evidence that Scotsmen of this period were interested in painting. Even James IV seems neither to have sought out artists nor to have bought their pictures.

But Scotsmen were interested in architecture. Now that methods of warfare had changed, the old solid towers and keeps were not so easily defensible and their discomforts therefore became intolerable. Men who had travelled realized that the new culture had material as well as aesthetic merits, with its emphasis on the individual's right to enjoy being himself, a person entitled to dignity, beauty and even some physical comfort in his surroundings. So nobles enlarged the living apartments in their older castles, sometimes by adding new wings, sometimes by ingeniously exploiting upper storeys. New buildings were more generously constructed, with finely decorated exterior façades, imposing outer doorways and larger windows, while indoor rooms were designed to dignified proportions, and fitted with large ornamental fireplaces. Much of Linlithgow Palace as you see it today dates from this period and the same is true of Falkland Palace. Many other castles were also partially rebuilt, Craigmillar for example, Huntley, Caerlaverock, Crichton, to mention only a few. French designs in structure and decoration were still sought after, but Scottish craftsmen were not enslaved to them. Their work was conditioned by the nature and site of the buildings they worked on, each with its individual character.

De Ayala, writing home to Ferdinand and Isabella, said that Scottish people lived in stone-built houses with glazed windows, that they burned coal in their hearths, had fine collections of continental furniture, and cultivated charming gardens. Susceptible to ladies' fashions, De Ayala specially admired the headdresses worn by Scottish women, the handsomest in all Europe. As he mixed only with court society and knew little about districts beyond central Scotland, we need not interpret his comments too generally, but he recorded accurately enough a rising standard of living in the south-east. On what it was based remains something of a mystery. De Ayala himself noted the deficiencies in Scottish husbandry, which on the whole failed to extract as much from the soil as should have been possible, except on some of the Cistercian properties. The burghs were still pursuing their traditional policies which tended to restrict rather

116

than to enlarge trade. There is room for much research still into this field, for it is clear that the King and his nobles could not have spent money so freely as they did if there had been no solid foundation to the nation's economy.

James' interests were not confined to cultural and recreative activities. He made courageous efforts to reduce the country to law and order. These indeed were needed in a land where it was possible for David Drummond to organize in 1490 the burning of a Strathearn church packed with his personal enemies. Drummond was executed, and so were a number of other trouble-makers. In the Border regions, disorder was continual and James established courts at Dumfries and elsewhere, with instructions that marauders were to be brought to trial and hanged.

He took more active measures in the Highlands and Islands than any of his predecessors, and actually made journeys in person right into the heart of this wild, uncivilized country, whose language, surprisingly, he could himself speak. No other medieval Scottish ruler is believed to have had the Gaelic. James abolished the Lordship of the Isles and forfeited to the crown all the properties of the fourth and last man to hold this title. He repaired and strengthened castles in key positions, such as Tarbert and Urquhart, he built new ones, at Loch Kilkerran and Inverlochy: these were to serve as bases for the administration of law and order. He revised the arrangements about Sheriffs and Sheriff Courts, increasing their number, so that the west and north-west should be adequately covered for judicial purposes. He used his fleet to intimidate those who disliked all this interference and he made a point of showing friendship towards as many Highland chiefs as he could, while sanctioning merciless punishment of those who were unruly.

His energetic and bold attempts, unequalled by his predecessors, did little permanent good. The Highlands were too inaccessible for any medieval King to bring them under control. The Highland line continued, therefore, as a frontier between two peoples who lived completely apart from each other and who developed quite different traditions. James IV has been criticized as 'ineffective' because he failed to make his writ run permanently in the Highlands and Islands. This seems hard criticism, as no

Government really succeeded in this difficult assignment until the second half of the 18th century.

What was James IV's measure as a political thinker or leader? He was sound enough in his efforts to control the uncontrollable within his own realms, but he seems to have had little discrimination when he came to consider political relationships with other countries. He believed Perkin Warbeck to be a genuine claimant for the English throne and risked a major war with England in 1497 with the purpose of dethroning Henry VII. Mercifully, war on the grand scale at this time was averted, though not because of any good sense on James IV's part. A later enthusiasm was to go on Crusade against the Infidel Turk, an out-dated ambition, which suggests that James' abnormal boyhood had prevented him from becoming fully adult in his approach to European problems. He was perfectly serious in his desire to go Crusading and it was with this in mind that he built his famous fleet. Wood was felled on Loch Lomondside, especially at Luss, and also throughout Fife, and it was bought from Norway and France. Seacoast towns were ordered to build twenty-ton vessels and James took a personal and furiously energetic interest in the whole business. The ship which gave him the greatest pleasure of all was the *Great Michael*. James told the English ambassador that she carried more weapons than the French ever brought to a siege, a remark which the Englishman considered 'a great crack'.

Some of James IV's admirals and sea-captains were of the first order. Sir Andrew Wood, who commanded *The Flower* and *The Yellow Carvel*, served James until he was an old man, always with distinction. There were three seafaring brothers who were equally celebrated—Andrew, Robert and John Barton—sons of a fine sea-captain who was ultimately taken prisoner by the Portuguese. They all carried out punitive measures against English pirates, also against Dutch and Portuguese marauders, and themselves indulged in a good deal of fairly successful piracy. At no period in medieval history did Scotland's maritime strength reach such a pitch as under James IV's direction.

The end of James IV and all that he stood for is the saddest story in all the tragic history of medieval Scotland. In 1511, almost all western Europe joined in a Holy League under the Pope and against France. Henry VIII, James' brilliant young brother-in-law, a king of immense promise at this time, joined the Holy League. Because of the long alliance between his own country and France, James decided, against the advice of some of his best counsellors, to take active part on behalf of the French: he hoped too that victory in this campaign would help him later in his Crusading plans. It ended in the horror of Flodden Field in 1513. James was killed in action, with thirteen Scottish earls, two bishops, two abbots, the dean of Glasgow, the provost of Edinburgh and thousands of Scotland's best young men of all ranks.

Since 1295, Scotland had known no reasonably long period unbroken by warfare. Repeated efforts had been made to secure peace by the negotiation of royal marriages; Malcolm III, his daughter Maud or Matilda, Alexander II, Alexander III, David II and James IV all married members of the English royal family. David I and James I married distinguished ladies of the English nobility, James II married Edward IV's widow and the Maid of Norway was betrothed to Edward I's son before her early death. In spite of these marriage treaties, the two countries fought each other unmercifully, and the wars, which afflicted the least prosperous part of England, wrecked the towns, villages, monasteries and farmlands of the districts most vital to Scotland's well-being. They also killed many of the best leaders and finest young men of a country so limited in population that such personalities were greatly needed and hard to replace. And they left Scotland with a deadly hatred for England.

Almost more essential to a medieval kingdom than consistent peace was the continuity of strong authority on the throne. It is startling to count up the protracted royal minorities which crippled the power of medieval Scottish monarchy. Malcolm IV was eleven when he came to the throne; Alexander III, eight; the Maid of Norway three; David II six; James I eleven; James II seven; James III eight. James IV was fifteen, by comparison quite a mature young man, but when he was killed at Flodden in 1513, James V was a baby a year old and this James died less than a week after the birth of his daughter and heiress, Mary. She became famous as Mary, Queen of Scots, and she was forced to abdicate when her son, James VI, was not yet two.

During the years between 1286 and 1513, there were therefore only brief intervals when an adult King of any strength was on the Scottish throne. So the great baronial families were able to pursue their selfish race for personal aggrandizement and grievously to retard Scotland's development. When the 16th century opened, Scotland was quite unprepared for the impact of the religious revolution which swept Europe, or for the redoubled efforts of England to reduce her to servitude. She was still a feudal country, with only a tiny middle class, and a limited share in international trade. Worse still, she had only the beginnings of a national culture, Renaissance thought had made little impact on her Universities, most of her people were illiterate, her religious leaders were corrupt, her constitutional machinery was controlled by vested interests.

The plain truth is that Scotland was about three-quarters of a century behind the times. In England, parliamentary institutions and local government by the early 1500s had given the lesser gentry and the leading burgesses some experience of responsibility, town life had prospered sufficiently to produce an influential middle class, feudal controls had been curbed by the economic changes of the 14th century.

Had James IV lived to bring up his son himself and to consolidate the improvements he had set going in his kingdom, Scotland's experience in the next hundred years might have been vastly better. The battle of Flodden was the worst tragedy the nation had known since Alexander III's sudden death.

PART TWO

The Reformation and the Covenant

CHAPTER 12

Religious and Political Turmoil

During the early 16th century, Protestantism was born and the Roman Catholic Church met the challenge. Luther's Theses against indulgences were published in 1517, Zwingli founded his Reformed Church in Switzerland during the 1520s, Calvin produced his *Institutes of the Christian Religion* in 1536. By 1541, Ignatius Loyola secured the Pope's recognition for his Society of Jesus and four years later the Council of Trent began a long campaign to strengthen the Roman Catholic position. Rivalry between the old and the new religions plunged all Western Europe into bitter controversy.

Nowhere in Europe was the Church so degraded as in Scotland. In 1549 and 1552, the Scottish Bishops held reforming Councils in a belated effort to set their house in order, and these openly admitted that the root of heresy had been 'the corruption of morals and profane lewdness of life in churchmen of almost all ranks, together with crass ignorance of literature and of all the liberal arts'. Archibald Hay, a relative of Beaton's, warned him that clergy were being ordained 'who hardly knew the order of the alphabet' and that priests 'come to the heavenly table who have not slept off last night's debauch'.

The priests knew Latin sufficiently to hurry through their offices by rote, but many of them could hardly repeat the Lord's Prayer or the Creed intelligibly. The dignity of worship which the ancient liturgies had been designed to foster could not exist in churches without educated or even reverent clergy, without choirs, without instructed worshippers. Churchgoers were observers of mangled rites which neither they nor the celebrants understood, they took no part in response, in prayer or in singing. So people went to Mass reluctantly or not at all.

The leaders of the Church were not fit to handle the situation. They blatantly ignored the rule of priestly celibacy, and this undermined their influence. Bishop Hepburn, 'the great dilapidator of the See of Moray', had nine children for whom he provided at the expense of the Church, and almost all his colleagues founded illegitimate families too. They were following the royal example in this.

James IV had several illegitimate sons. One of them, Alexander Stewart, he made Archbishop of St. Andrews at the age of twelve. This boy was also Abbot of Dunfermline and Prior of Coldingham. The properties which went with these appointments were held for him *in commendam*, a form of trust much in use, which gave the commendators all the financial advantages and none of the responsibilities attached to clerical life. Barons and bishops secured valuable properties *in commendam* for their protégés too, and the system encouraged pluralism. It became common for one cleric to hold several benefices simultaneously and to put in curates to do the work. These were some of Archibald Hay's men who scarcely knew the order of the alphabet.

Monastic communities were now very small. In the early 16th century, Melrose numbered twenty-three, Kinloss twenty, and these were comparatively high figures. Abbot Thomas Crystall of Kinloss was in fact a fine man, who had high ideals and improved the standards of his house. He was however an exception. Most abbots and priors were primarily concerned with economic problems and spiritually the monasteries were lax.

It was difficult for religious institutions to uphold the disciplines for which they had been founded, and it was also difficult for them to administer their properties wisely. In order to raise ready money which it badly needed, the Church let out its estates by feuing, and so bore all the odium of capitalism without retaining its advantages, since the rents steadily depreciated in value. At the same time, the Pope sanctioned heavy ecclesiastical subsidies to the Scottish crown. A corrupt State therefore became indebted to a corrupt Church and there remained no supreme authority untainted by abuse.

Religious leaders economized on current expenditure by neglecting to repair their buildings. All over the country, church walls crumbled and roofs leaked. By 1512 the little Cathedral on Lismore had become so ruinous that James IV suggested the See of Argyll should be moved elsewhere. Many other examples could be quoted. Protestant zeal of the wrong kind has been blamed for the destruction of many Scottish churches which had begun to collapse long before the new religion was known.

Ordinary people could not understand that the financial position of the Church was fundamentally unsound when they saw how some clerics lived. Adam Colquhoun, parson of Stobo, represented a type of priest who did untold harm. He lived with his two sons and their mother in luxurious comfort. His house in Glasgow was stocked with expensive furniture, feather beds, velvet, damask and silken hangings, gold and silver valuables, magnificent suits of clothes, armour and archery outfits, his kitchen with quantities of preserved meat, fish, groceries and wine. Besides being a collector of silver plate, he was a connoisseur in up-to-date novelties. He possessed the first cupboard recorded in Scotland, a striking clock, a set of Flemish carving knives, a fork, a silver toothpick and in his bedroom he had a parrot in a cage. When Colquhoun died, in 1542, his nephew claimed the inheritance, but in the legal case which followed, Adam's sons were formally legitimated, and they secured his entire fortune.

This was a time when plain people in country and town were living in poverty, when a bad harvest or an epidemic brought not hardship but starvation. Though Colquhoun's wealth was exceptional, many priests had private establishments where they brought up their children more comfortably than their parishioners could and it made for cynicism and embitterment among the laity. Most parish priests however were very poor, because they received only a pittance from the monastic houses or cathedrals which had appropriated the parishes and which absorbed most of the tithes and other revenues for other purposes. One effect of such poverty was that ordinary priests were often very ignorant, with the unfortunate result that the Church was weakest precisely where it ought to have been strongest—at the parochial level where it was most in touch with the people.

The inevitable consequences of a royal minority created harmful complications. After the débâcle of Flodden in 1513, intrigues among the nobles were fomented by James IV's unscrupulous widow, Margaret Tudor. The young James V was given no sound upbringing and in childhood was exposed to evil influences. In young manhood he thought himself a sincere Catholic, but he had an irresponsible attitude to religion and scant regard for integrity.

Sincere religious people were at a loss to know where to turn for the leadership they needed. It was the tragedy of the Church that it could not offer some of its best members the spiritual direction they were seeking. And there was a strong desire for purer spiritual teaching, for genuine worship at this time, as if, despite all the corruption they had seen and all the faulty teaching they had received, people had a spontaneous and natural hunger for religious truth.

Many of them found what they wanted in the Bible. This had not been studied in a scholarly way or used in personal devotions for hundreds of years. Within a decade of James IV's death in 1513, Scotsmen were eagerly absorbing it in a language they could understand. At first, a 14th century Wycliffite translation was used, with the archaic words altered by a Scot called Murdoch Nisbet. Much more easily assimilated however was the translation secretly printed at Worms in 1525, by the Englishman, William Tyndale. The Scottish Parliament made it illegal to handle this publication, but in spite of this Bibles were smuggled into the country.

One of the earliest leaders in the new Protestant movement of Scotland was a great-grandson of James II, a young man of much personal charm, named Patrick Hamilton. He met Lutherans in Paris and in Marburg and returned to St. Andrews in 1527, an active supporter of the new doctrines. He was the author of a little commentary, known as *Patrick's Places*. Like Tyndale's Bible, it became a best-seller.

Lutheran teaching therefore made its impact upon Scotland largely through print. Those who could read found refreshment of spirit in the beautiful prose of Tyndale's translation and in Patrick Hamilton's commentary. The purity of Christ's love, the transforming effect of the Crucifixion and the Resurrection, the assured promise of redemption for believers gave people an experience of new light, new freedom in the power of Christ.

Patrick Hamilton was a rich man with powerful connections, recently married, enjoying apparently every prospect of a successful career. Archbishop James Beaton of St. Andrews determined to make an example of him and he was arrested and ordered to recant. The Archbishop was forthwith faced not with submission but with a declaration of faith. 'As to my confession, I will not deny it for awe of your fire, for my confession and belief is in Jesus Christ. I will rather be content that my body burn in this fire for confession of my faith in Christ than my soul should burn in the fire of Hell for denying the same.'

So they burnt Patrick Hamilton in their fire at St. Andrews. Unfamiliar as yet with the technique of building such fires and hampered by squalls of rain, they took six hours to kill him. His serenity throughout the long torture shattered the complacency of everybody who saw it, hardened as people were to brutality. Somebody offered the Archbishop advice which he should have taken seriously. 'My Lord, if ye burn any more, except ye follow my counsel, ye will utterly destroy yourselves. If ye burn them, let them be burned in deep cellars, for the reek of Master Patrick Hamilton has infected as many as it blew upon'.

The people infected by the reek of Hamilton's fire were far more numerous than the Archbishop and his advisers could guess, nor did they know that members of the Augustinian and Dominican orders, also of the nobility, some of Scotland's keenest thinkers, were strongly attracted to the faith for which Hamilton had suffered.

The King himself never failed to encourage those who made open fun of religion. By 1537, when he was only twenty-four, James V was looking for a tutor to direct the education of an illegitimate son, a child called James Stewart. He chose George Buchanan, a scholar of prodigious learning, steeped in the new humanism, who had so far spent most of his life in Europe. James was enchanted by Buchanan's gift of satire, and urged him to publish his poems. These made mock of the Franciscans, and they were skilfully written, in no sense great poetry, but full of sarcasm and deadly invective. At this time, Buchanan was not much attracted to Protestantism, but he helped to inflame hostility against the Roman Catholics.

One of James V's Gentleman-ushers, named Sir David Lyndesay, also diverted him with poems in which the vices of the clergy were made amusing. In 1540, the King and the Court, with a number of Church dignitaries, assembled during Epiphany, at Linlithgow, for the first performance of Lyndesay's famous dramatic piece *Ane Pleasant Satyre of the Thrie Estaitis*. Richly entertaining, highly dramatic and pointed with topical reference, this play ridiculed the clerics who hated Chastity, revered Folly, faked relics and exploited paupers. James V and his entourage found it entirely delightful.

By this time, James V's uncle, Henry VIII of England, was the bitter enemy of the Pope, bent upon breaking the power of Rome in England. He wanted James V to marry his daughter, to give up the French alliance and to turn against the Pope. James V understood in no way the gravity of the religious crisis breaking upon Europe, but he disliked Henry VIII, and preferred the old links with Rome and with France. He married Madeline, the French King's daughter, and after her early death, Mary of Guise. This second wife belonged to the most powerful family in France. Of her seven brothers, the best known was the Cardinal Duke of Lorraine, who organized vigorous persecution of religious reformers in his own country, and for whose judgment Mary had sisterly respect. She was herself a woman of ability, endowed with the Guise brains and well accustomed to political intrigue.

When he discovered that James did not intend to oblige him, Henry enticed many Scottish noblemen into his own service, and used them in his efforts to wreck their country's wellbeing. He found it easy to do this, because James had alienated a number of them by his pro-French policy and by his readiness to depend on French armed assistance. Furthermore, Henry's dissolution of the English monasteries had enriched land-hungry subjects and there were Scotsmen who could hardly wait to enter upon similar good fortune. Secular greed for monastic property had much to do with the political disloyalty and the religious intrigue that were ugly features of this period.

Henry VIII had by now deteriorated into an evil tyrant, possessed by a fanatic's passion to dominate in every possible sphere. Exasperated by James' French sympathies, he organized an invasion of Scotland in 1542, which James wanted to arrest by a counter-invasion of England. The Scottish nobles saw in this merely a manoeuvre to support France and they refused to cross the Border. On November 24th, 1542, James' small army was defeated at Solway Moss. Two weeks later, his daughter and heir, Princess Mary, was born. Six days after that James suddenly died, aged thirty, and the baby was proclaimed Queen.

So Mary of Guise was the Queen Mother. She was confronted by an English King who now intended to absorb Scotland into his own domain, and who was not only an excommunicated man but also a megalomaniac. She was committed to Roman Catholicism, while Scotland was already shot through with the explosive forces of Protestantism. She was supported by powerful French interests, while many Scottish nobles were in the service of Henry VIII. The situation was complex and dangerous enough to tax the resources of the most gifted ruler.

Her most trusted adviser was David Beaton, Abbot of Arbroath and Bishop of Mirepoix in Languedoc. He had succeeded his uncle James Beaton as Archbishop of St. Andrews and, thanks to French influence, he had become a Cardinal. He was a man of the times, unscrupulous, immoral, but very able, and set against allowing Scotland to be swamped by England. He and the Queen Mother were disgusted by Henry VIII's proposal that the baby heiress of Scotland should be married to the English prince Edward, and especially by the conditions attached to the plan. Henry VIII wanted the little girl to be sent to England and brought up under his care: he demanded that he should be recognized as Lord-Superior of Scotland, and that key fortresses should be handed over to English garrisons. He was acting as if the evil genius of Edward I at his worst had found re-incarnation in himself and, like Edward, he had at his back a number of Scottish lords who were residing in England.

Enraged by the refusal of the Scottish government to accept such proposals of marriage, Henry launched on Scotland in 1544 and the following year the cruel invasions under the Earl of

Hertford which became known as the Rough Wooing. Leith was captured, the Border Abbeys destroyed, the Lothians ravaged, 243 villages and five market towns laid in ruins. The cruelties of the English in these campaigns did ineradicable harm. The Protestant cause became identified in many people's minds with Henry VIII's policy, people were revolted by all that he stood for: patriotism demanded subservience to Beaton, support of the Roman Catholics, adherence to the French alliance. Worse still was the legacy of hatred. The traditional hostility of Scots against Englishmen which spoiled the Union of 1707 and survived the 18th century had long roots in these terrible years from 1544 to 1547.

Henry VIII died in 1546, but his policy was continued by the Duke of Somerset on behalf of Edward VI and in 1547 the English victory at Pinkie Cleugh was the climax of the whole bloody business.

Meantime the Protestants were struggling to understand the new faith and to adjust themselves to its claims. Some of their leaders suffered Hamilton's fate, all of them lived in danger, and as many as could manage it went abroad. George Wishart for example left in 1538, under grave suspicion because he had started teaching from the Greek New Testament in Montrose Grammar School. After six years in England and on the continent, he came back, in 1544, when Cardinal Beaton's persecution of reformers was at its height. He preached then in Dundee, in Ayr, in village churches, in the fields. The theme he best loved was the liberation of the believer in Christ, as it is expounded in Romans 8.

When plague broke out in Dundee, he went back and ministered to the people who were suffering; then he moved to Leith. In 1546, Beaton's agents arrested him in Haddington. It was a time of acute political tension, when Protestants were considered traitors, working in the interests of the English. In March 1546, two weeks after Luther's death, Wishart was burned in St. Andrews, in the presence of the Cardinal.

Two months later, Beaton was murdered in his own castle. No news could have delighted Henry VIII more. He hated this active and intelligent statesman, because he thought that only Beaton could organize Scotland sufficiently to withstand him. The

Cardinal's murderers were young noblemen acting like gangsters and to secure themselves from retribution they fortified themselves within St. Andrew's Castle, where they remained under siege until July. During these weeks they were joined by a strange selection of sympathizers, one of whom they made into a kind of garrison chaplain. This was John Knox, a young priest who had met George Wishart two months before his death and had been greatly impressed and disturbed by him. Knox, like others who were interested in the Protestant view, could not help rejoicing over the Cardinal's death, although he had nothing to do with it, but he did not like the company he found in the castle, a rough, immoral crowd of ill-disciplined soldiers and hangers-on.

Mary of Guise was shocked by these events. She sent for help from France and in July 1546 the French fleet attacked St. Andrews Castle, overcame its defenders, and carried the leaders away to the horrible punishment of rowing in the galleys. John Knox was one of those who suffered.

The Queen Mother's policy was now concentrated on beating off the English, crushing Protestantism and safeguarding the future of her daughter. All three aims were wrapped up in the third. The little girl had been kept on Inchmahome island in the Lake of Menteith and then in the Castle on Dumbarton Rock. In 1548, she was sent to France.

The French King was well pleased with this arrangement. The child would be brought up at his court, and married to his son; Scotland would become a French dependency. Meantime the English were being beaten out of France and they were recalling their troops from Scotland, so that the Auld Alliance seemed firmer and more successful than ever. The Roman Catholic Council of Trent was making progress with its reforming decrees, the Protestant Princes in Germany were being beaten by the Emperor, Henry II of France was preparing edicts to crush the Huguenots. All seemed set for a Roman Catholic Europe under the domination of a French King who controlled Scotland and would soon absorb England too. The English King, Edward VI, was sickening for the tuberculosis which killed him, his sisters were illegitimate according to Catholic doctrine, the Queen of Scots was the next heir to the English throne.

The Reformation and the Covenant

Henry II of France was so reassured about the situation that early in 1549 he released the St. Andrews prisoners. John Knox therefore made his way to England, the only country except Switzerland where Protestantism seemed to have a chance of survival.

CHAPTER 13

Protestant Scotland

W hen John Knox left his forced labour early in 1549, it seemed that the Roman Catholic pro-French régime was permanently established in Scotland. In England, the security of all reformers depended upon the boy Edward VI, whose Protestant principles were as strong as the Roman Catholic loyalty of his elder sister and heir, Mary Tudor, but whose health was already undermined by a 'tough, strong, streining cough'.

The decade between 1549 and 1559 proved one of the most important in all Scottish history. The year 1560 was a turning-point which changed the whole course of events. In that year Mary of Guise died, the French alliance abruptly ended, permanent peace was made with England. Above all, the Protestant Church was established in Scotland. Even in the highest moments of faith, no reformer living in the 1550s could have anticipated such an outcome.

In this chapter, the developments which led to this extraordinary climax are described, the nature of the new Church discussed. The terrible débâcle of Mary, Queen of Scots, which followed the reformers' triumph and caused repercussions of incalculable significance is also recorded here. The dominant personalities of the period, so far as Scotland was concerned, were John Knox, Mary of Guise and Mary Queen of Scots.

In John Knox himself, a finely wrought, conscience-ridden and mentally tortured man, the tensions of the age were concentrated.

For almost five years after his release in 1549, Knox lived in England, where the Protestant Edward VI was King, and where he met all the leading reformers and especially Cranmer. He was highly thought of, appointed to a royal chaplaincy and offered a bishopric. When Mary Tudor came to the English throne in 1553, dedicated to the recapture of her country for Rome, Knox was one of many who left England. He went to Frankfurt-on-the-Main and then to Geneva. Already he had thought with fierce concentration about the meaning of Christianity. Now, in Calvin, he met a reformer whose powerful and logical mind helped him to work out his revolutionary ideas. Not until 1559 did he permanently settle in his own country. The foundations of the new church there were laid by other hands than his.

He was a man 'in spiritual torment', as Lord Eustace Percy puts it. There was agony in breaking loose from strong and even yet hallowed tradition; the revolt from the old faith cost him years of intellectual strife; his European outlook forced him to identify himself with problems from which men of the parish pump were spared.

Everywhere Knox saw ruin for the young Protestant Church. Reformers were being driven under by Mary of Guise in Scotland, by the Emperor in Germany, by Henry II in France, and after 1553 they seemed doomed to extinction in England. Only in Switzerland, a tiny island of resistance, embraced by almost impassable mountains but surrounded too by mighty Roman Catholic powers, did there seem any hope of Protestant survival. Within the ranks of the Reformers themselves there was no unanimity but stark disagreement, and they were weakened by the influences of those fellow-travellers who wanted to exploit religion in the interests of materialism. This background of agonizing tension and vicarious pain must be remembered when one reads of Knox's later policies in Scotland.

Mary of Guise was not only a Roman Catholic, but also, naturally enough, a French patriot, and like Knox at least to the extent that she saw the international significance of national policies. Logical, courageous, resourceful and infinitely hard-working, she co-operated with her brother, the Duke of Lorraine, to establish French control at all key-points in Scotland. Why? Because her daughter was to marry the Dauphin and become Queen, not only of Scotland but also of France, and ultimately of England too, for Roman Catholic Europe recognized her as heir to Edward VI's crown.

While Knox was battling his way to theological assurance and Mary of Guise was preparing for her daughter's future, Roman Catholic and Protestant leaders were trying to consolidate the faith of their supporters.

The Archbishop of St. Andrews summoned in 1549 and 1552 Reforming Councils. Their most impressive achievement was the production of a Catechism for priests to use when they were instructing their people. It dealt especially with the Ten Commandments, the Creeds, and the Sacraments, and it was reverently and beautifully expressed. Such a document in the hands of sincere priests could have done much to save the old Church, if only it had been produced half a century earlier. Its late appearance, under a French ruler, its association with corrupt and cynical men of immoral habits meant that for the time being it could do little good. By the 1550s, the damage was too severe, the political exploitation of the religious issue too far advanced for calamity to be prevented.

Meantime, the Protestants in Scotland were needing an order of worship in their own language, with which inexperienced religious leaders of no great educational background could replace the old Latin liturgy. They found what they wanted in the English Book of Common Prayer, published in 1549 and revised in 1552. This included large portions of the Bible, which were read or sung as a central part of every service and which enabled people to become familiar especially with the Psalter, the Gospels and the Epistles. It set out orders of service and also many short prayers suitable for use in public and private devotions, prayers collected from ancient sources and translated by Cranmer into English of unsurpassed beauty. The Sacrament of Holy Communion was the central act of worship and the Prayer Book stated clearly that while people were to receive the Bread and Wine kneeling, 'no adoration of the sacred elements is intended or ought to be done.' So the men who held to the Roman Catholic belief in transubstantiation could not join in the English celebration of Communion. But the Prayer Book at this stage imposed no rigid uniformity and it left both priests and laymen a certain freedom in worship. People of widely differing thought could join in the services with sincerity.

135

The Reformation and the Covenant

It is impossible to exaggerate the importance of the English Book of Common Prayer. Its dignity and reverence, its ordered rhythm and lucid prose so close to poetry, its spiritual insight and the depth of meaning in its prayers gave strength to generations of believers. In Scotland it was lovingly and reverently used for many years and it helped to shape Scottish Protestant thought, the first Service Book ever handled by Scottish laymen, who learned from it the central doctrines of the Christian faith.

Another work much loved by Scottish Protestants at this time was compiled by three brothers, James, John, and Robert Wedderburn. It was called *A Compendious Booke of Godly and Spiritual Songs*, or *The Gude and Godly Ballatis*. This was a collection of Lutheran hymns, with some metrical Psalms and some rather scurrilous poems, almost doggerel in nature. The Saltire Society has recently published a small volume containing a selection of these verses which influenced 16th century Scotsmen so much. In his book, *Worship in the Church of Scotland*, Dr. Maxwell shows the significance for Scottish Protestants of the Prayer Book and of the Wedderburns' hymns and psalms. 'For the first time in centuries, the voice of the people was once more heard in praise and worship of God. Except in great churches, the metrical psalms did not replace plainsong, they replaced silence.'

The tension between the old Church and the new grew more acute during the 1550s, for in spite of the Queen Mother's efforts, Protestantism was becoming stronger. The leadership came from the nobility, who were inspired by motives far from wholly religious, for political and economic advantage was clearly to be derived from a breakdown of the old religion. In 1557, a group of Scottish Lords drafted a document which has become famous in Scottish History. This was the First Covenant.

It was designed to promote 'the most blessed Word of God and His congregation', to provide 'faithful ministers', to defend both congregations and ministers from interference. The Lords proposed to persuade their Government to authorize the Book of Common Prayer, they emphasized the need for Bible Study and private worship and, above all, insisted that when the Sacraments of Communion and Baptism were celebrated, the Scots tongue must be used. By 1558, this Covenant was being taken round Scotland for signature by gentry and burgesses. It created an immense sensation because the procedure was unprecedented and much more because the proposals were revolutionary.

One explosive event followed another in 1558, while Scotsmen were signing the First Covenant. Mary Tudor died and the English throne passed to her half-sister, Elizabeth, who set about establishing a Protestant state religion, based on the Book of Common Prayer. The burning of Protestants therefore ceased in England. The last of the martyrs in Scotland died that year in St. Andrews—old Walter Myln or Mill, aged eighty-two. The citizens in St. Andrews were so shocked at his sentence that nobody would provide fuel for the fire or ropes to bind him to the stake and the Provost flatly refused to have anything to do with the affair. In the end the Archbishop's personal servants had to carry it through as best they might, and it caused a scandal throughout Scotland.

Four days after Myln's death in 1558, Mary Queen of Scots married the Dauphin. She was sixteen. Her subjects at home did not know that she had pledged her kingdom to France if she had no heir. They did know that her young husband had demanded the Crown Matrimonial, that he boasted himself King of Scotland, and they knew also that Mary of Guise was preparing to suppress the Covenant by force.

The country was now worked up to a fever of excitement. The danger was an outburst of violence such as had swept Germany in the early days of Luther's movement. Even the Queen Mother underestimated this risk and the Lords of the Congregation were totally unprepared for it. But the Protestants knew they needed a leader to weld them together and urgent messages were sent to John Knox to return. He came back to Scotland in 1559 and at once became the inspiration of Protestant activity and the architect of Protestant thought. His incredible capacity for concentrated, rapid work astonished everybody and during the next few months he helped to bring about profound changes in the Scottish way of life.

He was an inflammatory preacher whose prophetic message was not understood by people whom fear and hatred had embittered.

His sermons at once touched off an orgy of desecration, in which angry mobs, excited beyond all control, burst into action, and began senselessly smashing the altars, pictures and furnishings of monastic buildings and even parish churches. The extent of these outbursts has been exaggerated and much destruction wrought by other hands has been attributed to Knox's followers, but they were responsible for outrages in Scone, Perth, St. Andrews, Stirling, Linlithgow, Edinburgh and Holyrood—a sufficiently black indictment.

Knox and the other Protestant leaders were horrified. It was clearly the beginning of civil war. The Queen Mother had ample strength to annihilate the rebels, if she could mobilize her forces, and the outlook was very black. And then the incredible happened, so quickly that people could hardly keep up with events.

Henry II of France died from an injury received in a tournament in July 1559. His son Francis II therefore became King of France. He quartered on his arms the devices of Scotland and also, most misguidedly, of England. All Roman Catholic Europe supported him in this. His wife, Mary Queen of Scots, the great-granddaughter of Henry VII, was deemed by Rome to be the only surviving heir to Henry VIII whose claim was legitimate. Elizabeth, according to Catholic doctrine, had been born out of wedlock. Thus, for the first time in hundreds of years, the English sovereign had cogent reasons for seeking alliance with Scotland against the French, because both countries were now threatened by France. In an agony of suspense Knox supported negotiations for assistance from Queen Elizabeth.

Elizabeth was reluctant. She strongly disapproved of rebellion, as indeed did Knox himself, and she was deeply alienated by his recent publication of a most unfortunate work. This was *The First Blast of the Trumpet against the Monstrous Regiment of Women*, which denounced the notion that women were fit to be crowned monarchs. But it was plain that, now or never, the French claims to Scotland and to England must be refuted. So the irony of history brought about this strangest of partnerships. In January 1560, the English fleet appeared in northern waters to assist the Protestant Scots, a sight incredible to men who remembered the Rough Wooing. The Queen Mother's forces retired to Leith, where they were besieged by an English army co-operating with Scottish nobles. In the early summer, the Treaty of Leith or Edinburgh finished the business, and all French troops were ordered out of Scotland.

This would not have been the end of the story however, but for the death of Mary of Guise in June 1560. The significance of her hold on affairs is shown by the rapid changes which followed her death.

The Scottish Parliament was called. To it there came a better representation of lesser freeholders than ever before. Not until the 1690s was so much popular interest shown in any Parliament.

By a rapid succession of statutes, the authority of the Pope in Scotland was abolished and the celebration of Mass forbidden. Knox, with five other ministers, was asked to draw up a definition of the new beliefs, and they produced a document in four days. This was the Confession of Faith, an intellectual statement of Christianity as he understood it, which became the basis of Scottish Protestantism until 1647. That even Knox's dynamic mind could work so rapidly is surprising, though he was prepared for the sudden need by the years he had spent with Calvinists. There followed in a matter of weeks *The First Book of Discipline*, also the work of Knox and his colleagues. This set out the principles upon which the Scottish Church should be organized, and though it bore the marks of haste, it was expressed in terms of such authority that it was accepted almost without question, except as regards its far-reaching financial proposals.

Knox has been much misinterpreted and so has the Church which he helped to found. The Confession of Faith and *The First Book of Discipline* show clearly that he believed whole-heartedly in the sacramental nature of worship. Shocked as he had been by the degradation of the Mass, Knox wanted Communion to be the central focus in the life of the Church. He found authority for this in the New Testament, and believed it to be the principal means of grace for the Christian. Knox, like Calvin, believed in frequent Communion, but shortage of ministers and the prejudices of people who had been in the habit of communicating only once a year at Easter made this impossible, and the general rule in Scotland was that Holy Communion should be celebrated quarterly in burghs and twice yearly in country parishes. There were long periods, however, when in many places even this frequency was not attained. The celebration, however, was always recognized as a corporate action, in which the faithful should share, and all communicants were encouraged, after examination, to receive at every Communion service. Worshippers were seated at long tables, because this was believed to be nearer the Apostolic practice than kneeling.

The Bible was the basis of the Confession of Faith. Because people must not only know but understand the Scriptures, preaching was to be an important part of worship. Ministers were told to speak in Scots, in a loud clear voice so that all could hear.

The First Book of Discipline set forth the way in which the Church should manage its business. It gave laymen responsibility in religious matters which was quite new. Each parish was to appoint a Kirk Session of lay elders, whose task it was to assist the minister in oversight of the people and in all parish concerns. Superintendents, or itinerant ministers, were appointed, each with a district which coincided more or less with one of the old dioceses, and these superintendents had status and authority similar in many ways to that of bishops. From the first, a General Assembly met once or twice a year to settle matters affecting the whole Church.

This boldly democratic system was later completed by the formation of district Presbyteries, composed of ministers and elders representing the parishes. They dealt with some of the work which proved too difficult for the Sessions. The Presbyteries were given power to ordain ministers, and this was one of the most important breaks with Roman Catholic tradition, for in the Old Church, clergy were ordained by bishops. Between the Presbytery and the General Assembly came the Provincial Synod, composed of several Presbyteries. The Supreme Court was the General Assembly which eventually came to be composed of commissioners from the Presbyteries both ministers and elders.

This whole system of Church Government became exceedingly precious to Scottish Protestants, who ultimately did away with the office of Superintendent, but clung most tenaciously to the Sessions, Presbyteries and Synods.

The General Assembly flourished from the beginning. People took the liveliest interest in it and it gave them a means of expressing public opinion long needed in Scotland. In fact it took something like the place in national life which the House of Commons came to hold in England, though it was a far more representative and democratic body.

The Book of Discipline demanded that the wealth of the unreformed Church should be used to provide Scotland's parishes each with a minister's manse and salary, a fund for poor relief and a school. Knox was well aware that already much of the land formerly owned by monasteries had been secured by lay lords and commendators, often in collaboration with the abbots and priors themselves. 'With the grief of our hearts, we hear that some gentlemen are now as cruel over their tenants as ever were the Papists, requiring of them whatsoever before they paid to the Church, so that the Papistical tyranny shall only be changed into the tyranny of the lord or the laird.' This was what Knox wrote. Years earlier the poet Henryson had put it more suc cinctly: 'The worst wolves are lords that have lands as a loan from God.' In the introduction to the *Register of the Privy Council of Scotland* 1625-27, a list of the principal abbeys and priories with the names of their lay owners is set out, showing how well Scottish lords exploited the Reformation for their own material benefit.

It is essential to democracy, whether in Church or State, that those who take decisions must have some education. In the Protestant Church, which bases its teaching on the Bible and calls upon laymen to take their part, it is necessary for Church members to be at least literate. *The Book of Discipline* therefore stated that every parish was to have its school. Knox and his colleagues in fact wanted a free, compulsory, national system of education.

Nobody in Scotland had ever suggested such a revolutionary idea before. It was typical of these early Protestant leaders, who believed with Calvin that it was a moral duty to train the mind. The scheme never succeeded because Protestant nobles had effectively secured so much of the old Church's property and the new Church had no chance to share adequately in the spoils.

141

Many parishes in fact had no school till the second half of the 18th century. But do not let 20th century complacency overlook the astonishing originality of Knox's educational policy, unmatched in any contemporary society.

Knox's third great literary production was delayed until 1562. This was the Book of Common Order, a Service Book designed for laymen as much as for ministers, and based on one used in Geneva by English refugees. It took some time to supersede the English Book of Common Prayer, which was popular in Scotland until the 1570s, but once people became used to it they liked it and it passed through seventy editions between 1562 and 1637.

Later generations of Scottish Protestants cut completely adrift from this Service Book. It repays study. It sets out the Lord's Prayer, the Creed, the Ten Commandments, the Magnificat, the Nunc Dimittis and the Veni Creator. Strangely enough, unlike the English Book, it includes no Scriptures. No celebration of special festivals in the Christian year was allowed, so that even Christmas, Easter and Whitsun were passed by without recognition. This was of course in reaction against the Holy Days of Rome, but Scottish Protestants suffered spiritual loss in their neglect of these special periods of worship and recollection.

It is odd that 1314 is the best known date in Scottish history. Although the Battle of Bannockburn was glorious for Bruce, it heralded decades of frustration and fighting. The year 1560 is surely a much more momentous one. It ended three centuries of warfare with England. It saw the foundation of the Presbyterian Church. A nation's thoughts were radically changed by all that Parliament did in those brief weeks of 1560. And for those who grieve over the divisions among Christians, 1560 is a year of tragic significance, for then the breach between the old Church and the new was made permanent in Scotland.

There was one final shock in store for Europe before 1560 ended. When Christmas preparations were afoot, Francis II, King of France, died suddenly from a mastoid. Mary, Queen of Scots, not yet nineteen years of age, was widowed. There was nothing for her now but to return to Scotland.

By character and training Mary was hardly fitted to deal with what she had to undertake. Deprived since earliest childhood of her parents' company, of normal family life and of home security, she was almost uninstructed in the history and traditions of her country. She was more French than Scottish. She had even adopted the French form of her own surname, which she spelt Stuart. Famous for her beauty, strongly sexed, conditioned to gay court life, delighting in pleasure and also in intellectual stimulus, she was at home in the atmosphere of high-powered intrigue: devout according to her own light, she understood less readily the religious dedication of the spiritually-minded Protestants than the self-interest of the worldly ones. And when she came to Scotland this eighteen-year-old girl felt her isolation from the sunshine, the warmth, the palace life, the court festivities she had known during her childhood in France.

Her return to Scotland in 1561 was a moment of crucial opportunity. Had Scotland ever needed a balanced, wise, experienced monarch more desperately than then? Enlightened patience, mature judgment, firmness of purpose and tolerance of mind in the Scottish ruler could have preserved the nation in its wholeness and inaugurated the new era of religious growth without excessive embitterment or partisan politics. People are ready enough to recollect Mary's personal tragedy with hot resentment or cold criticism, according to their outlook. Not enough has been said about the nation's tragedy at this time of new beginnings when the very springs of national thought became poisoned at the source.

The middle-aged Protestant divines by whose courage the new beginnings had been shaped were nonplussed by Mary. The wonder is that for nearly five years a modus vivendi was somehow found. She insisted on hearing Mass regularly in Holyrood. Knox and the other Protestant leaders were deeply shocked by this. They were desperately afraid that such a royal example might bring a reaction in Scotland, and indeed in Europe, which would undo all their work and let loose again the evils they had striven to crush. And certainly Roman Catholic Europe did regard their Queen as a kind of Joan of Arc, a Crusader in a pagan land, fighting a lonely, holy war.

Mary was at a loss to understand why people in Scotland disapproved of her so much. Probably some of her happiest hours were those spent in the company of George Buchanan. He had returned to Scotland after many years on the continent, in 1561. He was more interested in humanist thinking than in religious controversy at this time, although he was by now a Protestant thoroughly trusted by Knox and a member of the General Assembly. He had a great love for France and the Queen used to read the classics with him, no doubt also enjoying his reminiscences of the country they both knew so well.

In 1565 she fell in love. Henry Darnley was the grandson of James IV's widow, Margaret Tudor, by a later marriage. He was about nineteen, attractive in appearance and very tall. They were married before Mary discovered his third-rate mind and total lack of perception. So for intelligent companionship Mary looked elsewhere, and within ten months of the marriage, Darnley was jealous of David Rizzio, an Italian musician.

Rizzio was murdered in Mary's presence by Darnley and a group of others. She was six months pregnant, and the next day she almost miscarried, and she became very ill. Her baby, the future James VI and I, was born three months later. Darnley's brutality had only just missed depriving two kingdoms of a monarch.

After that, Mary could not get over her repugnance for this odious second husband and one disaster followed another. He fell ill of smallpox in 1567, and while he was slowly convalescing, his house at Kirk o' Field near Edinburgh was blown up: next morning, amongst the wreckage cluttering the garden, his body was found—and his neck had been wrung.

Nobody knows exactly what happened, or how many agents were employed in the crime. Scotland was in no doubt as to who organized it however—James Hepburn, the fourth Earl of Bothwell, a Protestant of notoriously bad character. Within eight weeks, Mary had married this man.

What could have possessed her? Beautiful, sensitive, high-powered—why did she twice tie herself up with a contemptible character? The union with Bothwell cost her everything. Roman Catholics throughout Europe were scandalized by it, the Scottish Protestants outraged, George Buchanan no less than the rest. It brought about immediate war, for the nobles had no difficulty in raising troops to fight both the Queen and Bothwell. In June 1567, her soldiers retreated from Carberry Hill and she was forced to sign her own abdication. The baby James was crowned, Knox preached the Coronation sermon and Mary's Protestant half-brother James Stewart, Earl of Moray, one of James V's abler illegitimate sons, was made Regent.

Mary was imprisoned in Lochleven Castle, from which she made a dramatic escape in 1568, but another defeat followed, at Langside by Glasgow, and she made one more desperate decision. She appealed to Queen Elizabeth, secretly crossed the Solway and appeared on English territory as a suppliant for hospitality and assistance.

This was the last development Elizabeth wanted and it distracted her. She did not know what to do with such a guest, the heir-presumptive to the English throne, who had already made free to consider herself Queen of England; a Roman Catholic, the wife of her husband's murderer, a woman whom Scotland no longer wanted and whose presence in England was an acute danger. A hundred years later, in 1668, Henry Savage, Master of Balliol College, made the following comment on Mary's decision to go to England: 'The circumstances of her suffering, 'tis not my business to dispute or relate, but the event gives way to this note upon it, viz: How dangerous a thing it is, first to lay claim to a crown and afterwards to fly for succour to the head that wears it.'

Elizabeth kept Mary imprisoned in country castles and her advisers organized careful scrutiny of all her correspondence, which often contained incriminating documents. Meantime, it took the Protestant Lords almost five years to achieve a stable government in Scotland, and James VI was subjected to the most rigorous discipline ever endured by a Scottish King in childhood. The Protestants were determined to leave no stone unturned to ensure that this time they would educate their ruler in the way of their own choosing.

This final royal minority did Scotland endless harm. At a time of bold new thought, it is disastrous to have weakened leadership, because career-minded climbers, materialists, people devoted to intrigue of all kinds have such unusual opportunities.

The Reformation and the Covenant

The fight between Mary of Guise and John Knox for the nation's soul, followed by the anti-climax of Mary Stuart's personal calamities, set the scene for sordid developments during the childhood of the new King.

CHAPTER 14

Prelude to the Seventeenth Century

James VI was crowned in the summer of 1567, when he was thirteen months old. By the time he was four, his studies were being directed by George Buchanan, who had formerly made his conversation acceptable to the little King's mother.

When he began tutoring James, Buchanan was sixty-three, an advanced age for those times, his health was poor and his temper short. Although he had tutored a number of boys before, including a Stewart prince, he was unsuited to the care of small children. He could not stand noise and as the years went by he found schoolboy wit intolerable. He had learned his pedagogy in schools where thrashing was a normal part of each day's work and he did not change his method. Worse than this was his habit of making embittered reference to James' parents, especially his mother. James hated him and was afraid of him.

The King was systematically overdriven at books, for which he showed unusual ability. He quickly absorbed Latin and Greek, committed long passages of the Bible to memory, mastered much Calvinist theology and became probably the best-educated prince of his day. But it was a precocious learning, acquired during a lonely, abnormal childhood. Although a library of some six hundred books was collected for him during his childhood—probably a unique personal possession in those days—money was so short that James' royal apartments were shabby and by modern standards he was neglected. It occurred to nobody that the King should have any training in consideration of other people or in understanding the mentality of those with whom he would have to deal.

Buchanan vigorously drummed his political ideas into James' head. Kings were answerable to law, their authority was derived from the people, if they failed in their responsibilities their subjects were entitled to get rid of them. These were not original views. John Major and John Knox and many others had voiced them before. Because James was afraid of Buchanan he came to hate his political doctrines and, although he was never particularly loyal to his parents' memory, he resented the crude way in which Buchanan justified the Scots' rejection of Mary.

James grew up with fear on the doorstep. From 1563 till 1573, nobles who supported Mary Stuart's cause waged active war against those who wanted a Protestant régime and peaceful terms with England. There was a succession of Regents, who had impossible difficulties to contend with. The Queen's friends, and others too who wanted power, were always trying to get possession of the King's person. As a boy James more than once witnessed physical violence between his guardians and their enemies in his own home. The experience frightened and humiliated him.

One can understand James and his legacy best by considering his reaction to all this boyhood misery. In self-assertion against the adults who overruled him, he developed a brazen self-conceit. Starved of loving companionship as a child, he began in his early teens that series of emotional attachments with specially favoured men which caused scandal till his old age. Esmé Stuart, Seigneur d'Aubigny, was the first to awaken this side of James' nature and his was a wholly harmful influence, for he was both evil and charming.

More serious for both Scotland and England was James' reaction against Calvinism. He hated Presbyterian principles so much that in later life he could not think logically about them, and this hatred he bestowed also on Puritan ideas. All his adult life, he laboured to destroy the power of the Kirk and to force Scotsmen to adopt the ritual worship he came to love in the Anglican Church. And he became set on Episcopacy. The establishment of bishops in Scotland was one of his dearest ambitions from very early days.

Equally disastrous was James' reaction against Buchanan's political philosophy. It must have been a positive release of the spirit for James to realize, as he did in adolescence, that one need not believe in the sovereignty of the people. It was perhaps from Esmé Stuart that he first learned how some continental thinkers approached political philosophy, and how differently from himself continental rulers were trained to work out their responsibilities. One wonders whether old Buchanan realized how dangerous were the volumes of Jean Bodin which had been included in the King's library. They are difficult, indeed exasperating to read, but to James they were meat and drink. Bodin was a French philosopher of the late 16th century. The general purport of his teaching was that law is nothing else than the command of the sovereign, that sovereignty in fact consisted in the right to make law. From Bodin, James deduced that men are anything but equal and that democracy is a rebellion against nature because it encourages belief in an equality of man which does not really exist. True sovereignty, in fact, was only to be found in monarchy.

In defiance of Buchanan, James embraced the doctrines of Bodin and worked out his own theory of the Divine Right of Kings. This he explained in various books which he published, but especially in *The Trew Law of Free Monarchies*. His son Charles I adopted this book's teaching with a seriousness of purpose that led him to antagonize the most powerful classes in his kingdom. So James' revolt against Buchanan's political philosophy produced long-term results which did infinite harm.

Some writers have suggested that not even the most enlightened handling in childhood could have made James into a wise or balanced personality. But it is almost impossible to conceive of an upbringing more likely to bring out the worst in his nature.

James never knew his mother personally. She was imprisoned in England until his twenty-first year. In theory, he wanted to stand up for her, but he resented the inconvenience she caused him by her implication in plots against Queen Elizabeth. For James desperately wanted to be King of England. Only by this means did he see any chance of eluding forever the poverty and the humiliation he endured in Scotland. Anything Mary did to endanger his succession to the English throne irritated and even alarmed him. When at last she was executed in 1587, he was in a sense relieved, though of course he took it as a personal insult to himself that such a thing should have happened.

Queen Elizabeth had been most reluctant to allow this execution, which affronted all her sensibilities and was contrary to all her principles. Her ministers had the greatest difficulty in persuading her to agree to the measure, even though they were all sure that it was essential to Elizabeth's own life, for they had damning evidence of Mary's dealings with traitors.

The result of Mary's execution in Scotland was an emotional upheaval which Englishmen could never have foreseen and certainly never have understood. Though Mary Stuart had shocked Scottish public opinion and offended Scotsmen's religious scruples, though she had been forced by her own subjects to abdicate and few people had wanted her back, now that English hands had been laid upon her and she had been done to death by an English Queen's orders, a surge of loyalty to her and hatred against England swept through the country. People clamoured for vengeance and could not understand James' embarrassed inactivity about the matter. Border raids were organized and the whole thing became a national scandal. The execution of Mary Stuart, like the Rough Wooing organized in the 1540s by Henry VIII, left deep roots of bitterness.

For the first thirty years of James' reign, Scotland suffered cruelly from the lawlessness of the aristocracy. As a young man, James could no more assert his authority over the nobles than he could keep on good terms with the Kirk, and he was so desperately short of money that it was a problem even to meet tradesmen's bills. In the last decade of the century, James' position was so humiliating that he had to put up with barefaced insolence from those about him.

The country was tormented by the feuds and wrangles between Protestant and Roman Catholic lords. Of the latter, the Earl of Huntly was a principal leader. He was for awhile one of James' favourites and he pretended to take an interest in Protestant services, in order to earn more favours from the King. He was a barbarous, double-faced man, who conducted treasonable correspondence with Spain, to Queen Elizabeth's indignation, but James could hardly bring himself to disgrace Huntly, even when this was discovered. Later, Huntly carried out a dreadful murder. He killed the young Earl of Moray, a popular Protestant, and burned out the castle of Donibristle on the Forth where his victim was staying. Public opinion was utterly shocked by this and James himself had to bear much of the odium.

Huntly's chief enemy was the fifth Earl of Bothwell. This disreputable, and probably deranged, man was a nephew of Mary Stuart's third husband and a grandson of James V. He hated Huntly and the other Roman Catholic Earls and for years he made orderly government impossible. James was terrified of him, because he believed that Bothwell was endowed with supernatural powers. Three times, this extraordinary man made personal attacks on James in an effort to kidnap or injure him, twice in the King's own palace quarters.

At last in 1595, Huntly and Bothwell were both driven out of Scotland as exiles, and from this time onwards, James' position improved. His adviser Maitland died in that year and he took over the direction of affairs himself, showing a new and dogged determination to be master in his own land and to quell disorder.

In the midst of the worst upheavals, James had enjoyed a short spell of romance. He became betrothed to Anne of Denmark. In October, 1589, he went to Oslo, where she was stormbound on her journey to Scotland, and there he married her. He really enjoyed this episode, anxious though he was about the reception he would receive on his return, for there was as usual no money to spare for suitable celebrations. 'For God's sake', he wrote to a friendly minister, 'take all the pains ye can to tune our folks well now against our homecoming lest we be all shamed before strangers. Thus recommending me and my new rib to your daily prayers, I commit you to the only All-sufficient'. The arrangements worked out well enough to spare his blushes, and he really loved his new rib. Unfortunately, she proved to be silly and quarrelsome and she did not help him much. James found her most tiresome when their children were born because she wanted to have them under her own care. This he considered unsafe, owing to the very real risk that treacherous nobles might do them harm and he insisted that they should be brought up in other households of his own choosing. That was common practice amongst the aristocracy at the time, but the Queen disliked it and it estranged her from her husband.

One of the few encouraging events of these difficult years was the foundation of Edinburgh University in 1582. James liked to think himself responsible for this, but in fact the initiative and the endowments came from the capital's own citizens and the University was organized and controlled by the Town Council, which retained considerable authority, even to the appointment of Professors, until the 19th century.

While James was still at the very threshold of his troubled reign, Presbyterians began giving fresh thought to the organization of their beloved Kirk, and in doing this they accelerated the pace of controversy. In 1581, the *Second Book of Discipline* was declared authoritative by the General Assembly. This was inspired by the thinking of Andrew Melville, formerly Principal of Glasgow University, now Principal of St. Mary's College, St. Andrews. He was much more definite than Knox had ever been on the question of Episcopacy, which he condemned with the forthright severity James disliked so much in Presbyterians. Melville went so far as to urge that church courts should instruct civil magistrates in their jurisdiction 'according to the Divine Word'.

James naturally was much displeased by this development. In 1584, he persuaded Parliament to pass statutes which confirmed the appointment of bishops, and forbade convocations of ministers except with the King's consent. This legislation made James most unpopular. It was a shock to Presbyterians, the first in a long series of crises which aroused such emotions that it became difficult for people to think rationally about episcopacy. Within two years, James had to modify his position, and though bishops still held office, Presbyteries, Synods and General Assemblies were again allowed to meet.

Frightened by the possibility of losing their hard-won religious liberty, hardened by their hatred for all things Roman, ministers and laymen in the Kirk began to adopt a more extreme Calvinism. They insisted that, as God is no respecter of persons, all the elect are equal in His sight and they began too to depart from the dignified forms of worship set out in the Book of Common Order, adopting instead more extempore prayer. Many serious-minded Protestants were concerned about this change. John Spottiswoode was one of these, and his views are worth quoting. 'My judgment is and has been that the most simple, decent and humble rites should be choosed, such as is the bowing of the knees in resaving (receiving) the Holy Sacramente and others of that kinde, prophannesse being as dangerous to religion as superstition; and touching the government of the church, I am verily persuaded that the government episcopall is the only right and Apostolique form. Paritie among ministers is the breeder of confusion, as experience might have taught us, and for these ruling elders, as they are a mere human devise, so they will prove, if they find way, the ruin both of church and estate.'

Melville and Spottiswoode represent the two militant and opposed bodies of Scottish Protestants, now fully conscious of their beliefs and determined to stand up for them. The issue was not simply the virtues and defects of one form of Church govern ment over against another. It was complicated by the fact that the King saw in bishops appointed by himself an essential instrument of his own royal supremacy. This complication was intensified by the conflicts of the 17th century and it drove the cleavage between Presbyterian and Episcopalian so deep that its healing could not even be attempted until the 20th century.

The late 16th and early 17th century saw a strange revival of belief in witches. It is difficult to understand this hysteria or its causes, nor can one explain why Scotsmen were much more afflicted by it than Englishmen, prevalent as it was in England too. They attributed any sudden death of man or beast, and especially any suicide, to an alliance with the Devil on the part of some withered, senile woman. Witchtrials gave the men who conducted them ample chance to satisfy and even to stimulate sadistic impulses: the poor old crones often became demented under the prolonged interrogation and confessed to impossible sins before they were finally burned alive in public.

The King was fascinated by sorcery because he was afraid of it. Like other leading men of his day, he believed it was a Christian's duty to root out witchcraft and he published a treatise on the subject. It was called *Daemonologie* and described in some detail the techniques by which the Devil established his hold upon those who became enthralled to him. There were of course warlocks, male devotees, as well as witches, in this bondage to Satan, but

153

James declared that, because of Eve's surrender, the Devil had always been on 'homlier' terms with the female sex.

But the King was more enlightened than many Scots and he knew that delusion and hysteria could produce extraordinary states of mind. Unlike most people at that time, James could distinguish false from genuine evidence. He followed many cases in detail, with the result that he was able to expose a number of malicious attempts to incriminate defenceless victims, and he secured their release. He discovered that physical causes often explained strange behaviour and he was known to recommend rest and proper food and on one occasion, marriage, as the best cure. Some people think that James ultimately abandoned his belief in sorcery as a result of his investigations. However this may be, Scotsmen in general did not, and the torture of witches remained an ugly feature of the 17th century Scottish life.

It was unfortunate that in the closing years of the 16th century James not only set the tone for religious controversy, but also acquired a dangerous skill—the management of the Scottish Parliament. Because of the 15th century developments, described in chapter 10, it was relatively easy for him to establish complete mastery over the whole Parliament. He himself selected the Lords of the Articles. A full meeting of Parliament was of course summoned to 'elect' them, but the men chosen were his nominees. James then had all the ordinary members dispersed while the Lords of the Articles were at work, drafting legislation according to his instructions, and a full meeting was once more convened to vote for the statutes en bloc. So ordinary Scottish members could not influence the course of legislation at all, and indeed hardly understood its significance. All this was of course more or less in keeping with 14th and 15th century tradition, but it gave James a false sense of security and a very bad training for handling the totally different English Parliament.

During his adolescence and young manhood, James was much concerned about the succession to the English throne. He wanted it more passionately than he wanted anything else and he thought about it continually, sometimes with anxious doubt, sometimes with confident hope. There was in fact no other heir for Elizabeth and when at last the great old Queen died on March 24th, 1603,

James was proclaimed King of England without any opposition at all. He set forth for the magic south on April 5th, happy at last, delighted by the welcome he received at every stopping point along the Great North Road. His Queen followed later with the children and the Court became permanently based in England.

James positively basked in his new way of life. He appreciated the deferential, not to say obsequious, manners of English courtiers, who quickly learned that he could digest any amount of flattery: he was delighted with all the opportunities for hunting, and he found his large and gracious palaces entirely satisfying. At last, too, he was among people who had a proper regard for bishops, and he enjoyed the aesthetically pleasing ritual and the formal tone of the services he now attended. In a recent biography of James, David Harris Wilson says that he 'took the Church of England to his heart in a long rapturous embrace that lasted the rest of his life'. He continued to talk his broad Scots to the end of his days, but he was not in the least homesick: on the contrary, he felt released from an unloved bondage, and he only visited Scotland once during the remaining twenty-two years before he died.

He devoted some thought to Scottish affairs however. For one thing he was determined to unite the two Kingdoms in name and in fact. He introduced the title 'Great Britain', against strong opposition from his English subjects, who had no wish to sink their ancient identity in a new political creation. They also bluntly refused to contemplate organizing a joint Parliament with Scottish representatives at Westminster and still less would they consider allowing trade concessions to their brothers across the Border. James was disappointed about this. As a Christian King, he said, he did not want 'to be a polygamist and to have two wives . . . as God hath made Scotland the one half of this isle to enjoy my birth and the first and most unperfect half of my life, and you here to enjoy the perfect and last half thereof, so can I not think that any could cut asunder the one half of me from the other'. But he had to accept polygamy. It was perhaps a pity, for real union, together with parity in trading privileges, might have prevented many later troubles—but few people, apart from James and perhaps Francis Bacon, saw the matter in this light.

The King now succeeded in establishing a remote control over Scottish affairs which was more effective than the authority of any of his predecessors. He worked the Scottish Privy Council hard, sending them sharply worded instructions, which on the whole they faithfully carried out. 'This I must say for Scotland, here I sit and govern it with my pen, I write and it is done, and by a Clark of the Council I govern Scotland now, which others could not do by the sword'. This boastful remark was not far wide of the mark.

James' orders to his Council dealt frequently with the problem of lawlessness, which reached lengths one can hardly nowadays imagine. In 1612, for example, some of the Neish clan raided the Macnabs as they were about to enjoy Christmas dinner, and were able to escape with the roast to an island on Loch Earn, because they owned its only boat. Macnab's four eldest sons, urged on by their mother, carried their own boat from Loch Tay over to Loch Earn, caught the Neishes unprepared and in vengeance killed the whole family except two small children. They decapitated the corpses and took the heads back to their mother in a sack, to her great satisfaction, though they felt too tired to carry back their boat as well.

This was the kind of thing James was determined to stamp out. The Clan Gregor was possibly one of the worst hornets' nests: its neighbours, especially in the Loch Lomond area, had suffered endless misery from it. James authorized the complete extinction of this clan, whose name was abolished, and whose members were driven away from their homes by fire and slaughter, willingly carried out through the agency of traditional foes.

The Southern Hebrides were reduced to quiet in similar fashion; the Macdonalds of Islay suffered frightful punishment; and the notoriously evil 'Earl Pate', Patrick Stewart of the Orkneys, a cousin of the King who had ruled these islands with injustice and violence for years, was hanged. James' methods would hardly stand scrutiny from a constitutional or judicial point of view, except perhaps his treatment of Earl Pate, but he made Scotland a more peaceful and orderly country.

James' other aim in Scotland was of course to break the power of the Presbyterian Kirk. After 1603, for a number of years, the

General Assembly was forbidden to meet. In 1606, Andrew Melville and seven other leading Scottish ministers were summoned to England to discuss the religious situation in their country. They were subjected to insulting cross-examination and exhortation, which Melville would not suffer mildly. He was therefore imprisoned in the Tower for three years and then, like his nephew James, forbidden to return to Scotland; and the other six ministers were delayed in England much longer than they wanted to stay.

After this suppression of the Presbyterian leaders, James increased the powers of the Scottish bishops and also their numbers. By 1610, there were eleven of them and two Archbishops, one of whom was John Spottiswoode. They could enforce ecclesiastical law through the two Courts of High Commission, established for them in 1610 on the English model.

That Scottish people put up with such interference is surprising. It was partly because Andrew Melville was safely out of the way and their other leaders intimidated, partly because some of the Scottish bishops, Forbes of Aberdeen for example, were men of tolerance and wisdom. Mainly, however, it was because so far congregational worship had not been tampered with, and so ordinary people found their Sunday services unchanged and did not realize the new power of the bishops in Scotland.

In 1617, the King decided to come north himself and deal with religious matters. His visit did not endear him to his subjects in Edinburgh, who were angered by an organ and surpliced choristers suddenly appearing in Holyrood. James tried to make a representative group of ministers accept five considerable changes. These were that Communion should be received kneeling, that the festivals of the Christian year should be observed, that confirmation should be administered by bishops and not by ministers, that private Communion and private baptism should be allowed in the case of serious illness.

A General Assembly was summoned on the King's orders for 1618, and met in Perth. It was subjected to all the bullying that James could devise. So his Five Articles of Perth were sanctioned by the Kirk's highest authority. There was a furious reaction up and down the country. People were specially incensed by the order to receive Communion kneeling. Congregations and ministers boycotted the innovations so systematically that not even the Courts of High Commission could do anything to enforce them. Some twenty years were to pass before the General Assembly met again.

James' policies south of the Border do not fall within the scope of this book, but it is relevant to say that his experience of Scottish life and institutions, his vanity and his weaknesses of character made him ill-prepared to deal with the English situation.

When he met the English Puritan leaders at the Hampton Court Conference in 1604, for example, James assumed at once that they were of the same stamp as the Presbyterians he had hated in childhood, especially as they used some of the same religious terminology. He handled them with angry contempt and the Conference ended in recrimination. English Puritans had so far been milder in spirit and less extreme in principle than Scottish Presbyterians, and under more moderate guidance than James could give that Conference could have initiated a period of comprehensive tolerance. It was a tragedy for 17th century England that their new King's prejudices should have made him miss this unique opportunity.

In similar fashion, James fell foul of the English Parliament. He was indignant when he discovered that the Commons, meeting quite separately from the Lords, felt free to debate all legislation at leisure and openly to critize royal suggestions. The King was poles apart from his new subjects too, in that he had no personal pride in the seamanship of Elizabeth's great admirals like Sir Walter Raleigh, nor did he feel as they did towards Spain. Englishmen had never shaken off their fear of Spain and the Armada tradition was their great pride. James' idea that he would hold the balance of power in a peaceful Europe by negotiating both with France and with Spain suited his own vanity excellently but it horrified Englishmen who remembered the old days.

Possibly things would have worked out better had James' eldest son Henry survived, but this promising young man died before his father. By 1624, James was mortally ill, and affairs were under the control of his second son, Charles, and the royal favourite of the King's old age, the Duke of Buckingham. In 1625 he died. The Scots had gained nothing by the fact that they had given Great Britain her first King, except a complexity of problems which his successor was even less capable of interpreting wisely.

CHAPTER 15

The Making of the National Covenant

When Charles I became King, his subjects in the Highlands probably remained unaware of the fact for many months. Mountains and sealochs separate the north and west from the rest of the country and there were then no roads fit to carry wheeled traffic. The northern and western shires were unmoved by controversies which disturbed people elsewhere in Scotland and they were not even represented in the Scottish Parliament until the middle of the 17th century. Chieftains exercised their ancestral hold on their clans and administered their traditional forms of justice, clan loyalties were strong, clan feuds unforgotten, in spite of James I's strong hand. Economic conditions were primitive and standards of living much lower than people in the south realized.

In sharp contrast to the Highlands was the north-eastern area of Scotland. The people of Aberdeen consciously enjoyed the sense that theirs was the capital city of this prosperous district. In the mid-17th century the population in Aberdeen was probably about 8,750. They were relatively well-to-do people, because of their east coast sea-trade. They imported taffetas, calicoes, looking-glasses, swordblades and much else. They were proud of the peaceful and orderly way of life that was normally theirs, and proud too of their University.

The Border shires enjoyed more peaceful conditions after 1603. The old Border feuds abated, raiding became less common. In southern and central Scotland, in the north-east too, the landed gentry established at this period a prosperity they had not known earlier, a rough and homespun prosperity, but nonetheless enjoyable. It was based on traffic in Church properties and carefully planned marriage alliances, which enabled the Lords to live more spaciously, as one can see by the domestic architecture of the times. It is significant that in the Western Highlands there was apparently no such change in building as one can detect elsewhere and no improvement in personal comfort.

Agriculture was the chief means of making a livelihood. People lived as their forbears had done, by subsistence farming. For ordinary people, poverty was necessarily still a continuing nightmare. Village life was stifled by the jealous way in which the little burghs guarded their medieval monopolies, trade played only a small part in the national economy except on the eastern coastline, industry was hardly established at all. There was no banking system and currency had a very limited circulation. Scotland's middle class was a relatively small element in the nation.

At this time there seemed to be little conscious national feeling. So far as it existed, it was dormant, or perhaps masked. While Highlanders thought of clan before country at this time, many Scotsmen were more international than national in outlook. The nobles were in the habit of sending their sons to France and to the Netherlands for university and also for legal training. But the travelling Scot was to be found at every level of society. In particular, the armies of Sweden and France attracted all types of Scotsmen who joined up as professional soldiers in foreign service. A violent political or religious crisis was needed before a specifically Scottish national spirit would emerge once more.

There was no religious unity. Protestantism had reached Caithness and the Orkney and Shetland Isles through the traffic by sea, but it had not penetrated old Drumalban. The Western Highlands knew little of it, except in the Earl of Argyll's domains. Even the medieval Church had failed to establish an effective hold on parts of the north and west, so difficult were some of the glens to reach, and there were districts where the inhabitants must have been living in a state of near paganism. Early in the 17th century, however, priests from Ireland began a mission to the Islands and Western Highlands, and its success is marked by the devout and loyally Roman Catholic population which survives in certain districts to this day.

The strongholds of the Presbyterian Kirk were in southern and central Scotland. Here the ministers exercised an influence far beyond anything we can easily realize today. So long as they satisfied Calvinist consciences on matters of principle, all Protestant laymen were prepared to support their ministers staunchly. This was especially noticeable, when the Kirk was in danger. And danger seemed always near at hand. Ministers and laymen alike were obsessed by horror of Rome and fear of anything akin to Roman practice. They thought the Church of England was only a step removed from Rome, and bishops they resented as the agents of a supposedly romanizing King.

Only in one part of Scotland was Episcopacy firmly rooted. This was in and around Aberdeen, where a strong Episcopal tradition grew up. It is rather difficult to explain this. Perhaps it was partly geographical. Today it takes almost four hours to reach Aberdeen from Glasgow by train, and in the early 17th century the city was far removed from the militant Presbyterians of the south, and still farther from the sphere of Anglican interference. The bishops of Aberdeen generally maintained harmonious relations with the university officials and they were on good terms also with the local Kirk leaders. This goodwill was extended even to the Roman Catholic families and priests of the neighbourhood, who, fostered by the Gordon family's influence, were able to practise their religion without incurring hostility.

The way in which Presbyterians and Episcopalians and Roman Catholics maintained their way of life in the north-east suggests that religious intolerance need not have developed so acutely as it did later in the century. Possibly, if James I and his son had not tried to make church organization uniform throughout their kingdoms, members of these three Churches might have accepted each others' existence more readily.

There is ample evidence that spiritual issues meant everything to many of the militant Presbyterians in southern Scotland. It has sometimes been fashionable to decry piety of the 17th century Presbyterian type, on the grounds that it was skin-deep, a device to secure worldly advantage, a hypocrisy in fact. This is far from being true. Many ministers were imbued with the spirit of Samuel Rutherford, minister of Anwoth in Galloway. 'I desire not', he wrote in 1631, 'to go on the lee-side or sunny side of religion, or to put truth betwixt me and a storm: my Saviour did not so for me, who in His sufferings took the windy side of the hill'. This spirit of devotion was nurtured by prayer and Bible study and it bought no worldly advantage for those who cultivated it. Ministers were not alone in seeking this living relationship with Christ. Burgesses, lairds, shopkeepers, countryfolk, nobles— many of them were inspired by a faith, unostentatious but genuine, which enabled them ultimately to face almost impossible strain. Like Lord Warriston at the height of his success in the legal profession, they could say: 'God's consolations never run drye, ar ay tastye, and keeps men ever fresh, for they are a fountayne, not a pudle or a pond.'

Presbyterians were at one in believing that their religion should be the supreme influence in the land. They thought, as Andrew Melville had inspired them to think, that secular officials should be guided in matters of principle by the leaders of the Kirk. Only so could they hope for security in their faith. They were reluctant to accept episcopacy, partly because they knew that bishops were appointed by the King, and that the King would give the bishops political authority, which could mean the infiltration of Roman Catholic practices.

Into this situation in 1625 there came a King utterly incapable of understanding it. Charles I was more divorced from his Scottish subjects than his father had been. He spent all his life after his fourth year in England. He never even visited Scotland until 1633. He made friends with hardly anybody, least of all Scotsmen. He did not know what other people's thoughts were and it never occurred to him that there was any reason why he should. He lived in a world of his own, a cultivated, fastidious world, where painting, literature, formal manners and serenely conducted religious services were the things that mattered. If only Charles had been a reasonably wealthy country gentleman, with a well-appointed country house, a good-sized garden, a library, a stable, a quiet wife and a large family, he would have been happy and successful, a man with few friends perhaps, but enjoying widespread respect and upholding valued principles.

As it was, Charles I could no more understand Scotland than he could guess at the existence of nuclear energy. The pattern of Scottish life and the climate of Scottish opinion remained foreign to him all his days. He knew little about the Kirk and disliked what he knew. He had no notion of the hold the General Assembly had on people's affections, even though its meetings had been proscribed. He did not understand Highland clan loyalty, nor did he grasp the fact that traditional alliances held certain great Lowland families together. That Scots regarded England as a rich and ruthless neighbour, that they had bad memories dating back to Tudor invasions of Scotland, that they were deeply afraid of Roman Catholicism—none of these things occurred to this serious-minded, highly cultivated grandson of Mary, Queen of Scots.

Charles inherited his father's suspicion of democratic assemblies and by 1628 he had deeply offended the English Parliament. So incensed was he with this organ of the English body politic, that he ruled without it from 1629 until 1640, a feat which put him in a difficult position with regard to money matters. He had to finance his very expensive court and administration by methods which shocked people who had every wish to remain loyal to him.

Charles I was devout. And his religion was the religion of William Laud.

Laud was Bishop of London, later Archbishop of Canterbury. He had a great reverence for the authority of the Church of England, which he enforced through the Court of High Commission. He loved ritual and orthodox Anglican principles. He began a carefully planned campaign of church reform to bring even obscure parish priests into line with his own practice.

For English Puritans, this was a time of terrible difficulty. They were repulsive to Laud, because of their indecent insistence on the individual's right to interpret Christian doctrine and the Scriptures according to his own light. They condemned certain things in the Prayer Book as dregs of popery and they put great stress on the necessity of preaching. Their courage in the face of persecution became notorious and the Court of High Commission was busy with them continually. Their ministers were removed from their churches; open-air preaching was forbidden; physical torture and imprisonment were inflicted on them. Among these Puritans, who also hated Episcopacy, there grew up a lively sympathy for the Scottish Kirk.

The Making of the National Covenant

Although Charles had no love for Scotland, he devoted serious attention to its affairs. The most sincere of all Stuart kings, with the possible exception of James II, Charles was forced by the logic of his own thinking into a policy of imposing religious uniformity. Like his father, he believed himself to be invested with Divinely given authority. He thought he must use it to foster true religion: and he believed that political loyalty to the Crown could flourish only when all its subjects were united under one form of Church government. So he set himself to complete his father's task of bringing the Scottish Kirk into line with the Church of England. Within a dozen years, the leaders of the Scottish Kirk in their turn were trying to force the English nation to come into line with Presbyterianism. It was typical of the age to see no way but the one way, no safety other than the safety of uniformity.

Charles began by planning a re-organization of all the old Church properties, which had been for some eighty years in the hands of the Scottish gentry, and of the old Church tithes, which were also being enjoyed by laymen. These capital assets he proposed to use as provision for the maintenance of the clergy in Scotland.

Later, in 1633, Charles made a royal progress into Scotland and held a coronation service in St. Giles, Edinburgh. This service was conducted with full Anglican rites, which Charles believed the Scots would find so impressive that they would be completely won over to a Laudian view of ritual ceremony. In the same year the King founded the bishopric of Edinburgh. Not long after, he appointed Spottiswoode, Archbishop of St. Andrews, to be his Chancellor in Scotland.

The General Assembly had not been allowed to meet since 1618. Charles decided that the other democratic elements in the Kirk must be brought to an end too, and therefore he planned to abolish Presbyteries. At the same time, he and Laud took up with fresh vigour a problem which had troubled them both for some time—the Scottish form of Divine Service. It was clear to them that the English Book of Common Prayer was not acceptable in Scotland, though they could hardly see why, so they appointed a Commission to draw up a Revised Prayer Book for use in the Northern Kingdom. They thought they had offered a big concession in doing this, especially as a number of Scots were included among those who worked out the new Liturgy. They compiled a very fine Prayer Book.

One can never quite become accustomed to Charles I's ignorance of his own people or to his life-long habit of giving offence unawares. He did not know that his schemes to redistribute Church properties had enraged the Scottish gentry. He did not know that his coronation service had seemed like an act of paganism to Edinburgh people. He did not know that the Scots hated the thought of bishops being endowed with political authority. Least of all had he the slightest idea of how the Prayer Book would effect the situation.

The new Liturgy was read for the first time in St. Giles, Edinburgh, on July 28th, 1637. The Dean had hardly begun the service before there was an uproar of shouts from the congregation. Angry worshippers flung stools and Bibles about, and after they had been forced by armed guards to leave the cathedral the rioters banged on the doors and threw stones at the windows.

The outburst of fury was an expression of hatred against high-handed interference with religious liberty. As somebody wrote later, 'This new Book of Common Prayer is introduced and urged in a way which this Kirk hath never been acquianted with.' It was a beautiful Liturgy and its adoption would have been to the advantage of the Kirk in many ways, but it was doomed to rejection because it was identified with autocratic, remote control and it became a symbol of Roman Catholicism in thin disguise.

Public demonstrations were so violent that the Privy Councillors did not know what to do. They shut themselves up in Holyrood, which at a pinch could be defended against physical attack. They announced that the rioters were guilty of treason and worthy of death, but they also suspended the use of the Prayer Book. And then they composed a report of the matter to send to the King.

Charles had much else on his mind, and little attention to spare for Edinburgh's reaction to decently conducted public worship. He wrote his instructions to the Privy Council and they were perfectly straightforward. All who had protested against the Prayer Book were to be punished and the Book itself was to be taken into regular use.

'This I must say for Scotland, here I sit and govern it with my pen, I write and it is done, and by a clark of the Council I govern Scotland now . . .' So wrote James I. So thought Charles I. But this was one stroke of the pen too many. The Privy Councillors could not even begin to enforce the King's will in the matter.

Wild disorder continued in Edinburgh. In her book, *The King's Peace*, C. V. Wedgwood describes 'the Bishop of Brechin, tough and formidable, who glared at his congregation over a pair of loaded pistols while he conducted the service'. It became a risky proceeding for a bishop, or even a bishop's sympathizer, to appear in the Edinburgh streets. Of course, the rabble which chased and insulted these people was drawn from the barbarous vennels and closes of the city slums. It was headed as often as not by street women, harridans who understood nothing at all about orders of worship, but who loved to goad their men into a spirited fight. At the same time, however, petitions against the Prayer Book were appearing from many parts of the country, written in dignified incisive prose, the work of men who were fully capable of leading responsible opinion. The anger which inspired them was no emotion of the mob, but a new political fervour. But Charles persisted in sending orders that the petitioners should be dispersed and punished.

During the autumn and winter, representatives of the opposition formed a committee in Edinburgh known as The Tables. It was led by men with powerful connections, the Earls of Rothes and of Montrose. They had the support of many influential laymen, Lord Warriston for example, and ministers of first-class ability, such as Alexander Henderson of Leuchars. In sympathy with them were Lord Lorne, heir to the Earl of Argyll, and Sir Thomas Hope, both members of the Privy Council. Their hold on public opinion became very powerful.

When February 1638 came, the King decided to go off on holiday to Newmarket and enjoy some hunting. He did so with a relatively easy mind about Scotland, because, before setting out, he had despatched yet another proclamation. It was to be publicly announced in Edinburgh and other cities, that all the nobles who had resisted the Prayer Book were to submit to the King's will and to conform.

The proclamation was the spark that fired a totally unexpected explosion. Hundreds of demonstrators gathered at the Mercat Cross in Edinburgh in such a threatening temper that the only way of getting them to disperse was by asking their own leaders, Rothes and Montrose, to send them away. Even Charles was forced to see how slender his authority in Scotland had become when news of these scenes reached him in early March.

Far worse news however was to follow. On February 28th, in the Greyfriars Kirk at Edinburgh, the nobility of Scotland signed a document of which copies were soon made and signed on the two following days by many ministers and other delegates assembled in Edinburgh. The National Covenant was the document and it represented, in Lord Warriston's words, 'the great marriage day of this nation with God'.

The National Covenant had been drawn up by Lord Warriston and Alexander Henderson and other leaders, after months of thought and prayer. It incorporated a Confession of Faith, signed in 1581 by the twelve-year-old James VI; it detailed many Acts of Parliament for the establishment of the true religion and the maintenance of the Church's liberties; it included a protest against all the recent changes forced upon Scotland's Kirk; it ended with a vow of loyalty. 'From the knowledge and conscience of our duty to God, to our King and country, without any worldly respect or inducement——we promise and swear by the great name of the Lord our God to continue in the profession and obedience of the aforesaid religion; that we shall defend the same and resist all those contrary errors and corruptions according to our vocation and to the utmost that God hath put into our hands, all the days of our life.'

When Edinburgh's civic act of faith had been completed, copies of the Covenant were taken by mounted messengers to every part of Scotland and signatures were collected from all over the country, except the Catholic Highlands. It was then carried to Europe, to be signed by Scottish soldiers serving in foreign armies. It was supported by men of all classes and all ranks.

Cynics can claim that for political reasons skilled rascals whipped up the emotions of simple people and forced them to support the Covenant. Unquestionably many did so without in the least understanding what it was all about. We, who live in the 20th century, have every reason to appreciate that there are always people willing to sign documents in complete ignorance of their contents. And we know too that every movement attracts some knaves as well as a good many fools. But these were by no means the only influences behind the Covenant. Sincerity, courage, agonizing anxiety about the future, integrity, all went into its making. Among its authors and their best supporters were men who really loved their country and their religion. Charles had in fact precipitated exactly the crisis which could unite the Scottish people against him and he almost made the nation a unity. But he did not know this.

The Covenant expressed loyalty to the King and this was deliberate. The Scottish people had no wish to go against their sovereign, but they did think he was badly advised and they were desperate that he should know their thoughts. They probably did not realize that they had faced Charles with a challenge he could not ignore, but did not know how to meet.

CHAPTER 16

Scotland and the Civil War

The religious crisis of 1638 nearly achieved the impossible. For a few months it seemed as if the Scots were caught up in an all-embracing national purpose. From Edinburgh and the Lowlands there surged a wave of enthusiasm for the Covenant.

The driving force which inspired this movement came in large measure from James Graham, fifth Earl of Montrose. He was a Calvinist, but not at all a conventional one, for his was a tolerant, gay and generous spirit, he loved life and savoured its happinesses in friendship and in experience. By his personal charm and uncommon gift of leadership, perhaps too by his irrepressible sense of humour, he created a tremendous enthusiasm for the Covenant. His family seat was at Kincardine on the Ochil Hills and his influence extended through much of Perthshire and the east, but he carried the Covenant into Aberdeenshire too, the heart of Episcopalian territory, and even there he gathered a number of signatures.

In the west, the overwhelming power was that of Archibald Campbell, eighth Earl of Argyll, a different type of Scot, although he too was a single-minded Calvinist and as such distrusted all that Charles had been trying to do. His headquarters was at Inveraray and he controlled great stretches of the beautiful mountain country from Loch Awe to Loch Etive and across to Islay. While he was a dangerous enemy for Charles, he was also a dangerous colleague for Montrose, though this did not come to light in the early stages of the conflict.

Copies of the Covenant soon found their way to London, where nonconformists of all persuasions were stirred to great sympathy with the Scots. Charles realized that he was faced with a resistance that would yield to no persuasions, and in July 1638 he told his English Council that he would have to use force. This was easier said than done, as he had no standing army and his administration was riddled with inefficiency.

To give himself time for preparations, and hoping that his Scottish critics would quarrel with each other, the King sanctioned a meeting of the General Assembly, which was summoned in November 1638. A good many Covenanting Lords arrived, representing their congregations as elders. With them came bands of armed retainers. None of Aberdeen's Episcopalians dared to show face at all, nor were any bishops present, so the ministers of the kirk were well pleased. The King's Commissioner was the Duke of Hamilton, a London Scot who was most unpopular in his own country.

The Assembly of 1638 proved one of the most important in the century. So violent were its debates that after only a week Hamilton tried to dissolve it and he himself stalked out of it, but it continued in session without him. The Assembly deposed and excommunicated all the bishops, rejected the Service Book and appointed a Commission to enquire into abuses. The King declared that none of its decisions carried weight because in the absence of his Commissioner it was not a properly constituted body.

Enthusiasm for the Covenant received fresh impetus as a result of the 1638 Assembly, and the leaders found people eager to help in the preparations for war, which were now openly going ahead. Scottish officers and soldiers who had seen long service in continental armies returned home, and recruiting in the Lowlands and elsewhere was most successful. In Alexander Leslie the Covenanters had a first-class general whose experience had been gained under Wallenstein in Germany.

The King made two attempts to reduce the Covenanters by force, one in 1639, the other in 1640, and each was a humiliating disaster for him. On the second occasion, the Scottish army crossed the Tweed at Coldstream, led by Montrose, who waded the river in full kit three times to show the troops that it could be safely forded: they then marched in triumph to Newcastle, where they met with no resistance.

The failure of his efforts to crush the Scots forced Charles to summon his English Parliament. The members seized their chance to set out all their criticisms of the King's government since 1629 during which time he had ruled without any meetings of Parliament at all. Scottish commissioners, who were in London at this time, came to the premature conclusion that the English were pleased to have the Scottish army in their country and that they would be glad to adopt the Covenant.

Already, Covenanters in Scotland were falling foul of each other. A vindictive, intolerant spirit was abroad by now amongst some who wanted to enforce the Covenant, to make signature compulsory and to excommunicate any who stood out against it. Others were most uneasy about this bitterness, and saw that it could lead to religious tyranny of a very dangerous kind. At the same time, Argyll was making use of every chance to build up his own power. He was even talking of deposing the King, and it seemed that he wanted to organize a military dictatorship. Round Montrose a more moderate group was gathering, and it was known that he was out of sympathy with Argyll. He signed a pact with some of his supporters at Cumbernauld in Lanarkshire, re-affirming his belief in the Covenant but also his loyalty to the King.

In an effort to play off one faction against another, and to enlist Scottish support for himself, Charles agreed late in 1641 to all the decisions of the General Assembly of 1638. He was becoming more and more of an opportunist, and he still believed his enemies would quarrel so bitterly with each other that he would be able to re-assert his authority. Charles over-estimated his powers of intrigue. As he had never studied other people's thoughts, he did not know how their minds worked and he was wrong in thinking he could manipulate the factions arrayed against him.

He was not far wrong however in diagnosing disharmony among his enemies. When Civil War broke out in the harvest season of August 1642, there was friction in both his kingdoms among the people who hated him. The English Parliament and Army were hearing more than some people liked from the Independents, men of strong and sincere religious conviction who wanted much more individual freedom in religion than anybody else could approve. The Scottish Covenanters were divided less on principle but much more in practice. Montrose had no doubts as to his duty. Though still unchanged in his religious outlook and still loyal to the Covenant as he understood it, he was disgusted by the idea that he should take up arms against his King, and there were many like him, who had come to distrust the dogmatic views expressed by extremists. Argyll on the other hand was implacably hostile to the King and identified himself with the Parliamentary point of view: he too commanded support from many Scotsmen.

During the opening months of the war, events went ill for Parliament, whose leaders became desperately anxious. In 1643, therefore, they began to negotiate for active help from Scotland. Here was the chance for which Covenant men had been seeking. They consented to give Parliament military assistance by attacking the Royalist positions from the North, in return for which they were to be paid £30,000 a month for expenses. It was also agreed—and this was the marrow of the matter for the Scots —that there should be 'a reformation of religion in the Kingdoms of England and Ireland in doctrine, worship, discipline and government, according to the Word of God and the example of the best reformed churches, and that popery and prelacy should be extirpated'. The Scots hoped that by this treaty, which was called the Solemn League and Covenant, the English might be induced to bring their Church into conformity with that in Scotland, but the English Parliament interpreted the matter rather differently.

The Scottish Covenanters had been shocked when Laud had tried to impose his kind of religious uniformity throughout the land. They saw nothing inconsistent now in trying to enforce their own. This was because they believed that the Law of God must be supreme over the law of men, and throughout the 17th century the Covenant seemed to them to contain the Law of God. The Solemn League was a serious setback for Charles as it led to war on two fronts, which his forces could not sustain.

Meantime Parliament was giving attention to the spiritual wellbeing of the country, which in their view had been so gravely damaged by Laud, and it appointed the Westminster Assembly to give it advice. This Assembly, which in later days would have been described as a Parliamentary Commission, consisted of 121 English clergymen and 30 laymen, some of whom were Members of Parliament. Once the Solemn League and Covenant was ratified, the General Assembly was invited to send five ministers and three laymen to represent Scottish opinion in these deliberations.

The Westminster Assembly, despite a good deal of wrangling among its members, produced four documents of great importance. The Confession of Faith set out religious principles which were Calvinist in nature; the two Catechisms, known as the 'Larger' and the 'Shorter', were designed to help ministers and elders in their duty of instructing the young in Christian belief; the Directory of Public Worship gave orders of service which were to replace the English Book of Common Prayer. It was expected that England, Scotland and Ireland would all adopt these publications and so the desired uniformity throughout the three kingdoms would come about.

In fact, the Westminster Assembly's work exercised little influence in England except among the Congregationalist and Baptist Churches, but it did have a lasting effect in Scotland. For many generations Scottish ministers and Church members based their religious thinking and their worship on the Westminster documents, which have indeed become part of the Scottish Presbyterian's inheritance, though many devout members of the Church of Scotland would be astonished to realize that English influence predominated in the drafting of them.

Another publication which, after it had been revised, received the approval of the Westminster Assembly, was a metrical version of the Psalms by Francis Rous, a Cornish Member of Parliament, who was Provost of Eton. Further revision was carried through in Scotland over a period of several years, with the result that the Metrical Psalter, which came into use in 1650 with the authority of the General Assembly, bears little trace of Rous. The metrical Psalms have become an essential part of Presbyterian worship and they are still used too in some of the English Nonconformist Churches.

After the Solemn League and Covenant was signed, Parliament reorganized its army, under Cromwell's direction, and from 1644 onwards it was clear that Charles was doomed. With Scottish help—and it was worth much, because the Scottish soldiers were experienced and well-disciplined—Parliament's forces defeated the King's at Marston Moor in 1644. The following year, Charles met with fresh disaster at Naseby.

The only thing Royalists could rejoice over in 1644 and 1645 was the news from Scotland. Montrose had taken up arms for the King and was gathering a formidable army in his support. The story of his year of victories has become one of Scotland's sagas. He defeated the Covenanters at Tippermuir and captured Perth in autumn 1644. He campaigned in Speyside and caught Argyll unawares at Fyvie. He went to Blair Atholl and thence, in dreadful winter weather, forced his way over the barren mountains westwards and attacked the Campbells at Argyll's own stronghold of Inverary, so unexpectedly that Argyll himself only escaped by rising from his dinner table, embarking on his boat and sailing away down Loch Fyne to the sea. After an appalling winter's march, Montrose defeated Argyll's people once more at Inverlochy and here again their chief left them to their fate and made off by boat. Nobody who has even the slightest knowledge of all this wild country or of winter conditions in the Highlands, can fail to marvel at Montrose's generalship and at the physical endurance of his troops.

The Covenanters in Scotland were in despair by 1645 and they sent for English help. But Montrose captured Dundee, won fresh victories at Alford, near Aberdeen, and at Kilsyth, and finally established his hold both on Edinburgh and also on Glasgow. He met with his first defeat in September 1645 at Philiphaugh, but he still hoped to redeem the King's fortunes in Scotland, when he heard that Charles had surrendered to the Scottish army at Newark, in England. A condition of this surrender was that Montrose should disband his followers and leave the country. This was in May 1646.

It was a frightful blow for Montrose. Charles was at his old game of playing off one set of enemies against another and he was now seeking the support of Argyll. He thought he could do this because the Independents in the English army had become so hostile to Presbyterianism that there was no chance of Parliament honouring the promises the Scots considered they had made in the Solemn League.

Montrose went to Norway, deeply disillusioned, but with his personal reputation high, and his hold on Scottish affections extraordinarily strong, even in the districts where he had carried out his already legendary campaigns. Only amongst Campbells was he unforgiven.

The Scottish army in England was unfortunately placed. Since Marston Moor, their services had become less necessary to their allies, and the Covenant was most unpopular among the English soldiers. Moreover, the Scots were short of money; their expenses had been heavy, in the region, they estimated, of half a million pounds, and they had not yet received the payments promised in the Solemn League. Though they held Charles I, they could not make him accept the Covenant. Had he done so, they could have raised enthusiastic and effective help for him in Scotland, but it was more than he could swallow, even in his extremity. Stalemate had been reached, and so the Scottish leaders handed him over to the Commissioners of Parliament, accepted a promise of £400,000 towards their expenses, and made their way back to Scotland. They were dismayed when Charles declared that they had sold him.

And then, most curiously, there was a reaction among some of the Scots, who began to think that if Charles were re-instated things might improve. The Earl of Lauderdale, and others, visited him secretly and assured him of Scottish military aid if he would undertake to make England Presbyterian for a trial period of three years. Charles agreed, though with some modifying conditions. The treaty was called the Engagement, and the lords who negotiated it became known as the Engagers. Many Covenanters were bitterly angry with the Engagers, who seemed to be diluting the implications of the Covenant.

Meantime, Montrose was still abroad, much cast down in spirit because of all that he had seen and suffered and because he knew very well that the end was not yet. He was in Brussels when he learned, in February 1649, of the King's execution. When he was told of this, the shock was such that he fainted.

His great enemy, Argyll, was also profoundly moved. It had seemed logical enough to him that he should fight against Charles in collaboration with the Parliamentary leaders, but when Englishmen executed his King, Argyll was incensed. Like Montrose, he at once offered his services to Prince Charles, who was then eighteen years old, and he had him proclaimed King in Edinburgh. The Prince was not at all like his father in character, but unfortunately he believed, as Charles I had done, in playing one set of people against another. So he negotiated both with Argyll and also with Montrose, perhaps without fully realizing how furiously the former longed to bring about the downfall of the latter.

Montrose went to Orkney as the Prince's representative and thence crossed to Thurso to begin recruiting in Sutherlandshire, well aware that the cause was now almost hopeless. At Assynt he was betrayed by a laird who had offered him hospitality. He was then taken in miserable and humiliating circumstances to Edinburgh and put on trial for treason to the Covenant. In June, 1649, he was hanged, drawn and quartered. This horrible climax may have given Argyll some satisfaction. It established Montrose forever in the affections of those Scots who saw in him a man without bitterness or self-pity, capable of selfless devotion to a King unworthy of such service. His sentence was ordered by the Edinburgh Committee of Estates, men of his own country and his own religion.

After Montrose's disaster, Prince Charles had no option but to trust to Argyll. He came to Scotland and accepted the Covenant, a gesture which was not misunderstood by the Scottish leaders, for they knew that he did not intend to fulfil his word. But a coronation ceremony was arranged for him in Scone and it was Argyll himself who placed the crown on his head. Everybody present knew that not one of the principals in this stately scene trusted any of the others.

Already Charles II's supporters had been defeated by Cromwell at Dunbar, in 1650. The following year they met with an even worse disaster at Worcester. So the newly crowned King went on his travels and lived abroad for nearly nine years. During this period, Cromwell set up the most efficient, just and successful government Scotland had experienced in centuries. It was also the most hated.

It took Cromwell's troops from twelve to eighteen months to establish the military control which he considered a necessary beginning. By August 1652, resistance was at an end and already the Scots were becoming accustomed to the idea that their country had been united with England in a Treaty of Union. Thirty Scottish members were later selected as representatives in a national Parliament at Westminster. This startling departure from history and habit seemed perfectly natural to Cromwell, who had no patience with illogical or cumbersome political arrangements. He was in no doubt that a full Union would make for better administration, more effective control over those who might wish to make trouble, and also considerable economic benefit for Scotland.

Sir Thomas Urquhart of Cromarty, a most odd individual who translated Rabelais and wrote books on Trigonometry, offered some advice about this Union. He recommended that 'it be not heterogeneal (as timber and stone upon ice stick sometimes together) bound by the frost of a conquering sword, but homogeneated by naturalisation and the mutual enjoyment of the same privileges and immunities'. Urquhart had some attractive ideas. He begged the English not 'to maintain the charge of an everlasting war against the storms of the climate, the fierceness of discontented people, the inaccessibility of the hills and sometimes universal penury, the mother of plague and famine; all which inconveniences may be easily prevented without any charge at all, by the sole gaining of the hearts of the country'. Cromwell's officers in Scotland had difficulty in gaining the hearts of the country however, and one wonders what effect such a miracle would have had on the inaccessibility of the hills, let alone the storms of the climate. Robert Blair made a shorter and sadder comment. 'As for the embodying of Scotland with England, it will be as when the poor bird is embodied with the hawk that hath eaten it up.' This was the general view of the Scots. One of Cromwell's officers wrote with naive surprise, when the Union was proclaimed at the market cross in Edinburgh: 'Soe senceless are this generation of theire owne goods that scarce a man of them showed any sign of rejoycing.'

Cromwell appointed seven Commissioners, four English and three Scottish, to supervise the administration of justice. Their work surprised the Scots. 'To speak treuth, the Englisches were more indulgent and merciful to the Scottis, nor was the Scottis to their awin countriemen and nychtbouris, as wes too evident, and thair justice exceidit the Scottis in mony things, as wes reportit. They also filled up the roumes of the justice courtes with very honest clerkis and members of that judicatery.' New sheriffs were commissioned for all the Scottish counties, and special care was taken to put an end to violence and disorder in the Highlands. After some three or four years, it was said that 'a man could ride all over Scotland with a switch in his hand and £100 in his pocket, which he could not have done these 500 years'.

Cromwell deeply offended the General Assembly with whom he had little patience. He wanted to allow freedom of worship to all except Episcopalians and Roman Catholics. This new idea, and others too, shocked the Assembly, which was set on the Covenant's principles first and foremost. 'In the bowels of Christ', Cromwell wrote, 'think it possible you may be mistaken.' As the Assembly could think no such thing, Cromwell forbade it to meet. Small wonder that he was hated by Presbyterians.

The administration of Scotland, both during the Common-wealth, which lasted till 1653, and also thereafter under Cromwell's Protectorate, was based on military authority. At one time there were as many as nine regiments in Scotland. Five large permanent garrisons were established at Inverlochy, Inverness, Perth, Ayr and Leith; and a great many much smaller garrisons occupied old castles and country houses. The cost was so great that the most crushing taxation Scotland had ever known was laid upon a people already suffering from poverty which moved the English officers to pity. The Generals were appalled by the 'multitudes of Vagabounds, masterfull Beggars, strong and idle persons' wandering over the country, unemployed and without hope of finding material security. General Monck, who was Cromwell's commander-in-chief in Scotland, saw that most of the

£10,000 per month that he was supposed to raise in taxation must come from the struggling little burghs. He objected to it all very much. The burghs he said should be 'tenderly and carefully cherished', not bled white by such terrible exactions. This financial burden hit the common people very hard.

Naturally enough, Scottish people deeply resented the new arrangements which cut across precious traditions and subjected everybody to a discipline sanctioned by armed force. Cromwell's political idealism was too much for his contemporaries: believing in toleration and democracy, he was driven by the tensions of his day into establishing a rigidly enforced dictatorship. People in Scotland did not realize that their English neighbours disliked it all as much as they themselves. Anglo-Scottish relations, already much poisoned by bad memories of James I and Charles I, deteriorated still further under Cromwell.

The Marquis of Argyll was one of the few who made the best of it. Typically, and ingeniously, he came to satisfactory terms with Cromwell, despite his dealings with Charles II in 1649. On all his wide domains, only at Dunstaffnage and at Dunnolly were English soldiers posted, and he managed to maintain a certain independence which gave him a more comfortable existence than any other leading noble.

When Charles II was restored to his father's throne in 1660, there was a wave of emotional rejoicing all over Scotland. People irrationally believed that at last things would settle down, and that there would be an end of military dictatorship, interference with normal daily life, civil war and all the other evils. There was to be terrible disillusion.

CHAPTER 17

The Persecution of the Covenanters

Charles II was not vindictive and he was no religious fanatic. Bloodthirsty revenge on his family's opponents did not appeal to him and he disapproved of religious persecution. But he was determined not to offend those upon whom his security in England depended. He therefore agreed that fifteen of the surviving leaders who had been responsible for his father's execution should themselves suffer the same fate.

Argyll, whom Charles had made a Marquis in 1649, expected to be honoured when the man he had crowned in Scone was restored to the throne. Charles' advisers meant to get rid of him however, and the ingenuity of the great Marquis was at last defeated. They could not convict him as a regicide, but they executed him for treason. He received much more considerate treatment during his trial than Montrose had been allowed.

During the whole twenty-five years of his reign, Charles II never visited Scotland. He appointed a Privy Council, as his father and grandfather had done, which worked in Edinburgh, but whose Secretary was a London Scot, always based on the English capital. At the beginning of his reign, this Secretary was the Earl of Lauderdale, the Engager. Once an ardent Covenanter, he now held very different views.

The Scottish Parliament was summoned to meet in Edinburgh in January 1661, and the King's agents saw to it that this Parliament was efficiently packed with men of Royalist views. It cancelled all legislation carried through since 1633. This implied the restoration of bishops and also of the system of patronage, abolished in 1649, whereby ministers were chosen by the land-owner and not by the congregation.

Ministers admitted to the parishes since 1649 were required to seek out their patrons and ask to be formally presented and

181

then to secure admission to their charges from the bishop of the diocese. About 300 ministers refused to submit to the regulations and abandoned their churches and manses. They formed almost one-third of the total number of ministers and the authorities had some difficulty in finding substitutes for them. The main centre of opposition was in the south-west where, in many places, the people forsook the parish churches and resorted to their former pastors in kitchens and barns, and later in the open fields and on the hillsides.

The Privy Council began to fine people who refused to attend the services in the parish churches, and to encourage parish ministers to make lists of absentees, so that these fines could be enforced. It also decreed that 'outed' ministers were not to live within twenty miles of their former parishes or within three miles of any royal burgh, so that it became difficult for their supporters to keep in touch with them. And then troops were quartered in the areas where resistance was strongest, especially in the shires of Ayr, Lanark, Dumfries and Galloway.

Meantime the newly appointed bishops were trying to make the best of a very awkward situation. Some of them, like Patrick Scougall in Aberdeen and Robert Leighton in Dunblane, were men of real piety and much wisdom, but on the whole they had not the qualities or the leadership to make Episcopacy any more palatable than formerly. Most unpopular of them all was Archbishop Sharp of St. Andrews.

By 1665, the illegal services in the farms and fields, known as conventicles, were so numerous that the Government made absurdly severe efforts to crush them by force. The punishments were made steadily harsher, until the Covenanters were goaded into raising a pathetic and ill-organized little rebellion. A number of them marched in pouring rain and squelching mud through Ayrshire and Lanarkshire to Rullion Green, on the outskirts of Edinburgh. Here in November 1666 they were hopelessly routed. Fifteen leaders were hanged in Edinburgh, others in Glasgow and Ayr, many more were imprisoned and subjected to torture by an instrument known as the Boot.

In 1669, Lauderdale himself came north as the King's Commissioner and tried a new policy of winning the Covenanting ministers by issuing Letters of Indulgence which offered them parish appointments on rather less stringent conditions. While some of the ministers accepted them, others refused, on the grounds that Covenant principles were still in danger and the Government had no right to legislate for the Church. Those who continued their resistance were treated more severely than ever. By armed force they were hunted out and rounded up with their lay supporters and put in specially prepared prisons, such as that on the Bass Rock, where many of them died in great misery. For years and years the odious oppression went on and so did the resistance.

At last violence produced the inevitable reaction. In 1679, Archbishop Sharp was shockingly murdered by a group of Covenanters who came upon him driving home to St. Andrews in his coach. Shortly after the King's troops, commanded by John Graham of Claverhouse, a relative of the great Montrose, were surprisingly defeated by an armed mob of Covenanters at Drumclog, on the borders of Ayrshire and Lanarkshire. This led to terrible retribution. Charles II's illegitimate son, the Duke of Monmouth, was sent to quell the disorder, and at Bothwell Bridge he carried out his mission. The Covenanters were mown down by the Government troops, and after the battle was over, twelve hundred were taken prisoner. They were herded into an improvised concentration camp in the churchyard of Greyfriars, Edinburgh, for many weeks on end. About a third of them were cowed by this and took oaths to submit to the Government, and so were sent home. Others obdurately refused and of these many died and some were executed, but about two hundred and fifty were condemned to slavery in the West Indies and loaded onto a transport ship. Perhaps fortunately for them, this vessel sank in a storm near the Orkneys and they were drowned. After another Indulgence, the policy of repression was renewed, the persecutions were accelerated, and the early 1680s became known as the Killing Time.

The stories of Covenanters who underwent all this shocking misery have been told and re-told. Descendants of these people naturally accord them the highest place in family regard and tradition. The fundamental point is overlooked very often however.

How, why, did men and women stand it? And how, why, did they do so for such long years? Unquestionably, their strength was derived from their Calvinist faith. They believed that they were predestined to grace and that they would be given the blessings of those who had 'come out of great tribulation', who would be 'before the throne of God' to all eternity. Many of them died, not with Spartan fortitude, but with joy.

Relief came at last in an absolutely unexpected way. When Charles II died in 1685, he was succeeded by his brother James, Duke of York, who became a Roman Catholic. So bitter were the controversies in which he involved himself with his English subjects that, late in 1688, he threw in his hand and left the country. The English at once declared that this 'abdication' meant that he had forfeited all right to the throne. They invited his Protestant daughter Mary and her husband, William of Orange, to become the rulers of the country in his place, and this great change is known in English history as the Glorious Revolution. In England it was almost a bloodless revolution. Though William III was never much liked, Protestants were thankful to have him, and they saw to it that he came on conditions thoroughly understood and well hedged about by sanctions.

For Scotland, the Revolution meant an abrupt end to the Killing Time and to all the miserable hounding of Covenanters that had bedevilled everything for so long. Early in 1689 a Scottish Convention of Estates agreed that William and Mary should become King and Queen and declared that there should be no more bishops. Later the same year, Episcopal government was in fact abolished and in 1690 the Westminster Confession of Faith was once again adopted: the Presbyterian government of the Church by General Assemblies, Synods, Presbyteries and Kirk Sessions was confirmed; and patronage was again set aside.

A most important constitutional change was also brought about in 1690, one which had been long needed in Scotland. The Committee of the Lords of the Articles was abolished. This meant that the Scottish Parliament was at last free to discuss legislation as a Parliament should, and in consequence its work became more vigorous and influential, because the King could not interfere so effectively as hitherto. Not enough emphasis has been laid on

184

this side of the Revolution Settlement in most histories of Scotland.

It was impossible for the Revolution to be 'bloodless' north of the Border. Stewart loyalties were strong in the Highlands, and Graham of Claverhouse raised enthusiastic support for James among the clans. General MacKay was sent with Government troops to suppress this outburst, but unfortunately for them their route took them through the deep, narrow gorge of Killie-crankie, to this day a grim, wild spot. Claverhouse waited for MacKay at the head of the gorge, with his men in an advantageous position in the cliffs above. The success of the Highlanders was complete and in a matter of hours MacKay's forces had been almost annihilated. But Claverhouse himself was killed, and without his leadership, his forces were ill-handled, and soon after were themselves defeated in the grounds of Dunkeld Cathedral beside the River Tay.

William III's position was now assured in Scotland. On the whole people were thankful for it, though the country was too exhausted and poverty-stricken with the results of three terrible decades to show much enthusiasm. Apart from certain West Highland clans, only the most extreme Covenanters grudged William his success. They formed a hard core of implacable and obstinate dissent, the nucleus from which sprang a number of splinter groups in the 18th century Presbyterian Church, and to them the Revolution meant nothing but the betrayal of their principles. In their view a State-sponsored Church was a disaster: and the Covenant should have been made compulsory by the supreme authority of the Kirk. But there were too few of these fanatics to hinder the establishment of William's authority.

Of the Highland clans, the Glencoe Macdonalds were the most reluctant to accept the inevitable. The horrible tragedy that befell them spoiled the success of the Revolution and made one more black and disgraceful memory for Scotsmen of the 1690s.

The Chiefs who had fought against the Government were offered pardon on condition that they took an oath of allegiance before January 1st, 1692. For this purpose, MacIan Macdonald of Glencoe arrived at Inveraray, his nearest point of civil administration, on January 2nd. His lateness was due partly to his own procrastination, partly to the snowstorm which held up his difficult journey from Fort William. By January 2nd, the Sheriff-depute had temporarily left his Inverary headquarters. But he returned on January 5th and took Macdonald's submission.

The Master of Stair reported to the authorities that by January 1st the Macdonalds had not subscribed the oath. Hereditary enemies of the Macdonalds now seized upon the moment as a chance of wiping out old grievances, which were numerous, because this family had indeed been a lawless, marauding lot. William III was therefore induced to sign a document authorizing the annihilation of the Glencoe Macdonalds. His defenders have always alleged that he never read it—and certainly he had the bad habit of allowing correspondence to accumulate and then rapidly going through it, signing papers he had not digested.

In February, 1692, Campbell of Glenlyon was instructed to go to Glencoe and billet his men on the Macdonalds, which he did. For a week, the Campbell troops lived on good terms in the small Macdonald community of that exposed mountain glen, and then at 5 o'clock one morning, they turned upon their hosts and began, under stringent orders, an attempt to murder them all. Tradition tells many tales of Campbells evading the horrible task, warning individuals up and down the glen to escape while the going was good, but thirty-eight of the one hundred and fifty adult men living there were murdered and others lost their lives afterwards in the snowbound mountain region where they tried to hide.

The scandalous affair created angry reaction up and down the country from Ballachulish to London. No public disaster, no official or semi-official crime, had ever made people so furious or so disgusted before. Some historians have suggested that the Glencoe massacre was no worse than earlier attempts to liquidate unruly clans, such as James I had perpetrated against the Loch Lomond MacGregors. But the betrayal was unforgivable to a Highland people, where proper treatment of those who are admitted to one's home was traditionally matched by the principle of respect for the man who has given another his hospitality. Nor could public opinion overlook the fact that the Macdonalds had taken their oath, and a four days' lateness seemed a minor matter in those unpunctual days, so that there was left no excuse for justifying the massacre as a punishment merited by disaffection. The whole affair blackened the reputation of William's government in Scotland for many years.

As one thinks about the thirty years following the Restoration of Charles II in 1660, one realizes that it formed one of Scotland's most unhappy periods. Irreparable harm was done. Charles II's Government was afraid of treason, afraid that if legal regulations were disregarded, the State would be endangered. It was influenced by men who were unfitted to form a reliable judgment either on the state of public opinion in Scotland or on the right way to handle religious dissent, and so the policy of barbarous repression was adopted and nobody had the wisdom or courage to stop it.

Had there been wiser counsels in Westminster and in Edinburgh, the Presbyterians and Episcopalians might have found a modus vivendi and their divisions would thus have been much less damaging in the following centuries. As things worked out, however, the results of religious persecution made it impossible for Presbyterians and Episcopalians to trust each other. The bitterness between them had been artificially inflamed to such a point that religious intolerance seemed almost a moral duty.

The sadness of it all becomes more poignant when one recalls that at this time the two parties had much in common. In order of worship and in religious principle they were more similar than people nowadays realize. Both preferred to receive Communion seated at long tables; neither as a rule observed the Christian festivals of the year; both upheld Sabbatarian principles, and administered severe moral discipline; each was suspicious of organ music but devoted to the metrical Psalms. As an English army chaplain stationed in Scotland put it—'The difference between the Episcopalians and the Presbyterians can scarcely be discerned in their worship and therefore we the more admire that the two parties so much disagree between themselves when they appear to the world so much like brethren.'

The brotherliness detected by the English chaplain did not survive the Killing Times. In revulsion against the authority which had sanctioned all that terrible suffering, Presbyterians developed a bitter hatred for everything English, forgetting that the persecution had been approved and largely administered by Scots. Anger and pain make for irrational judgment, and it is not surprising that the children of Covenanters identified Anglican and Episcopalian principles with the English way of life. They adopted the mistaken idea that everything Anglican was hostile to their own traditions and to spiritual wellbeing. So Presbyterians now became narrower in outlook than the founders of their Reformed Kirk had been, and they came to regard the Creeds and Doxologies as liturgical devices that should be expurgated from their services and many even rejected the Lord's Prayer as an 'obnoxious prelatic superfluity'. In the 18th century services were composed of long sermons and extempore prayers, with Bible readings which were too often selected from the Old Testament and expounded with emotion rather than scholarship. There was little in all this that was in keeping with the Book of Common Order and with the principles of John Knox and his associates.

The 20th century has seen a growing desire among many Christians for union between the Churches. In Scotland, this ecumenical movement has been impeded by the long-term results of controversies now three centuries past, inaccurately recollected and emotionally rather than rationally interpreted. It is difficult to exaggerate the harm done by those who directed the religious policy in Scotland of Charles II and James II.

The King who came to power as a result of the Revolution in 1688 and 1689 was unaware of all these tensions. He was a European and he thought in continental terms. To William III, the separate political and economic administration of two such small countries as England and Scotland seemed absurd. Like his predecessors James I and Cromwell, William believed that there should be full union. Pre-occupied with his international worries, he could not carry through even the preliminary steps towards such a change, but as he lay dying in 1702, he sent a recommendation to Parliament: 'Nothing can contribute more to the present and future peace, security, and happiness of England and Scotland than a firm and entire union between them.'

The way in which this unlikely event was achieved is described in the following chapter.

PART THREE

The Eighteenth and Nineteenth Centuries

CHAPTER 18

The Union of 1707

That Scotland and England became united in 1707 is one of the oddest facts in British history. In the last decade of the 17th century everything seemed to be militating against any such event; yet thinking people were beginning to realize that political and economic union would indeed offer both partners real benefit. This opinion was encouraged by two strange and unconnected developments—the Darien scheme and the ill-health of Queen Anne's son.

The Darien affair was largely the work of a Dumfriesshire man named William Paterson, who had a flair for associating himself with novel projects, and had amassed a fortune in London. He was one of the original directors of the Bank of England, founded in 1694, and he took a hand in organizing North London's new water supply, led from the Hampstead and Highgate hills. He had also travelled a good deal in the West Indies and New England.

In June 1695, Paterson helped to found the Scottish Africa and India Company. He advertised it with such zest that he secured £300,000 from English investors, and subscriptions from Hamburg and other European centres, besides promises of £400,000 in Scotland. High hopes were centred upon the project amongst Scotsmen, who believed it would bring them a trade revival, and there was furious indignation when the English government suddenly repudiated it and all English contributions were accordingly withdrawn.

To Paterson such a setback was merely a goad to further effort. He now made Scotland his headquarters and began to charter Dutch vessels, to buy stores and to accumulate goods for export. The scope of his endeavours had to be reduced because of the English withdrawal, and so the Darien isthmus was

191

selected for its beginning. The company directors planned a settlement there for colonization and trade. They pictured it as a world emporium, for did not the isthmus command access both to the Pacific and to the Atlantic Oceans? Here a new Caledonia would retrieve Scotland's economy, provide markets for world trade, careers for the young, dividends for the old and glory for everybody.

One wonders whether Paterson was unaware that Darien belonged to Spain, that the English government was negotiating with the Spanish, that any Scottish success in the isthmus would lead to hostilities. Had he no knowledge of Darien's swamps, flies and fevers? Did he really expect customers for the bonnets, serges, huckabacks, stockings, bobwigs, periwigs and gridirons which were loaded onto his vessels?

The three ships of Paterson's first Darien expedition sailed in 1698 and he himself was a member of the company. Before news of the disasters encountered by this advance party had reached Scotland, a second expedition was on its way. On arrival, this new group of 300 settlers found that famine and disease had almost obliterated the first contingent, that there was nowhere to live, nobody to sell to, and no protection from fever. A few months later, a third expedition set forth, still without information about the calamities of the first two. There were brief hostilities with Spanish forces, after which a handful of survivors managed to struggle home, despite shipwrecks and other distresses.

Scotland had subscribed almost a quarter of a million, nearly a third of her total cash circulation. Every penny of this was lost, all the ships and their cargoes squandered. Two thousand young men had died.

The disaster brought it home to Scotsmen that even though Scotland and England were ruled by one sovereign, as had been the case since 1603, the Scots would never be able to develop their material wellbeing properly while their country remained economically separated from England. The Darien tragedy had used up all Scottish capital and it would be years before any more could be available. Sheer want drove men with business knowledge to a new political viewpoint about union. They realized that

Scotland, with limited resources and little influence, needed what England, strong and alienated, was determined not to give.

Queen Anne's personal tragedy provided the smaller country with the only bargaining power which could modify the larger country's policy. She had given birth to seventeen children: only the Duke of Gloucester survived. In 1700, at the age of eleven, he also died. England therefore had to face the prospect of Anne's own death, without a direct heir.

The principal danger, of which English statesmen were acutely aware, was a second Stewart Restoration, and this the ruling Whigs were determined to prevent. The country was now predominantly Protestant, and James Edward, the son of James II, was a Roman Catholic. Parliamentary institutions had become essential to the English way of life, and Stewarts had proved themselves to be evasive of constitutional limitations. In 1701, therefore, the Act of Succession was passed, to ensure that the crown should go to Protestant George, Elector of Hanover, and the great-grandson of James VI and I. The next and urgent step was to secure the agreement of Scotland in order, as Bishop Burnet of Salisbury put it, that 'the back-door' might be 'shut against the attempts of the pretended Prince of Wales'.

Here was Scotland's weapon. The English so little understood their neighbours that it was a matter of conjecture whether the Scots would prefer a Roman Catholic or a Protestant succession. This was because they knew that loyalty to the Roman Church and to the Stewart family was assured in the Highlands, also among many Scottish nobles; on the other hand the strength of the Reformed Kirk in the Lowlands and among townsfolk was not fully understood in London. And political leaders in Scotland played for time so that English anxiety about the 'back-door' was aggravated, especially when war began against France in 1703.

The Scottish Parliament, lately released from the paralysis formerly laid upon it by the Lords of the Articles, acted with spirit. Most of its members were Presbyterian and most of them knew that a Stewart succession would lead to disaster. They were not prepared, however, submissively to follow England's lead and for months heated debate raged over the questions of succession, separation and federation. Andrew Fletcher of Saltoun declared that if union under one sovereign must continue, it should be much modified. Burnet said that his proposals amounted to 'setting up a commonwealth, with the empty name of King'. These proposals included automatic royal consent to parliamentary bills, the appointment of all highly placed officials by Parliament, and parliamentary sanction for declarations of war and peace.

At last, the Scottish Parliament showed how far they were prepared to collaborate with the English over the succession, by the Act of Security, passed in 1704. This stated that the Scots would not decide who was to be their next sovereign during the lifetime of Anne, and that while they would give the crown to the nearest Protestant descendant of the royal line, in no case would Hanover be acceptable without safeguards for Scottish political institutions, religion and trade. It also made provision for a military force to be trained in defence of the country. This Act aroused furious reaction in England, and at first the royal assent was refused. Two other Acts emphasized the new strength of Scotland's bargaining powers. One embodied Fletcher's suggestion of parliamentary sanction for declarations of war and peace, which in effect took foreign policy out of the control of the sovereign; the other legalized the import of French wines, duty-free.

England was now deeply involved in hostilities against France, and as an incentive the Scots flung in the threat to withhold supplies for maintaining strongholds and defences along their coasts. The back-door seemed to the English half-open already, and, reluctantly, Anne's ministers conceded that she should give her assent to the Act of Security, because of the danger if French ships were allowed access to Scottish ports.

In March 1705, the English produced their counterblast, the Aliens Act, by which Scotsmen were to be treated as aliens, unless they agreed to the Hanoverian succession by Christmas Day the same year. This meant that Scots would be forbidden to send their linen and cattle over the Border, and they would be cut off from supplies of English horses, woollen goods and weapons. Such a situation would naturally have led to even more deplorable poverty in Scotland. The Aliens Act was a vicious move, but it suggested that Commissions should be appointed to discuss 'firm and entire union'.

Less than a month after this Act had inflamed Scottish feelings to a pitch of hatred, an English sea-captain called Green, with two of his crew, was executed on the sands of Leith, on a charge of piracy. This was partly because a short while earlier a Scottish ship called the *Annandale* had been seized in the Thames by the London authorities for trespassing on East India Company preserves; still more potent an incentive was the common belief in Scotland that Green had been responsible for atrocities inflicted upon another Scottish vessel, ill-named *The Speedy Return*. Storms of anger convulsed the Edinburgh mobs, who were determined to have blood revenge on Green, although the charge against him was substantiated only by false evidence, so that soon after his execution his innocence became a well-established fact.

In the heat of this crisis, while London opinion was seething over the tragedy of Captain Green, while Edinburgh was letting loose a spate of anti-English pamphlets, while many serious-minded people were dreading bloodshed, the Commissioners were appointed. The atmosphere could hardly have been worse. Yet the moment had arrived when at least each side had something to offer and something to sacrifice. If Scotland would agree to the Hanoverian succession, and if England would concede commercial equality, Union would have some chance of success. By the end of 1705, responsible opinion on both sides was aware of this fact.

Once it was agreed that negotiations should be undertaken, thirty-one Scottish nobles and thirty-one English Commissioners were without delay appointed by the Queen. It is to their great credit that they approached the difficult work seriously and decisively, each side making adjustments in order to find a feasible compromise where opinions clashed, because at this late date each side believed that the Union was essential to the future peace of both countries.

The two Commissions worked separately, except for one meeting, and they communicated with each other in writing. They completed their draft of the Treaty in rather less than three months. In October 1706, the final session of Scotland's last Parliament met to consider the terms in an Edinburgh seething with anti-unionist mobs. Violent scenes occurred also in the streets of Glasgow and Dumfries, while hostile addresses flowed in from many shires and also from royal burghs. But there was support for the measure too, from the nobility, from businessmen and from ministers. With only slight modifications, the Treaty was finally passed in the Scottish Parliament on January 16th, 1707. Thereafter the measure was debated at Westminster in the final English session of the last English Parliament, with much less heat and much less delay. Finally the Act of Union received royal assent on May 1st, 1707. It was described by Mar as 'a solid fundation for putting the countries on one bottome to all posterity.'

The two Parliaments were both brought to an end, and the newly constituted Houses of Lords and Commons were created to form the new supreme legislative body for the United Kingdom. The question of representation was complicated, because England was not only the larger partner but also much the richer. The ratio of wealth was probably about 38:1, and of population about 5:1. In the end it was agreed that there should be 513 English members to Scotland's 45 in the House of Commons, a ratio of 11:1, and that there should be 16 Scots peers to England's 190.

The Treaty made no change in the religious systems of the two countries. Statutes were passed for the purpose of recognizing the Churches of Scotland and England, and these were incorporated in the Acts which ratified the Union. Without this safeguard, designed to make sure that their religion was 'effectually and unalterably secured', Scottish Presbyterians would never have allowed the Union to come to pass.

The legal traditions of the two countries were also safeguarded. Scottish law courts were to continue as before, the heritable jurisdictions and legal rights enjoyed by clan chieftains were unaltered, nor was any adjustment suggested for royal burgh privilege. Appeal from Scottish courts to certain named English courts was forbidden, but no reference was made in this regard to the House of Lords, an evasion which was to cause trouble later on.

Scottish ships, whether foreign-built or otherwise, were classed as British, so that the old sting of the Navigation Acts was

removed forever. Standardized coinage, weights and measures
were adopted, on English lines; although English customs and
excise were to become the basis of future British tariffs, Scotland
was exempted for the duration of the war from any increase of
the malt tax, and for seven years from higher impositions on salt.

The most complex of the Articles of Union dealt with financial
matters, and they illustrate, as do those dealing with commerce
and trade, the effort made by the Commissioners to negotiate a
fair deal for the Scots, now that the Union had become essential.
By 1697, England had a National Debt of some £14½ million,
which increased year by year until in 1714 it amounted to over
£36 million. This money represented loans, or investments, made
through public subscription, largely by such privileged organizations as the East India Company and the Bank of England.
The loans were regarded as permanent, and annual dividends on
them were paid by the Government, on the security of national
taxation. The system marked a considerable advance in financial
policy and offered reasonably safe investment for capital, and
great convenience to the Government. On the other hand, by
the time of the Union the Scottish public debt was less than
£200,000. Thus Scottish taxation would in the following years
be partly devoted to the payment of annuities on National Debt,
for which the Scots had no responsibility. The Commissioners
agreed therefore that trusted Scottish mathematicians should be
employed to work out an assessment of Scottish loss from this
source. A figure of almost £400,000 was finally arrived at. The
sum, termed the Equivalent Money, was sent up to Edinburgh
in bullion and exchequer bills. It was used to compensate Scottish
merchants for private losses caused by the change in coinage, to
discharge the public debts of the Crown in Scotland, to encourage
Scottish industry and fisheries, and also to repay as far as possible
those who had suffered loss through their Darien investments.

There was little enthusiasm for the Treaty. One historian has
stated that 'most of the subjects of the new united kingdom were
ignorant of the Union or unmoved by it'. Even the Equivalent
Money made a bad impression. The dragoons detailed to guard
the waggons dragging this curious load northwards were abused
and pelted by Northumbrians, who were enraged at the sight of

English gold crossing the Border, and abused and pelted again in Edinburgh because people thought the great sealed boxes contained only stones and useless paper. The mud slung at those unfortunate soldiers from both southerly and northerly critics perhaps symbolizes a good deal of later abuse. Certainly it was not long before the habitual mistrust between the two sections of the new United Kingdom found fresh means of expression.

Critics of the Union have often declared that the Scottish Commissioners were bribed by the English government to accept it. In fact, these thirty-one Commissioners spent four months in London during 1706 and they were given handsome grants to cover their expenses, which must indeed have been considerable, while various state officials had arrears of salary made up. Almost all who received such reimbursement were fully committed to the Act before any payments were agreed, and the whole transaction was publicly debated in Parliament. By 18th century standards of public integrity there was no question of bribery and even by modern standards it would be hard to prove the charge.

In recent years, it has become fashionable to belittle the Treaty of Union, to dwell upon its more irksome consequences and to question the motives of those who worked to achieve it. Some 20th century Scottish Nationalists regard the whole thing as a great betrayal. But as one reconsiders the circumstances in which it was worked out, one can see that the Commissioners on both sides acted in good faith to establish what was essential for the future welfare of both nations. And they had no precedents to help them. Inexperienced as both Scots and English were in handling the problems which arise when two nations seek a common way of life, they could look to no other similar union for enlightenment. Thus they had to concentrate upon what seemed to be of fundamental importance, and to work out as best they might a daring and unusual political experiment, whose consequences could only be surmised. Some of their decisions show insight and wisdom—the recognition of the Scottish Church and the maintenance of the two separate legal systems for example, also the assessment of the Equivalent Money. More impressive still is the fact that, both to England and to Scotland, Union was now a fundamental necessity. For the sake of its assured continuance, the English abandoned the commercial monopoly they had so tenaciously maintained hitherto. For the same purpose, and also to rescue their people from economic disaster, the Scots embarked upon organized collaboration with a people whom they had formerly found hostile and unyielding.

Those who decry the Treaty and criticize its makers would do well to consider the only available alternatives. These were renewed warfare at worst, ill-defined and uneasy federation at best. Each of these expedients would have made Stewart restoration more likely and so would have led to fresh religious conflict, and probably also to economic disaster. Each would have deprived both nations of the stimulus produced by partnership with a vigorous and gifted neighbour. The Treaty of Union, on the other hand, gave Scots and English alike the chance to develop economic stability during the 18th century and at the same time to foster their own special characteristics.

But the question still remains, why has the Union aroused angry, even emotional criticism amongst Scottish people from time to time since 1707 and especially in the 20th century?

Perhaps this may be explained by its two most serious defects. Included in its terms there was no scheme for altering the balance of representation in Parliament, should the balance of population or wealth become changed. Thus when Scottish contributions to the Treasury increased, and when Scottish people formed a larger constituent in the total British population, it did not occur to the Government that there should be more Scottish members sent to Westminster, until 1832. Even then no rational principle of increasing the Scottish membership was worked out, and only in 1884 was the northern partner in the United Kingdom adequately represented. The other defect was more fundamental, more difficult to rectify and even less readily understood in England. Sovereignty is a precious thing. The Scots now lost it. However well they might be represented at Westminster, in terms of numbers they would necessarily always be in the minority. So decisions about Scottish affairs, the spending of national resources on Scottish administration, would always be controlled by a legislature overwhelmingly English.

CHAPTER 19

Jacobites

The half-century from 1695 onwards formed a wretched period in Scottish history. There was the Darien disaster. Then there was James Edward's rebellion of 1715. Thirty years after that, the families who had already suffered so much endured the terrible losses of Culloden, and the privations caused by Cumberland's policy of suppression. Much hostility and some hardship came through the Government's financial measures. Religious animosities were once more aroused. The Scottish people were insufficiently represented both in the House of Lords and also in the House of Commons.

The troubles began with misunderstandings about religion. In 1711, an Episcopalian clergyman called Greenshields was punished by the Court of Session for using the Book of Common Prayer. This man set off an explosion by appealing to the House of Lords, now by implication the supreme court of appeal for the whole country. So soon therefore was the test case launched which the framers of the Treaty had hoped to evade. The House of Lords reversed the findings against Greenshields, put through a Toleration Act in support of Episcopalians; and ordered all Presbyterians and all Episcopalians to take an oath abjuring the Pretender.

Worse aggravation followed in the Patronage Act of 1712. This restored the right of landowners to appoint the ministers to churches situated on their properties. No piece of legislation could have contravened more flagrantly the spirit in which the Treaty of Union had been drawn up, no misunderstanding of Presbyterian principle could have produced more resentment. The religious emotion evoked by this Act aroused both hatred of the English arrogance in handling ecclesiastical affairs, and much dissension within the Church of Scotland itself. Not until 1874 was it abolished.

Scottish anglophobia was stimulated by other insults to Scottish pride. In 1711, the Duke of Hamilton was given the additional and British title, Duke of Brandon. He expected a seat in the House of Lords as a peer of the realm, but it was decreed that no British title should give a Scottish peer the right to this honour, also that Scots who became peers of Great Britain should thereby lose their right to vote for their sixteen representatives in the Upper House. Thus the most distinguished members of the Scottish aristocracy were disfranchised.

There were economic grievances too. The tax on salt was increased and this damaged Scottish fisheries. The Malt Tax was re-assessed in 1713, in order that the excise on Scottish malt might be brought more into line with that of the much richer English product. Home-brewed ale was produced all over the country at that time, when tea and coffee were hardly known, wines and spirits far too costly. The uproar caused by the proposed increase in the excise on malt was so great that the regulation was allowed to remain a dead letter for a dozen years, but Scottish anger was not lessened by this procrastination.

There were repercussions all over the country. As early as 1710 Parson Wodrow of Eastwood wrote: 'The Jacobites are mighty uppish . . . They talk of nothing but Resignation, Restauration and Rescission, their three R's, and they talk their King will be over, either by Act of Parliament or by invasion by August nixt. They boast mighty, which I hope will ruin their cause.'

The only people in the United Kingdom who were consistently against these three R's were the English Whigs and a proportion of the Presbyterian Lowlanders. In fact most of the Tory leaders were in touch with James Edward, even though they affirmed their loyalty to Anne. So strong was Jacobite feeling that, when Queen Anne fell ill in 1714, there was danger of the Hanoverian Succession being annulled by a coup d'état. The proclamation of George I was due to the rapid and cool-headed action of Shrewsbury, a Whig leader who was appointed Lord Treasurer by Anne only a few hours before her death. 'A wonderful dash to the

Jacobites' wrote Wodrow of this proclamation. 'Had the Queen lived a little longer they think their schemes would have taken effect. However the Lord hath broken the snare and we are escaped.' George himself, like his English advisers, knew the escape had been by a narrow margin.

At this time James Edward was twenty-six years of age. All his life had been spent abroad, mainly on French territory, and as his father died when he was thirteen, he was much influenced by his Italian mother, Mary of Modena. Had James Edward become King, therefore, he would have seemed as foreign to the British as did George I. If he had been willing to renounce his Roman Catholicism and to declare himself a Protestant, the crown would have been his, probably without bloodshed, but he was not prepared to secure his inheritance on such terms. Further he must have imagined that a second Stewart restoration was feasible without resorting to any such policy, for malcontents of all parties corresponded with him, and as he never visited either Scotland or England he could hardly have realized the odds against him.

By the time George I had been on the throne a year, he had inspired little affection for himself among his new subjects, while James Edward could boast many supporters in south-west England, in Oxford, in Northumberland, in London itself, as well as in Scotland. The failure of the enterprise on the English side was due to the well-timed action of the Government in arresting prominent Jacobites. The sudden departure of the Duke of Ormonde, who went abroad at the critical moment, had a good deal to do with the collapse of the movement too, as he was its acknowledged leader. His failure of nerve, or lack of judgment, in going off at this point left James Edward's supporters without a commander-in-chief on the spot, so that few of their movements were co-ordinated.

The Scottish rising was led by the Earl of Mar. He summoned a gathering at Braemar, ostensibly for 'hunting', and there on September 6th, 1715, he proclaimed James VIII and III as King. At the same time he made a public statement to the effect that the Union had proved a blunder, by which Scotland's 'ancient liberties were delivered into the hands of the English'. The ideals he had entertained eight and a half years earlier, when he had supported Queensberry and acted as Commissioner for the Treaty, Mar thus publicly renounced and thereby gave his critics one more reason for nicknaming him 'Bobbing John'.

A large number of chieftains came out to join Mar from the shires of Ross, Inverness, Banff, Aberdeen and Perth, also from parts of northern Argyllshire, from the Lothians and from Galloway. The burghs of Inverness and Inveraray remained Government strongholds, as did Glasgow, with most of the central Lowlands and Fife. Late in September, the Pretender learned with some surprise of the Scottish developments, for he had expected the main effort to come from south-west England.

'Bobbing John' proved himself to be no leader. In the early weeks of the revolt he commanded far more men than the Government. He captured Perth almost at once, and made it his head-quarters. Had he then advanced upon Stirling, he could have secured the road to England, and with an immediate move across the Border, or a concerted drive on Edinburgh, he could have won further success before winter set in, and this would have brought him more supporters. However he chose to remain in Perth, and to divide his army, part of which he sent to Galloway.

Meanwhile Argyll was organizing Government forces in Scotland. This very able soldier made sure of Stirling, with the help of a contingent from Glasgow and Paisley, and immediately afterwards consolidated the defence of Edinburgh. On November 14th, 1715, the forces of Mar and Argyll met in battle on Sheriff-muir, a desolate upland above Dunblane. The Jacobites out-numbered their opponents, but the battle ended indecisively, as each right wing scattered its immediate enemies and flung itself into disorganized pursuit. A Jacobite officer summed it up as follows: 'Thus ended the affair of Dumblain, in which neither side gained much honour, but which was the entire ruin of our party.'

Sheriffmuir did prove to be virtually the end. Within a few days of the engagement, the half-hearted efforts of the Jacobites in northern England were crushed at Preston. From now on, with winter's ordeals threatening their families, short of many necessary supplies and without effective leadership, the

Highlanders began to go home. Desertion depleted the Pretender's armies so much that when at last James Edward arrived at Peterhead in mid-December, he found that Mar had lost about half the troops he was believed to command. James Edward's late arrival and pessimistic outlook depressed his followers. He had every reason however to be depressed himself by the attitude of his undisciplined and unco ordinated supporters. On February 4th, 1716, he left again for France, accompanied by Bobbing John, who preferred not to await events in Scotland.

Many Jacobites believed things would have been different had French help been forthcoming, and these regarded the death of Louis XIV, in September 1715, as a major disaster. In fact, Louis XIV would certainly not have given effective help, at least until James Edward had proved himself supreme, as France could not have faced the renewal of war with England which this policy would have brought about. The true causes of the failure in 1715 lay in the Jacobites' lack of a leader, who could both co-ordinate the scattered resources and also exact loyal obedience. In short raids and guerrilla tactics the Highlanders excelled, but in strategic movements on alien ground over a period of several months, they were not reliable. Further, there could be no unanimous support for James Edward in a predominantly Protestant country while he continued in his Roman Catholic loyalty. The same difficulties were to arise again thirty years later.

The aftermath of the revolt makes dreary reading. Some hundreds of Scottish Jacobites were transported to the plantations, and nineteen peerages were forfeited by Act of Attainder, so that although only two of the leaders were executed, many Scotsmen had to go into exile. An attempt was made to disarm the Highlands, with the result that loyal clans handed in their arms while those who had supported James Edward successfully hid most of their more efficient weapons for future use. Throughout all these proceedings, Scotsmen resented the fact that their whole nation was stigmatized, although George I had been loyally supported by many of the clans and by most of the Lowlands.

The influence of Sir Robert Walpole on the affairs of the realm did nothing to improve the situation. His long tenure of office lasted from 1721-42. During this time, he set himself to extract more national income from customs and excise and he never troubled to study Scottish ideas or traditions. In 1725 he determined to put into effect the changes in the assessment of salt which had been made statutory in 1713. The result was an outburst in Glasgow, where so far the support for the new régime had been consistent since 1707. The mobs destroyed the magnificent mansion of Daniel Campbell, the member of Parliament for the Glasgow group of burghs, and put up a spirited fight against the town guard.

Such an outburst could in no way prevent the law from being fulfilled, but this one was long remembered as a patriotic display, and it caused even more popular sympathy with smuggling. From now onwards, French wines were regularly brought to inlets all along the East coast and even to the Solway, and so were brandy, tea and cambrics. The nation's attitude to smuggling was well illustrated in 1736, when the Edinburgh folk yet again broke out, this time to lynch Captain Porteous. The cultured and broadminded minister, Alexander Carlyle, described Porteous as a man 'elated' by being 'admitted to the company of his superiors' proud of his 'skill in manly exercises, particularly the golf', insolent, rough and of violent temper. When he was in charge of the execution of a well-known smuggler, Porteous was insulted and pelted with mud by the crowd, a common enough occurrence when these odious hangings were carried out. Losing his temper, he fired on the densely packed mob, and a number of people were killed. Although he was imprisoned for this outrage and condemned to death, rumours got round that he might be reprieved. In consequence 'Persons unknown, with the greatest secrecy, policy and vigour', forced his prison, 'executing his sentence upon him themselves, which to effectuate cost them from eight at night till two in the morning; and yet this plot was managed so dexterously that they met with no interruption, though there were five companies of a marching regiment lying in the Canongate'.

The affair became a public scandal. In Parliament, the view was taken that Edinburgh should be disgraced, because of the disorder which the authorities had possibly countenanced and certainly failed to quell. In the end, the Lord Provost was expelled from his office, never to be allowed to hold a public position again, and Edinburgh was fined £2,000. Scottish public opinion was enraged by these decisions, just as English public opinion had been enraged by the lynching of Porteous.

All things English were now under suspicion, but more harmonious relationships might have developed through the increased travel and trade between the two countries. Charles Edward however hankered to proclaim his father as King. He landed in July, 1745, on the island of Eriskay, with two Scotsmen, four Irishmen and one Englishman. The enterprise was a hopeless one from the start, although in the early stages Charles Edward brought to it an enthusiasm and an assurance which almost made it seem feasible.

As usual, the Jacobites hoped for French help. In 1744, France had declared war on Britain, already deeply involved in the War of the Austrian Succession, and Louis XV had invited Charles Edward to Paris, for discussion about a Stewart restoration. Shortly before the Prince embarked, the British had met with defeat at the Battle of Fontenoy. Louis XV was prepared to follow this up by creating a second front, for the embarrassment of his foes, in Scotland. Charles Edward's interpretation of the events was optimistic in the extreme, and he expressed his hopes in a letter to Louis XV. 'May I not trust . . . that this signal victory which your Majesty has just won over your enemies and mine (for they are one and the same) has resulted in some change in affairs; and that I may derive some advantage from this new blaze of glory which surrounds you?'

Scottish Jacobites were reluctant and dubious. Soon after Charles Edward's arrival in Scotland, Macdonald of Boisdale begged him to go home. 'I am come home, Sir,' was the reply, 'and I will entertain no notion at all of returning to that place from whence I came; for that I am persuaded my faithful Highlanders will stand by me.' The Prince managed to persuade Lochiel, Chief of the Cameron clan, to join him, and this had an immediate effect on others; indeed, but for Lochiel's decision, the whole project might well have petered out. On August 19th, the standard was raised at Glenfinnan, James VIII and III was once again proclaimed King, and the Prince set forth towards Edinburgh, gathering supporters as he went.

Sir John Cope was in charge of the inadequate Government forces and, knowing that it would be some time before he could be reinforced, he determined not to risk another Killiecrankie. His withdrawal was sensible enough, but he chose an odd direction for his retreat, making for the north and leaving the road to the capital open. In mid-September Charles Edward marched exultantly into Edinburgh where he was 'mett by vast Multitudes of people, who by their repeated shouts and huzzas express'd a great deal of joy to see the Prince'. Cope meantime reached Aberdeen, embarked his men on board ship and brought them south to Dunbar, whence he gloomily set forth to recover what lost ground he could, although he was still short of supplies, arms and even cash to pay his troops. The Jacobites, who were at their best in these circumstances, came out from Edinburgh in strength and on 21st September met and routed Cope's army after a brief engagement at Prestonpans. This victory elated the Prince's supporters and brought him many reinforcements. 'The Prince', recorded Lord Elcho, 'from this Battle entertained a mighty notion of the Highlanders, and ever after imagin'd they would beat four times their number of regular troops.' In a triumphant letter to his father, Charles Edward wrote: 'The men I have defeated were Your Majesty's enemies, it is true, but they might have been your friends and dutiful subjects when they had got their eyes open to see the true interest of their country, which I am come to save and not to destroy. For this reason, I have discharged all public rejoicings.'

Had this campaign been staged half a century later, the Prince would probably have made an immediate drive over the Border. These however were days of slow motion warfare, inevitably, because communications were so poor. As Mar thirty years earlier had remained in Perth during the precious autumn weeks, so Charles Edward now stayed in Edinburgh for well over a month. In the first week of November, a bad time of year for starting a war, he began his march southwards with nearly eight thousand men. They came from the same areas and the same clans as those who had supported his father, with some additional groups, such as the Frasers of Lovat. Old Simon Lovat, the head of the clan, refused at first to commit himself, and negotiated with both sides, waiting to see who would win before acclaiming or disowning his heir, who went out under his instructions.

Many clans were firmly hostile to Charles Edward throughout the affair. These included Campbells, Mackays, Munros, Macphersons, Grants, McLeods, MacNeills and some of the MacDonalds. Of those who joined the Prince, few could have understood the issues at stake. These men marched because their chieftains told them to, and perhaps also in hope of booty. Years later Lord Cockburn recorded the story of a Highlander who was asked whether he had not always considered it absurd even to try to dethrone the Hanoverians. 'Na, Sir!' was the reply, 'I ne'er thocht aboot it. I just ay thocht hoo pleasant it wad be to see Donald riflin' London.'

On November 8th, the Prince's army reached Carlisle and then pushed on to Preston. By a feigned advance upon Wales, they shook off the pursuit of Cumberland, who had been sent to intercept them. Once again a road to a capital was open, and the Jacobites made use of it, but by the time they reached the Midlands they were suffering from familiar difficulties. When was French help going to materialize? Why had only about 300 Englishmen joined them? What would the Londoners do? With these questions in mind, Charles Edward's advisers fell to quarrelling, while his Highlanders decided that winter in England offered little reward, that 'riflin' London' seemed a remote possibility and that they would be better at home.

The decision to retreat was taken against Charles Edward's wishes. Lord Elcho, who was present, said that he 'fell into a passion and gave most of the Gentlemen that spoke very Abusive Language, and said that they had a mind to betray him.'

His instinct was to press on. Many historians have believed that his instinct was right and that, had he gone on to London, his immediate campaign might have been successful, though ultimately his cause could hardly have survived. Once the Jacobites turned north, their luck was out. People who had been friendly when the army was marching south were now hostile, supplies were not to be had, the wintry weather impeded everything, discipline weakened and desertion increased. The army retreated to Dumfries, then to Glasgow, where they forced the merchants to supply them with quantities of clothing. In January 1746, Charles Edward won his last success at Falkirk, where he dispersed a Government force, but he did not follow the victory up and he made no effort to get back to Edinburgh. Instead he went further north.

Only misery now lay ahead for the Jacobites. They had served their turn as far as Louis XV was concerned, for large numbers of British and Continental troops had been withdrawn from Flanders. These troops were sent to Scotland under the Duke of Cumberland, George II's favourite son. This Prince, now twenty-five years of age, was enjoying a reputation described by Horace Walpole: 'The soldiers adore him, and with reason; he has a lion's courage, vast vigilance and activity and, I am told, great military genius.' Later, Walpole changed his opinion, as did many another.

Cumberland made for Aberdeen, where he spent six weeks in methodical preparation. With him was his aide-de-camp, young Wolfe, later famous as the conqueror of Quebec. In April 1746, with a well-armed and experienced force, they caught the Jacobites on Drummossie Moor, east of Inverness, near Culloden House. Charles Edward's men were exhausted with forced marches and lack of food and sleep. They were taken by surprise and cornered, to face driving wind and rain. Their divided leadership and inadequate weapons made them easy prey for their enemies and they suffered a devastating defeat. Duncan Forbes, the Laird of Culloden, was the Lord President of the Court of Session, a man of justice who valued peace and had devoted himself at great personal cost to the Government. That the ghastly slaughter carried out came to be known by the name of his family home must have been bitter indeed for Forbes. He loathed bloodshed, and he did all he could to restrain Cumberland from the brutal excesses which followed.

Cumberland on the other hand detested Jacobites, with almost pathological fervour. After the battle he ordered that all stragglers were to be killed and that no mercy was to be shown, even to the wounded. As one contemporary record baldly puts it, 'everybody that fell into their hands gott no quarters, except a few who they reserved for public punishment.' The Duke organized a systematic burning of homes, including remote hovels, and he had thousands of cattle rounded up for confiscation. The disaster he inflicted on the Highlands caused terrible destitution. Duncan Forbes he described as 'that old woman who spoke to me of humanity'.

Charles Edward made his escape towards the west, while Cumberland's butcheries were inflicted on those who went north or north-west. The Prince was given such wonderful help on his sad journeyings at this stage that in songs and poems and historical romances the story has been made a classic, and justifiably, for the £30,000 reward offered to the man who captured the Prince represented untold wealth.

Flora Macdonald's share in his adventures won her respect and renown. After she had secured his embarkation at Portree, she was arrested and sent to London, for her Highland boatmen talked injudiciously, even though many of their countrymen were silent. She spent some months in the Tower, was released, and later lionized in London, whose inhabitants had a good eye for the spectacular. Her head was unturned by this publicity, and she went home again, to marry Alan Macdonald of Kingsburgh. When Samuel Johnson met the two of them at their own home in 1773, he was immensely taken with her personality and he deeply regretted her emigration to North Carolina the following year. She and her husband made a stand for the Hanoverians during the American War of Independence, and experienced as exciting adventures in support of George III in the New World as Flora had gone through for the Stewart Prince in Skye: ultimately they got back to Kingsburgh. Her portrait by Allan Ramsay may be seen in the Bodleian Library at Oxford; the painter's sure touch has revealed the gentleness, the sympathy and the courage which in youth had comforted the Prince and in middle age had stolen old Johnson's heart.

After 1746, Jacobitism was finished, although the authorities in London did not realize it. The Government had been so shocked that every effort was now made to crush the already moribund movement. One hundred and twenty people were executed, including the 78-year-old Lovat, whose foxy behaviour brought him no advantage and caused him to be mourned much less than the rest. Over eleven hundred were transported or exiled, and nearly seven hundred died in filthy gaols. The High lands were disarmed, this time with scrupulous and undiscriminating care; the confiscation of weapons and bagpipes was imposed throughout the Highlands, to the exasperation of the many clansmen whose loyalty to the Government had been consistent. The most absurd ruling of all was that the wearing of the tartan was forbidden—'no more than a chip in the porridge', and 'not worth a halfpenny', as Forbes contemptuously exclaimed, but none the less an unrealistic and silly prohibition devised by distant Englishmen and calculated to exacerbate bitter feelings. The estates of the Jacobite chieftains were confiscated for administration by the Government, until 1784, when heirs of the families were reinstated.

A more telling piece of legislation, which had permanent results, was the abolition of heritable jurisdictions, in right of which civil and criminal justice had been summarily dispensed by the heads of certain Highland families for many centuries. The abolition of this anomaly was a necessary prelude to establishing the King's Courts and the normal judicial routine in the High-lands. As G. M. Trevelyan put it: 'The King's writ must run in the glens.' Contemporary letters suggest that the Judges found their new spheres of activity exacting and bizarre, not least because of the misadventures which befell them as they journeyed over rough tracks and negotiated fords across the rivers which swirled through their enlarged circuits.

The two rebellions poisoned the relationships between England and Scotland just when there was some hope of improvement. The inept interference from London with Scottish religious problems and the equally unfortunate fiscal policy caused a lot of resentment, naturally enough, but in spite of these mistakes, economic conditions in Scotland did gradually improve in the early years of the 18th century and confidence in a supposedly equal partnership might have been established. But the repressive measures carried out in Scotland after the rebellions, and especially the presence of English soldiers on Scottish soil, made a permanent and a very bad impression. The whole thing smelt of conquest. Popular sentiment and popular literature—both powerful forces—romanticized the Jacobites, not so much because the Scots really wanted the Stewarts back as because they hated the English. The Union of the two countries would have been far more successful but for this.

After about 1750 however there came a marked change in the Scottish scene, because now, for the first time since 1286, when Alexander III's horse stumbled in the darkness and flung his master over the cliff-edge, Scotland was relieved of the nightmare of war on her own territory. At last, long-stifled vitality found outlet, in original and vigorous form. From about 1750 onwards, the Scottish share in British and in imperial developments became more and more significant. This may be illustrated from the history of agriculture, industry and transport; it is apparent in Scottish literature, art and architecture, in religious thinking and educational planning: almost more strikingly so in exploration, missionary work and colonial enterprise.

Too often it is assumed that Scotland's true greatness may be found in medieval times or even in the more remote past, to which periods sentimentalists are inclined to attribute romance of an altogether fictitious nature. The truth is that, in facing the demands and seizing the opportunities offered by the new way of life opening out from the mid-18th century onwards, Scottish people entered upon a renaissance not always accorded its rightful emphasis. Certainly it was tarnished by the grim and materialistic squalor in which it was nurtured, marred by much physical and mental suffering, vitiated by greed and heartlessness. This dark side of modern history must be admitted: and it must be recognized as characteristic of many countries other than Scotland. It was the price at which was bought the adjustment to unprecedented tensions, the growing-pains of modern society; gradually it became recognized as such and then men gave their minds to this challenge also, with results which are not yet fully realized in the 20th century.

In the following chapters the bold achievements of Scottish courage and intelligence are set out and the record shows that, once freed from the fear of crippling internal warfare and of foreign invasion, Scotsmen could take a leading place on many frontiers, physical and intellectual.

CHAPTER 20

Agriculture

Scotsmen living in the Lowlands and the Borders enjoyed a rather better standard of living even as early as 1707 than those in Argyllshire and the north and west. Even so, their families, like those of all other agricultural workers in Scotland, were held in chronic bondage to unrewarding labour. This was because medieval techniques were followed with little adaptation and so the soil yielded poor results. Malnutrition sapped people's strength and burdened their lives.

Traditional designs in domestic architecture did not help matters. People lived in one-roomed cottages, built of loose stones, turfs and clay, thatched with heather, ventilated by one door but no window and no chimney. Such hovels were in use till the end of the 19th century in the Highlands, though elsewhere rather better homes began gradually to appear. Admirers of the poet Burns will recall that his father, William Burnes, himself built the cottage where in January 1759 he was born; and that the little building collapsed in a violent storm less than a week after the baby's arrival. William then rebuilt it, and the second structure withstood all subsequent gales and today is one of the most frequently visited centres of tourist traffic. It represents a more roomy and comfortable style of living than agricultural workers could afford at the time of the Union.

The terrible poverty of the Scottish countryside, caused by unenlightened farming methods, was suddenly worsened at the end of the 17th century, because in 1696 there began a dreadful series of bad summers. For seven consecutive years there were destructive rainstorms in July, August and September, the harvesting months, and in each of these years winter came early and proved severe. This calamity coincided with the financial disasters of the Darien scheme.

The destitution in Scotland at this time was vividly described by many writers, both Scottish and English. In 1698, Andrew Fletcher of Saltoun expressed his bitterness in terms somewhat confused by emotion. 'There are at this day in Scotland, besides many poor families very meanly provided for by the church boxes, with others who by living on bad food have fallen into various diseases, 200,000 people begging from door to door. These are not only in no way advantageous, but a very grievous burden to so poor a country. And though the number of them be perhaps double to what it was formerly, by reason of the present great distress, yet in all times there have been about 100,000 of those vagabonds, who have lived without any regard or subjection either to the laws of the land or to those of God and Nature.' An anonymous author wrote in 1747: 'If we cast our Eye over all the counties in Scotland and look into the wretched and low Condition of the Common People and Poor, we will find some famished for want of Bread; others dispirited for want of Employment; not a few starved with Cold and Nakedness; and many whole families throughout every County, especially in and about Villages, commonly remain in a languishing, nasty, slothful and useless condition, uncomfortable in themselves, and unprofitable to the Proprietors of the Grounds.'

Even the men who were not dispirited for want of employment in the early 18th century were short of many necessaries, because wages were so low. Labourers in 1730 were earning 40/- a year and by 1760 this figure had risen only to 60/-, so that although food was cheap, standards of life were miserable. The lairds were also hard put to it to maintain reasonable comfort in their families, since much of their rent was paid in kind and, being perpetually short of cash, they had nothing to invest and no means of undertaking improvements.

One fundamental and rarely acknowledged reason for such continuing poverty was that Scottish soil lacked lime. Even nowadays, the value of lime is probably not fully appreciated. In the 18th century, few landowners understood how badly their acid soil needed calcium in one form or another: and transport was so difficult that not even the best-intentioned farmers could have carried lime to their properties in sufficient quantity.

Agriculture

The collapse of the monastic system had done away with the landowners who were best able to make a success of their farms. Their properties had fallen into the hands of lairds who knew little or nothing themselves, while until the mid-18th century their tenants persisted in the run-rig system of early medieval times. The outfields were alternately scourged and neglected; the infields were divided into hump-backed rigs; and each man had to tramp around his neighbour's intervening rigs in order to reach his own scattered holdings. Seed was still broadcast by hand; winnowing was done out of doors on windy days; grinding continued as a daily chore for the women, who used querns, unless there was a local mill, in which case the tenant always had exorbitant dues to pay. The old, heavy, Scottish plough pursued its slow progress until the 1790s or even later, surface-scratching half an acre a day to a chorus of shouts and yells from the four or five men and women who directed it and controlled its eight or ten oxen. The astounding fact is that these underfed and ignorant people did for many generations somehow succeed in supporting their families. It is equally astonishing to realize how rapidly in some areas the transition from the outmoded run-rig system to more adequate methods of production was effected.

For these improvements, better transport was the first necessity to make proper manuring possible, and drainage a strong second, since much of Scotland's best soil was lying waterlogged in the channels between the rigs, or in uncultivated valley marshes. Along with these could be listed afforestation on a national scale, for Scotland had built and burnt her woods away, with the result that rain and wind had done much deadly work in shifting top-soil and laying bare the rocky structure of the Scottish hillsides.

Clearly initiative in the use of fertilizers, the planning of drainage, tree-planting and the like could be undertaken only by moneyed landowners, or by wealthy tenants enjoying the security of long leases. Most Scots leased their holdings on uncertain tenure for one or two years at a time: such men could not undertake longterm improvements, for if they did so, their rents were raised in proportion to the increased prosperity, or else they were turned off their holdings when their leases expired.

Soon after the Union, landed gentry began to realize the scope for agricultural developments. As early as 1723, the Honourable Society of Improvers in the Knowledge of Agriculture was founded, the first organization of its kind in Scotland. Its members planned to collect and publish information, to give advice and to support all enterprise in agricultural projects. From this time onwards, Lowland and Border landowners began to take a more active interest in farming techniques, and numerous other societies were founded by enthusiastic agriculturalists. They pooled their information, discussed their experiments, criticized what they had observed on their continental travels, and often found occasion to comment unfavourably on the work being done by landowners over the Border. These Scottish pioneers in agriculture were spared some of the delays which their English contemporaries had to face, because tenant rights in Scotland were not buttressed by traditional or legal safeguards. At the end of a man's lease, the tenant could be turned off with scant ceremony, so that the term 'enclosure' north of the Border came to mean merely the process of building dykes or walls around the owner's land, and it should not be confused with English 'enclosure' which involved sanction by Act of Parliament.

A considerable literature on farming topics naturally began to develop. James Donaldson was the first of such Scottish writers. In 1697 he published his *Husbandry Anatomised*. Donaldson suggested enclosure of the rigs, so that people's property might become geographically compact, he wanted more fertilization, with a regular system of resting the fields between crops, and he believed in potato culture. He also said that far too many head of cattle were being maintained on indifferent pasture, and he therefore suggested reducing livestock.

Donaldson's book was followed in 1699 by Lord Belhaven's *The Countryman's Diary* and, during the next century or more, by a quantity of pamphlets and other publications, all dealing with agricultural improvement. In some districts the new methods were ignored or despised, in others this literature was eagerly sought, even by people struggling against adverse conditions with little or no capital behind them. One such was the poet Burns, who found himself in 1784 responsible for a family of brothers and sisters, on the death of his father. Burns moved them to a new holding, at Mossgiel in Ayrshire, where he threw himself into the task of making the little farm pay, and he read all the agricultural literature he could lay hands on. Sixty years earlier nobody in such a position would have dreamed of reading anything.

One of the first individuals who began practising new methods was the Earl of Peterborough's daughter, who married Lord Huntly in 1706. She took the bold step of bringing English ploughmen with their ploughs all the way up to the Gordon estates, and began a campaign of draining, tree-planting, fallowing and haymaking. Her enterprise proved infectious, so that some of her neighbours began to undertake similar improve ments.

A contemporary of Lady Huntly was Sir Archibald Grant, son of Lord Cullen. In 1717, on the occasion of his marriage, Grant's father presented him with the poverty-stricken estate of Monymusk, twenty miles from Aberdeen. This was no fatherly gesture, as Lord Cullen had been regretting his recent purchase of these lands. Grant was an Edinburgh advocate and a Member of Parliament, so he could not settle on his new property until 1734, but he corresponded with his factor and other responsible employees.

In his first year, Grant spent £1,200 on enclosing his fields, building dykes, draining and tree-planting, with such success that between 1726 and 1731 his nurseries provided, for sale or transplantation, over a million trees of various kinds. The cultivation of trees improved his property, for the plantations acted as windbreaks. This prevented wholesale erosion of the soil by gales and so enhanced the value of the adjoining fields. At the same time, valuable supplies of Scottish timber were developed, in a period when Scandinavian wood was being imported at high costs.

In 1726, Grant brought an English farmer called Thomas Winter to his estate and this man supervised the cultivation of turnips by the drill, and also instituted hoeing. Turnips provided winter fodder for the undernourished cattle, so that the stock began to improve. At the same time better grain could be produced on fields where turnips had recently been grown, because the hoeing dealt with weeds. Monymusk was one of the first Scottish estates where turnips were properly used, and Grant was well ahead of many English improvers in this matter. The English prophet of turnip culture, whose preaching was rapidly adopted in progressive areas, was Jethro Tull, author of the classic, *Horse-Hoeing Husbandry*. This book, privately issued in 1731, was published in 1733. Grant bought a copy for 10/6d in 1736, by which time he had little to learn from it, and neither he nor his Aberdeenshire friends accepted all its findings.

Grant was one of the earliest Scottish improvers to insist upon regular use of lime. In adopting this method of improving his soil, he was doing his country a significant service, as it enabled him to grow wheat, a crop hardly known in Scotland before the Agricultural Revolution, although afterwards it was successfully produced on many Border and eastern farms. Grant's success in wheat production was also due to his rotation of crops, in which turnips were followed by wheat, beans and oats.

Grant made time to talk freely with his tenants and by personal conversation to stimulate their own initiative. Gradually he parted with those who were obstructive, while to those who were enthusiastic he gave long-term leases. In studying Grant's work, one is reminded of the great Coke of Norfolk, whose similar achievements a century later have attracted much wider publicity. Grant left in Monymusk one of the best-farmed and most beautiful estates of Scotland, and Lord Cullen's wedding gift proved to be more valuable than the donor himself would have dreamed possible.

Many other landowners transformed their estates by similar methods during this century, for example the Earl of Stair, who had property in West Lothian and in Galloway. He concentrated on roots, grasses, sainfoin and lucerne, all pioneer crops, but his most famous achievement was his great scheme of afforestation in Galloway, where he planted half a million trees, and where his woods still remain, a living testimony to his foresight, and a most beautiful heritage. Later in the century, Lord Kames became famous for the work he did in Berwickshire, and also in Perthshire. These two counties gained almost more than any others by the changes introduced, although throughout the Borders, in extensive areas near the east coast, in Morayshire and in Aberdeenshire, the new methods brought about a dramatic transformation. For the last two centuries some of these estates have been hard to rival in standards of husbandry and quality of output.

As rents and profits increased, small landowners and lairds took to enjoying spells of Edinburgh life, and so the more luxurious city ways spread into the countryside and provincial towns. After about 1760, Lowland farmers' wives began buying china dishes to replace pewter and wooden ware. By this time too, tea was used in all classes of society, to the disgust of Duncan Forbes, Alexander Carlyle and others, who regarded it as a demoralizing drug. About 1765, George Robertson noted that farmers were looking for carpets, exchanging their old boxbeds for four-posters with pleasantly checked curtains, furnishing their apartments 'in a more dashy style', purchasing sofas and elegant pianofortes. In 1790, the minister of Kilsyth reported a change in fashions. 'Formerly the most respectable Scottish farmers used to wear nothing but Scotch cloth of their own making, plaiding, hose and bonnets. Now the servant men on holidays wear nothing else than English cloth, cotton and thread stockings and hats . . . Every maid servant wears silk bonnets and cloak, and generally muslin or printed gowns and thread stockings. So that the men and women are more gayly dressed than their masters and mistresses were formerly.'

From medieval times there had always been a demand in England for Scottish cattle. There were famous cattle trysts at Crieff and at Falkirk, to which beasts were driven incredibly long distances. The drovers maintained a nomadic way of life as they journeyed over the Borders towards the south, following the ancient drove roads, and their story is admirably told in A. R. B. Haldane's *Drove Roads of Scotland*. English dealers bought Highland cattle eagerly, because although they were small, skinny animals, and although they lost weight on their long marches, a period of fattening on the richer southern pastures transformed them: their beef carcases had a particularly succulent flavour which was much appreciated in London dining-rooms. In the

219

early stages of their journeys, the cattle were saved many miles of land travel because they swam some of the estuaries, such as Lock Fyne, but the rough wayfaring was so hard on their feet that they had to be shod. North of Cambridge, on the Huntingdon Road, there is a little public house called the Travellers' Rest. It was one of many stopping places for the Scottish droves, and in the field behind it hundreds of small cattle shoes cast by the beasts have been unearthed.

The quality of Scottish stock greatly improved towards the end of the 18th century. This was partly the result of enclosure by dykes, which enabled owners to keep their herds separate from those of other people, but much better winter fodder became available as more turnips and grasses were sown, and this naturally improved the quality of the animals. The demand in England increased towards the end of the 18th century. Fully 100,000 beasts were driven over the Border each year during the Napoleonic wars, and the trade was well maintained after the wars came to an end.

Much information about 18th century Scottish farming may be found in the famous *Statistical Account of Scotland*. This massive work was planned by Sir John Sinclair, the owner of large estates in Caithness, a man with a fanatical love of statistics, who had carried out improvements on his own property and accumulated an encyclopaedic knowledge of agriculture. The Statistical Account was a national survey, based on information extracted from parish ministers, each of whom was issued with a questionnaire and asked to provide a description of his parish, its economic background and its contemporary conditions. The Account ran to twenty-one Volumes, published from 1790 onwards. It contains vividly expressed evidence of the agricultural advances made in the parishes where enclosure had been carried out, also of the consequent rise in expenditure and improvement in living standards.

Sir John persuaded the Government to constitute the Board of Agriculture in 1793, and he became its first President. He made himself rather unpopular, as he was a bombastic man with little sense of humour and he was always harrying people to undertake grandiose schemes; indeed Sir Walter Scott nicknamed him Cavaleiro Jackasso. But he did a great deal for the nation's food production during the war and he was the first person to understand the value of statistics in public investigations. His immense labours proved so valuable that in 1845 a second Statistical Account was published in 15 volumes; and now, during the 1950s, a third and much more comprehensive one is in process of publication.

Farm implements were slow to change during the 18th century. It was not until 1764 that James Small, a Berwickshire man, invented a swing plough which could be manipulated by one man with a pair of horses. Progressive farmers were quick to see its advantages, because the furrows it cut were deeper and cleaner than those of the old Scotch plough. Nonetheless, the old model died hard and was used in remote corners of some counties until the 19th century was well advanced. During the 1770s, Andrew Meikle of Dunbar produced a horse-drawn threshing machine, which was soon adapted to water power. The notion of artificially creating a wind shocked a number of people who declared that Meikle's invention was of the Devil, but by the end of the century it had been adopted on many farms. Early in the 19th century, a Scots minister called Patrick Bell devoted his engineering tastes to the construction of a mechanical reaper. This entirely novel machine cut the grain and bound it into sheaves which were flung out into a line as the reaper made its way across the field. The original models were pushed, not pulled, by horses.

During the Napoleonic wars, Britain needed much more home-produced food, so that progressive Scottish farmers who made use of new methods and new machines were sure of ready markets and high prices. The incentive to modernize all husbandry made a great difference south and east of the Highland line.

In the Highlands however the picture was very different. The Statistical Account shows that by 1790 little enclosure had taken place in the north-west and west of Scotland, where indifference to new-fangled ways persisted throughout the 18th century. Indeed to cross the Highland line was almost like entering another country. The crofters carried out their ancient agricultural rites on scattered pockets and patches of land, and in some

places, Arrochar for example, people used the ancient Highland
digging-stick, or caschrom, until 1810 and even later.

Cut off from all but immediate neighbours by boulder-strewn
hills, long narrow sea-lochs, and sodden peat mosses, the
Highland people were lethargic in mind and slow in movement,
partly because they and their families suffered chronically from
the agues, rheumatisms and skin diseases of the ill-housed and
the ill-fed. Ironically enough, part of the trouble was that in
those glens that were populated at all, there were too many of
these peasants, whose primitive methods of cultivation could
not produce sufficient food to maintain their large families.
Statistics concerning prisoners captured during the Forty-Five
show that the average Highlander in Charles Edward's army was
a man of poor physique, about 5 feet 4 inches in height, though
he had proved himself capable of enduring excessive fatigue
when campaigning in his own country.

That some of the least promising districts could be made to
prosper was proved after the Second Jacobite Rebellion. By an
Act of 1752, some forty Jacobite estates were forfeited and
annexed to the Crown, to be administered by a Board of Commissioners. The hanging of James Stewart on account of the
Appin murder has probably become the most widely known event
connected with these proceedings, which is regrettable, however
much one may enjoy the stirring narrative in *Kidnapped*, because
enlightened work was done by the Commissioners, who were
entitled to more recognition than they were accorded.

The forfeited properties varied in economic conditions from
the potentially wealthy Breadalbane estates in Perthshire to the
beautiful but unproductive possessions of Lochiel and Lovat in
the west; the people who lived on them were wretchedly poor,
but such was their loyalty that many of them paid their
rents twice over, as they insisted on sending money to their
exiled chieftains, although they also had to pay rent to the
Board.

The Commissioners astonished the people at the start by paying
all the proven debts of the banished owners. Sheafs of claims
remain in the records, and they reveal, often in poignant detail,
the miserable conditions in which the people were living. The

Glasgow Cathedral: Robert Paul, Foulis Academy, 1760.

By courtesy of the Mitchell Library, Glasgow.

Commissioners carried out surveying, roadmaking, bridge-building, and much afforestation. They even built schools, because the people were illiterate and their homes remote from those already in existence. Gradually the estates were given back to the heirs of the families; in 1784 all the remaining ones were returned, on condition that the money spent by the Government in meeting debts was repaid. In the end the total sum came to over £90,000, all of which was given to public works and charitable organizations in Scotland.

It was demonstrated, therefore, that the adoption of Enlightened methods could bring much advantage, but Highlanders by temperament and by habit resisted change. Famine recurred in 1740, 1756, 1766, 1778 and, with sharply increased severity, in 1782, but only in the last two decades of the century did turnip cultivation, the key to all farming progress, become at all general in the Highlands.

Meanwhile resistance had been made with similar obstinacy to potato culture. Potatoes were grown in Ireland, and also in England, long before they were adopted in Scotland. R. S. Salaman has dealt with this subject in his fascinating book entitled *The History and Social Influence of the Potato.* It was not until after the Second Jacobite Rebellion that potatoes were much cultivated in Scotland, though some Lowland farmers had introduced them rather earlier. Salaman shows how popular this cheap, easily produced food became in a relatively short time, particularly when the food shortages of the Napoleonic wars became acute. By the second decade of the 19th century, potatoes formed 'the main food for nine months of the year in some parts of Scotland.'

Sinclair's Statistical Account has many references to the changes effected by turnip and potato culture. Where these two roots were cultivated in alternation with grain crops, prosperity steadily developed, indeed proper use of turnips and other roots was the hallmark of the up-to-date farmer by 1790. But there are also depressingly consistent reports that in backward and poverty-stricken places, such as the majority of Highland villages, people were substituting potatoes for grain in their fields, a retrograde policy. Sir John Sinclair, like many other experts of the day, probably failed to see the danger. 'It is difficult to conceive', he wrote, 'how the people of the country could have subsisted, had it not been for the fortunate introduction and extensive cultivation of this most valuable plant.' 'This most valuable plant' was too much relied upon among the really poor however.

While therefore the century following the Second Jacobite Rebellion was a period of much advance in the south and east, there were ominous developments in the Highlands. The chieftains, deprived of old privileges and stripped of power, tended to become absentee landlords, interested only in the extraction of rents. Many of these men were faced with an almost insoluble problem. The mountainous regions in the west and north-west cannot produce good arable crops, and they have always proved difficult as pastoral areas because cattle cannot survive a winter on some of those storm-wracked hills. In the latter part of the 18th century, landowners began to realize that Blackface sheep can stand up to such conditions, while Cheviots, which are not quite so hardy, do well in the glens. And so the fashion set in for sheep-farming.

In order to clear large areas for sheep-walks, these landowners forced their tenants to give up their holdings, and the most popular method at first was the simple one of raising rents. The naturalist Thomas Pennant was one of the many travellers in Scotland who remarked on this. He wrote in 1771: 'The rage of raising rents has reached this distant country . . . Here the great men begin at the wrong end with squeezing the bag before they have helped the poor tenant to fill it by the introduction of manufactures. In many of the isles this already shows its unhappy effect and begins to depopulate the country, for numbers of families have been obliged to give up the strong attachment the Scots in general have for their country and exchange it for the wilds of America.'

The higher rents forced some tenants to reduce their plots and to live almost wholly on potatoes, but many thousands, driven to despair, sought the more drastic alternative of emigration. Johnson was horrified by the numbers of people preparing to emigrate when he toured the Hebrides in 1773, and he shrewdly pointed out that generous landowners, 'of more prudence and less rapacity', caused no such 'epidemical fury of emigration'. It is believed that between 1760 and 1808 some 12,000 people left the Highlands for America and at least 30,000 for the Colonies. The depopulated farmlands they left behind became vast sheep-walks, which the chieftains found much more advantageous, because of the reduction in wage bills, and the existence, especially during the wars, of ready markets for meat and wool.

Some crofters were able to keep going at home during the Napoleonic wars by working at kelp. Largely used in the manufacture of soap and glass, kelp is an alkaline ash, one ton of which could be made by burning twelve or more tons of seaweed. During the wars the demand for kelp was much increased by the difficulty of importing the foreign alkaline substances, such as barilla, which were preferred in peacetime. By 1800, kelp was priced at £22 a ton; an enormous, though unskilled, labour force was needed both on the west and east coasts to collect the seawrack, lay it out to dry and burn it. An industrious family could earn about £7 a year at this unattractive work, the main profits of which went to the owners and employers. The boom outlived the wars which produced it by eight years. In 1823, the import tax on barilla was removed and the price of kelp dropped from £22 to £2 per ton. The wretched families who had been relying on the artificially high price were ruined and could no longer put off the only alternative to starvation at home and so they too emigrated.

The practice of driving out the crofters became so common during the Napoleonic wars and the following period that almost every county has sad and sometimes shameful records of such procedure, undertaken by landowners who saw in sheep-farming the only solution to their problems. You can still come across pathetic little mounds of grass-grown rubble which mark the sites of old villages. Hounam in Roxburghshire is an example, but far more frequently one finds such relics in the Highlands.

Of all the clearances, those of Sutherlandshire have become the most notorious. They have been described by many writers and they have provided material for furious controversy. From 1811 to 1820, some 15,000 people were evicted by the second Duke

P   225   G.S.S.

of Sutherland, through his factor James Loch. Eyewitness accounts of the unsavoury process make distressing reading. Donald Sage, minister of Achness in Strathnaver, saw the evictions, which were followed by the burning of the people's cottages. His grief and anger may be understood because at least 1,600 people were turned out of Strathnaver in one day at short notice. 'On the Sabbath, a fortnight previous to the fated day, I preached my valedictory sermon in Achness, and the Sabbath thereafter at Achnabuiaghe. Both occasions were felt, by myself and by the people from the oldest to the youngest, to be among the bitterest and most overwhelming experiences of our lives.'

It should be emphasized that the Sutherlandshire hills are enormous structures of rock and boulder, with patches of soil fit only for sheep farming, so that the crofters living among them had been for generations hopelessly poor. Their removal by Loch was organized thoroughly and ruthlessly, in an effort to turn the land over to more profitable use. Literally thousands of the families were transferred to the coast, where they built themselves fresh hovels and lived on the products of the potato plots which were allotted to them there. They made the best of it by working at the kelp on the seashore, but when this industry collapsed in 1823 great numbers of them embarked in the emigrant ships.

The steady flow of Scots to the New World received sharp acceleration in 1846, when the Potato Blight spread its poison into the crops of farmers all over Scotland. This brought about specially serious results in the Highlands, where within a few months whole districts were stripped of food resources. Relief schemes were organized by the Government, by the churches, by citizens of Glasgow and Edinburgh, by public-spirited chieftains such as Macleod, Mackenzie and Mathieson, but none of these efforts could prevent a national disaster. Faced with starvation, embittered by the death through famine of the weakly members of his family, many a Scot gave up all hope of making good at home. Thus the tide of emigration swelled and, in a year, 106,000 people left Scotland. The less adventurous crowded into the cities of the industrial belt, in search of relief, along with many thousands of Irishmen who were suffering from the same calamity and who believed that on Clydeside they would find work and wages.

Meantime, in Scotland's richer and more prosperous areas of the south and east, men were able to develop a material security such as they had never known before. Shorthorns, Ayrshires and Galloway cattle became well-known for their quality and commanded high prices. In 1829 the Royal Highland and Agricultural Society began to hold its shows, and dealers came from far and wide to make purchases and to study the improved breeds. First and foremost among these was the Aberdeen Angus. Magnificent specimens of the most famous herds were exported to the Argentine and to other foreign markets. This was the period too when Clydesdale horses made their name.

The golden age of Scottish agriculture was in the mid-19th century, when ley-farming began to be adopted. The great Border farms, and also many of those in central Scotland, were particularly well suited to this system, which is profitable only in areas where rich grass can be successfully laid down. The rotation of crops is extended to a cycle of six or eight years, of which half are given to consecutive seasons of grasses, carefully selected and nurtured. How astonished the advocates of this system would have been, had they realized that it was regularly practised by the Cistercian monks of Cupar Abbey in the 15th century!

Scottish owners and farmers developed some of the richest land in Britain to such a pitch of husbandry that their grain, seed-potatoes and fatstock became famous literally all over the world. Carefully constructed byres, comfortable farmhouses, extensive woodlands and, above all, the fields of first-class crops testified to the success of the new ways; so did the crowded stock-markets, the dignified bank-houses and the well-run county academies for the younger generation. The historian of Scotland's 19th century could make a heartening narrative of material progress if he neglected consideration of the emigrants huddled together in those overcrowded sailing ships which beat their way across the Atlantic. Those thousands of Highlanders left the land they loved, the way of life they knew, bitterly resentful. Nobody knew how to deal with the desperate problems which drove them away.

The Eighteenth and Nineteenth Centuries

The tide of emigration was not stemmed until the once over-populated glens of the north and west had become almost deserted, so that the problem of depopulation became one for 20th century economists and politicians to solve. The Scots who made their way into Canada and America concentrated all their gifts of endurance and courage, all their mental and physical energy, on the task of building a fresh way of life in the cities and on the prairies. That they succeeded so well, and made such a magnificent contribution to the growth of the new communities, should not mask the calamity which destroyed a whole section of Scottish society.

CHAPTER 21

Transport

One result of the Roman failure to make permanent settlements in Scotland was that roads only appeared by gradual stages in medieval times, as a result of the passage of men and beasts. Road maintenance was never the responsibility of any reliable body of people until the 17th century, and when repairs were carried out, methods were perfunctory. Ruts and pot-holes were filled with loose stones or sand, and the ridges roughly levelled off. The whole operation was rendered useless by the next rainstorm.

The Tweed was crossed by only two bridges, one at Peebles, one at Berwick, with forty miles of unspanned river flowing between them. The further north you penetrated, the less you were likely to find any means of crossing water, other than ford or ferry. On one of his preaching tours, Wesley was nearly drowned with his horse in the Tay, while on another he took a severe ducking in the Solway, and in 1784 Lord Braxfield, who was riding his circuit, had to go twenty-eight miles up the Findhorn before he could find a safe place to cross. Lord Cockburn wrote from personal experience: 'There was no bridge over the Tay at Dunkeld, or over the Spey at Fochabers, or over the Findhorn at Forres. Nothing but wretched, pierless ferries, let to poor cottars, who rowed or hauled or pushed a crazy boat across, or more commonly got their wives to do it.'

Goods were transported on horseback, because wheeled traffic was not to be had, and even coal was carried in panniers by horses. In the 1750s and 1760s, horse-drawn, wheeled carts were an exciting new development, but their expense seriously affected prices. Coal costing 10d. per cartload at the Monkland pits commanded twice that sum when it reached Glasgow, twelve miles away; and the poor condition, both of horses and of road

MAP 7.
SOME ROADS AND CANALS IN THE EARLY INDUSTRIAL REVOLUTION

Inverness
Peterhead
R.Findhorn
R.Spey
R.Don
Monymusk
Aberdeen
Fort Augustus
Caledonian Canal
R.Dee
N.Esk
Dalwhinnie
S.Esk
Dalnacardoch
Fort William
R.Tay
Dunkeld
Crieff
Craignish
Crinan Canal
Aberfoyle
Helensburgh
R.Forth
Dumbarton
Forth and Clyde Canal
Leith
Greenock
Port Glasgow
Monkland Canal
Edinburgh
Glasgow
Coatbridge
Berwick
R.Clyde
Peebles
R.Tweed
Kilmarnock
Troon
Selkirk
Ayr

Φ.Γ.

Carlisle
R.Eden

Canals.............   Wade's roads........

0   10   20   40   80   100 Miles

0 10 20   40   60   80   100   120   140 160 Kilometres

surfaces, is revealed in the fact that a cartload was only seven hundredweight. One carrier working the forty miles between Selkirk and Edinburgh took two weeks to complete his return journey; he found that he made the best progress by wading his horse and cart along the bed of the Gala River, a safer and easier route than was afforded by the main road. He used to be seen off by all his neighbours coming out to cheer. Landowners on the North-East coast found it more profitable to ship their grain to London than to transport it even ten miles inland, and when wealthy Scots made their way to London they sent the heavy luggage by sea with the servants. Scottish literature of the 18th and early 19th centuries is crammed, both with references to the frustrations of inland travel, and also with ample evidence that, one way or another, anybody who meant to get about did so, whatever the inconveniences involved.

The first large-scale scheme of road-building was initiated for military reasons. The misadventures of government troops during the First Jacobite Rebellion compelled the authorities in London to believe that something must be done. To General Wade therefore was assigned the task of constructing highways in central and north-east Scotland.

Wade began in 1725 and during eight consecutive summers he worked with some 500 soldiers, who were paid in Royal Bank notes, carried to them at regular intervals by clerks on horseback. His problems of discipline and commissariat in the remote and wild hills were as complex as any faced by contemporary officers serving in European areas, but despite all obstacles he completed forty bridges, also 500 miles of roads, most of which were about sixteen feet wide.

Wade's two points of departure were Crieff and Dunkeld; the two lines he carried north from these points met at Dalnacardoch, whence he drove a single road over the mountains to Dalwhinnie. There he divided the route again, making one branch towards Fort Augustus, and a second, by the Spey Valley, to Inverness; a third road linked Inverness, Fort Augustus and Fort William. The scheme covered mountainous areas and precipitous heights hitherto never crossed by properly surfaced roads.

Wade's achievement is rightly famous, and his hump-backed bridges, and narrow, steeply graded highways, now generally bypassed, are considered a national heritage. His work did not however solve the real problems of the day, as, with military rather than economic or commercial concerns in mind, he penetrated the Highlands at only two main entrances. The beginnings he made were followed up after the Forty-Five by another scheme of military roads, which covered almost 800 miles and included something like 1,000 bridges. The inhabitants of the areas thus opened up thought poorly of the whole enterprise. Ramsay of Ochtertyre recorded a typical countryman's view: 'In 1761, I was in company with Peter Graham of Rudivous, a lively man, past fourscore. The conversation turning upon roads, he said he saw no use of them but to set burghers and redcoats into the Highlands none of whom in his father's time would have durst venture beyond the Pass of Aberfoyle.'

With the rising ambitions of landowners and farmers, and also the increasing population in the towns, public irritation over the poor communications began to be aroused, in spite of Peter Graham and his kind. In 1751 the first effective Turnpike Act was passed, for the district of Edinburgh, and some 350 other local Turnpike Acts followed. This development led to hundreds of miles of roads being built. They were financed largely by the tolls taken from travellers at the regularly placed turnpikes, those five-barred structures which straddled the new highways and were supervised from little toll-houses—there were no less than ten turnpikes on the thirty-four mile stretch from Glasgow to Ayr. The roads were administered by trusts or companies, which employed distinguished engineers like Rennie and Macadam. Their well-metalled surfaces enabled wheeled traffic at last to travel with relative speed and safety.

In 1802, the Government commissioned the great Telford to report on roads, bridges and fisheries in the Highlands. This was part of a campaign to arrest the steady emigration which had already reached alarming proportions. Telford's survey did nothing to lessen public anxiety. He recommended schemes far more ambitious than anything undertaken elsewhere and he urged that the cost should be met largely by the State, as the works in question were 'exceptional and extraordinary.'

The Government accepted most of Telford's recommendations, with the result that 920 additional miles of roads and many bridges were made, while at Wick, Aberdeen and Peterhead, and at other harbours, there were big reconstructions. All these projects were directed by Telford, expenses being met half by the State, half by local assessment, with the help of some considerable gifts from the Duke of Gordon, the Duke of Atholl and other landowners.

During the second half of the 18th century, as a result of road-building, the great days of the mail coach began. In 1749 the first vehicle to run between Glasgow and Edinburgh set out twice a week, and it covered the forty-four miles in just under two days. In 1760, after the introduction of the turnpike system, the journey could be achieved in a day and a half, by a coach affectionately christened 'The Fly', so delighted were its proprietors with its speed. Passengers from Edinburgh reached Holytown on the first evening, where they had 'as comfortable quarters as double-bedded rooms in the inn could afford, there to repose and recover their breathing after the fatigue of twelve hours' jolting on a solid hand made road, a little rough no doubt from the stones being somewhat of the largest, and having travelled no less than 33 miles. . . The two Flies made out very correctly three journeys betwixt them in the course of a week; that is thrice going to Glasgow, and thrice to Edinburgh; six journeys in all.' These recollections from the diary of George Robertson were offset by some less flattering passages. 'In wet weather' the tracks became 'sloughs in which the carts and carriages had to slumper in a half-swimming state, whilst in time of drought it was a continued jolting out of one hole into another.'

It was not till 1760 that an Edinburgh coach service to London became regularly available and then there was only one service per month. Glasgow folk had no direct contact with London till 1788, so that for nearly thirty years they had first to make the two days' preliminary run to Edinburgh and then, duly rested no doubt by a night in a double-bedded room, set out for the south. When the first Glasgow coach trip was advertised the cost was

£4 16s. 0d., and the time sixty-five hours. In 1798, Aberdeen followed on with an independent service to London.

These facts show how isolated folk in Scotland were, alike from each other and from their English neighbours. The same thing is illustrated by the postal arrangements, which were re-organized after 1707 on a more business-like basis. A general Postmaster was appointed in Edinburgh at a salary of £200 a year; with the help of an accountant and two clerks he was able to handle easily all the mail entering and leaving the Capital, and for ten years deliveries were distributed by one letter-carrier. Even as late as 1780 only six post-boys were needed. The arrival of a letter was an event worth comment, and in Glasgow a gun was fired when the daily quota of letters had been sorted and was ready for distribution.

Ambitious commercial firms soon began to press for better use of Scotland's numerous inland waterways and for the construction of canals. Such goods as china—now in demand because of the new-fashioned coffee and tea—did not improve by being hauled about on horseback, while coal and manufactured goods soared in price as one horse-drawn mile dragged after another.

A canal connecting the Forth and Clyde was proposed in the times of Charles II, but the idea was dismissed because of the cost. After the Union it was revived, and Defoe was greatly taken with it and looked forward to the time when men 'shall not only feel the want of it, but find themselves inclinable as well as able to effect it'. In 1764 Smeaton drew up two alternative plans and in 1768 work was begun. By 1775, the proprietors of the scheme had spent all their money, the American war had started, the tobacco trade was collapsing, a financial panic had undermined confidence, and work on the canal came to an end. In 1784 however, the Government made a grant of £50,000 from the revenues of the Forfeited Estates and at last, in 1790, the whole magnificent venture was completed. In the 35 miles of the canal, which was eight feet deep, there were thirty-nine locks to negotiate the rise from sea level to a summit of 156 feet; and vessels of 19 feet beam and 68 feet keel could pass through it. The 80-ton sloop *Agnes* sailed from Leith to Greenock to celebrate the inauguration of the new waterway.

In the same year, 1790, a shorter but almost more important canal was opened. This was the Monkland Canal, designed to make available the rich supplies of coal in the Coatbridge area, because hitherto there had been no suitable transport to carry them to Glasgow. James Watt undertook the construction of the Monkland Canal, at a salary of £200 a year, with a staff consisting of one clerk, who assisted him in the tasks of surveying, planning, costing and supervising. After years of delay, it was completed and joined at Port Dundas to the Glasgow branch of the Forth and Clyde Canal. To-day, in 20th century conditions, this twelve-mile stretch of waterway is not only useless, but a positive menace to the safety of the children at play, who are the only people interested in it, but a century and a half ago it brought much financial gain to landowners and industrialists on the Lanarkshire side of Glasgow.

In 1803, another famous Scottish canal was designed by Telford, as part of his general scheme to improve Scottish transport. This was the Caledonian Canal, a gargantuan undertaking upon which almost a million pounds were spent over a period of seventeen years. In the end, this canal was 60 miles in length and no less than 40 of these miles were provided by the great inland lochs which form a diagonal rift across north-west Scotland. At the western end there were eight miles covering a drop of 90 feet; Telford built 8 locks for the negotiation of this gradient, dubbing the completed series 'Neptune's Staircase'. At the other end of the canal, a huge lock extended for almost half a mile into the sea. The purpose of the Government in undertaking all this was to make the dangerous passage round northern Scotland unnecessary. Samuel Smiles put it as follows: 'The Pentland Firth, which is the throat connecting the Atlantic and German Oceans and through which rolls its long majestic waves with tremendous force, was the dread of mariners.' A case was quoted to Parliament of an Inverness vessel sailing for Liverpool on Christmas Day, which reached Stromness Harbour in Orkney on January 1st there to be storm-stayed till mid-April. Another witness told of two vessels setting forth on the same day from Newcastle, one for Liverpool via the Pentland Firth, the other for Bombay via the Cape of Good Hope, and the latter reached her destination first. Thus the Caledonian Canal was much desired and Telford spent many years with hundreds of labourers working upon it, but financially it never paid, a fact which nearly broke the heart of its designer: his cheerful, optimistic nature suffered no more hurtful experience than the failure of this tremendous enterprise.

There were a number of other canals constructed during this period in Scotland, of which perhaps the Crinan Canal is best known, because it shortens the dangerous run from the Clyde to the Western Isles. All the canals were used for transport of heavy goods, but almost all were regularly patronized also by passengers who were encouraged to enjoy their trips by the advertising agents of the day. In 1823, an Edinburgh publisher produced a guide-book of 82 pages called *A Companion for Canal Passengers betwixt Edinburgh and Glasgow*. It gave 'a complete account of all the interesting objects that are seen along the lines of the two canals; such as towns, villages, gentlemen's seats, works of art, ancient structures and scenes of former wars.' Tourist traffic was beginning to make its appearance and to be recognized as a source of profit.

Of all the inland waterways developed at this time, the Clyde was the most important, and the work done upon it has remained as a permanent investment for commerce and industry. In 1755, Smeaton made a report for the city magistrates on the state of the river between Glasgow and Renfrew. He described twelve large shoals, one of which lay 400 yards below Glasgow bridge, leaving a depth of only 15 inches, while four others left only 18 inches. After nine years' delay, Golborne was commissioned to make a similar survey, and his report showed that, owing to neglect, the river was in 'a state of nature' and had spread its meandering waters further still across the adjacent meadows. In 1773, Golborne was given a contract by the city and he undertook to create a navigable stream giving a depth of six feet right up to Glasgow itself. He constructed jetties and walls and he organized regular dredging: by these means he gave the river a depth of 6 feet 10 inches, outdoing his promise by nearly a foot, but by 1781 the Clyde's own movement towards the sea in the narrowed channel had produced a depth of 14 to 22 feet. The artificial maintenance of this channel has been continued ever since. In

1809 the Clyde Navigation Trust was founded to keep the channel clear. This organization still exists, and has carried out its original function throughout its history by regular dredging and excavation.

The results of these enterprises were soon apparent. In the heart of Glasgow, there had been until 1773 a riverside meadow where the broom grew so charmingly as to leave us the name of the Broomielaw. Here people pastured cattle, hung out their laundry, and shouted at boys wading over to the other side of the river. All ships, shipping, quaysides and dock work were out of sight at Port Glasgow, at least 16½ miles away. Visitors to Glasgow in this enviable period were delighted with its pleasant air, its gardens, fruit-trees, spacious streets, and the attractive villages within reach for those who enjoyed an evening walk— Govan for example, and Partick. The united efforts of Golborne, Rennie and Telford were successful in inaugurating a transformation which was financially an overwhelming success. Quays, docks, harbour equipment, warehouses and shipbuilding yards were created so that the shipping brought to the Broomielaw increased within Telford's own lifetime from nothing at all to over a million tons a year. He died in 1834, long before the steamer had ousted the sailing ship, and when each vessel was incomparably smaller than would be the case to-day; these figures illustrate the passing of the old, pleasant riverside city and the emergence of the blackened, noisy centre of overcrowding we now know.

The expansion of overseas commerce, which burst upon all Scottish ports, but upon Glasgow with especial force in the early 19th century, was accelerated by the development of steamships. For some twenty years William Symington and his partner, Patrick Miller, laboured on their plan of building a steam-propelled vessel and at last their dreams were fulfilled in 1802, when they launched their *Charlotte Dundas* on the Forth and Clyde Canal. Her performance astonished the crowds who turned out to see, for she towed two barges, each loaded with 70 tons of cargo, and she covered 20 miles in the record time of six hours. The Canal proprietors objected to the 'agitation of the water' created by her wash however and, in defence of their precious banks, they put an end to her career as a substitute for the horse on the towing path.

Henry Bell, originally a wheelwright, was the second British engineer to succeed in this sphere. His Clyde-built *Comet* was launched in 1812. She had a three horse-power engine, she covered four miles per hour, she had on board a library of classical literature, and she was the pride of Helensburgh, whose schoolmaster was her first Commander. Bell himself was Provost of the town, where with his wife's help he ran the Baths Hotel, now known as the Queen's Hotel; it commands a splendid view of the Clyde and the course taken by the *Comet*. The little vessel plied between Glasgow and Greenock, afterwards extending her run to Fort William via the Crinan Canal, until she was wrecked in 1820 off Craignish Point in Argyllshire. Two other very early paddle-steamers were the *Industry* and the *Trusty*, both of which were bought in 1815 by the recently founded Clyde Shipping Company. This firm has continued in business ever since and in 1956 published an interesting history of its services to Scottish transport.

The first steamship to cross the open sea was the *Marjorie*, one of nine similar vessels built on the Clyde in the last two years of the Napoleonic wars. By the end of 1823, 95 steamers had been built in Scotland, 72 on the Clyde; and 40 had been sold out of the country.

Shipbuilding therefore laid hold upon Scottish yards and soon iron began to be boldly incorporated in the great structures which carried goods all over the world. The crossing of the Atlantic under steam was achieved in 1838, by the *Sirius*, built the previous year at Leith, engined in Glasgow. She was 178 feet in length and she made the journey in eighteen days on 450 tons of coal, carrying forty passengers, of whom eleven were ladies. Her arrival in New York was celebrated by much publicity and by an official visit to the ship, at which the Mayor of New York made a speech. The excitement of the occasion was greatly increased by the arrival of the Bristol-built *Great Western*, a vessel of double the size, only a few hours after the *Sirius*.

The beautiful wooden sailing ships on the tea run to the East therefore had powerful rivals, but they held their own for many a year. Numbers of them were built in Aberdeen, such as the

Port-Glasgow from the South-East: Robert Paul, Foulis Academy, 1768.

By courtesy of the Mitchell Library, Glasgow.

famous *Thermopylae*, whose maiden voyage from the Thames to Melbourne was in 1868. The following year, the *Cutty Sark*, built in Dumbarton, began her long career. For twenty-six years she made journeys to the East and her speed became the talk of seafarers all over the world. From 1888 to 1893 there was a last magnificent boom in the construction of these ships, in which the Clyde took a leading part. One of the bold adjustments in design at this time was the use of steel for certain parts of the vessels. By the last decade of the 19th century, however, the tramp steamers had won the day and only fanatics could claim that there was any future for sailing ships. The beautiful *Cutty Sark* was sold away to Portugal, where, under the name *Ferreira*, she was used as a cargo-boat for nearly thirty years. She plied to West Africa during the 1914-1918 war and was still sailing in 1922, when she was bought by a British owner called Captain Dowman, whose widow presented her to the Thames Nautical Training College in 1938. In 1954 she was moved to Greenwich, where she may still be seen, the swiftest, the longest-lived and the last of a wonderful succession. Meanwhile, ocean-going steamers increased in number, tonnage and commercial profit. Scotland had a large share in the new shipbuilding industry, which became closely linked with the heavy metal industries, as more and more iron was needed in the construction of steamers, until steel replaced it.

Owing to the sudden development of the railway, inland waterways attracted less business from the 1830s onwards and finally became liabilities rather than assets. Wagonways for the transport of coal were in use both north and south of the Border for a long time before railways, as we know them, appeared. There was one at Alloa, originally constructed in 1771, and another at Little Govan which dated from 1778. The best known was the so-called railway from Kilmarnock to Troon, opened in 1810, and built at a cost of £50,000 to carry the Duke of Portland's coal from the collieries to the sea. This line was used by many business people in Ayrshire for the carriage of timber, grain, lime, and even passengers. On all these early 'railroads', the trucks were horse-drawn, and much better speed could be made by the horses than on the highways.

One year after the famous Stockton-Darlington line was completed, the first genuine Scottish railway was opened, from Monkland to Kirkintilloch. This line was 10 miles in length, with passing places here and there, and it linked the Monkland collieries with the Forth and Clyde canal. Other early railway lines were also built as feeders to canals, or as supplementary routes. The Glasgow-Garnkirk railway ran beside the Monkland Canal and was designed primarily for the haulage of coal. It was opened in 1831, with much flourish, as George Stephenson himself came to drive the first engine, which was named after him in honour of the occasion. The cost of carrying coal from Monkland to Glasgow was immediately halved, with the result that landed proprietors who were fortunate enough to find coal seams on their properties began to make enormous profits.

These early railways were designed for the carriage of goods, but, as in the case of the canals, passengers swarmed to enjoy this novel type of journeying. The 'carriages' in which they travelled had no covering and were provided only with the hardest of benches. All the same, people were eager to make use of the railways, boasting to each other of the incredible speeds at which they travelled, and enduring with apparent delight the smoke and smuts through which they rushed at 16-20 miles an hour: sixty-two thousand people travelled thus on the Glasgow-Garnkirk line in its first year, which shows what a complete change was taking place in the nation's habits, for even a decade earlier it would have been impossible to imagine so many people on the move. Passenger traffic was organized on methods similar to those used for highway coaches. People could hail the trains and board them where they wished; drivers blew their horns on approaching a road crossing; any owner of a wagon might hitch it on behind the train, for a given fee, provided it was clearly labelled with his name on the outside.

It soon followed that trunk lines were designed as well as a network of local routes and in 1835 citizens of Edinburgh and Glasgow began to interest themselves in a railway linking their two great cities. In their prospectus, they made the bold claim that such a railway would bring '200,000 persons more along its line into daily, nay, it may be said hourly, communication . . . It is impossible to see the extent to which it may go.' Sea-side holidays soon became a practical proposition for the Scot and his family. In 1836, a line from Glasgow to Paisley and thence to Ayr was proposed, partly to open up a fresh industrial area, partly for reasons set forth by the proprietors in their prospectus. 'A Railway to the sea-coast of Ayrshire would enable seabathing visitors to reach it with certainty in about one hour, in place of their spending as at present five to eight hours in an uncertain and tedious voyage. It is reasonable therefore to suppose that the sea-bathing quarters on the coast of Ayrshire which at present are considerable, would become still more fashionable resorts and in this way that a new traffic in the carriage of passengers along the line would also be created.'

Horse-traction was forgotten and locomotives were used on all railway lines by mid-century, the period of railway mania, when many small companies built short lengths of line, independently of each other and in suicidal competition. 'Britain is at present an island of lunatics, all railway-mad,' Lord Cockburn wrote in 1845. 'The patients are raving even in the wild recesses of the Highlands.' The absurd rivalries led to a number of bankruptcies and gradually to some amalgamations. A national gauge was then adopted, so that all railway lines were the same width apart and trucks could be used in any part of the country. A comprehensive system of safety regulations was also worked out, particularly for signalling, which in the earlier days had been primitive to a degree. By 1850, it was possible to travel from London to Glasgow and also from London to Aberdeen by train.

The Scottish contribution to the vast changes in transport throughout the kingdom in the 18th and 19th centuries was very considerable, particularly among roadbuilders and shipbuilders: John Rennie was the architect of the London Docks, the East India Docks and Waterloo Bridge; John Macadam invented a road surface which was universally adopted and his name has became part of the English language; Bell of Helensburgh, Scott of Greenock, Denny of Dumbarton, Robert Napier of Glasgow form only one group of many Scottish engineers, internationally renowned, on whose work Britain's lead in the new seafaring methods was founded.

Of all these giants, Thomas Telford was perhaps the most interesting. Laughing Tam was his nickname as a boy; Laughing Tam he remained all his life. His father, a shepherd in the little-known hills of Kirkcudbrightshire, died when his son was a baby. The boy began life as a working stonemason, doing odd jobs in the neighbourhood. When he died, in 1834, he was known all over Europe. He had been consulted in Sweden, Russia and Austria; he had built the Ellesmere Canal and rebuilt much of the Grand Trunk Canal; he had bridged the Menai Straits, the Clyde, the Tay and many other rivers; he had worked on harbours, docks and roads all over the United Kingdom. All his life Telford's sunny and compassionate nature made him beloved, and richly he enjoyed his friendships, particularly with Robert Southey, who gave him the nickname of 'Pontifex Maximus', because of his bridge-building. He was at heart a poet and a philosopher, for he read and wrote poetry all his days, and he always maintained an idealistic view of his profession. Shortly after the Battle of Waterloo, Telford wrote to a friend: 'During the war just brought to a close, England has not only been able to guard her own land, and to carry on a gigantic struggle, but at the same time to construct canals, roads, harbours, bridges—magnificent works of peace—the like of which are probably not to be found in the world. Are not these things worthy of a nation's pride?'

The changes in transport which took place north of the Border during this period are remarkable enough when we consider them in relation to Scotland alone. It is interesting to consider them in relation to Britain as a whole. Throughout the country, the pattern, though perhaps not the timing, is similar. In the early days of the great roadbuilders, people were able to take to the highways by coach, carriage and cart. Thus the inns and hostelries of the 18th century made their name. The second stage was the period when inland waterways were developed and a new race of British workmen came into being, the bargees and their families. After the turn of the century came the invention of steamer and railway engine. It followed that many of the fine old inns, with their dignified and bustling discomfort, fell into decay, for the railways passed them by, outmoding travel by road and also depriving the canals of much business; it also followed that by mass movements of goods and folk, by high speculation and huge turnover of capital, both countryside and city centre were utterly transformed. The home life, the business and recreative pursuits of Scottish folk were affected by the great changes in transport during these two centuries more than by any development other than the industrial revolution with which they were linked.

CHAPTER 22

Industry

The immediate effects of the Union upon Scotland's economic life brought about some unfortunate developments, because Scottish industries at once suffered from the competition of the more advanced and highly organized English producers, especially in the woollen business.

It was in commerce that recovery first began, because the Navigation Acts no longer excluded Scottish ships from the colonial markets, and a vast new sphere lay open to men of initiative. The almost chronic state of war between Britain and France during this period gave Glasgow its opportunity, as the Clyde was safer than the Mersey or the Bristol Channel, and it saved miles of uncertain sea travel. From the 1720s onwards, Glasgow merchants began to import quantities of tobacco from the New World in their own ships. In 1724, over four million pounds of it were brought up the Clyde, fully three-quarters of which were re-exported. It was largely because of this annually increasing commerce in tobacco that people began to insist that the Clyde must be made navigable so that ocean-going vessels could come right up to the city, instead of berthing at Port Glasgow.

William Cunninghame was the richest of all the magnates at this time. He secured the fine estate of Lainshaw, in Ayrshire, and for his Glasgow residence bought a site on Cow Loan, the old lane by which the city cowherd had hitherto driven the people's cattle to pasture each day. Here he spent £10,000 on the only one of the great mansions still to be seen in something like its original form. It is incorporated in the Royal Exchange, now used as a Public Library, and the old homely Cow Loan is Queen Street. Cunninghame realized that the American war, which broke out in 1775, would reduce supplies of tobacco and he bought up all that he could lay hands on, only selling when it reached the shattering price of 3/6d a pound. Thus, out of the utter ruin which because of the war fell suddenly and completely upon this trade, he made an even larger fortune; but he was the last to do so.

In 1771, Spenser published his *English Traveller*, a book which contains a description of such men as Cunninghame. 'Many of the merchants acquire vast fortunes and they have such an inclination to business that little besides it ever engages their attention. Those that trade to Virginia are decked out in great wigs and scarlet cloaks, and strut about on the Exchange . . . like so many actors on the Stage.' By 1777, this particular stage no longer existed. Instead of some 46 million pounds of tobacco, much less than ½ a million came up the Clyde that year and the city was faced with economic crisis.

The capitalists in Glasgow were quick to turn their wealth to other uses however. Already the staple industries of the 19th century had made beginnings, both in the west and in the east. After the collapse of the tobacco trade, five main types of enterprise were developed in Scotland, namely textile mills, iron foundries, coal mines, engineering shops and shipyards.

The textile industry was the first to become established. During the years when tobacco accounted for so much Scottish business, linen was steadily absorbing capital. Soon after the Union, and under the terms of the Treaty, steps were taken to foster the production of linen-yarns and materials. In 1727, a Board of Trustees for Manufactures was set up by Act of Parliament, with £6,000 a year to spend from government grants, to stimulate Scottish industry. To linen was allocated £2,650 per year.

Elizabeth Mure of Caldwell recorded in old age some early recollections, dating from about 1727. The following passage illustrates the state of affairs in linen production before and after the Board's early efforts. 'At that time there was little bread in Scotland; Manefactorys were brought to no perfection either in linnen or woolen. Every woman made her web of wove linnen and bleched it herself; it never rose higher than 2/- the yard, and with this cloth was everybody cloathed. The young gentlemen, who at this time were growing more delicat, got their cloth from

Holland for shirts; but the old were satisfied with necks and
sleeves of the fine, which were put on loose above the country
cloth . . . A few years after this wevers were brought over from
Holland and manefactorys for Linnen established in the West.'

Elizabeth Mure's 'manefactorys' were started by the Board
of Trustees, who brought in foreign weavers and flax-dressers, to
give instruction about the methods best suited to the production
of this difficult crop. Linen was successfully established in many
places from Aberdeen to Paisley, and it began soon to be in
demand abroad. In 1742 the first of a series of Bounty Acts was
passed, to subsidize linen exports. As demand and profit consequently increased, so craftsmanship developed, with the result
that linen of a much finer quality was produced in Scotland for
sale to America, the West Indies and elsewhere.

The Scottish linen workers of the 18th century were cottagers
and farmers, who carried out their craft on their own premises,
with their own hand-made wheels and frames. It was a life of
hard work and some financial anxiety, but it afforded them
independence. Capital was provided by agents, who distributed
flax to the spinners and collected the yarn, which they gave out
to weavers. These agents were employed by men of small means,
who had difficulty in securing credit, in maintaining steady
markets and in accumulating sufficient supplies of currency. The
Dukes of Queensberry and Argyll, with other leading gentry,
therefore founded the British Linen Company, to assist these
people with the organizing side of their business. This Company,
founded in 1746, started branch banking in Scotland and later,
when its other services were no longer needed, the banks were
carried on: they are still familiar, under the original title, to all
Scots folk.

The Statistical Account of 1790 shows that many hundreds of
men and women were still employed upon the production of linen
by hand, for craftsmanship resisted mechanization longer in this
than in any other field of the textile industry. Stout Holland
sheetings and shirtings, umbrella linens and linens for window-
blinds, shawlcloths, calicoes and muslins, wide brown and white
country linens 'chiefly used for hat-linings' are listed for Perth:
fine lawns and damasks for Glasgow: coarse linens and bleached

canvas, much needed by the Royal Navy, for Fife: 'bagging, canvas and osnaburghs' for Kincardineshire: muslin for Cambuslang, table-linen for Dunfermline, twisted thread for Paisley. But the prosperity in this characteristically 18th century craft began to decline soon after 1790 because mechanically produced cotton was soon to become supreme, both in home and in foreign markets. As early as 1814, Sir John Sinclair wrote of the great distress caused by the decreasing demand for linen. The minister of Colinton in Midlothian reported in 1840: 'Spinning has almost wholly disappeared. Thus the old are cut off from employment within the power of age and suited to its disposition . . . which used to keep time from becoming a burden and to supply the necessaries of life.'

This report was typical, and only in a few places, such as Dunfermline, did the linen industry survive after about 1820, for cotton soon became the 19th century's most successful textile. The *Annals of Commerce*, published in 1785 by Macpherson, show that already cotton had become popular and also much cheaper than linen. 'Women of all ranks from highest to lowest are clothed in the British manufacture of cotton, from the muslin cap on the crown of the head to the cotton stocking under the sole of the foot . . . With the gentlemen, cotton stuffs for waistcoats have almost superseded woollen cloths, and silk stuffs I believe entirely.'

The earliest ventures in cotton manufacture were made during the latter years of the 18th century in England. In 1765 Hargreaves invented his spinning jenny. Ten years later another Englishman, Samuel Crompton, completed his new spinning machine, known ever since as the 'mule'. His first one was fitted with 48 spindles, which could produce fine yet strong threads, suitable for weaving firm material of light texture. About the same time, Thomas Arkwright was at work upon the harnessing of industry to water power. The jennies and mules were handdriven machines which could manipulate many spindles simultaneously: for some years they were used to make yarn for the weft, while Arkwright's water-frames produced the warps. Later the mules were adjusted to water-power too. During the last twenty years of the 18th century the cotton industry developed in

Lancashire and within a short time it made its appearance in Scotland.

The first successful Scottish cotton mill was opened in Rothesay on the island of Bute, in 1778, a two-storey building with machinery for a thousand spindles. In Renfrewshire and Lanarkshire, other mills were set up where cotton yarn was spun on jennies or mules, modelled on those installed south of the Border a few years earlier. At first the machinery was hand-driven, but soon in Scotland, as in England, water began to be used from swift-flowing hill streams; and factories began to invade the uplands. The old cottage industry was doomed.

Though most people knew little of what went on in these mills, it was plain that cargo upon cargo of raw cotton was coming up the deepened Clyde, also that quantities of cotton yarn were annually available for manufacture. New industrial magnates began to dominate the business world and thousands of workers' dwellings were rapidly built. Schools and churches were not provided in many of these industrial schemes, which consisted of meanly designed tenements, built as cheaply as possible without expensive amenities such as proper sanitation.

David Dale is perhaps the best known among many Scottish names associated with the early years of this industry. Dale began in Paisley as a linen weaver, later he became a dealer and employed large numbers of linen workers. In 1786 he entered upon a vigorous career in the new textile business, by founding his famous cotton mills at New Lanark, and afterwards he started similar works at Newton Stewart, at Catrine, by the Dornoch Firth and in Blantyre—it was at this last that David Livingstone was later to be employed during his toilsome childhood.

Like the tobacco lords before them, cotton kings lived luxuriously. Dale built himself a fine house of gracious and attractive proportions near Glasgow Green, which survived until 1954, when the City Council ordered its demolition, to make space for a neighbouring school's playground. Dale made this Glasgow home his headquarters and devoted his time to directing the mercantile side of his business, with managers to run the mills. At New Lanark, Dale employed William Kelly, a man of some distinction, for it was he who first adapted the mule to water-power in Scotland. Later, another industrialist made his name at this centre, Robert Owen of Manchester who became Dale's son-in-law and bought the New Lanark mills. In a bold attempt to run factory life on humanitarian lines, Robert Owen anticipated many reforms which were to be adopted in the 20th century.

From 1795 onwards, spinning mules were constructed to work over 150 spindles each, but weaving defeated inventors of machinery for a surprisingly long time. Weavers therefore continued to work by hand on the old-style frames and to command an enviable position even after the turn of the century. They secured high wages and worked in their own homes, employed by mill-owners, whose travellers distributed yarn and collected in webs, just as was done in the old days. 'Then was the daisy portion of weaving', wrote William Thom of Inverurie. 'Four days did the weaver work, for them four days was a week, as far as working went, and such a week to a skilful weaver brought 40/-. Sunday, Monday and Tuesday were of course jubilee, lawn frills gorged freely from under the wrists of his fine blue, gilt-buttoned coat. He dusted his head with white flour on Sunday, smirked and wore a cane. Walked in clean slippers on Monday, Tuesday heard him talk war bravado, quote Volney, and get drunk. Weaving commenced gradually on Wednesday.' Thousands of looms were worked by these aristocrats of industry, but machinery was ultimately to prove too strong. In 1807, a power-loom was set up at Catrine, and soon more appeared.

It was not until after 1840 that hand loom weaving was finally ousted, because the early power looms could not make fine materials, but during the '20s and '30s the competition of the new machines reduced the weaver's wages, depriving him of frills, cane and clean slippers, and finally in the '40s driving him altogether out of business, after a period of acute distress. On May 19th, 1848, the *Wiscassit*, an old whaling schooner, now square-rigged for the merchant service, sailed from the Broomielaw for the United States. On board was William Carnegie, one of the defeated weavers of Dunfermline, with his wife Margaret and his sons Andrew and Tom, all in great distress over their departure, but all perfectly clear that the Old Country could offer them only penury. Of Andrew Carnegie, Scots all over the world were later to hear much. Thousands of his countrymen went to the New World in similar circumstances and there built up for themselves a new way of life.

For nearly three-quarters of the 19th century, cotton mills worked to capacity and commanded an enormous market, both at home and abroad. Their prosperity was in no way threatened by work done in other branches of the textile industry, important as some of them were. Galashiels and Hawick were ideally situated for the traditional woollen manufacture, because the great Border sheep farms gave good supplies of Cheviot wool, while the Tweed and the Gala provided water power. During the Napoleonic wars, this area was developed by industrialists who introduced machinery adapted from the cotton mills. Two pieces of good luck favoured the proprietors of these new woollen factories. One was that Sir Walter Scott, then at the height of his literary fame, liked to wear locally made shepherd's plaid, which therefore became fashionable. The other was the highly profitable in-accuracy of a London clerk, who substituted for 'tweel'—the accepted name of Scott's favoured material—the word 'tweed.' This accidental error was ingeniously exploited and the new name came to stay, and to give city men all over the United Kingdom a pleasant feeling of literary distinction when they sported suits associated with the poet's well-loved river. The Waverley novels also stimulated the demand for tartan, legalized since 1782, and a number of towns in the east of Scotland built up flourishing businesses in the production of tartans, commercially designed to satisfy the public.

Another interesting local industry was centred at Paisley, where in 1802 shawls began to be made, in imitation of those produced in India. At first cotton was used, later spun silk, later again, a mixture of silk and wool. Local craftsmen attained a wonderful skill in designing the intricate and exquisitely delicate colourings of these shawls, which were worn by ladies of wealth for many years. Such work could not be done by power looms and until the shawls went out of fashion Paisley remained one of the few successful strongholds of craftsmanship. Not until about 1880 was the day of this attractive garment over; thereafter the

Paisley workers had to concentrate once again on the making of twisted thread.

Throughout the formative years of these textile industries, that is to say from 1770 onwards, a new source of power was being examined. This was steam. The dominant personality in the story of steam as an agent of production was another Scot of world-wide distinction, James Watt. Telford referred to him affectionately as the 'steam-engine man from Glasgow', although he was born and brought up in Greenock.

This great inventor suffered all his life from the allied ailments of indigestion, indecision, self distrust and pessimism. He was an only child and his boyhood in Greenock was rather miserable, owing to ill-health and failure to make friends. In his teens, Watt discovered Geometry, his first source of creative happiness. He spent his nineteenth year in London, training to become a mathematical instrument-maker, after which in 1757, at the age of twenty-one, he found work in Glasgow University. In 1763, Watt was asked by Professor Anderson to repair for use in the Natural Philosophy class, an 'atmospheric steam-engine', commonly known as a 'fire-engine'. This was a steam-driven machine which had been invented some fifty years earlier by Thomas Newcomen, a Devonshire man; it was used for pumping water out of mines. Watt realized when he examined Professor Anderson's model that its defect was in the loss of steam by condensation, indeed the engine could only be kept going for a very short time, because the boiler could not supply sufficient steam. It took Watt the best part of two years to find the remedy for this weakness and he finally reached his solution in the middle of a Sunday walk on Glasgow Green. To put his theory of a separate condenser into practice cost several more years of experiment, during which time he became well-known as a civil engineer. At last, in 1769, his patent was sealed for 'a new invented method of lessening the Consumption of Steam and Fuel in Fire-Engines'.

In 1775, when the American war was ruining the tobacco trade, and Crompton was completing his work on the mule, Watt went into partnership with Matthew Boulton, at the Soho Works of Birmingham. This firm began the manufacture of the new steam engines. They were first employed in the Cornish mines, for pumping water out of the way, and Watt had to visit Cornwall to supervise their erection and the training of the workmen who handled them. Boulton persuaded Watt during the 1780s to make further experiments on the use of steam power, in order that it might be used, not only in mines, but in the new mills, to drive machinery. The rotary engine was the result of Watt's busiest and most productive years, and this could be used to drive forge-hammers by steam power.

In spite of his chronic scepticism, Watt had succeeded in releasing a major force of incalculable importance. The industrialists of the English Black Country seized upon it. In Scotland, partly because of the almost unlimited supplies of water power, the steam engine was not taken into general use until after the Napoleonic wars. The subsequent changes in economic and industrial organization were largely conditioned by developments in the iron industry.

Until the mid-18th century, iron foundries in Scotland, as in England, burnt charcoal. This was one of the reasons why Scottish hillsides had been denuded of trees. The shortage of fuel became so serious that for some years iron ore was actually transported at colossal cost to wooded areas, so that the industry became very much dispersed. In the 1720s for example, furnaces were lit at Invergarry, Taynuilt and Inveraray, by Lancashire ironmasters, who leased considerable expanses of forest from Macdonell, Lochiel, the Duke of Argyll and the Earl of Breadalbane. Roads, wharfs, even boats had to be built for the transport of the ore to these remote places. 'The industry of smelting and refining was literally fleeing to the wilderness to escape destruction.'

The wilderness was not needed for this particular service after 1750, because in that year an Englishman called Abraham Darby discovered how to use coke for smelting iron. Foundries now began to be established near the coalfields, as people had become accustomed to carrying ore to the source of fuel supply, but it soon became evident that in many areas rich iron seams were to be found almost alongside the coal. The foundries expanded since demands for iron were increasing on every side, and the new method of smelting made production much more profitable.

Industry

The earliest Scottish iron foundry to use coke was the famous Carron Iron Works, set up at Falkirk in 1759, a strange development in a town hitherto chiefly remarkable for its enormous autumn Cattle Trysts. Although the Company had severe setbacks to face in its early years, it gradually developed into one of the largest ironworks in Europe and it still exists today. One of its founders was John Roebuck, an Edinburgh Doctor of Medicine, who became a captain of industry. He was an important influence in the life of James Watt, as he saw how immensely valuable steam power could be in working iron and through his influence one of Watt's engines was installed at Carron in 1767. 'The steam-engine man from Glasgow' was much encouraged by Roebuck, at a period when he was almost engulfed by his difficulties.

The Seven Years' War was in full swing till 1763, so that supplies of iron from Sweden and Russia were not available, when the demand for armaments was at its height. The forges and mills connected with the Carron foundries manufactured cannon, at first with small success, though later their productions became world-famous. It was cannon from these foundries which formed part of the armour of Nelson's *Victory*. Wellington's field guns in the Peninsular campaign were made there too; they were known as 'carronades'. Agricultural implements and household goods were also made for export to many European dépots and to the plantations. Iron-rod for nails was something of a side-line, but it enabled the 'naileries' to do a tremendous trade in these homely articles, with the result that the old hand-made heather pegs were superseded except in Highland districts, where they served their turn for at least another century.

In 1784, Henry Cort of Portsmouth worked out a system of forging iron with raw coal; he also invented a process of groove-rolling, which eliminated one stage hitherto essential to the preparation of forge iron. His work had immediate results all over the country. In Scotland, the Carron foundries increased in size and scope while new works were opened near Glasgow, in Lanarkshire and in Ayrshire. Within twenty years of Cort's success, there were twenty-nine furnaces at work in the Scottish Black Country. Almost all of them were blast-furnaces, employing engines similar to those designed by James Watt.

The demand for labour was enormous, but so was the supply of destitute incomers to the cities from the Highlands. The employees had to learn new skills and to live in unfamiliar surroundings and they handled dangerous equipment. No legislation protected them and suffering became an inevitable feature in the lives of their families.

During the early years of the 19th century, iron was in greater demand than ever before. It seemed impossible to produce enough for the manufacturers of components used in factory machinery, railway lines, engines of all kinds, bridges, ships, locomotives, and innumerable pieces of equipment for industrial and domestic use, let alone for the armament firms.

Some 20,000 tons of pig-iron were produced every year during the Napoleonic wars, and during the 1820s the output increased sharply. This was because the valuable blackband ironstone of the Monkland area was discovered and also a new process of working it, known as the hot-blast. James Neilson of Shettleston invented this in 1828 and it meant that the fuel consumption needed in smelting each ton of iron was reduced by about 75 per cent. William Baird's Gartsherrie works were opened in the same year, the first of a new series of firms almost all in the Monkland area, and by 1847 Scotland was producing 25 per cent. of all the pig-iron smelted in Great Britain. By 1857, Scottish mines reached the figure of $2\frac{1}{2}$ million tons a year.

This immense development, together with the adoption of steam power, created a new situation in the coal mines. Coal had been known and used in Scotland from medieval times. In 1790, a Stirlingshire minister recorded his belief that coal had been worked in his parish for 500 years, more or less continuously, and the Culross mines had a long history too. An English traveller visited them in 1618 and was astonished by what he saw. 'In the space of eight and twenty years, they have digged more than an English mile under the sea, so that when men are at work below, an hundred of the greatest ships in Britain may sail over their heads.'

During the 17th and most of the 18th century, coal-mining was confined to a few areas in Fife, Ayrshire and Lanarkshire where, for the most part, only surface coal was worked. A few thousand tons were sent annually by sea to London, a certain amount was used for domestic purposes in Glasgow and Edinburgh, but the main function of coal was the traditional one, dating from the middle ages—to provide fuel for the salt-pans. Colliers like salt-workers were 'thirled', that is, bonded to their tasks. Cockburn's Whig principles were outraged by this traditional curtailment of personal freedom. 'They could not be killed or tortured, but they belonged, like the serfs of an older time, to their respective industries, with which they were sold as part of the gearing.' Legislation in 1775 and 1799 put an end to this enslavement, which had gone on from one generation to another since medieval times.

The expansion of industry in the latter part of the 18th century naturally increased the demand for coal, so that new pits were opened and old seams deepened. It was to make more coal accessible that the early canals and wagon ways were constructed and, by 1790, ministers had a good deal to say about local mines when they prepared their records for the Statistical Account. The parson at Kilsyth for example wrote as follows: 'Coal has been wrought for ages and is still abundant, I trust inexhaustible . . . The coal in the west barony is one of the best I ever saw. It burns clear, lasts long, gives a good heat, and cakes so that the very dross of it is valuable . . . The manner in which the coals are wrought is by pick and wedge; boys and sometimes girls are employed to draw the skiffies below ground . . . The expences attending the work are very considerable . . . It is to be hoped that a great deal of this will be saved, for there is a small steam engine immediately to be set up. This will easily do the work of a number of men, and save an enormous expence.'

During the first half of the 19th century, many new mines were developed and old ones extended, in Ayrshire, Lanarkshire, the Lothians and Fife. By 1854, Scottish mines were producing $7\frac{1}{2}$ million tons a year and quantities of coal were exported. The output mounted steadily and in 1900 reached 33 million tons.

The wealth of coal and iron contributed to the establishment of the Scottish engineering industry. Machines and tools of all kinds for the factories and mills were manufactured, equipment for agriculture, transport, armaments, and later on locomotives.

Again, great quantities of these goods were sold abroad. They went to Europe, the Middle East, the Far East, and all parts of the Empire, and supplanted textiles as Scotland's major export.

The engineering industry was concentrated in and around Glasgow and by the Clyde, with important branches at the Carron works and in Fife—naturally enough, as it had to be as near the sources of coal and iron supply as possible. The Second Statistical Account, published in the 1840s, showed that one-third of Scotland's manufacturing labourers lived in Lanarkshire. Some 19,000 of them were in Glasgow; the overcrowding in the workmen's quarters of the city became appalling.

Shipbuilding on the other hand was more dispersed, indeed for a considerable period a greater tonnage was produced at Aberdeen, Leith, Port Glasgow and Greenock than in the Glasgow yards. In the 1830s however the balance began to change, because steamships were now regularly ordered by such firms as the P. & O. Company. The Cunard Company was founded, with many Glasgow shareholders, and the first four vessels used in its service were built on the Clyde, with engines made by Robert Napier. Soon after this, iron was adopted as a basic material for shipbuilding. Because Glasgow was a centre both of the iron industry and of engineering, it followed that the iron ships and their engines were built on the Clyde, which became a joint head-quarters for many branches of heavy industry and for shipbuilding. In 1877, two steel paddle-steamers were built at Govan by John Elder and, during the next twenty years, steelworks began to take the place of the iron foundries.

By the year 1877, exactly a century and a half had elapsed since Elizabeth Mure's interest had been aroused in the 'mane-factorys' established by the Board of Trustees. During this period, Scottish ways of life had been completely disrupted and a new society had evolved, a society which bore little resemblance to that in which Elizabeth Mure and her friends had been brought up. The Industrial Revolution which precipitated the upheaval caused many political repercussions and it was also accompanied by a quickening interest in ideas, in art and in literature, which gave Scotland, and especially the capital, a decisive influence in Western Europe.

CHAPTER 23

Cities, Citizens and the Arts

Defoe described Glasgow in 1727 as 'one of the cleanliest, most beautiful and best built cities in Great Britain'; nine years later McUre said it was 'surrounded with cornfields, kitchen and flower gardens, abounding with fruit of all sorts, which, by reason of the open and large streets, send forth a pleasant and odoriferous smell'. Barely 13,000 people lived there, in the small area between the Cathedral at the upper end of the High Street and the College at the lower. Close to the College buildings were the meadows, with their fringe of broom by the riverside, and the Clyde was a placid and beautiful stream, crossed by only one ancient bridge, below which fishermen were able to pursue successful sport, and children to go paddling. The absence on Glasgow streets of drunkenness and brawling was attributed by an 18th century Professor to the people's religion, which 'though of a gloomy and enthusiastic cast makes them tame and sober'.

These 'tame and sober' Glaswegians were satisfied with homes of primitive simplicity. While the well-to-do rented small, badly lit flats, the poor lived in hovels, and for everybody the daily carrying of water from the city's wells was an accepted piece of routine. There were no clubs, no coffee-houses, few public functions and little organized pleasure. Going out at night was not attractive when the streets were unlit, garbage collection spasmodic, and social enjoyment so limited in scope.

Over in Edinburgh, people lived in similar conditions, though here there was less space, less fresh air and no pleasantly 'odoriferous smells' from orchard or garden. The capital was confined within the area of the old city walls, for the North Loch was not completely drained until 1820 and it was a barrier to expansion. About the time of its disappearance, Lord Cockburn described this 'loch' as a 'nearly impassable fetid marsh, a stinking swamp, open on all sides, the receptacle of many sewers and seemingly of all the worried cats, drowned dogs and blackguardism of the city'.

For lack of ground space, Edinburgh people made their homes and did their business in tall and narrow houses, sometimes twelve storeys high. The close-packed dwellings were crowded together on each side of the High Street and the Cowgate, from which branched off cobbled wynds and stone-paved vennels, all incredibly filthy.

Many authors have made acid comments on the dirt of the capital. After the uncomfortable months he spent there in 1707, Defoe summed up the situation rather more charitably than most: 'Were any other people to live under the same unhappiness, I mean as well of a rocky and mountainous situation, thronged buildings from seven to ten or twelve storeys high, a scarcity of water, and that little they have difficult to be had, and to the uppermost buildings far to fetch, we should have as dirty a London or Bristol as Edinburgh; for though many cities have more people in them, yet I believe there is no city in the world where so many people live in so little room.' Over a century later, Lord Cockburn dropped a characteristic remark, 'Though standing in a rainy country, Edinburgh has always been thirsty and unwashed.'

The overcrowding led to a genial if insanitary way of life, in which everybody knew everybody. The two or three storeys above street level were occupied by titled and professional families, while huddled in the upper ranges were the poorer working people. The narrow stone staircases, ill-lit and never cleansed, were shared by all and sundry, judges, aristocracy, children, coal-porters, clerics, water-carriers, Musselburgh fish-wives, sweeps, message-boys and many more. Unceremonious pushing and jostling became natural to Edinburgh citizens on these staircases and on the narrow, mile-long thoroughfare of the Canongate and the High Street. This cobbled road was the city's spinal cord, the very centre of its life, linking Holyrood Palace at the lower end with the great battlemented, rock-founded Castle which still towers above everything else. 'Upon this street, twice every day,

Glasgow from the South: Robert Paul, Foulis Academy, circa 1758.

By courtesy of the Mitchell Library, Glasgow.

there are seldom fewer than 1,500 people walking' was the evidence of Forbes of Culloden, when he was speaking in the House of Commons about the Porteous Riots. Most of the City's few shops were concentrated here, in the Luckenbooths, near St. Giles, where shopkeepers used the street itself for their stalls and counters.

Throughout Scotland people suffered from malnutrition, from the all-pervading filth and from the lack of piped water. Tuberculosis, fevers, epidemics and smallpox ran riot in the towns and also invaded rural areas, so that bereavement was a constant affliction. In Kirkwall, the principal town of the Orkneys, there lived in the latter years of the 17th century a sculptor, much in demand for rectangular grave slabs, which he decorated with skulls and crossbones and what he deemed suitable verse. One of the jingles reads as follows:

> *'Agnes nine children boor unto hir mate,*
> *Six died befor their sire, by cruel fate.'*

These lines seem crude enough, but the craftsman's obvious horror of death is plainly revealed in the pathetic phrases he selected for his many clients, and the tragedy of Agnes was characteristic of an age when people had no knowledge of how to safeguard children's health. And things did not improve as the 18th century wore on. From 1790 until about 1851, child deaths in Glasgow accounted for over 50 per cent. of the total.

For many years, Edinburgh remained the most populated city in Scotland, but gradually linen and tobacco began to attract more people to Glasgow. New streets were laid down, colourful and creaking signboards appeared to advertise the increasing number of shops and by mid-century hackney coaches were in demand. In 1775, the Saracen's Head, Glasgow's first hotel, was opened at the eastern end of the city; eight years later the Black Bull in Argyle Street began business, and it was in the smoking rooms of these establishments that Glasgow men began to develop club life. By the end of the century, some of the more prosperous families were living in self-contained houses instead of two-roomed flats, though they were still without water, which was laboriously fetched in buckets from the city wells until 1804. In this year, William Harley set up great cisterns in the appropriately named Bath Street and began delivering halfpenny stoups of water by pony-cart. Glasgow's cornfields and orchards were nearly all obliterated by warehouses, factories, streets and terraces, for the city's population numbered well over 70,000.

The expansion of Edinburgh was slow in starting, for even when George Street and Brown Street were constructed in 1765, their fine new houses were regarded as inconveniently far from the centre of things, because the North Loch lay between them and the old city. During the 1770s, work was at last begun on draining it and filling it with earth and shingle, a process which took some fifty years to complete: to link the Old Town with the new streets, the North Bridge was built across the famous old gully.

When people with capital and social position realized how easy of access the New Town had become, they moved out of their cramped quarters in the Canongate, the Lawnmarket and the High Street, with the sad result that the network of buildings round St. Giles, the heart of the old capital, was allowed to fall into dilapidation. High society set up much more expensive homes in George Street, Queen Street and Charlotte Square. 'There, when the great exodus was made across the valley, and the New Town began to spread abroad its draughty parallelograms, and rear its long frontage on the opposing hill, there was such a flitting, such a change of domicile and dweller as was never excelled in the history of cities: the cobbler succeeded the earl; the beggar ensconced himself by the judge's chimney; what had been a palace was used as a pauper refuge.' So wrote R. L. Stevenson in his rather lugubrious little book on Edinburgh. The New Town bears to this day the dignity and graciousness bestowed upon it by its principal designer and architect, Robert Adam, cynical though R.L.S. chose to be about it. And Charlotte Square is no more draughty than the old High Street.

During the years which followed the Second Jacobite Rebellion, there developed a gradual awakening of interest in literature and the arts. The origins of this development belong to the early years of the 18th century, when the stimulus came from certain family groups.

Cities, Citizens and the Arts

One famous centre of literary interest was in a most unlikely place—a wigmaker's shop, on the High Street of Edinburgh. Its owner was Allan Ramsay, a man with an insatiable appetite for books, especially books on poetry. His background was a remote, windswept village called Leadhills, on the uplands of Lanarkshire, where his father had been superintendent of the gold and lead mines belonging to the Earl of Hopetoun, and where he had received very little education. Until he was fifteen, Ramsay's acquaintances were the children of miners, men who lived as semi-slaves, bonded to their masters, deprived of legal rights, and often ill from the effects of lead-poisoning. In 1700, he went to Edinburgh, to be a wigmaker's apprentice: there he later married and became, in the course of about a dozen years, the father of ten children. Only three survived infancy, the eldest of whom was named Allan, after his father.

The family lived at first on High Street, where Ramsay dealt with his customers and made his wigs, but he enjoyed far more the trade in satires and verses which became the absorbing interest of his life. During these years he wrote poetry himself, and finally he moved his books to a shop in the Luckenbooths, where in 1725 he opened the first circulating library in Edinburgh. The squat, stout, merry little barber-poet became a well-known and popular figure, who attracted to his premises citizens and visitors of all kinds, delighting them both with his wares and with his wit. One of these visitors was the poet John Gay, who came to Edinburgh in 1725 and became a personal friend.

About this time, Ramsay decided to found a theatre, and he financed and designed a building for this purpose in Carubber's Close, but the project could not survive the disapproval of the church. Ministerial strictures however failed to prevent him from providing his customers with French romances, London publications, Dryden's comedies and many classical works as well, nor could it stem the flow of his own writing, which included not only poems but also the charming pastoral opera called *The Gentle Shepherd*. In 1740 Ramsay retired from his bookshop, to devote his leisure to reading, and moved into an oddly constructed house, known as 'Guse-pie', which became something of a jest

261

in the city, and which was the scene of a considerable skirmish in the Forty-Five.

Allan Ramsay the younger grew up in an atmosphere of books: from his earliest days he was interested in literature, particularly in Horace, and he also learned Italian, French and German. His gift for painting must have surprised his father and he himself wanted to achieve literary rather than artistic distinction. In the summer of 1736 he set forth on the Grand Tour, and in Italy he began to study painting seriously. He settled in London for a while on his return, but during the 1740s he worked often in Edinburgh, making use of a studio in his father's home. He did not stay at Guse-pie long, for he spent much of his time abroad and in London, and until 1765 or 1766 an astonishing number of the aristocracy sat to him for portraits. Although he employed assistants to carry out much of the routine work, very many pictures of his own may still be seen today. Ramsay liked to paint people in splendid dress, but he achieved simplicity in design and serenity in pose, and he had a gift for revealing personality. The graciousness and dignity of the 18th century at its best may be understood if one studies such portraits as those of his wife, Margaret Lindsay, of Mrs. John Sargent and of Lady Susan Fox-Strangways. His royal portraits are more magnificent but less intimate and not so satisfying, perhaps because he turned out so many in quick succession.

All his life, the younger Ramsay longed to make his name as a writer and a patron of literature. In 1754 he founded the Select Society for Encouraging Art, Science and Industry, an enterprise typical of the age when people set themselves seriously and unself-consciously to create a culture. Adam Smith and David Hume both gave Ramsay's society their support and for a while it brought a number of distinguished men together, Lord Kames for example, John and James Adam the architects, William Robertson, George Dempster, John Home, and later Boswell, all men who contributed to the brilliant life of Edinburgh. In his latter years, Ramsay gave up painting, with the curious result that his obituary notice in the *Gentleman's Magazine* made no mention of his portraits. After 1784, when he died, his work was forgotten and it was not until the 20th century that the true value of his painting was re-discovered. Exhibitions of Scottish Art in Glasgow and in London during the late 1930s made him known once more, and to a much larger public than he ever reached during his lifetime.

The Luckenbooths library was not the only unlikely quarter of the capital which produced artists. Allan Ramsay discovered a gifted young man working as a coachbuilder's apprentice on heraldic decorations for the carriages of the gentry. This was Alexander Nasmyth, whom Ramsay took to London to do background work on his portraits. Nasmyth was a person with independent views and in 1778, at the age of twenty, he returned to Edinburgh, where he was successful as a painter of portraits and landscapes, a designer of formal parks and gardens, and also as an architect. Nasmyth's two sons and six daughters all became artists too and regularly exhibited their works in the capital.

Among many other Scottish painters, but outclassing them all, was Henry Raeburn, whose portraits rank with those of Reynolds. He spent almost all his life in the city of his birth, working with enviable happiness and prosperity, and giving his sitters personal, undivided attention, for, unlike Ramsay, he did not believe in employing assistants. On the occasion of the royal visit to Edinburgh in 1822, organized by Sir Walter Scott, George IV knighted Raeburn, whom he sincerely admired.

Meantime in Glasgow, Andrew and Robert Foulis, both graduates of Glasgow University, developed a skill hitherto lacking north of the Border. This was the art of printing, in which Scottish standards had so far been deplorable, for even the Bible was produced in miserable type with numerous misprints. These brothers set up the famous Foulis press, which gave Scotland a series of exquisitely printed classical texts, whose accuracy far exceeded anything known before. Probably their most valuable production was a four-volume folio Homer, still considered one of the finest pieces of Greek printing to be seen; they also published good texts from the works of Sophocles, Aristotle, Horace, Cicero and many more. Andrew and Robert were Printers to the University of Glasgow, and they established a bookshop and a printing press in the quadrangle of the University itself. Just as the elder Allan Ramsay's place of business became a focal point for booklovers and writers, so the Foulis press attracted scholars and thinkers from many places.

These brothers, like the elder Ramsay, had a castle in the air. In 1753, when the theatre in Carubber's Close had already proved a lost cause, Andrew and Robert launched in Glasgow an Academy of Arts, upon which they lavished care and money. In this enterprise they failed as completely as Ramsay, for Scottish people were not yet sufficiently interested in painting and sculpture to support the Academy, nor was the scholarship of the two founders so sound in the selection and purchase of pictures as in the publication of classical texts.

It is rather sad that men who gave so much to the literary world were embittered in their latter years by the collapse of such idealistic schemes as the Carubber's Close theatre and the Glasgow Academy of Arts. Nonetheless, the Academy gave a number of young men their chance, some of whom stood by the Foulis brothers when financial troubles engulfed them. Such was David Allen, the son of quite humble folk in Alloa. His gift for painting found expression when he reached the height of his powers in humorous character studies, but he also became a popular portrait painter in an age that had no photography and when people loved sitting to artists. His designs for Allan Ramsay's *Gentle Shepherd* made him renowned in literary and musical circles too.

Much, perhaps too much, has been made of the 18th century Englishman's distaste for Scotland and the Scots. The English aristocracy of the period were delighted to have their portraits done by Ramsay and Raeburn, English scholars to study their classical texts in the Foulis editions: at the same time it became common for English congregations to worship in the buildings of one famous Scot and for English noblemen to live in the mansions of another. James Gibbs and Robert Adam were both distinguished architects and no account of the period can be made without taking both men into consideration.

James Gibbs, the son of an Aberdeenshire Roman Catholic, was born in 1682, and brought up at a time when people of his persuasion were hemmed in by every legal stricture that could be devised. When he was twenty he went to Holland as a student of architecture and there he met the 11th Earl of Mar, soon to become known as Bobbing John. In Gibbs the Earl recognized a man of great gifts, and he gave him money to go to Rome. Here he worked for a time under Pope Clement XI's surveyor-general; altogether he spent ten years in Italy, after which he settled in London.

Gibbs was fortunate. He enjoyed the patronage both of Mar and of Argyll; he also arrived in London when an ambitious church-expansion scheme was afoot and he at once secured commissions. He designed St. Mary-le-Strand, completed the adjacent St. Clement Danes, where Samuel Johnson later worshipped, and built the present St. Martin-in-the-Fields, perhaps his most distinguished work. Gibbs also built the Radcliffe Library in Oxford, in Cambridge the Senate House and the beautiful block of buildings in King's College, which stands at right angles to the 15th century chapel. His buildings were in keeping with the traditions of his day and yet they were designed with originality. 18th century architecture in Britain represents some of the finest work achieved since the Rennaissance and Gibbs was one of those Scots who contributed much to its development.

Robert Adam was a member of another Scottish family which attained international distinction at this time. His father, William Adam, made a name for himself as an architect in the classical style for which Gibbs did so much. He brought four able sons into his profession, John, Robert, James and William, of whom Robert was by far the most gifted. Robert left Scotland in 1754, to travel as Allan Ramsay had done in France and Italy, and in 1758 he set up a home for himself and his brothers and sisters in London.

From 1758 onwards, Robert Adam was in constant demand among owners of country houses, which he rebuilt or enlarged, combining dignity in proportion with delicacy in detail and ornament. Kedleston in Derbyshire, Compton Verney in Warwickshire and Syon House in Middlesex are three famous works of this sort, though there are many others, and he was responsible too for a number of new mansions which he designed and carried out from the foundations. In every case, Robert devoted his artistry and scholarship as much to interior as to exterior design: his ceilings, staircases, fireplaces and doorways are still to be seen in houses whose structure has often been mutilated in later years by much less gifted architects. Culzean Castle in Ayrshire is a fine example of his work and one of the few such houses he designed north of the Border.

Robert Adam's influence on city architecture was almost more permanent in its effects. The Admiralty Screen, Whitehall, is one of his best-known works, but he was prolific in his designs for town houses, large and small, as well as for whole streets and squares and boldly massed blocks. Many of his structures are now spoiled by subsequent alterations and by neglect, but you can still see some in St. James's Square and Grosvenor Square and in other London streets.

In Edinburgh, Robert was commissioned to build the beautiful Register House and to design much of the New Town. Some of the houses in Queen Street and Castle Street are his, and Charlotte Square would have been one of his most splendid achievements had it been completed according to his plans, but unfortunately only the north and south blocks were built as he meant them to be. He was also asked to rebuild Edinburgh University, but he died in 1792 before his plans were fulfilled. The influence of Robert Adam and his brothers was perhaps greater than that of any other Scottish family; architects all over the country took up their ideas and for at least a century the basic structure, the interior decoration and the outer façade of many buildings were modelled on Adam designs.

During their earlier years when they lived in Edinburgh, William Adam's sons made many friends, who also became well known. One was a cousin, William Robertson, a man of massive intellectual ability, much personal charm and astonishing industry. He was a popular man, at the very centre of Edinburgh society and on intimate terms with Allan Ramsay, Robert Adam, Lord Kames, Adam Smith, David Hume and many another.

The next two chapters refer in more detail to Robertson, but here it is worth quoting Horace Walpole's comments upon him when they met in London, after the publication of Robertson's *History of Scotland.* 'How could I suspect that a man under forty,

266

whose dialect I scarce understood, and who came to me with all
the diffidence and modesty of a very middling author, and who I
was told had passed his life in a small living in Edinburgh—how
could I suspect that he had not only written what all the world
now allows to be the best modern history, but that he had written
it in the purest English and with as much seeming knowledge of
men and courts as if he had passed all his life in important
embassies?' The first edition of this History sold out in a month,
and nobody was more surprised by his success than Robertson
himself. Lord Cockburn as a boy used to play with Robertson's
grandson and he affectionately recalled the old scholar directing
the children's attention to the best fruit on his favourite cherry-
tree—'a pleasant-looking old man, with an eye of great vivacity
and intelligence, a large projecting chin, a small hearing-trumpet
fastened by a black ribbon to the lapel of his coat, and a rather
large wig, powdered and curled'.

David Hume the philosopher was a close friend of the Ramsays,
of Robertson and also of the Adam brothers, whose mother, however, had her doubts about him, because he was a sceptic. Hume
was the greatest of the sceptics. He carried much further than
Descartes had been able to do the philosopher's task of calling in
question accepted beliefs. The perennial philosophy of Christendom had been profoundly inspired by Plato's teaching that the
truest knowledge is derived, like mathematics, from insight into
the logical implications of self-evident propositions. It was
believed that logic can give us knowledge of the existence of God.
Hume's criticism showed that this system breaks down, that pure
logic gives rules of thought, but not knowledge of existing reality.
He developed a system of his own which claimed to show that all
our knowledge is derived from reflection upon the experience that
comes to us through the senses and through feeling. This system
is itself open to criticism, but Hume's empirical method introduced a fresh line of enquiry and he remains today a dominant
influence in philosophical speculation.

Hume was mortified by the reception accorded to his great
philosophical works, his *Treatise of Human Nature*, which, as he
said himself 'fell dead-born from the press' in 1739, and the
Enquiry Concerning the Principles of Morals, published in 1752.

But he continued to write, always with distinction, over a range of interests so wide and so novel that his influence can be seen in the works of Kant, Adam Smith, Bentham and Comte. Hume never failed to please as a man, and he enjoyed exuberant popularity in France, where he held diplomatic appointments for some years. On his return to Edinburgh, he became a prominent leader in the splendid group of writers living there, 'the Socrates of Edinburgh' as George Dempster called him in one of his letters to Adam Fergusson.

David Hume had a young cousin, whom he befriended and from whom he received much kindness. This was John Home, who insisted to Hume's disgust in spelling his name with an 'o'. He was an ordained minister with a charge at Athelstaneford, but he devoted his leisure to writing plays. In 1754, to the immense delight of secular opinion, but to the horror of the General Assembly, Home's tragedy *Douglas* was produced at the Canon gate Theatre in Edinburgh.

This was a succulent piece of news for George Dempster to send to Adam Fergusson. 'Nothing', he wrote, 'ever afforded more entertainment to this country than the "Douglass", Mr. Home's tragedy. The novelty of a play being writ by a member of the Church, by a Scotsman, and first represented in Scotland, has given rise to a vast deal of fun. And paper bullets have been flying with great vehemence ever since.' Solemn censure was passed on all the ministers who disgraced themselves by going to see this performance, and William Robertson, then at the beginning of his ministry, was one of only eleven members in the General Assembly who thought this condemnation absurd. Home had to give up his church, but this proved no great financial sacrifice, as Lord Bute negotiated a royal pension for him. His cousin, David Hume, praised *Douglas* to the skies, like other contemporaries, including, most curiously, John Wesley, who read it in 1757 and thought it well written. Posterity's judgment has not upheld the views of Hume and Wesley in this matter.

In 1773 Samuel Johnson came to stay in Edinburgh at the Boswell's flat in St. James' Court, High Street. Mrs. Boswell made him innumerable cups of tea and showed off her baby Veronica, who flattered him by appearing to listen to his conversation, although she was only four months old. Dr. William Robertson was invited to breakfast—a meal Johnson always specially enjoyed in Scotland—and to dinner came all the other celebrities whom Boswell could collect. While Johnson complained of the smells in the High Street, he appreciated the conversation in St. James' Court, to his host's naïve delight. The two set off for their Hebridean tour on August 18th and travelled north to Inverness by St. Andrews and Aberdeen, then west to the islands, in conditions which would daunt most holiday-makers today, but Johnson in his sixties seemed to thrive on the experience. They recorded their impressions, each in his own characteristic prose, and as the 20th century has an insatiable appetite for everything Boswell wrote, the Highland tour is now a classic.

Edinburgh citizens were accustomed to the visits of celebrities, but an unparalleled sensation was created on November 28th 1786, when Robert Burns wearily rode into the Grassmarket, on a borrowed pony. His *Poems, Chiefly in the Scottish Dialect* had been published at Kilmarnock in the spring of the year. The small volume of poems and songs won immediate recognition, as Robert Heron, Burns' first biographer, recorded: 'Old and young, high and low, grave and gay, learned and ignorant, all were delighted, agitated, transported. I was at that time resident in Galloway, contiguous to Ayrshire, and I well remember how that even plough-boys and maid-servants would have gladly parted with the wages they earned the most hardly and which they wanted to purchase necessary clothing, if they might but procure the works of Burns.'

In London and in Edinburgh, the Kilmarnock edition aroused as much enthusiasm as in Ayrshire and Galloway. The poems captured the spirit of the Scottish countryside and its people in a dialect whose fresh and musical rhythm was enhanced by vivid and rather earthy turns of phrase. Burns delighted people too with his shrewd and witty analysis of character, his strong sympathy for common folk, his sense of the ridiculous and, above all, with his gift of crystallizing beauty in lines which were at once terse and exquisite. When people learned that this poet had been born in an Ayrshire cottage which his father had built himself, that by city standards he had hardly been educated at all, that his life had been spent in working on a farm, they were more 'agitated and transported' than ever, and his arrival in Edinburgh in 1786 led to a period of lionizing such as Burns could hardly have anticipated in his wildest dreams.

A new edition of the poems was necessary and for this Burns chose as his literary agent William Creech. The premises used by Creech for bookshop and publishing house were situated in the Luckenbooths, below those formerly held by Allan Ramsay, senior, and like his predecessor, Creech made his shop the centre of literary and intellectual society. Here Burns met as many distinguished people as in the drawing-rooms of the capital and in more congenial circumstances, for he soon wearied of the social engagements which people pressed upon him. Early in 1787, he set out for a tour of the Borders, and though he returned to Edinburgh for some months during the following winter, he never settled there. He died in Dumfries in 1796, only ten years after the publication of his first volume, the victim of an agonizing heart disease which contemporary medicine could not relieve. By the time of his death, fellow-countrymen all over the world were singing his songs and reciting his verses, so that Tam o' Shanter, Holy Willie and many more of his characters were loved and quoted, and the Lowland Scots in which he wrote had won a sure place in the nation's literature. Nobody else painted Scottish folk and their ways in such vivid Scottish language, with one exception—Walter Scott.

Walter Scott was born in 1771, one of a family of nine, of whom only four survived infancy. He had poliomyelitis as a baby, which left him with a limp and made his childhood rather miserable. Because of his poor health, he was sent to stay for long periods on a farm in the Borders. In this environment his physical constitution was built up so that in manhood he could ride and walk longer distances than most of his friends, and here too he discovered folk-lore. The ballads and stories of the district excited him greatly and he spent more time than his father would have approved in collecting and memorizing them, an activity which brought him into contact with many strange characters whom he afterwards described.

Scott's love of Border traditions found expression first in *The Minstrelsy of the Scottish Border*, published in 1802, a collection of ballads which he edited with scholarly devotion. His introduction was packed with fascinating information and, as at least forty-three of the poems had never been printed before, the volume created a great stir in Edinburgh. In January 1805, *The Lay of the Last Minstrel* appeared, the first of his longer poems, and it went through edition after edition. People were ready for a fresh conception of poetry and in Scott's work they found it, for he could combine incisive narrative with lyrical passages of haunting, delicate beauty, and while he seemed to be a genius in the art of lament, he could also write with a headlong, rhythmic speed which can still make the reader catch his breath. *Marmion* and the *Lady of the Lake* followed soon after from the pen of this 'rattle-skulled half-lawyer, half-sportsman', as Scott described himself, and it is hardly possible to exaggerate the effect these works had in reviving people's enjoyment of poetry.

On July 7th, 1814, an anonymous novel in three volumes was published in Edinburgh, priced at a guinea. This was *Waverley*. Three weeks later Walter Scott embarked on the Lighthouse yacht with R. L. Stevenson's grandfather for one of the happiest holidays he ever enjoyed, and he had reason to be in high spirits. Edinburgh was consumed with curiosity as to the authorship of this romance, so rich in eccentricity and whimsical reminiscence; and Scott had amused himself by starting some false trails before he set off.

Cockburn wrote of Edinburgh's reaction to the book: 'The unexpected newness of the thing, the profusion of the original characters, the Scotch language, Scotch scenery, Scotch men and women, the simplicity of the writing and the graphic force of the descriptions—all struck us with a shock of delight'. The author could not maintain his secret for long and the mystery became one of Edinburgh's jokes as one after another the novels in the series captivated the reading public. Hitherto novels had not been written in a style likely to command much respect or popularity, while social history and antiquarian research had hardly been begun. Scott's writing let a flood of light upon a new field of interest, and while he gave the 19th century fresh literary forms, he also showed people that historical scholarship can uncover romantic pictures of life in the past.

Scott was incapable of malicious or narrow-minded judgment and he was the best of companions. After his death, Cockburn's affection for him found expression in words which still give one a most vivid impression of his personality. 'Dear Scott! . . . It is a pleasure, which the next generation may envy, that I can still hear his voice and see his form. I see him in the Court, and on the street, in company, and by the Tweed. The plain dress, the guttural, blurred voice, the lame walk, the thoughtful heavy face with its mantling smile, the honest, hearty manner, the joyous laugh, the sing-song feeling recitation, the graphic story—they are all before me a hundred times a day.'

One of Scott's many friends was Sydney Smith, the English clergyman, who came to Edinburgh as the tutor of young Michael Hicks Beach. This lad's father had wanted him to make the Grand Tour, but Napoleon's activities prevented it and so he sent him to Edinburgh. The fact was that, although barely half a century earlier Englishmen had been wont to express contempt for Scotland, they were now eagerly coming to Edinburgh to find the culture hitherto sought on the continent. Lord Palmerston, the third Marquis of Lansdowne and many other young men from the south had their early training there and carried home with them friendships and memories which drew nostalgic reminiscence from them ever afterwards.

None of them however could compete with Sydney Smith's radiant genius for enjoyment, which made him immensely popular. It was largely owing to Smith's irresistible enthusiasm that the Friday Club was founded, a society which met weekly at Fortune's Tavern for dinner, price £2 a head. Among the original members was Lord Cockburn. Cockburn was a bit of an eccentric, with independent views on gardens, politics and everything else. His dogged upholding of democratic ideas delayed his promotion, until he was made Solicitor-General in the Whig ministry of 1830. Cockburn had a relish for observing and describing human beings and their institutions, so that his *Memorials* are a mine of racy, astringent, charitable comment upon Edinburgh in its heyday. As well as Cockburn, Sydney

Smith rounded up Walter Scott, Henry Brougham, Dugald Stewart and old James Watt, along with other renowned personalities, and riotous evenings at the Friday Club were spent in gales of laughter at Smith's outrageous jests. Francis Jeffrey and Francis Horner were two with whom he became specially intimate and in 1802 these three launched the *Edinburgh Review*.

Journalism at the time was considered an inferior profession because newspaper men were not free to publish unbiassed views, and even the recording of contemporary events was restricted by the reactionary attitude of the Government. The French Revolution intensified this. After 1789 even the mildest of reforms was dreaded by people whose social position afforded them security, lest with a little relaxation of traditional laws a whole spate of revolutionary changes might follow. Nobody who wanted a successful career dared express sympathy for any kind of underdog. Prisoners being tried for their lives were allowed no counsel, the Slave Trade flourished, savage game laws were condoned, lunatics were chained and beaten, chimney-sweeps were allowed to endanger the lives of small boys in the interests of property-owners, suffrage was strictly limited, Roman Catholics suffered many restrictions. To found a periodical which would challenge such scandals and put forward liberal views was a risky venture. Only writers of exceptional quality could successfully have carried the enterprise through. From the beginning Francis Jeffrey and Sydney Smith attracted such writers and paid them much larger fees for articles than was usual in those days.

Too many people remember the Review chiefly for its savage attacks upon the Lake Poets and upon certain religious movements, and there is no doubt that Smith and his friends did publish scathing criticisms. On the other hand, the Review gave scope to some first-class writers and it brought its readers into sympathy with new points of view. The need for political and social reform was made clear to many people who previously had been satisfied with the existing situation because they knew nothing about the way in which less fortunate human beings were living. A liberal-minded Englishwoman called Mrs. Fletcher recorded in her autobiography: 'I, who knew Edinburgh both before and after the appearance of the Review, can bear witness to the electrical effect of its publication on the public mind and to the large and good results, in a political sense, that followed its circulation.'

One result of Smith's initiative in launching the *Edinburgh Review* was that other periodicals shortly followed, such as the *Quarterly* in 1808 and *Blackwood's* in 1817, both in the Tory interest. Also in 1817 there appeared for the first time *The Scotsman*, a weekly paper sold at 10d, which reached a much wider public than the quarterly journals and which exercised an influence of incalculable importance during this troubled period of the 1820s and 1830s.

During the 19th century, the writings of J. G. Lockhart, Scott's son-in-law and biographer, of Thomas Carlyle and of R. L. Stevenson made a permanent contribution to literature and enhanced Scottish prestige in the world of letters. There is no doubt however that the great days of Edinburgh made the period 1760 to 1830 remain unique in the country's literary and cultural history. G. S. Pryde, in a recent history of Scotland, suggests that 'the brilliance of Edinburgh's Athenian age was fatally dimmed by the death of Scott in 1832', and certainly the loss of this great figure deprived society of one unrivalled influence. But this was not the whole story. From time to time in history one particular generation becomes renowned because more than the usual proportion of people are endowed with noble gifts of mind and heart, and through this brought to new-found enjoyment of each other. This was what happened in the latter part of the 18th century, when for several decades the Scottish capital was a focal point of thought and letters and art, and when Scottish authors and thinkers exercised an influence far beyond their own country. But no society seems to be able to live at this level for an unlimited span. Perhaps inevitably the magical energy spent itself, and from about 1830 onwards, though Scotland produced many men and women of distinction, the former brilliance and zest gradually became diluted. Cockburn felt this, but he explained the change simply by the re-opening of Europe after the Napoleonic wars, an event which drew people away from Edinburgh to Paris and to other continental cities. 'A new race of peace-formed youths came on the stage but with little literature

The Heart of Midlothian: W. & A. K. Johnston, 1852.

and a comfortless intensity of political zeal; so that by the year 1820, the old thing was much worn and there was no new thing of the same piece to continue or replace it.' He admitted that much remained to make Edinburgh unique, but he reiterated nostalgically 'The exact old thing was not.'

CHAPTER 24

Religion

In Scotland, during the 18th century, people had more regard for religion than their English neighbours. Rational detachment and cynical indifference were not yet making it difficult for Scotsmen to accept the Christian faith. Presbyterians indeed were immensely proud of their traditions and of the fight their forbears had made to establish them. Except in districts where ministers could not penetrate because of long distances or impossible geographical conditions, Scotsmen enjoyed grappling with doctrinal problems and discussing spiritual principles. It was partly a matter of temperament, but partly too it was because life in Scotland was harder, conditions more rigorous, personal suffering more constant, so that for many people the hereafter seemed to be worth more attention than the here and now. In London and the south-east of England, there were more amenities, more amusements, more physical comforts, more distractions, so that there people tended to become more readily sophisticated and to create for themselves artificial pleasures. All this militated against the influence of the Church. But this tide of sophistication reached Scotland later and slowly.

Because people attached such importance to religion, Scottish ministers exercised great influence. People looked to them for guidance in matters of principle, for advice in dilemmas, and for an example in standards of daily living. The reverence accorded to ministers did not exempt them however from much acid criticism, especially from the elders, who took themselves seriously and relished their duty of seeing that the minister behaved as he should.

The minister's first task each week was of course to prepare the Sunday sermon. Listening to this gave many people their one weekly diversion and it was always closely followed and much commented upon. The congregation sat on uncushioned benches in draughty, unheated buildings for two hours each Sunday morning, and if the minister preached more briefly, the elders lost no time in reprimanding him. Preaching, like praying, was supposed to be done without reference to written notes, and to be guided by spiritual light at the moment of delivery. Sermons and prayers were charged with strong emotion, for the Scots are emotional people, and in the 18th century ministers and congregations found an outlet in corporate worship.

The Church of Scotland observed neither Christmas nor Easter, but special efforts were made to keep the Communion season, which was celebrated in country parishes only once a year. Often several parishes would organize a series of Communion Services in one church after another and to these gatherings, sometimes three or four in succession, people from all over the countryside would flock, camping out for the night in barns, or wherever they could, if their journey had been too long for them to get home the same day. Even in wet weather, such Services were conducted out of doors because no church building could hold the large numbers of people.

The ministers worked hard. Apart from preparing sermons and conducting services, they were responsible for Poor Relief and religious discipline in their parishes, and they had to supervise the local school. The laborious deliberations of the Kirk Session took up much of their time too.

And they had to visit their people. It is easy to overlook the strain involved by this. In October 1955, the minister of Kilfinnan and Kilbryde reported to the Dunoon Presbytery that in twelve months he had journeyed 1,290 miles in Sunday travel and 8,200 miles in weekday travel, an arduous way of life indeed, conditioned by a large and scattered country charge. How did his predecessors manage, with neither car nor bicycle? What of the 18th century ministers in Urquhart? This Inverness-shire parish was thirty miles long, ten to twelve wide, and diagonally intersected by a great boney mountain ridge. Ardnamurchan was another mountain parish of great size, Kilmorack a third, and there were of course many more like them. Long exhausting journeys on horseback in dirty weather and across rough country formed a regular part of the Scottish minister's life.

Many ministers received slender emoluments. Often they were paid partly in kind, with bolls, pecks, firlots, even lippies of meal and bere. They all had a manse and most of them a few acres of glebe. In cash, some received as little as £5 to £10 a year, hardly more than farm labourers: Collace in Perthshire was one of these very poorly paid charges. The average stipend was about £40, as in Sorn, Ayrshire, Abercorn near Edinburgh and many others. Doune was exceptional in paying £100 to £150.

Ministers were glad to get to the General Assembly in Edinburgh. Here they could meet people other than their own parishioners, listen to matters of national importance being discussed, renew friendships and replenish their bookshelves at Allan Ramsay's bookshop in the Luckenbooths. Above all, they could worship in one or other of the city churches and hear somebody else preach, a rare inspiration for an 18th century minister.

During this period, everything Anglican and most things English were under suspicion. The Church of Scotland's services were consequently impoverished because public opinion demanded the omission of the Creed, the Doxology, even the Lord's Prayer, all of which were regarded as Episcopalian devices, though all had been included in the Book of Common Order and Knox would never have dreamed of doing without them.

Singing in church was led by the 'up-taker of the psalm', an official later known as the Precentor, who was often the schoolmaster. 'Up-taking' meant singing the Psalm line by line, the congregation following line by line alternately with the leader, a custom which made the musical part of worship a dreary discipline, especially as for many years there were only twelve accepted tunes. Hymns as we know them did not appear until the early 19th century and they were a development from the Paraphrases, which began to be used in 1781.

In the middle of the 18th century, a change in church music was initiated by Sir Archibald Grant, the agricultural reformer, He instructed the local schoolmaster to select a choir of children with good voices, to train them in choral singing and on no account to let them drone. Practices were held in Sir Archibald's library, where he had an organ—and he must have been unique in possessing such an instrument and putting it to such a use. In 1753, Grant heard of an English soldier called Thomas Channon, stationed at Aberdeen. Channon had a gift for choral work and for getting people to sing. The Synod of Aberdeen arranged his discharge from the army, and Grant secured and financed his services. This Englishman started a movement which spread throughout Aberdeenshire, thence to Edinburgh, and gradually transformed church music. In 1761, John Wesley visited Sir Archibald and recorded in his diary: 'About six, we went to church. It was pretty well filled with such persons as we did not look for so near the Highlands. But if we were surprised at their appearance, we were more so at their singing. Thirty or forty sang an anthem after the sermon, with such voices as well as judgment, that I doubt whether they could have been excelled at any cathedral in England.'

No cathedral in England could have rivalled the choir practices of Sir Archibald's church. It was thought irreverent to sing the words of Scripture except at services, so practice verses were composed for use in rehearsal. One paid tribute in happy vein to Sir Archibald himself:

> '*How lovely is thy dwelling-place,*
> *Sir Archie Grant, to me;*
> *The Home-park and the policies,*
> *How pleasant, Sir, they be.*'

The sincerity of the ministers and their congregations was genuine, and their faith deep-rooted. Their strong religious convictions gave them spiritual resources which they all sorely needed. One sad feature of the 18th century, however, was that the Kirk Sessions used their authority with censorious intolerance and little compassion. The man or woman convicted of Sabbath-breaking, 'horrid swearing' or immorality was subjected to humiliating cross-examination by the Session and afterwards made to stand out before the whole congregation for solemn rebuke by the minister. Sometimes this punishment was continued for several Sundays running, and the culprit was further abased by being made to wear sackcloth garments. These acts of penance were enjoyed by the righteous who witnessed them.

The democratic nature of congregational government led to a good many disagreements and to some major controversies. There was bitterness of feeling about Lay Patronage, the legal right of landowners to appoint the ministers to churches on their own properties, which was restored by Act of Parliament in 1712. While it would be too much to say that this Patronage Act caused most of the ecclesiastical trouble in Scotland during the following decades, it certainly was an important contributory factor. During the 18th century, a number of groups withdrew from the National Church, and these seceding bodies could not maintain their own unity, so they in turn also became divided. They were popularly known by such quaint names as Burghers and Anti-Burghers, Auld Lichts and New Lichts. Scotsmen are by nature intolerant, and they have generally valued truth above unity. These smaller churches provided an orthodoxy of preaching and a warmth of fellowship which were often lacking in the Established Church, and their numbers were swollen by the General Assembly's high-handed enforcement of patronage against the will of dissatisfied congregations. They did not escape the rigid outlook and the intolerance characteristic of struggling minorities, but as time went on most of them did develop political and ecclesiastical principles which were fundamentally liberal.

Some parts of Scotland had hardly been reached by the Reformation, and there were areas in the north-west where Roman Catholicism was still the religion of the majority, and where the priests enjoyed some immunity from the Penal Laws. Poverty-stricken and ill-educated as these men were, they found it impossible to reach, let alone to teach many of their people. After the Forty-Five, efforts were made to carry out Protestant missions in these distant corners of Scotland, by such organizations as the Scottish Society for Propagating Christian Knowledge. This Society published the first Gaelic New Testament in 1767, a measure which was frowned upon by Hanoverians, for Gaelic was the language of Jacobitism and as such, they said, should be suppressed. Samuel Johnson expressed scorn for this point of view, and declared that the Scriptures should be denied to nobody on such grounds.

Religion

Elsewhere than in the Highlands, Roman Catholics had to worship in secret, deprived even of the common rights of citizenship, because of their political associations with the Stewarts. In 1779, measures of emancipation were proposed, but these produced such fanatical outbursts in London, Edinburgh and Glasgow that another half-century had to elapse before toleration was extended to Roman Catholics. Their influence counted for little in the country as a whole, though a courageous nucleus braved all difficulties to maintain their faith. The mid-19th century saw a considerable increase in their numbers, because the Act of 1829 abolished the Penal Laws, but also because there developed an enormous labour market in the industrial south, to which flocked crowds of workers from Ireland, driven from their homes by the Potato Famine of 1846.

The Church of Scotland and the minority sects were almost as hostile to Episcopalians as to Roman Catholics. The Revolution Settlement of 1689 stimulated violence against Episcopalian priests and some two hundred parsons were driven out of their benefices, and numbers of chapels destroyed. Only in the north and north-east were the Episcopalians comparatively unmolested. for here there was a traditional support for this way of worship.

In the south, and particularly in the capital, popular prejudice against the Episcopalian Church was strongest. Priests were driven to all sorts of expedients in the effort to conduct their services, as Covenanters and Nonconformists had been in the 17th century. James Greenshields led his small congregation in an Edinburgh flat, with one inside wall removed to join up two rooms, and it was here that he was discovered using the Book of Common Prayer. In consequence he was confined in the Tolbooth during some twelve months, until in 1711 the House of Lords ordered his release. The Toleration Act of 1712 legalized the Episcopal form of worship, so long as it was conducted by parsons who had abjured the Pretender, but this many refused to do, and their Jacobite sympathies brought them into constant trouble.

While some of the Episcopalian priests struggled on in the effort to maintain their congregations by holding frequent celebrations of the Sacraments for tiny groups of worshippers,

281

others found a living by becoming chaplains or tutors to families among the gentry; in the south their numbers steadily declined, although their hold on Aberdeenshire and other northern counties was fairly well maintained. The Forty-Five produced a fresh set of Penal Laws designed still further to restrict their activities. Even those priests who abjured the Pretender were under relentless suspicion. Bishops, clergy and laymen of the Episcopal Church in Scotland lived in chronic poverty, disliked by Presbyterians of all ranks, and excluded from the Universities. Not until Charles Edward died in 1788 did their position improve and only in 1792 were the Penal Laws against them repealed.

Interesting comments on the religious life of Scotland during the second half of the 18th century are recorded in the journals of John Wesley. Between 1751 and 1789 this tireless evangelist made twenty-two preaching tours north of the Border. Book in hand, for he was a peripatetic reader, he travelled on horseback with 'a loose rein', generally in the months of April and May and often in execrable weather. Wesley almost always found a ready hearing, and sometimes, especially 'by the riverside' in Glasgow, he preached to many thousands. People were prepared to endure exposure to harsh rainstorms and biting winds rather than relinquish the quest for the spiritual enrichment which Wesley strove to give them. He was impressed by the Scottish appetite for solid doctrine and plain speaking, nonplussed by the apparent lack of response to evangelistic appeal. Though Wesley made a number of friends in Scotland and became attached to some of the Methodist societies he founded there, he never felt quite at ease with Scottish people. 'I admire this people,' he wrote. 'So decent! So serious! And so perfectly unconcerned!'

Until about the middle of the century, the General Assembly frowned upon organized amusement, especially the theatre, as John Home discovered in 1754. Only thirty years later Alexander Carlyle described quite another state of affairs. 'It is remarkable that in 1784, when the great actress, Mrs. Siddons, appeared in Edinburgh during the sitting of the General Assembly, that court was obliged to fix all its important business for the alternate days when she did not act, as all the younger members, clergy as

Religion

well as laity, took their stations in the theatre by three in the afternoon.'

This relaxation of traditional disapproval for the theatre was due partly to the impact of economic and social developments, but partly to the influence of the Moderate group in the Church which became dominant during the second half of the century.

The leader of the Moderates was Dr. William Robertson, the historian, who in his young days had protested against the Assembly's reaction to Home's theatrical ambitions. In riper years Robertson's scholarship came to be respected all over Europe and in 1762 he became Principal of Edinburgh University, and the following year Moderator of the General Assembly, of which he was the most influential member. Among Robertson's many friends were the economist Adam Smith, the novelist Tobias Smollett, and the sceptic David Hume.

Despite the draining away of evangelical fervour into the smaller groups, the Anti-Moderate or Evangelical party in the Church of Scotland persisted, and it was ready to take advantage of the change in atmosphere brought about by the French Revolution. The excesses of the period seemed to be due in part to the free thought which was the logical outcome of Moderate ideas. In some circles, therefore, there developed a reaction from the cult of reason towards the traditional, the romantic and the mystical. In others, the revolutionary idea of the rights of man produced a democratic fervour, secular rather than religious in nature.

Once again, patronage became a burning question, but only as part of a larger programme. The Evangelicals realized that the changes in agriculture and industry, which were making for the increase of population and its concentration in towns and cities, had brought about a situation in which a new policy was required by the Church. Parishes in industrial areas now needed to be sub-divided, and many new churches clearly were needed too, as well as new schools. If people were to be drawn into these new churches, they must be made to feel that they had at least some say in the choice of ministers.

By 1834, the Evangelical party was dominant in the General Assembly, and succeeded in putting through the famous Veto

Act. This said that if a majority of the male heads of families in a parish disapproved of the patron's nominee, that should be sufficient ground for his rejection. Thomas Chalmers, the leader of the Evangelicals, considered this Act conservative in tone. His idea was to make the call of the people important in the appointment of ministers, but not to encourage popular agitations for well-liked ministers.

The Veto Act of 1834 brought about a crisis. It was challenged in the case of Auchterarder and some other parishes, and the law courts declared that it could not constitutionally be upheld. To the Evangelicals, this was an invasion of the church's spiritual jurisdiction by the civil courts, and so the question of patronage became merged in the deeper question of spiritual independence.

Would Parliament provide a way out of the deadlock by legalizing the Assembly's Veto Act? More than one political leader framed a measure designed to satisfy both Church and State: but the government in London took the typically English view that an Established Church must pay for its privileges by being definitely subject to the Crown in Parliament. When it appeared that their claims were not going to be met, the majority of the Evangelicals prepared for a break with the State connection. This event, known as the Disruption, took place in May 1843, when some 474 ministers, more than a third of the total number, followed by about the same proportion of the people, formed the Free Church of Scotland. They gave up their former churches, manses and stipends.

The congregations who supported them had to find buildings, and financial resources, also to establish colleges for the training of their clergy. They met with unexpected sympathy from powerful quarters and subscriptions were forthcoming in such quantity that within a few months they were able to set about practical organization. Thomas Chalmers became the first Moderator of the new Assembly, a fact which gave the Free Church much prestige and strength.

This Disruption revealed a wonderful quality of faith and self-sacrifice in its supporters, but it was a tragedy, for it took most of the ensuing century to heal the breach, and even now the scars are hardly out of sight. The Tory Government of 1843 did something to make amends, though it was done too late. The Benefices Act was passed, and this provided that objections to the nominees of patrons were to be taken into consideration, also the character and number of the objectors. By another Act, the establishment of new parishes in crowded industrial districts was made much easier. Not until Disraeli's time, in 1874, was Lay Patronage completely abolished.

During the rest of the 19th century, the Scottish Presbyterians fell into three main groups—the Church of Scotland, the new Free Church and the United Presbyterian Church. This last was formed in 1847, as the result of a series of re-unions between groups which had seceded in the 18th century. Although these three dominant organizations were not separated by any differences in doctrine, much sectarian bitterness between them led to waste of energy and initiative, which should have been devoted to Christian work, but which in fact found expression in competitive church-building and denominational controversy.

Religion influenced considerable sections of Scottish society until the very end of the 19th century. It was fashionable amongst respectable circles to go to church, and as physical comfort was now more in evidence in people's homes, it began to be expected at worship, so churches were re-constructed: curiously enough, while roofs became rain-resistant, walls draught-proof and pews cushioned, services, and especially sermons, became shorter. On the whole the large middle class maintained the habit of supporting the churches and so did some of the more prosperous artisans and skilled workers, but many thousands of the really destitute never took part in organized religion.

One cannot read the story of the Church in the 19th century without regret. Religious partisanship absorbed high-principled and devout Scotsmen at a time when a different attitude was desperately needed. G. M. Trevelyan says that this period in England was one when the Bible had 'a rival in the ledger' and certainly the same might be said of Scotland. Highland landowners, factory proprietors, business men, iron magnates, industrial leaders and property-owners were engrossed in money making. Many of them were enjoying wealth. The artisans in trades exposed to periodic depressions, the unskilled labourers and those who for a variety of reasons had fallen out of the labour market altogether were suffering destitution of a kind Scotland had never yet seen. The disease-ridden slums were inhabited by hordes of families who earned wages which could not buy them sufficient food to maintain health, and by a submerged population which maintained a precarious existence through devices such as begging, theft and prostitution.

Individual ministers and church members worked here and there with magnificent self-dedication in the interests of slum-ridden parishes; the General Assembly of the Free Church sponsored enquiries into such problems as the housing of working people, the bothy system, the excessive facilities for drunkenness; Temperance Societies were organized both by the Roman Catholic and by the Protestant Churches; Sunday Schools, Ragged Schools and some orphanages were founded. Yet the Church as a whole was timid about being involved in political controversy, its members reluctant to face the terrible problem of wealth and its proper use by Christians. So religious people were inclined to indulge in generalities, while ministers offered too little leadership and guidance to their congregations on subjects like the administration of house property, responsibility for employees and the fair distribution of material riches. The evil effects of the all too frequent divorce in the life of prominent Christians between individual piety and economic and political action have still a baneful influence on the religious situation in Scotland.

CHAPTER 25

Education

One of the ideals envisaged by John Knox was that the Church should assume responsibility for education. Believing like Calvin that unlettered people could hardly sustain an enlightened Christian faith, he set great store by his plans for the foundation of grammar schools and arts colleges in all the towns, together with village schools for even the smallest parishes. Unhappily for Scotland, Knox's plans were not fully carried out, although efforts were made by the Scottish Parliaments during the 17th century to meet the country's need for more schools. The last of these, a statute passed in 1696, required heritors in each parish to find a commodious school building and to settle a salary of £10 on the schoolmaster; but the arrangements were not completed and so, during the difficult opening years of the 18th century, there were parishes which possessed no school at all.

In the more fortunate areas where parish schools did exist, boys, and sometimes also girls, from the age of about six or seven were taught to read. Methods used were simple enough and changed little during the years. The training of Scottish children, both at home and at school, was carried out with the help of frequent and faithfully administered thrashings, which most Scots regarded as essential to moral and intellectual progress.

The abler boys at the age of nine or ten could go on from the parish school to a grammar school in the nearest burgh, which would often be under the care of only one man; in the larger establishments, where there were two or more masters, one would take charge of a class of three or four consecutive years, handing it over at the top of the school to the Rector.

The geologist Hugh Miller, who was born in 1803, wrote an autobiography called *My Schools and Schoolmasters*. It is a most readable and entertaining account of rural life in a fishing community on Cromarty Firth, and it describes the author's education in a single-teacher school, which sent a steady stream of boys to Scottish Universities. To prepare their best pupils for this, schoolmasters, even at the cost of neglecting the less able, would spare neither time nor trouble. Boys went up to the Universities at the age of thirteen or sometimes even twelve, there to live as boarders or in lodgings. Thomas Carlyle was fourteen when he walked the hundred miles from Ecclefechan to Edinburgh in 1809, in order to read for his degree. Because Latin was necessary for students, schoolmasters grounded their bright boys in this subject day in and day out, indeed some of the schools included little else in the curriculum—though it was on a matter of English spelling that Hugh Miller literally came to blows with his teacher.

Lord Cockburn went to Edinburgh High School in 1787, when he was about eight years old, and there he remained for six years. During the first four years he was beaten almost daily, although being afraid of his master he always had his work well prepared; things improved somewhat in the last two sessions when he moved into the Headmaster's class, but he never voluntarily read even fifty pages of a book until he left school, and throughout the whole period he was taught nothing but Latin. It should be added that he became later a voracious reader of classical literature and an advocate of Latin as a valuable school subject if properly taught.

Scottish people have always attached great importance to education and even in the early 18th century many who were not professional educationists were realistic in their thinking about it. They were proud of the tradition which sent even the poorest boys to Universities, if they were of the right intellectual calibre, but it was common knowledge that schools were insufficient in number, uneven in quality and as a rule inexpressibly dull, except for the small number of really gifted boys. In the country, as soon as the spring days began to lengthen, the children dis appeared from school, because they were needed in the fields and lessons therefore seemed irrelevant.

It was characteristic of the nation that laymen and ministers, business men and town councillors, merchants and manufacturers, all gave serious thought, and also a good deal of money, to widen the scope of education during the very years when the results of the Jacobite troubles and of the economic revolution might well have blinded people to such concerns as the training of children. In the year of the Union, Glasgow appointed James Muir, at a salary of £100, to teach mathematics and navigation, subjects which were adopted in the Writing or Commercial Schools, and in the Academies founded in many other cities during the 18th century. Book-keeping, surveying and natural philosophy were also introduced into these new foundations which were designed to educate boys for business, seafaring, commerce and engineering.

This departure from the traditional emphasis on Latin was specially noticeable in burghs like Ayr, Dundee, Perth and Dumfries where new industrial developments were taking place, but Elgin and Inverness also experimented on similar lines: technical training and qualifications for a practical career obviously began to influence thought as soon as the effects of economic change became apparent, and the success of Scotsmen at this time in seafaring, engineering and surveying made its mark on school-planning remarkably early.

While burgh councillors were developing these new Academies, wealthy merchants who had amassed large fortunes in the tobacco trade and in other business enterprises made generous endowments for charitable purposes, especially for the support of the aged and the very young. In a number of cases, both age groups were catered for in the same establishment and so there developed the famous Hospitals and Hospital schools which were designed in part as almshouses 'for the aliment and maintenance of old men and women', in part as schools for city orphans. George Watson's in Edinburgh was founded in this way, so was James Gillespie's at the very end of the 18th century. Like the similar foundation of the Hutcheson brothers, set up in Glasgow as early as 1640, these schools survive to this day, though the almshouses they supported have long since been closed.

No such leadership was available to deal with the much more difficult problems of the country districts and especially of the Highlands. Here it was the Church that took the initiative, when the attention of the General Assembly was called to the state of affairs in the north and west. The Assembly carried out some enquiries and was so shocked by what it discovered that sanction was willingly given to the foundation of a new organization. This was the Society for Propagating Christian Knowledge, launched in Scotland in 1709, and not to be confused with the society of similar name founded in England in 1698.

It set up schools in the more remote parishes where the ministers had the most difficulty in covering their work. The first was established on the island of St. Kilda where 'nothing had been taught for many a dark and dreary generation but the art of catching fish and solan geese for the wretched support of mere animal life'. Here Alexander Buchan worked for eighteen years, until he died in an epidemic which swept the island. Buchan was exceptional, as most of the schools were designed to be of a temporary nature and the masters were supposed to move on after only two or three years. The rules of the Society required them to be regularly inspected by at least two ministers of the local presbytery, to ensure that reasonable standards were maintained. Boys and girls of all ages up to twenty-one attended these schools, mainly in the winter months, and they learnt to read and sometimes to write, though the latter accomplishment was rather unusual; their teachers also conducted services for them and instructed them in religion.

Between 1715 and 1795, over 300 such schools were founded. Although the salaries paid were meagre—about £6 sterling a year—and the buildings and equipment pitiful, this achievement was a remarkable one for a voluntary society dependent upon private subscriptions. The work was recognized as more essential than ever after the Forty-Five, yet in 1758 as many as 175 Highland parishes possessed neither school nor teacher. The General Assembly put the facts bluntly enough by referring to 'the many Thousands in this Church and Nation, especially in the Highlands and Islands, who live in Barbarity and Ignorance'.

The parish ministers themselves were well aware of the facts and plainly stated them in their contributions to Sinclair's Statistical Account, published in the 1790s. Entries from all over the country emphasized how inadequate were schoolmasters' salaries, which varied from £10 to £25, and amounted to much less than sums earned by mechanics in industry; they also commented on the miserable school buildings, and on the number of children out of reach of any educational amenities at all. To quote only two of many such records, the minister of Dowally, Dunkeld, wrote: 'There is no salary for a parish schoolmaster here, by consequence there is no parish school.' From the minister of Fossaway and Tulliebole came the comment: 'Parochial schoolmasters commonly receive a good education, are a body of men of great importance to the country and certainly deserve much better encouragement from the landed proprietors than at present they receive.' The concern of the Church continued after the Napoleonic wars, when the movement of population was already causing unmanageable new social problems, and in 1824 the General Assembly appointed a permanent Education Committee which opened 200 schools in the course of a few years.

When the Disruption took place in 1843, an extraordinary situation developed almost overnight. Evangelical influence was strong among schoolmasters, and nearly 400 joined the United Free Church. For this imposing corps of teachers the Evangelicals set up new schools in astonishingly quick time, while in the older schools their places had to be filled by other people. Thus a notable expansion of education came about in the 1840s and 1850s. Scotland's one Government Inspector of Education joined the Free Church too.

So did Scotland's pioneer in the training of teachers. This was David Stow. By 1843, his indefatigable efforts to bring about an improvement in the moral standards of the poor had already given the Church of Scotland a Sunday School Movement and a Teachers Training College. After 1843 Stow was the driving force behind the new Assembly's educational policy and under his guidance two more Training Colleges were opened.

In spite of all these developments, the country's educational system was quite unable to cover the field by the mid-19th century. In rural districts, but still more in the great areas of newly opened mine, mill and factory, literally thousands of children were growing up without any education at all.

Boys and girls were employed in the factories and mills from the age of five and six, a fact upon which the press not infrequently commented; journalists were vociferous in their statements that there was nothing in the factory system which could be considered prejudicial to people's health—even the *Edinburgh Review* of the 1840s published articles to this effect.

As they worked thirteen or fourteen hours daily, the children could not go to the parish schools even where these existed. A pamphlet published by George Lewis in 1835 was entitled *Scotland a half-educated Nation*, but really this caption suggests an over-optimistic attitude. In 1839, St. David's Parish, Dundee, with an industrial population of 9,000, had one public school staffed by one unsalaried teacher, dependent for his living upon the fees brought by his pupils—fees which would amount to a few pence per week per child. There were a few small private schools as well, and between them all, one-third of the children aged 5 to 14 in this parish were having reasonably regular tuition. In 1846, 54 per cent. of Glasgow's children were at school, but in the Gorbals parish, a district of incurable poverty, 93 per cent. of the children were attending no school whatever. After 1833, efforts were made to arrange two hours of 'education' for children each day after the work in the factories had been completed, but on all sides the evidence was that the pupils arrived in the evening so exhausted by the hours spent on their feet in the bad atmosphere of their workrooms that they could give no attention; and parents loudly proclaimed that these children would have been far better in their beds than yawning over books.

Children in the industrial cities were therefore illiterate, overworked and deprived of healthy recreation. As their homes were tiny slum dwellings, such leisure as they had was spent roaming round the streets in gangs. Juvenile crime was common, and society dealt with it pitilessly. Children were sent to prison on charges which nowadays would qualify them for a period of supervision under a Probation Officer, and they were even transported to Botany Bay. In autumn 1837, the *Glasgow Courier* reported that Joan Alexander, aged 13, stole twenty-nine yards of cotton print and a green apron. She was transported for seven years. The same paper told a few weeks later of four boys who each stole a silk handkerchief by pickpocketing, and they too were sentenced to seven years' transportation. Entered as 'a little boy' was John McColgan, who was transported for house breaking in Dobbies Loan, Glasgow—he had removed a shutter from a window in order to steal blankets—and Robert Kirkwood of Beith had a similar sentence for stealing two shovels and two spades. Respectable people seemed unaware of the iniquitous treatment given to such children, victims of a society which could neither educate nor care for them.

Until the middle of the 19th century, the development of education in Scotland was largely due to the efforts of the Church, but thereafter the State gradually began to take over responsibility in this sphere. In 1856, an Education Department was set up by the Government and a number of Commissions appointed to investigate conditions in Scottish schools. One such Commission, appointed in 1864 under the Duke of Argyll, estimated that of the total child population in Scotland, that is 92,000 children, some two-thirds were enrolled in no school of any kind. This bombshell led to the Education Act of 1872, which brought about a completely changed situation. Every parish and burgh was now to appoint a School Board and education became compulsory for children up to the age of thirteen. In 1885, the Scottish Education Department became a department of the Scottish Office and from that time onwards the Secretary for Scotland handled educational policy. Except in the comparatively small number of independent schools, the State thus became responsible for carrying out the idea entertained so long before by John Knox, and gradually Scotland became a literate country. How horrified he would have been had he realized that his ideal of a school in every parish would take 300 years to achieve, and how much more horrified by the notion of State-run secular education!

In the period following the Union, Scotland still maintained her five universities—one each in St. Andrews, Glasgow and Edinburgh, two small rival institutions in Aberdeen. Their expansion was hindered by political restlessness, by poverty, by the loss of life caused in the rebellions, and later by the emigration of Scotland's more enterprising families. In spite of all this, there was considerable re-organization in the universities during the 18th century, of which one early example was the abolition of the regenting system. This arrangement, to which Andrew Melville had long ago objected, meant that the Regents, that is the university teachers, moved with their classes through the full range of the seven subjects for four consecutive years. By 1727, regenting had been abolished both in Edinburgh and in Glasgow, though it lasted longer in the other Universities, and from the time of the Union onwards a series of Chairs was founded, which enabled men of distinction to concentrate wholly on their own special subjects.

Outstanding among these early Professors was Francis Hutcheson, who held the Chair of Moral Philosophy at Glasgow from 1729 to 1746, a period when the influence of the 17th century Thomas Hobbes was still strong. Hobbes, who was a materialist and a very powerful thinker, believed that people are dominated by fear and self-interest and will only act for the public weal under pressure of these very instincts. Accordingly, he adopted the view that the State should be so organized that from selfish motives men will wish to obey the laws, a doctrine which tended to create a sceptical and disillusioned attitude. Religious thinkers, on the other hand, were under the spell of Calvinism and therefore they frowned on all worldly activities, even those associated with intellectual and aesthetic pursuits. Hutcheson rejected both these views: unlike those who followed Hobbes, he believed that man is endowed with a moral feeling which can enable him to choose the good and reject the evil, that the impulse to do good and to act benevolently is as potent as the impulse to fend for oneself at the expense of others; in contrast to those of the Calvinist school, he held that aesthetic appreciation is as essential to full spiritual growth as intellectual integrity. Unlike his colleagues, Hutcheson delivered his lectures not in Latin but in English. The very many young men who came under his influence were enriched by his enlightened approach, and he did much to prepare the way for the intellectual awakening which took place in the latter half of his century.

Education

Hutcheson's most distinguished successor was Adam Smith, who held first the Chair of Logic, then that of Moral Philosophy, at Glasgow from 1751 to 1763, a period which he afterwards described as the happiest of his life. Adam Smith had few, if any, equals among the thinkers of his day. His *Wealth of Nations*, published in 1776, laid the foundations for the modern study of Political Economy and it is still a sine qua non in the training of economists. With no accurate statistical data upon which to work, Smith set out and interpreted a whole range of basic facts hitherto ignored and he exposed a number of myths which had long been reverenced as truth. Until his day, for example, people had taken it for granted that money and wealth were identical, that free trade and free enterprise would lead to chaotic reduction of profits, that the prosperity of one country must automatically reduce that of its neighbour—the influence of this last notion is well seen in the reluctance of Englishmen to give Scotland any share in commercial activity when the Treaty of Union was being negotiated. The principles which were expounded in the *Wealth of Nations* won almost immediate recognition, in fact the work of Adam Smith led to far-reaching changes in the legislation, the foreign policy and the economic administration of Great Britain. Glasgow University did not lose touch with this brilliant man, for he was made Rector in 1787.

Famous days for Edinburgh University began in 1762, when Professor William Robertson, whose influence on the Moderate party in the Church was so pronounced, entered upon his thirty-one years of service as Principal. He wrote massive historical studies on England, Scotland, Charles V, America and, in his old age, on India. These works earned him a European reputation, partly because of the splendid prose in which they were written, partly because historical scholarship was so rare at the time. Among his most enthusiastic admirers were Edward Gibbon, Samuel Johnson, Horace Walpole and Catherine II of Russia.

Robertson reformed the management of the University Library, and with courageous optimism he launched a huge scheme of re-planning the dilapidated and inadequate College buildings. His cousin Robert Adam was employed to design two stately quadrangles, a hall, a chapel, a set of classrooms, and above all the new Library. The architect's death in 1792, Robertson's death in the following year, shortage of funds and the effects of the Napoleonic wars held up these ambitious schemes, and the work was not completed till the 1820s, when the architect Playfair carried out some of Adam's plans on a modified scale.

Cockburn's unhappy days in Edinburgh High School have already been mentioned. In 1793, when he was fourteen, he went up to Edinburgh University, and there began to attend lectures in Logic delivered by Professor Finlayson. 'Until we heard him, few of us knew that we had minds,' was Cockburn's grateful comment. Even better things were in store, for soon he started going to Dugald Stewart, Edinburgh's most distinguished philosopher, and of him he wrote: 'To me Stewart's lectures were like the opening of the heavens. I felt I had a soul.' These were only two of the brilliant men who were attracted to the capital at this time and there were many more, all inimitably described in Cockburn's *Memorials*—Adam Ferguson, Hugh Blair, John Robison and the rest of them. Robison was perhaps the most picturesque of the lot—'a pigtail so long and thin that it curled far down his back: and a pair of huge blue worsted hose without soles and covering the limbs from the heel to the top of the thigh, in which he walked and lectured, seemed to improve his wise elephantine head and majestic person.' All but Robison were what Cockburn called 'great peripatetics'. Their academic grove lay in the Meadows—'under these trees walked and talked and meditated all our literary and scientific and many of our legal worthies.' These walkers and talkers were responsible to a great degree for Edinburgh's reputation during the Napoleonic wars as a city of scholarship.

Throughout the 18th century, and in fact well on into the 19th, Professors and students all lived on the minimum of material security. In 1708 the Professor of Botany in Glasgow was allotted the salary of £30 a year; the Professor of Anatomy in Edinburgh started with £15. Adam Smith became Professor of Logic in Glasgow with £44 10s. 0d. a year: the Rev. Hugh Blair, Professor of Rhetoric at Edinburgh, with £70. Blair built up an unrivalled reputation as a preacher and his published sermons created such a sensation, in England as well as in Scotland, that they came to be considered as part of the literary revival of the period. George III granted Blair a pension of £200 and he then discovered that he could afford his own carriage. He is believed to have been the first Presbyterian minister in Edinburgh who ever rose to such luxury.

If Professors were expected to live on narrow means, students felt the pinch even more acutely. When Pryse Lockhart Gordon, a son of the manse, went up to Aberdeen at the age of fourteen in 1776, his total expenses for six months' board, tuition fees, travel expenses and incidental extravagances amounted to £17 4s. 3d. This adolescent complained that his grandfather thought him a spendthrift, on the ground that in his day, sixty years earlier, he had never exceeded £12 per session. It is rather touching to find in Gordon's meticulous accounts 13/- to Sweety Nell, an old woman who sold lollipops, 1/4d. for shuttlecocks, 6d. for a fine because he threw a snowball at the sacrist and £1 16s. 0d. for extra food to supplement the college meals, while fees to the Professors of Greek and Latin came to £2 6s. 6d.

It was in such conditions that the Medical Schools of Glasgow and Edinburgh established their reputation. In 1726, Edinburgh instituted four medical Chairs, in addition to that of Anatomy, which already existed; and in 1746 the Royal Infirmary was opened as a teaching hospital. After this, the capital became famous far beyond the boundaries of Scotland for the excellence of its medical training and men came from all over the Empire, and also from Europe, to take their medical degrees there. Until 1834, they all had to present their theses in Latin. Glasgow was expanding its school of Medicine at this time too, although it was still a much smaller city than Edinburgh, since by 1755 its population was less than half that of the capital, and there was no teaching hospital until 1794. Professor William Cullen and Professor Joseph Black each established in Glasgow a reputation as a distinguished teacher of Chemistry, but both were glad to accept appointments in Edinburgh where wider scope was afforded. Incidentally, in Glasgow, men who wanted to study Chemistry had to become medical students, as there was no Professor there for this subject.

The need for vigorous leadership in medical research and surgical skill became greater than in any previous period. In Glasgow's vast industrial growth, factories, mills and shipyards were the scene of many ghastly injuries to workmen handling dangerous tools in dirty surroundings: their wounds were often already infected by the time they reached hospital. Surgery was carried out in such primitive conditions that death from hospital gangrene was a most likely risk, even if the operation to be performed were comparatively simple and no previous infection had complicated matters.

In 1860, an Englishman was appointed to the chair of surgery in Glasgow. This was Lord Lister, who initiated a new approach to surgery, based on his knowledge of Pasteur's researches, so that antiseptic conditions were made compulsory in his operating theatre, with the result that by the exclusion of bacteria risks of infection were immeasurably reduced. Senseless prejudice among the conventional surgeons of the day delayed Lister's recognition, but ultimately his methods were accepted and untold numbers of lives were thereby saved. One of Lister's critics, ironically enough, was James Young Simpson, Professor of Midwifery at Edinburgh, who had himself met with ferocious hostility. He had introduced the use of anaesthesia, a measure which orthodox people regarded as contrary to the laws of God and of nature because, in reducing pain, chloroform would eliminate an essential feature of human experience.

From the early years of the 19th century onwards it became increasingly evident that the Scottish University system was in urgent need of reform. There had been constant friction ever since the 16th century over the administration of Edinburgh University, by the terms of its foundation under the jurisdiction of the Town Council. This municipal control limited the freedom needed by research specialists and academic experts, whose attitude was not understood by the bailies and magistrates. The co-existence of two rival establishments in Aberdeen became more and more absurd, for neither could really flourish, yet this was a centre where a vigorous university life was greatly needed. The Disruption of 1843 complicated everything, because a number of professors and other officials followed the lead of

Dr. Chalmers, who held one of the Edinburgh chairs in theology, and the loss of their services was difficult to cover. An Act of 1690, still in force, required every Professor to sign the Westminster Confession of Faith and in so doing to promise loyalty to the Established Church. From the mid-19th century onwards, it would have become much more difficult to find properly qualified men willing to do this.

From the point of view of the students' attitude to university opportunities, much also needed to be done. As there was no entrance qualification and no encouragement to complete degree courses, many young men openly idled their time and, after spending several years at a university, went down with no qualifications, with little advantage derived from the frittered years, but in many cases with some irresponsible habits.

During the 1850s, the constitution of Scottish Universities was reformed by a series of Acts of Parliament. The two institutions at Aberdeen were amalgamated, Edinburgh was released from municipal control, the religious test was abolished except for Principals and theological professors, the status of all professors raised by increases in salary. Scottish students were given several incentives to work harder, including a new Honours degree course, which carried considerable importance as a qualification in professional careers. All these reforms helped to make the Universities a more valuable influence in the nation's life, and although a man could still take several years to amass enough examination passes for his degree, far more students now began to come up with the ambition to make a success of scholarly study.

The expansion of the Universities after these reforms was perhaps most noticeable to the general public in the sphere of Science, in which Glasgow now began to take a much more prominent part than in earlier days. Lord Kelvin was appointed to the Chair of Natural Philosophy at Glasgow in 1846 when he was twenty-two, and he held it until 1899. During this long period of service, he worked on new fields of research and he combined encyclopaedic knowledge with inventive skill, so that his scientific knowledge was applied to practical life. Submarine telegraphy and the provision of heat and light by electricity are only two examples of work in which he made an international reputation.

Little mention has been made so far in this chapter of the education of girls, for the excellent reason that, until the second half of the 19th century, little effort was made by Scotsmen to educate their daughters. In 1695, the Merchant Maidens' Hospital was opened as an orphanage for girls in Edinburgh, and in 1704 a similar institution called the Trade Maidens' was established. The spinning schools set up by the Board of Trustees for Manufactures in the middle years of the 18th century gave some technical instruction to a small proportion of girls, and some were also taken into the schools of the S.P.C.K. Co-educational too were many of the burgh schools, so that sisters sat under the dominies along with their brothers, at least until their parents decided that their daughters' time would be more usefully spent in the house, the dairy or the fields. Well-to-do families employed governesses and there were a few small seminaries for ladies in some of the towns. Not until the Education Acts of the 1870s, however, were girls considered on an equal basis with boys in the nation's educational scheme. From that time until now, there has been much more co-education in Scotland than in England, even at the secondary level, and the number of girls' schools is still relatively much smaller north of the Border than south of it. During the last three decades of the 19th century, some girls' schools were founded, such as St. Leonard's; and some of the older merchant company foundations started separate establishments for girls, Hutchesons' for example in Glasgow, George Watson's in Edinburgh.

The struggle for the entry of women into the Universities began also in the 1870s. An association for the Higher Education of Women was founded in Edinburgh and a number of women began attending courses of lectures in the Universities. They presented themselves for examination, but there were no powers whereby they could be granted degrees. As long as they confined their interests to the Arts Faculties, these seekers after learning met with reasonable sympathy, but the attempts of Miss Jex-Blake and some of her friends to qualify in Medicine caused a minor crisis and shocked reaction was registered by public opinion. This brave lady finally qualified herself in Ireland and in 1886 founded a School of Medicine for Women in Edinburgh, where the authorities held out against the admission of women to the University Medical School until 1916. St. Andrews offered a diploma called the L.L.A. (Lady Literate in Arts) from 1876 and many women took advantage of this during the thirty-four years of its existence. In 1893, however, an ordinance was passed giving women the right to attend the same classes as men in all the Scottish Universities and to graduate in the same way.

The many changes and reforms which were introduced into Scottish schools and Universities during these two centuries sometimes came to maturity long after they were badly needed, so that the problems which were solved only by slow stages always gave place to fresh and more complex difficulties. Looking back over the story, however, one can see certain consistent principles at work, of which the most impressive has been the conviction that in a democratic country as many individuals as possible, no matter what their family circumstances, should have the opportunity to enjoy the widest scope in education. That this education should be based on an academic foundation was assumed until the 20th century, for Scottish people long retained their desire for the knowledge to be derived from books and their respect for the value of an intellectual point of view.

CHAPTER 26

Parliament and Politics

Stalwart in character, forthright in speech, happy in controversy, Scots of all people should have found much to attract them in politics. Yet the 18th century has been described by Dr. G. S. Pryde as 'one of deepest political apathy'.

Why did Scottish M.P.s play so small a part in Parliamentary affairs? Why were people in the constituencies so ill-informed and so indifferent to elections and electoral issues? Why did the nation have to wait till the Napoleonic wars for a full contribution of Scottish energy and intelligence in affairs of state? The Union certainly gave Scotland a disproportionately small number of representatives, 45 in the House of Commons, 16 in the House of Lords: and in the 18th century Scottish business never had its rightful place in the agenda at Westminster. Neither of these facts however explains the 'deepest political apathy' which continued for nearly a hundred years.

The trouble was caused by the marriage of a medieval electoral system to the newly matured parliamentary régime of the United Kingdom.

The Commissioners for the Union assumed, reasonably enough, that the traditional Scottish methods of election should be continued; indeed, had these been interfered with, Scottish opinion would have been outraged. It occurred to nobody that Scottish parliamentary traditions dated in the main from the 15th century; or that they had been devised to suit a population of rather less than a million people, among whom few were qualified to hold political responsibility, fewer still desirous of doing so.

What were these electoral arrangements? And why was reform so long delayed?

Parliament and Politics

Thirty of Scotland's forty-five members were allocated by the Treaty of Union to the shires, of which there were thirty-three. Twenty-seven therefore were given a member each, six shared the remaining three shire members between them. The right to vote for these thirty representatives was confined to landholders whose property was held directly from the Crown—royal tenants-in-chief in fact. This was in keeping with 15th century tradition. As only a small number of landholders held their properties in this way, many lairds of good standing exercised no political rights at all. In 1788, the number of voters in Bute was 12, in Ayrshire—a large county—214. By 1821, when the population was just under two million, barely 3,000 enjoyed the county franchise. It was easy for the Government to secure the shire votes, by offering their supporters posts in the East India Company and in other branches of public service, even by giving such appointments to friends and relatives of the voters. Scottish landowners were glad to take advantage of this, the Government built up its majority in the House of Commons, and not until the 1780s or the 1790s did any appreciable number of Scots see anything wrong in the system.

While thirty seats in the House of Commons were reserved for Scottish shires, fifteen were allocated to the burghs. Again by feudal tradition, only royal burghs were represented, towns which had received their charters from the Crown. There were 66 of these, some large and influential, others small and diminishing. To divide 66 by 15 is a tiresome exercise in mental arithmetic, an impossible one in political organization. A cumbrous solution was worked out. While Edinburgh was honoured with one burgh representative all her own, the other 65 towns were divided into 14 districts or groups, each containing several civic centres, but represented by one member, whose election was perforce carried out by delegates.

Excluded altogether from the burgh franchise were large industrial towns, like Paisley and Greenock, because they had no royal charter. Among the royal burghs, no difference was recognized between, for example, Glasgow whose population in 1821 was 150,000 and Rutherglen with 10,000. So the developing business and industrial interests would have been ill represented

303

in any case. But the situation was made much worse by the ruling that only Town Councillors could vote. There were on average only about twenty of these in any burgh, and vacancies had been filled since the 15th century by co-option. The Councils were therefore self-elected bodies, sometimes consisting of one family's members and friends. While bribery by means of hard cash probably occurred rarely in shire elections, it was common in the burghs, where the councillors were often indebted to some powerful noble.

Even if Scotland had been given double her number of members in the new British Parliament of the 18th century, with such an electoral system she would still have been ill represented. On the other hand, if her 45 M.P.s had been elected in a manner less tied up with feudal usage, they could have made a powerful bloc in the House and therefore influenced legislation. In fact the contribution of Scotsmen to the business at Westminster consisted only in the provision of a solid supply of pro-Government votes on all controversial issues—a result not to be foreseen by the Commissioners in 1707, but eagerly put to advantageous use by the Crown's most powerful ministers later in the century. The 'management' of Scotland—an odious term which significantly seemed to cause little comment—had been reduced to a fine art by the 1780s.

These facts alone would explain a condition of 'deepest political apathy'. There were other circumstances however which contributed to it. Members from Scotland did not feel at home in Westminster, where they were looked upon as odd and indeed rather comical figures, and where they had difficulty in making themselves understood. It took them fully ten days to reach London, where they had to maintain expensive establishments at their own charges.

George Dempster, Member for the Perth group of burghs, managed quite well as long as he was single, because he held some good shares in the East India Company, and though he resented party discipline when the House divided, he was faithfully present as a general rule. In 1775 however he married, and wrote as follows to his friend Adam Fergusson: 'I have great doubts if I shall be in town this winter, and although perhaps at bottom my only reason for not coming is an unwillingness to leave my dear wife on a bleake Scotch hill by herself and my inability to bear the expence of a London jaunt and residence en famille, yet I have more solid and manly ones without which the first would not have operated. I have long thought . . . that unless one preserves a little freedom and independency in Parliament to act in every question and to vote agreeably to the suggestions of one's own mind, a seat in Parliament is a seat on thorns and rusty nails.'

Few of Dempster's constituents would be any the wiser about his decision not to attend Parliament that winter. As newspapers were scanty and ill informed, especially in Scotland, ordinary people did not know what was being said in Parliament or by whom.

Between 1707 and 1789 only three Scotsmen reached Cabinet rank, and their total service amounted to less than ten years. The first Scot to attain high office and to hold it for a long time was one who perfected the art of managing Scottish elections to a degree attained by no previous individual. His services to the Government were therefore so important that he was worth promotion. That he was also an exceedingly able man made him the more successful. He was Henry Dundas, who became later in life the first Lord Melville.

Dundas was very gifted. He was also kindly in disposition, impenitently Scots in diction, phenomenally ambitious and capable of more sustained hard work than one could believe possible. He was not an original thinker and he did not believe that any change in the political set-up could do good. In 1766, when he was twenty-four, Dundas became Solicitor-General for Scotland, eight years later Lord Advocate. In 1782, he was made a Privy Councillor and Treasurer of the Navy, a post which he held for many years, and which ultimately proved his undoing.

The position of Dundas became even stronger in 1783, when Pitt became Prime Minister, for these two were close friends. In 1784, Dundas introduced Pitt's India Bill: under its terms, he became the most powerful member, and subsequently President of the Board of Control for India, a responsibility which he shouldered with infinite personal care until 1801. In spite of this, Dundas accepted the post of Home Secretary in 1791, just when the unrest caused by the impact of the French Revolution was at its height. Indefatigable and supremely confident, he undertook in addition to his other work the War Office and the direction of operations against Napoleon, for some six or seven years. From 1782 onwards therefore, he wielded immeasurable authority, and among all his other commitments he found time to organize Scottish elections with scrupulous care and success.

Lord Cockburn, a consistent Whig during the long period of Tory ascendancy, said of Dundas, 'his business consisted in laying forty-five Scotch members at the feet of the Government.' Dundas would probably have found little objection to this statement, except that to his regret he only once achieved more than 39. He was certain that Pitt could not manage the nation's affairs without his support and he entertained no criticism of the unreformed constitution. The control he established over Scottish elections was based on his friendships with all the great land-owners—to many of whom he was related—and also with the leading business men, lawyers and Town Councillors. He relied too on the literally innumerable offices and posts which were in his gift. Lord Cockburn listed 'the pulpit, the bench, the bar, the colleges, the parliamentary electors, the press, the magistracy, the local institutions' as being under the control of this 'absolute dictator of Scotland', who now became known as Harry the Ninth. Cockburn could have added an equally comprehensive list of appointments in India, where the 'Scotticization' practised by Dundas caused much criticism.

It was the American War of Independence which first stirred Scotland into awareness of politics. Criticism of its conduct led to debate upon the merits of the Government responsible, and thence to enquiry about the electoral system which had thrown up such a Government. A movement was launched to check the abuse of fictitious votes in the shire elections. Efforts had indeed been made before with no result, but in 1782 twenty-three counties sent delegates to a meeting in Edinburgh to draft a bill dealing with the scandal.

At the same time the Whig advocate, Archibald Fletcher, organized a drive to reform municipal government. Throughout the 1780s, committees met, reports were published, petitions lodged: the corrupt state of the burghs was revealed. Some towns were deeply in debt, others almost bankrupt, all were ill-provided with public works, there was no legal authority competent to audit burgh accounts, the self-elective councils had fallen into the hands of dishonest family cabals. That these councillors were the only persons entitled to vote inflamed public opinion, especially amongst the Whigs, who were now aware of the grave social evils caused by the Industrial Revolution and who therefore wanted fundamental reform.

Dundas headed off all these various pressures by procrastination. He was largely responsible for the repression during the 1780s of all attempts at reform. Had Scottish democracy reached a more mature state, had their elections been even a little less shackled, Scotsmen might have succeeded in improving municipal government before the cataclysm of the French Revolution. Their success would have been infectious and other reforms might have followed.

The French Revolution set off the dynamite. Poets and artists, advocates and professors, ministers and business men in Scotland hailed it with delight, Scottish working-men took it up as the beginning of a new age. Everybody wanted news, and there was a sudden demand for newspapers. It was in English journals that Scotsmen first read long extracts from Burke's *Reflections on the French Revolution*, a work which stimulated an outburst of talking, writing and debating in Scotland.

In 1791 and 1792 there followed the two parts of Tom Paine's inflammatory gospel, *The Rights of Man*, available at 2d. each. Again, no part of Britain welcomed this heady mixture with more enthusiasm than Scotland, indeed it was claimed that Bunyan's *Pilgrim's Progress* was now forever superseded as the cottagers' favourite. The equality of man and his natural rights were discussed in almost every household, nor did the philosophy lack its poet. Burns delighted the democratically minded by such verses as the following, from 'Man was Made to Mourn':

> *If I'm design'd yon lordling's slave,*
> *By Nature's law design'd,*
> *Why was an independent wish*
> *E'er planted in my mind?*
> *If not, why am I subject to*
> *His cruelty or scorn?*

Even better known was 'Is there, for honest Povetry', which included:

> *Ye see yon birkie ca'd a lord,*
> *Wha struts and stares and a' that,*
> *Tho' hundreds worship at his word,*
> *He's but a coof for a' that,*
> *For a' that and a' that,*
> *His riband, star and a' that,*
> *The man of independent mind*
> *He looks an' laughs at a' that.*

During the 1790s, Harry the Ninth found Scottish affairs more difficult than any previous 'manager'. People were on fire with excitement over the new ideas. Even religious circles were affected by an unprecedented outburst of zeal for lay preaching and foreign missions; and hot denunciations of the slave trade flowed forth in support of Wilberforce. Agitation was exacerbated by the Tory policy on agriculture, for this condoned the enclosures for sheep-farming, and it also upheld the Corn Bills, which virtually excluded foreign wheat and caused home produce to soar in price.

In 1793 the war against France broke out and was denounced by certain factions in Scotland, where popular disturbances made conditions in all the big cities unpredictable, and where contacts with Jacobins were being fostered. The Government was also alarmed by the rapidly growing political organizations of the day, the Corresponding Societies and the Association of the Friends of the People. Their aims were to reform the British constitution, to extend the franchise, to shorten Parliaments, to increase the hold of the public over its chosen leaders.

Dundas and his underlings mistakenly supposed that all these political associations identified reform with revolution. The Society of the Friends of the People was supported by serious-minded Whigs like Archibald Fletcher, who would have nothing to do with violence and whose methods were quite alien to those of the more extreme reformers. One of the tragedies of the time was that during the 1780s, when necessary political reform could have been peaceably introduced, it was stifled, and that during the 1790s its prophets were identified by Tories with leaders of street fights and shouters of unpatriotic slogans.

The Reel o' Tullochgorum: Walter Geikie, (1795–1837).

By courtesy of the Mitchell Library, Glasgow.

Parliament and Politics

In 1793, the Government announced that it was seditious to possess or disseminate any of Paine's publications, and a series of notorious State trials began, which continued intermittently for nearly thirty years of repression. Most scandalous of all were the trials of Muir, Margarot, Gerrald and Skirving. They were leaders in the Scottish Corresponding Societies and suspected of Jacobinism, the ogre of the age and equivalent in official eyes to bare faced treason. In 1793 these four men were convicted and sent to Botany Bay for fourteen years each, a vicious sentence unprecedented in judicial annals and in any case of doubtful legal validity. The proceedings were conducted in Edinburgh by Lord Braxfield, who made use of packed juries, Government spies, subsidized press agents and vitriolic declamation. His name now ranks in history with that of Judge Jeffreys.

In the result, Paine's works became much more popular in Scotland, but the political organizations were driven underground, the electoral abuses continued, and deep, dangerous hatred of the Government festered everywhere, nourished by acute economic distress. Dundas remained unshaken in his satisfaction as to the Government's policy. His grip on the Scottish electorate was probably at its height in 1796, for in spite of the problems of the war, and of India, his tireless industry achieved in that year's General Election the return of at least thirty-nine Government 'yes-men' out of the forty-five Scottish M.P.s.

Pitt's administration was interrupted in 1801 by the brief and inglorious service of Addington, whose fall in 1804 ushered in another spell of the old régime, with Dundas again in high office as First Lord of the Admiralty. In 1805, however, the Commissioners of Naval Inquiry published their shattering tenth report. This revealed that while Dundas had been Treasurer of the Navy the Paymaster had speculated on a huge scale, and to his own large profit, with Navy funds. His financial transactions included loans to his chief, Dundas. Dundas was therefore impeached, that is to say, tried before the House of Lords, on the charge of improper handling of public funds. Naturally such a development cost him all his public offices and unleashed a pack of noisy denigrators who voiced the country's pent-up resentment.

Dundas was acquitted on all charges, a decision which some people considered a gross miscarriage of justice. In Scotland it was greeted by general and sincere rejoicing, for one of the strangest facts about Dundas was his popularity in his own country, in both the main political camps. Whigs as well as Tories north of the Border were convinced that if irregularities had taken place Dundas had allowed them inadvertently, since he was never personally greedy for cash, he was far too busy to examine the Paymaster's proceedings, and had he been minded to filch public moneys he could have done so on a much vaster scale. His acquittal therefore was acclaimed with neighbourly celebrations, and during the remaining five years of his life Dundas recovered a good deal of the respect he had formerly enjoyed. Nonetheless, his fall was a portentous affair, and heralded a new era, for never again did any one man achieve such an asphyxiating grasp on the political machine.

After Napoleon's defeat, Britain entered upon one of the most agitated post-war periods of national malaise recorded in her history. The troubles were economic, caused by the strain of twenty-three years of war, and by the Industrial Revolution. Great hopes were set on electoral reform, and every effort was now renewed to achieve this.

When at last the long-needed Reform Bill of 1832 did become law, it introduced some effective changes for Scotland. Eight new burghs were created, so that after this there were 53 Scottish Members. In the re-allocation of seats, Edinburgh and Glasgow were given two members each; some non-royal burghs were recognized, among them Paisley and Greenock; Dundee, Aberdeen and Perth were given one member each. In these ways, some recognition was made of industrial expansion and so the business element now had a voice at Westminster. The franchise was at the same time widened to include in the burghs all householders who paid £10 in rates; while in the shires, owners of property valued at £10, with occupiers of land worth £50, and leased for not less than nineteen years, were also given the vote.

Scorn has been poured on these changes by some historians, on the grounds that they benefited only the middle classes and excluded all the workers in mine, mill, factory and field. This criticism is at once valid and unrealistic. The middle classes were indeed given the right to vote, while the working people in Scotland had to wait for it, like those in England, till 1867 and 1884, when they got it by stages. The delay was unfortunate in many ways, but understandable. It is unrealistic to blame people for moving at the contemporary pace. Not until the mid-19th century did Britain divorce electoral responsibility from property qualifications, and indeed it was not until much later that the country's educational system was sufficiently advanced to carry anything like universal suffrage for men. Until the schools and the social services were developed, and secret ballot introduced, the vast majority of working people on both sides of the Border could have been cruelly exploited in the exercise of votes, by employers and others who already had too much power over them. Had the right to vote been given to all and sundry in 1832, it is open to question whether the 19th century problems caused by social and economic tension would have been more equitably handled.

Complete re-organization of municipal government followed the reform of Parliament. That this was necessary has already been shown: it now became urgent because of the eight new burghs formed in 1832, for which no traditional constitution existed, and because if all the £10 householders were to assist in electing M.P.s, burgh elections could obviously no longer be confined to a charmed circle. By the Act of 1833 therefore, councillors were also to be chosen by £10 householders, at annual municipal elections, and each year one-third of each burgh council was to resign. This marked a real advance in the popular conception of local government, and gone forever were the days when self-elected bodies of councillors could neglect municipal well-being, filch the public funds, and rest assured that no legal authority could audit their accounts.

Because of the reforms in parliamentary and local government, Scottish people became much more interested in politics. There was some purpose in it all now that their representatives could exercise real influence. In reaction against the years of Tory mismanagement, the burghs voted almost solidly Liberal, and so did some of the shires, for something like fifty years. In the

311

1880s, the Irish Home Rule controversy altered things, but till then the Liberal Party's ascendancy at Westminster was rarely interrupted: its strength derived to a great degree from the consistent backing of the Scottish constituencies.

Scottish people quickly took the Liberal principal of Free Trade to their hearts. North of the Border, Duncan McLaren was the inspiration of the campaign to abolish the Corn Laws, and Cobden and Bright had no more effective colleague on this project anywhere in the United Kingdom. They wanted to do away with the protective taxes on foreign grain, so that bread could become cheaper, in the interests of the working people in the cities. It was ironical that this reform, so ardently desired by the Liberals, was achieved in 1847 when the Conservatives were in power for a short time under Sir Robert Peel. His own party was hotly indignant with Peel for this daring change of policy, but he never regretted it because the dreadful Potato Famine of 1846 made it urgently necessary to provide cheap food quickly. After this, the Liberals' faith in Free Trade was stronger than ever.

Duncan McLaren's status was still further enhanced by his fight for a second Parliamentary Reform Bill. He wanted working men to be given votes, and he was determined too that Scotland should have more representatives. He worked up enormous enthusiasm for these ideas in Scotland and he made some most telling speeches in the House. But again it was a Conservative Government, this time under Disraeli, which brought in the new Electoral Reform Bill in 1868. By this, votes were given to burgh householders, and Scottish members were increased in number from 53 to 60.

Included among new voters both in Scotland and in England, there were now thousands of industrial employees, many of whom were illiterate. For this reason, important educational reforms were set going, so that there could be a larger number of schools, and school attendance was made free and compulsory up to the age of twelve. A revolution in the nation's ideas and habits was represented by this ruling, which aroused grave criticism, but even the sceptics thought that men who were entitled to vote should be able to read. The schools which were opened in the 1870s and 1880s were grim establishments and the teaching administered in them was often very poor in quality. But until their thirteenth birthdays children were now kept out of the mills and shops and factories; though nobody could claim that they were being educated towards political responsibility, small boys were at least spared some physical strains.

To give the vote to thousands of industrial wage-earners was no democratic measure while elections were conducted in public by counting hands, because people could be so readily intimidated by their employers. Gladstone's Secret Ballot Act of 1872 was therefore a most necessary sequel to the Reform Act of 1868. It remained now to give agricultural workers the same rights as their relatives in the cities, and this was done by the Liberal Government of 1884, which introduced manhood suffrage. So far the idea of votes for women was confined to a few visionaries, deemed by society at all levels to be unstable and worth no serious consideration. The 1884 Act again increased Scotland's representation at Westminster, from 60 to 72. Thus, in G. S. Pryde's phrase, Scotland was at last accorded 'her proper share by population'.

The great changes in the political scene stimulated some important developments in journalism, which was also affected by speedier transport.

In the early years of the 19th century, Scottish newspapers provided dull reading, at least by modern standards. This was partly because they were always late with their information, a fact which could not be helped until the railway and the telegraph improved communications. Scottish editors relied for all but local news on excerpts from the English press, sent north with the mails, and the news they published was almost unadorned by any comment. *The Newspaper in Scotland*, by R. M. W. Cowan, a book full of interest, shows that until the franchise was widened journalism was necessarily a disappointing business—'to harangue a voteless public with leading articles would have been merely beating the air.' Uninspiring as they seem to us, the newspapers were however eagerly read. While the circulation was limited— the *Glasgow Herald* in 1815 was bought by about 1,100 people— copies were borrowed and handed on from house to house, until they must have been almost thumbed to pieces.

When *The Scotsman* was founded in 1817, it was a weekly paper, costing 10d. a copy, a sum equivalent to almost the whole of a working man's daily wage. It made an immediate impression, because it carried a front-page leader and because it adopted a bold and fresh approach, supporting unorthodox ideas about Church and State, and attacking vested interest in both. It was the first newspaper which showed the privileged classes how unpopular they were and for what reasons, though even this progressive organ was complacent about industrial conditions.

Not until the days of railway mania could Scotland support a daily newspaper. The first in the field, founded in 1847, was the *North British Daily Mail.* The main interest was political, though public executions were popular items and always described in lurid detail. Then as now, the reading public liked murders, atrocities and abnormalities to be well documented. J. Y. Simpson's discovery of chloroform in 1847, by contrast, passed almost unnoticed.

The repeal of stamp duties and taxes on advertisements and on paper, all carried through in the 1850s, led to an immediate expansion in journalistic enterprise. In 1852, Scotland had 75 newspapers, in 1856, 105. Many of the newly founded ones were dailies, some published at a penny each, some running to as many as eight pages. Some were local, some national. Every kind of political opinion was now reflected in the press, which could provide ample information and comment upon parliamentary affairs, especially after 1861, when Scottish agents for the first time were allowed independent access to the Press Gallery in the House of Commons.

Had George Dempster lived to see these things happen, he might have found fresh reasons for declaring that a seat in Parliament was one on 'thorns and rusty nails', but the days of political apathy were over, so far as Scotland was concerned. The reform of the electoral system and the development of journalism meant that men of all occupations and every rank could take an active share in the political controversies of their day.

CHAPTER 27

Poverty

The new resources made available during the Industrial Revolution were not so manipulated as to increase the well-being of society as a whole, indeed misery seemed to develop in proportion to man's power over natural forces. As the pace of industry accelerated and population grew, horrifying epidemics swept across the whole United Kingdom, some of a familiar nature, some hitherto uncommon.

Scotland's share in the troubles of the age was complicated by the traditional architecture of her towns, which invited rather than checked epidemic infection; the mass migrations of Highlanders and Irishmen contributed to the congestion in the cities; inflexible systems of law and local government made public control of abuses and relief of destitution doubly difficult. Poverty seems to have been worse in Scottish towns than anywhere else at this time. Many decades elapsed before even well-intentioned and compassionate thinkers fully diagnosed the causes of the trouble or understood its implications.

Scottish urban architecture was influenced by continental designs and also conditioned by the intractable nature of local weather and geography. For reasons of defence and because of steep hillsides, towns were too compact, and tall stone tenements were crammed together in narrow streets. Water for all purposes had to be fetched from public wells or bought in stoups from vendors, then carried up precipitous lanes and stairways. Garbage could only be disposed of by its owners throwing it out of their windows or dumping it in their backyards, around which were clutters of pigsties, stables and dairies. As the population increased, slaughter-houses and tanneries multiplied in ground-floor premises, adding to the traditional accumulations of filth and smells. The farmers who lived nearby knew how valuable much of this heterogeneous sewage and dung could be to them as manure for their fields and they came and bought it by the cartload. People therefore literally treasured their filth in steaming, sodden middens which they piled at their doors with ash and other rubbish, precious capital upon which to rely for the rent.

Burgh councils made repeated attempts to keep the main thoroughfares reasonably clean, but no effort was spent on the networks of vennels and wynds or on the staircases. The tall, solid tenements proved a deadly legacy to the 19th century, becoming more and more impregnated with dirt and vermin: to introduce water-pipes and water-closets to buildings of such height involved far greater expense and skill than was needed for houses or cottages. That people were able to make money from their dunghills meant that there was obstinate opposition to housing reform.

In periods of rapid industrial development, the population of towns always tends to increase at a sharpened pace. This was so in Scotland, as elsewhere in Britain. New building however was not undertaken to anything like the necessary extent, and so people began the disastrous habit of sub-letting and sharing their dwellings, landlords allowed mean hovels and sheds to be thrown up in the backyards, while cellars and basements were rented for all kinds of unsuitable purposes.

The upward trend of the population in the cities was accelerated by the Highland evictions, which sent thousands of destitute families to add to the congestion. These were Gaelic speakers, who had difficulty in making themselves understood and were accustomed to rural ways. Cut off from their traditions, reduced already by privation to poor health, perplexed and disillusioned, they had everything against them in the competitive scramble for house-room and employment.

Along with the Highlanders, came the Irish, in even worse case. Shipping companies brought them at specially reduced rates and disembarked them in hordes every week, especially during the early 19th century. By 1831, there were 35,554 Irish people in Glasgow alone, and they came in even larger numbers after the Potato Famine of 1846. These people were Roman

Libberton Wynd: Walter Geikie, (1795-1837).

By courtesy of the Mitchell Library, Glasgow.

Catholics, and like the Highlanders quite unprepared for the particular miseries of city life, though they were well accustomed to desperate poverty.

In 1740, just over 17,000 people were living in Glasgow: by 1791 the number had grown, through industrial progress, to 66,000—a figure well below that of Edinburgh, where there were between 80,000 and 90,000 people. After the turn of the century, Glasgow's industrial expansion was speeded up because of the heavy industries, and during the same years the influx from the Highlands and from Ireland became unceasing: by 1831 therefore, there were nearly 203,000 people in Glasgow, which was now the most highly populated city in Scotland, and thirty years later the figure, almost doubled, had reached 395,503. Other cities in the industrial belt had the same kind of experience, though the scale and speed of the increase naturally varied. Common to them all however was the insoluble problem of poverty and distress.

The early 19th century was a transition period, when processes were rapidly changing, and artisans were liable to find themselves on the street without notice and with no chance of finding another job of their own type. The early stages of automation made many skills redundant and when new inventions deprived people of their accustomed work there was no question of compensation or assistance. The unemployed were offered no guidance by the authorities, and their numbers were swollen by those crowds of unskilled labourers who were thrown out of work by the unpredictable rhythm of over- and under-production. Even when the poorer people were in regular work they were paid on such miserable scales that they recruited all possible members of their families to the task of earning, although this damaged the health of all but the most robust.

The invention of lighter machines meant that women and children could be used in processes formerly reserved for men. The introduction of gas lighting early in the 19th century lengthened the working day in the factories. As the mills became more fully mechanized, much larger numbers of workers were employed, so that relationships between employers and operatives became steadily less personal, factory discipline more rigid and inhumane.

In the 1830s, children from six and seven upwards were employed in the cotton mills at 1/6d. to 2/- a week. A Select Committee of the House of Commons heard evidence in 1832 about the conditions in which children were working. Before this Committee, Peter Smart, overseer of a Dundee flax mill, described children rising from bed at 4 a.m., walking to work, which began at 4.55, and continuing all day till 7.30 p.m. A millowner at Duntruin admitted that the children in his mill had to be beaten with straps to keep them at their tasks. Those whom he employed were orphans from Edinburgh, housed in a bothy which was locked and barred all night, to prevent their running away, and no clock was allowed on the premises lest the older ones should notice when they were doing overtime. These are not isolated incidents: evidence shows that it was quite as common to find such things happening in Scottish as in English factories. Children were also used in coal-mines, where they worked fourteen hours daily in the East, eleven to thirteen in the West, often in the dark and often standing in water. Examples of this were quoted in Parliament during the debates preceding the passage of the Mines Act in 1842.

Women were employed in the coal-mines as hauliers, to drag trucks on all fours along the narrow passageways from the coal face to the cages: these dark passages were often deep in slush and their gradients sometimes reached 1 in 6 or 7. Hugh Miller, the Cromarty geologist, quoted cases of women weeping bitterly with the effort of dragging coal in this way, and other writers in the early 19th century expressed their horror at seeing girls and women crying under their loads. The Mines Act of 1842 put a stop to the employment of women and children underground.

Women were employed much more than men in the textile industries, but they also worked in mills and factories of many kinds. The normal day's work lasted 13 or 14 hours, and 17 was not unknown. Women's wages in the early 19th century generally varied from 4/- to 8/- a week, but in periods of slump they would drop. In 1851 a factory inspector reported that many women were earning as little as 3/-. The fact that female labour was so regularly used helps to account for the heavy incidence of sickness among small children, as infants who were too young to go

318

to work had to be cared for by the very old or by nobody at all. In 1861 the Registrar-General stated that 25 per cent. of children under one year died in the families of cotton operatives: the equivalent figure for agricultural workers, whose women had more chance to look after their babies, was 12 per cent.

Men's wages varied from one industry to another and reacted also to the swing between over- and under-production. In 1825 an Aberdeenshire weaver earned 13/- a week, with which he fed and clothed a family of six, paying school fees for three and 10/- a year for pew rent in church. By 1836 the same work brought him in 8/- and the price of meal had risen. During the 1830s and 1840s weavers' wages dropped to 4/- and 5/-, while mechanics could earn anything up to 18/-. Railway navvies in 1838 were paid 10/-, in 1853 12/-. The purchasing power of money was much greater in the 19th century than now, but men's wages were not related to any subsistence level; indeed the idea that a subsistence level existed, that wages which fell below it would make for malnutrition, was unknown until the 20th century.

The factory buildings had no lavatories, wash-rooms, first-aid centres or feeding arrangements; ventilation was not understood, heating not provided, except in textile mills where it was necessary for the texture of woven goods. Modern knowledge of time and motion in relation to industrial fatigue had yet to be born. With inadequately fenced machinery and ill-planned scaffolding, men working 60-70 hours a week were liable to accidents, but no compensation for injury was given nor could casualties be treated on the spot.

During the first two decades of the 19th century, a unique effort to reform factory conditions was made at New Lanark by Robert Owen, David Dale's Welsh son-in-law. Owen encouraged his employees to form friendly societies for the assistance of the sick and bereaved, and he organized a store where goods of reasonable quality could be bought at 75 per cent. of the normal price. He also undertook strenuous efforts to make houses, streets, lanes and workshops in New Lanark much cleaner. His campaign was remarkably successful and refuse and filth no longer collected at every corner and doorway; lime-washing of buildings was introduced, water made available for personal

319

hygiene. Somehow this remarkable man won the confidence of his people and he contrived to induce in them a certain pride in their community and craft. Owen's reforms reduced drunkenness and improved general health. In the face of indignant expostulation from other industrialists, he reduced the working hours in his mills to 10¾ per day and he refused to engage children below the age of ten. For these youngsters, he started a huge school which was run on principles quite new to Scots people. Corporal punishment and angry reproof were not allowed, music, dancing and drill were taught, history, geography and botany included in the curriculum, visual aids largely employed. The expenses involved were met from the profits of the factory store.

Much of Owen's work was far in advance of his times. His views on labour management and factory organization aroused angry criticism among the leaders of industry at home and he was discredited because he wanted legislation to prevent more than ten hours being worked per day in the mills; also because his religious views were unorthodox.

In spite of his humanitarian methods he made himself wealthy and had he remained in Scotland he might have convinced people that it pays to consider the welfare of factory hands. Unfortunately, obsessed with the desire to found an ideal society, he departed to America, where he started a community at New Harmony, Pittsburg.

The general conditions in Scottish industry went from bad to worse, and working people turned to the form of escape most easily available. Drunkenness among adults and teenagers became so common that revolting scenes were everyday occurrences in the city streets and also in the barracks and bothies of rural workers. Hugh Miller began his working life as a stonemason's apprentice, when he was about fourteen, just after the Napoleonic wars. The heavy labour exhausted him. In his book, *My Schools and Schoolmasters*, he later described how he and his companions sought and found relief in the 'ardent spirits of the dram-shop', which 'gave lightness and energy to both body and mind and substituted for a state of dullness and gloom one of exhilaration and enjoyment. Usquebaugh (whisky) was simply happiness doled out by the glass and sold by the gill'. This kind of happiness brought its own reaction and caused much harm; and it was sought more in Scotland than anywhere else in the United Kingdom. In 1840 seven pints of spirits were consumed per head per annum in England, 13 in Ireland and 23 in Scotland. The *Scotsman* published in 1853 a set of figures cynically termed the 'drunken statistics' which suggested that Glasgow was three times more drunken than Edinburgh and five times more so than London.

Why should Scottish working people have been more given to excessive drinking than their English neighbours? It was partly because Scottish housing was worse than English and a higher percentage of people were thankful to find anywhere to go after work other than their overcrowded, smelly little homes. By tradition too, it has always been harder to remain sober after an hour or so in a Scots pub than in an English one. In the Scottish licensed house, the bar was the most important piece of furniture, the sale and rapid consumption of liquor the prime activity: there was much less sitting about, chatting, playing skittles and general passing of time than in similar English establishments. The rigid administration of Poor Relief, much more stringent in Scotland than in England, offered no adequate help to the destitute: during the Napoleonic wars and the epidemics, breadwinners in vast numbers of families were lost. Drink seemed the only alleviation available, and it was recklessly used.

It is understandable that health could not be maintained among working-class families and that illness was chronic and virulent among them. They suffered from deficiency diseases through lack of nourishment, because their diet consisted almost entirely of farinaceous foods, particularly porridge and potatoes. Pregnant women remained at work till the last possible moment, even when they were hauling heavy weights. Their babies were born in their own filthy dwellings because there was not enough provision for midwifery in the hospitals; and by reason of rickets —which can be caused by malnutrition—these women often suffered from deformities of the pelvis, which made delivery very difficult. As soon as they possibly could, the mothers would struggle back to work, so that the children really had no chance.

Crippling bone diseases and unsightly skin eruptions were every-day matters in the city slums, where children and young people died regularly of illnesses nowadays no longer considered deadly. In certain industries, notably mining and cotton-spinning, the prime killers of young adults were lung complaints, though tuberculosis was everybody's enemy and a lethal agent even among the well-to-do.

The health problem which probably frightened people most was the curse of epidemics. Smallpox was the most familiar of these from the 17th century onwards, and it broke out over and again in the 18th, sweeping the Highlands and raging in the slums. It killed more young children than any other disease and was brutally termed 'the poor man's friend', so effectively did it reduce the families of the destitute. Inoculation was used fairly extensively from the 1730s onwards, but this was dangerous in itself as it often brought on full-scale attacks of the disease, and it certainly proved no check. Between 1744 and 1763, 10 per cent. of all deaths in Edinburgh, one death in every six in Kilmarnock, were caused by this loathsome 'poor man's friend'. Only when the great physician, Edward Jenner, hit on the technique of vaccination was the disease brought under control. Between 1801 and 1806, 10,000 people in Glasgow were vaccinated free of charge, and there was a dramatic drop in the scale of smallpox mortality. People soon became casual and careless about vaccination however and then fresh outbreaks would occur, as in 1817 and 1818.

The illness termed 'fever' was dreaded as much as smallpox. This generic term covered typhus and typhoid and other allied infections. It was always active in the overcrowded city districts, but from time to time, in cycles which became ominously shorter, mass epidemics of it would break out, with death rates far surpassing anything else except cholera. This additional scourge originated in the Far East, infected Europe and reached England early in 1831. Like the Black Death of medieval times, cholera pursued its path northwards, and in October 1831 it began its work in Glasgow. During 1832 its effects were such that cholera news in Britain that year superseded all other and even distracted attention from the public excitement over the Reform

Bill. Cholera re-appeared at intervals, particularly in 1848 and 1849 and again, with savage results, in 1853; by 1866 it was still busy in Glasgow. In 1867, a Public Health Act was framed with special reference to Scotland in order to improve sewage control and sanitation in general—a measure brought about because the cholera scourge was so serious.

Even though life was considered a cheap commodity, people gradually became aware that the mortality rates were worth study. In 1755, a minister called Dr. Webster distributed questionnaires on vital statistics to colleagues in Highland parishes. In the result he estimated that half the people born in these parishes died before reaching the age of eleven, and a quarter of the remainder died before their forty-third birthdays. Child mortality remained as a national problem for long after Webster's day. In 1790, 63 per cent. of all the deaths in Scotland were among children; after vaccination was introduced there was some improvement, but by 1838 child mortality still accounted for over 50 per cent. of the whole figure for Scotland. In 1842, the average length of life in Britain was 46 years, in British cities as a whole, 38 years : in Glasgow it was 30.6 years.

While the picture was black enough as a general rule, there were special places and dates for which the vital statistics were really frightening. Between 1833 and 1839—a bad period as regards public health—the mortality rate for England and Wales was 1 in 48, for Scotland 1 in 45, for problem parishes such as St. David's, Dundee, 1 in 32. During the cholera year, 1832, it reached 1 in 21 in Glasgow, where 1 in 24 or 26 was common enough throughout the 1830s. The evidence of the fever years began to frighten the public, for it became evident that the death-dealing diseases had no proper respect for persons. Begin as they might and usually did in poverty-stricken tenements, the epidemics had no difficulty in penetrating the adjacent stairs and closes leading to the houses of the rich and the influential.

The city doctors of the 19th century spared no pains to publish the truth as they saw it. One cannot but admire the medical men who tended the very poor during those terrible decades. Many of them committed their findings to paper and the anger in which they wrote flares up at the reader who looks through the reports with any sensitivity. Medical opinion was emphatic that epidemics were caused by housing structurally unfit even for animals; that infectious illness multiplied in the slum areas because of the lack of drains and sewers; that the fields irrigated with city filth, such as those adjacent to Holyrood House, were poison dépots for infected air; that people who were herded together like beasts and at the same time undernourished and overworked were bound to fall ill once any virulent germ was at work. The doctors also emphasized that the years of fever epidemic often coincided with those of economic slump when unemployment became common and malnutrition bordered on starvation.

Among business men and employers there was strong prejudice against interference with conditions in the factories and the city slums. They were afraid that efforts at reform would deprive them of financial profit by reducing production, but they were also very much influenced by Adam Smith's successors. 'Laissez faire' was the basis both of the Liberal Party's free trade principles and also of its distaste for regulating the interaction of supply and demand in business. This meant that statutory reform was long in coming, which suited the industrialists very well. Not until the end of the 19th century did ordinary people of middle-class upbringing begin to realize how terrible were the abuses needing reform: and even then far too many were apt to adopt the attitude that 'such things must be' in a modern community. As the great Whig Solicitor-General Lord Cockburn asked himself in the 1830s: 'Are not millions of starving people the necessary sloughs of a very manufacturing nation?'

Meanwhile there was no machinery of local government to set going the wholesale campaigns needed in the cities. Until 1833, burgh councils were not empowered to undertake local administration of health and hygiene, and it was not for some decades after that date that people became courageous or experienced enough to tackle it. Even then the rigidities of the law held up much progress, property-owners defended themselves by every traditional and legal means, and only when a building was in such a state that collapse was imminent could it be termed, according to Scottish usage, a 'nuisance' within the technical meaning of the word.

When fever epidemics, and finally cholera scares, at last shocked the authorities into action, there was hopeless confusion. The Government issued orders for the streets to be cleansed, dwellings lime-washed, patients admitted to hospital, contacts isolated, vagrancy prohibited. Instructions flowed, and were often, as is their way, contradictory; often too, there existed in the towns no official body legally competent to carry them through; nor were there enough hospital beds, or proper means by which to enforce quarantine. The end of the story was always that, once the particular crisis in question passed over, all the preventive measures were dropped and the situation was restored to the status quo till the next outbreak. But the evidence of the medical profession accumulated and was endorsed from other sources. In 1840, Captain Miller, Chief Constable of Glasgow, reported to the British Association, then meeting in the city, that they could see there 'an accumulated mass of squalid wretchedness which is probably unequalled in any town of the British Dominions'. Not long after, the great British sanitarian, Edwin Chadwick, stated that he had never seen misery equal to Glasgow's in any other British city, and reckoned it worse than anything to be found in Europe: second to Glasgow, he ranked Edinburgh.

Poor Relief was meanly administered in Scotland. The principles on which it was organized had been set out in 1579, in an Act designed both to stamp out vagrancy and begging and to assist 'pure, impotent and aged persones'. Kirk sessions had charge of such relief as was given and their funds came from church collections. Voluntary giving for the poor was emphasized as the duty of Christians and there was an almost fanatical hostility to any kind of centrally organized or assessed tax for the purpose. The genuine poor were sharply distinguished in the public mind from able-bodied idlers, who were disqualified from assistance and supposed to be packed off to the parishes of their birth. The people who were considered needy were divided into two categories: the 'ordinary' poor, namely the old and disabled, and the 'occasional' poor, those normally able-bodied who were temporarily impeded by sickness. It never occurred to the authorities that anybody actually in work could be classed as 'poor', even though wages were so low. This was one of the reasons why destitution among unskilled labourers and their families was for so long unalleviated. Money grants were allotted by the Kirk Sessions to the 'ordinary' poor, on a scale designed to cover only rent, or part of it. Other necessities were supposed to be met by private charity, though for this nobody was supposed to beg. In no case was assistance given unless the poor concerned had been three years resident in the parish, a qualification often difficult to prove. In 1839, St. David's parish, Dundee, had 161 persons receiving relief, out of an industrial and impoverished population of 9,000, in which almost every sixth family was fatherless and therefore supported by a widow. Grants were given at the rate of 1/- or 1/6d. per head per week to persons who would have qualified in England for 4/- to 7/6d. The 'occasional' poor were given nothing, on the grounds that they should draw on reserves accumulated during periods of employment!

There was no tradition of institutional assistance in Scotland, where by 1839 there were only four poorhouses, three in Edinburgh and one in Paisley, though there were some 'hospitals' designed for the support of the aged. The only practical relief measures adopted by the authorities took the form of soup-kitchens which were set up in the cities during years of acute famine, such as 1783. In these periods Parliament sent thousands of pounds to northern and western parishes for the purchase and distribution of meal, while the soup-kitchens were busy in the cities. Towards the end of the 18th century there were times when over 10,000 people in Edinburgh were being fed at the public cost. These efforts were always regarded as temporary measures and discontinued at the earliest possible moment. Nobody thought that any permanent plans were called for to prevent the chronic want which was accepted as a normal feature of Scottish life in ordinary times.

Ingrained in the public mind was the idea that a man only became destitute or unemployed if he was lazy or immoral. Politicians did not understand the nature of the new industrial society, in which workers were at the mercy of economic forces that they could not control: unemployment was a national affliction, set going often enough by international trends, with results which no individual could avert by personal effort.

The religious leaders of the day did not understand either. The best ministers were deeply shocked by the conditions in the city parishes, but in the main they restricted their efforts to one field—that of Temperance. In this connection, clergymen of all denominations did achieve notable successes. There were 30,000 Irishmen connected with Temperance Societies run by Roman Catholic priests in Glasgow during the early 1840s. Sabbath School and Ragged School Movements were founded too, but the clergy fell far short of the medical practitioners in their general grasp and understanding of the social problems in their parishes.

Dr. Chalmers, the Moderator of the first United Free Church Assembly in 1843, exercised an influence over other Scottish ministers which must have retarded progress for many years. He diagnosed the nation's ills as flowing from 'deep inner dereliction of duty' and his remedies included the subdivision of larger parishes, a drive to improve day schools and Sabbath schools and the encouragement of 'saving' amongst the poor—'saving' when one earned 8/- or 10/- a week he evidently considered quite feasible. He thought that the abolition of the Corn Laws and the reduction of taxes on necessities would help, but the main part of the business, as he saw it, consisted in the building up of respectable habits. He declared each parish should maintain its own poor, that relief should be based on voluntary gifts locally collected by the charitable, that only those paupers who asked for help should be given it, after careful investigation. He had no understanding at all of the social interdependence now obtaining in industrial nations, nor of the great economic and social metamorphosis through which he was living; with an idealized picture of the old country parish in his mind, he set his face against the organization of properly planned relief by secular central authorities.

As early as 1817, Dr. Chalmers expressed his views, which no later experience caused him to modify. 'Which is nobler, to struggle with the difficulties of your situation, or to lay open your house and your circumstances to the scowl of the official inquisitor?' The *Glasgow Chronicle* took up this question in the following terms: 'This means in plain English: Is it nobler to suffer your wife and children to die of hunger in a world which God has stocked for your support, or to abate your pride so far as to solicit relief from the charity which religion inculcates and law has confirmed?' Chalmers' answer to this was that to take away a man's independence by giving him state-administered assistance would do his personality far more harm than physical wretchedness could inflict. He was also deeply impressed by the natural charity of the poor towards the poor. He was in charge of St. John's Parish, Glasgow, for many years, and in this huge slum district he did personal visiting assiduously, along with many voluntary assistants. They all paid tribute to the way in which the destitute tried to help each other and they all believed that this neighbourliness would be destroyed by state welfare schemes. Chalmers greatly influenced the founders of the Charity Organization Society in England, and he was supported in his hostility to officially organized welfare by a paper as avowedly liberal and progressive in its politics as *The Scotsman*.

At last, in January 1840, a different point of view was expressed, by a man well qualified to state it. This was Dr. W. P. Alison, who had had long and valuable experience of medical work in Edinburgh's slums. His pamphlet was called *Observations on the Management of the Poor in Scotland and its Effect on the Health of the Great Towns*. He exposed the evils so well-known to him and to his colleagues. He declared that expert, central administration of the Poor Law was needed, together with the provision of workhouses, improved hygiene, compulsory poor rates and— most significant and most distasteful to contemporary opinion— regular relief for the able-bodied unemployed.

All this was startling enough for thinkers of Chalmers' school. It was followed by a Commission of enquiry in 1843 and 1844, which examined the conditions described by Alison, and which led to a Poor Law Amendment Act for Scotland in 1845. This did *not* introduce relief for the able-bodied unemployed. It did however create a central Board of Supervision in Edinburgh charged with the general administration of poor relief in Scotland. Parish Boards were set up, each to appoint an Inspector of the

Poor, and to work in collaboration with the Central Board. It was also arranged that poorhouses should be built in all the big cities for the care of the destitute—and greatly did those poorhouses come to be hated, so rigorously were they run.

At last, too, Scotland was obliged to accept the principle of a legal poor rate, which was to be used for the assistance of those who were desperate, but who did not qualify for entry to a poorhouse. The sums paid were so niggardly that, by comparison, even the small pittances allowed in England seem generous, but they were an improvement on previous forms of assistance. Sometimes help was given in kind, as in the case of widow Ann Christie of South Uist. She was paralysed and she had four young children. Between November 18th, 1846, and February 19th, 1847, when she died, she received 10 pecks of meal. Her horse and her weaving-loom were sold after her death for £2 15s. 0d. to meet funeral expenses—she had no other saleable possessions as she had parted with everything else to find food for the children, who most illegally helped her by begging. The problem of poverty in Scotland was not solved by the Act of 1845 because it still had not dawned upon people that poverty could only be dealt with by wholesale raising of wages. Reformers were beginning to think in terms of relieving distress, but not of preventing it.

The Scottish Poor Law Amendment Act was passed at the time when the Chartist Movement was at its height. This had been founded in England by people who were disgusted both by the 1832 Reform Bill, which left the working classes without the vote, and by the English Poor Law of 1834, which put a stop to the supplementing of low wages with payments from the rates. The Chartists believed that only by radical reform of Parliament could social justice be achieved for the workers, because not until workers themselves were elected to the House of Commons would legislation to relieve poverty be countenanced. Their programme demanded votes for all adult males, secret ballot—to prevent employers and landowners from exploiting those under their power—equal electoral districts, payments of salaries to M.P.s, the abolition of property qualifications of M.P.s, and annual Parliaments. All these principles except the last have long since been adopted as rational bases of democratic government, but when they were first set out in the People's Charter conservative opinion was profoundly shocked.

Scottish Chartists took the proposals seriously and many recruits were drawn into the movement. Its story was very different from the parallel one in England. The Scottish middle classes were much attracted to the proposed reforms and Chartism drew them into closer sympathy with the working people, of whom however only the more prosperous and reflective were interested. Meetings, lectures and mass demonstrations were organized and supported all over the country, and two Chartist newspapers flourished for a number of years. One of these, the *True Scotsman*, actually had a wider circulation for a while than the original Edinburgh *Scotsman*. Chartist churches were founded, and these tried to link religion and politics: they even started schools, organized adult education, and launched a rather successful Temperance drive.

Throughout the short life of this movement, the Scottish branches insisted that peaceful propaganda and moral persuasion only must be used, and there was very much less extremism and violence associated with Chartism north of the Border than south. The reason for this difference was that in Scotland the explosive ingredients for a violent movement were missing. The really miserable were too miserable, too far down the abyss of suffering, to have the energy for such an affair as Chartism. This was why it was taken up by the middle classes and the more prosperous artisans rather than by the genuine poor. In England, the Poor Law of 1834 was considered so reactionary that industrial workers were stung into a fury of hostility which only needed the publication of the Charter in 1838 to become red-hot. Nobody was accustomed to public assistance in Scotland, indeed the grimly inadequate terms of the 1845 Act brought alleviation rather than disappointment, so that there was one factor the less for revolution.

Chartism collapsed in 1848, in the fiasco of the great Petition lodged at the House of Commons and instantly discredited because so many signatures appended to it were found to be faked. The movement left its mark in Scotland because it awakened people to new ideas and introduced them to fresh experience, but it did not touch the problem of poverty. The Factory Acts of 1833, 1844 and 1847, however, did something for young people and children. Hours of labour were modified a little, some educational facilities were made statutory, factory inspectors were appointed. These reforms were restricted to certain branches of industry only, inspection and penal action were grossly insufficient, and employers quickly found out how to evade them. The Mines Act of 1842 was a much more important advance because it put an end to the dreadful use of women and children in the pits.

The squalid city slums increased in extent and misery, and became breeding-grounds for sickness and crime, all through the 1840s and 1850s. In 1861, the census revealed that 35 per cent. of Scottish families lived in one room, whose average measurements would be 9 or 10 feet square, 7 or 8 feet high: 37 per cent. lived in two such rooms: 7,964 families lived in single rooms containing no window, but depending for ventilation and light upon the chimney and the door. An account was published in 1862 of the Middle Meal Market Stairs in Edinburgh, where 'there are 59 rooms, almost all separate dwelling houses, entered by a steep, dark, stone stair common to the whole. In these dwell 248 individuals (adults 197, children under five, 51) divided into 56 families and in this huge congress of dens there is no water, no water-closet, no sink.'

It was in 1862 that the first Medical Officer of Health in Scotland was appointed, fifteen years after the first such officer in England. Both were Scotsmen—Dr. William Duncan began his service in Liverpool in 1847, Dr. Henry Littlejohn in Edinburgh in 1862. Dr. Littlejohn had already published stringent criticisms of the treatment meted out to the poor. 'The pittances that are given to paupers, through the proverbial economy of the Boards representing the ratepayers of our City, are only intended to allow of life being maintained at a legal flicker and by no means at a steady flame.' His words could have been equally well applied to the treatment of the poorhouse inmates. In 1860, the average weekly cost per head of providing all necessaries for these people, including fuel, light, clothing and food, was 4/5½d. *The Scotsman* estimated that expenditure on food amounted to 3½d. per head per day and commented: 'We express a grave doubt whether aged, sick and broken-down paupers can be sufficiently fed on 3½d. a day.'

During these years, Scottish prisons and lunatic asylums were crammed with people whom no Court of Law to-day would relegate to any such institution. Many of the asylums were very small and were run for personal profit under private management. Solitary confinement, corporal punishment, even chains, were in regular use, and the 'patients' were left in indescribable neglect, short of food and clothes and bedding, in rooms and cells which were always filthy. In the prisons a larger food allowance was permitted than in the poorhouses, but prisoners of all ages and both sexes were herded together in overcrowded quarters and the degrading conditions were such that men and women who had served sentences came out more vicious and more skilled in crime than when they went in.

Although the main body of public opinion tolerated these scandals with equanimity or indifference, the working-men themselves made immense efforts to fight for better conditions. During the first three decades of the 19th century, Trade Unions began to develop in the industries which had been longest mechanized, namely various branches of the textile group. The Unions were formed by working-class initiative and management with two aims in view: one was to contribute funds, by weekly subscriptions, for the assistance of sick and injured members and for widows and children; the other to organize joint pressure on the employers for higher wages. Following on the Unions of spinners, weavers and other textile workers came similar organizations among colliers, metal workers, builders and railwaymen. Always their efforts were directed to securing higher wages, and to this end they tried to stage strikes which would paralyse the mills and force the employers to agree on better wage-scales. Led by men inexperienced in such affairs, these strikes were often ill-timed and badly co-ordinated. They sometimes lasted for weeks on end. They very rarely succeeded. Ultimately the workers had to go back to their jobs, if they were still available, at the old or even at worsened wage-scales.

Poverty

The employers were afraid of the Unions and afraid of the strikes, although until the very end of the 19th century their position was relatively impregnable. They had capital behind them, and the strikers had not; they had the law and its corps of magistrates and justices on their side, and the strikers had not; they could break the strikes by importing yet more Irish labour, and the strikers had no similar weapon. The Unions therefore fought a losing battle till nearly the end of the century, and a deadly tradition of hatred grew up. Public opinion was against the Unions not only because industrialists dreaded any rising costs of production, but also because any kind of collective bargaining smelt of radicalism. By the end of the century, suspicion and hostility had long roots so that, when the balance of power shifted and the Unions became strong enough to insist on what they wanted, their attitude towards employers and consumers was as unrelenting as that of the industrialists had been in their heyday. The technique of arbitration and the art of personnel management developed too late, and while in the early decades of the Industrial Revolution moderate concessions would have eased everything and made for a much better spirit on every side, the abuse of power by the employers in fact led to the bitter feuds and the Red Clydeside of the 20th century.

CHAPTER 28

The Scot Abroad

Sir Walter Scott once spoke of 'the national disposition to wandering and adventure'. From early medieval times the Scot was well known all over Europe. In the 18th century all who could afford it sent their sons on the Grand Tour, through France into Italy and back through Germany. Sir Archibald Grant explained to his son the purpose of this. 'To goe too early abroad before qualified for conversation, observation and comparissons, I apprehend to be lost time and expense, at least in great degree, whereas reall improvement and usefull friendships may and probably will be the fruits if previously qualifyed. Setting out with proper stock will probably yield more of both in one year than several years would doe without it.' The stock which Sir Archibald wanted his son to acquire before setting out included the study of British History and Geography, and some mastery of French, Latin and Greek. The letters of George Dempster to his friend Adam Fergusson in the 1750s give a vivid impression of the impact of these journeys on the fortunate young men who made them. George Dempster's letters are always good reading.

After the Union, the contribution of the Scots to Britain's influence abroad, and in particular to the development of the Empire, was altogether out of proportion to the size of their own country. They travelled and talked and worked and wrote their way from one continent to another, and everywhere they were to be found in positions of high responsibility. In this book, the story can only be illustrated from typical careers of Scots in diplomacy and administration, in the armed forces, in emigration and exploration and in missionary enterprise. Time would fail to tell of the Scot as engineer, gold prospector, man of business, doctor, novelist.

The Scot Abroad

During the early 18th century, it was difficult for Scots to obtain diplomatic employment abroad, because Sir Robert Walpole disliked them and filled all possible posts with Englishmen. After 1760 there came a marked change however. Between 1760 and 1789, one-seventh of all diplomatic appointments went to Scotsmen, a high proportion at a time when Scottish population was still less than one-seventh of that in England. From 1763 onwards there was nearly always a Scot in charge of the embassies in Austria, Prussia, Poland, Russia and Sweden, also at Constantinople and Naples, while many Scots served in west European cities and in far distant islands. The English press published some sour comment on this infiltration of northerners, for it was at its height during years when Scotsmen were still unpopular in London's political circles.

Scots were well-suited for foreign diplomatic service, because they readily adjusted themselves to strange conditions and unfamiliar company and they were willing to live for years on end in remote middle eastern capitals and semi-barbarous islands. Their philosophical attitude to difficult climates and unhygienic conditions may have been due to the discomfort in which many of them spent their boyhood at home. Their professional success was helped by their flair for foreign languages, in which Englishmen did not distinguish themselves; indeed it was rare to find an English diplomat fluent in any language other than French, while Scotsmen abroad could frequently speak Dutch and German as well. Scottish schools and Universities emphasized Latin and used the continental pronunciation, so that when necessary a Scot could fall back on this and make himself understood without employing an interpreter. A good many interested themselves also in oriental tongues, like Alexander Burnes, the descendant of Robert Burns the poet, and this enabled them to carry out useful negotiations in Persia, China and India.

Many families built up a tradition in the diplomatic corps. The 9th Baron Cathcart and his son were both ambassadors in St. Petersburg for quite long periods. The 7th Earl of Elgin, who transported the famous Parthenon marbles to London, served at the court of the Emperor Leopold in 1790 and afterwards in

Brussels and Berlin; both his sons were distinguished diplomats, indeed the elder became Governor-General first of Canada and afterwards of India. Sir Robert Keith was ambassador in Vienna and St. Petersburg during the 1760s, and he was followed in Vienna by his son, a brilliant linguist fluent in at least seven languages. The 1st Earl of Minto, his son, his brother, and his nephew all held posts of the highest importance in many parts of the world.

While Scotsmen were making their mark in the embassies, they were also to be found in administrative posts, as soldiers and as civilians. Some of them showed initiative and originality which shocked the authorities at home. One of these was Lachlan Macquarie.

Lachlan Macquarie arrived in New South Wales late in 1809, with a long record of distinguished military service behind him. His biographer, M. H. Ellis, describes him as 'yellowed with fever, blotched with curative aids, racked with long courses of mercury, saddened under the strain of grief and marked in every way with the evidences of twenty years in the tropics'. His instructions were to clean up the situation caused by the mismanagement of Governor Bligh, the man whose name will always be remembered in connection with the mutiny on the *Bounty*, but who had probably done more harm than anywhere else in the convict settlement at Botany Bay.

Macquarie's was the first rational administration of this miserable corner of the Empire. His powers seemed rejuvenated by the challenge of his new responsibilities and he set about creating a more normal society. Roads and public works were built on a lavish scale, agricultural improvements encouraged, pioneering and exploration stimulated. Convicts who had served their time were admitted to high positions in society and treated as equals, though delicately nurtured officials bitterly complained about having to receive communion in Church, kneeling beside such riff-raff. Corporal punishments were reduced, drinking habits attacked, a great hospital erected, courts of justice re-organized, land settlement in small lots offered to emancipated convicts, a bank, schools and a printing press established.

The expenses caused by these projects stimulated furious criticism from the Government; Britain was still struggling to pay its way through a war of survival, and the authorities at home could see no excuse for spending so much. In an effort to meet his expenses, Macquarie became involved in financial transactions which brought him to disgrace, and his great services were not recognized till much later. He ended his days in bitterness and poverty. Macquarie's work however did bring permanent and good results to New South Wales. Many thousands of Scots were among those who explored and surveyed and farmed there and elsewhere in Australia, and their names may be seen in plenty on the maps, as indeed is the case in New Zealand and in Canada.

The East India Company at this time was employing great numbers of Scotsmen. In the 18th and 19th centuries, this Company undertook not only vast commercial projects, but also the administration of enormous areas, where conquest and political control had followed on mercantile enterprise. After the terrible Mutiny of 1857, the Company was wound up: the responsibility of government became the direct concern of the British Parliament, and administration on the spot was carried out through the Indian Civil Service, staffed in the main by British officials, till the end of the 19th century.

The British conquest of India is an achievement not to be justified in terms of the modern ethic of self-determination, which even yet is not fully realized. No such ethical notions troubled the heads of Scots or Englishmen or Indians till comparatively recent years: the continent had long been accustomed to wars of conquest by the time the British became involved in them.

The British administration of India attracted some of the best manhood this country had to give, though of course there were rogues and swindlers too, upon whom it is fashionable in some circles nowadays to concentrate at the expense of the better ones. Many were animated by high ideals: these wanted to establish justice, incorruptibility, a better material standard of living for the peasant, and to eliminate such gross cruelties as the burning of widows and infanticide. They were interested in trade and in religious toleration for Hindu and Moslem alike: in general they were less interested, until the 1860s, in education and in the great civilization of India. Very few of them shared the Brahmins' intense preoccupation with philosophy. As the 19th century wore on they became concerned with public health and gradually in the possibility of self-government for India. They found it easy to be compassionate about the peasant, much harder to respect the banya (the small-scale man of business). It has always been difficult for the Briton to appreciate the qualities of people cleverer than himself and the Hindu is often very clever. The merit of British administration has been the consistent efforts to establish peace, order, general justice and a rising scale of prosperity. Its outstanding defect has been the lack of interest in the thoughts and feelings, the dignity and aspirations of the people administered.

Within the limits of temperament and training, the British went far towards the realization of the ideals they set themselves in India. To this achievement, the Scot, with his colossal capacity for work and his strong intellectual endowment, made a contribution described by Professor Dewar Gibb as 'massive and continuous'.

There was a Dumfriesshire stonemason called Allan Cunningham, born in 1784, who became a minor poet. Of his four sons, three made their names in India. Joseph entered the Bengal Engineers and wrote a history of the Sikhs; Alexander became a major-general, also in the Bengal Engineers, later Director-General of the Indian Archaeological Survey (from 1870 till 1885) and he published works on Indian Geography and Numismatics; Francis joined the Indian Army and produced editions of Ben Jonson and Marlowe.

Many Scottish families could produce similar records. The Indian Civil Service was staffed at every level by Scots. They took an impressive part in the work on the great canals, railways and telegraph installations which so greatly mitigated famine, and they shared too in medical and agricultural research. There were many Scottish Governors of provinces, and of the Viceroys, three were Scots—two Earls of Elgin and Lord Minto—and Dalhousie was a half-Scot.

During the 18th and 19th centuries, military and naval service took Scotsmen abroad as much as diplomacy and administration. From 1707 onwards, Lowland regiments served in Europe and in America under many well-known generals, but Highland names were missing till the 1760s. This of course was because the authorities were afraid to give martial training and equipment to people suspected of Jacobite sympathies. Duncan Forbes of Culloden was one of those who deeply regretted this attitude. He was sure that the Forty-Five could have been much curtailed or even prevented had regiments been formed from the loyal Highlands clans. In this view he was fortified by the record of the Black Watch, the one exception to the general rule. Formed in George I's reign from some independent companies of Campbells, Grants, Munros and others of Hanoverian interest, this regiment fought in Europe during the 1740s and won immediate recognition for steadiness and courage.

The Seven Years' War strained Britain's resources to the utmost and the elder Pitt decided at last to enlist Highlanders. In 1766 he made his well-remembered statement on the subject in the House of Commons. 'I sought for merit wherever it was to be found. It is my boast that I was the first Minister who looked for it and found it in the mountains of the north. I called it forth and drew into your service a hardy and intrepid race of men . . . They served with fidelity as they fought with valour and conquered for you in every part of the world.' During the American war, more Highland regiments were brought into being. One of the best-known was the 73rd, raised in 1777 by Lord Macleod, a former Jacobite, who had seen military service in Sweden. The 73rd made its name in India and in the Peninsula.

In 20th century circumstances, it seems fantastic that a man should spend seven to ten thousands of pounds from private resources in order to raise and equip a battalion for national service, while simultaneously exhausting himself on unpaid administrative work in its organization. This was how the British Army was expanded to meet the crisis precipitated in 1793 by Napoleon, and many Scotsmen hastened along with others thus to impoverish themselves in the nation's interests. During the latter part of the 18th century some fifty new Scottish regiments were raised, by private initiative, including the Gordons, Camerons, and Argylls. They fought in the West Indies, in European and Eastern theatres of war, most of them have proud records of their share in the campaigns of Egypt, the Peninsula and Waterloo, and some of their officers attained international reputation.

The naval side of the story is equally interesting. No Scot lives very far from the sea, so indented is the long, crumpled coast-line, and in days when life on dry land presented intolerable disadvantages, life at sea attracted young men in plenty, especially from the islands of the north and west. Long accustomed by the Hudson's Bay men and by traditional deep-sea fishing sagas to the notion of seafaring, these islanders joined the Navy in great numbers, especially during the Napoleonic wars. In 1809 it was believed that from the Shetlands and the Orkneys, upwards of 5,000 men were serving at sea and there were innumerable others as well, from both coastal and inland shires. Ill-fed, battened down in filthy sleeping-quarters, coarsely treated and mercilessly punished by old-style public floggings, these sailors were also irregularly paid, until reforms were belatedly introduced in the early 19th century. But Scottish seamen were found in every kind of vessel all over the world, they took part in all the naval actions fought against Napoleon, and later they shared in some bizarre adventures whose repercussions were far-reaching.

Some of the best-known Scottish sailors came of military families: these included Sir Patrick Campbell, brother of General Sir Colin Campbell, Sir Graham Moore, brother of Sir John of Corunna, and Sir Basil Keith, brother of the great soldier and diplomat. Others came of seafaring families which gave many famous names to the fleet, such as Admiral Duncan of Camperdown, Sir Richard Strachan and Sir Thomas Cochrane. The career of Cochrane was extraordinary and took him into strange spheres. Few individuals can have had a hand in so many different kinds of success, few overcame such dreadful reversals of fortune.

Public service in the diplomatic corps or the armed forces generally led to retirement at home in Scotland. Emigration was quite another matter: it involved permanent settlement in a new country. All through the 18th century this was going on, but it was much more in evidence after the Seven Years' War, which came to an end in 1763. Some Scottish regiments never returned: Fraser's Highlanders, for example, remained in America, sure that there they would have a better chance of making a living than in Scotland. They were more fortunate than later settlers, because they made their homes in places where thriving communities were already established. Their letters dwelt upon the best features of the new life and encouraged others to join them, while propaganda by Scottish landowners and their agents, and later also by shipping companies, intensified the campaign to send the crofters away.

The ship-owners took advantage of the situation. Vessels therefore left which were neither seaworthy nor properly equipped and grossly overloaded. Loss of life was caused when cholera made its way among the overcrowded travellers, and also by shipwreck. In February 1848, Labouchere reported in the House of Commons that of the 106,000 Irish and Scots who had emigrated in the previous year, 12,200 had died at sea or immediately after arrival, while a further 7,100 had failed to survive their journey for more than a few weeks.

Those who did survive tended to settle as far as possible in family groups. Round Quebec were large contingents from Arran; in the Cape Breton district people from Skye: in Nova Scotia families from Ross-shire. In 1815 a settler in New Caledonia wrote to his nephew: 'I suppose there is two hundred Scotch families in this township of respectable people. Your mother will meet with more of her relations here than in Breadalbane.' By the time this letter was written, Gaelic had become a prevailing language in parts of Upper Canada and the Red River Valley, as well as in Cape Breton, Prince Edward Island and a number of other areas.

Some of these emigrants fared much better than others. Those who had the worst experiences were the ones who made their way into country hitherto undeveloped, where they had to build up a new life without the help of any established services.

A typical story was published in 1823 by a John McDonald who went to New Lanark in Upper Canada. It is tempting to quote at length from his short book, which ran through five editions in less than a year, for he describes so much that one wants to know, although there is an undertone of complaint in his writing which is not characteristic of his countrymen.

The crossing from Greenock took six and a half weeks, in atrocious weather, and by the time the ship made Quebec most of the passengers were ill with various infections, though none developed cholera. Then began the laborious journey up the St. Lawrence, first by steamer, afterwards in the flat-bottomed boats used on the upper reaches of the river. Everybody lacked equipment and suitable clothing, so that camping in the open at nights, after days spent largely in hauling boats and baggage over the rapids, caused much illness and many deaths. The last 74 miles were covered overland, across ground rough enough to overturn the waggons.

McDonald wrote of the excessive humidity, the 'noisome exhalations of immense woods', the torrents of rain, the mosquitoes, the snakes, but above all of the continual exposure. When at last, in the month of August, the survivors reached New Lanark, they had to prepare for a winter of five to six months' continuous frost and snow; the nearest town was sixty miles away; draught animals were hard to come by; there were shortages of food, warm clothing and necessaries of all descriptions. McDonald admitted that the prospect of ultimate prosperity was high, but he said that the initial hardships exceeded anything he had ever imagined, and he was continually depressed by the frightening death-roll and, not less, by the irreligious materialism of his fellow settlers. He wrote with disgust of the flattering accounts 'so industriously published' of Upper Canada and stated that all the truth which had been written about it 'would not cover one half of the lies which had been told'.

While he was preparing his book for the press, 'industrious propaganda' continued, and many more Scots were persuaded to set forth on journeys as hazardous and as inadequately planned as McDonald's, some into the wilds of Canada, others to various parts of the United States. Their contribution to the development of the New World was most significant. Driven from their own country by want, they devoted to the new communities, of which they became foundation members, all the drive and initiative which at home had been crushed but which now were stimulated to the full.

Many Scotsmen were attracted to the Hudson's Bay Company, and by about 1800 three-quarters of its servants were Orcadians and so were most of its officials. They operated from a base called York Factory, which was situated on Hudson's Bay, and their purpose was to trade with the Indians, from whom they bought furs for export to Europe. The life was hard and rough, but it brought out the fine qualities of the Orkneymen. As boatmen, fishermen, hunters and carpenters these island folk were unrivalled: they could face privations without complaint and they learned to handle the nomad Indians with confidence and justice. In Stromness, at the northern end of the little street that runs along the shore side of the town, you can see an old well, now sealed up, from which the Hudson's Bay vessels took in their last supplies of water before heading across the Atlantic. They watered there each summer for over two centuries and carried with them untold numbers of men from all the islands.

The North West Company was a rival fur-trading firm, founded in 1783, to work the same area as the Hudson's Bay men. The two organizations hated each other and fighting broke out between them before they were finally amalgamated.

Sir Alexander Mackenzie is probably the most famous of the North West Company's officials. His boyhood home was at Stromness and like so many islanders he went to Canada as a young man. He spent a number of years at Fort Chipewyan, in Hudson's Bay territory, and later carried out two tremendous ventures in exploration. The first one took him in 1789 to the Arctic Ocean, the second in 1792 to the Pacific by way of the Rocky Mountains. Mackenzie's fortitude and success as an explorer were matched by his skill in personal relationships with the men in his crew and with the many unfamiliar Indian tribes through whose land he passed. The negotiations he had to conduct with these Indians demanded of him endless patience and skill and he always avoided arousing hostility. Mackenzie wrote up his journeys himself, most beautifully. Professor Dewar Gibb describes his journals as 'the most unpretentious record of dangerous exploration ever written'.

While the stream of emigration to Canada continued throughout the 19th century, Scotsmen were simultaneously making their way in huge numbers to the United States. Some were seasonal workers, who spent seven or eight months each year working as stone cutters or builders and then returned to Scotland until the following season, but far more were genuine emigrants. Agricultural labourers, carpet workers, weavers, jute and linen operatives poured into New England during the first half of the 19th century, to be followed in the second by as many engineers, iron and steel workers, coal-miners and shipbuilders.

The most famous of them all was Andrew Carnegie, whose parents struggled against the inevitable in Dunfermline for years after it had become clear that weaving as they had known it was finished. Carnegie's enormous success in iron and steel gave him control over a vast network of business firms, newspapers and railroads, and it also made him a household name throughout the Western World. His generous use of wealth added to his prestige, for there was magic in the story of the telegraph boy who worked his way up from the poorest beginnings and ultimately gave away hundreds of thousands of dollars, both in Scotland and in the country of his adoption. The libraries and research centres, the endowments, loans and scholarships which he financed on both sides of the Atlantic make an almost fantastic climax to his story and have enabled great numbers of his fellow countrymen to start life better equipped than he did himself.

Meanwhile Africa was laying its spell upon British explorers. Among the Scotsmen who went there, the name of Mungo Park will always be honoured because of his explorations in Nigeria. Although this gifted and most unusual man ended his life in terrible circumstances—he was killed in Timbuctoo in 1810— many of his countrymen followed him to West Africa and became associated with the British developments on the Lower Niger.

The French Revolution stimulated among religious people an unexpected reaction to Africa and the Far East. Hitherto, little or no missionary work had been done by the British, but in 1792 the Baptist Missionary Society was founded in England and three years later the London Missionary Society.

The Scot Abroad

The notion that every man has an equal right to the Gospel of Christ caught on in Scotland, and Missionary Societies were founded in Glasgow and Edinburgh, enterprises which were frowned upon in powerful quarters. In May 1796, the General Assembly of the Church of Scotland drew up the following resolution: 'To spread abroad among barbarians and heathen natives the knowledge of the Gospel seems to be highly preposterous, in so far as it anticipates, nay, reverses the order of Nature.' This statement illustrates the fear of liberal ideals engendered by the French Revolution, and the difference in attitude between men bred in the 18th century and in the 19th.

Despite the opposition of highly influential religious leaders, many Scottish workers went abroad under the London Missionary Society, which was undenominational, and therefore attracted people of varying persuasions. The Society's first field of operations was in Tahiti and it attracted a high proportion of Scots, but its work expanded very rapidly into Africa, India and the Far East.

The great period of Scottish missionary work came after 1843, when the Disruption brought about a revival of religious zeal throughout the country. By this time the Church of Scotland itself was active in the mission field, for the reactionary dictum of the General Assembly in 1796 was soon abandoned. There is no doubt however that in the mid-19th century the Free Church and the United Presbyterian Church gave the greatest support to missionary and educational enterprise, and they sent their members all over the world.

John Philip, a Congregational minister from Aberdeen, started his missionary career in 1819, when he was well over forty; it was a series of explosions. He has been described as the Elijah of South Africa, the 'outspoken and indefatigable champion of the blacks', a man who horrified Britain by the revelations he publicized about the slave trade, and who was loathed by the Boers for those revelations. During his thirty stormy years abroad, Philip spent himself in the cause of the Hottentots and the Bushmen, thundered against the sale of liquor to native peoples, and revolutionized the organization of the London Missionary Society.

Contemporary with Philip was Robert Moffat, who reached Africa in 1816. Moffat gave fifty-four years to Africa, living for most of the time at Kuruman in Bechuanaland, and like Philip he became a devoted friend to the Hottentots. He reduced the Bechuana tongue to writing and translated the Bible and other religious literature into it, a prodigious work for one who never ceased making extensive and incredibly arduous journeys.

Of Robert Moffat's son-in-law it is difficult to write, for so much has already been written in many different languages, and he has attracted the admiration and indeed reverence of Christian thinkers throughout the world. No account of Scottish history however would be defensible if it lacked some reference to this intellectual and spiritual giant, in whose background one can see many threads of Scotland's story woven together. David Livingstone's family passed through at least three of the vicissitudes which afflicted his nation. His great-grandfather died at Culloden, a Jacobite; his grandfather had to leave his holding on the island of Ulva, because of the economic drive which sent so many country folk to the cities; David himself was caught up in a third national upheaval, the Industrial Revolution, and from the age of ten he worked at the jennies in the Blantyre cotton mills. Like many Scotsmen, he was brought up in a home that was short of money but sensitive to religion, and he shared with his countrymen the traditional reverence for the classics. With his early savings he bought a Latin primer, which he propped up in front of him on his machine. As a boy, he caught the idealism of the age and determined to become a doctor and go to China, under the London Missionary Society which attracted him because of its non-sectarian principles.

Livingstone was directed however to Africa, a decision to which he was somewhat reconciled after his first meeting with Robert Moffat, whose daughter he subsequently married. Moffat advised Livingstone to avoid the well-established missionary centres and go further north, to places described by the historian Latourette as 'vast reaches' as yet 'untouched by the faith and where on any clear morning there could be seen the smoke of a thousand villages in which the name of Christ had not been heard'.

Moffat did not expect Livingstone to follow this advice quite so enthusiastically as he did. Like Mungo Park, Livingstone had a passionate desire to explore. His travels included journeys across the Kalahari desert, up the unknown Zambesi River, across to the western coast; his discoveries included Lake Nyasa, Lake Mweru, Lake Bangweolu and the Victoria Falls. He wanted to make possible a vast extension of knowledge, and of mission work; all his travelling days were pre-occupied with his urge to put on record scientific information and at the same time to preach the gospel of Christ. By his journeys, he hoped too to open up new channels of commerce which could give traders a profitable substitute for the slave traffic, and it was this hope which drove him from the heart of Africa to the western coast. This ideal fired the imagination of many other Scotsmen, in particular of John Kirk, who was able to go far towards achieving it.

Perhaps the Scot whose spirit was most akin to Livingstone's was Mary Slessor. Like him she passed much of her childhood working in a factory, and during the long hours spent in the Dundee weaving-shed she too kept a book propped up beside her. As an eleven-year-old she worked from 6 a.m. till 6 p.m. at the weaving and also carried out many household chores at home, helping to support her sisters and brother, and to conceal from the neighbours the fact that their father was a habitual drunkard. From early childhood she was deeply religious and she soon became devoted to the missionary ideal.

In 1876, three years after Livingstone's death, Mary Slessor went to Old Calabar in Nigeria, where she developed some surprising qualities of character. Drunken natives, infuriated chieftains, rioting strangers, degraded women, she faced with forthright courage and spontaneous affection. They called her 'Ma' and allowed her to box their ears, confiscate their firearms, fight their insect pests and criticize their primitive habits. Under the influence of her terse yet fluent scoldings, these people found themselves obliged to give up murdering twins and flogging women. Even such practices as human sacrifice, the torture of slaves and trial by poison were gradually abandoned as a result of her astonishing vitality. Her life was constantly endangered by her determination to save life, and most especially she did battle for women, in a society which deemed them to be inferior animals. Her success may be measured by the demand which arose in so many of her villages for a 'White Ma to teach our women book and washing and machine'. Her versatility may be gauged from her recipe for cement-making: 'I just stir it like porridge, turn it out smooth with a stick, and all the time keep praying, "Lord, here's the cement, if to Thy glory, set it" and it has never once gone wrong'. Her courage seemed to grow from year to year, as she endured repeated illness, solitude, hostility, in surroundings which teemed not only with people made grossly cruel by ignorance and superstition, but also with snakes, ants, leopards, hippopotamuses and crocodiles.

During all these years when Scottish initiative was so evident in Africa, there were important developments in the Far East, in India and in the Pacific Islands. Men and women went abroad from the 1840s onwards in such strength that Christian work in all these areas was permeated by Scottish and Presbyterian ideals. In the *History of Church Missionary Societies*, Eugene Stock states that 'Scotland has given a far larger proportion of its ablest and most cultured men to Foreign Missions than any other country in the world'.

A 'national disposition to wandering and adventure' is compatible with fierce and loving pride in one's own country. By their lavish expenditure of ability outside Scotland, the explorers, and administrators, missionaries and many others made generous and substantial contributions to the welfare of many peoples. But they never lost their sense of nationality, or their nostalgic love of their own countryside. One may ask why they did not find an outlet for their tremendous ability and energy at home, but how can a man satisfy his urge to wander, his craving for adventure, in the streets and banks and factories of the city where he was born? It has been to the lasting benefit of many countries that the Scots could not do so and it has given their nation an international perstige that could have been achieved in no other way.

PART FOUR

Scotland since 1870

CHAPTER 29

Economic Developments

The purpose of this chapter, and of the two which follow, is to set out some of the facts which explain the present social and economic state of affairs in Scotland, and to put forward reasons for some of the thoughts and feelings of Scottish people today. The wars which broke upon the world during the years between 1870 and 1945 are not described, nor is the Scottish contribution to the British war efforts, substantial and important though it was. In so short a book, it is impossible to deal with this enormous subject, though the effect of the great conflicts on life and thought in Scotland is suggested.

It seems best to begin by describing some of the economic developments, then to show how changes in social life came about and after that to touch upon public opinion. Throughout the whole discussion Scotland must be considered in relation to Britain and indeed to the world in general, because in modern conditions no country can be understood if it is studied as an isolated unit.

A long and terrible depression in farming destroyed the prosperity of agriculturalists in Britain during the years following 1870. This was the heyday of Free Trade. Housewives could buy relatively inexpensive meat, cereals, butter and cheese imported from the New World, Denmark, Australia and New Zealand. All these countries could produce food of good quality more cheaply than Britain because they had more favourable conditions of climate and soil, and the shipping of such goods was revolutionized by steam and refrigeration. City workers and town-dwellers badly needed cheap food, but the fierce competition from abroad was too much for British farmers. The only ones who could continue successfully were those who had both particularly productive soil and also capital to invest in the new heavy machinery, ploughs, binders, threshing-machines and the like.

South of the Border, the total area of land under farming hardly decreased, but many English agriculturalists turned to pasture. There was much more stock-breeding, especially in cattle, because this involved less outlay in wages and in general upkeep than grain. In the United Kingdom as a whole, some $4\frac{1}{2}$ million acres formerly used for crops other than grass were withdrawn from arable cultivation between 1875 and 1916.

Scottish economy was now so bound up with that of Britain as a whole, that the general depression in agriculture could not fail to affect it. Some farms in the Borders and in central and eastern Scotland still made a success of grain production; and cattle-breeding, both for beef and for dairy products, flourished in Ayrshire and Galloway. On the whole, however, Scotsmen found the most economical thing to do was to rear sheep, so the acres devoted to sheep-farming increased steadily every decade. Land so used is close-cropped and the herbage in a difficult climate can therefore suffer. In any case, the proper balance between arable and pasture was destroyed, quantities of fodder and fertilisers had to be imported, land that could have been ploughed with good results went out of cultivation. Whereas in 1800 there had been about half a million Scotsmen employed on farms and crofts, by 1900, when the total population had trebled, land workers had decreased in number by half. South of the Border the flight from the land was not nearly so marked as this.

The general movement to the cities and the outward flow of emigrants continued throughout the forty years following 1870. Both were fed especially from the Highlands and Islands, where a contributory factor was the fashion for deerstalking. Land-owners found it most profitable to preserve their properties for this purpose and about two million acres were therefore enclosed for game, of which fully a third could have been farmed success-fully. This land was engulfed by bracken, pests thrived on it, the deer multiplied and wandered on to adjacent farm properties in search of food, especially during winter.

The crofters had the worst of it. They were smallholders in the Highlands and Islands, who lived on tiny stretches of rough country, many of them on the shores of estuaries and sea lochs far removed from the centres of administration. Their rents in some cases amounted to only a few pounds annually, but by tradition they had no security of tenure, no written leases, and in consequence no incentive to improve their holdings. The roads leading to their crofts were bad, their amenities poor, their miserable little plots were mismanaged and they had to eke out a subsistence by fishing and weaving. Most of them abandoned the effort to grow oats or turnips; they concentrated instead on potatoes and kept a few sheep and a cow or two. Many utterly lost heart and gave up the struggle to find even the minimal rents they owed; their young people left for the cities and embarked on the emigrant ships. Lethargic as these crofters were, beaten by poverty and climate and circumstance, they did not go under without protest. The bitterness of feeling among them caused some ugly outbreaks of violence in the 1880s, when, for example in Skye and Lewis, there were organized riots, because crofters who were behind with their rent were being evicted.

The Government appointed a Commission to enquire and report about the crofters' distress, under Lord Napier and the Duke of Argyll, and the result of this was the Crofters' Holdings Act, passed in 1886. It gave these smallholders legal security of tenure, subject to very reasonable conditions, so that they should no longer live under fear of eviction, and it entitled them to compensation for any permanent improvements they made if they did themselves decide to leave their holdings. Rents were revised and in many cases much reduced, and arrears for some of them were cancelled.

The Act would have been more beneficial had all the recommendations of the Commission been fully carried through, but it did bring good results. The crofters now began to take the initiative in improving their houses, steadings and dykes, and even in planning some crop rotation. But it came too late, and conditions were too hard. The crofting districts needed piped water supplies, electricity and a wholesale scheme of improved roads, all of which were gradually introduced, but not until the 20th century was well advanced.

The most noticeable and rapid improvements date from 1943, when the North of Scotland Hydro-Electric Board was set up. Its work has unquestionably brought new amenities of the greatest importance to the crofters. In the interval, men and women continued to book single tickets by rail and sea. Nearly a quarter of Scotland's population lived in the Highland counties in 1881: fifty years later, less than one-tenth. The Commissioners who investigated the situation in 1883 were impressed by the character of the people they met: they wrote of the 'decency, courtesy, virtue and even mental refinement' of crofters inhabiting the squalid black houses. Scotland lost citizens she could ill spare in the depopulation of those areas.

In the cities, the half-century from 1870 onwards proved a most crucial time. There was such rapid and impressive change that to cross from the rural areas into the industrial belt was like entering a different country.

All over the world, capital goods, the raw materials and machines that make the articles we buy over the counters, were becoming the basis of industrial organization. In Scotland, too, heavy industry took possession, especially in the land between the Forth and the Clyde. From the engineering works of this industrial belt, quantities of machines, machine tools, boilers, locomotives, metal equipment of all kinds were sent to customers in all parts of the world. With these exports there went abroad specialists skilled in their use, to demonstrate how they were made and how they should be handled and repaired. There were to be long-term results of British success in this direction: as R. C. K. Ensor puts it, 'we were equipping our customers to cease buying from us.'

It was in marine engineering and in shipbuilding that Scotland specially succeeded. This meant that Glasgow dominated the economic scene, because of the concentration of shipyards and machine-shops on the Clyde. John Brown & Co. in particular became famous because of the battleships, cruisers, merchant vessels and luxury liners the firm built, but there were many other Clydeside builders too, whose ships became familiar on all the oceans—for example Stephen of Linthouse, and the Fairfield Shipbuilding & Engineering Company.

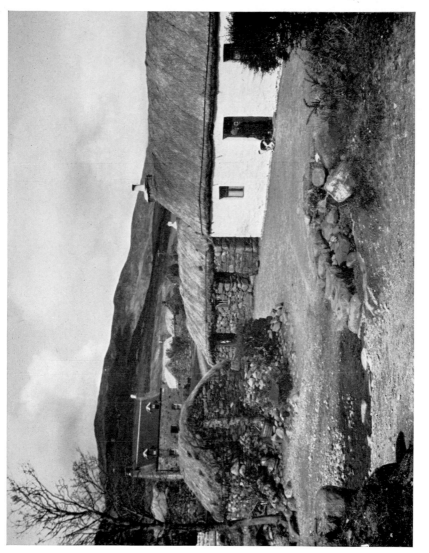

The Crofting Village of Keills, Isle of Jura.

Photo. Douglas Scott 1956.

Ships, like machines and locomotives, were now being made very largely of steel. The processes involved in the production of finished steel were worked up to a high standard of efficiency in Scotland during the 1880s and 1890s. Steel production combined with shipbuilding brought wealth into the country to an extent never experienced before and at the turn of the century the promoters and senior officials of the successful plants must have thought that prosperity had come to stay. On the other hand, the resources of iron ore, still needed for so many processes, were becoming exhausted and by 1900 considerably more iron ore was imported from abroad than could be produced at home, a marked change from the early 1860s.

Oil was available for processing in the black shale fields of the Lothians and Fife. It was refined into paraffin and other products and the oil works employed many thousands of workers until the last thirty years of the 19th century when American, Burmese and other foreign companies were able to send better and cheaper oils into Europe. The Scottish industry survived this competition by concentrating on other substances in the shale, such as ammonia and tar. In 1913 about £165,000 net profits were made in this way.

As yet neither oil nor electricity could compete with coal. All branches of industry and transport were dependent on it, and domestic consumption was very high. In 1854, the year's output in Scotland was 7½ million tons, in 1908 it reached 39 millions, of which more than a third was exported. The coalfields were concentrated in Lanarkshire, Ayrshire and Fife. Many of them had been in use for a long time and were therefore old-fashioned in design and equipment, and it was almost impossible to modernize the working of such mines, because the old cuttings, shafts and passages determined the nature of later developments. Nonetheless, mechanical improvements had been made since the bad early days. Coat-cutting machinery, electrical equipment for lighting, signalling and ventilation, small underground railways and steam haulage were among these.

As soon as the World War broke out in 1914, an artificial boom stimulated industry all over the United Kingdom. There was a sharply accelerated demand for textiles, because uniforms, blankets and cotton products for webbing and the basis of tyres were needed in enormous quantity for the armed forces. The munitions drive meant that in iron and steel works there was almost unlimited scope for expansion. The crisis imposed terrific strain on the Scottish industrial belt which contributed enormously to the war effort. This was true in textiles, in chemicals, in coal, but it was specially evident in engineering and most of all shipping. Clydeside and other yards were under hectic pressure to make good the losses of the fleet in battle and from submarines.

The emergency strained the farming areas to an almost comparable degree. By 1914, Britain was importing something like two-thirds of her food supplies. This obviously meant disaster, because of the naval blockade and the attacks of submarines on the merchant fleet. Emergency plans were drafted to increase the production of all kinds of food, but especially cereals, at home. County Agricultural Executive Committees were formed and the Ministry of Food set up. By the end of 1917, over 280,000 extra acres had been ploughed in England and Wales. This was a tremendous feat. Men were being called up into the forces all the time and the fields had to be tilled by about one-third of the normal number of labourers, though women did their turn and prisoners-of-war were employed on the work as well. There was heavy anxiety in the whole business for farmers, who dreaded a sudden drop in prices once the war was over, which might leave them committed to long-term capital investments in the land, with a new and much higher wage scale for labourers.

Scotland made a very big contribution to this food production drive. Much of her land could never be put under cereals because it is so mountainous and poor, and much had deteriorated to a dangerously low level in recent decades, but 51,000 extra acres were ploughed up for the production of wheat, oats and root crops. The harvests were good and somehow they were taken in, though such a high proportion of Scots joined up that the labour problem was acute. Transport difficulties prevented full use being made of the fish, eggs and dairy produce of the more remote parts of the country which were isolated by roads of severe gradient and unreliable surface. The prices commanded by the grain however were high and there was a brief appearance of prosperity on some of the farms which could produce cereal crops. This was to prove short-lived.

When peace came, the economic life of the world was completely disrupted: and the financial arrangements set in motion by the Treaty of Versailles did nothing to help matters. Britain was by now so bound up with Europe and America that, when trade cycles or sudden disaster brought boom or slump elsewhere, the British were bound to suffer with everybody else. And in the early 1920s there began a long trade depression. There were periods of alleviation when the full seriousness of the situation was somewhat masked, but the downward trend of business and commerce continued till 1929, when America's Wall Street collapse shook the security of her customers throughout the world. For some three or four years after that there was the most appalling stagnation in trade and everywhere people suffered. From about 1933, improvement slowly began. By 1939, that slow drive towards greater prosperity had not had time to take full effect—but re-armament cured unemployment.

Very soon after the First War, it became obvious that people could no longer afford to buy British manufactures, and that we were not going to recover markets lost during the war. On the contrary, our own shops began to sell cheap foreign products—textiles, bicycles, household gear, equipment of many kinds—with which our producers could not compete.

Scotland suffered with the rest of the country. There was a brief revival in the shipyards immediately after the war, because the merchant fleet needed repair and replacement. This did not last and, before long, recently launched merchant ships appeared in the Gareloch and elsewhere, lying up unused, because there was no business for them to do. The depression hit the engineering trade equally hard. Shipbuilding and steel production are so enormously costly that they respond more violently than most other industries to international slump, because when people sense that bad times are coming they at once cancel orders for new heavy equipment. Had Scottish industry been geared to the making of small articles, and the consumer goods used and constantly replaced in daily life, the disaster would not have been so acute.

By 1931, the output of pig-iron in Scotland dropped to less than a quarter of what it had been in 1920; so did the production of steel ingots and castings. In 1913, the Clyde shipyards had completed in twelve months very nearly 760,000 tons of shipping: in 1933, the figure was 56,368, a drop of over 700,000 tons. Coal production by the 1930s was about a third of what it had been before the war.

Fully three-quarters of the Scottish people were living in the confined region of the industrial belt where the heavy industries had absorbed the major part of capital and labour. It was almost impossible to rescue the economy of such a district, but the problem was aggravated by the agricultural depression too. Scottish farmers suffered, just as they had dreaded doing, from the falling prices of the 1920s, and many of them went bankrupt.

Most of the industrial belt was officially classified as a Depressed Area. In 1934, the Government Commission, appointed to enquire into the Depressed Areas, issued a report on the West Lothian Coal and Shalefield, the Ayrshire Coalfield, Cowdenbeath and Lochgelly in Fife, districts round Falkirk, Port Glasgow and Alexandria and the whole of Lanarkshire, excluding Glasgow, which was treated as a separate problem. In this highly industrialized and over-populated area, there were whole districts which had lost their one and only industry, so that the inhabitants had literally no alternative employment, and up to 60 per cent. of them were out of work. Almost two-thirds of Scotland's unemployed were concentrated in this terrible region, but there was unemployment in many other places too, especially in the fishing towns round the North Coast, where competition from Norway and elsewhere was complicating the issue.

Many thousands of the unemployed remained without work for several years. Children left school at fourteen and could not find jobs, so that young people in the Depressed Areas grew up without the discipline and incentive of work, frustrated, embittered, and often crushed in spirit. The Carnegie United Kingdom Trust published in 1937 a short survey called *Disinherited Youth* in which are summarized the main facts about unemployment between the ages of 18 and 25 in Glasgow, Liverpool and Cardiff. It is a most sensitively written document, full of understanding, at once compassionate and realistic. It shows with terrible lucidity how deeply the experiences of the 1930s embittered a whole generation of young men and women. Educated people suffered with uneducated, skilled with unskilled, and it cost them their confidence in themselves, in society, in the future, in religion.

For the first few months of unemployment, people drew Insurance Benefit, after that they were put onto Unemployment Assistance, for which they had to report twice weekly at the local Labour Exchange. In 1920, a man drew 15/- a week, a woman 12/-, boys 7/6d., girls 6/6d.; children at school, up to the age of sixteen, were allowed 1/- a week. Thus a man, his wife and one child had to live on 28/- a week, finding rent, fuel, clothing and food for all three.

These figures did not improve as the years went by, because the Government wanted to reduce the expense caused by the 'dole'. It was because of this that the Means Test was introduced as a condition of Unemployment Assistance. The Means Test was a worse indignity than reporting at Labour Exchanges, for people with any spirit or independence. If families joined together and shared a home to reduce overhead costs, the Means Test led to their Unemployment Assistance being reduced to the point when a grown man would draw so little as 3/- or 4/- a week. It led to subterfuges of many kinds, to the break-up of family life and to deep resentments which moulded the character of children in their early years. It was one of the most unhappy features of the long-drawn-out disaster.

One cannot escape the fact that much of the suffering and still more of the frustration and embitterment caused by the Depression could have been mitigated if a better tradition had grown up among the owners and managers during the decades between 1870 and 1920. Materialists on the make were responsible for much social injustice and for gross misuse of resources. Callous and careless mistakes were made, sincere and well-intentioned errors of judgement accepted, bold measures of relief obstructed.

And yet the policy of having Unemployment Assistance at all marked an important change. In earlier periods of depression, nothing of this kind had been done. Older wage-earners regarded it as something to be thankful for. The Means Test itself would not have borne so hardly on people but for the fact that it was applied by untrained Labour Exchange officials who had little skill in such work.

The magnitude of the disaster was due to the fact that people had not yet understood how to manipulate the economic laws of a world-wide community. In 1936, J. M. Keynes published his *General Theory of Employment, Interest and Money,* just when F. D. Roosevelt was launching the New Deal in America, and these two men did more than anybody else to show how government finance, capital investment and public works can be used to tide a country over a period of slump. The collapse of the 1930s was irretrievable, but Keynes in Britain and Roosevelt in America helped to ensure that future crises would be differently handled.

CHAPTER 30

Political and Social Change

The curse of Britain at the end of last century was poverty. It was worse in Scotland than almost anywhere else. Unless one has envisaged what it was like, the political and social changes of the last eighty years cannot be understood. It can best be seen by considering first the houses in which the poor had to live and then the food they could afford to buy.

In cities, towns, villages and clachans, Scottish wage-earners had been expected over a period of many decades to rear their families in one-roomed dwellings.

The Highland crofter inhabited what was known as a 'black house', built of stone, without lime, roofed with heather thatch, provided with one door, no chimney and no window. A beginning was made in the 1860s to replace these hovels by something better, but by 1914 there were still some in use. In well-appointed farms, unmarried labourers were put to live in bothies, tiny single-roomed apartments built alongside the byres in the farm-yard, to be shared by several men for eating and sleeping.

In the cities, tall stone tenements housed great numbers of families in 'single-ends', one-roomed flats, with outside sanitation shared by the whole building, and no piped water for anybody. In 1888, one person in every four of Glasgow's population lived in a 'single-end'.

All the cities of the industrial belt expanded, swallowing up nearby villages and making them into slums. By 1911, nearly 9 per cent. of all Scots people lived in one-roomed houses; in Glasgow and Dundee, 50 per cent. were officially termed 'over-crowded', which meant there were more than two people per room, so that at least seven would inhabit a two-room and kitchen flat. Even in 1951, about 30 per cent. were still in one or two-roomed dwellings and in Glasgow nearly a tenth of the people lived in

361

Scotland since 1870

'single-ends'. It was a continual and heart-breaking struggle to keep up a decent standard of family life in one room where not only cooking, sleeping and washing had to be done, for also in this one room sickness, childbirth and death had to be witnessed even by small children. Small wonder that there was so much chronic disease. People in such conditions could not even stack kitchen utensils or store food properly, so that they could certainly never nourish their families adequately. Small wonder too that illegitimacy was an everyday matter and that there was more drunkenness in Scottish cities than elsewhere in Britain.

Thomas Ferguson, in his book *Scottish Social Welfare* 1860-1914, shows that standards of living improved in the better farming districts after 1870. He also describes investigations in Dundee and Glasgow in the early 1900s which revealed how miserably poor was the normal diet of working people in cities. Families living on less than 20/- a week simply could not feed their children well enough, and there were many such families. Similar facts are recorded in *Food, Health and Income*, a short work published in 1936 by John Boyd Orr. He set out statistics which show that, in the early 1930s, 50 per cent. of the British nation were living on less than 20/- per head per week, and that in these families less than 8/- was spent on food for each member each week. One person in ten had a total income of less than 10/- a week, of which less than 4/- was spent on food, and there were people spending as little as 2/-.

Boyd Orr showed that in the higher income groups much more milk, eggs, fruit, vegetables, meat and fish were eaten; people spending less than 10/- a week each lived on potatoes and bread, cheap jam, margarine and tea, to which Scottish workers added a good deal of porridge. Nutrition in childhood affects growth. In 1933, children of well-to-do families reached a height as much as $5\frac{1}{2}$ inches more than that of children in poor families, and with this obvious physical difference went less easily detected variations in health and stamina.

'In animal husbandry', wrote Boyd Orr, 'an optimum standard, far from being utopian, is regarded as good practice. Every intelligent stock farmer in rearing animals tries to get a minimum diet for maximum health and fitness. A suggestion that he should

362

use a lower standard would be regarded as absurd. If the children of the three lower income groups (from 10/- to 20/- a week) were reared for profit like young farm stock, giving them a diet below the requirements for health would be financially unsound. Unfortunately, the health and physical fitness of the rising generation are not marketable commodities which can be assessed in terms of money.'

The food rationing of the Second World War represented a much higher standard of nourishment for working people in Boyd Orr's three lowest income groups—half the British population—than they had ever experienced before. In Scotland, the working people of the industrial belt had been consistently under-nourished throughout the period following 1870. Medical Officers of Health and doctors working in slum districts had been saying so for years and years.

Today it is an accepted principle in Britain that people cannot be allowed to go without the basic necessities of life. The poverty accepted by earlier generations shocks us. Why was it tolerated by a wealthy and supposedly Christian community? How did it come about that changes were at last made?

Part of the trouble was that well-to-do people in the 19th century did not know what poverty meant. Till the end of the century, little was done to investigate the facts about it or to bring them home to people in authority. If you read the Parliamentary Debates recorded in Hansard, you will find that the view of many members could be summed up in the words—'Depend upon it, the sufferings of the poor are greatly exaggerated.'

While many people were ignorant about the problem, or indifferent to it, those who could have done something about it were influenced by theories which militated against reform. One of these was derived from the writings of Adam Smith and Ricardo, reinforced by the Utilitarians and the Manchester School. This taught that the prices of everything, including labour, are determined by demand, by the fluctuations of the market; and that if you interfere with this process of price-fixing, you make things worse. Therefore if wages were raised beyond the minimum at which you could hire labour, the price of the product would rise, the expansion of demand would be arrested and this would bring neither you nor your workers any advantage. Poor Law orthodoxy was another influence against reform. According to this, the relief of poverty by donations of money, whether through public or private channels, increases the supposed inclination of the poor to live by begging rather than by work.

This ignorance and these theories were gradually broken down. Well-to-do women of high intelligence were still excluded from professional life, but they were permitted to go into Social work and what they saw for themselves, at close quarters in the homes of the very poor, they freely disclosed. Beatrice Webb was the most famous of these women, but there were many others in her generation. The Charity Organization Society made a study of poverty which helped to change public opinion. The Settlement movement, notably at Toynbee Hall in East London, brought into the poorest districts of the great cities highly educated young men, destined for positions of authority in the Church, the Civil Service, politics and the professions. They went to live in the settlements and got to know the slum-dwellers as friends. The experiences of all these individuals, their publications in journals, their pressure on public opinion, led to the great social surveys of Charles Booth in London and Seebohm Rowntree in York. Among these young men were some still prominent in public affairs, like William Beveridge and Clement Attlee.

The press contributed to this process of enlightenment, especially the *News Chronicle*, which ran a campaign against sweating. The Royal Commission on this subject revealed conditions which shocked people very deeply in the early 1890s. In the Rutherglen Chemical Works near Glasgow for example, a twelve-hour day and a seven-day week were worked, day and night shifts alternating. This state of affairs inflamed people who by now had become much more aware of the scandal of poverty.

During these years, the nature of the electorate became very different. In 1884, all adult men were allowed to vote, both for Members of Parliament and for Town Councillors. After 1889, County Councils were established to administer county districts, and soon Parish Councils were also set up, all popularly elected. So people who had never before been able to exercise influence could now share in the choice of responsible representatives both in local and in national government.

And this was the period too when the Trade Unions were gathering power and extending their influence from skilled to unskilled trades. Though Trade Unionism did not become so strong among Scottish working men as among English in the last decades of the 19th century, they did make progress and their influence began to count for something. The Scottish Union leaders were men of great ability and strength. They worked not only in Scotland and for Scottish Unions but also in England where Keir Hardie and Alexander Macdonald, for example, did a great deal for the coal-miners' organization, in the belief that a nation-wide mobilization of workers' resources was needed.

The Union leaders were determined to get the hours of work reduced and to secure a rise in wages, both reforms which were long overdue, and they realized that only by fighting for their rights could they secure success; in the late 19th and early 20th centuries therefore there occurred many tragic strikes, a few of which were followed by slight improvements in working conditions. Employers of labour made a bad showing in these years. Most of them were careless about the lives and safety of their workers, especially in the mines. They resisted, with all their might, the very just wage claims put forward by the Unions. Their behaviour fostered the idea that class warfare between employer and employed was natural and inevitable.

The leaders of labour were led by their chequered story of success and failure to the conclusion that only by entering politics could they make any real progress, and because of the recent electoral reform they discovered that they could organize the working-class vote. They wanted to secure by legislation such reforms as the eight-hour day, a national minimum wage, arbitration courts for the settlement of wage disputes, state insurances against accident and sickness. They also believed that the means of production—the mines, heavy industries, railways and so on—must be nationalized, because only so did they think the community could be safeguarded against vested interest and private gain.

In Scotland these ideas were eagerly fastened upon. One of the first Labour M.P.s was Keir Hardie, a fine man, who won everybody's respect and who knew from personal experience what the extremes of poverty could do to a family. The Labour Party, like the Trade Union Movement, owed much in these years to Keir Hardie and a number of other Scottish leaders, Alexander Macdonald and Alexander Campbell in particular. It was in no small measure due to the co-operation of these Scottish leaders that the Labour Party gained in power more quickly then might have been expected. By 1905, it had won twenty-nine seats in the House of Commons, and as the years went by it succeeded in exercising a formidable influence in Parliament. Its success was built up by a Scot, whose leadership counted enormously in his earlier years, though later he lost the confidence of many Labour members—Ramsay Macdonald.

An epoch-making attack, the first of its kind, was made upon poverty by the Liberal Government of 1905. It was led until 1908 by the Glasgow-born Scot, Sir Henry Campbell Bannerman, and after his death in that year by H. H. Asquith. R. C. K. Ensor describes Campbell Bannerman as a man whose nature was 'to move persistently to the left', and also as one who had qualities of the first order—'shrewdness, steadfast will, directness of purpose and unselfish devotion to his party's cause'. His name became 'the watch word of the radicals and of the young'. His rare statesmanship was shown in his handling of the South African situation. Field Marshal Smuts, years later, said that Campbell Bannerman's negotiations in 1906 led to the evolution of the Commonwealth, a piece of work unequalled in imperial records for nobility and originality. But his government made history too by its programme of social reform, which itself brought in a new era. Campbell Bannerman enlisted the services of some extraordinarily able colleagues, and after his death Asquith was no less successful in his appointments. Among these men were Winston Churchill and Lloyd George.

The Liberals produced legislation to improve the position of smallholders, to safeguard merchant seamen, to extend workers' compensation. They started Old Age Pensions, free school meals for necessitous children and regular medical examination of all children in State Schools. Winston Churchill was responsible for the Trade Boards Act of 1909, which initiated a system of consultation between employers and employed about wage rates, in an attempt to put an end to sweating. Though it was started in a very limited way, its success led to much more widespread use of the system later on. Also in 1909, Labour Exchanges were set up. W. H. Beveridge was appointed to organize them. He probably knew more than anybody at that time about unemployment, because he had made a scientific and authoritative study of it. He had in fact already formed some of the conclusions to which he held all his life and in which he continually educated public opinion. He designed the Labour Exchange to assist unemployed and casually employed men in their search for work. They were not used at first so much as Beveridge had hoped, because employers were obstructive in the early stages, but they became much more effective in later years. So the medieval method of hawking labour from door to door began to die out.

More important than any other measure was Lloyd George's National Insurance Act of 1911. This made regular contributions by employers and employed in certain trades compulsory, so that men who fell out of work or became ill might receive insurance benefits. It was the beginning of a completely new approach to the handling of poverty in Britain.

Today when the welfare point of view is so widely accepted, it is difficult to realize what a revolution took place between 1905 and 1911. One can estimate the extent of the change by reading such reminiscences as those of Hugh Miller. His young manhood was spent in the middle years of last century: thoughtful, compassionate, intellectual as he was, he took for granted conditions which seem to the modern reader barbarous. Osgood Mackenzie's *A Hundred Years in the Highlands* shows the same sort of thing. Still more revealing are the terrible records of accident and disaster in the mining and engineering industries.

When the First World War broke out, the shortage of munition workers became so acute that wages rose suddenly and dramatically, indeed these people had never handled so much money before. They became much more conscious of their rights and of their power to enforce those rights. At the same time, many well-to-do British boys aged eighteen and nineteen went into trench warfare as subalterns. A high proportion were killed, but the survivors came back filled with respect for the private soldiers beside whom they had fought. These young men believed that class feeling in industry could and must be overcome. Though they were not at first in positions of authority, their point of view made an impression and these were the men of influence during the 1930s and 1940s.

And then the great Depression came and poverty was once again the nation's scourge. But by this time people had outgrown the classical economic theory that you cannot effectively interfere with economic process by means of Government action. So the unemployed who had used up their insurance benefits were given the assistance described in the last chapter. Minimal as these payments were and insufficient for the maintenance of health, they were nevertheless paid out on the principle that the community is responsible for its members when calamity comes to them.

The climax of half a century's work towards comprehensive welfare came during the Second World War. William Beveridge was asked to be Chairman of an inter-departmental Committee, to clear up inconsistencies and gaps in what Churchill described as 'our incomparable system of social insurance'. A better choice of chairman could not have been made. All his life Beveridge had worked at the problems of poverty, want and unemployment; he had already published original views on these subjects; he had adopted without reserve the principles set out in Eleanor Rathbone's book on Family Allowances. Instead of patiently working at the detailed administration of Workmen's Compensation, Health and Unemployment Insurance, Old Age and Widows' Pensions, Beveridge suddenly came out in 1942 with an entirely new scheme. He produced the plan for a complete system of social security, the blue-print of the Welfare State.

The Beveridge Report captured the imagination of the electorate in this country and in the Forces overseas. The General Election of 1945 returned a Labour Government, supported by an overwhelming majority. There is no doubt that one reason for this was that men and women, hitherto right of the centre in political outlook, now wanted Beveridge's plan to be implemented. So at last, in 1948, a National Health Service and a complete system of National Insurance were put on the Statute Book.

In a history of Scotland, one is justified in expecting to find some record of how events worked out in Scotland. This chapter has been largely concerned with a movement of public opinion and with legislation which affected Britain as a whole. Scottish people were involved for the most part because they were British rather than because they were Scottish. This trend in affairs had weighed on the minds of prominent Scotsmen for a long time.

During the 20th century, the machinery of government became vastly more complicated. The improvement in Social Welfare was won and maintained by prolonged legislative work in Parliament: it was administered by whole new phalanxes of officials employed in the enlarged offices of local Government organizations. The nationalization of industry was carried through after the Second World War by the Labour Cabinet and the necessary legislation was so cumbersome that it was found to override traditions of importance in many parts of the country. Democracy which undertakes the duties of a Socialist State must be served by a bureaucracy and a top-heavy bureaucracy at that.

Scottish people had long been exasperated by matters of urgency to them being held up by the congestion at Westminster. It seemed that it was impossible even to erect in a Glasgow side-street a notice saying 'No Thoroughfare' without applying to London and being kept waiting for months on end.

There was good reason for the angry frustration which grew up in Scotland. People felt that Scottish concerns were shelved, that Parliamentary debating time on Scottish matters was much too brief, that evidence submitted by Scottish representatives was neglected, that Government grants for projects north of the Border were niggardly, that congestion at Westminster was unduly holding up the administration of Scottish business.

Some of the difficulties so far as Scotland was concerned had been understood at quite an early stage and efforts were made to meet them. In 1885, the Earl of Rosebery was given the post of Under-Secretary at the Home Office with Scotland as his special charge. This was because people felt that nobody was really responsible for Scottish affairs and that it was now necessary to revive the old idea, long since in abeyance, of a special Parliamentary Secretary for Scotland.

Rosebery found his new appointment anything but satisfactory because he had neither time nor opportunity to handle Scottish affairs adequately. Within less than a year he succeeded in getting a further change made, and he was supported on both sides of the House in doing so. A Scottish Office entirely distinct and separate from the Home Office was formed, under the direction of a special Minister, who was given Cabinet rank (in 1892), and who was assisted by a whole staff of officials, themselves Scots. Further, in 1894, all Scottish members of the House of Commons were formed into a Scottish Grand Committee whose business was to discuss Bills concerning Scottish affairs.

These changes were well intended, but they proved disappointing. The Scottish Office was in London, four hundred miles distant from the country whose affairs it was supposed to run, its senior members were inaccessible and overworked, and the Grand Committee—which became a Standing Committee permanently established—was not empowered to debate the Scottish Bills in principle, but only in practical application.

The removal of the Scottish Office to Edinburgh in 1939 was therefore very literally a step in the right direction. At St. Andrew's House in their own capital city, citizens of Scotland could now meet the Senior Civil Servants who were administering their affairs and thrash things out with them in discussion.

But Scottish thinkers were still indignant about the way in which their country was being run. Delays at Westminster constantly obstructed proper consideration of Scotland's particular problems, which were indeed very different from many of those affecting England and Wales, and which involved special knowledge of background and current development. It irked people very much too to realize that, even if the wheels of Government moved without any obstruction at all, there was no constitutional way in which Scotsmen could influence legislation in principle at a formative stage, even when it concerned principally or only their own institutions. Scottish Members numbered 70 in a House of over 500. They therefore could not exercise real influence. So an unprecedented measure of devolution was worked out, a most interesting political experiment. In 1948 the Scottish Standing Committee was given authority to examine all Bills affecting Scotland at the second reading and to make recommendations; it was also empowered fully to discuss financial estimates in connection with projects proposed for Scotland. The Committee was to include all the 70 Scottish M.P.s with ten to fifteen others, appointed to ensure that its political composition was approximately in line with that of the House of Commons as a whole.

These changes in Scottish administration are so recent that it is not easy to say how far they will solve the problem. There are some who think they hardly touch it. The views of these critics are discussed in the next chapter.

CHAPTER 31

The Background to Contemporary Thought

I
t is a bold thing to try to understand the mood of a people at any particular period in history, most of all a contemporary period. Nonetheless it is sometimes of value to consider the influences which have contributed to it and in this chapter the cultural, political and religious movements of the last eighty years are discussed. It is impossible for these movements to be completely or comprehensively described, and much of what has to be said is more a matter of opinion or of interpretation than of history, because it is all so recent and because one is personally involved.

Lord Cockburn complained in the early 19th century of a falling-away in the cultural life, and declared that he found the new race of politically minded young men excruciatingly dull. Perhaps he was indulging himself a little in the prerogative of the older generation which always thinks young men are not what they were; perhaps, as was his habit, he had diagnosed the mind of the times with exactness and understanding.

The 19th century proved to be a time when British writers produced prose that will always live, and poetry of the highest and near-highest quality. On the other hand, the artists and architects could not touch the standard set by their predecessors. Ugliness was tolerated, indeed admired, both indoors and out, even ladies' fashions became over-decorative and unbecoming and everywhere people seemed satisfied with material rather than aesthetic values. As Cockburn said: 'The exact old thing was not.'

In Scotland, the spirit of the times was as apparent as in England. Critics of Scottish history have tried to explain it by saying that the Presbyterian Church discouraged the arts, or that Scotland was overshadowed by England, but the trouble lay elsewhere. You cannot read the records of Queen Victoria's time in Scotland without seeing where Scottish energies were being concentrated. In his book *Economic Developments in Victorian Scotland*, W. H. Marwick describes industrialization as 'an influence more hostile to culture than Calvinistic Puritanism or English domination'.

Regrettably, Scotsmen who employed architects had apparently unlimited resources, except when they were planning working-class houses. Their sham Gothic and sham baronial structures are with us still and there is little comfort either in looking at them or living in them. The lovely work of Robert Adam and his generation was despised and the careful restoration of ancient buildings, especially churches, by people with insufficient knowledge often spoiled them. Mid-19th century artists painted, as their public wished them to do, innumerable Highland Cattle, Stags at Bay and Sheep in Twilight. In Thomas Carlyle and R. L. Stevenson, Scotland had two authors who won recognition, but from about 1870 onwards novelists became obsessed with misdirected romanticism. So there emerged what has been rudely but justifiably called the 'Ben and Glen' or 'Kailyard' style of writing. People's power of appreciation seemed to be blunted. They sought no new forms of expression and they mishandled the old ones.

Towards the end of the century however a fresh inspiration came into Scottish painting, especially through the work of Robert Scott Lauder, who as painter and teacher gave a whole generation of artists a new directions and a new standard. Some of his pupils went to London, where their work was at once influential, Orchardson, for example, and McWhirter. The most important of them all was William McTaggart who grew up speaking Gaelic near the village of Machrihanish, and who spent most of his life in Scotland. His chief interest was in the effect of light and atmosphere, especially on the surface of the sea and on clouds. He was in fact an Impressionist, though he was an original one, who formed his style before the French school became well-known.

In the last twenty years of the century, a group of artists, centred on Glasgow and known as the Glasgow School, began to produce pictures of quite a new kind. Among them were W. T. MacGregor and E. A. Hornel.

These artists abandoned the convention of narrative pictures. They were interested in rich colour, bold composition, decorative pattern, and they handled paint in daring original ways. There was no defect of craftsmanship in their work however as there was with some of their would-be successors. D. Y. Cameron, Muirhead Bone and James Guthrie were all artists of this school who survived both wars, but whose influence was important well before 1914. The fine work done by these three contributed very much to the revival in art. Another aspect was represented by Pittendrigh Macgillivray, the sculptor, and yet another by Charles Rennie Mackintosh and Robert Lorimer, both architects.

Mackintosh was perhaps the most successful of them all. The bold and massive lines of his buildings combined strength with proportion, they were in keeping with the best traditions of earlier Scottish architects and yet the designs were original and stimulating. Admirers of Scottish baronial styles were not pleased, but Mackintosh's work is refreshing to see because it has dignity and there is nothing insincere or bogus about it. He was greatly admired on the continent, where his influence can be detected in much modern work.

The Glasgow School was not the only sign of a reviving culture. From the turn of the century onwards, Scotsmen began to influence the literary forms of the day in many directions. In 1901, George Douglas Brown brought admirers of the Kailyard style down to earth with his tragic story of Scottish village life, *The House with Green Shutters*, a book which made an immense impression. A. J. Cronin and George Blake in the 1930s wrote powerful novels about the city and the river in industrial Scotland. J. M. Barrie, Neil Munro, Compton Mackenzie, Eric Linklater were all prose writers who covered a wide range and produced work of lasting value. Edwin Muir's poetry was of a higher order than any Scot had written for a long time. As novelist, historian, biographer, John Buchan won himself a place in the affections of a very large public, both in Scotland and far afield. These are only some of the well-known names associated with the literary side of this new Scottish Renaissance.

During the forty years preceding the First World War, a ferment of new ideas was also at work among politicians and economists. Until the 1880s the Scottish electorate had been almost consistently Liberal, except of course in some of the shires, where landowners and farmers always voted Conservative. The Radical groups in the cities worked against the tide of public opinion, in their support of the ideals the Chartists had tried to achieve, and it was difficult for them to make headway, so entrenched was the Liberal establishment. In the 1880s, the balance between Liberals and Conservatives was suddenly disturbed. The upheaval, which shocked the complacency of old-style politicians, was partly due to the Irish Home Rule crisis, partly to the appearance of the new Labour Party.

Scottish people had no love for the Irish. They had seen too much of them in the slums of the industrial areas for one thing, and they dreaded their religious influence for another. To grant Home Rule to a predominantly Roman Catholic Ireland would mean that the Ulster Presbyterians, who were largely of Scottish origin, would be submerged. So Gladstone's Irish schemes met with a very critical reception in Scotland, where many former Liberals broke away during the 1880s and 1890s, to become either out-and-out Conservatives, or Liberal-Unionists who were willing to vote with Conservatives. Although the Liberals survived the shock of this long controversy, and returned to power in full force in 1906, they never recovered their old supremacy in Scotland.

While some Liberals were turning to Conservative leadership, others were attracted to Socialism in general and to the rising Labour Party in particular. Working people supported Keir Hardie and Cunninghame Graham and the rest of them, for reasons suggested in the last chapter, but the new movement received much impetus too from an increasing number of professional and middle-class men and women. There was much more awareness of the need for social reforms towards the end of the 19th century and the seriousness and thoroughness with which the Fabians set out their doctrines made a deep impression in Scotland as well as in England. Sidney and Beatrice Webb and Graham Wallas brought in a totally new way of thinking about society and politics.

Socialism was one new dynamic force which undermined the hold of orthodox politicians north of the Border. The uproar over

Irish Home Rule contributed to the rise of another. People began to say that, if Home Rule were being seriously considered for Ireland, there were good reasons why it should be seriously considered for Scotland too. The proposition did not arouse emotions or passions comparable with the outbursts over the Irish question, but Scottish M.P.s and their constituents were becoming more and more indignant about the congestion of business at Westminster. The bottleneck was doing Scotland harm and people felt that this should not be tolerated. In 1889, G. P. Clark, the Member for Caithness, moved a resolution in the House of Commons that Scotland should have a National Parliament for 'the management and control of Scottish affairs'. Similar resolutions were raised each year till 1895 and always voted down. General irritation began to grow more pronounced and it was not allayed by the creation of the Scottish Secretary-ship and the Scottish Standing Committee. But as yet there was no widespread or nationalist fervour about the matter and business leaders in Scotland, especially those of the industrial belt, were against anything that might weaken the Union.

When the Liberal Government of 1905 came in, support for Home Rule in Scotland became much stronger. There was no suggestion that the sovereignty of the Imperial Parliament should be impaired, but far more people now wanted a scheme of devolution, by which a Scottish Parliament should handle Scottish business. Bills framed to implement such a scheme were introduced several times between 1908 and 1914 when, because of the outbreak of war, the matter was dropped.

During the great Depression of the 1920s, feeling about Scottish Home Rule suddenly became much more pronounced. People trying to live on Unemployment Assistance, those subjected to the Means Test, and others who were moved to angry compassion by the terrible destitution in Scotland were inclined to think that the suffering was due in part to Westminster's habit of shelving Scottish business, although conditions on Tyneside and in South Wales were in fact even more acute. Furious comment was published about the negative attitude of the Government towards the Scottish Fisheries, which were suffering from foreign competition: about the refusal of a subsidy to farmers producing oats, while wheat-growers, of whom there were relatively few in Scotland, were generously assisted: about the limitation laid upon Scottish sugar-beet development. The Scottish railway system was amalgamated with England's in 1921 and this led to the closing down of railway workshops at Kilmarnock and Inverness. There was resentment too over such events as the closing of works at Lennoxtown by the Calico Printers' Association, which was interpreted as an effort to rescue some of Lancashire's lost prosperity, also over the removal of textile machinery from the Clyde Spinning Company of Glasgow to Oldham. People felt that English business interests always had better treatment than Scottish.

All these grievances added up to something more than pre-war dissatisfaction had fastened upon, and during the 1920s there was a fresh spate of Home Rule Bills for Scotland. In 1934, two organizations interested in the problem merged and the Scottish Nationalist party was thus formed. No longer was the concern limited to releasing Scottish administration from the congestion at Westminster. Responsible thinkers now wanted a system which would give Scotsmen authority and control to initiate and draft legislation and to order the financial requirements of it. Extremists were enthusiastic for the Union to be ended. Moderate Nationalists saw no need for this, but were emphatic that fundamental re-adjustment was needed.

There was more to it, however, than legal or financial reform would meet. There was strong feeling now that Scotland was becoming anglicized. Education, the radio, the press, the English chain-stores which were buying up Scottish family firms, the influence of the Civil Service, even of the Trade Unions with their London-based head offices—all these things were undermining the traditions of Scotland, overriding Scottish interests, moulding the ideas and changing the speech of the rising generation north of the Border. In the work of the artists and architects of the Glasgow School, whose standing was now very high, Nationalist sympathizers saw plain evidence of a new Renaissance in culture. In poets such as Hugh McDiarmid and novelists such as George Blake the country was finding a new literary stimulus. The Saltire Society, founded in 1936, was one result of this revival and its success was very significant. This Society sought to foster Scottish literature, music and art, to encourage the study of Gaelic, also of Scottish history and archaeology. The out-and-out Nationalists had as yet limited support, but in their desire to preserve Scottish culture and to gain more control over Scottish administration, they had a great deal of sympathy both in their own country and beyond it.

When the Second World War began, the Scottish Nationalist Movement made little headway, because again such interests seemed of smaller moment to most people than the world's crisis. As soon as peace was made, the tide of Nationalist feeling began to flow once more, with new strength. There were fresh reasons now for Scotsmen to criticize the constitutional status quo. The Welfare State was designed to abolish poverty, to safeguard the health and to ensure the education of everybody's children. It vastly enlarged the bureaucratic controls which all stemmed from Westminster. Less than ever did it appear that Scotsmen would make or implement the decisions which would condition the lives of Scotsmen.

There was great indignation when the naval dockyard at Rosyth was closed and the services at Prestwick Airport curtailed. Britain had been glad enough to use these places in wartime, because of their good geographical situation. Why should they be cut off from the movement of capital and business to the great impoverishment of Scotland as soon as peace came? And Scottish people were exasperated by the long delay of the Government in voting money to build a Forth Bridge for road traffic. To southerners, it seemed a wild extravagance. Those whose business took them northwards up the east side of Scotland found powerful arguments in the expense and frustration of the extra miles they had to drive inland, and in the inadequacy of the car ferry service. There had been support for a Mersey Tunnel, to assist road traffic, why not for a Forth Bridge? Scottish opinion was exasperated by the bland way in which an overwhelmingly English legislature seemed prepared to obstruct measures for which politicians hundreds of miles away could not see any urgency, but which were in fact necessary. And it irritated the Nationalist sympathizers when statutes framed in the interests of

England were embellished with complicated codicils which were supposed to make them applicable also to Scotland.

It became obvious that many people who had hitherto been indifferent were now urgently anxious to see a change made in the administrative if not in the legislative set-up. It was in deference to this feeling that the Government enlarged the scope of the Scottish Standing Committee in 1948. That this did not satisfy Scottish Nationalists was made plain the following year when they produced their significantly named 'Scottish Covenant'. This pledged its signatories—of whom some thousands were enrolled in a few weeks—'in loyalty to the Crown and within the framework of the United Kingdom to do everything in our power to secure for Scotland a Parliament with adequate legislative authority in Scottish affairs'.

The extreme Nationalists draw criticism and censure upon themselves because the Press cannot resist making copy out of their sillier gestures. This should not mask the fact that very many people of proved wisdom and undoubted patriotism are now sympathetic with the more moderate Nationalists. British institutions have never been static, over-organized, bonded to fixed theories, in fact they have erred in the opposite direction. Their great merit has been their capacity for development as circumstances have changed. There is unquestionably room for further change now. It is beyond the capacity of neither Scots nor English to work out a fresh system of government and social organization that would bring fresh satisfaction to both, and such re-thinking need not involve a separation which would undoubtedly impoverish each side.

No assessment of Scottish thought in the last eighty years or so could be attempted unless religious opinion in the country were taken into account. Until the First World War, the hold of organized religion continued to be stronger north of the Border than south of it. Church-going, family prayers, and Sunday School for the children formed part of normal routine for a high proportion of people. This did not include the very poor, the lowest paid navvies and labourers in mine, mill and shipyard— Hugh Miller had noticed in the 1840s and 1850s that these people had no religious connections, and their children and grandchildren as a rule did not form any. This was because cities had expanded rapidly, already existing churches could offer no pew accommodation to incomers, and new churches were not built soon enough in sufficient numbers. The working-class districts in the overcrowded industrial areas often had little mission-halls, run by Church members from 'west-end' congregations; but these could not meet the need and so, in Scottish as in English cities, the very poor were not able to form a tradition of church-going.

Scottish theologians and ministers have made a very great contribution to the Biblical Scholarship which in the last eighty years or so has counted for so much. A fresh understanding of the meaning of Christianity has been the result. In the strength of this, the challenge of Darwinism has been understood. The re-thinking of Christian doctrine which has been stimulated has enabled many leaders in intellectual life, especially in the Universities, to find that their desire to follow Christ was not incompatible with intellectual integrity: and among these a number of prominent scientists have been included. Scottish thinkers have taken a most constructive part in this re-interpretation.

But this fresh approach to religion was not passed on effectively to the general run of laymen, in the first two decades of this century. Sermons rarely touched upon Bible Scholarship, exciting and enlightening as it was. Too many people therefore tacitly assumed that to be a Christian meant tolerating in religion modes of thought no longer respected in science and literature, while others accepted orthodox and traditional teaching without thinking about it independently at all.

On their very doorsteps, Scottish Church people could see misery and destitution, disease and distress. They must have known that in Europe and the East the sum of human pain exceeded anything they themselves could really understand. Somehow these things were accepted. But when the 1914 War broke forth, many Christians in Scotland, as in England, found their faith suddenly assaulted. It seemed impossible to them that a loving God could contenance such tragedy.

The War made a profound and terrible impression on all kinds and classes of people. From every city, village, clachan and glen,

Scotsmen were drafted to all the great battle fronts, they served in thousands in the Army, the Royal Navy, the Merchant Navy, the Royal Flying Corps. The casualties suffered by Britain and the Commonwealth during those four years cost a whole generation a great proportion of its finest people, many of them hardly adult, and Scotland's share in this was terribly high. The oldest regiment of the line in the British Army, the Royal Scots, suffered over 11,000 casualties. This was no exception to the general rule. Earl Haig himself was a Scot and his countrymen served and died in every rank of all the services. The deprivation caused by such loss of life and health in so small a nation made it infinitely difficult for those who survived to reconstruct their country's way of life.

The war years caused a complete break with formerly unques tioned traditions. People were suddenly pitchforked out of familiar surroundings and well-loved homes into circumstances of acute danger, and terrible daily strain. Those who remained at home were subjected also to quite new distresses and soul-destroying pressures. Families were divided, children neglected, home life disrupted. In the upheaval, people reacted with resentful and embittered distaste against the society which had precipitated the disasters. Many of them also turned against the Church and its teachings, about which they were disillusioned. Some of the younger generation blamed the Church for having failed in its mission, others dismissed it as obsolete, irrelevant.

The confusion of mind amongst these young people was one symptom of the nation's trouble. They thought they wanted to think independently, but they lacked both the training and the concentration this demands. They thought they wanted freedom from authority, so that they could make their own decisions, emancipated from old restrictions of principle and tradition, but really they were longing for authoritative direction they could respect. They thought they were done with idealism, that the war had proved the hollowness and the sham of all idealisms, but they discovered in themselves a hunger for new ideals. The one obvious fact from which nobody could escape was that security of any sort, emotional, material or political, was apparently beyond the grasp of everybody. Amongst young people so disillusioned and so lacking in stability, Communist enthusiasts were able to make rapid headway. Communism offered an ideal, a gospel, a crusade, an all-embracing purpose, companionship, authority, discipline. Its weaknesses in logic and in historical interpretation, its duplicity, its cruelty, its usefulness to dictators bent on exploitation—none of this was easily apparent to people brought up in the conditions of spiritual confusion and industrial disaster which followed the war.

By this time, many older people had lost confidence in themselves and in their beliefs. They did not trust themselves to give their children guidance even about basic moralities. In homes and schools, teaching about truth and generosity, integrity and courage was often neglected. Religious instruction in particular reached a new low level, and many children whose parents and grandparents had been God-fearing grew up quite ignorant even of the simplest facts about Christianity. Organized religion seemed for a while to have little chance of survival, church attendance decreased steadily and Sundays were devoted by most people to pleasure or to chores about the house.

The pace of life militated against recovery from this sickness of the spirit. By motor coach, car, train and plane people were on the move, both at work and in leisure-time. Even during the depression, when hunger marches, Labour Exchange queues, destitution up and down every street seemed to be breaking people's hearts, commerce laid hold upon the universal craving for distraction. Dance-halls, public-houses, night clubs and the like exploited the need for time-killing and escape. The radio and the film poured a whole new cacophony of noise into the ears of young and old. And there was loneliness too. The old neighbourliness of village and town was replaced by the impersonal character of huge cities, where people travel great distances to work and lose interest in local community life.

In these very years of apparent failure there became evident some signs of a renaissance in religion. The work of the Student Christian Movement had led, especially in Scotland, to a renewal of interest in Foreign Missions. Young, intelligent missionaries coming out from Universities where they had experienced a sense of union with Christians of other denominations, found the divisions of Christendom in the mission fields intolerable. A returning tide of vitality from these mission fields reinforced the desire at home for Church reunion.

As early as 1900, the Free Church and the United Presbyterian Church had joined together under the name of the United Free Church. Again, in 1929, the Church of Scotland and the United Free Church made a successful union, and in doing so they greatly strengthened their position. Unfortunately, in both cases there was a minority which continued as a separate organization.

This union between Presbyterians has been symptomatic of a new desire among Christians to stand together and face together the challenge of the new paganism, the materialism, the ideologies which are threatening civilization. The World Council of Churches has held a number of conferences in recent years, notably one at Amsterdam in 1948, to which representatives from many nations and many branches of the Christian Church came. The work of the World Council aroused much interest in Scotland, as it did in England. In view of this development it was natural that the two leading branches of the Protestant Church in Britain should wish to draw together. And so, in spite of some important differences in doctrine and tradition, the Church of Scotland and the Church of England have been holding discussions together. The result has been the publication of a preliminary report by a joint body of representatives from both sides in 1957. There is a long way to go before a solution can be worked out which will satisfy the rank and file in these two great national churches, but it is a sign of the times that they are seeking to emphasize the principles they hold in common.

The abandonment of conventional church-going has not really been a loss to the church. There is more sincerity and vitality among its members and adherents today and this is apparent in their activities. In Scotland, as in England and France, Industrial Chaplains have been appointed to work in the factories and this seems to meet a real need, and to elicit a real welcome. The Iona Community has contributed to a recovery among ministers and laymen of the sense of Christian fellowship transcending class: it has afforded a fresh experience of the strength gained in corporate devotions and a new conviction of the mission of the Church. The same hunger for religious guidance is met with on the Housing Estates, especially among young people whose parents have no religious teaching to offer them. One fact which should not be overlooked is that the Roman Catholic Church claims to be growing steadily in numbers, and is probably justified in this claim, though exact statistics are difficult to establish.

The renewed interest in religion has been much fostered by the Religious Department of the BBC. And it has also been stimulated by the Scottish theologians. During the years of the Second World War and since, Christian scholarship has reached the lay public of Scotland in terms which can be more readily understood than in any previous period. This is much needed. The advances in scientific research have given mankind a far greater control over the forces of nature, but they have not given anybody renewed confidence in man himself or in his destiny. The materialism of the age is beginning to produce its own reaction and some people are now more willing to turn to spiritual resources.

And what of the future? Poverty, the ancient and continuous enemy of Scotland, has been virtually abolished in the short period since the Welfare State was inaugurated in 1948. Even in unemployment, no Scottish worker, or his family, suffers now as men did formerly when they were drawing regular wages.

New anxieties are pressing upon many who hold Scotland in high regard. As in England, there has developed with increasing material prosperity an ominous irresponsibility. Everywhere people seem to be more conscious of their rights, their physical comfort, their immediate securities and pleasures than of their due share in the nation's work, their contribution to its wellbeing. The Trade Unions of to-day are fighting, not for the basic welfare of their members, nor for the status of working people in the world as a whole, but for a steadily steepening rise in wage scales, designed to secure monetary advantage in the immediate situation. In pressing for this, the Trade Unions are showing no more understanding of economics or social justice than did the employers of the bad old days; they are trying to substitute one privileged class for another, without regard to the economic laws which affect the nation as a whole, or to the economic condition of the masses in under-developed territories of Asia and Africa.

The enormous and impersonal organizations which to a great extent have ousted family firms and suppressed private enterprise seem to be in a fair way towards eliminating individual initiative and submerging in a mass of colourless mediocrity the brains and courage of younger generations. On matters of principle, individuals are far too ready to remain silent, to go with the crowd, to take the path of least resistance, and in this way to condone policies and behaviour patterns of which they really disapprove. This has often been the case in the strikes which have done such damage to the Scottish firms upon whose stability the country's future must in great measure depend.

Is it not the case too that Scotland has become infected with the notion, which has done much harm elsewhere in recent years, that people should be treated as if one and all were alike in ability, in common sense, in intellectual stamina? This is plainly not true. But Trade Unionists, politicians, educationists, journalists are all endeavouring so hard to give equal opportunity to everybody—a justifiable purpose within limits—that they are in danger of trying to give the *same* opportunity to everybody. It has become almost an indecency to suggest that those who are specially gifted, those who carry heavy or important responsibility, those who can do what others cannot attempt, should be given any advantage or status other than what is accorded to the rest. Carried much further, such an approach will iron out individuality, frustrate initiative and quench the very qualities which in research and enterprise are vital even for economic progress, let alone for fulness of life.

Scottish people claim to be proud of their history. One wonders whether they are proud of the right things. There is an unreal flavour, a fantasy element, in the fashion for idealizing, indeed almost idolizing, a handful of popular characters—Mary, Queen of Scots, for example, Charles Edward and Robert Burns. These people have been made into symbols of something for which they never really stood, and Scotsmen will talk with abandoned romanticism about them, often without any real knowledge of what they were like. Such idolizing of figures of the past may be interpreted as the sentimental escape of men who are subconsciously aware that they have lost control of their own country in the present, and are reacting in opportunist fashion to forces directed upon them from without. Even in the serious study of the past, a sphere where Scotsmen themselves ought primarily to be concerned, not nearly enough original research has yet gone into certain topics of absorbing interest—for example the origins of Scottish Trade Unionism, the Parliamentary and judicial institutions of Scotland, the local traditions of parishes up and down the country.

The habit of going away from Scotland still exercises its traditional hold upon her citizens. Sir Walter Scott said in his day that they went in search of adventure. It seems that many nowadays go for no such reason. They go in search of security. And those who go, or who live in hopes of going, include some who cry out most loudly that Scotland does not have a fair deal in the Union. Many English people are puzzled by this attitude. To them it is plainly apparent that Scotland is a country of surpassing beauty with many natural advantages all its own, that Scottish people inherit qualities and traditions of the highest value, that the Scot's courage and humour and regard for principle make him a first-rate colleague. One asks oneself the question—loving their country as they so justly do, why do they not devote their many gifts to its service instead of seeking their personal fortunes elsewhere?

There is great comfort in knowing that you belong to a splendid nation, and this is one comfort that no Scot can lack. On the other hand, it is not sufficiently realized, on either side of the Border, that Scotsmen and Englishmen have much in common. In principle and belief, in love of freedom and respect for individuals, in traditions of democracy and culture, in zest for adventurous living and for creative thinking, Scotland and England share a great heritage. With such resources of mind and spirit, these two peoples, given that they develop more awareness and realism in their attitude to each other as well as to themselves, could together offer the world of to-day and to-morrow a leadership needed at this moment in history more than ever before. One may well finish a history of Scotland by asking, 'What of the future?'

A Selected list of Books

ALAN O. ANDERSON: *Scottish annals from English Chroniclers*, A.D. 500–1286. London, 1908.

ALAN O. ANDERSON: *Early sources of Scottish History*, A.D. 500–1286. Edinburgh, 1922.

CECIL ASPINALL-OGLANDER: *Freshly Remembered, The Story of Thomas Graham, Lord Lynedoch*. London, 1956.

JOSEPH BAIN: *The Edwards in Scotland*, 1296–1377. Edinburgh, 1901.

E. W. M. BALFOUR-MELVILLE: *James I, King of Scots*, 1406–37. London, 1936.

E. M. BARRON: *The Scottish War of Independence*. (2nd edition). Inverness, 1934.

J. W. BAXTER: *William Dunbar, a biographical study*. Edinburgh, 1952.

R. T. BERTHOFF: *British Immigrants in Industrial America*, 1790–1950. Cambridge (Mass.), 1953.

G. F. BLACK: *The Surnames of Scotland: their origin, meaning and history*. New York, 1946.

JAMES BOSWELL: *Journal of a Tour to the Hebrides with Samuel Johnson*. London, 1928.

P. HUME BROWN: *George Buchanan, humanist and reformer*. Edinburgh, 1890.

P. HUME BROWN: *Early travellers in Scotland*. Edinburgh, 1891.

P. HUME BROWN: *Scotland before 1700 from contemporary documents*. Edinburgh, 1893.

P. HUME BROWN: *History of Scotland*. Cambridge, 1899.

GEORGE BRYCE: *Mackenzie, Selkirk, Simpson*. (Makers of Canada. Anniv. ed., 9). London, Toronto, 1926.

JAMES BULLOCH: *Adam of Dryburgh*. London, 1958.

ROBERT BUTCHART: *Prints & Drawings of Edinburgh. A descriptive account of the collection in the Edinburgh Room of the Central Public Library*. Edinburgh, 1955.

RONALD G. CANT: *The University of St. Andrews: a short history*. Edinburgh, 1946.

ANDREW J. CAMPBELL: *Fifteen centuries of the Church in Orkney*. Kirkwall, 1938.

H. M. CHADWICK: *Early Scotland: the Picts, the Scots and the Welsh of Southern Scotland*. Cambridge, 1949.

V. G. CHILDE: *The Pre-History of Scotland*. London, 1935.

V. G. CHILDE: *Scotland before the Scots*. London, 1946.

V. G. CHILDE: *Skara Brae, a Pictish village in Orkney; with chapters by T. H. Bryce and D. M. S. Watson*. London, 1931.

A Selected List of Books

V. G. CHILDE and W. D. SIMPSON: *Illustrated guide to ancient monuments in the ownership and guardianship of the Ministry of Works. Vol. VI. Scotland.*

J. STORER CLOUSTON: *A history of Orkney.* Kirkwall, 1932.

HENRY, LORD COCKBURN: *Memorials of his time.* Abridged and edited with notes by W. F. Gray. (Scottish Classics, 1). Edinburgh, 1946.

JOHN D. COMRIE: *History of Scottish Medicine.* London, 1932.

LORD COOPER: *Select Scottish cases of the thirteenth century.* 1944.

REGINALD COUPLAND: *Welsh & Scottish nationalism.* London, 1954.

JAMES COUTTS: *History of the University of Glasgow,* 1451–1909. Glasgow, 1909.

R. M. W. COWAN: *The newspaper in Scotland: a study of its first expansion* 1815–1860. Glasgow, 1946.

ALAN D. CUTHBERT: *Clyde Shipping Company Limited.* Glasgow, 1956.

DANIEL DEFOE: *A tour thro' that part of Great Britain called Scotland.* (*Vol.* 4 *of A tour thro' the whole island of Great Britain*). Dublin, 1746.

GEORGE DEMPSTER: *Letters of George Dempster to Sir Adam Fergusson* 1756–1813. Edited by James Fergusson. London, 1934.

A. V. DICEY and R. S. RAIT: *Thoughts on the Union.* London, 1920.

WILLIAM C. DICKINSON: *John Knox's History of the Reformation in Scotland.* London, 1949.

JOHN DOWDEN: *The Celtic Church in Scotland.* London, 1894.

JOHN DOWDEN: *The Medieval Church in Scotland.* Glasgow, 1910.

JOHN DOWDEN: *The Bishops of Scotland.* Glasgow, 1912.

JOHN A. DUKE: *The Columban Church.* Edinburgh, 1957.

JOHN A. DUKE: *History of the Church of Scotland to the Reformation.* Edinburgh, 1957.

A. H. DUNBAR: *Scottish Kings,* 1005–1625. Edinburgh, 1899.

ANNIE I. DUNLOP: *The life and times of James Kennedy, Bishop of St. Andrews.* Edinburgh, 1950.

ANNIE I. DUNLOP: *The Royal Burgh of Ayr; seven hundred and fifty years of history.* Edinburgh, 1953.

DAVID E. EASSON: *Gavin Dunbar, Chancellor of Scotland, Archbishop of Glasgow.* Edinburgh, 1947.

MALCOLM H. ELLIS: *Lachlan Macquarie, his life, adventures and times.* Sydney, 1952.

HENRY G. FARMER: *A history of music in Scotland.* London, 1947.

CHARLES R. FAY: *Adam Smith & the Scotland of his day.* Cambridge, 1956.

THOMAS FERGUSON: *The dawn of Scottish social welfare.* London, 1948.

THOMAS FERGUSON: *Scottish social welfare,* 1864–1914. Edinburgh, 1958.

THOMAS FERGUSON: *The young delinquent in his social setting, a Glasgow study.* London, 1952.

THOMAS FERGUSON & J. CUNISON: *In their early twenties, a study of Glasgow youth.* London, 1956.

JAMES FERGUSSON: *Alexander III, King of Scotland.* London, 1937.

JAMES FERGUSSON: *Argyll in the Forty-Five.* London, 1951.

JAMES FERGUSSON: *Lowland Lairds.* London, 1949.

W. IAN R. FINLAY: *Art in Scotland.* London, 1948.

W. IAN R. FINLAY: *Scotland.* London, 1957.

A Selected List of Books

CHARLES H. FIRTH: *Scotland and the Commonwealth.* (Scottish Hist. Soc.) Edinburgh, 1895.

CHARLES H. FIRTH: *Scotland and the Protectorate.* (Scottish Hist. Soc.) Edinburgh, 1899.

DAVID HAY FLEMING: *The Reformation in Scotland: causes, characteristics, consequences.* London, 1910.

J. R. FLEMING: *A History of the Church in Scotland,* 1843–1929. Edinburgh, 1927.

FORFEITED ESTATES PAPERS 1715–1745. Scottish History Society, 1st. Series, Vol. 57.

FORTUNA DOMUS: *A series of lectures delivered in The University of Glasgow in Commemoration of the Fifth Centenary of its Foundation.* Glasgow, 1952.

T. B. FRANKLIN: *A History of Scottish farming.* London, 1952.

HOLDEN FURBER: *Henry Dundas, first Viscount Melville,* 1742–1811. London, 1931.

J. G. FYFE: *Scottish Diaries & Memoirs* 1550–1746 *and* 1746–1843. Stirling, 1942.

WALTER GEIKIE: *Etchings, Scottish Character and Scenery.* Edinburgh, 1885.

A. DEWAR GIBB: *Scottish Empire.* London, 1937.

ROBERT GIBBINGS: *John Graham, Convict,* 1824; *an historical narrative.* London, 1937.

FREDERICK GOLDIE: *Short History of the Episcopal Church in Scotland, from the Reformation to the present time.* London, 1951.

S. GORDON and T. G. B. COCKS: *A People's conscience. Six typical enquiries* (1729–1837) *by Select Committees of the House of Commons.* London, 1952.

H. G. GRAHAM: *The Social Life of Scotland in the Eighteenth Century.* London, 1937.

ALEXANDER GRANT: *The Story of the University of Edinburgh, during its first three hundred years.* London, 1884.

MRS. ANNE GRANT of Laggan. *Letters from the Mountains, being the real correspondence of a lady* (*A. Grant*) *between the years* 1773 *and* 1807. London, 1807.

ISABEL F. GRANT: *Everyday life on an old Highland farm* 1769–1782. London, 1924.

ISABEL F. GRANT: *The Social and economic development of Scotland Before* 1603. Edinburgh, 1930.

ISABEL F. GRANT: *The economic history of Scotland.* 1934.

MALCOLM GRAY: *The Highland economy,* 1750–1850. Edinburgh, 1957.

A. R. B. HALDANE: *The drove roads of Scotland.* London, 1952.

HENRY HAMILTON: *The Industrial Revolution in Scotland.* Oxford, 1932.

HENRY HAMILTON: *Selections from the Monymusk Papers,* 1713–55. (Scottish Hist. Soc.) Edinburgh, 1945.

JAMES E. HANDLEY: *The Irish in Scotland* 1798–1845. Cork, 1943.

JAMES E. HANDLEY: *The Irish in Modern Scotland.* Cork, 1947.

JAMES E. HANDLEY: *Scottish farming in the Eighteenth Century.* London, 1953.

A Selected List of Books

R. K. HANNAY: *The College of Justice; essays on the institution and development of the Court of Session.* Edinburgh, 1933.

G. D. HENDERSON: *Religious life in seventeenth century Scotland.* Cambridge, 1937.

G. D. HENDERSON: *Presbyterianism.* Aberdeen, 1954.

ROBERT HERON: *Observations made in a journey through the western counties of Scotland in autumn of* 1792. Perth, 1793.

JOHN HIGHET: *The Churches in Scotland to-day, a survey of their principles, strength, work and statements.* Glasgow, 1950.

HUDSON'S BAY RECORD SOCIETY. Vol. XIV.

COSMO INNES: *Sketches of Early Scottish history and social progress.* Edinburgh, 1861.

COSMO INNES: *Scotland in the Middle Ages.* Edinburgh, 1860.

GEORGE PRATT INSH: *The Company of Scotland, trading to Africa and the Indies.* London, 1932.

GEORGE PRATT INSH: *The Scottish Jacobite Movement; a study in economic and social forces.* Edinburgh, 1952.

SAMUEL JOHNSON: *Journey to the Western Islands.* London, 1775.

T. JOHNSTON: *History of the working classes in Scotland.* Glasgow, 1923.

JAMES KEITH: *Fifty years of farming.* London, 1954.

JAMES KINSLEY: *Scottish Poetry, a critical survey.* London, 1955.

G. A. F. KNIGHT: *Archeological light on the early Christianizing of Scotland.* London, 1933.

H. M. KNOX: *Two hundred and fifty years of Scottish education.* Edinburgh, 1953.

J. G. KYD: *Scottish population statistics.* (Scottish Hist. Soc.) Edinburgh, 1952.

A. C. LAWRIE: *Early Scottish charters.* Glasgow, 1905.

J. LEES-MILNE: *The age of Adam.* London, 1947.

T. C. LETHBRIDGE: *Herdsmen and hermits: Celtic seafarers in the northern seas.* Cambridge, 1950.

WILLIAM McCOMBIE: *Cattle & cattle breeders.* Edinburgh, 1886.

D. F. MACDONALD: *Scotland's shifting population,* 1770–1850. Glasgow, 1937.

JOHN McDONALD: *Voyage to Quebec and journey from thence to New Lanark in Upper Canada.* First Edition 1823.

A. M. MACEWEN: *The Thistle and the Rose; Scotland's problem to-day.* Edinburgh, 1932.

DAVID MACGIBBON and THOMAS ROSS: *The ecclesiastical architecture of Scotland.* Edinburgh, 1896.

AGNES MURE MACKENZIE: *History of Scotland* (6 vols.) new edition. Edinburgh, 1957–58.

OSGOOD MACKENZIE: *A hundred years in the Highlands.* New edition. London, 1949.

W. C. MACKENZIE: *Andrew Fletcher of Saltoun, his life and times.* Edinburgh, 1935.

W. M. MACKENZIE: *The medieval castle in Scotland.* London, 1927.

W. M. MACKENZIE: *The Scottish burghs.* Edinburgh, 1949.

J. B. MACKIE: *The life and work of Duncan Maclaren.* Edinburgh, 1888.

A Selected List of Books

JOHN DUNCAN MACKIE: *The University of Glasgow, 1451–1951, a short history*. Glasgow, 1954.

ROBERT L. MACKIE: *A short history of Scotland*. London, 1931.

ROBERT L. MACKIE: *King James IV of Scotland, a brief survey of his life and times*. Edinburgh, 1958.

MARTIN MARTIN: *Description of the Western Isles of Scotland circa 1695*. London, 1703.

HUGH MARWICK: *Orkney*. (County Book Series.) London, 1951.

W. H. MARWICK: *Economic developments in Victorian Scotland*. London, 1936.

CYRIL MATHESON: *Henry Dundas, first Viscount Melville, 1742–1811*. London, 1933.

DAVID J. MATHEW: *Scotland under Charles I*. London, 1955.

WILLIAM L. MATHIESON: *Church and reform in Scotland 1797–1843*. Glasgow, 1916.

W. D. MAXWELL: *A history of worship in the Church of Scotland*. London, 1955.

H. W. MEIKLE: *Scotland and the French Revolution*. Glasgow, 1912.

H. W. MEIKLE: *Scotland, A description of Scotland and Scottish life*. London, 1947.

GEORGE MENARY: *The life and letters of Duncan Forbes of Culloden, Lord President of the Court of Session, 1685–1747*. London, 1936.

HUGH MILLER: *My schools and schoolmasters*. Edinburgh, 1905.

DAVID MILNE: *The Scottish Office, and other Scottish government departments*. London, 1957.

E. C. MOSSNER: *The Life of David Hume*. New York, 1943.

DAVID MURRAY: *Early burgh organization in Scotland*. Glasgow, 1924.

WALLACE NOTESTEIN: *The Scot in history*. London (printed U.S.A.), 1946.

C. A. OAKLEY: *The second city*. London, 1946.

J. W. OLIVER & J. C. SMITH: *A Scots anthology from the Thirteenth to the Twentieth Century*. Edinburgh, 1949.

THEODORA PAGAN: *The Convention of the Royal Burghs of Scotland*. Glasgow, 1926.

MILLAR PATRICK: *Four centuries of Scottish Psalmody*. London, 1949.

HESKETH PEARSON: *The Smith of Smiths*. London, 1934.

THOMAS PENNANT: *A tour in Scotland*. Chester, 1771.

LORD EUSTACE PERCY: *John Knox*. 1937.

CHARLES A. PETRIE: *The Jacobite Movement*. London, 1948.

STUART PIGGOTT: *Scotland before history*. London, 1958.

DAPHNE D. C. POCHIN MOULD: *Scotland of the Saints*. London, 1952.

F. M. POWICKE: *Ailred of Rievaulx and his biographer Walter Daniel*. London, 1950.

GEORGE S. PRYDE: *The Treaty of Union*. London, 1950.

ROBERT S. RAIT: *The Parliaments of Scotland*. Glasgow, 1924.

ROBERT S. RAIT: *The Universities of Aberdeen*. Aberdeen, 1895.

ROBERT S. RAIT & G. S. PRYDE: *Scotland*. (Second Edition). London, 1954.

REPORTS OF THE ROYAL COMMISSION ON THE ANCIENT MONUMENTS OF SCOTLAND.

R. L. G. RITCHIE: *The Normans in Scotland*. Edinburgh, 1954.

A Selected List of Books

GEORGE ROBERTSON: *Rural recollections.* Irvine, 1829.

ROYAL MUSICAL ASSOCIATION: *Music of Scotland,* 1500–1700. London, 1957.

R. N. SALAMAN: *The history and social influence of the Potato.* Cambridge, 1949.

L. J. SAUNDERS: *Scottish Democracy* 1815–1840, *the social and intellectual Background.* Edinburgh, 1950.

W. D. SIMPSON: *The historical Saint Columba.* Aberdeen, 1927.

W. D. SIMPSON: *The Celtic Church in Scotland.* Aberdeen, 1935.

JOHN SLEZER: *Theatricum Scotiae.* London, 1693. Reprinted, with the life of the author and large additional illustrations by John Jamieson. Edinburgh, 1874.

ALISTAIR SMART: *The life and art of Allan Ramsay.* 1952.

MRS. ELIZABETH SMITH OF BALTIBOYS: *Memoirs of a Highland Lady,* 1797–1827. Revised and edited by A Davidson. London, 1950.

SAMUEL SMILES: *Lives of the Engineers.* London, 1904.

THOMAS SOMERVILLE: *My own life and times,* 1741–1814. Edinburgh, 1861.

The (Old) Statistical Account of Scotland (1791–99).

The New Statistical Account of Scotland (1845).

The Third Statistical Account of Scotland (1951–   ).

MARGARET STUART: *Scottish family history.* Edinburgh, 1930.

M. W. STUART: *The Scot who was a Frenchman (The Regent Albany).* London, 1940.

ANDREW SYMSON: *A description of Galloway.*

CHARLES S. TERRY: *The Scottish Parliament,* 1603–1707. Glasgow, 1905.

HUGH THOMSON: *Highways & Byways in Galloway and Carrick.* 1916.

ARTHUR C. TURNER: *Scottish Home Rule.* Oxford, 1952.

JOHN WARRACK: *Domestic life in Scotland,* 1488–1688. London, 1920.

WILLIAM J. WATSON: *History of the Celtic place-names of Scotland.* Stirling, 1922.

C. V. WEDGWOOD: *Montrose.* London, 1952.

C. V. WEDGWOOD: *The King's Peace,* 1637–1641. London, 1955.

C. V. WEDGWOOD: *The King's War,* 1641–1647. London, 1958.

DAVID H. WILLSON: *King James VI & I.* London, 1956.

J. A. WILSON: *A contribution to the History of Lanarkshire.* Glasgow, 1936.

A. P. WOOLLACOTT: *Mackenzie and his voyageurs.* London, 1927.

DOROTHY WORDSWORTH: *Recollections of a Tour in Scotland* A.D. 1803. London, 1874.

LESLIE C. WRIGHT: *Chartism in Scotland.* Edinburgh, 1953.

Index

Index

Dunbar, William, poet, 110, 111, 112
Duncan, King of Scotland, 47
Duncan, son of Malcolm III of Scotland, 50, 52
Dundas, Henry, first Lord Melville, 305, 306 et seq.
Dupplin Moor, Battle of, 1332, 89, see map 6, facing 85

Eanflaed, wife of King Oswy, 43
East India Company, 303, 304, 337
Edgar Atheling, 48, 52
Edgar, King of Scotland, 52, 53
Edinburgh Review, The, 273, 292
Edinburgh University, 152, 293, 295 et seq.
Education Act, 1872, 293
Edward I, King of England, 74, et seq., 91, 129
Edward II, King of England, 81, 82, 83, 85
Edward III, King of England, 88, 89
Edward VI, King of England, 129, 131, 133, 134
Edward the Confessor, 47, 48
Elder, Sir John of Govan, 256
Elgin, 8th Earl of, see Bruce, James
Elizabeth I, Queen of England, 137, 138, 145, 149, 150, 154
Elliot, Sir Gilbert, 1st Earl of Minto, 336
Elphinstone, William, Bishop of Aberdeen and founder of Aberdeen University, 105, 113
Emigration, eighteenth century, 224 et seq.; nineteenth century, 341 et seq., 352; twentieth century, 386
Engagers, 176
Engineering, 255, 256, 354
English Book of Common Prayer, 135, 136, 165
Episcopalian Church, 162, 171, 187, 188, 200, 281, 282
Equivalent Money, 197, 198
Erasmus, 107, 113
Erskine, John, eleventh Earl of Mar, 202, 203, 204, 207, 265

Factory Acts, 331
Falaise, Treaty of, 68
Fergus, Lord of Galloway, 61, 69
Fergus MacErc, 37
Ferguson, Professor Adam, 296
Ferguson, Thomas, *Scottish Social Welfare*, 362
Fergusson, Adam, correspondent of George Dempster, 268, 304
Fitzalan, Walter, Steward of Scotland and Lord of Renfrew, 69
Fitzalan, Walter, Steward of Scotland and son-in-law of Robert I, 87

Five Articles of Perth, 1618, 157
Fletcher, Andrew of Saltoun, 214
Fletcher, Archibald, Whig Advocate, 306, 308
Flodden, Battle of, 1513, 119, 126
Fontenoy, Battle of, 1745, 206
Food-rationing in the Second World War, 363
Forbes, Duncan, of Culloden, 209, 219, 259, 339
Forth Bridge for road traffic, 378
Foulis, Andrew and Robert, printers, 263
Francis II, King of France, 137, 138, 142
French Revolution, influence of, 273, 283, 305 et seq., 344, 345

General Assembly, 157, 171, 179, 282, 283, 290, 291, 345
George, David Lloyd, 366, 367
George I, 193, 201, 202, 204
George II, 209
Gibb, Professor A. D., *Scottish Empire*, 338, 343
Gibbs, James, architect, 264, 265
Glasgow Academy of Arts, 264
Glasgow Herald, The, 313
Glasgow School of Painting, 373, 374, 377
Glasgow University, 105, 293, 294, 295, 297, 299
Glencoe, massacre of, 185, 186
Graham, James, Earl, later Marquis of Montrose, 167, 170, 171 et seq.
Graham, Sir Robert, murderer of James I of Scotland, 102
Grant, Sir Archibald, of Monymusk, 217, 218, 278, 279, 334. For Monymusk, see map 5, facing 61
Greenshields, the Rev. James, 200, 281

Hadrian, 27
Hadrian's Wall, see map 3, 31
Hakon, Earl of the Orkneys, 63
Hakon, King of Norway, 71
Haldane, A. R. B., *Drove Roads of Scotland*, 219
Halidon Hill, Battle of, 1333, 89, see map 6, facing 85
Halyburton, Andrew, 115
Hamilton, Patrick, died 1528, 126
Hampton Court Conference, 158
Hardie, James Keir, Trade Union Leader, 365, 366, 375
Harlaw, Battle of, 1411, 98
Henderson, the Rev. Alexander, 167, 168
Henry, I, King of England, 53, 54, 65
Henry II, King of England, 68, 69
Henry III, King of England, 71, 91

395

Index

Henry V, King of England, 98
Henry VI, King of England, 98
Henry VIII, King of England, 119, 128 et seq., 150
Henry, son of David I of Scotland, 55, 68
Henryson, Robert, poet, 110, 111
Hepburn, James, Bishop of Moray, 124
Hepburn, James, Earl of Bothwell, 144
Home, the Rev. John, *Douglas* 262, 268, 282
Honourable Society of Improvers in the Knowledge of Agriculture, 216
Horner, Francis, *Edinburgh Review*, 273
Hudson's Bay Company, 343
Hume, David, philosopher, 262, 266, 267, 268, 283
Hutcheson, Francis, Professor in Glasgow University, 294

Indian Civil Service, 337, 338
Industrial Chaplains, 383
Ingibjorg, wife of Malcolm III of Scotland, 48, 50, 52
Iona, 38, 39, 40, see map 4, facing 35
Iona Community, The, 383
Irish Home Rule, 312, 375, 376
Iron industry, 252, 254, 355, 356, 358
Isabella, wife of Edward II of England, 85

James II, King of England, 184, 188
James I, King of Scotland, 92, 96, 97 et seq., 119
James II, King of Scotland, 97, 119
James III, King of Scotland, 97, 104, 106, 108, 119
James IV, King of Scotland, 97, 107, et seq., 119, 120, 124, 125
James V, King of Scotland, 119, 126, 127, et seq.
James VI and I, King of Scotland and King of England, 120, 145, 147 et seq., 162
James Edward, son of James II, 193, 200 et seq.
Jeffrey, Francis, *Edinburgh Review*, 273
Jenner, Edward, discover of vaccination, 322
Jex-Blake, Dr. Sophia, 300
Joanna, wife of David II of Scotland, 85, 88, 90
Johnson, Samuel, 210, 268, 269, 280, 295
Johnston, Archibald, Lord Warriston, 163, 167, 168
Justiciars, 58

Kames, Henry Home, Lord, 266
Keith, Sir Robert, 336, 340
Keith, Sir Basil, 340
Kelvin, William Thomson, Lord, 299
Kennedy, James, Bishop of St. Andrews and founder of St. Salvator's College, 105, 106
Kenneth McAlpin, King of Dalriada, 46, 47
Keynes, J. M., later Lord Keynes, 360
Killiecrankie Pass, 185
Killing Times, 183, 187
King's College, Aberdeen, 113
Knox, John, 131, et seq., 137 et seq., 188, 287, 293

Labour Exchanges, 359, 367
Labour Party, 366, 375
Largs, Battle of, 1263, 71
Laud, William, Archbishop of Canterbury, 164, 173
Lauder, Robert Scott, artist, 373
Lauderdale, Earl of, see Maitland, John
Leith, Treaty of, 139
Leslie, Alexander, Earl of Leven, 171
Letters of Indulgence, 183
Lewis, George, *Scotland a half-educated Nation* 292
Liberal Party, 312, 375, 376
Liberal Reforms, 1908–1911, 367
Linen industry, 245, 246, 247
Lismore, isle of, 40, 125, see map 4, facing 35
Lister, Joseph, surgeon, later Lord Lister, 298
Littlejohn, Dr. Henry, 331
Livingstone, David, 346, 347
Lochiel, Donald Cameron of, 206
Lockhart, J. G., biographer of Scott, 274
Lollius Urbicus, 27
Lords of the Articles, 101, 154, 184
Lorne, Lord, see Campbell, Archibald
Loudoun Hill, Battle of, 1307, 81, see map 6, facing 85
Loyola, Ignatius, 123
Luther, Martin, 113, 123

Macadam, John, road builder, 241
Macbeth, 47
Macdonald, Alexander, Trade Unionist, 365, 366
Macdonald, Flora, 210
Macdonald, J. Ramsay, 366
McDonald, John, emigrant to Upper Canada, 341, 342
Macgillivray, Pittendrigh, sculptor, 374
Macintosh, Charles Rennie, architect, 374
Mackenzie, Sir Alexander, explorer, 343

Index

Mackenzie, Osgood, *A Hundred Years in the Highlands*, 367

Mackie, R. L., *James IV of Scotland*, 110, 111, 112

McLaren, Duncan, politician, 312

Macquarie, Lachlan, Governor of New South Wales, 336

McTaggart, William, artist, 373

Maes Howe, 19, 63, see map 2, facing 25

Magnus Barelegs, King of Norway, 52, 53

Maid of Norway, 74, 75, 119

Maitland, John, Earl of Lauderdale, 176, 181, 182

Major, John, *The History of Scotland*, 114, 148

Malcolm II, King of the Picts and Scots, 47

Malcolm III, King of Scotland, 47 et seq., 119

Malcolm IV, King of Scotland, 68, 119

Malt Tax, 1713, 201

Mar, Earl of, see Erskine, John

Margaret, wife of James IV of Scotland, 108, 109, 110

Margaret, wife of Malcolm III of Scotland 48–51, 62

Marston Moor, Battle of, 1644, 175, 176

Marwick, W. H., *Economic Developments in Victorian Scotland*, 373

Mary of Guise, wife of James V of Scotland, 128, 129, 131, 132, 134, 138

Mary, Queen of Scots, 119, 120, 129, 131, 133, 137, 138, 142, 143, et seq., 149, 150, 385

Matilda, daughter of Henry I of England, 65

Maud, daughter of Malcolm III of Scotland, wife of Henry I of England, 53, 65, 119

Maxwell, W. D., *A History of the Church in Scotland*, 136

Medical Schools, 297

Megalithic settlers, 19

Meikle, Andrew, inventor, 221

Melancthon, Philip, 113, 114

Melville, Andrew, reformer, 152, 157, 163, 294

Merchant Gilds, 103

Metrical Psalms, 174

Miller, Hugh, *My Schools and Schoolmasters*, 287, 288, 318, 320, 367, 379

Mines Act, 1842, 318, 331

Missionary enterprise, 344 et seq.

Moffat, Robert, missionary, 346, 347

Monck, George, 1st Duke of Albemarle, 179

Mons Graupius, 26

Montrose, Earl, later Marquis of, see Graham, James

Mousa, Broch, 23, see map 2, facing 25

Muir, Edwin, poet, 374

Mure, Elizabeth, of Caldwell, 245, 246, 256

Myllar, Andrew, printer, 112, 113

Myln, Walter, died 1558, 137

Napier, Robert, shipbuilder and engineer, 256

Naseby, Battle of, 1645, 175

Nasmyth, Alexander, artist, 263

National Health Service, 369

Neilson, James of Shettleston, 254

Neville's Cross, Battle of, 1346, 89

Newcomen, Thomas, inventor, 251

Niall of the Nine Hostages, 36, 37

Norham-on-Tweed, 76, see map 6, facing 85

North of Scotland Hydro-Electric Board, 354

North West Company, 343

Northampton, Treaty of, 1328, 85

Oban, 17, see map 1, facing 21

Oil, Scottish shale oil industry, 355

Ordericus Vitalis, 51

Orkneyinga Saga, 45

Oswy, King of Northumbria, 43

Otterburn, Battle of, 1388, 90, see map 6, facing 85

Overcrowding, 331, 361

Owen, Robert, New Lanark, 249, 319, 320

Paine, Tom, *The Rights of Man*, 307, 309

Paisley, shawls, 250

Park, Mungo, explorer, 344

Parliaments in Scotland, fourteenth century, 87, 90; fifteenth century, 100, 101, 102, 103; 1560, 139; early seventeenth century, 154; 1661, 181; 1690, 184; early eighteenth century, 193

Paterson, William, Darien scheme promoter, 191, 192

Patronage, Lay, 200, 201, 283, 284, 285

Pennant, Thomas, naturalist, 224

Percy, Lord Eustace, *John Knox*, 134, 391

Philip, the Rev. John, missionary, 345, 346

Philiphaugh, Battle of, 1645, 175

Picts, 21, 22, 26, 27, 28, 33, 36, 38, 39, 46

Piggott, S., *Scotland Before History*, 18

Pinkie Cleugh, Battle of, 130

397

Index

Poor Law Amendment Act, 1845, 328, 329
Poor Relief, 321, 325, 326, 329, 364
Porteous Riots, 205, 259
Prestwick Airport, 378
Primrose, Archibald, fifth Earl of Rosebery, 369, 370
Protectorate, 179
Pryde, Professor G. S., 274, 302
Public Health Act, 1867, 323

Ragman Rolls, 78
Raeburn, Sir Henry, artist, 263, 264
Railways, 239, 240, 241
Ramsay, Allan, (senior), 261, 263, 264, 270, 278
Ramsay, Allan, painter, 210, 261 et seq.
Randolph, Thomas, nephew of Robert I of Scotland, 81, 88, 89
Reform Bills, 1832, 310, 329; 1867, 312; 1884, 313, 364
Rennie, John, civil engineer, 237, 241
Resby, James, died 1407, 96
Ring of Brodgar, 21, see map 2, facing 25
Ritchie, R. L. G., *The Normans in Scotland*, 55, 57
Robert I, King of Scotland, 77 et seq., 88, 89, 91
Robert II, King of Scotland, 89, 90, 91
Robert III, King of Scotland, 91, 92
Robert of Normandy, 50, 51
Robertson, George, diarist, 219, 233
Robertson, Dr. William, 262, 266, 268, 283, 295, 296
Roebuck, Dr. John, industrialist, 253
Rognvald, Earl of the Orkneys, 45
Rognvald, Earl of the Orkneys, founder of St. Magnus Cathedral, Kirkwall, 63. For Kirkwall, see map 2, facing 25
Rollo, Conqueror of Normandy, 45
Romans, 26 et seq.
Rosebery, Earl of, see Primrose, Archibald
Rous, Francis, M.P., Provost of Eton, 174
Royal Musical Association, *Music of Scotland*, 110
Rullion Green, skirmish at, 1666, 182
Rutherford, the Rev. Samuel of Anwoth, 162
Ruthwell Cross, 41

Sage, the Rev. Donald, 226
St. Aidan, 40, 41
St. Andrews University, 98, 293
St. Ambrose, 35
St. Augustine, 42
St. Bernard of Clairvaux, 59, 61
St. Columba, 35, 37–40

St. Cuthbert, 40, 65
St. Godric of Lincoln, 64
St. Kentigern, 39
St. Maelrubha, 35, 40, 41
St. Martin of Tours, 35
St. Moluag, 35, 40, 41
St. Ninian, 35, 36
St. Ninian's Isle, 41, see map 2, facing 25
St. Oran, 37, 38
St. Patrick, 36, 37
Salaman, R. S., *The History and Social Influence of the Potato*, 223
Saltire Society, The, 377
Sauchieburn, Battle of, 1488, 106
Scotsman, The, 274, 314, 328, 330, 331, 332
Scott, Sir Walter, 220, 250, 263, 270, 271, 272, 273, 334, 386
Scottish Africa and India Company, 191
Scottish Nationalist Movement, 376, 377, 378, 379
Scottish Office, The, 370
Scottish Standing Committee, 370, 371, 376, 379
Select Society for Encouraging Art, Science and Literature, 262
Sharp, James, Archbishop of St. Andrews, 182, 183
Sheriffmuir, Battle of, 1715, 203
Sheriffs and Sheriff Courts, 58, 100, 117
Shipbuilding, 238, 239, 256, 354, 355, 356, 357
Simpson, Sir J. Y., physician, 298
Sinclair, Sir John, 220, 223, 247, 290
Siward, Earl of Northumbria, 47
Slessor, Mary, 347, 348
Small, James, inventor, 221
Smeaton, George, engineer & surveyor, 234, 236
Smith, Adam, economist, 262, 266, 283, 295, 296, 324, 363
Smith, the Rev. Sydney, *The Edinburgh Review*, 272, 273, 274
Smuts, Field Marshal, 366
Society for Propagating Christian Knowledge, 280, 290
Solemn League and Covenant, 173, 174, 176, 177
Solway Moss, Battle of, 1542, 129
Somerled, Lord of Argyll, 69
Spottiswoode, John, Archbishop of Glasgow, 152, 153, 157
Statistical Accounts of Scotland, 220, 221, 223, 246, 255, 290, 291
Steam Power, 252
Steamships, 237, 239, 256
Steel, 256, 355, 356, 357
Stephen, King of England, 65, 66
Stevenson, R. L., 260, 274, 373

Index

Stewart, Alexander, son of James IV of Scotland, 124
Stewart, James, Earl of Moray, 145
Stewart, Patrick, Earl of the Orkneys, 156
Stirling Bridge, Battle of, 1297, 79, see map 6, facing 85
Stow, David, educationist, 291
Stuart, Esmé, Seigneur d'Aubigny, 148
Student Christian Movement, The, 382
Sutherland clearances, 225, 226. For Sutherland, see map 4, facing 35
Sweated labour, 318, 319, 364
Synod of Whitby, 43

Tacitus, 26
Telford, Thomas, engineer & surveyor, 232, 233, 235, 242
Temperance Societies, 286, 327
Tertullian, 28
Thorfinn the Mighty, 48
Tobacco trade, 244, 245
Trade Unions, 332, 333, 365, 366, 384, 386
Transportation, 293, 309, 336
Treaty of Versailles, 357
Tull, Jethro, *Horse-hoeing Husbandry*, 218
Turgot, biographer of Margaret, Queen of Scotland, 51, 53
Turnbull, William, Bishop of Glasgow and founder of Glasgow University, 105
Turnpike Acts, 232
Tyndale, William, 126

Unemployment, 1930s, 358, 359
Urquhart, Sir Thomas of Cromarty, 178

Veto Act, 1834, 283, 284
Vikings, 41, 44 et seq.
Vitrified Forts, 23, see map 1, facing 21

Wade, Field-marshal George, 231, 232
Wade's Roads, see map 7, facing 231
Wallace, William, 79
Walpole, Horace, 209, 266, 295
Walpole, Sir Robert, 204, 335
Wardlaw, Henry, Bishop of St. Andrews, 98
Warriston, Lord, see Johnston, Archibald
Watt, James, 235, 251, 253, 273
Weaving, 249
Wedderburn, James, John and Robert, *The Gude and Godly Ballatis*, 136
Wedgwood, C. V., *The King's Peace*, 167, 392
Wesley, John, 268, 279, 282
Westminster Assembly, 173, 174
Westminster Confession of Faith, 174, 184
Wheelhouses, 28
William the Lion, King of Scotland, 68, 69, 70
William III, King of England, 184, 185, 188
William of Malmesbury, 63
William of Normandy, King of England, 45, 48, 50, 51, 65
William Rufus, King of England, 51, 52
Wilson, D. H., *James VI and I*, 155
Wishart, George, died 1546, 130
Witchcraft, 153
Wodrow, the Rev. Robert of Eastwood, 201
Wood, Sir Andrew, sea-captain, 118
World Council of Churches, 383

399

Palgrave Study Skills

Authoring a PhD
Business Degree Success
Career Skills
Critical Thinking Skills
e-Learning Skills (2nd edn)
Effective Communication for Arts and Humanities Students
Effective Communication for Science and Technology
The Exam Skills Handbook
The Foundations of Research
The Good Supervisor
How to Manage your Arts, Humanities and Social Science Degree
How to Manage your Distance and Open Learning Course
How to Manage your Postgraduate Course
How to Manage your Science and Technology Degree
How to Study Foreign Languages
How to Write Better Essays (2nd edn)
IT Skills for Successful Study
The International Student Handbook
Making Sense of Statistics
The Mature Student's Guide to Writing (2nd edn)
The Palgrave Student Planner

The Postgraduate Research Handbook (2nd edn)
Presentation Skills for Students
The Principles of Writing in Psychology
Professional Writing (2nd edn)
Researching Online
Research Using IT
Skills for Success
The Study Abroad Handbook
The Student Life Handbook
The Student's Guide to Writing (2nd edn)
The Study Skills Handbook (3rd edn)
Study Skills for Speakers of English as a Second Language
Studying the Built Environment
Studying Economics
Studying History (3rd edn)
Studying Mathematics and its Applications
Studying Modern Drama (2nd edn)
Studying Physics
Studying Programming
Studying Psychology (2nd edn)
Teaching Study Skills and Supporting Learning
Work Placements – A Survival Guide for Students
Write it Right
Writing for Engineers (3rd edn)
Writing for Nursery and Midwifery Students

Palgrave Law Masters

Series Editor: Marise Cremona

Company Law (6th edn) Janet Dine and Marios Koutsias
Constitutional and Administrative Law (6th edn) John Alder
Contract Law (7th edn) Ewan McKendrick
Conveyancing (3rd edn) Priscilla Sarton
Criminal Law (5th edn) Jonathan Herring
Employment Law (6th edn) Deborah J. Lockton (Spring 2008)
Evidence (3rd edn) Raymond Emson
Family Law (6th edn) Kate Standley (Spring 2008)
Housing Law and Policy David Cowan

Intellectual Property Law (5th edn) Tina Hart, Linda Fazzani and Simon Clark (Spring 2008)
Land Law (5th edn) Kate Green and Joe Cursley
Landlord and Tenant Law (5th edn) Margaret Wilkie, Jill Morgan and Godfrey Cole
Law of the European Union (3rd edn) Jo Shaw
Law of Succession Catherine Rendell
Legal Method (6th edn) Ian McLeod
Legal Theory (4th edn) Ian McLeod
Social Security Law Robert East
Torts (3rd edn) Alastair Mullis and Ken Oliphant
Trusts Law Charlie Webb and Tim Akkouh (Spring 2008)

Studying Law

Second edition

Simon Askey
Deputy Director
External LLB Programme
University of London, UK

and

Ian McLeod
Visiting Professor of Law
School of Social Sciences and Law
University of Teesside, UK

Associate Senior Research Fellow
Institute of Advanced Legal Studies
University of London, UK

palgrave
macmillan

First published 2006
Second edition published 2008 by
PALGRAVE MACMILLAN
Houndmills, Basingstoke, Hampshire RG21 6XS and
175 Fifth Avenue, New York, N. Y. 10010
Companies and representatives throughout the world

PALGRAVE MACMILLAN is the global academic imprint of the Palgrave
Macmillan division of St. Martin's Press LLC and of Palgrave Macmillan Ltd.
Macmillan® is a registered trademark in the United States, United Kingdom
and other countries. Palgrave is a registered trademark in the European Union
and other countries.

ISBN-13: 978–0–230–57311–6
ISBN-10: 0–230–57311–8

This book is printed on paper suitable for recycling and made from fully
managed and sustained forest sources. Logging, pulping and manufacturing
processes are expected to conform to the environmental regulatons of the
country of origin.

A catalogue record for this book is available from the British Library.

10 9   8   7   6   5   4   3   2   1
17 16   15 14 13 12 11 10 09 08

Printed in China

Contents

Preface

Law teachers and examiners often complain that many students fail to do themselves justice. More particularly, they complain that although many students have learned a great deal of law, they have simply not mastered the skills of using the law to deal with the kind of tasks that they have to perform. While these skills may be practised and developed in the context of tutorials and seminars, they must ultimately be demonstrated in assessed work of one kind or another. Additionally, for those students who go on to pursue careers with a law element (whether in the legal profession or elsewhere) these skills will continue to be invaluable in the much longer term.

This edition continues the basic structure of the previous one by beginning with an introduction to some basic ideas which underpin both law itself and the English legal system, before explaining how lawyers find and cite the sources of law. (In Chapters 2 and 3 we have taken the opportunity to rearrange some of the material on European Community law.) There is then a discussion of the basic principles of legal method, followed by a new chapter on how to read law reports and statutes. The case we have chosen in relation to law reports is *Henthorn v Fraser* [198] and we are grateful to The Incorporated Council of Law Reporting for England and Wales, Megarry House, 119 Chancery Lane, London WC2A 1PP, publishers of The Law Reports and The Weekly Law Reports, for permission to reproduce the report. The statute we have chosen is the Dealing in Cultural Objects (Offences) Act 2003, the original text of which was printed under the superintendence and authority of the Controller of Her Majesty's Stationery Office, being the Queen's Printer of Acts of Parliament. The Act is Crown copyright and is reproduced by permission. After a chapter on how to write good English (in which we have taken a somewhat less didactic tone), the final three chapters explain how to answer essay questions and problem questions, and how to make oral presentations. The chapter on oral presentations now includes guidance on mooting.

Additionally, of course, we have tried to eliminate the infelicities which inevitably seem to afflict first editions.

Although we have each been responsible for originating individual chapters, we have jointly revised the whole book. Accordingly, convention requires that, publicly at any rate, we must each accept full responsibility for any remaining defects. Naturally, this will not stop us privately blaming each other if any such matters are subsequently brought to our attention.

We are grateful to John Marston of the Department of Law at de Montfort University, whose comments on the draft of this edition have resulted in the final version being significantly improved; to Jacqui McLeod for helping to read the draft manuscript and the final proofs; to Suzie Burywood and Karen Griffiths of Palgrave Macmillan, for their cheerful support at all times; and to Ian Kingston for taking care of the copy-editing and typesetting.

If this book helps students to find their feet in the early stages of their studies, and to develop their skills in such a way as to improve their performance in assessed work, we will have achieved our aim.

Simon Askey
Ian McLeod
November 2007

1 Studying Law: What's it All About?

What law does, how it does it and how it should do it, are all basic questions that have engaged the minds of philosophers and lawyers for more than two thousand years. For students with the right aptitude, who are prepared to work hard at developing their analytical and linguistic skills, the academic study of law offers the possibility to engage with challenging questions such as these and to develop the kind of transferable skills which many employers value highly.

Introduction

What is law *about*?

The best way to approach the academic study of anything is to ask: *what is this subject about*? This question may be important for two reasons.

First, those who start to study a subject like law without giving at least some thought to its nature are likely to find themselves adrift upon a vast ocean of apparently random – and therefore confusing – detail. Some knowledge of the nature of law, even if only in outline, will help to provide a framework within which you can organise and understand as much of that detail as possible. More particularly, this understanding will enable you to see how the detail contributes (or, in some cases, fails to contribute) to the coherence of the body of law as a whole.

Secondly, it will give you an important insight into how you will be required to think and the intellectual skills you will need if you are to study the subject successfully.

So, returning to the initial question, what is law *about*? We will approach this question by asking two further questions:

- What does law do? and
- How does it do it?

We will consider these questions in turn.

What does law do?

Although there is a great deal of academic debate about the nature of law, for the moment we can assume that law consists of a body of *rules*. In practice, of course, those rules will need to be *made*. Additionally, having been made, the rules will need to be *interpreted*, *applied* and *enforced* in a wide variety of factual contexts; and they may need to be *changed* from time to time. It follows, therefore, that there must also be a set of *institutions* whose function it is to make, interpret, apply, enforce and change the law. There are many such institutions, with Parliament, the courts, central government and local authorities being among the most obvious examples.

The fact that law involves both rules and institutions still leaves open the question of what it is that law actually *does*. An outline answer to this question is that *law regulates social conduct with a view to enabling (or at least helping) people to live peaceably in a well-ordered society*. In practice, this means that the law must *identify* the *duties* and *powers* of both *government* and *individuals*, as well as *enforcing* the *duties* and *regulating* the *exercise* of the *powers* in both cases.

More specifically, constitutional law deals with the allocation of power between different institutions (such as central government departments like the Home Office) and local authorities (such as county councils and London borough councils) as well as a range of other public bodies (such as the Environment Agency). Once constitutional law has allocated public powers to various institutions, administrative law seeks to control the way in which those institutions exercise their powers.

Moving to the level of relationships between individuals, the range of law is truly vast. Taking only a few examples at random, the law regulates matters as varied as:

- the ownership and transfer of property and rights in property;
- the creation, functioning and winding-up of companies and business partnerships;
- the right to privacy;
- the rights of people who are not British citizens to enter the United Kingdom and their status when they have done so; and
- the relationships which arise from marriage and cohabitation.

Of course, these categories are by no means watertight. (For example, marriage may well affect existing property rights, or bring new ones into being, or both.) However, the vastness of the law's range is seldom reflected in the way students are introduced to it, which generally relies very heavily on a few traditional categories.

Of all the categories of law which regulate relationships between individuals, the two which you are most likely to encounter at an early stage are *contract* and *tort*, which may sometimes be put together to form the bulk of a single subject called *obligations*. (The idea of *contract* is probably obvious even to non-lawyers, but it may be worth saying that the word *tort* describes particular kinds of unlawful conduct, such as trespass, negligence, libel and so on, where the legal relationship between the parties arises simply as a matter of law, rather than arising from an agreement between them.) The placing of these subjects at an early stage within your studies is far from arbitrary. The fact of the matter is that they underpin many of the specialised subjects which you will encounter later on. They are, therefore, literally *foundational* in nature.

So far, we have approached the question *'What is law about?'* in terms of *'What does law do?'*, but this is only a partial answer because it still leaves the more practical question of *'How does law do it?'*.

How does law do it?

Introduction
One useful way of approaching the way in which law functions is through the distinction between *criminal* law and *civil* law.

The distinction between criminal law and civil law
Criminal law prohibits certain types of anti-social conduct such as murder, rape, theft and dangerous driving. By way of contrast, civil law deals with conduct which, while still anti-social, is rather less so, such as breaching contracts and trespassing on other people's land.

The policy decision as to whether a specific type of conduct should be classified as criminal or civil will depend on how harmful to society and its members the conduct in question is thought to be. In order to understand how this policy decision is made, it will help if you first understand the practical consequences which flow from something being classified as either *criminal* or *civil*.

The first practical consequence is that, in the case of *criminal law*, the state itself (acting mainly through the police and the Crown Prosecution Service, but sometimes through other institutions such as local authorities) will investigate allegations of illegality and also bring legal proceedings. On the other hand, where conduct is classified as a *civil wrong*, it is left entirely up to the victims to assemble the evidence and formulate the legal arguments which will be necessary in order to support their claims, and to decide whether to bring proceedings in the courts.

The second practical consequence is that where guilt is either admitted or proved in criminal proceedings, the court will impose sanctions which will be enforced automatically. Moreover, these sanctions will usually be intended, in principle, to be either punitive (such as fines), or reforming (such as probation) or perhaps even an uneasy combination of the two (such as imprisonment). The fact that the courts exercising criminal jurisdiction may also be able to award compensation for financial loss represents only a small exception to the general nature of criminal sanctions. In practice, they make such awards only in very straightforward cases, leaving the victims of crime to pursue more complicated claims by way of civil actions.

On the other hand, where judgment has been obtained in civil proceedings, it is left entirely to the victims to decide whether to enforce whatever orders the courts may make. Moreover, these orders will very seldom be intended to be either punitive or reforming, but will focus instead on compensating claimants or protecting them against further wrongdoing; or, sometimes, both.

By way of an example, suppose your neighbour erects a fence in such a way that it trespasses on your garden. If you choose not to enforce your rights, no official or agency of the state will force you to do so, or do so on your behalf. Suppose, however, that you have chosen to enforce your rights and that the court has made orders in your favour, requiring your neighbour to remove the fence from your garden and pay you damages. Although you have obtained two remedies, you may well decide that all you really want is to have the use of your garden back. If this is so, you may well decide to require your neighbour simply to move the fence, without also requiring the payment of damages. The law leaves this choice entirely up to you.

As a final footnote to the distinction between criminal and civil law, it is worth saying that a single piece of unlawful conduct may be both criminal and civil. For example, suppose A assaults B. A may be successfully prosecuted in a court exercising criminal jurisdiction, where the result may be some kind of penalty such as a fine. Whether or not there is a successful prosecution, B may sue A in a court exercising civil jurisdiction and, if successful, obtain damages.

If you think it strange that a claim for damages may succeed where a prosecution has failed, you may be immediately congratulated on having read the text carefully and critically. However, the answer is quite straightforward. In a *criminal* case the prosecution needs to produce evidence which is convincing enough to prove that the defendant is guilty *beyond a reasonable doubt.* In *civil* cases, on the other hand, claimants can succeed on evidence which is significantly less convincing, because the standard of proof in civil cases is only *the balance of probabilities.* In other words, claimants in civil cases need only show that it is *more likely than not* that what they allege to have happened did actually happen.

Law and justice

Introduction

The proposition that law is about enabling (or, at least, helping) people to live peaceably in a well-ordered society, is only a starting point. Much depends on how peace and good order are established and maintained. Societies that are based on abuses of fundamental human rights will often use law as an instrument of violence and oppression against their citizens. These societies (so-called *police states*) will undoubtedly be peaceful and well-ordered, but they can scarcely be called *just.* Thus, within a few, short sentences – and taking only one example – we have identified the need to consider not only *law* but also *justice.*

At this stage two further questions arise. First, how do we identify what we mean by *justice*; or, in other words, *what is the content of justice?* Secondly, once we know what we mean by *justice*, we need to ask *what is the relationship between law and justice?*

The content of justice

Introduction

We will begin our consideration of the content of justice with the importance of respecting and protecting fundamental human rights. The difficulty is that, although this can reasonably be considered to be at least one aspect of justice, what it actually requires in any given case may be a great deal less clear.

For example, does it follow that a society which prohibits racial discrimination in the field of employment must prohibit the proprietors of Chinese restaurants from employing only Chinese waiting staff, where they think this form of racial discrimination is necessary in order to provide their establishments with the ambience which their customers enjoy?

Similarly, although admittedly by way of a more extreme example, most people would say that they support freedom of religion and worship. However, suppose a group of people chooses to revive the religious beliefs which formed the foundation of the Central American Aztec civilisation before the

European conquest. These beliefs required the offering of human hearts and blood as nourishment for the sun god. Does a commitment to respecting and protecting freedom of religion mean that we must accept the right of this group to practise human sacrifice? When answering this question, is it relevant to ask whether the victims are themselves followers of the faith who are happy to die in the service of their god.

Even leaving aside questions involving fundamental human rights, it is not difficult to imagine situations where the requirements of justice are less than obvious. Suppose a thief (T) steals property from its owner (O) and sells it to a buyer (B), who genuinely and reasonably believes T to be its owner. If the property is traced to B, does justice require that B should be allowed to keep it, or that it should be returned to O? You may argue that the answer to this question is unimportant, because if B is allowed to keep the property, O will have the right to obtain compensation from T. Alternatively, if the property is returned to O, B will have the right to obtain compensation from T. In either case, therefore, it seems that the innocent victim will be protected and that the loss will fall, as it should, on the guilty party. In the real world, however, experience shows that T will either have vanished or lack the means to pay any compensation to anyone. In practice, therefore, in the vast majority of cases, either B or O will have to stand (or, perhaps, share) the loss, even though they are both innocent victims of T's criminal conduct.

As you might expect, the law does, in fact, have answers to all these questions, but we will not pursue them here. What we will do instead is to pick up a methodological point and consider three different ways of identifying the content of justice in specific *types* of cases. Our first approach is based on *economic* considerations, our second on *psychological* considerations, and our third on a more general idea which is commonly labelled *public policy*, and which may appear in a variety of forms.

An economic approach to justice

An economic approach to justice may be illustrated by the problem that arises when a car crash occurs at a junction between a major road and a minor one, where the view of drivers emerging from the minor road is restricted by an overgrown roadside hedge. More particularly, if a car emerging from the minor road collides with a car on the major road, can the driver of the emerging car lay at least part of the blame on the local highway authority, which could have cut back the hedge in such a way as to improve visibility at the junction? Assuming there is no relevant case law or statute, and that the court must, therefore, approach this question at the level of principle, there are likely to be two opposing arguments.

On the one hand, it can be argued that a driver who encounters a particularly dangerous situation on the road should exercise a correspondingly high degree of care. Furthermore, any liability which the court imposes on the driver will, in reality, almost always fall on the driver's insurance company rather than on the driver personally. (For the present purposes, since we are discussing the matter at the level of principle, we can ignore the possibility of the loss of any no-claims bonus which the driver may have earned, as well as any excess which he or she may have to pay.) On the other hand, it can be argued that if the local community at large (acting in this case through the local highway authority) has allowed a dangerous situation either to arise or continue (or both), it is only fair that the local community at large should accept at least some financial liability for accidents which then occur. If it is agreed that such liability is fair in principle, each individual case will simply require the apportionment of liability between the driver and the local highway authority, in the light of all the facts.

If you stop to think about these two arguments for a few moments, it becomes obvious that the problem may be seen in largely economic terms. More particularly, the cost of any liability which falls on the driver will be borne by the driver's insurance company – or, more accurately, by the other policyholders and shareholders of the driver's insurance company, who may suffer, respectively, from increased premiums and reduced dividends. The cost of any liability which falls on the local highway authority will ultimately be borne by the local community at large through the increases in council tax which will be necessary to enable the local authority to pay either insurance premiums or damages. Where insurance cover does exist, the reality of the matter is that the court has to decide how the losses should be allocated between two insurance companies (or, again more accurately, between their respective policyholders and shareholders).

On the basis of a purely economic analysis, therefore, the question requires the economic efficiency of both alternatives to be assessed so that an informed choice can be made between them. On this view, it follows that the interests of justice become the same as the interests of economic efficiency.

You may, of course, object that the judges who decide such cases lack the skills and knowledge which would equip them to undertake the relevant economic analysis with the same expertise that professional economists would bring to the task. While this is no doubt true, those who argue for the requirements of justice to be identified by reference to economic considerations may make two responses. First, expert evidence could be used here, as it is in many other cases involving technical matters. Secondly, and more fundamentally, most people would probably accept that the concept of justice is an ideal that we should strive to attain. This being so, it would be unfortunate if we were to limit our perception of the scope of the concept merely because of the inability of the legal system to attain the ideal in its fullest form.

Finally, if you wish to pursue the arguments in cases such as this, you could usefully read *Stovin v Wise (Norfolk County Council, Third Party)* [1996] AC 923, where the House of Lords, by a majority of three to two, reversed the decision of the Court of Appeal, reported at [1994] 1 WLR 1124.

A psychological approach to justice

Turning to the psychological approach to justice, the law of murder allows for the defence of provocation. In reality, this is only a partial defence because its effect is to reduce the conviction from murder to manslaughter. However, this reduction is enormously significant in practice because a sentence of life imprisonment is mandatory for murder, while being merely the maximum for manslaughter.

The essence of provocation is a sudden and temporary loss of self-control at the time of the defendant's fatal act. One problem which commonly arises from this is the need to decide whether the defendant's reaction was reasonable in the light of the victim's conduct. More particularly, can a successful plea of provocation be based on a *course of conduct* by the victim, even though the *final event* which triggered the defendant's fatal response may have been comparatively minor? While, as a matter of law, this question can arise in any type of case where provocation is pleaded, in practice it is typically found in cases where women, having been victims of domestic violence over a period of time, finally kill their abusive partners. In such cases, the law recognises battered woman syndrome as a variety of post-traumatic stress disorder. In other words, a background of abusive conduct leading up to a fatal act may render a plea of provocation credible, even though there would be no reasonable relationship between the fatal act itself and the actual incident which triggers it, if each was viewed in isolation from the other.

Finally, if you wish to pursue the arguments on the domestic violence aspect of this discussion, you could usefully read the decisions of the Court of Appeal in *R v Thornton* [1992] 1 All ER 306 and *R v Ahluwalia* [1992] 4 All ER 889.

A public policy approach to justice

For an example of a situation in which some people would think about the requirements of justice in terms of public policy, suppose A is injured and becomes unfit for work as the result of an accident for which B is responsible. Also suppose that A belongs to an occupational pension scheme which pays out ill-health benefits. A's loss of income will be the difference between the earnings which he or she would have received but for the accident, and the pension which he or she does actually receive as a result of the accident. In other words, to allow A to receive damages based on the total loss of earnings, *as well as receiving the pension*, would result in over-compensation.

On the other hand, if the damages are reduced to take account of the pension, B has to pay less than he or she would have paid if A had not invested in a pension scheme which included ill-health benefits. This would mean that B has become the true beneficiary of A's investment in the pension scheme. While this solution avoids over-compensation, that fact that A receives no benefit from his or her pension contributions is not only intrinsically unfair, but is also contrary to that aspect of public policy which encourages people to take responsibility for their own future needs.

In fact, the law prefers the element of over-compensation and does not, therefore, require the damages to be reduced on account of the pension.

Finally, if you wish to pursue the arguments which arise in cases such as this, you could usefully read *Parry v Cleaver* [1970] AC 1, where the House of Lords, by a majority of three to two, reversed the decision of the Court of Appeal, which is reported at [1968] 1 QB 195.

The relationship between law and justice

Introduction
Having considered the topic of the *content of justice*, we can now turn to the second of our further two questions, namely *what is the relationship between law and justice*? We will approach the topic by considering some broad schools of thought in legal theory.

Legal theory is a very broad area of study and most individual legal theorists have concentrated their efforts on only one or two aspects of the whole subject. Since lawyers love to classify everything, it is not surprising that they classify legal theorists. Traditionally, many theorists have approached the relationship between law and justice in terms of the relationship between morality and law. We will consider both these positions in turn, beginning with the traditional classification which divides legal theorists into two groups, one of which argues for what is known as *natural law*, while the other one argues for what is known as *positivism*.

Natural law
Although all natural law theorists emphasise the role of morality in relation to law, closer consideration reveals that the *natural law* position as a whole can be further subdivided into two.

The first sub-group consists of those theorists who advance a *strong* version of natural law, by arguing that something which appears to be a law (for example, in the English legal system, an Act of Parliament) is nevertheless not truly a law if it is unjust. (In this context, the word *unjust* is normally used to mean something like *violating the moral principles according to which humankind should live.*)

The second sub-group consists of theorists who advance a *weak* version of natural law. These theorists accept that whatever the legal system asserts to be a law is, by definition, truly a law, while nevertheless insisting that the *desirability* of all laws must be assessed by reference to the requirements of natural law.

In very general terms, older versions of natural law theory tend to be of the strong kind, while more modern versions tend to be of the weak kind. However, both versions share a common problem, namely *what are the requirements of natural law*? Or, to put it another way, *what is the content of the moral principles according to which humankind ought to live*? Or, yet again, to link the matter even more clearly to our previous discussion, *what is justice*?

Very broadly speaking, if we go back to the beginning and regard all natural law theorists as a single group (disregarding for the present purposes the distinction between those who advance the strong and the weak versions) they will once again fall into two sub-groups. This time, however, the basis of the division between them will be different.

Members of one sub-group argue that the requirements of natural law (and therefore the content of justice) may be identified by reference to religious beliefs of one kind or another. Members of the other sub-group argue that it is possible to identify the requirements of natural law through the exercise of human reason alone, and that there is no need to introduce religious belief into this process.

All we can safely conclude at this stage, therefore, is that there may be significant disagreements, even between natural law theorists, as to what justice truly requires in a given situation. Each side to a dispute may genuinely believe that it has justice on its side, while disagreeing fundamentally as to what this means in terms of how their dispute should be resolved.

Positivism

The second main group of legal theorists regards the *existence* and the *desirability* of a law as being two quite distinct matters. For these theorists (who are generally known as *positivists* because they emphasise law as it is *posited* or *laid down*), anything is truly a law if it has been laid down as a law according to the formal requirements of the legal system in question. To return to the earlier example, within the English legal system, the provisions of an Act of Parliament are, by definition, law. However, it would be a serious mistake to conclude that the positivists' emphasis on the formal requirements of a legal system means that they are interested only in law and not in justice. The positivists' position is rather that separating the processes of *identifying* and *evaluating* laws is important for a number of reasons.

Among the positivists' reasons for separating questions as to the nature of law from questions as to the nature of justice is that, as we have seen, the nature of justice is such that disagreement as to its requirements will often arise. From the positivist viewpoint, therefore, any definition of law which depends on the concept of justice is bound to lead, in some cases at least, to disagreement as to whether an alleged law is truly a law at all. Since law is an essential element in the fabric of society (because it enables – or at least helps – people to live peaceably in a well-ordered society), it follows that questioning the very existence of something which appears to be a law may amount to undermining, at least to some extent, the basis of society itself.

Before moving on, it is worth emphasising again that the positivists' insistence on separating questions of the existence of laws from questions of their desirability does not exclude argument as to whether particular laws are just or unjust, or as to what the law on a particular subject ought to be. The positivist position is simply that the two matters should be dealt with separately.

How real is the distinction between natural law and positivism?
At this stage you may well be wondering what, if anything, is the difference between *weak versions of natural law* and *positivism*. The answer lies in the fact that, while many positivists accept that conclusions as to the requirements of justice rest on the moral principles according to which humankind should live (and therefore differ from natural lawyers only as to the point at which this consideration becomes relevant), others rely on matters which would find no place in natural law theory, such as the *economic, psychological* and *public policy* considerations which we discussed at pp. 8–9.

Choosing between natural law and positivism
While positivists may challenge natural lawyers on the basis that if natural law were truly natural, it should be possible to formulate a single, universally agreed and coherent account of its requirements, so natural lawyers may challenge positivists on the basis that their concept of law is, in essence, law without values. If you study legal theory (which you may encounter under a variety of names, including *jurisprudence* or *legal philosophy*) in more depth, you may well conclude that there is something in both criticisms.

If your temperament is such that you like clear-cut categories and are therefore uneasy about living with doubt, you will probably align yourself with one or other of the theoretical positions, while persuading yourself that the objections to it are either unsound or relatively unimportant.

On the other hand, if your temperament is such that you can happily accommodate matters of doubt, you may prefer to avoid aligning yourself absolutely with either position. In this case, you will probably be saying (on the basis of your further study of individual legal theorists) that many members of each group have something useful to say about the nature of law, the nature of justice and the relationship between the two. If this is indeed your view, you will probably also conclude that to insist on applying an uncompromising label to yourself (and to other people) is a sign that you attach more importance to labels than to the substance of the theories which those labels describe.

● Some distinctions between the academic study and the practice of law

Some people who become law students never have any intention whatsoever of entering the legal profession. Some others have professional aspirations when they become law students, but change their minds during the course of their studies. Finally, of course, there are those law students who do become practising lawyers (either solicitors or barristers) in due course. Whichever category you think (or know) you fall into, while you are a law student you will often be dealing with law as it works in practice, but you will be doing so from an academic perspective, with no practical consequences flowing from your analyses, criticisms and conclusions. It follows that you need to be aware of some of the major differences between being a law student and being a member of the practising profession.

Perhaps the central point of distinction is that practitioners have clients who are hoping to achieve certain outcomes. Those outcomes will vary from routine, low-profile matters such as making a valid will, to exceptional, high-profile matters such as bringing, or defending, legal proceedings involving issues of high constitutional principle. Whatever the clients' desired outcomes may be, however, practising lawyers act on their clients' instructions, provided those instructions do not require the doing of anything which is either illegal or contrary to their code of professional conduct.

Of course, lawyers may advise clients as to what outcomes are most likely to be achievable, and perhaps also as to which are most likely to be genuinely in the clients' best interests; and clients may change their minds in the light of such advice. But clients are never obliged to accept advice, no matter how sound that advice may be. Newcomers to the law frequently ask whether a lawyer is bound to accept instructions. The answer is that solicitors are always free to decline to accept instructions, although commercial considerations are such that very few solicitors will turn away work of a kind which they usually undertake. On the other hand, barristers are required by their code of professional conduct to accept any instructions within a field of law in which the individual barrister practises and for which a proper fee is offered.

Law students, on the other hand, in common with their teachers, enjoy greater freedom, being subject to neither commercial reality, clients' instructions or the rigours of the codes of professional conduct which bind practitioners. Of course, neither law students nor their teachers are entirely free from constraints. Students who wish to succeed must keep their examiners reasonably happy, while teachers who wish to remain employed, and to progress in their careers, must keep both their students and their employers reasonably happy. In reality, however, these constraints are much less limiting than those which apply to practitioners.

An important aspect of the freedom enjoyed by law students is the possibility of *criticising* the law. Although practitioners may, of course, also indulge in the intellectual exercise of criticising the law, in the purely practical world of appearing before courts and negotiating with other lawyers, they are almost always limited by what the law on a particular point simply *is*. Admittedly, in cases involving statute law it may be possible to achieve startling results by the imaginative use of creative techniques of interpretation, while those who practise in the highest courts may have the opportunity to influence the development of the law through the doctrine of binding precedent. (Both these points are discussed further in Chapter 7.)

However, the fact remains that, under the British constitution, it is simply impossible for any court to quash an Act of Parliament. Additionally, while it is not impossible for the Appellate Committee of the House of Lords (that is, the House of Lords as the highest court of appeal) to depart from one of its own previous decisions, in practice it may refuse to do so even if it considers the previous decision to be wrong. (The doctrine of binding precedent is discussed in more detail in Chapter 7.) On the other hand, students may cheerfully write essays, while their teachers may equally cheerfully give lectures and write books and articles, arguing that particular aspects of the law are wrong in terms of legal principle or are unjust and should be changed.

Another important distinction between the worlds of academe and practice is that students are presented with fact situations on which they are asked to advise. You will investigate the techniques involved in answering such questions when you get to Chapter 11, but for the moment the essential point is simply that students are given a set of facts to which they must apply the relevant law. In practice, though, most cases turn entirely on disputes as to the facts, with both parties agreeing about which principles of law will be relevant when the issues of fact have been resolved. Of course, in some cases the process of resolving factual disputes may involve issues of law in the form of the law of evidence, which deals with the way in which disputed facts may be proved. However, in practice, arguments on the law of evidence are relatively rare, with most factual disputes being resolved on the very simple basis of *which witnesses does the court believe*?

The skills required for success as a law student

Law students require a variety of aptitudes and, to use a more specifically practical word, skills. Reduced to their most basic, what is required is an aptitude for hard work coupled with an analytical mind which enjoys the challenge of expressing difficult ideas clearly. Furthermore, there is no escaping the fact that much of the hard work will involve a great deal of reading and note-taking; and much of this will, at least in the short term, be heavy going and unexciting. However, if undertaken properly, this work will, over a period of time, accumulate into a substantial body of knowledge, which can then be applied to the key tasks of writing essays and solving problems by way of both coursework and examination.

A useful approach to effective reading and note taking is the SQ3R technique, the stages of which are:

- survey ;
- question;
- read;
- recall (*or* recite);
- review.

The aim of the SQ3R technique, which was first promoted by the American psychologist Francis Robinson in 1941, is to help you read purposefully in order to create a mental framework of the topic as you read. We will discuss the techniques of researching, planning and answering both essay and problem questions in Chapters 10 and 11. For the moment, however, we shall confine ourselves to showing how the SQ3R technique can help you to study a topic simply in order to understand it, rather than to research, plan and write a piece of written work.

To begin your consideration of a chapter in a book or an article in a law journal, for example, you will *survey* the whole piece by skimming through the pages, paying particular attention to any introductory summary and conclusion, as well as to the headings and subheadings which break up the text. Having understood the structure of the piece as a whole, you will then *question* what value it has for you, by asking whether it reinforces, extends or contradicts your existing knowledge of the topic. Assuming that you wish to proceed further with the piece, you will then *read* it properly, making appropriate notes. If you find yourself copying out any passages word-for-word, be careful to use quotation marks round the relevant passages and to note their precise location. If, at some later stage, you wish to incorporate these passages into pieces of written work, you will then have no difficulty in citing your source accurately, in order to avoid laying yourself open to an allegation of plagiarism. (Plagiarism, which is a form of cheating, is discussed at pp. 160–163.)

At this stage, and by way of a slight digression from the SQ3R technique itself, it may be worth saying that your notes will become a very personal part of your resources. Some people rely simply on a careful structure of headings and subheadings, while others use graphics (such as boxes, circles, different colours and connecting arrows) to create emphasis, illustrate links and raise questions. There are only three really important things to bear in mind:

- You must be able to understand your notes easily when you come to re-read them.
- They must be structured in such a way that they help you to generate a mental map of the topic.
- Do not take the easy option of simply highlighting or underlining what you see as the key sections of a text, rather than making notes from them, because:
  - note-taking is an important skill which you may well need in the future (for example, when attending meetings or when taking instructions from clients); and it can be acquired and developed only through practice; and
  - the act of note-taking makes you decide for yourself how the main points of the material can best be summarised. The crucial point here is that the mental activity which this involves is an invaluable part of the learning process; and

- your notes will be an important resource when you come to write coursework essays and revise for examinations. In the context of coursework, as we shall see at p. 162, working from notes is a very helpful way of avoiding plagiarism (or cheating), while in the context of examinations, almost everyone finds they can revise most effectively from materials which are in their own handwriting rather than from the printed page (whether or not it is enhanced by highlighting or underlining).

Returning specifically to the SQ3R technique, the *recall* stage is a way of embedding in your mind what you have read. If you are reading a particularly complex chapter or article, you might find it helpful to read just part of the text, take a short break, and then test your ability to recall the basic concepts, arguments or core facts of the material you have just read. For a less complex text, you might do the recall stage a day or two later. Recall should be done without looking at the notes you made during the *reading* stage. One way to consolidate your thoughts is to write a summary of the material while you are *recalling* it; or alternatively you could create a diagram such as a flow chart or algorithm, or simply recite what you know out loud. The method you choose will very much depend on your learning style and temperament. The key thing is to use a method that helps you to instil in your mind what you have read, while also developing your understanding of the material.

Finally, you will *review* what you have been reading, in order to reinforce your understanding and to check that you have not missed anything of importance. The *review* can take place at anytime after the *recall* stage. In most cases (as with the *recall* stage itself) the time when you *review* your material will depend on how difficult you found the reading. Simple material can be quickly noted and then reviewed days later. Complex material may need to be *read* and *recalled* in short sections, and then *reviewed* in longer sections, all on the same day.

Organising yourself to read in this way can take a great deal of self-discipline, but the SQ3R technique remains a popular method of effective reading. While you may find the system laborious at first, it has the advantage of helping you read actively, questioningly and effectively. The pressures of academic life are such that you can never read everything in detail. Learning to read purposefully now will be hard work, but it will save you a great deal of time and effort later on.

It is important to emphasise the need for hard work as an essential part of studying law, because far too many students are tempted to think that they can succeed by relying on what they imagine to be their natural ability, without bothering to add the expenditure of effort. To take an analogy, some people prefer the more or less instant gratification which comes from watching a television adaptation of a classic novel to the rather more laborious process of reading the novel itself. Those who prefer watching television to reading the book are less likely to study law successfully, unless they rapidly acquire a taste for text-based materials.

It is also important to emphasise that studying law is a cumulative process. This means that you must *absorb*, *understand* and *retain* at least the main principles of every subject that you study, so that you will be able to apply them to other subjects later on. For example, you will need a sound grasp of foundation subjects such as contract law and administrative law before you can progress successfully to subjects such as employment law and environmental law.

Incidentally, it is often said that lawyers neither know nor need to know any more law than other people, but that they simply need to know where to look it up. While it is, of course, true that many lawyers do frequently look things up, there are various reasons why it is quite simply untrue to say that they neither know nor need to know any more law than other people do.

The first point is that, in common with members of other learned professions, lawyers are expected to know a lot of material. There are several reasons why this is so.

First, as a matter of psychology, clients are unlikely to have much confidence in lawyers who plainly know no law.

Secondly, lawyers who have to spend time on getting themselves onto an equal footing with their more knowledgeable competitors before they can start spending time on the key task of giving advice or providing other professional services will have to charge more than their competitors charge. It follows that lawyers who do not know the law will be at a commercial disadvantage against competitors who do know a lot of law, since those who know the least will have to charge the most.

Thirdly, having found the law, you need to be able to understand it. This requires both a good grasp of that area of law known as *legal method* (so that you can understand and apply the sources you have looked up), and a wider knowledge of the law relating to various topics. After all, there is no point in looking up a legal rule which seems to dispose of your case if you are unaware of another and more authoritative rule which will prevail. An example may help.

Suppose your client's widowed mother has died without leaving a will, and that your client is her only child. If you simply look up the Act of Parliament dealing with inheritance of property in situations where there is no will, you will conclude that your client is entitled to inherit the whole of his or her mother's estate. However, suppose that your client killed his or her mother. This may have been by murder or manslaughter, or, perhaps more probably, by being the driver of a car in which the mother was a passenger and which was involved in an accident for which your client was responsible and as a result of which the mother died.

The Act of Parliament which lays down the rules of succession where there is no will makes no mention of the fact that those rules are subject to an additional set of rules which seek to prevent people benefiting from their own wrongdoing. The additional rules, which originated in the courts but have since been developed by another Act of Parliament, may or may not (depending on all the circumstances of the case) prevent your client from inheriting. It follows that a lawyer who merely identifies the first Act of Parliament, but who is unaware of the additional rules contained in both case law and the later Act of Parliament, may give bad advice.

Fourthly, there will be many occasions in professional practice when it is simply impossible to look up the law, and lawyers must, therefore, rely on their legal knowledge. For example, they may be in a meeting with clients, or appearing as advocates in court, when only a few textbooks may be available, and pressure of time may mean that even these can be used only to jog the memory, rather than as sources on which to base research.

Quite apart from a capacity for hard work, law students require good linguistic and analytical skills. Although these may sound like, and in some cases will indeed be, two distinct skills, in practical terms they often merge into one. For example, take an Act of Parliament which, among other things, prohibits the possession of obscene articles for publication for gain, except where publication is

> justified as being for the public good on the ground that it is in the interests of science, literature, art or learning, or of other objects of general concern.

Clearly this exception would apply to the depiction of nudity in classical art and to the publication of photographs of human genitals in medical textbooks. But what about cases involving articles which are plainly obscene on any sensible meaning of the word? Can the defence argue that such articles are nevertheless lawful because they help some people to release their frustrations through sexual fantasies (with a consequent reduction in the number of sexual offences) and that this is plainly an object of general concern?

A linguistically perceptive response to this question would proceed on the following lines. If the exception applies to *any* 'objects of general concern',

why did Parliament specify the preceding categories (namely 'science, literature, art or learning')? Is it not reasonable, therefore, to interpret the words
'other objects of general concern' as being limited to other things *of the same
kind* as those which are specified? Thus the argument for the defence does
not justify the application of the exception.

Furthermore, and quite apart from purely linguistic considerations, when
the content of the argument for the defence is analysed, it becomes plain
that what is really being claimed is that the availability of obscene articles
can be justified simply on the ground that they are obscene. It is difficult to
see how anyone could reasonably regard this as a credible interpretation of
an Act of Parliament which was passed in order to subject obscene articles
to very strict controls.

As a final point on the need for good language skills, it may be useful to
consider a classic legal anecdote. The story is told of a judge who, having listened patiently to an advocate who was making a long and learned submission, said: 'Well, Mr Smith, having listened to all you have had to say, I must
confess that I am none the wiser'. 'Perhaps not, my Lord', replied the advocate, 'but at least your Lordship is better informed'. Whether or not you find
this funny may be a good indicator of whether you are sufficiently sensitive
to nuances of meaning to be likely to succeed as a law student.

Conclusion

Both law and justice are complex subjects which require a great deal of careful analysis if you are going to discuss them sensibly.

Having read this chapter, you may be fired with enthusiasm and impatient
to read the rest of this book and pursue your study of law. Alternatively, you
may have found it dense, difficult and – to put it bluntly – either boring or
incomprehensible, or both. Whichever category *you* fall into is less important than the fact that you will have benefited from reading it.

If you fall into the first category, you are likely to enjoy both the remainder
of this book and the rest of your time studying law.

If you fall into the second category, you are likely to find the study of law
rather heavy going and unrewarding.

Regardless of these (unless you have found this chapter totally incomprehensible, in which case you might be best advised to try to persuade your
college or university to allow you to change your course), you should, at the
very least, have developed some insight into the question with which we
began: what is law, and the study of law, *about*?

Finally, if you did not find the anecdote about being none the wiser but better informed even slightly amusing, you may be among those who conclude that legal humour is not very funny.

2 The Sources of English Law

There are three domestic sources of English law, namely the common law (which is developed by the courts), statutes (which are enacted by Parliament) and delegated legislation (which is made by people acting under the authority of Parliament). European Community law is also an important source of English law, especially through the doctrines of direct applicability and direct effect. Under the Human Rights Act 1998 (HRA), the European Convention on Human Rights (ECHR) is, strictly speaking, a source of substantive law only in relation to public authorities. Nevertheless, the ECHR is of enormous practical importance because of the way in which the HRA requires English courts to approach the decision-making process in cases involving almost all the rights which the ECHR protects.

Introduction

For all practical purposes, the sources of English law are the common law, statute law and delegated legislation, and European Community law. We will discuss each of these in turn, but before we do so it is worth commenting that the omission of the European Convention on Human Rights from the sources of English law is intentional. The reason for this omission is that, strictly speaking, under the Human Rights Act 1998, the Convention is a source of English law only to the very limited extent that it is unlawful for public authorities to breach those articles of the Convention which the Act classifies as 'Convention rights'.

However, it would be seriously misleading to suggest that the Convention is unimportant in English law, because in addition to the duty which it imposes on public bodies (and which we have just noted), the Human Rights Act 1998 requires all courts to:

- have regard to the law of the Convention in all cases involving 'Convention rights', and
- to interpret all English legislation in such a way as to give effect to 'Convention rights' wherever it is possible to do so, even if the legislation in question pre-dates the Act itself.

We will return to the Convention and the Human Rights Act in more detail in Chapter 5, but it is never too early to understand that, in many situations, you will have to consider *three legal systems* (namely domestic English law, European Community law, and the law of the European Convention on Human Rights), and the ways in which they interact with each other, if you are going to have a proper understanding of the law as it is administered by the English courts.

Common law and statute law

Introduction
An initial difficulty with the phrase *the common law* is that it has a variety of meanings, with the correct one in any given context depending on that context. Thus it may be contrasted with *statute law*, *equity* and *civil law*. For the moment, we will use the phrase *the common law* in its most general sense of *judge-made law*, by way of contrast with *statute law and delegated legislation*. Within our discussion of this meaning of the phrase, we will explain the origins and meaning of *equity*, leaving only the distinction with *civil law* to be dealt with briefly at the end of our discussion. However, as we shall see, the phrase *common law* may also be used in a narrower sense, in which it contrasts with *equity*.

Common law, equity, statute law and delegated legislation
Common law is that part of the law which is contained in the decisions of the courts, rather than being made by Parliament. Of course, an important part of the status of any system of *law* is that it must be *binding*. In the case of the common law, bindingness flows from the doctrine of *binding precedent*, which is one of the main topics discussed in Chapter 7.

Historically, the common law originated in the King's courts. More particularly, it emerged from the practice of the King's judges, who travelled round the country when administering the law, adopting what they considered to be the best legal rules from each area and enforcing them in other areas as well. Thus, at a time when communications were such that there could be wide variations between laws in different localities, the King's judges used their powers to minimise those variations and enforce a single set of laws that were *common* to the whole country. In other words, they created the *common law*.

Although, as we shall see in Chapter 7, the modern version of the doctrine of binding precedent is surprisingly flexible, in earlier times the common law valued uniformity above flexibility. Consequently, there were many situations in which the common law lacked the flexibility to produce fair results in individual cases. It was to counter this tendency of the common law that the doctrines of *equity* emerged.

Equity originated in the office of chancery, whose head was the Lord Chancellor and whose function it was to issue the writs that were the documents used to begin actions at common law. What happened was that the office of chancery began to introduce a more flexible system of rules, which operated alongside the rules of common law but were much more geared to producing results that were consistent with what was thought to be good conscience. This parallel system came to be called *equity*, and in due course its operation and development came into the hands of the Lord Chancellor's court, namely the *court of chancery*.

To take a straightforward example of how the relationship between the common law and equity worked (and, indeed still does work), suppose that you agree to sell me an 'old master' painting, but you then decide not to go through with the deal and refuse to deliver the goods even though I am ready, willing and able to pay the price we have agreed. The only remedy the common law can offer me is damages. However, in cases like this, the subject matter of the contract is unique and therefore no amount of money will enable me to go out and buy an equivalent painting. Equity, on the other hand, has developed a remedy (called *specific performance*) for cases like this. If I obtain an order for specific performance against you, you will be obliged to perform our contract and deliver the goods I have agreed to buy. If you fail to comply with the order, you will be in contempt of court and may be sent to prison.

A moment's thought will show you that, since the whole purpose of having the two systems of common law and equity was to get different answers to the same question, it was inevitable that the courts of common law and chancery would find themselves at loggerheads. Returning to the example we have already considered, if you are ordered to pay me damages at common law, and you comply with the order, that will be an end of the matter. However, if equity also orders you to perform the contract, and you fail to do so, you could be imprisoned for contempt of court.

The rule that emerged to deal with conflicts of this kind was that where the two systems conflicted, equity was to prevail over the common law. Since the Judicature Acts of 1873–75, both common law and equity have been administered by the same courts; but, as this jurisdictional change did nothing to avoid conflict between the two systems, there is still a maxim to the effect that where equity and the [common] law conflict, equity prevails.

Perhaps an even more important aspect of equity's creativity than the invention of additional remedies may be found in its invention of the law of trusts. While it is difficult to produce a totally accurate definition of the word *trust*, the idea which underlies all trusts is simple enough, namely that property is owned by one person (or a group of people) for the benefit of another person (or a group of other people). The person or people who own the property is (or are) called the *trustee* (or *trustees*), while the person or people who have the benefit of the property is (or are) called the *beneficiary* (or *beneficiaries*). Because the beneficiaries have the benefit of the property, they are sometimes said to be the *beneficial owners*, even though the common law regards the trustees as being the *legal owners*.

If trustees use trust property for their own benefit, equity will hold them to account. Indeed, one equitable remedy is known as *account* because it compels defendants to account for – or, in other words, pay back – their wrongful profits.

Strictly speaking, this explanation of the nature of a trust is defective, because trusts need not benefit people, but may exist for the benefit of animals and other things, such as the maintenance of buildings. However, the outer limits of the nature of trusts cannot be pursued here. All that need be said is that, historically, wealthy families found that trusts provided a very important way of managing their property. In the modern world, however, the main importance of trusts is that they provide the legal frameworks for the operation of pension funds and unit trusts.

Having seen how judge-made law as a whole contains the contrasting systems of common law and equity, we can now move on to the distinction between judge-made law as a whole, and law made either by Parliament or by someone else acting under authority conferred by Parliament.

Statute law and delegated legislation

Although the courts are still developing the common law, the main sources of English law are now statutes and delegated legislation.

Statutes, as their alternative name *Acts of Parliament* makes plain, are made by Parliament itself. However, in a modern, fast-moving and complex society, Parliament cannot possibly generate all the legislation that is needed. Therefore many statutes delegate to other people or bodies (typically, but by no means exclusively, Secretaries of State and local authorities) to make a great deal of detailed law in order to supplement that which is contained in the statutes themselves. Delegated legislation takes many forms, but the most common are statutory instruments (which are usually made by Secretaries of State) and byelaws and compulsory purchase orders (both of which are usually made by local authorities).

Statutes, along with certain Orders made by the Privy Council when exercising the Royal Prerogative on behalf of the Crown and certain enactments of the Scottish Parliament, the Welsh Assembly and the Northern Ireland Assembly, are called *primary* legislation. Laws made by people or bodies acting under authority conferred on them by Parliament are called, variously and interchangeably, *secondary*, *subordinate* or *delegated* legislation. Only statutes come within the doctrine of the legislative supremacy of Parliament, for the very simple reason that they are the only form of legislation made by Parliament.

Common law and civil law

As we have seen, the phrase *common law* is sometimes used generally to mean judge-made law as distinct from statute law, and sometimes more specifically to mean that part of judge-made law which originated in the King's courts, as distinct from that part of judge-made law known as *equity*.

A fundamentally different contrast may be made between *common law* and *civil law*. The contrast in this context is between the English legal system (together with those countries whose legal systems are derived from it, such as Australia, New Zealand and the United States of America) on the one hand, and the legal systems of the states of continental Europe on the other, whose legal systems are derived from Roman Law.

One of the most important functional distinctions between common law and civil law systems is that the latter have no doctrine of *binding* precedent. (The doctrine of binding precedent is discussed in Chapter 7.)

Finally, it is important to notice that the use of the term *civil law* discussed here has nothing whatsoever to do with the distinction between *civil* law and *criminal* law which is discussed in Chapter 1.

European Community law

Introduction

By way of a preliminary to our discussion of Community law, it will be useful to explain what is meant by the *European Community* and to clarify the common confusion between the European *Community* and the European *Union*.

The meaning of European Community
Originally, there was only the European Coal and Steel Community, which was created by the Treaty of Paris 1951. This community, which came into being in 1953, was established for a fixed term of 50 years. Accordingly it no longer exists, although its functions have been taken over by the European Community, to which we now turn.

In 1957 two Treaties of Rome established two further communities, namely:

- the European Economic Community, as it was originally called, before the Treaty on European Union 1992 (the Maastricht Treaty) renamed it as the *European Community*; and
- the European Atomic Energy Community (which is also known as Euratom).

Currently, therefore, there are two communities, namely Euratom and the European Community, of which only the latter need concern us.

The Treaty of Rome, which established what is now the European Community, is commonly known simply as the *EC Treaty*.

European Community law or European Union law?
Despite the fact that the Treaty on European *Union* renamed the European Economic *Community* as the European *Community*, the *Community* and the *Union* are not interchangeable concepts.

The key point is that the *Community* is only one component of the *Union*. More particularly, the *Union* consists of *three pillars*, namely:

- the two Communities (which, for these purposes, are taken together as a single pillar):
- a common foreign and security policy; (CFSP); and
- police and judicial cooperation in criminal matters (PJCCM).

Additionally, and crucially, the Community is a *legal* entity which has a legal system, while the *Union* is still at a somewhat less formal stage its evolution, in which it is a *political* entity. The correct usage is, therefore, European *Community* law, rather than European *Union* law. Support for this conclusion may be derived from the fact that the full title of the European Court of Justice (or ECJ as it is commonly known) is still the Court of Justice of the European Communities (which is abbreviated to CJEC). (The jurisdiction of the Court is outlined at p. 59, but it may be worth saying at this point that the inclusion of the plural *Communities* in the Court's full title reflects the fact that its jurisdiction covers Euratom as well as the European Community.)

Unfortunately, and inexplicably, the inaccurate usage (of European *Union* law) has been adopted by practically every commentator in the media, together with the authors of practically all the academic textbooks in the field.

Although the basic distinction between the *Community* and the *Union* is clear, the waters have started to become slightly muddied. More particularly, art. 8 of the EC Treaty (which was inserted by the Treaty on European Union and was *not* renumbered by the Treaty of Amsterdam) provides that people holding the nationality of a member state are automatically also citizens of the *Union*, and accordingly have certain rights as a matter of *Community* law.

Perhaps fortunately, the distinction between the *Community* and the *Union* will become a matter of history when the Treaty of Lisbon replaces the *Community* with the *Union*. The Treaty is due to be signed in December 2007, after which (assuming it is ratified by all the member states), it will come into force in 2009, on a date to be specified. The *Union* will then have legal – rather than merely political – status, and there will be a Court of Justice of the European *Union*. However, even before the Treaty comes into force (and even if it does not do so), you may prefer to use the technically incorrect expression *European Union law*, rather than risk annoying your lecturers, tutors and – most importantly – examiners, by using the technically correct, but inexplicably unfashionable, expression *European Community law*.

The Community Treaties

The Community Treaties, which created and have subsequently modified the structure and functioning of the European Community, are clearly a source of Community law. The principal Treaties, with their commonly used abbreviations, are:

- the Treaty of Rome 1957 (originally known as the EEC Treaty, but now known simply as the EC Treaty);
- the Maastricht Treaty 1992 (the Treaty on European Union or TEU);
- the Treaty of Amsterdam 1997 (the ToA); and
- the Treaty of Nice 2001 (ToN).

We will not pursue the detailed content of any of these Treaties here, except to say that the ToA renumbered many of the articles of the EC Treaty.

Although there is some variation of practice between commentators, the Community's own practice is to cite the renumbered version first, with the original number (prefixed by *ex*) following in brackets – for example, art. 234 [ex 177] EC.

Under art. 249 [ex 189 EC] there are three other types of Community instruments which are binding (and which are, therefore, sources of law), namely:

- Regulations;
- Directives; and
- Decisions.

We will consider the nature of each of these sources in turn, before considering how they impact on the English legal system.

The nature of the Treaties

The Treaties are often said to be, or to be the equivalent of, a constitution. While this is not wrong, it may be misleading, because the Treaties contain a great deal more detail than is usual for constitutions. However, we need not debate the question of terminology here: the Treaties are plainly a source of law.

The nature of Regulations

Regulations, which are the form of Community law that most closely resembles statute law within the English legal system, are plainly a source of law.

We will come to the effect of Community Regulations in English law in a few moments, but it is worth noticing at this stage that, despite their similarities, English statutes differ from Community Regulations in one important respect. Under the doctrine of the legislative supremacy of Parliament (see Chapter 3), the English courts have no power to quash Acts of Parliament, because it is Parliament and not the courts which are supreme. On the other hand, there is nothing to stop the European Court of Justice quashing individual Regulations which it finds to be unlawful.

The nature of Directives

Directives have no equivalent within the English legal system. Directives are instructions from the Community to the member states requiring them to achieve certain legal results within their national legal systems, but leaving it for each member state to decide how this should be done. Each Directive will specify a date by which member states must comply with its terms.

It is clear from the nature of Directives that they are not a source of law in the same way as the Treaties and Regulations are sources of law, because they depend on member states for their implementation. Nevertheless, there is plainly a sense in which they are sources – even if only conditional sources – of law, because they bind member states to produce specific legal consequences.

The nature of Decisions

Decisions are addressed to member states or to individuals and are binding upon those to whom they are addressed. Therefore they are plainly a source of the law which applies to those states or individuals.

How Community law enters English law

Introduction

The whole of Community law was received into English law by s. 2(1) and (4) of the European Communities Act 1972. However, in order to understand this statement fully, we must investigate two doctrines of Community law that have no equivalents in English law, namely *direct applicability* and *direct effect*.

- Direct applicability

    A provision of Community law is said to be *directly applicable* if it becomes part of the law of member states *automatically*; or, in other words, without any action on the part of member states.
- Direct effect

    A provision of Community law is said to be *directly effective* if, and only if, it creates rights which are enforceable in the courts of a member state at the instance of people who are aggrieved by breaches of the provision.

Most people's immediate reaction when they first encounter the distinction between *direct applicability* and *direct effect* is one of puzzlement. How can a provision of Community law enter the legal systems of member states without also creating rights which are enforceable in the courts of those states? After all, is it not one of the prime functions of courts to enforce all the law in all cases? Understandable though this puzzlement is, in reality it flows from not thinking the topic through with sufficient rigour.

Even if we limit ourselves entirely to the English legal system, many laws do not give rise to rights that are enforceable in the courts. For example, I have the *power* (or *capacity*) to enter into contracts, such as a contract to buy a book. However, if I choose to exercise that power by buying a book written by author A rather than a competing title written by author B, nobody can argue that I have infringed the rights of author B.

The direct applicability and direct effect of different forms of Community law

Since some forms of Community law are only directly *applicable*, while others are also directly *effective*, we obviously need to know which is which. We will consider the treaties, regulations, directives and decisions in turn, but before doing so we will refine the basic question before adding two further ones.

The refinement involves rephrasing the basic question so that it becomes:

- Which forms of Community law are *capable* of being directly effective?

The first additional question is:

- Supposing we are dealing with a form of Community law that *is capable* of being directly effective, how do we know whether this particular provision *actually is* directly effective?

The second additional question is:

- Supposing the particular provision of Community law actually *is* directly effective, against whom can it be enforced? (If it can be enforced by a private individual or organisation against the state, its direct effect is said to be *vertical*. If it can be enforced by a private individual or organisation against another private individual or organisation, its direct effect is said to be *horizontal*.)

To answer this additional question, we need to understand what is meant by *the criteria for direct effect*.

The criteria for direct effect

It is obvious that people who seek to enforce their legal rights in court must be in a position to say what they claim those rights to be. In terms of Community law, the technical terminology that covers this point is *the criteria for direct effect*. Reduced to their essentials, the criteria for direct effect are basically the commonsense requirements that the provision of Community law in question must be both:

- clear and precise in its expression (so that the court can know what it is being asked to enforce); and
- self-contained (in the sense that its implementation must not depend on the exercise of discretion by the public authorities of member states).

If we decide that a particular provision of Community law is of a type which is *capable of direct effect*, and that it also *satisfies the criteria for direct effect*, so that it is, therefore, *actually directly effective*, we then come to the second additional question posed above:

- is the direct effect:
  - only vertical; or
  - both vertical and horizontal?

A provision's direct effect will be only *vertical* if a private individual or organisation can enforce it only against the state. Its direct effect will also be *horizontal* if a private individual or organisation can also enforce it against another private individual or organisation.

Although this statement may seem rather dense on a first reading, it is, in fact, underpinned by some very clear logic. Both treaty articles and regulations present no difficulties: they are both directly applicable and capable of having direct effect. Furthermore, there is no reason to limit their direct effect; and, therefore, in the interests of making Community law as effective as possible, their direct effect is both vertical and horizontal. However, matters are less obvious when it comes to Directives.

As we have seen, Directives require member states to take some action, and therefore they are not directly applicable. However, where a member state fails to implement a Directive by the due date, the result will be that people within that state will be deprived of rights which they would have had if the state in question had complied with its obligations under Community law.

Where this situation arises, therefore, if a person brings an action against the member state which is in default, that state may well reply: *but you do not have the rights you are seeking because we have not implemented the Directive*. However, such a reply would be a clear violation of the fundamental principle of justice that nobody should be allowed to gain advantage from their own wrongdoing, and therefore the Court of Justice has held that, under these circumstances, the Directive can be enforced against the defaulting member state. (*Grad v Finanzamt Traustein* [1970] ECR 825.) In other words, it will have vertical direct effect.

However, if an action is brought against another private individual or organisation, the same logic will not apply. After all, it is not the fault of any private individual or organisation that the state has not complied with its obligations under Community law, and therefore the argument based on gaining advantage from wrongdoing does not even get off the ground. In other words, the potential direct effect of Directives can only ever be vertical, and not horizontal.

By way of example, suppose a Directive requires employers to provide free annual eyesight tests for all their employees who drive motor vehicles. If a member state fails to implement this Directive by the due date, government employees could enforce the Directive against the state, but employees of private organisations could not enforce it against their employers, because the failure to implement the Directive is not their employers' fault.

The EC Treaty does not make Decisions directly applicable, but it does make them binding on the people to whom they are addressed. As the Court of Justice said in *Grad*, the effectiveness of Decisions would be seriously reduced if the courts of member states could not treat them as part of Community law. In other words, Decisions are both directly applicable and capable of vertical direct effect.

This leaves the question of whether their direct effect is *only* vertical, or both vertical and horizontal. Although the Court of Justice has never been called upon to decide this point (which is, therefore, presumably of little importance in purely practical terms), there is no reason, in principle, to withhold horizontal direct effect from Decisions. For example, where a Decision addressed to a company has the consequence that one of its contracts is void because it is contrary to Community law, the other party to the contract should be able to rely on the voidness in an action against the company. Any other conclusion would mean that the company to whom the Decision is addressed would gain an advantage (in this case, a valid contract) by breaching the Decision which rendered the contract void.

A tabular summary

The whole topic of direct applicability and direct effect is summarised in the following two tables.

Table 1

	Directly applicable?	*Capable of direct effect?
Treaty Articles	Yes	Yes
Regulations	Yes	Yes
Directives	No	**Yes
Decisions	Yes	Yes

*A provision which is *capable* of having direct effect will not *actually have* direct effect unless it also satisfies the *criteria for direct effect*.
**Provided the Directive has not been implemented within the time allowed.

Table 2

	Capable of vertical direct effect?	Capable of horizontal direct effect?
Treaty Articles	Yes	Yes
Regulations	Yes	Yes
Directives	Yes	No
Decisions	Yes	Probably

Indirect Effect

Finally, even where Community law lacks direct effect, it may still have an *indirect effect* on the laws of member states, in the sense that a relevant provision of Community law may influence the interpretation of existing national laws of member states. This proposition is sometimes known as the *von Colson principle* or the *Marleasing principle* after the leading cases of *von Colson v Land Nordrhein Westfalen* [1986] 2 CMLR 430 and *Marleasing SA v La Comercial Internacional de Alimentacion SA* [1992] 1 CMLR 305.

Resolving conflicts between English law and Community law

One inevitable consequence of the entry of Community law into English law is that, from time to time, specific provisions of the two systems will conflict with each other. It is clearly established that these conflicts will be resolved in favour of Community law, but we will postpone further discussion of this matter until we come to the topic of the supremacy of Community law in the next chapter (see pp. 46–49).

European Convention on Human Rights

The European Convention on Human Rights and its effect on the English legal system are discussed in Chapter 5.

Conclusion

In order to be confident of your ability to understand the way in which English law works, you need a good working knowledge of three legal systems. More particularly, in addition to understanding domestic English law, you need to understand both European Community law and the law of the European Convention on Human Rights.

The sources of domestic English law are the common law (using this phrase in its broad sense to mean all judge-made law, including equity), together with statute law and delegated legislation.

It is technically inaccurate to speak of European *Union* law rather than European *Community* law, but its inaccuracy has not prevented this usage from becoming very firmly established.

The principal sources of European Community law are the Community Treaties, together with Regulations, Directives and Decisions. The doctrines of direct applicability and direct effect govern the ways in which Community law impacts upon the domestic English law.

The law of the European Convention on Human Rights, and the operation of the Human Rights Act 1998, are discussed in Chapter 5.

3 The Constitutional Context of English Law

A constitution provides the legal structure for the governance of a state. The British constitution is underpinned by the doctrines of the legislative supremacy of Parliament, the rule of law and the separation of powers. However, it is practically unique in not being contained in a single written document. Membership of the European Community involves a voluntary limitation on the legislative supremacy of Parliament; but the Human Rights Act 1998 does not try to limit the legislative supremacy of Parliament in any way.

Introduction

In this chapter we will pick up and develop the point (which we introduced briefly at p. 2) that constitutional law is concerned with the allocation of public (or governmental) power between different institutions and people. We will begin by considering the nature of constitutions generally, before looking more closely at the British constitution.

What is a constitution?

Introduction

Every state must have a constitution in the sense of a body of legal rules (usually supplemented by a collection of informal practices which are called *constitutional conventions*), both of which will reflect certain underlying political doctrines and will provide a framework for the governance of that state. While it is obvious that both the underlying doctrines and the content of the rules and practices will vary from one state to another, it is also true, if less obvious, that the way in which those doctrines, rules and practices are presented will also vary from one state to another.

Written and *unwritten* constitutions

Almost all countries have what are called *written constitutions*, in the sense that there is a single document containing at least the most important formal rules, which may be expressed in varying degrees of detail. In the context of this meaning of the phrase *written constitution*, the British constitution is usually described as being *unwritten*. However, it is important to note that this is a technical usage of the word *unwritten*. More particularly, it does not mean that the rules are not written down anywhere, but simply that they are not written down in one place. In fact, almost all the formal rules of the British constitution are written down, either in the judgments of the courts or in Acts of Parliament, while the underlying doctrines and almost all the informal practices are described in sources ranging from textbooks on constitutional law and political science to the memoirs of politicians. From time to time, the doctrines and informal practices may also be recognised by the courts

The factual inaccuracy of the term *unwritten constitution* leads some people to reject the *written/unwritten* terminology altogether, preferring to use the terms *codified* and *uncodified* instead. Since *codified* means *brought together in a single document* (or at least in a small number of documents), while *uncodified* means *not brought together in this way*, there is much to be said for this usage. However, this does not exhaust the possible variations of terminology, since some people prefer to speak in terms of *formal* and *informal* constitutions. From your point of view, however, all that really matters is that you are able to understand whatever usage you may come across.

The relationship between *constitutions* and *law*

Since the constitution validates the exercise of power by governments, two questions arise, namely:

- What validates the constitution? and
- What is the relationship between government and the constitution?

One of the best brief answers to these questions, at least from the viewpoint of the political tradition which is usually known as *liberal democracy*, may be found in the words of Tom Paine, the 18th century English radical:

> A constitution is not the act of a government, but of a people constituting a government, and *a government without a constitution is power without a right* ... *A constitution is a thing antecedent to a government;*

and a government is only the creature of a constitution. (The Rights of Man, 1790; emphasis added.)

In short, therefore, the constitution comes before, and validates, the government, rather than the government coming first and then validating the constitution. It follows that, since law is the product of *governmental processes* (using that phrase loosely for the moment), we can adapt Paine's words and say that the *constitution is a thing antecedent to the law*.

One crucial function of any constitution is to identify the person who, or the body which, exercises supreme power within the state. Different constitutions take different views of this matter, with variations in constitutional histories between different states usually providing the explanation for how the matter has been resolved in each case. Some states, such as the United States of America, place this ultimate power in the Supreme Court. On the other hand, perhaps the most important doctrine of the British Constitution is that this ultimate power lies with Parliament. At this stage, therefore, it is appropriate to turn our attention to the underlying doctrines of the British Constitution generally.

The underlying doctrines of the British constitution

Introduction
There are three underlying doctrines of the British constitution, namely:

- the *legislative supremacy of Parliament*;
- the *rule of law*; and
- the *separation of powers*.

If your course includes a more detailed study of the British constitution, you will consider each of these doctrines in some detail at that stage, but whether this is so or not, it will be useful for us to consider them each briefly here.

The legislative supremacy of Parliament
The *legislative supremacy* (or, as it is sometimes called, the *sovereignty*) *of Parliament*, has been at the heart of British constitutional law for over three centuries, since the Glorious Revolution of 1688. The idea of the *legislative supremacy of Parliament* is simply that

- Parliament can pass any legislation it wishes to pass; and
- only Parliament can repeal legislation which Parliament has passed.

However, three points must be made if this statement is not to be seriously misleading.

First, it is essential to grasp that *Parliament* is *not* the same thing as the *House of Commons*. More particularly, for something to be an *Act of Parliament*, it must normally have been passed by both the House of Commons and the House of Lords and must always have received the Royal Assent from the monarch. The exceptional situation lurking behind the word *normally* in the previous sentence arises where a special procedure, which is contained in the Parliament Acts 1911 and 1949, is invoked. The details of this procedure are complicated, but its effect is simple: the House of Lords may delay legislation for one year, but cannot veto it. The only exceptions are Bills which the Speaker of the House of Commons certifies as being *money bills* – which are exempt even from the one year delaying power – and bills to prolong the life of Parliament, which are exempt from the provisions of the Parliament Acts altogether, and which can, therefore, still be vetoed by the House of Lords. The Parliament Acts procedure is very seldom invoked, although notable examples of its use include:

- the Parliament Act 1949, which was itself passed under the provisions of the 1911 Act and which reduced the Lords' delaying power from two years to one;
- the War Crimes Act 1991, which permits United Kingdom courts to try people charged with certain war crimes, provided they were, on 8 March 1990, or have subsequently become, British citizens or residents of the United Kingdom, the Channel Islands or the Isle of Man; and
- the Hunting Act 2004 which creates an offence of hunting wild mammals with dogs.

Secondly, the fact that something – in this case the legislative power of Parliament – is *legally* uncontrolled does not necessarily mean that it is *totally* uncontrolled. More particularly, in a liberal democracy, it is extremely unlikely that Parliament would use its powers in a way which would be universally viewed as being oppressive or unjust in any other way. Furthermore, there are two relevant constitutional conventions, namely that *the House of Lords usually defers to the House of Commons*, and that *the monarch does not withhold the Royal Assent*. The combined effect of these conventions is that, in purely practical terms, the political party that dominates the House of Commons will also very largely dominate the whole of the legislative process.

Thirdly, in *Factortame Ltd v Secretary of State for Transport (No 2)* [1991] 1 AC 603, the House of Lords accepted that when Parliament passed the European Communities Act 1972, it effectively surrendered part of its sovereignty, to the extent that whenever English law and Community law conflict, Community law prevails.

By way of contrast to this third point, and although we will not pursue the protection of fundamental rights until we come to Chapter 5, it may be worth noting here that the Human Rights Act 1998 contains nothing which limits the continuing legislative supremacy of Parliament. More particularly, s. 4(5) of the 1998 Act expressly provides that where a United Kingdom statute is found to be in breach of a *Convention right* (as defined by s. 1(1) of the Act), neither the outcome of the case, nor – more importantly in the present context – the continuing validity of the offending statute will be affected.

Two further, but unconnected, points may usefully be made by way of conclusion.

First, the doctrine of *the legislative supremacy of Parliament* is limited, as the phrase itself indicates, to Acts of *Parliament*, and therefore the doctrine does not apply to *delegated legislation*, which can be – and frequently is – quashed by the courts. (We have already considered the topic of delegated legislation in Chapter 2; but, very briefly, you will recall that it is legislation made by some person or body other than Parliament, to whom Parliament has delegated the power to legislate.)

Secondly, Parliament's power to repeal Acts of Parliament may be exercised either expressly or impliedly. The idea of express repeal requires no comment, but it is worth noticing that implied repeal occurs where two statutory provisions are so fundamentally incompatible that one must give way to the other. In this situation, Parliament is presumed to have been aware of the earlier provision, and therefore is also presumed to have intended that the later one should repeal it.

The rule of law

Introduction
The doctrine of the rule of law states what is essentially a political ideal, namely that government should be conducted according to law, rather than discretion. It comes in two versions, namely *formal* and *substantive*. We will consider each in turn.

Formal versions of the rule of law

One of the most famous statements of a formal version of the rule of law comes from AV Dicey, the leading Victorian commentator, who said that it requires

> the absolute supremacy or predominance of regular law as opposed to the influence of arbitrary power, [with the resulting exclusion of] the existence of arbitrariness ... or even of wide discretionary authority on the part of the government. (*The Law of the Constitution*, first published in 1885.)

While Dicey's version has an obvious and immediate appeal, on reflection it can be seen to be a substantial overstatement: the process of government inevitably requires the exercise of discretionary – and sometimes wide discretionary – authority. Nevertheless, Dicey was right to identify the dangers of discretionary powers, even though it would be impossible, in practical terms, to eliminate them. What really matters, therefore, is not that discretionary powers should be eliminated, but that:

- whatever limits are imposed upon discretionary governmental powers, they are identified by law;
- there are legal mechanisms for dealing with complaints that government has exceeded those limits; and
- the courts can provide remedies where government has exceeded those limits.

Furthermore, and even before the question of the extent and control of discretion arises,

- laws must be made in accordance with the procedures laid down by the constitution.

Of course, it is implicit in what has just been said that those who advance purely formal versions of the rule of law exclude from the scope of the doctrine any concern with the *content* of the law, provided the relevant formalities have been observed. Thus an absolute dictatorship whose laws systematically differentiated between the rights of its subjects on the grounds of their race, sex, sexual orientation or religious beliefs could easily comply with the rule of law in a purely formal sense, while being seriously lacking in terms of its content, according, at any rate, to the generally prevailing standards of contemporary western democracies. It is this aspect of the matter which leads many political and legal theorists to prefer *substantive* versions of the doctrine.

Substantive versions of the rule of law
By way of contrast with their *formal* counterparts, *substantive* versions of the rule of law require more than mere compliance with the relevant formal criteria: they rely upon the idea of the rule of law for the additional purpose of providing the basis for certain substantive rights.

Obviously, substantive versions of the doctrine present problems which their formal counterparts do not encounter, since there may be sincere, legitimate and reasonable disagreements as to which substantive rights the law should recognise and uphold. For example, does allowing same-sex marriage represent a proper respect for individual autonomy by allowing people to make up their own minds as to what constitutes the good life? Or does it represent an insidious undermining of the traditional view of marriage as the union of one man and one woman, and thus indirectly undermine society itself by undermining one of its most important building blocks, namely the family?

While arguments such as these may be both interesting and important, once the doctrine of the rule of law becomes inextricably linked with the content of the law, there is clearly a danger that those who lose such arguments on particular issues will feel that the rule of law has let them down; and they may, therefore, become alienated from society as a whole. Where this happens, those who prefer the formal versions of the doctrine will argue that the substantive versions have not only failed to deliver on their own terms, but – even more seriously – have undermined the whole enterprise of law as an agent of social cohesion. In other words, the formalist argument will be that the substantive argument has helped to destroy that which it appeared to be advocating and defending.

How strict is the formal/substantive distinction?
Although the distinction between formal and substantive versions of the rule of law, as outlined above, appears to present a straightforward choice between two alternatives, it can be argued that a formal version may require rather more than mere compliance with formalities, without forfeiting its status as a formal version. The argument to this effect is that law must, in its very nature, be capable of guiding conduct; and therefore it follows that *any* version of the rule of law must have *some* substantive content. As a bare minimum, for example, legal acts performed by public bodies and officials should be guided by rules which are open, stable, clear and general; and

there must be independent judges, giving decisions in courts in which anyone can bring proceedings and to which the public have access in order to see how the law is administered.

On this view of the matter, therefore, the distinction between formal and substantive versions of the rule of law is more a matter of degree than a straight choice between two alternatives.

The separation of powers

The doctrine of the separation of powers is usually attributed to the 18th century French political philosopher Montesquieu, and more particularly to his book *L'Ésprit des Lois*, although the origins of the idea can actually be traced back to classical antiquity.

The doctrine divides all forms of power exercised by the state into three categories, namely *legislative*, *executive* and *judicial*, with the nature of each being as follows:

- legislative power involves *making* law;
- executive power involves *administering* the law, in the sense in which governmental agencies and officials administer it; and
- judicial power involves *interpreting and applying* the law in the sense in which the courts interpret and apply it.

Having identified these three types of power, the doctrine then requires that no more than one type should be exercised by a single body or official. So, for example, the legislature that makes the law should not also interpret it and apply it in individual cases. Similarly, executive bodies and officials who administer the law should not have the power to make authoritative decisions as to what the law means and how it is to be applied in individual cases. Furthermore, the courts which interpret and apply the law should not also make it.

Although it is important to note that the British constitution has never reflected this strict version of the doctrine, the basic idea of the separation of powers retains considerable practical importance in several ways. One of the most obvious examples of this importance lies in the field of judicial review (which, as we will see at p. 52–53, is the process that requires the court to decide whether a *decision-making process* is *lawful*, but without asking whether the *decision itself* is *right*). The case of *R v Birmingham City Council ex parte Sheptonhurst Ltd* [1990] 1 All ER 1026 provides a useful example of judicial review in action.

The case was one of several similar ones in which the court was concerned with the refusal of local authorities to renew expiring sex shop licences that had been granted under statutory powers. In each case, the local authority had concluded that the appropriate number of sex shops in the relevant area was nil, and therefore all applications for licences would be refused, even though, on the facts of each of the cases which were before the court on this occasion, there had been no change of circumstances since the previous licences had been granted.

The court held that when considering an application for renewal of a sex shop licence, a local authority must *have regard to* the fact that a licence had previously been granted. However, provided it does have regard to this fact, its decision to refuse to renew a licence will *not* be perverse simply because there has been no change in the character of the relevant locality or in the use to which any premises in the vicinity are put.

The crucial point in the court's approach to cases such as this is that the legislature is not only supreme but must also be taken to know that a local authority is a democratically elected body, whose membership changes from time to time in line with the changing views of the local electorate. It is not surprising, therefore, that what is 'appropriate' may be perceived differently by different elected representatives at different times. Equally, it is not surprising that the court, being aware of the doctrine of the separation of powers, should decide not to intervene.

Although the constitutional basis of the *Birmingham* case is readily apparent, the courts are also clearly aware that there are cases where the doctrine of the rule of law does require them to intervene. As Farwell LJ said, in *R v Shoreditch Assessment Committee ex parte Morgan* [1910] 2 KB 859, 880:

> It is a contradiction in terms to create a [decision-maker] with limited jurisdiction and unlimited power to determine such limit at its own will and pleasure – such a [decision-maker] would be autocratic, not limited ...

Nevertheless, the court remains conscious that its constitutional role is limited. For example, in *R v Hillingdon London Borough Council ex parte Puhlhofer* [1986] AC 484, which arose in the context of local authorities' statutory duties in cases of homelessness, Lord Brightman said (at p. 518):

> My Lords, I am troubled at the prolific use of judicial review for the purposes of challenging the performance by local authorities of their functions under the Act ... Where the existence or non-existence of a fact is left to the judgment and discretion of a public body and that

fact involves a broad spectrum, ranging from the obvious to the debatable to the just conceivable, it is the duty of the court to leave the decision of that fact to the public body, save in a case where it is obvious that the public body, consciously or unconsciously, are acting perversely.

Perhaps the most important thing for you to take away from the discussion so far is that, when it comes to real cases, there is often a degree of tension between the basic doctrines underlying the British constitution. When should the courts be primarily conscious of their limited status according to the doctrines of the legislative supremacy of Parliament and the separation of powers, and therefore refuse to intervene in a particular case? Alternatively, when should they assert themselves as the guardians of the rule of law? Finally, to what extent is it relevant – as will often be the case – that the decision-maker whose conduct has resulted in the case being brought to court, is democratically accountable? (In other words, when should the court take the view that the existence of a *political* mechanism of control is sufficient to justify the court in refusing a *legal* remedy?)

The limited nature of the separation of powers in the British constitution
So far we have mentioned only in passing that the British constitution does not reflect a strict version of the doctrine of the separation of powers. Until recently, the most complete breach of the doctrine lay in the status of the Lord Chancellor as a member of the legislature, the executive and the judiciary. However, the current practice is that the Lord Chancellor (who, since May 2007 has occupied that ancient office together with the new office of Secretary of State for Justice) does not sit as a judge. (Indeed, the office of Lord Chancellor will be abolished altogether in the foreseeable future.) We will, therefore, move swiftly on to consider what are probably the three most important ways in which the British constitution fails to reflect the doctrine, namely:

- the domination of the legislature by the executive;
- the status of the Appellate Committee of the House of Lords as the highest court of appeal in the English legal system; and
- the power of the courts to make law through the doctrine of binding precedent.

Taking these in turn, we can begin by developing a point that we made when discussing the meaning of the word *Parliament* (see p. 38). As a matter of political reality, all members of the government (or, to use the terminology which better fits the separation of powers, the *executive*) will sit in Parliament (or, again to use the terminology which better fits the separation of powers, the *legislature*). Furthermore, the vast majority of them will sit in the House of Commons. In other words, the political party which forms the government will usually dominate the House of Commons, and will, therefore, also effectively dominate the legislative process. The only exception to this proposition is that a government with only a very small (or perhaps even non-existent) majority in the House of Commons will be very dependent on the loyalty of its back-benchers. Since this may limit the range of legislative proposals which the government chooses to bring forward, it is not wholly fanciful to say that, in this situation at least, the legislature is exercising some control over the executive. However, this situation is relatively unusual.

Turning to the second point, no strict version of the doctrine of the separation of powers could tolerate the degree of overlap between the *legislative* and *judicial* functions which inevitably flows from having a committee of the House of Lords (which is, after all, one of the Houses of Parliament) as the highest court of appeal. (Admittedly, this defect will soon be remedied by the creation of a Supreme Court, which will probably happen in 2009.)

Thirdly, the courts (that is to say, the *judiciary*) make law (that is to say, *legislate*) through the doctrine of binding precedent. However, as we shall be considering this doctrine more closely in Chapter 7, we will say no more about it at this stage.

Clearly, therefore, there are various ways in which the functioning of the separation of powers as an underlying doctrine of the British Constitution is not as straightforward as it may appear to be at first sight. However, all those bodies and officials who perform public decision-making functions are aware of the terms of the doctrine, and will, despite its qualified nature in the British context, treat it as constraining their freedom of action in at least some contexts.

● **Devolution to Scotland, Wales and Northern Ireland**

The Scotland Act 1998 created the *Scottish Parliament*, the Government of Wales Act 1998 created the *National Assembly for Wales* (which is commonly known simply as *the Welsh Assembly*), and the Northern Ireland Act 1998 created the *Northern Ireland Assembly*. All three statutes devolve certain legislative powers to the bodies which they create, with the powers of the Welsh Assembly having been extended by the Government of Wales Act 2006. The mass of detail in each of these devolutionary schemes need not be pursued here.

● The European Community dimension

Introduction

We have dealt with the sources of European Community law, and its reception into English law, in the previous chapter (see pp. 27–33). However, the fact that we are now discussing the constitutional context of the English legal system makes it appropriate to deal here with the basic question of the supremacy of Community law over the laws of the member states; and, more particularly, its supremacy over English law.

The supremacy of Community law over the laws of the member states

From a very early stage in the development of the European Economic Community (as it then was), the Court of Justice established the supremacy of Community law over the laws of the member states. As the Court put it, in the leading case of *van Gend en Loos* [1963] CMLR 105, 129:

> The Community constitutes a new legal order ... for whose benefit the states have limited their sovereign rights.

Very shortly afterwards, in *Costa v ENEL* [1964] CMLR 425, the Court said (at pp. 455–456):

> The reception within the laws of each member State, of provisions having a Community source, and more particularly of the terms and of the spirit of the Treaty, has as a corollary the impossibility, for the member State, to give preference to a unilateral and *subsequent* measure against a legal order accepted by them on the basis of reciprocity
> ...
>   The transfer, by member States, from their national orders in favour of the Community order of the rights and obligations arising from the Treaty, carries with it a clear limitation of their sovereign right upon which a *subsequent* unilateral law, incompatible with the aims of the Community, cannot prevail. (Emphasis added.)

Part of the justification for the supremacy of Community law over national law lies in the Court's insistence that Community law must apply uniformly in all member states.

> In accordance with the principle of the precedence of Community law, the relationship between provisions of the Treaty and direct applicable measures of the institutions on the one hand and the

national law of the member states on the other is such that those provisions and measures not only by their entry into force render automatically *inapplicable* any conflicting provision of current national law but – in so far as they are an integral part of, and take precedence in, the legal order applicable in the territory of each of the member states – also preclude the valid adoption of new national legislative measures to the extent to which they would be incompatible with Community provisions.

Indeed any recognition that national legislative measures which encroach upon the field within which the Community exercises its legislative power or which are otherwise incompatible with the provisions of Community law had any legal effect would amount to a corresponding denial of the effectiveness of obligations undertaken unconditionally and irrevocably by member states pursuant to the Treaty and would thus imperil the very foundations of the Community. (Emphasis added. *Italian Finance Administration v Simmenthal* [1978] 3 CMLR 263, 283.)

Furthermore, it is clear from *Internationale Handelsgessellschaft mbH* [1972] CMLR 255, that Community law prevails even over a fundamental doctrine of a member state's constitution. The facts were that a German company argued that a Community Regulation was invalid because it infringed the principle of proportionality, which was a fundamental principle of the German Constitution, and the Constitution contained nothing which would give supremacy to Community law. Although the Court of Justice decided, on the facts, that there had been no breach of the principle of proportionality, the Court took the opportunity (at p. 283) to re-emphasise the supremacy of Community law:

The law born from the Treaty [cannot] have the courts opposing to it rules of national law *of any nature whatsoever* ... the validity of a Community instrument or its effect within a member state cannot be affected by allegations that it strikes at either the fundamental rights as formulated in that state's constitution or the principles of a national constitutional structure. (Emphasis added.)

The Community doctrine of the supremacy of Community law clearly raises a difficulty in relation to the United Kingdom. One side of the argument may be outlined thus:

- The United Kingdom courts should not uphold United Kingdom legislation which is inconsistent with Community Law, because (at least in the case of legislation passed after the European Communities Act 1972), the doctrine of *implied repeal* will operate to repeal, at least as far as is necessary for the instant case, that part of the 1972 Act which provided for the law of the Community to prevail over the law of the United Kingdom. (The doctrine of *implied repeal* is explained at p. 39.)

The other side of the argument may be outlined thus:

- when passing the 1972 Act, Parliament made Community law part of English law; and
- it is a basic doctrine of Community law that it shall prevail over any inconsistent laws of member states; and
- *Internationale Handelsgessellschaft mbH* (see above) shows that this basic doctrine prevails over even the most basic constitutional doctrines of member states.

The House of Lords resolved the matter in *Factortame Ltd v Secretary of State for Transport (No 2)* [1991] AC 603. In the context of a decision that came down in favour of the second argument, Lord Bridge said (at pp. 658–659):

If the supremacy within the European Community of Community law over the national law of member States was not always inherent in the EEC Treaty, it was certainly well established in the jurisprudence of the Court of Justice long before the United Kingdom joined the Community. Thus, whatever limitation of its sovereignty Parliament accepted when it enacted the European Communities Act 1972 was entirely voluntary. Under the terms of the 1972 Act it has always been clear that it was the duty of a United Kingdom court, when delivering final judgment, to override any rule of national law found to be in conflict with any directly enforceable rule of Community law. Similarly, when decisions of the Court of Justice have exposed areas of United Kingdom law which failed to implement Council Directives, Parliament has always loyally accepted the obligation to make appropriate and prompt amendments.

Finally, the case of *Thoburn v Sunderland City Council* [2002] EWHC 195 Admin [2003] QB 151 must be noted. In the context of an appeal by way of case stated to the High Court, Laws LJ expressly rejected the possibility of relying on the doctrine of implied repeal where a later statute conflicts with the European Communities Act 1972. The basis of his decision was that there is a category of 'constitutional statutes' (including Magna Carta, the Bill of Rights 1689, the Human Rights Act 1998, and – crucially in the present case – the European Communities Act 1972) which *'by force of the common law* cannot be impliedly repealed'. (Emphasis added.) In passing, it may be worth noting that, while this decision may well be correct in relation to the narrow point of the inapplicability of the doctrine of implied repeal in relation to the European Communities Act 1972, the House of Lords has doubted whether there is a category of statutes which can properly be described as 'constitutional'. (*Watkins v Secretary of State for the Home Department* [2006] UKHL 17, [2006] 2 AC 395.)

The European Convention on Human Rights

The status of the European Convention on Human Rights within the British constitution is discussed in Chapter 5. All that need be said here is that no issues concerning the legislative supremacy of Parliament arise from the way in which the Human Rights Act 1998 makes the Convention relevant to the English legal system.

Conclusion

The word *constitution* is used in two senses. In one sense it means the body of rules and informal practices which provide for, and control, the governance of the state. In another sense, it means a single document which sets out at least the most important of those rules. Every state must have a constitution in the first sense. In practice, almost all states also have a constitution in the second sense. However, there is no single document containing the British constitution, which is, therefore, described variously as being *unwritten*, *uncodified* and *informal*.

Despite the informal way in which the British Constitution is presented, it clearly functions within a framework provided by the three doctrines of the legislative supremacy of Parliament, the rule of law and the separation of powers.

The European Communities Act 1972 has added the doctrine of the supremacy of Community law to the doctrinal basis of the British constitution. By way of contrast, the Human Rights Act 1998 does not affect the legislative supremacy of parliament.

The law of the European Convention on Human Rights, and the operation of the Human Rights Act 1998, are discussed in Chapter 5.

4 The Jurisdictions of the Principal Courts

Most of the principal English courts exercise both criminal and civil jurisdictions and do so both at first instance and on appeal. The High Court also exercises a supervisory jurisdiction by way of judicial review. Questions of Community law raised in domestic courts may be referred to the European Court of Justice under the preliminary reference procedure. The European Court of Human Rights may order a state to pay compensation where there has been a breach of the Convention, but it cannot enforce that order.

Introduction

In order to understand some of the material in this book, you will need also to understand, at least in outline, the jurisdictions of the principal English courts as well as the courts of the European Community and the European Court of Human Rights. (In this context, *jurisdiction* simply means *the power to hear a case*. In other contexts – see, for example, p. 83 – it means the geographical area which is subject to the court's power.) To begin with, you will simply have to *learn* some of the detail, which will no doubt seem tedious. However, as you become immersed in the study of law, you will find that you rapidly acquire the ability to refer to the right court in the right way.

The principal statutes governing the jurisdictions of the English courts are the Magistrates' Courts Act 1980, the Supreme Court Act 1981, the County Courts Act 1984, the Courts and Legal Services Act 1990 and the Civil Procedure Act 1997. (Other statutes deal with the sentencing powers of criminal courts and the administration of various courts, but these topics are beyond the scope of this book.)

● The three types of jurisdiction

Introduction
The courts exercise three types of jurisdiction, namely *at first instance*, *on appeal*, and *supervisory*, where the proceedings are by way of *judicial review*.

Jurisdiction at first instance
Cases which are being heard for the first time are said to be *at first instance*. In these cases the court will have to identify those facts which are agreed and make findings of those facts which are not agreed, before deciding what the relevant law is and applying that law to the facts in order to reach a decision.

Jurisdiction on appeal
A challenge to a decision reached at first instance will be by way of *appeal*. The court which hears the appeal is said to have *appellate jurisdiction*. An appellate court which upholds an appeal will normally be able to substitute its own decision for the one that was reached at first instance. The exception to this proposition is that in appeals *by way of case stated* (see below), the appellate court will usually be limited to sending the case back to the lower court for further consideration in the light of the appellate court's judgment. However, in some circumstances, even where an appeal is by way of case stated, the appellate court can direct the lower court to reach a specific decision.

Supervisory jurisdiction
The High Court has, for many centuries, *supervised* the way in which some lower courts and administrative decision-makers exercise their decision-making powers. This jurisdiction is called *judicial review*. Although a claim for judicial review may, at first glance, seem to be much the same as an appeal, closer examination reveals a crucial difference. In judicial review, the court will be considering the *legality of the decision-making process* that produced the earlier decision, rather than the *correctness of the decision* itself. One consequence of this is that, even if the court upholds a claim for judicial review, its most extensive power will usually be limited to quashing the decision and requiring the decision-maker to reconsider the decision on a lawful basis. The exception to this proposition is that where a lawful decision-making process could result in only one possible decision, the court that upholds the claim for judicial review may simply make that decision itself, without involving the original decision-maker.

Although the essence of the distinction between *appeal* and *judicial review* is quite clear, it will be apparent from what has been said that there is some overlap between *appeal by way of case stated* and *judicial review*. The explanation for this is complex and involves delving into legal history. We will simply note it and pass on.

The hierarchy of the courts

Introduction

The hierarchy of the courts, including for these purposes administrative tribunals and statutory inquiries, is best represented as a diagram.

European Court of Justice	(European Court of Human Rights)
House of Lords	(Judicial Committee of the Privy Council)
Court of Appeal	
High Court	
Crown Court	County Courts
Magistrates' Courts	
(Administrative Tribunals and Public Inquiries)	

Magistrates' courts

The jurisdiction of the magistrates' courts includes both civil and criminal elements. It is almost entirely exercisable only at first instance, but some very limited elements of civil jurisdiction involve hearing appeals.

The magistrates' civil jurisdiction at first instance does not include either contract or tort, but does include a very mixed bag of aspects of administrative law. These relate especially (but not exclusively) to the topics of highways and public health, and are largely left over from the time when the magistrates exercised many of the functions that are now exercised by elected local authorities.

Similarly, the appellate jurisdiction of the magistrates is almost entirely limited to administrative law, with a particular focus on appeals against certain decisions of local authorities in matters such as public health, highways and licensing.

When sitting as family proceedings courts, the magistrates' civil jurisdiction is at first instance only, and includes a variety of aspects of child welfare and family law, but does not include divorce.

The magistrates' criminal jurisdiction includes both trials (including guilty pleas) and sending people to the Crown Court, either for trial or for sentence. When sitting as youth courts, the magistrates' criminal jurisdiction involves defendants who are under the age of 18.

Most magistrates are not legally qualified (or, to use the more formal vocabulary, and putting it the other way round, they are *lay*) and are not paid for their services. However, some are both legally qualified and employed on a full-time, salaried basis. The latter were known for many years as *stipendiary magistrates*, but are now known as *District Judges (Magistrates' Courts)*. In practice, lay magistrates tend to rely heavily on their legal advisers for advice on the law, although technically they decide both the law and the facts.

Magistrates have no particular style and title as such, although they may put *JP* after their names. (*JP* stands for *Justice of the Peace*, which is an alternative, somewhat more formal and ancient, synonym for *magistrate*.) When addressing a bench of magistrates, the formal mode of address is *Your Worships*, but in practice many advocates address the entire bench through the chair, in which case the form of address is *Sir* or *Madam*, as the case may be.

The Crown Court

The Crown Court's jurisdiction includes both civil and criminal elements, and is exercisable both at first instance and on appeal.

The Crown Court's civil jurisdiction at first instance does not include either contract or tort. It is principally concerned with residual aspects of administrative law, particularly in relation to highways, and dates very largely from the time when the magistrates, sitting either in Petty Sessions (which are now known as magistrates' courts) or at Quarter Sessions, performed many of the functions which are now performed by local authorities. (Quarter Sessions were abolished and replaced with the Crown Court by the Courts Act 1971.)

The Crown Court's criminal jurisdiction at first instance covers those cases which have been transferred from the magistrates' courts and is exercised by trying those defendants who plead not guilty and sentencing those who plead guilty. It also includes dealing with people whom the magistrates have committed for sentence. A Crown Court trial is conducted by a judge and a jury, while sentencing on a guilty plea is done by a judge sitting with magistrates.

The Crown Court's appellate jurisdiction in both civil and criminal cases consists almost entirely of hearing appeals against decisions of the magistrates; and therefore, once again, the civil side does not include contracts and tort. In criminal cases, the appeals may be against either conviction or sentence. Appeals against conviction are by way of re-hearing, which means that there is a full trial, with the witnesses giving their evidence again, as they did in the magistrates' court. Appeals are heard by a judge and jury. The prosecution cannot appeal to the Crown Court against an acquittal by the magistrates.

Judges of the Crown Court are known as *circuit judges*. Their formal style is *His* (or *Her*) *Honour Judge Blank*, which may be abbreviated in writing to *HHJ Blank*, or *HH Mary Blank*. More informally, but very commonly, a circuit judge may be described as *Judge Blank*. Circuit judges are addressed as *Your Honour*.

County Courts

The County Courts' jurisdiction is entirely civil, and is exercisable almost entirely at first instance. However, it does have a very limited appellate jurisdiction, arising especially (but not exclusively) in relation to a range of decisions made by local authorities concerning certain aspects of housing law.

In contrast to the civil jurisdiction of both the magistrates' courts and the Crown Court, the County Courts' jurisdiction includes contract, tort and divorce.

Circuit judges are also County Court judges, and therefore the details given above, in relation to style and mode of address, need not be repeated here.

The High Court

Although the High Court is nominally one court, it functions as three separate units, namely the Queen's Bench Division, the Chancery Division and the Family Division.

Its jurisdiction includes both civil and criminal elements, with some elements being exercisable at first instance and some being exercisable on appeal. The Queen's Bench Division's jurisdiction at first instance is entirely civil, and includes cases in contract and tort. The Queen's Bench Division's

appellate jurisdiction (which is by far the largest part of the appellate jurisdiction of the High Court as a whole) takes the form of appeals by way of case
stated from magistrates' courts, and from the Crown Court when that court
is exercising its appellate jurisdiction. Appeals by way of case stated can
raise points of law only. In procedural terms, the court whose decision is
being appealed sends the Queen's Bench Division a written statement of the
facts of the case, as they were either agreed by the parties or found by the
court, together with the court's understanding of the relevant law, and the
way in which that law applied to those facts. The Queen's Bench Division
then says whether the lower court got the law, and its application to the
facts, right or wrong. It will then usually send the case back to the court from
which it came, telling it either what decision it should make, or leaving it to
come to its own decision in the light of the law as it was found to be on the
appeal. Sometimes, particularly in minor cases where a substantial period of
time has elapsed in waiting for the appeal to be heard, the High Court will
content itself by giving judgment on the relevant point of law, without
sending the case back at all.

The Queen's Bench Division also has a *supervisory* jurisdiction, which, as
we saw at p. 52, is simply another way of saying it has jurisdiction by way of
judicial review. This jurisdiction, which in practice almost always involves
cases decided by a magistrates' court (but can also arise from decisions of a
Crown Court exercising its appellate jurisdiction) covers both civil and
criminal cases,

The Chancery Division has only civil jurisdiction, and deals with cases
involving property, wills and associated matters. It is almost entirely at first
instance, although it does include a few types of appeal from the County
Courts.

The essence of the Family Division's jurisdiction is self-evident from its
title, and includes divorce.

High Court judges are technically known as *puisne judges*. (*Puisne*, pronounced *puny*, does not indicate lack of power but is simply an old word for
junior.) Their formal style is always written as *Blank J* but is always spoken as
Mr (or *Mrs*) *Justice Blank*. Describing a High Court judge as *Judge Blank*, or
even as *Justice Blank* (without the *Mr* or *Mrs*) is the sort of error which marks
you out either as someone who is uneducated in the law or as someone who
cannot be bothered with detailed accuracy. You would be foolish to project
either of these images of yourself into the mind of whoever is marking your
work. (We will explain how to deal with the titles of judges in Chapter 12, in
the context of mooting.)

The Court of Appeal

Although the Court of Appeal is nominally one court, it is divided into a Criminal Division and a Civil Division. The principal jurisdiction of both Divisions is – perhaps obviously – appellate.

The Criminal Division hears appeals from the Crown Court against either conviction or sentence or both. It also has a limited quasi-appellate jurisdiction, hearing certain types of cases which are referred to it by the Attorney-General or the Criminal Cases Review Commission. These cases arise from acquittals by juries, sentences passed by the Crown Court which the prosecution consider to be too lenient, and convictions which are alleged to have been miscarriages of justice.

The Civil Division hears appeals from both the County Courts and the High Court.

The Lord Chief Justice, who is also the Head of the Judiciary, presides over the Criminal Division of the Court of Appeal, while the Master of the Rolls presides over the Civil Division. The other judges of the Court of Appeal are formally known as *Lord Justices of Appeal*. The written styles of the Lord Chief Justice and the Master of the Rolls are, respectively, Lord (or Baroness) Green, CJ and Lord (or Baroness) Grey, MR; or, where the Master of the Rolls has not yet been granted a peerage, Sir John (or Lady Mary) Grey, MR, but the spoken usage is to give the title in full: for example Lord Green, Lord Chief Justice. The other judges of the Court of Appeal have the written style of Blank LJ, which is spoken as *Lord* (or *Lady*) *Justice Blank*.

The House of Lords (and the Supreme Court)

The House of Lords has a residual and very limited jurisdiction at first instance – for example, in relation to disputed peerage claims. However, when the phrase *the House of Lords* is used in a judicial context, it almost always means the *Appellate Committee of the House of Lords*. As its title indicates, the Committee's jurisdiction is appellate. More particularly, it hears appeals in criminal cases from the High Court, and in both civil and criminal cases from the Court of Appeal. It may also occasionally hear appeals in civil cases directly from the High Court, where permission has been given to leap-frog over the Court of Appeal.

Members of the Appellate Committee are, in practice, specifically appointed to that position, although, strictly speaking, peers who hold or have held high judicial office are also eligible to sit. Those who are specifically appointed are formally known as *Lords of Appeal in Ordinary*. The first, and so far only, female Law 'Lord' is Baroness Hale of Richmond. Whether the phrase *Law Lady* becomes generally accepted appears to be largely academic, since the Appellate Committee will be replaced by the Supreme Court – probably from some date in 2009 and almost certainly during the life-time of this edition of this book. Lords of Appeal in Ordinary are known by their titles (for example, Lord Grey and Baroness Green) with no distinction between the written and spoken forms. Judges of the Supreme Court will, in common with their American counterparts, be known as *Justices of the Supreme Court*.

Finally, by way of a footnote, it is worth noting the distinction between the *Appellate Committee* (which we have just been discussing) and the *Appeals Committee*, which also consists of Lords of Appeal in Ordinary, but the func-tion of which is to deal with petitions for permission to appeal to the House of Lords, rather than with the appeals themselves.

The Judicial Committee of the Privy Council

The Judicial Committee of the Privy Council is principally concerned with both civil and criminal appeals from certain Commonwealth countries, although the number of countries preserving this avenue of appeal has diminished over the years.

Additionally, it has jurisdiction over a wide range of appeals relating to disciplinary proceedings brought by various professions, such as doctors, dentists and opticians, as well as dealing with a variety of admiralty and ecclesiastical matters, and constitutional matters arising out of devolution to Northern Ireland, Scotland and Wales.

Membership of the Judicial Committee of the Privy Council is largely the same as membership of the Appellate Committee of the House of Lords, but with the addition of senior judges from those overseas countries which still retain the right of appeal to the Privy Council.

Oral usage is the same as in the High Court, the Court of Appeal and the House of Lords, so the detail given above need not be repeated here; and, once again, the examples given in the context of High Court judges may be easily adapted.

Rights of appeal and permission to appeal in the English courts

Whether there is any right of appeal in a given situation will always depend on the relevant statutory provisions. These provisions contain a mass of practical detail which need not concern you in your early days as a law student.

However, in very general terms, there will often be one appeal on either (or both) the facts and the law, with the possibility of a further appeal on the law only.

Many rights of appeal may be exercised only where permission to appeal is granted. Depending on the context, permission may be granted either by the court whose decision is being challenged or by the court that will hear the appeal if permission is granted.

Administrative tribunals and statutory inquiries

Finally, within the context of the domestic English legal system and before looking at three European Courts, we must notice *tribunals* (or administrative tribunals as they are traditionally known) and *statutory inquiries*. While these are, as their titles indicate, not courts, they should nevertheless be included here because they both typically connect with the hierarchy of the courts through appellate processes, or, sometimes, judicial review.

The European Court of Justice and the Court of First Instance

The Court of Justice of the European Coal and Steel Community was established in 1954, and renamed as the Court of Justice of the European Communities in 1958. Since 1989 there has also been a court known as the Court of First Instance, although this title is somewhat misleading if it is understood to suggest that all cases start there, with a subsequent right of appeal. While it is true that an appeal from the Court of First Instance may lie to the Court of Justice, it is also true that many cases begin in the latter court. The identity of the court in which cases will begin is subject to detailed rules, but the essence of the scheme lies in distinguishing between cases according to their significance and complexity.

The mass of detail surrounding the jurisdiction of these courts need not be pursued here. Suffice it to say the bulk of the jurisdiction involves two categories of cases. First, either one of the institutions or a member state may allege that one of the other institutions or member states is in breach of Community law. Secondly, where a point of Community Law arises in a case before a court of a member state, that court may (and sometimes must) seek the opinion of one of the Community's courts, in order to enable it to give its own judgment. This is known as the *preliminary reference procedure*. In the Court of Justice, the procedure is governed by art. 234 of the EC Treaty (which was art. 177 until it was renumbered by the Treaty of Amsterdam), while in the Court of First Instance the procedure is governed by art. 225 of the Treaty (as amended by the Treaty of Nice).

Although any of the parties to the proceedings before the court of the member state may ask the court to refer a question of Community law to one of the Community's courts, no party ever has any right to insist that a reference shall be made. Furthermore, once a case has been considered by one of the Community's courts, it will return to the court that made the reference, which will then give its judgment in the light of the reply to the reference. It is therefore wrong to describe the preliminary reference procedure as an *appeal*.

Individuals, and organisations such as companies and local authorities, have only very limited rights of access to the Court of Justice, although they do have somewhat wider access to the Court of First Instance.

Judges of both Courts have the style of *judge* and are described and addressed accordingly.

The European Court of Human Rights

Although the protection of fundamental rights is discussed in Chapter 5, it is convenient to note here that the European Court of Human Rights, which sits at Strasbourg, hears complaints alleging infringements of the European Convention on Human Rights. A party who is dissatisfied with a decision of an English court may complain to the European Court of Human Rights, but this will involve entirely new proceedings and is not an appeal against the English decision.

The principal remedy available in the European Court of Human Rights is merely a declaratory judgment that a breach of the Convention has occurred. Additionally, however, the court may award compensation, but there is no mechanism to enable such an award to be enforced if the state against which the order is made fails to comply.

Judges of the European Court of Human Rights have the style *judge*, and are described and addressed accordingly.

Conclusion

The system of courts within the English legal system is hierarchical, with each court exercising one or more of three jurisdictions, namely first instance, appellate and supervisory.

In addition to the courts of the domestic English legal system, the European Court of Justice (together with the Court of First Instance) and the European Court of Human Rights must also be taken into account.

5 The Protection of Human Rights and Fundamental Freedoms

The importance of protecting human rights and fundamental freedoms is now taken for granted in the liberal democracies of the western world. The Human Rights Act 1998 (HRA) gives special status in English law to most of the rights and freedoms which the European Convention of Human Rights protects, and calls these 'Convention rights'. The HRA has therefore greatly reduced the need to rely on the common law for such protection. The HRA does not affect the legislative supremacy of Parliament, but it does allow the higher courts to make declarations of incompatibility in respect of statutes which breach 'Convention rights' and to quash almost all delegated legislation.

Introduction

This chapter considers the way in which English law protects, or fails to protect, *human rights and fundamental freedoms* (a phrase which is usually abbreviated simply to *human rights*). It will consider both the common law and statute law, with the emphasis in the latter context being on the Human Rights Act 1998.

Protection of human rights by the common law

Although there is no doubt that the common law is capable of protecting human rights, there is equally no doubt that it cannot be relied upon to do so, as the following three cases will show.

The first case is *R v Lord Chancellor ex parte Witham* [1998] QB 575, where the Lord Chancellor (acting with the concurrence of the Lord Chief Justice, the Master of the Rolls, the Vice-Chancellor and the President of the Family Division) had exercised a statutory power to increase court fees quite substantially, and to remove an exemption from fees for people on income support. Even though the new rules contained a power for the Lord Chancellor to reduce or remit the fees in individual cases on the ground of undue financial hardship, the High Court granted a declaration that he had exceeded his statutory powers. The basis of this decision was simply that the effect of the increases would be to exclude many people from access to the courts.

The second case is *Malone v Metropolitan Police Commissioner (No 2)* [1979] Ch 344, where a man who had been convicted of handling stolen goods complained that the police had tapped his telephone during their investigation. Sir Robert Megarry V-C held that the telephone tap had been lawful because the law did not restrict this kind of activity by the police. Although he could have done so, he was unwilling to find that Malone had a right not to have his telephone tapped, simply so that he could then hold that that right had been infringed. The creation of such rights, according to the judge, is a matter for Parliament, not the courts.

The third case, *R v Secretary of State for Social Security ex parte B and Another* [1997] 1 WLR 275, shows that the judges may disagree among themselves on matters of human rights even within a single case. The Secretary of State had made certain regulations under the Social Security (Contributions and Benefits) Act 1992. The content of the regulations was such that some asylum seekers, who would previously have been eligible for benefits while their applications for asylum were being assessed, would, in the words of Simon Brown LJ (at 292), be reduced to 'a life so destitute that to my mind no civilised nation can tolerate it'. However, Neill LJ dissented, on the basis that the regulations had been aimed primarily at, and would principally affect, people who were not genuine asylum-seekers. Furthermore, although the regulations would 'also have a very serious effect on a considerable number of genuine asylum-seekers and those who might be hoping to obtain exceptional leave to remain', the Secretary of State had not crossed 'the threshold of illegality', bearing in mind not only the 'objects to be achieved by the legislation and its results' but also the need 'to strike a balance' in 'the allocation of the resources made available to him'. (See p. 283.)

Statute law other than the Human Rights Act 1998

Of course, the common law is not the only – or even the main – vehicle for developing the law. However, statutory intervention in relation to specific areas of human rights law (such as discrimination on the grounds of race and sex) has been haphazard, and appears to have resulted more from perceived political need than from any fundamental concern with the principle of equality.

The European Convention on Human Rights

Introduction
The European Convention for the Protection of Human Rights and Fundamental Freedoms (which is commonly referred to simply as the *European Convention on Human Rights*, which in turn is commonly abbreviated to *ECHR*) was agreed in 1950 by the states of Western Europe.

The ECHR is a product of the *Council of Europe* (rather than the *European Community*) and is enforced by the *European Court of Human Rights*, which sits at *Strasbourg* (rather than the *European Court of Justice*, which sits at *Luxembourg*). Despite the obvious importance of the provisions of the ECHR, successive British governments, of both major political persuasions, consistently refused to introduce legislation giving its provisions any status in English law, on the basis that English law was perfectly capable of protecting human rights anyway. However, in 1997 the newly elected Labour government put an end to this consensus by introducing the Bill that became the Human Rights Act 1998 (HRA).

Some key concepts under the European Convention on Human Rights
It is important to notice that, with the exception of the prohibition of torture or inhuman or degrading treatment or punishment by art. 3, all the rights and freedoms guaranteed by the Convention are subject to some kind of limitation or qualification. Of particular interest in this respect are arts 8 to 11, which may all be restricted by law to such extent as is 'necessary in a democratic society' for the reasons set out in each of the articles. (For the full text of the articles, see Appendix 1, at pp. 212–217.) It is useful to notice, therefore, that in a case concerning homosexual relationships, the Court of Human Rights identified 'tolerance and broad-mindedness' as two of the 'hallmarks' of a democratic society. (*Dudgeon v United Kingdom* (1982) 4 EHRR 149, [53].)

Turning to the phrase 'necessary in a democratic society', in *Handyside v United Kingdom* (1976) 1 EHRR 737, [48], while upholding the law relating to the forfeiture of obscene publications, the Court said that 'while the adjective "necessary" ... is not synonymous with "indispensable", neither has it the flexibility of such expressions as "admissible", "ordinary", "useful", "reasonable" or "desirable"'. More positively, in *Olsson v Sweden* (1989) 11 EHRR 259, [67], while finding that the then current state of Swedish law provided no basis for the practice of social workers of restricting parental access to children who were in public care, the Court said:

> According to the court's established case-law, the notion of *necessity* implies that an interference corresponds with a *pressing social need* and, in particular, that it is *proportionate* to the legitimate aim pursued. (Emphasis added.)

These cases provide a useful introduction to two of the Strasbourg court's key concepts, namely the *margin of appreciation* and the doctrine of *proportionality*. Taking these in turn, the *margin of appreciation* is the area for the exercise of discretion that the Strasbourg court accepts must remain with national legal systems. In *Handyside* (above) the Court said (at [48]–[49]):

> By reason of their direct and continuous contact with the vital forces of their countries, state authorities are in principle in a better position than the international judge to give an opinion on the ... "necessity" of a "restriction" or "penalty" .... It is for the national authorities to make the initial assessment of the reality of the pressing social need ...
>
> Consequently art. 10(2) leaves to the contracting states a margin of appreciation. This margin is given both to the domestic legislator ("prescribed by law") and to the bodies, judicial amongst others, that are called upon to interpret and apply the laws in force.
>
> Nevertheless, [the Convention] does not give the contracting states an unlimited power of appreciation. The court, which ... is responsible for ensuring those states' engagements, is empowered to give the final ruling on whether a "restriction" or "penalty" is reconcilable with [a Convention right or freedom] .... The domestic margin of appreciation thus goes hand in hand with a European supervision. Such supervision concerns both the aim of the measure challenged and its "necessity"; it covers not only the basic legislation but also the decision applying it, even one given by an independent court.

Secondly, the doctrine of *proportionality* requires that the *means* which are used must be proportionate to the *ends* which are to be achieved, because, in the words of the Court in *Soering v United Kingdom* (1989) 11 EHRR 439, [89]:

> Inherent in the whole of the Convention is a search for a fair balance between the demands of the general interest of the community and

the requirements of the protection of the individual's fundamental rights.

● The Human Rights Act 1998

The scheme of the Act

The scheme of the Human Rights Act depends on the core concept of *Convention rights*. However it is important to understand that, under s. 1(1) of the HRA, the phrase *Convention rights* does not include all the rights guaranteed by the Convention, but only:

> the rights and fundamental freedoms set out in –
> (a) articles 2 to 12 and 14 of the Convention, and
> (b) articles 1 to 3 of the First Protocol, and
> (c) articles 1 and 2 of the Sixth Protocol,
> as read with articles 16 to 18 of the Convention.

More particularly, the concept of Convention rights does not extend to arts 1 and 13, which deal, respectively, with securing Convention rights to everyone within the courts of the contracting state and providing effective remedies in national courts.

Articles 16 to 18 of the Convention respectively:

- permit restrictions on the political activities of aliens;
- prohibit any interpretation of the Convention that would permit the destruction or limitation of the rights and freedoms guaranteed by the Convention; and
- require that the restrictions permitted by the Convention shall be applied only for the purposes for which they were created.

A summary of Convention rights

The full text of the articles and protocols which guarantee Convention rights within the terms of the HRA is set out in Appendix 1 (see pp. 212–217), but may be summarised as follows:

art. 2	the right to life;
art. 3	prohibition of torture or inhuman or degrading treatment or punishment;
art. 4	prohibition of slavery and forced labour;
art. 5	the right to liberty and security of the person;

art. 6   the right to a fair trial;

art. 7   freedom from the imposition of retrospective criminal liability and punishment;

art. 8   the right to respect for private and family life;

art. 9   freedom of religion;

art. 10   freedom of expression;

art. 11   freedom of assembly and association;

art. 12   the right to marry and found a family;

art. 14   prohibition of discrimination in enjoyment of rights under the Convention.

First Protocol

art. 1   the right to property;

art. 2   the right to education;

art. 3   the right to free elections.

Sixth Protocol

arts 1 & 2   prohibition of the death penalty.

Section 1(2) makes the operation of these articles subject to *derogations* and *reservations*. Schedule 3 contains *derogations* relating to terrorist activity and a *reservation* relating to preserving efficient instruction and training, and avoiding unreasonable public expenditure when seeking to satisfy the right of parents to ensure that their children are educated 'in conformity with their own religious and philosophical convictions'.

The status of Convention rights in English law

Introduction

The starting point, and one which cannot be emphasised too strongly, especially because it is repeatedly misrepresented in the media, is that, in the words of Lord Clyde in *R v Lambert* [2001] UKHL 37, [2002] 2 AC 545, [135], 'the Act did not incorporate the rights set out in the Convention into the domestic laws of the United Kingdom'. What the Act does do, however, is to identify most of those rights, which it then labels 'Convention rights' and upon which it then confers a special status which has a variety of consequences. It is that status and those consequences which we will now examine.

Section 2 of the Act provides that any court or tribunal which has to determine any question in relation to a Convention right 'must take into account' the case-law of the European Court of Human Rights. Strictly speaking, as Laws LJ and Poole J pointed out in *Gough and Another v Chief Constable of Derbyshire* [2001] EWHC Admin 554, [2002] QB 459, [32], s. 2 means what it says, and therefore the duty of the court is 'to take account of Strasbourg jurisprudence, not necessarily to apply it'. However, cases in which the courts refuse to apply Strasbourg jurisprudence are likely to be few and far between, bearing in mind the view of Lord Slynn in *R (Alconbury Developments Ltd) v Secretary of State for the Environment, Transport and the Regions* [2001] UKHL 23, [2003] AC 295, [26]:

> In the absence of some special circumstances it seems to me that the court should follow any clear and constant jurisprudence of the European Court of Human Rights. If it does not do so, there is at least a possibility that the case will go to that court, which is likely in the ordinary case to follow its own constant jurisprudence.

Interpretation and validity of English legislation
Section 3(1) of the Act provides that

> so far as it is possible to do so, primary and subordinate legislation must be read and given effect in a way which is compatible with the Convention rights.

As a result of s. 3(2) of the Act, s. 3(1) applies to all legislation, whatever its date of enactment, including legislation which was passed before the 1998 Act. However, also as a result of s. 3(2), the court's inability to find a compatible interpretation under s. 3(1) does not affect the *validity* of any *primary* legislation, nor of *delegated* legislation where the terms of the Act under which it is made are such that the incompatibility is inevitable. (In practice, *primary* legislation almost always means Acts of Parliament, although occasionally it may also mean certain instruments made by the exercise of the royal prerogative.) As we saw at p. 25, *subordinate legislation* is simply another form of words for *delegated legislation*. On the assumption that both primary legislation made in exercise of the royal prerogative and Acts protecting delegated legislation made under them will both be very rarely encountered in practice, the effect of these provisions is therefore to introduce a new principle of interpretation of general (but not quite universal) application. This principle of interpretation preserves the legislative supremacy of Parliament, while making practically all delegated legislation quashable on the ground of incompatibility with Convention rights.

The duty imposed on public authorities
Section 6 of the Act makes it unlawful for a public authority to act in a way that is incompatible with Convention rights. For these purposes, the expression *public authority* is defined as *excluding* both Houses of Parliament but as *including* courts and tribunals, as well as 'any person certain of whose functions are functions of a public nature'. The effect of s. 7 of the Act is that a person who wishes to establish that there has been a breach of the duty under s. 6 may do so either proactively by claiming judicial review, or reactively by way of defence to proceedings brought by, or at the instigation of, a public authority.

Declarations of incompatibility
Although the Act contains nothing to diminish the legislative supremacy of Parliament, s. 4 does give a court at (or above) the level of the High Court the power to make declarations of incompatibility where primary legislation conflicts with Convention rights. Such declarations have no effect on the parties to the cases in which they are made, nor on the continuing operation or validity of the provisions in respect of which they are given. However, under s. 10 of the Act, they may result in the provisions being amended or repealed by remedial orders. (These remedial orders will typically take the form of delegated legislation, in order to avoid the pressures on time which beset the government's legislative programme. However, where the declaration of incompatibility relates to an Order in Council made in exercise of the royal prerogative, the remedial order may be in the form of a further Order in Council.) Section 10 also provides that remedial orders may be made following adverse findings by the European Court of Human Rights.

Statements of compatibility
All Bills are scrutinised by a Joint Committee of both Houses of Parliament, to check whether they contain any provisions which would, if enacted, breach any Convention rights. Furthermore, Ministers who are in charge of Bills in either House of Parliament must, before the Second Reading of the Bill, do one of two things. The first, and overwhelmingly more common possibility, is a statement of compatibility, to the effect that the Bill contains nothing that is incompatible with Convention rights. The second possibility is that, even though the Minister is unable to make a statement of compatibility, the House is nevertheless being invited to proceed with the Bill. The latter alternative does not arise very often, but the Bill which became the Communications Act 2003 was one particularly interesting exception. The issue was whether political advertising should be banned from the broadcast media. Although such a ban would appear to breach the right to freedom of

expression under art. 10 of the European Convention on Human Rights, as interpreted by the European Court of Human Rights in *Vgt Verein Gegeng Tierfabriken v Switzerland* (2002) 34 EHRR 4, the government took the view that the ban was nevertheless justified. The government's reasoning was that, in the absence of a ban on all political advertising, the wealthiest political interests would dominate the advertising carried by the broadcast media. When viewed in this way, a degree of interference with freedom of expression could be seen as the lesser of two evils.

Conclusion

English law has always been capable of protecting human rights but has not always shown that it can be relied upon to do so.

The European Convention for the Protection of Human Rights and Fundamental Freedoms, which came into force in 1953 and is usually known simply as the *European Convention on Human Rights* or *ECHR*) has never been incorporated into English law by Act of Parliament. However, the Human Rights Act 1998 creates and defines an English law concept of *Convention rights*, and provides that in cases where Convention rights are relevant, English courts must take into account the law as developed by the Court of Human Rights (which sits at Strasbourg and interprets and applies the ECHR); and, wherever it is possible to so, must also interpret Acts of Parliament in such a way as to make them compatible with Convention rights. The Act also provides that it is unlawful for public bodies to act in ways which are incompatible with Convention rights.

The European Court of Human Rights applies a number of concepts, including *restrictions which are necessary in a democratic society*, the *margin of appreciation* and *proportionality*.

6 Finding and Citing the Sources of Law

The law can change on an almost daily basis. In the English legal system, the courts develop the common law on a case-by-case basis, with Parliament using statutes to make more comprehensive changes. Textbooks, journals, casebooks and statute books are, at best, aids to understanding the primary sources of cases, statutes and European materials, but they are never replacements for reading those primary sources. Developing the research skills to find and use both paper-based and electronic resources will help you keep up to date, while citing your sources in accordance with the standard conventions will help you to communicate this information to others.

Introduction

As a student, you will have to consult many books, journals, law reports, statutes and European materials in order to find the law. You will not always have a great deal of time to search for the law you need. Knowing, therefore, where to find the relevant law, and how to search for it, is a skill well worth learning at an early stage of your law studies.

We will examine the materials you are most likely to use in your studies, including both paper-based and electronic materials. Increasingly, the electronic resources available are Internet-based, although you may also still encounter some sources on CDs and DVDs. All modern students of law must, therefore, have at least basic IT skills which they can develop, if necessary, while acquiring knowledge of the specialist legal sources.

● Libraries and learning resource centres

In many institutions, the current trend is for *libraries* to be part of *Learning Resource Centres*, or *Integrated Learning Resource Centres*, in order to emphasise the fact that sources of knowledge are no longer exclusively paper-based. However, for convenience and brevity, this chapter will refer only to *libraries*, leaving readers to translate the terminology to fit the style of their own institutions.

While different libraries may use different systems to organise their stock of books and other materials, most libraries arrange their stock according to a classification system, with books usually being grouped together according to their subject matter. (Some books may be housed on open access shelves, with others being retained in short-loan, reference-only or reserve sections, to which only the librarians have access.) It is also common for books to be located separately from journals, law reports and other media, such as CDs, DVDs and microfiche.

When searching for material, your first port of call should be the *library catalogue*. Although some specialist collections still use card-based and microfiche catalogues, in most modern libraries the catalogue will be electronic. Electronic catalogues can always be accessed from dedicated computer terminals in the library itself, but may in many cases also be accessed via the Internet.

Using the library catalogue to search for materials is a better way of identifying whether the library has the resources you need than physically browsing the shelves. This is because much of the library's stock will, at any given time, be in use by other readers, either within the library or on loan. Online catalogues usually allow you to reserve books which are currently out on loan, and this will often be the easiest (and sometimes the only) way to get hold of a popular text during term time.

If you are living away from home during term time, it is worth checking what arrangements for vacation access your college or university library has with other colleges and universities. In each case, of course, if you are to make good use of any other libraries to which you have access, you will need to spend some time familiarising yourself with the way they are organised.

● Textbooks, casebooks, statute books and journals

Introduction
Textbooks will usually be your basic learning resource. For most subjects, your lecturers will specify a textbook or a choice of textbooks, and you will

be expected to buy one of these. You may also be expected to buy a casebook and a statute book, and to supplement all your books by reading articles in a variety of journals.

Textbooks and casebooks

The idea of a textbook is very straightforward. Most textbooks cover conventional subjects (such as criminal law or land law), but some are wider in their scope. The most extreme version of width of scope is *Halsbury's Laws of England*, which is an encyclopaedic work running to more than 50 volumes, including a comprehensive updating service.

The distinction between textbooks and casebooks is that textbooks contain the authors' statements, explanations and criticisms of the law, while casebooks contain extracts from the judgments of the courts and, where relevant, statutes and other materials, together with linking commentary and criticism. While casebooks are, on the whole, very useful aids, because the editor has done the work of sifting through the cases in order to decide which ones to include, as well as sifting through each individual case to decide which are the key passages in the judgments, they have two major limitations.

First, if a case is fundamental to your understanding of a particular area of law, you should not simply rely on what someone else thinks are the key points in the case, but you should read the whole case before deciding for yourself what it is really about. For example, the editor of a casebook may simply note that there was a dissenting judgment, without reproducing any of it. In practice, however, it is not uncommon for dissenting judgments to be adopted as *ratio* either by an appellate court in the same case, or by another later court which is free to depart from the earlier decision within the limits set by the doctrine of binding precedent.

Secondly, if you progress to practising the law professionally, you will often have to read entire cases for yourself in order to identify precisely those propositions for which they are – and are not – authority. This kind of analysis requires legal skills of a high order, which can be gained only by extensive experience and repeated practice. It is never too early to start acquiring and developing these skills.

Statute books

In addition to textbooks and casebooks, there are various series of statute books aimed specifically at students. These contain statutes relating to particular topics, such as criminal law, land law or employment law, and contain those statutory excerpts which the editors consider to contain the key legislative provisions relating to the topic. It is always worth checking at the start of your course whether you can take statute books (or photocopies of the statutes themselves) into your examinations. You will often find that you are permitted to do so, provided that the text is clean in the sense of being free from notes of any kind. If this is so in your college or university, it will obviously be in your own financial interest to avoid making notes in your statute books while you are studying. Otherwise, you will have to make the unpalatable choice between not taking your statute books into the examination, or buying new copies for that purpose. (Even if you are not permitted to take annotated statute books or statutes into your examinations, you may be permitted to underline and highlight, and put edge markers on the pages. It is important that you should clarify at a very early stage whether your college or university permits any – or all – of these devices.)

Choosing books

You will be expected to buy your own copies of any books which are prescribed as essential reading. Student numbers are such that no library will be able to afford to stock sufficient copies of these basic books for every student to be able to borrow a copy.

When your lecturers recommend one specific book (whether it is a textbook, a casebook or a statute book), your wisest course of action is to buy that particular book rather than an alternative. This is because the lecturer will almost certainly have tailored the content of the course with the basic readings in mind, and if you buy a different book it is highly unlikely that it will cover the material in exactly the same way and in the same order as the recommended text. This means that you could waste a lot of time working out if (and where) the material in the designated text is covered in the alternative you have bought. Of course, none of this means that you should not *read* other books. You will often find that reading more than one book enhances your understanding of a topic, as well as giving you the opportunity of impressing your examiners by saying that 'while author X argues such and such, it is worth noticing that author Y takes the contrary view and argues so and so'. However, the realities of students' finances are such that *buying* multiple texts is, quite simply, not usually an option

Finally, if your lecturers recommend books which they have written, do not assume that they are simply feathering their own nests at your expense. The economics of academic authorship simply do not work that way. In terms of pounds-per-hour, most academics would be better off spending their evenings and weekends stacking shelves in supermarkets rather than writing textbooks. The real reason why most academics write textbooks is that – rightly or wrongly – they feel frustrated by the quality of the existing books at the appropriate level in their subject areas.

Journals

To supplement your textbooks, you are likely to be referred to articles in legal journals. Most of these will deal with particular topics, such as criminal law or property law (such as the *Criminal Law Review* and the *Conveyancer*) in greater detail than is possible within textbooks. Some journals, however, such as the *New Law Journal* and the *Solicitors Journal* provide wider (if necessarily more superficial) coverage of the contemporary legal scene. Perhaps the most important quality of all journals, whatever their scope may be, is that they can be more up-to-date than textbooks, casebooks and statute books.

One particularly useful section of many journals contains short case notes. Even in the most academically heavyweight journals, these are seldom more than three or four pages long, and often run to no more than a page or two. These case notes can be an excellent introduction to some of the more complex recent developments in the law. Additionally, by referring to back numbers, you can see how cases which are now accepted as leading authorities were viewed at the time when they were decided.

Online resources

Textbooks, casebooks and statute books are seldom, if ever, available online, although some books are supported by companion websites which provide updating services between editions, and some publishers sell online access to individual chapters of some of their books.

By way of contrast, many of the journals held by college and university libraries are also accessible online as subscription services. You are likely to have access to some of these *via* intranet or Internet portals (also known as *gateways*), but since the range of relevant journals will vary from one institution to another, all that can usefully be said here is that you should familiarise yourself with what is available to you.

Additionally, there are some online journals and information resources which are freely accessible to anyone with access to an Internet connection, as we will now demonstrate. However, we can do no more that give a brief taste of what the Internet has to offer. With this mind, and also having regard to the fact that the content of the Internet is rapidly changing, we will focus on websites and portals which are part of established academic projects, and are therefore likely to be available for some time.

One useful starting point is the law portal on the Intute social sciences pages, available at `http://www.intute.ac.uk/socialsciences/law/`. Essentially this is a portal to global legal resources, but each link is described and evaluated, making the data somewhat more useful than that available on many websites.

Another useful starting point is the Lawlinks website (available at `http://library.kent.ac.uk/library/lawlinks/`), maintained by the University of Kent at Canterbury. This site is organised by subject headings and provides an annotated list of websites.

Although very few full-text journals are available free online, the Electronic Law Journals Project based at the University of Warwick does provide free access to three titles. These are the *Journal of Information Law and Technology* (available at `http://www2.warwick.ac.uk/fac/soc/law/elj/jilt/`), the *Law, Social Justice and Global Development Journal* (available at `http://www2.warwick.ac.uk/fac/soc/law/elj/lgd/`) and the *Entertainment and Sports Law Journal* (available at `http://www2.warwick.ac.uk/fac/soc/law/elj/eslj/`) . All three journals are peer-reviewed and full-text versions of articles published in them are available free to download and print. Other journals, including all the journals published by the Oxford University Press (available at `http://www.oxfordjournals.org/`) provide searchable online indexes, together with tables of contents and abstracts of some articles, while restricting access to full-text articles to subscribers. Although searching for an article in this way will not produce the full-text version, it is nevertheless much quicker than browsing through volumes of journals on library shelves (assuming both that your library takes the journal in question and that it happens to be on the shelf when you are browsing).

Finally, two general points might be usefully made. First, one consequence of the fact that the best online resources are regularly updated is that links and URLs do not always endure in the same way as paper-based materials. Secondly, the accuracy of a great deal of information posted online is questionable. Taking these points together, you need, therefore, to consider keeping copies of valuable resources you discover online (in case they are gone when you next visit the site); and to develop a critical approach to using online sources. A useful resource for developing an effective and evaluative approach to online research is the set of interactive tutorials for legal research on the Intute website (available at `http://www.vts.intute.ac.uk/he/tutorial/lawyers`).

The status of textbooks and journals

The textbooks you will read are likely to have been written specifically for students; and the material they cover, and the limited detail into which they go, will reflect this. If you go on to practise law, you will encounter rather grander tomes designed especially for practitioners. Whatever the breadth and depth of a textbook, and however impressive it is in terms of size, you must always remember that no modern court will ever regard any textbook as being an authoritative source of law in the same way that cases and statutes are authoritative sources of law. The same is true of journal articles.

This modern view of the non-authoritative status of learned authors may be contrasted with the attitude taken in some cases by judges in earlier centuries, when statements made by authors such as Glanvill in the 12th century through to Blackstone in the 18th century were often treated as being binding statements of law. Of course, the modern approach does not disqualify the courts from seeking assistance from the best available scholarship: it merely preserves the constitutional position (which is explained in Chapter 2) as to what does, and does not, count as a source of law.

Applying this principle to your activities as a student, it follows that you may treat the views of authors as being persuasive when you are presenting a piece of coursework or an examination answer. However, you should be careful to use those views as supplements to your legal arguments, rather than as substitutes for the careful citation of judicial decisions and statutes. Similarly, when citing from casebooks, you must cite the report of the case itself, rather than the extract from the casebook, because it is the views of the judges, and not the views of the casebook editor, which carry weight. (You will remember that the nature of casebooks is that they contain extracts from judgments. The original reports, on the other hand, may also contain passages casting doubt on the extracts selected by the casebook's editor.)

Law reports

Introduction
The effective operation of the system of binding precedent (which we mentioned briefly in Chapter 2 and will consider more fully in Chapter 7) depends on the availability of reliable reports of the courts' decisions. However, before giving any further consideration to law reports, it will be useful to consider how cases are named.

Conventions in case names
The usual convention when naming a case is that the name of the party who is initiating the current stage of the proceedings will be placed first. So

if Smith is suing Jones for breach of contract, the case will be *Smith v Jones*. If Smith loses and appeals, the case will still be *Smith v Jones* on appeal, but if Jones loses and appeals, the case will become *Jones v Smith* on appeal. However, this statement of the usual convention must be qualified in two ways.

First, the modern practice in the House of Lords is for the case name to revert to whatever form it had at first instance, irrespective of who is the appellant.

Secondly, case names in criminal law are usually given in the form of *R v Smith*, whether at first instance or on appeal. The *R* stands for either *Rex* or *Regina* (meaning *King* or *Queen*) depending upon the sex of the monarch who was reigning at the time of the case.

Thirdly, some proceedings give rise to case names in special forms. One of the most common examples is judicial review, where historically the application to the court was made by the Crown on behalf of the real applicant. Although this is now pure fiction, the case names continue to reflect the original practice. For many years, the form was, for example, *R v Secretary of State for Whatever ex parte Smith*. However, the current usage, pursuing the same example, is *R (on the application of Smith) v Secretary of State for Whatever*, or, more briefly, *R (Smith) v Secretary of State for Whatever*.

Other exceptional usages include cases involving the estate of someone who has died, which are often given the name of the deceased, preceded by the word '*Re*', which means 'in the matter of'. So if Smith has died, a case dealing with the estate may be reported as *Re Smith*. A similar form is often used when cases deal with the welfare of children, except that the convention there is to use only initials, as, for example, in *Re SA (A Minor)* (where SA are the initials of the person concerned) in order to preserve anonymity. Another exception sometimes arises in cases involving ships, which are sometimes named after the ship or ships involved. (See, for example, the alternative name for *Ellerman Lines Ltd v Murray*, which is given at the end of the next paragraph.)

Sometimes a case may appear in two series of law reports under two different names. References to such a case may give both names, linked by the abbreviation *sub nom* (meaning *sub nomine*, or *under the name of*). For example, you may encounter the following: *Ellerman Lines Ltd v Murray* [1930] All ER Rep 503, *sub nom The Croxteth Hall, The Celtic* 47 TLR 147. In this example, the editor of one series has used the names of the parties, while another has used the names of the ships involved in the case.

The range of law reports

Introduction

Strictly speaking there is no 'official' series of law reports, but in practice the reports published by the Incorporated Council of Law Reporting for England and Wales, a non-profit-making body founded and run by the legal profession, are often referred to as the 'official' reports.

The leading series of law reports

The law reports published by the Incorporated Council are predominantly general series in terms of their subject matter, and include Appeal Cases (AC), Chancery Division (Ch), Family Division (Fam) and Queen's Bench Division (QBD). The Appeal Cases cover the decisions of the House of Lords and the Judicial Committee of the Privy Council. The reports named after the three divisions of the High Court cover not only cases heard in those divisions but also appeals arising from them which go to the Court of Appeal. (As we saw in Chapter 4, criminal appeals from the Queen's Bench Division go straight to the House of Lords, and are therefore reported in the Appeal Cases.) Additionally, the Incorporated Council publishes the *Weekly Law Reports* (WLR). This is a general series which, as its name implies, is published weekly, before being bound as three volumes for each year. Those cases which the editor considers to be least important appear in volume 1, while the rest appear in volumes 2 and 3. In due course, the cases from volumes 2 and 3 appear again in the Appeal Cases, Chancery, Family and Queen's Bench series, where they benefit from the inclusion of outlines of the advocates' arguments.

The Incorporated Council's two specialist series are the *Industrial Cases Reports* (ICR) which contain only cases involving employment law, and the *Business Law Reports* (Bus LR) which cover a wide range of topics such as banking law and intellectual property law under the broad heading of business law.

The Incorporated Council's website, http://www.lawreports.co.uk, contains some useful resources, including *WLR Daily*, which provides brief summaries of important cases within 24 hours of judgment being given.

As well as the law reports published by the Incorporated Council, there are many commercially published series of law reports. The commercially published series you are most likely to encounter is the *All England Law Reports* (All ER) which was traditionally a general series appearing in weekly parts, before being bound as four volumes for each year. (Unlike the *Weekly Law Reports*, no significance attaches to the placing of a case in any particular volume.) After many years as an entirely general series, the All England Law

Reports embarked on a modest programme of diversification which has produced two sub-series. These cover European Community cases and commercial law cases, and are cited as All ER (EC) and All ER (Comm) respectively. However, most of the commercially published series of law reports are whole-heartedly specialist, with many covering quite small areas of law, such as *Housing Law Reports* (HLR) and *Road Traffic Reports* (RTR).

The headnotes in some law reports refer you to other relevant sources of law. The leading series of law reports which contains this kind of material is the *All England Law Reports*, which give any relevant references to other works published by the same company, principally *Halsbury's Laws of England* and *Halsbury's Statutes of England*.

The headnotes in most series of law reports do not contain summaries of the advocates' arguments, but the principal series of the Incorporated Council for Law Reporting for England and Wales (namely the *Appeal Cases* (AC), *Chancery Division* (Ch), *Family Division* (Fam) and *Queen's Bench Division* (QB) reports) do so. (See p. 79 for the contents of each of these series.) Summaries of the advocates' arguments do not appear in the other series published by the Incorporated Council, namely the *Weekly Law Reports* (WLR), the *Industrial Cases Reports* (ICR) and the *Business Law Reports* (Bus LR), nor in the commercially published full-transcript law reports (the leading example of which is the *All England Law Reports* (All ER)), nor in any of the series of short reports. (For the distinction between full-transcript and short reports, see pp. 81–82.)

The fact that most series of law reports do not include summaries of the advocates' arguments may be taken as an indication that they are less than essential. However, you may find them useful if you are mooting (and especially if you know that you are likely to lose on a point of law), because they may suggest lines of argument that you could adopt and, where necessary, adapt. If this tactic succeeds, you will at least have arguments of truly professional quality, which may help you to succeed as the best mooter. You will also find that moot judges will intervene at least once in respect of each advocate, as a means of testing each individual's ability to deviate from a set script. (Mooting is dealt with in more detail at pp. 205–210.)

The headnotes in some series of law reports list the cases cited in the judgment, together with a separate list of those cited in argument by the advocates but not referred to in the judgments. These case lists have two purposes.

First, they provide a research list of cases on similar subject matter which may lead you to more appropriate authorities for a legal problem or issue which you need to solve. However, the availability of electronic databases has reduced the importance of case lists for this purpose.

Secondly, knowing which of the cases that do not appear in the judgment were nonetheless cited to the court can be particularly useful if you already have a detailed knowledge of the relevant area of law and you are surprised to see that a particular case is not mentioned in the judgment. Knowing the case was cited in argument means that you can reasonably assume that the court considered the case to be irrelevant. If, on the other hand, you know that a case was not cited in argument (or if you do not know whether it was cited in argument) you may have an uneasy suspicion that the ensuing decision may not be of the highest quality. In itself, of course, the fact that the court was unaware of a case may mean nothing. For example, if a particular case had been cited, the court might have been able to distinguish it. (For an explanation of distinguishing, see p. 96.)

You will find a list of some of the most common abbreviations for series of law reports (together with abbreviations of the titles of many journals) in Appendix 2, but a more comprehensive index of abbreviations, which can be searched by abbreviation or title, is maintained by the University of Cardiff. It is available at http://www.legalabbrevs.cardiff.ac.uk/.

Full transcript and short reports
It is important to notice the distinction between *full transcript* and *short* reports. Full transcript reports, such as the *All England Law Reports*, together with all the series published by the Incorporated Council for Law Reporting and many other series, consist of the full transcripts of the courts' judgments, together with a headnote. We shall return to a more detailed analysis of full transcript law reports in Chapter 8, where we explain how to read a law report, but for the moment it is sufficient to comment briefly on the nature and status of headnotes.

The most important part of the headnote is the law reporter's summary of the case. However, it is essential to notice that, while headnotes are generally accurate, they are only an individual's summary and have no legal status whatsoever. It follows that you rely on them at your peril. The headnotes of some series of full transcript law reports contain only the law reporter's summary, but others contain a variety of other material, such as outlines of the advocates' arguments, including lists of the cases on which the arguments were based, in argument and in the judgment, together with references to extraneous material which the law reporter thinks may be relevant. The summary part of a headnote can take one of three forms.

First, it may be *fully propositional*, consisting only of the reporter's version of the proposition (or propositions) of law which the court formulated in order to dispose of the case, without any attempt to summarise the facts.

This kind of headnote is appropriate where the facts are very detailed, but a full grasp of them is not necessary to an understanding of the law established by the case.

Secondly, it may be *fully narrative*, which means it tells the story of what happened (thus providing a statement of the relevant facts), before stating the court's ruling as to the relevant law, and then, finally, applying the law to the facts, in order to produce a decision. (The headnote to the report of *Henthorn v Fraser* [1892] 2 Ch 27 (CA), which we will analyse in Chapter 8, takes this form.)

Thirdly, it may be a compromise between the first two styles, consisting of a brief statement of context, followed by a statement of law on which the decision was based. A headnote of this kind would read something like:

> In a dispute as to whether a contractual offer can be revoked after an acceptance has been posted but before it has been received, the court held ...

This style of headnote may be called *semi-propositional*.

Unlike a full transcript report, a short report consists only of the reporter's summary. Again, these are generally accurate, but without the full transcript immediately to hand, you have no easy way of checking whether this is so in individual cases; and, in any event, no summary can ever do justice to all the subtleties of the full judgment. It follows that, as with the headnotes to full transcript reports, you rely on short reports at your peril. However, some short reports (for example, those which appear in the *Criminal Law Review*) do have the advantage that they are accompanied by commentaries which criticise the decisions, or assess their significance, or both. These commentaries are particularly useful in relation to recent decisions, which are unlikely to be discussed in the current edition of the textbook you have been advised to buy.

Citing law reports

Both the High Court and Court of Appeal have indicated, in the *Practice Direction (Judgments Form and Citation)* [2001] 1 WLR 194, that where 'a case has been reported in the official (*sic*) Law Reports published by the Incorporated Council ... it must be cited from that source'. Although in this respect the *Practice Direction* was merely repeating a long established principle, it also broke new ground for the Administrative Court and the Court of Appeal by introducing what are called *neutral citations* of, together with *paragraph numbering* within, judgments, in order to facilitate reference to their published versions on the Internet. Neutral citation has since been extended throughout the High Court by the *Practice Direction (Judgments: Neutral Citation)* [2002] 1 WLR 346, and it has also been adopted by the House of Lords. Where a neutral citation exists it should be cited first followed by a citation of the best available law report. The following examples show how neutral citations work:

Gregg v Scott [2005] UKHL 2
Awberry v Marley Building Materials [2005] EWCA Civ 16
Gill v Sandhu [2005] EWHC 43 (Ch)

In these examples, *Gregg v Scott* is the second numbered judgment of the House of Lords in 2005, *Awberry v Marley* the sixteenth numbered judgment of the Court of Appeal (Civil Division) in 2005 and *Gill v Sandhu* the forty-third numbered judgment of the Chancery Division of the High Court in 2005. The decisions of the High Court and Court of Appeal deal only with English law (applicable in England and Wales; hence the 'EW'), whereas the House of Lords has jurisdiction over the United Kingdom as a whole, and over England and Wales on the one hand and Scotland on the other hand as two other, separate jurisdictions. Since *Gregg v Scott* dealt with the unified jurisdiction, it is designated as *UK*.

The convention when citing law reports in print is to *italicise* the name of the case and to provide the full citation at least once. You should apply the *italicising* convention to any word-processed work that you are required to submit. In examinations, which will, of course, be handwritten, the whole script will be in a form of italics. The convention here is that you should <u>underline</u> case names. In coursework, you should apply the convention of providing a full citation at least once for each case. In examinations, however, no one will expect you to have memorised case references. Beyond this, it is difficult to be dogmatic, since some lecturers will expect you to know the year of the case, while others will regard even this as being an unnecessary burden on your memory.

Sometimes you may wish to be more specific in your citation by providing what are called *pinpoint citations* or *pinpoints*. The pinpoint will be a paragraph number (which is cited using square brackets) or a page number. For example, if you needed to cite the fifteenth paragraph from *Gregg v Scott* (above) and had not cited the case previously, you would write: *Gregg v Scott* [2005] UKHL 2 [15]. If you had already fully cited the case you would simply write: *Gregg v Scott* [15]. In judgments delivered before the introduction of neutral citations which lack paragraph numbers, you will have to cite the case as published in the law report you consulted; the pinpoint will be the page number. So, for example, if you wanted to cite Lord Atkin's famous 'neighbour test' in *Donoghue v Stevenson*, instead of simply citing the report and expecting the reader to work through all sixty pages, you would write: *Donoghue v Stevenson* [1932] AC 562 (HL) 566. Where you quote from a judgment and need to identify the judge, this detail can be added in round brackets as in, *Donoghue v Stevenson* [1932] AC 562 (HL) 566 (Lord Atkin). In these examples we have followed the *Oxford Standard for the Citation of Legal Authorities* (known as OSCOLA and available at http://denning.law.ox.ac.uk/published/oscola.shtml) and included the abbreviation for the court in which the case was decided round brackets.

A point of general importance when citing law reports is the distinction between square brackets and round brackets. Sometimes a date in a reference is in square brackets, as in [2004] 3 WLR 113, and sometimes it is in round ones, as in (2004) 39 EHRR 15. Where the date is in square brackets, it is an essential part of the reference: the reference 3 WLR 113 is useless, because the *Weekly Law Reports* have been published since 1953, and each year has a volume 3 with a page 113. A date in round brackets, however, is not an essential element of the reference. Therefore, although it is usual practice to include the year, as in (2004) 39 EHRR 15, the reference 39 EHRR 15 would be completely adequate to locate a case since each annual volume of the *European Human Rights Reports* is numbered, so there will only ever be one volume bearing the number 39.

Cases from other jurisdictions follow their own conventions; the full version of OSCOLA provides comprehensive guidance on citing international materials. Because of their impact on English law, the decisions of the European Court of Justice (ECJ) and the European Court of Human Rights require a particular mention. Judgments of the ECJ should be cited using the assigned case number followed by the case name and (where it is reported) the case reference in the official *European Court Reports* (ECR). Since 1989, following the creation of the European Court of First Instance, cases are numbered and prefixed by court, with 'C' indicating the ECJ and 'T' indicating the Court of First Instance. The *European Court Reports* are similarly divided, with ECR I indicating a decision of the ECJ and ECR II indicating a judgment of the Court of First Instance. Thus, a citation such as C-98/01 *EC Commission v United Kingdom* [2003] ECR I-4641 indicates (from the 'C' prefix to the case number and the 'I' following ECR) a decision of the ECJ.

Citing decisions of the European Court of Human Rights is more problematic. The guidance and usage of the court is that cases are cited by name, application number, the abbreviation ECHR and the year and volume number of the relevant official report. Where a paragraph number within a judgment is cited, it is preceded by the '§' symbol. Thus, *Pretty v United Kingdom* no. 2346/02, § 61, ECHR 2002-III would be a reference to paragraph 61 of application number 2346/02 reported in volume 3 of the official reports for 2002. In practice, however, you are likely to find that if a case is reported in the *European Human Rights Reports* (EHRR) that citation is given, and where the case is not reported in the EHRR the application number is cited. The *Pretty* case would therefore be cited as *Pretty v United Kingdom* (2002) 35 EHRR 1 or (if it were not reported in EHRR) Application 2346/02 *Pretty v United Kingdom*.

Online resources

Some series of law reports are now available online as subscription services, and many colleges and universities subscribe to services such as LexisNexis, Westlaw and Justis either as an intranet service (available on your college's or university's networked computers) or via password-protected portals, allowing students to have access from any Internet connection. Since the resources available are constantly increasing, and the methods of accessing them will vary from one institution to another, you will need to check the position in your own college or university.

The fundamental advantage of these electronic databases is that they are searchable by citation, by party names and by keywords, which makes the process of locating a case a great deal quicker than browsing through volumes of law reports. Furthermore, some online databases provide additional features such as case summaries and annotations indicating whether a particular case has been applied, approved, overruled or doubted in later cases; and some even allow educational users to download cases.

The number of free online resources has increased significantly over recent years. For example, since 1996 all decisions of the House of Lords have been posted online within hours of being delivered. The judgments (available at http://www.publications.parliament.uk/pa/ld/ldjudgmt.htm) are grouped in years, and within each year they are organised alphabetically. (Incidentally, on the same site you will also find the official report of proceedings in Parliament, known as *Hansard*.) Most of the decisions of the Court of Appeal and an increasing number of High Court judgments as well as decisions of the European Court of Justice and the European Court of Human Rights are available on the British and Irish Legal Information Institute (BAILII) website (available at http://www.bailii.org/).

Generally speaking, however, the weakness of the databases with free access lies in their search facilities. For example, the House of Lords site has only limited search facilities (available through the *advanced search* on the Parliament site: http://www.parliament.uk/), although BAILII is somewhat more sophisticated. As far as the European sites are concerned, the entire case law of the European Court of Justice (available at http://curia.eu.int/en/content/juris/index.htm) is searchable online as are the decisions of the European Court of Human Rights (available at http://www.echr.coe.int/echr/).

● Statutes

Introduction
Although the early development of English law depended to a great extent on the common law, there is no doubt now that statutes – a word which is interchangeable with the phrase *Acts of Parliament*, or, simply *Acts* – are now the principal source of English law.

Citing statutes
There are three ways of citing statutes.

First, there is citation by year and chapter number. In the case of the Energy Act 2004, for example, this form of citation is '2004, c.20', which indicates that it was the twentieth statute to receive the Royal Assent in 2004. The year and chapter number will be found in the heading of the statute.

Secondly, there is citation by the long title. The long title appears at the start of a statute and may be quite substantial. For example, the long title of the Energy Act 2004 is:

> An Act to make provision for the decommissioning and cleaning up of installations and sites used for, or contaminated by, nuclear activities; to make provision relating to the civil nuclear industry; to make provision about radioactive waste; to make provision for the development, regulation and encouragement of the use of renewable energy sources; to make further provision in connection with the regulation of the gas and electricity industries; to make provision for the imposition of charges in connection with the carrying out of the Secretary of State's functions relating to energy matters; to make provision for giving effect to international agreements relating to pipelines and offshore installations; and for connected purposes.

Thirdly, there is citation by the short title – for example, the Energy Act 2004.

Although citation by year and chapter number is the most formal method, followed by citation by long title, in practice citation by short title is far and away the most common method. There are two reasons why this should be so. First, compared with citation by year and chapter number, short titles have the advantage that they provide at least some indication of the statute's subject matter. Secondly, compared with citation by the long title, short titles have the advantage that they involve the use of only one short phrase.

Finding statutes

The authoritative version of any statute is the Queen's Printer's copy published by Her Majesty's Stationery Office. Individual statutes are available from the Stationery Office and all statutes are published annually as Public and General Acts and Measures. The real problem with the Queen's Printer's copy of a statute is that it will not be updated in the light of any amending legislation which Parliament may subsequently pass. It follows that the text of the Queen's Printer's copy of an Act may no longer be accurate when you refer to it.

Two commercially published series, namely *Current Law Statutes Annotated* and *Halsbury's Statutes of England*, provide annotations to the text, explaining the effect of the statute and its relationship to other relevant areas of Law. *Halsbury's Statutes* also provides an updating service.

The most recently introduced means of accessing statutes is the UK Statute Law Database, which is mentioned under the next heading.

Online resources

Current Bills before Parliament are published on the Parliament website (available at http://www.parliament.uk/bills/bills.cfm), where it also possible to track the progress of Bills through Parliament. The text of Public and General Acts of Parliament (from 1988 onwards) and Local Acts (from 1991 onwards) and UK Statutory Instruments (from 1987 onwards) are published on the Office of Public Sector Information website (available at http://www.opsi.gov.uk/acts.htm). The site also includes legislation passed by the Scottish Parliament, the National Assembly for Wales and the Northern Ireland Assembly.

The documents published on the Office of Public Sector Information site are Queen's Printer's copies, and are, therefore, not updated. The UK Statute Law Database under the auspices of the Ministry of Justice (available at http://www.statutelaw.gov.uk/) has begun to address this difficulty. Official revised editions of primary legislation in force on 1 February 1991 and primary and secondary legislation enacted from then onwards are available on their website. Several online subscription services, such as the LexisNexis Butterworths *Legislation Direct* and Westlaw UK's *United Kingdom Law in Force*, also provide amended and annotated statutes.

Conclusion

The common law is constantly changing and developing; Acts of Parliament frequently amend other Acts of Parliament in various ways; and the European Community and the European Court of Human Rights are both active. Keeping up-to-date with legal developments is, therefore, essential. New electronic resources are likely to be developed, and the scope of existing ones is likely to change. The resources we have examined here, both electronic and paper-based, do not by any means cover all that is available, but they do direct you towards some solid, and hopefully enduring, starting points.

7 Legal Method

Law, like anything else expressed in language, requires interpretation. Once interpreted, the law then has to be applied to the facts of a particular case. In the English common law, this process of legal reasoning requires an understanding of the doctrine of binding precedent, including the concepts of *ratio decidendi* and *obiter dicta*, and the way in which the courts approach the task of legislative interpretation.

Introduction

People often begin studying the law with the belief that a lawyer simply has to find the right page of the right book in order to discover the answer to any question of law. However, as this chapter will show, there are two reasons why this view is fundamentally misconceived. First, the sources of law need to be *interpreted* and then *applied to the facts* of the case. Secondly, many lawyers are argumentative by nature, and this tendency often comes to the fore when they are representing their clients. Therefore, it is not altogether surprising that they frequently disagree either as to the interpretation of the law, or as to the correct legal principle to be applied to a given set of facts, or as to both interpretation and application. Some people see this as bending, or attempting to bend, the rules. In reality, however, it is more accurately seen as an indication of the intrinsic flexibility of many legal rules. The truth of the matter is that there are many situations in which it is totally misleading to regard the law as consisting of a set of essentially rigid 'rules' which, unless the court decides to 'bend' them, will always dictate the outcome of any dispute to which they apply.

The scope for alternative answers to the same question, and the willingness of lawyers to argue for any of them, may be illustrated by the old story of someone who wants to know the result of adding 1.1111 to 2.8888. When put to a mathematician, the question receives an unqualified answer: '3.9999'. When put to an engineer, it receives a rather lengthier reply:

'strictly speaking, the answer is 3.9999; but engineering is a practical subject, and for all practical purposes the answer can be said to be 4, so I will say 4'. When the question is finally put to a lawyer, it receives the following reply: 'What do you want it to be?' In other words, if the issue arose in a legal context, the lawyer would be able and willing to argue for whichever answer advanced the client's case.

Turning to the law itself, we saw in Chapter 2 that the principal sources of English law are:

- the common law which is contained in the decisions of the courts, and which has developed through the doctrine of binding precedent;
- statutes which are made by Parliament, and delegated legislation which is made by other people acting under authority given to them by Parliament;
- and European Community law;

with the European Convention on Human Rights, as made applicable to English Law by both the common law and the Human Rights Act 1998, also providing some significant influence, even though it is, strictly speaking, a source of law only in relation to public authorities.

The bulk of this chapter will consider the techniques of legal method which are applicable to each of these sources, but before doing so it will be helpful to outline the nature of legal reasoning generally. This requires an explanation of the form of reasoning known as a *syllogism*, because syllogistic reasoning is central to legal method.

Syllogistic reasoning

The form of syllogistic reasoning is best explained by a simple example:

If $A = B$
And if $B = C$
Then $A = C$.

The first line of a syllogism is called the *major premise*, the second line is called the *minor premise*, and the third line is called the *conclusion*.

Putting this into a specifically legal context, the major premise will be a proposition of *law*; the minor premise will be a proposition of *fact*, and the conclusion will be the *decision* in the case. For example:

It is an offence to exceed the speed limit in a motor vehicle on a public highway (*major premise/proposition of law*)
Exceeding the speed limit in a motor vehicle on a public highway is what the defendant did (*minor premise/proposition of fact*)

therefore

It is an offence to do what the defendant did – or, in other words, the defendant is guilty (*conclusion/decision*).

In reality, of course, simply being able to identify the form of reasoning as syllogistic tells us very little. What we really need to know is how we can identify and formulate:

- the correct proposition of law (the *major premise*); and
- the facts to which the proposition of law must be applied (the *minor premise*).

The answer to the first question is:

- by applying the techniques of legal method.

The answer to the second question is:

- by evidence establishing the facts which are in dispute.

As it is only the first question which falls within the scope of this book, it is to this that we will now turn.

The common law and the doctrine of binding precedent

Introduction

As we saw in Chapter 1, there are various ways of thinking about *justice*, but at a very basic level most people would probably accept that justice requires similar cases to be dealt with in a similar way. So there is nothing surprising in the fact that judges in developed legal systems tend to follow each other's decisions. What is unusual about the common law system is that, theoretically at least and in certain circumstances, judges are *bound* to follow decisions made in earlier cases.

A system which guarantees consistency between decisions in similar cases will also meet another important requirement of any fair legal system, namely making it possible for lawyers to advise their clients with reasonable confidence as to the legal position. However, a strict system of *binding* precedent also has the disadvantage of causing excessive rigidity, which may not only make it impossible for the courts to respond sympathetically to the particular subtleties of an individual case, but may also prevent the courts from introducing desirable developments into the law.

Although the conflict between the advantages and disadvantages of the system of binding precedent are often presented in the form of a conflict between certainty and predictability on the one hand and flexibility and justice on the other, such an analysis is too superficial to be genuinely helpful. More particularly, as we have seen, sufficient certainty to enable reasonable predictability is itself a part of, rather than being opposed to, justice. The problem, therefore, is not one of resolving a conflict between certainty and predictability on the one hand, and flexibility and justice on the other. It is about striking a broadly acceptable balance which will normally require the courts to follow earlier decisions, while allowing a degree of flexibility in cases where the courts consider this to be appropriate.

We will now consider how the doctrine of binding precedent (which is sometimes still known by the Latin tag *stare decisis*), attempts to strike this balance. (*Stare decisis* may be roughly translated as *to stand by decisions*.) As we will see, there are two elements to the doctrine. One requires us to analyse the hierarchy of the courts, while the other requires us to analyse individual judgments into their component parts. We will begin with the hierarchy of the courts.

The hierarchy of the courts

A working statement of the doctrine of binding precedent could be:

> All courts bind all lower courts, and the Court of Appeal also binds itself, as does the House of Lords (although the position in both the Court of Appeal and the House of Lords is subject to some exceptions).

The hierarchical structure to which, broadly speaking, this statement refers may be illustrated by repeating the diagram which you first encountered at p. 53. However, when reading the text, you will see that those bodies whose names appear in brackets do not fit neatly into the mainstream of the doctrine of binding precedent.

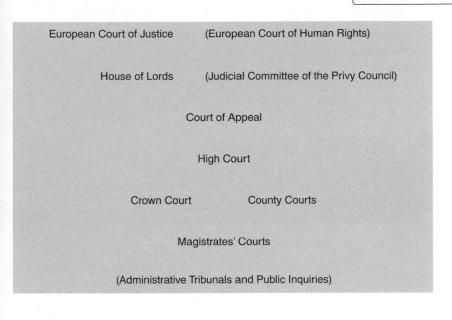

European Court of Justice   (European Court of Human Rights)

House of Lords   (Judicial Committee of the Privy Council)

Court of Appeal

High Court

Crown Court   County Courts

Magistrates' Courts

(Administrative Tribunals and Public Inquiries)

Decisions of the European Court of Justice are binding on English courts. Strictly speaking, however, as we shall see below, the Court is not bound by its own decisions, although in practice it does tend to follow them.

The status of decisions of the European Court of Human Rights within the English legal system is complex and can only be fully understood in the light of the Human Rights Act 1998. Very briefly, however, and at the risk of some over-simplification:

- at common law the English courts have always been willing to have regard to the provisions of the European Convention on Human Rights, but without feeling themselves bound by an instrument which is not actually part of English Law;
- under the Human Rights Act 1998, English courts:
  - must *take into account* any relevant decisions of the European Court of Human Rights; but
  - are not bound to follow them.

Decisions of the Judicial Committee of the Privy Council are never, strictly speaking, binding on any court. However, the fact that there is a very substantial overlap between the membership of the Appellate Committee of the House of Lords and the Judicial Committee of the Privy Council, means that many Privy Council decisions are treated for all practical purposes as having the same status as House of Lords authorities. The Court of Appeal may even choose to follow a decision of the Judicial Committee of the Privy Council sitting with more than its usual tally of five members and consisting entirely of Law Lords, rather than following a decision of the House of Lords. (See *Attorney-General for Jersey v Holley* [2005] UKPC 23, [2005] 2 AC 580.)

The Privy Council tends to follow its own decisions but is not bound to do so.

The Court of Appeal is basically bound to follow its own decisions, but there are exceptional situations in which it is free to depart from them. The authorities are not altogether clear, but the exceptions may be more flexible in the Criminal Division than in the Civil Division.

The self-bindingness of the High Court depends on which jurisdiction it is exercising:

- when dealing with appeals (i.e. where the correctness of a decision made by another court or other decision-maker is being challenged) it binds itself; but
- at both first instance (that is, when dealing with trials) and in judicial review (that is, when dealing with challenges to the legality of the decision-making processes of another court or other decision-maker, as distinct from challenging the correctness of the resulting decision) its own decisions are only persuasive (which means that it may choose to follow an earlier decision but is not bound to do so).

The Crown Court, county courts and magistrates' courts are not bound by their own previous decisions.

As tribunals (or administrative tribunals as they are traditionally known) and public inquiries are not courts at all, it is not surprising that, generally speaking, they do not create binding precedents (although they are subject to the doctrine of binding precedent in the sense that they are bound to follow the law as it is stated to be by the courts). They do, however, have a natural tendency to follow their own previous decisions. Similarly, public inquiries are not subject to the doctrine. In their case, there is the additional point that they are often very heavily concerned with finding the facts on which a final decision is to be based, which means that the idea of precedent would be of relatively little use anyway.

The elements of a judgment: *ratio decidendi* and *obiter dictum*
Having dealt with the hierarchy of the courts, the idea of bindingness must be explored in a little more detail. As a preliminary, however, it is worth

emphasising that the doctrine of binding precedent is not concerned with the position between the parties to the case which creates the precedent, but is concerned with the provision of rules of law which can then be applied by all later courts; and, more particularly, will actually be *binding* on some of them.

The first point is that not every part of a judgment will be binding. To identify the binding part, a judgment must be analysed into two constituent elements: *ratio decidendi* and *obiter dicta*. The binding part is the *ratio decidendi*, which may be translated as *the reason for the decision*. The remainder of the judgment will be *obiter dicta*, which may be translated as *sayings by the way*.

The plural of *ratio decidendi* is either *ratios decidendi* or (sticking more faithfully to the original Latin) *rationes decidendi*, according to personal preference. The sentence in the previous paragraph which used the phrase *obiter dicta* required it to be given in its plural form: the singular is *obiter dictum*. It is conventional to speak of *ratio* and *dictum* – and their respective plurals – without using the other part of each phrase. The word *obiter* may be used on its own as either an adjective or an adverb, but should never be used as a noun. In other words, a statement by a judge may be said to be *obiter* (using the word as an adjective) or to be made *obiter* (using the word as an adverb) but never to be *an obiter* (because this would be using the word as a noun).

Identifying the *ratio*

It follows from what has been said that one of the main tasks facing you whenever you read a case is to identify its *ratio*. The first point to be made is – at the risk of stating the obvious – that where there is only one judgment, the *ratio* of that judgment will be the *ratio* of the case, while if a multi-judge court divides into a majority and a minority, the *ratio* of the majority will be the *ratio* of the case. However, these propositions take us nowhere in relation to the key task of identifying the *ratio* of a judgment in the first place.

The difficulty of identifying the *ratio* of a judgment arises from the fact that judges who are deciding cases are usually going to be principally concerned with resolving the issues between the parties. Therefore, any statements of the law which judges make in the course of their judgments will be conditioned by the circumstances of the cases they are deciding, and the fact that their decisions will be subjected to detailed analysis in later cases will usually be of secondary importance to them. The point was well made by Lord Halsbury LC, when he said:

> The generality of the expressions which may be found ... are not intended to be expositions of the whole law but govern and are

qualified by the particular facts of the case. (*Quinn v Leathem* [1901] AC 495, 506.)

However, it is not all the facts that will be relevant when interpreting a judgment, but only the *material* facts. Or, putting this another way, when looking for the *ratio* of a case, it is necessary to identify the *material facts* which influenced the formulation of the legal rule on which the decision is based. A useful way of testing the materiality of a fact is to ask: *if this fact had either not been present or had been present but different, would the decision still have been the same*? If the answer to this question is *No*, it follows that that fact must be material. Ultimately, the materiality (or non-materiality) of a fact can only be determined in the light of all the circumstances of a real case. However, in general terms it can be said that facts as to the time and place where things happened, the identity of people and things, and the amount of property involved (including sums of money) will be presumed to be *not* material unless all the circumstances of the case are such that they justify the opposite conclusion. For example, there may be a crucial distinction in some cases between things which happened in a public place and things which happened in a private place. (But even here, the question of precisely *which* public – or private – place is unlikely to be material.)

If the judge in a later case decides that the facts of an earlier case were *materially different* from the facts of the case before him, he can perfectly properly *distinguish* the earlier case. This is not a question of interfering with the authority of the earlier case in any subsequent cases which may be genuinely similar. It is simply a question of deciding that the earlier case is not relevant to the case which is currently being decided, and is not, therefore, a binding authority.

The importance of the technique of distinguishing cases must be stressed, since it is an important way in which judges seek to achieve results which they feel to be appropriate to the cases which they decide. No totally reliable formula for the identification of material facts exists, but an example may help to show how distinguishing can work in practice.

The case of *Burgess v McCracken* (1986) 150 JP 529, arose from the commercial activities of a professional photographer in a public park. His method of business was to get people to agree to have their photographs taken. He then took their photographs, noted their names and addresses, and received a deposit. He subsequently sent them the photographs through the post, and they sent him the balance of his fee. It was important to know whether what he did amounted to *trading in the park*, because if it did he was committing an offence. A magistrates' court acquitted him on the basis that an earlier case (*Newman v Lipman* [1951] 1 KB 333) had decided that exactly the same conduct in a street did not amount to the offence of *trading in the street*.

However, in *Burgess* the prosecution appealed to the High Court, where it was held that there was a legally relevant distinction between streets and parks. The court said that the offence in relation to streets was intended to prevent obstructions of the kind that can arise when traders set up stalls to display their goods. Street photographers do not do this; therefore they do not commit an offence. On the other hand, people go into parks for relaxation and recreation, therefore the offence in relation to parks has a wider purpose, which includes protecting people from annoyance. In the context of a park, therefore, the mere absence of obstruction did not justify an acquittal. (This pair of cases also provides a neat illustration of the truth of the proposition that a decision on the meaning of a word for the purposes of one statute will not be binding as to the meaning of the same word for the purposes of another statute. As we have just seen, in reality, this proposition is simply an example of distinguishing.)

As a means of avoiding a consequence which they feel to be wrong, judges may be tempted to distinguish earlier cases on artificial grounds. Indeed, some people may feel that *Burgess* itself is an example of artificial distinguishing. However, leaving aside the merits of individual examples, the fact that artificial distinguishing does take place must be recognised. Similarly, it must also be recognised that this undermines the predictability of the legal system, because judges vary in their willingness to resort to artificiality. The responsibility of the judges when considering whether to distinguish an earlier case is well explained by Robert Goff LJ, in *Elliott v C* [1983] 1 WLR 939, 947:

> In my opinion, although of course the courts of this country are bound by the doctrine of precedent, sensibly interpreted, nevertheless it would be irresponsible for judges to act as automata, rigidly applying authorities without regard to consequences. Where therefore it appears at first sight that authority compels a judge to reach a conclusion which he senses to be unjust or inappropriate, he is, I consider, under a positive duty to examine the relevant authorities with scrupulous care to ascertain whether he can, within the limits imposed by the doctrine of precedent (always sensibly interpreted), legitimately interpret or qualify the principle expressed in the authorities to achieve the result which he perceives to be just or appropriate in the particular case. I do not disguise the fact that I have sought to perform this function in the present case.

At first sight this attitude may seem to amount to a total denial of the doctrine of binding precedent. However, you will have noticed that Robert Goff LJ did indicate that there are 'limits imposed by the doctrine', and that in the result, he actually felt unable to achieve the outcome which he perceived to be just or appropriate, saying he was 'constrained ... by authority' to reach a conclusion which caused him 'unhappiness'.

A litigant who is disappointed, either by artificial distinguishing or by a failure to undertake real distinguishing, will be in the same position as any other disappointed litigant, and will have no remedy other than pursuing any avenues, whether by way of appeal or judicial review, that the legal system may offer.

It should be apparent by this stage that legal method can be a great deal more flexible than many people assume it to be. One of the classic textbooks on jurisprudence expresses the dynamism of the concept of *ratio* in literally graphic terms:

> If we think of the rule of law as a line on a graph, then the case itself is like a point through which that line is drawn. (Fitzgerald, P. J., *Salmond on Jurisprudence*, 12th edn, 1966, p. 170.)

This flexibility of binding precedent leads to a very important conclusion, namely that it can be seriously misleading to talk simply of the *ratio* of a case. In reality, there are two *ratios*. The first in time is the *descriptive ratio*, which describes the reasoning leading to the decision in the earlier case. This *ratio* can, of course, be identified immediately after that judgment is given. The second *ratio* is the *prescriptive ratio*, which is formulated by a court in the process of making a later decision, and is then developed by a series of subsequent cases. This *ratio* is called *prescriptive* because it *prescribes* the principle of law which is binding on the later court. (You may find it puzzling that it is the later court which decides what it is going to be bound by, since this seems to go against the essential idea of being bound. However, as you progress through your study of law you will see that – puzzling or not – this is, in fact, how the doctrine of binding precedent operates.)

Having established that the flexibility of precedent is, in practice, largely due to the technique of distinguishing previous cases so that they can then be disregarded, coupled with the possibility of interpreting and applying their *ratios* in such a way as to produce just outcomes, we can now turn to the concept of *dictum*.

Assessing the weight of *obiter dicta*

Although, as a matter of definition, *dicta* are not binding, it does not follow that they are entirely irrelevant. They can be said to have *persuasive authority*, meaning that a later court may choose to follow them, even though not obliged to do so. An important point here is that the degree of persuasiveness varies greatly. In fact the stage may be reached where there is little practical distinction between *ratio* and *dicta*. The explanation of this will be found in a consideration of the reasons why, in strict theory, *dicta* are not binding.

Two factors are relevant. First, where a point is not central to the case, the advocates who appear will usually not argue the law, or if they do argue it, they will do so with less thoroughness than they would give to the main issues. Secondly, a judge who says something *obiter* will usually not have given the matter the same consideration as he would have done if it were more central to the decision. It follows from these two factors that, if a point has been fully argued, and the court did give it very careful attention, there is no real reason why the court's views should not be treated as being authoritative. An example may be useful.

In *Hedley Byrne & Co Ltd v Heller & Partners Ltd* [1964] AC 465, the facts were that the defendants had made an incorrect statement to the plaintiffs about the creditworthiness of a third party. The plaintiff relied on this statement and lost money as a result. The question was whether the defendants were liable to pay damages to the plaintiff. One complicating factor was that the defendants had expressly stated that they were giving the advice 'without responsibility'. In other words, they were making it clear that they would not consider themselves liable for any loss which resulted from their advice.

The House of Lords said that, in principle, the defendants ought to be liable. On the facts, however, the defendants had disclaimed liability, and therefore the plaintiffs failed to recover damages. If this is analysed into *ratio* and *dictum*, it will be apparent that the *ratio* was that the defendants had disclaimed liability. Since this was all that was necessary for the decision, all the rest of it must have been *obiter*. Nevertheless, the decision on the point of principle has been both generally accepted, and subsequently developed. The attitude of later courts faced with this kind of *dictum* may be found in the words of Cairns J:

> Where five members of the House of Lords have all said, after close
> examination of the authorities, that a certain type of tort exists, I
> think that a judge of first instance should proceed on the basis that it
> does exist, without pausing to embark on an investigation whether

what was said was necessary to the ultimate decision. (*WB Anderson & Sons Ltd v Rhodes* [1967] 2 All ER 850, 857.)

The fact that *dicta* are of varying degrees of authority, from the almost worthless to the very strongly persuasive, leads some people to adopt a sub-classification into *gratis dicta a*nd *judicial dicta*, with the former being much less weighty than the latter. There is no harm in this terminology, provided you do not allow it to lead you into the trap of thinking that all *dicta* fall fairly and squarely into one category or the other. The truth of the matter is that there is a spectrum of possibilities, from the mere throwaway comment which is worth practically nothing in terms of precedent to the fully argued and carefully considered opinion, the weight of which is indistinguishable from the weight of a *ratio decidendi*; and, in reality, most *dicta* fall somewhere in the middle ground between these extremes.

Legislation and legislative interpretation

Introduction
Since the Industrial Revolution, social and economic changes have occurred at such a rate that the common law, whose development is dependent on the random process of suitable cases coming before the courts, has been unable to keep pace with the needs of the society it serves. As a result, statutes (which are also known as primary legislation) and delegated legislation have become the major source of English law.

As we saw in Chapter 3, it is a matter of fundamental English constitutional doctrine that Parliament is legislatively supreme. In other words, Parliament can enact any statute it wishes and only Parliament can repeal whatever Parliament has enacted. There may be significant debate over the extent of the power (if any) of one Parliament to bind its successors, and over the relationship between European Community law and English law, but neither of these matters need be pursued for the present purposes.

What does need to be considered is the interpretation or construction of statutes and delegated legislation. In passing, it is worth noticing that judges use the terms *interpretation* and *construction* interchangeably on most occasions, and they can generally be taken to mean the same thing.

Communication and interpretation
Essentially the drafting and interpretation of statutes and delegated legislation is simply an exercise in communication. Having decided what it wants

to do, Parliament, or those whom Parliament has authorised to make delegated legislation, communicates the result to the world at large, including the courts which have to enforce it. However, the processes of legislative drafting and interpretation create more than usually acute problems of communication because they involve a vital question of the balance of constitutional power between the courts and the legislators.

The evolution of the current approach to legislative interpretation
There are, and always have been, several principles which the courts use to guide themselves in the task of legislative interpretation. For example, where a statute which creates a criminal offence is open to two or more meanings, there is a presumption that Parliament intended the courts to apply the meaning which is most favourable to the defendant. (*Dickenson v Fletcher* (1873) LR 9 CP 1.) Similarly, there is a presumption that Parliament did not intend legislation to operate retrospectively. (*L'Office Cherifien des Phosphates and Another v Yamasita-Shinnihon Steamship Co Ltd: The Boucraa* [1994] AC 486.) However, principles such as these will, in their nature, apply to relatively few cases, so we shall now turn our interpretation to the evolution of what is currently the single most important guide to legislative interpretation, namely the *purposive approach*.

Historically, when statutes were a relatively minor source of English law, the predominant principle of interpretation was the *mischief rule*, or the *rule in Heydon's Case* (1584) 76 ER 637, which may be stated as follows:

> For the sure and true interpretation of all statutes ... four things are to be discerned and considered:
>
> 1st   What was the Common Law before the making of the Act?
> 2nd   What was the mischief and defect for which the Common Law did not provide?
> 3rd   What remedy the Parliament hath resolved and appointed to cure the disease of the Commonwealth?
> 4th   The true reason of the remedy; and then the office of all the judges is always to make such construction as shall suppress the mischief and advance the remedy, and to suppress continuance of the mischief ... according to the true intent of the makers of the Act.

However, as statutes became increasingly important sources of law, and as Parliament became increasingly democratically validated during the 19th century, the courts relegated the mischief rule to the status of a long-stop, to be invoked only when all else failed. Instead, they started to rely primarily on the so-called *literal rule* of interpretation, which, in the words of Lord Blackburn, required them to give statutory words their *literal* or *plain* meanings, except where these led to

> an inconsistency or an absurdity or inconvenience so great as to convince the court that the intention could not have been to use them in their ordinary signification,

in which case the courts could invoke the so-called *golden rule*, which would

> justify the court putting on them some other signification, which though less proper, is one which the court thinks the words will bear. (*River Wear Commissioners v Adamson* (1877) 2 App Cas 743, 764.)

While this approach may sound perfectly reasonable in the abstract, it is in fact deeply flawed, because it assumes that words have *literal* or *plain* meanings. While there are, no doubt, instances where this is so, there are also very many instances where it is simply not true.

Take two examples. First, imagine a poster in a shop window which reads: *Last Week – Everything Half Price*. On a purely linguistic basis, this could mean that the sale finished at the end of the previous week (and that, therefore, everything has now gone back to being full price). But commonsense tells you this is not what the poster means, and that the message it is seeking to convey is that this is the *final* week of the sale. The second example requires you to name the last King of England. On a purely linguistic basis, you could reply that no answer is possible because, being unable to foretell the future, you cannot possibly know who will be the last (in the sense of *final*) King of England. But this response would never occur to most people, who would assume they were being required to name the *most recent* King of England (and would, therefore, say George VI).

While this pair of examples may seem trivial, it does show that the simple, everyday word *last* can mean either *final* or *most recent*, and – crucially – that the correct choice of meaning is *not to be found in the word itself, but in the context in which it is used*. Thus, any approach to interpretation in terms of *literal* or *plain* meanings is based on a fundamental misunderstanding of the nature of words and their meanings.

Eventually, the courts came to appreciate the importance of context when interpreting words. As Stamp J said, in *Bourne v Norwich Crematorium Ltd* [1967] 1 WLR 691, 696:

English words derive colour from those which surround them. Sentences are not mere collections of words to be taken out of the sentence, defined separately by reference to the dictionary or decided cases, and then put back again into the sentence with the meaning which one has assigned to them as separate words so as to give the sentence or phrase a meaning which as a sentence or phrase it cannot bear without distortion of the English language.

More particularly, the courts came to appreciate that the *purpose* underlying the legislation is an essential element in the context of the statutory words:

If one looks back to the actual decisions of [the House of Lords] over the last thirty years one cannot fail to be struck by the evidence of a trend ... towards the purposive construction of statutory provisions. (Lord Diplock, in *Carter v Bradbeer* [1975] 1 WLR 1204, 1206-1207.)

An example of the power of purposivism may be useful. In *R v Pigg* [1983] 1 WLR 6, the point at issue was whether the defendant's conviction for rape should be upheld or quashed. He had been convicted on a majority verdict, under a statutory provision in the following terms:

A court shall not accept a majority verdict of guilty unless the foreman of the jury has stated in open court the number of jurors who respectively agreed to and dissented from the verdict. (Section 17(2), Juries Act 1974.)

What actually happened in *Pigg* was that the foreman merely said that ten jurors had agreed to convict the defendant. The clerk of the court then said: 'ten agreed to two of you'. The foreman made no reply. Holding that the proceedings had complied with the statutory requirement, Lord Brandon, with the agreement of the other Law Lords, said (at p. 13):

the precise form of words by which such compliance is achieved, so long as the effect is clear, is not material.

The conviction was, therefore, upheld. Lord Brandon appears not to have been concerned that his interpretation resulted in the upholding of the conviction, even though this ran counter to the basic proposition that criminal statutes should be interpreted strictly in favour of the defendant. Perhaps Lord Brandon's abhorrence of the offence weighed more heavily with him than did any traditional ideas of fair play for the defendant.

European Community law

Precedent in the European Court of Justice
Although European Community law lies within the civil law tradition, and therefore has no doctrine of binding precedent, it does exhibit a strong tendency to follow its own previous decisions. For example, in *Da Costa* [1963] CMLR 224, when dealing with a preliminary reference from a Dutch court, under what was then art. 177 of the Treaty of Rome, the court said (at p. 238):

> The questions of interpretation posed in this case are identical with those settled ... [in the earlier case of *van Gend en Loos* [1963] CMLR 105] ... and no new factor has been presented to the court.

In these circumstances the [national court] must be referred to the previous judgment.

Legislative interpretation in the European Court of Justice
The civil law tradition has always been purposivist (or to use the word which that tradition itself generally uses, *teleological*) in its approach to legislative interpretation. It has never fallen into the trap of literalism. Two passages from *van Gend en Loos v Nederlandse Administratie der Belastingen* [1963] CMLR 105, which is one of the most important cases in the whole of Community Law, indicate the approach of the European Court of Justice.

> The objective of the EEC Treaty, which is to establish a common market, the functioning of which is of direct concern to interested parties in the Community, implies that this Treaty is more than an agreement which merely creates mutual obligations between the contracting states. This view is confirmed by the preamble to the Treaty which refers not only to governments but to peoples. It is also confirmed more specifically by the establishment of institutions endowed with sovereign rights, the exercise of which affects member states and also their citizens. ((1963) CMLR 105, 129.)

On the basis of this, together with a detailed consideration of the case itself, the court concluded:

> It follows ... that, according to the spirit, the general scheme and the wording of the Treaty, art 12 [of the Treaty of Rome] must be interpreted as producing direct effects and creating individual rights which national courts must protect. ((1963) CMLR 105, 130.)

The European Court of Human Rights

Precedent in the European Court of Human Rights

As with the European Court of Justice, the European Court of Human Rights is firmly located within the Civil Law tradition. However, and again as with the European Court of Justice, although it has no doctrine of *binding* precedent, the Court of Human Rights 'usually follows and applies its own precedents, such a course being in the interests of legal certainty and the orderly development of the Convention case-law', while being ready to depart from its own previous decisions where there are 'cogent reasons' for doing so, including the need to 'ensure that the interpretation of the Convention reflects societal changes and remains in line with present day conditions'. (*Cossey v United Kingdom* (1991) 13 EHRR 622, 639, in which the Court refused to depart from its decision in *Rees v United Kingdom* (1987) 9 EHRR 56, where it had held that the United Kingdom was entitled to refuse to allow transsexuals to have their birth certificates amended in order to show their acquired sex.)

Legislative interpretation in the European Court of Human Rights

It is a well-established principle of international law, currently contained in the Vienna Convention on the Law of Treaties 1969, that treaties 'shall be interpreted in good faith in accordance with the ordinary meaning to be given to the terms of the treaty in their context and *in the light of its object and purposes*'. (Emphasis added.)

The preamble to the European Convention on Human Rights Treaty makes it plain that its object and purpose are 'the maintenance and further realisation of Human Rights and Fundamental Freedoms'. Furthermore, the Court's decision in *Wemhoff v Federal Republic of Germany* (1979-80) 1 EHRR 55, shows that where the wording of the official texts of the Convention cannot be reconciled with each other, the 'object and purpose' of the Convention will be decisive.

Conclusion

Legal method is much more flexible than many students think when they first approach the law. Good lawyers examine the relevant sources of law with a view to trying to construct an argument which will favour their clients' interests.

When dealing with the common law, a great deal of flexibility arises from the concepts of *ratio decidendi* and *obiter dictum* and the status of each in terms of bindingness and persuasiveness.

Both the European Court of Justice and the European Court of Human Rights come from the civil law tradition, which means that neither of them has a doctrine of binding precedent

When dealing with legislation, a great deal of flexibility arises from the fact that many words have a variety of meanings, and that even apparently plain words can be interpreted in unexpected ways when regard is had to their purpose. More particularly, the English courts no longer approach the task of legislative interpretation in a literal way, preferring to give greater importance to the purpose of the legislation.

Another consequence of the fact that both the European Court of Justice and the European Court of Human Rights come from the civil law tradition is that they both approach legislative interpretation in a purposive way.

8 Reading Law Reports and Statutes

Cases and statutes are the principal building blocks of English law. You must, therefore, be able to read them both confidently. In relation to both sources, you must be familiar with the way the text is likely to be laid out. In relation to law reports, you must be able to identify the *ratio decidendi* of a case and assess the weight of *obiter dicta*. In relation to statutes, you must always try to identify the purpose of the Act, and be aware that (almost always) some words and phrases will be defined by the Act itself, while others will be left open for interpretation by the courts.

Introduction

We noted in Chapter 2 that the English legal system is a common law system, which means that a great deal of the law has been created, and some of it continues to be developed, by the courts when deciding individual cases. Indeed, there are still some significant areas of law – such as the tort of negligence – which remain relatively untouched by statute and which are, therefore, largely dependent on the courts for their continuing development on a case-by-case basis.

Nevertheless, despite the continuing importance of the common law, statutes now create a far greater volume of law than judicial decisions do. It follows, therefore, that you must rapidly acquire the ability to read both cases and statutes. Quite apart from anything else, statutes have to be interpreted by the courts. This point divides into two sub-points. First, the principles of statutory interpretation are themselves part of the common law rather than having been enacted by Parliament. Secondly, under the doctrine of the separation of powers (which is explained at pp. 42–44) it falls to the courts to decide the definitive meanings of individual statutes, and these decisions may then bind other courts in later cases arising from the same statutes.

Of course, you may be tempted to rely on the few lines in a textbook which purport to tell you what a case decides or what a statute means; and there is no doubt that textbooks can be very useful as a means of gaining a bird's-eye view of a topic. However, when it comes to more detailed study, whether by way of preparation for tutorials or essays, or when assembling a body of notes from which you will be able to revise for examinations, there is no effective substitute for reading the cases and statutes themselves.

In this chapter we are going to do two things. First, we shall take a substantial extract from the report of the Court of Appeal decision in *Henthorn v Fraser* [1892] 2 Ch 27 (which is a leading case in the law of contract) and explain how you can get the maximum value from the time and energy you will invest in reading it. More particularly, there are two aspects to this part of the chapter. Our first aim is to help you find your way around a typical law report in terms of identifying its elements and understanding its structure. Our second aim is to illustrate how the *ratio decidendi* of a judgment can be identified and how the weight of *obiter dicta* can be assessed. Of course – and recalling the distinction between the *descriptive* and *prescriptive* meanings of the word *ratio*, which is explained at p. 98 – all we can do at this stage is to identify the *descriptive ratio*, since it is only the judges in later cases in which this one has been cited who can identify the *prescriptive ratio*.

Secondly, we shall take the Dealing in Cultural Objects (Offences) Act 2003, which is a very short, modern statute, in order to illustrate both the basic structure of a simple statute and some points of statutory interpretation.

Reading Law Reports

Introduction

You will very shortly come to an extract of a report of the case of *Henthorn v Fraser*, where the issue was whether a person who has offered to sell certain property to another person can withdraw (or, to use the technical term, *revoke*) that offer after the other person has put his acceptance of the offer in the post but before the prospective seller has received it.

We have taken the report from The Law Reports, where it appears in one of the volumes which contain decisions of the Chancery Division of the High Court and decisions of the Court of Appeal arising from appeals against those decisions. (In fact, as you will see when you read the report carefully, this particular case was heard at first instance by the Vice-Chancellor of the County Palatine of Lancaster. This court of chancery no longer exists but it was the local equivalent of the High Court – to which its jurisdiction passed when it was abolished – so nothing turns on this particular historical oddity.)

We have reproduced the report in substantially the same form as that in which it was originally published, subject to the following alterations.

First, it has been sufficient for our purposes to reproduce only the headnote and the judgment of Lord Herschell. However, if you read the original report you will see that both the other judges concurred. More particularly, Kay LJ delivered a fully reasoned judgment, while Lindley LJ simply delivered a short statement of his concurrence.

Secondly, as well as being selective in relation to the text, we have also edited it in three other ways. The first, and most obvious, aspect of our editing is that we have inserted text boxes at various points in order to provide a commentary on either what has just been said, or what is about to be said, in the text. Additionally, we have modernised some of the typography. Finally, we have expanded the footnotes by including explanations of the case references.

Reading the case for the first time

Since you cannot realistically hope to absorb all the details on your first reading of a case, at this stage you should read the text fairly quickly in order to acquire an overview of what the case is about and how the court approached its decision. *However, you should not, at this stage, slow yourself down by reading the text boxes.* On your second and subsequent readings, when you know roughly what the case is about, you will be in a better position to understand both the text and the text boxes. Even on your first reading, however, there is one detail you should make a point of noticing. It is only from the point (on p. 30 of the report) where you find '1892. March 26. LORD HERSCHELL', that you are reading the actual words of the judgment (all the previous text having been provided by the law reporter). This is significant because it is only the judgment which contains the definitive version of the facts and the authoritative statement of the law.

The report and the boxed commentary

| 2 Ch | CHANCERY DIVISION | 27 |

HENTHORN v FRASER

On the top line is the page heading. Here it tells you the volume (2), report series (Chancery Division) and page number (27) of the Law Report you are reading. It does not, however, tell you that it is a decision of the Court of Appeal, since Chancery Division reports include first instance decisions of the High Court (Chancery Divison) as well as appeals which arise from those decisions.

Below the page heading is the name of the case. The topic of case names is discussed more fully at p. 77, but since this case involves an appeal, it is reasonable to assume that the appellant's name comes first, followed by the respondent's. One odd aspect of this particular case-name is that the respondent is given as *Fraser* (who, according to the report, was the secretary of the building society) rather than as being the building society itself. The report does not explain this, but since nothing turns on this detail we can safely ignore it.

1892 March 3, 26

These are the dates on which the court dealt with the case. The fact that two dates are given (March 3 and 26) suggest that the case was heard on the earlier date but the court did not give its judgment immediately, preferring to give careful consideration to the arguments which it had just heard. This is confirmed at the start of Lord Herschell's judgment (towards the foot of p. 30 of the report) where the law reporter expressly identifies March 26 as the date of the judgment. The technical way of describing what is happening when this kind of delay occurs is to say that the court *reserves judgment*. Headnotes sometimes indicate that judgment was reserved by including the abbreviation *cur adv vult*. This represents the Latin phrase *curia advisari vult*, which translates literally as *the court wishes to be advised*, although, in reality, the court will be advising itself rather than seeking any outside assistance.

Lord Herschell, Lindley and Kay, LJJ

These are the names of the judges who decided the case. (The abbreviations of judicial titles are explained in Chapter 4.)

Contract by Letters – Acceptance of Offer by Post – Time of Acceptance – Withdrawal of Offer.

These are the catchwords (which are sometimes known as the keywords). They provide a very general idea of what the case is about. They seldom extend beyond three or four lines, and they always appear in italics.

The reporter's summary of the case comes next and is the part of the headnote which you will find most useful. In this case, the headnote is fully narrative. (The three possible styles of headnote are explained at p. 81.) This headnote is unusual because it contains two summaries of the facts, with the second being a little more detailed than the first. It is much more usual for the law reporter to decide which facts are worth including and then include them in a single summary.

H, who lived at Birkenhead, called at the office of a land society in Liverpool, to negotiate for the purchase of some houses belonging to them. The secretary signed and handed to him a note giving him the option of purchase for fourteen days at £750. On the next day the secretary posted to H a withdrawal of the offer. This withdrawal was posted between 12 and 1 o'clock, and did not reach Birkenhead till after 5 p.m. In the meantime H had, at 3.50 p.m., posted to the secretary an unconditional acceptance of the offer, which was delivered in Liverpool after the society's office had closed, and was opened by the secretary on the following morning:

Held, that where the circumstances under which an offer is made are such that it must have been within the contemplation of the parties that, according to the ordinary usages of mankind, the post might be used as a means of communicating the acceptance of it, the acceptance is complete as soon as it is posted.

Held, that in the present case, as the parties lived in different towns, an acceptance by post must have been within their contemplation, although the offer was not made by post.

Held, that a revocation of an offer is of no effect until brought to the mind of the person to whom the offer was made, and that therefore a revocation sent by post does not operate from the time of posting it.

Held, therefore (reversing the decision of the Vice-Chancellor of the County Palatine), that a binding contract was made on the posting of H's acceptance, that the revocation of the offer was too late, and that H. was entitled to specific performance.

IN 1891 the Plaintiff was desirous of purchasing from the Huskisson Benefit Building Society certain houses in Flamank Street, Birkenhead. In May he, at the office of the society in Chapel Street, Liverpool, signed a memorandum drawn up by the secretary, offering £600 for the property, which offer was declined by the directors; and on the 1st of July he made in the same way an offer of £700, which was also declined. On the 7th of July he again called at the office, and the secretary verbally offered to sell to him for £750. This offer was reduced into writing, and was as follows:–

"I hereby give you the refusal of the Flamank Street property at £750 for fourteen days."

The secretary, after signing this, handed it to the Plaintiff, who took it away with him for consideration.

On the morning of the 8th another person called at the office, and offered £760 for the property, which was accepted, and a contract for purchase signed, subject to a condition for avoiding it if the society found that they could not withdraw from the offer to the Plaintiff.

Between 12 and 1 o'clock on that day the secretary posted to the Plaintiff, who resided in Birkenhead, the following letter:

"Please take notice that my letter to you of the 7th instant, giving you the option of purchasing the property, Flamank Street, Birkenhead, for £750, in fourteen days, is withdrawn, and the offer cancelled."

This letter, it appeared, was delivered at the Plaintiff's address between 5 and 6 in the evening, but, as he was out, did not reach his hands till about 8 o'clock.

On the same 8th of July the Plaintiff's solicitor, by the Plaintiff's direction, wrote to the secretary as follows:-

"I am instructed by Mr. James Henthorn to write you, and accept your offer to sell the property, 1 to 17, Flamank Street, Birkenhead, at the price of £750. Kindly have contract prepared and forwarded to me."

This letter was addressed to the society's office, and was posted in Birkenhead at 3.50 p.m., was delivered at 8.30 p.m. after the closing of the office, and was received by the secretary on the following morning. The secretary replied, stating that the society's offer had been withdrawn.

> The procedural history of the case is given next, in very brief outline. The headnote of a more modern law report may well contain a more detailed procedural history, including, for example, dates of previous hearings. The procedural history is tedious and – in the vast majority of cases – of very little interest to anybody, least of all to students on academic courses.

The Plaintiff brought this action in the Court of the County Palatine for specific performance. The Vice-Chancellor dismissed the action, and the Plaintiff appealed.

Farwell, QC, and TR Hughes, for the appellant:

> The names of the advocates, and summaries of their arguments, come next. Both sets of advocates refer to the same cases but they construct different legal arguments based on those authorities. (For a list of the law reports which contain summaries of the advocates' arguments, see p. 80.) As Lord Herschell demonstrates here, judges are perfectly willing to interrupt advocates.

We say that a binding contract was made when the Plaintiff's letter of acceptance was posted: *Dunlop v Higgins* (1); *Harris's Case* (2); *Adams v Lindsell* (3). We do not dispute that, though

(1) 1 HLC 381 (i.e. reports of House of Lords before the introduction of the abbreviation *App Cas* – see below).
(2) LR 7 Ch 587 (i.e. reports of cases in the Court of Chancery, which is now the Chancery Division of the High Court, and which would now appear under the abbreviation *Ch*).
(3) 1 B & Al 681 (i.e. Barnewall & Alderson, the reporters who produced this series).

the option was given for fourteen days, it could be withdrawn within that time: *Dickinson v Dodds* (1); but if a binding contract is entered into, there cannot be a withdrawal. Where an acceptance is to be signified by doing some particular thing, as soon as that particular thing is done there is a contract: *Brogden v Metropolitan Railway Company* (2). Where it must be in the contemplation of the parties that an answer will be sent by post, the posting an acceptance makes a contract. In the case of *Household Fire and Carriage Accident Insurance Company v Grant* (3) it was considered that, according to the usages of mankind, an acceptance would be sent by post; and it was held that posting an acceptance made a contract, though the acceptance was never received. Here, as the parties lived in different towns, it was to be expected that the Plaintiff would post his answer. In *Byrne v Van Tienhoven* (4) a withdrawal was held too late which was not received till after the offer had been accepted, though it was posted before the acceptance; and so in *Stevenson v McLean* (5) it was held that a withdrawal of an offer was of no effect until it reached the other party.

Neville, QC, and PO Lawrence, for the Defendant:

We submit that the Vice-Chancellor has drawn a correct inference – that there was no authority to accept by post; and if that be so, the acceptance will not date from the posting. *Dunlop v Higgins* (6) went on the ground that it was the understanding of both parties that an answer should be sent by post. In *Brogden v Metropolitan Railway Company*, Lord Blackburn puts it on the ground "that where it is expressly or impliedly stated in the offer that you may accept the offer by posting a letter, the moment you post the letter the offer is accepted." It would be very inconvenient to hold the post admissible in all cases. Here, Liverpool and Birkenhead are at such a short distance from each other, that it cannot be considered that the Plaintiff had an authority to reply by post. If the offer had been sent by post, that would, no doubt, be held to give an authority to reply

(1) 2 ChD 463 (i.e. reports of the Chancery Division of the High Court, before the introduction of the current abbreviation *Ch*).
(2) 2 App Cas 666, 691 (i.e. reports of House of Lords' decisions which would still appear in the Appeal Cases reports but which would now be abbreviated to *AC*).
(3) 4 ExD 216 (i.e. reports of the old Exchequer Division of the High Court, which no longer exists).
(4) 5 CPD 344 (i.e. reports of the old Common Pleas Division of the High Court, which no longer exists).
(5) 5 QBD 346 (i.e. reports of the Queen's Bench Division of the High Court before the introduction of the current abbreviation *QB*).
(6) 1 HLC 381 (see above).

30   CHANCERY DIVISION   [1892]

by post; but the offer was delivered by hand to the Plaintiff, who was in the habit of calling at the Defendants' office, and lived only at a short distance, so that authority to reply by post cannot be inferred. The post is not prohibited; the acceptance may be sent in any way; but, unless sending it by post was authorized, it is inoperative till it is received. Suppose, immediately after posting the acceptance, the Plaintiff had gone to the office and retracted it, surely he would have been free.

[LORD HERSCHELL: It is not clear that he would, after sending an acceptance in such a way that he could not prevent its reaching the other party. Possibly a case where the question is as to the date from which an acceptance which has been received is operative may not stand on precisely the same footing as one where the question is whether the person making the offer is bound, though the acceptance has never been received at all. More evidence of authority to accept by post may be required in the latter case than in the former.]

Dickinson v Dodds (1) shows that a binding contract to sell to another person may be made while an offer is pending, and that it will be a withdrawal of the offer.

[LORD HERSCHELL: In that case the person to whom the offer was made knew of the sale before he sent his acceptance.]

Farwell, in reply.

At this point we leave the headnote and move on to the judgment itself. Lord Herschell begins by identifying the facts of the case. However, they are not all *material* facts. For example, the legal issue in this case does not depend on the location of the property or the precise times at which things happened (although the times would have been material if they were such that the building society had been able to communicate its withdrawal of the offer – and had in fact done so -- before Henthorn posted his acceptance). (*Material facts* are explained more fully at p. 96.)

1892. March 26. LORD HERSCHELL:

This is an action for the specific performance of a contract to sell to the Plaintiff certain house property situate in Flamank Street, Birkenhead. The action was tried before the Vice-Chancellor of the County Palatine of Lancashire, who gave judgment for the Defendants. On the 7th of July, 1891, the secretary of the building society whom the Defendants represent handed to the Plaintiff, in the office of the society at

Liverpool, a letter in these terms:- "I hereby give you the refusal of the Flamank Street property at £750 for fourteen days." It appears that the Plaintiff had been for some time in negotiation for the property,

(1) 2 ChD 463 (see above).

and had on two previous occasions made offers for the purchase of it, which were not accepted by the society. These offers were made by means of letters, written by the secretary in the office of the society, and signed by the Plaintiff there. The Plaintiff resided in Birkenhead, and he took away with him to that town the letter of the 7th of July containing the offer of the society. On the 8th of July a letter was posted in Birkenhead at 3.50 pm, written by his solicitor, accepting on his behalf the offer to sell the property at £750. This letter was not received at the Defendants' office until 8.30 pm, after office hours, the office being closed at 6 o'clock. On the same day a letter was addressed to the Plaintiff by the secretary of the building society in these terms: "Please take notice that my letter to you of the 7th inst. giving you the option of purchasing the property, Flamank Street, Birkenhead, for £750, in fourteen days, is withdrawn and the offer cancelled." This letter was posted in Liverpool between 12 and 1 pm, and was received in Birkenhead at 5.30 p.m. It will thus be seen that it was received before the Plaintiff's letter of acceptance had reached Liverpool, but after it had been posted. One other fact only need be stated. On the 8th of July the secretary of the building society sold the same premises to Mr Miller for the sum of £760, but the receipt for the deposit paid in respect of the purchase stated that it was subject to being able to withdraw the letter to Mr. Henthorn giving him fourteen days' option of purchase.

From Lord Herschell's summary of the facts, we can identify the following as being material: (1) the seller offered to sell certain property to the buyer, for a fixed price within a specified time; (2) the buyer accepted the offer, at the set price and within the time limit, using the post to communicate his acceptance; (3) before receiving the buyer's acceptance, the seller revoked the offer, once again using the post as the means of communication.

In the next part of his judgment, Lord Herschell turns to the legal issues in the case. The first issue concerns the revocation of the offer. By identifying a series of cases which establish that postal acceptance of an offer is effective as soon as it is posted, Lord Herschell explains why he thinks the same principle does not apply to postal revocations of offers.

If the acceptance by the Plaintiff of the Defendants' offer is to be treated as complete at the time the letter containing it was posted, I can entertain no doubt that the society's attempted revocation of the offer was wholly ineffectual. I think that a person who has made an offer must be considered as continuously making it until he has brought to the knowledge of the person to whom it was made that it is withdrawn. This seems to me to be in accordance with the reasoning of the Court of King's Bench in the case of *Adams v Lindsell* (1), which was approved by the Lord Chancellor in *Dunlop v Higgins* (2), and also with the opinion of Mellish LJ in *Harris's Case* (3). The

(1) 1 B & Al 681 (see above).
(2) 1 HLC 381, 399 (see above).
(3) LR 7 Ch 587 (see above).

32   CHANCERY DIVISION   [1892]

very point was decided in the case of *Byrne v Van Tienhoven* (1) by Lindley LJ, and his decision was subsequently followed by Lush J.

The grounds upon which it has been held that the acceptance of an offer is complete when it is posted have, I think, no application to the revocation or modification of an offer. These can be no more effectual than the offer itself, unless brought to the mind of the person to whom the offer is made.

Lord Herschell then turns to the second legal issue he has to settle, namely whether acceptance of an offer is complete once it is posted. This is quickly resolved by reference to the binding precedent of *Dunlop v Higgins*. However, there remains a sub-issue of whether the postal rule applies to all cases or only in particular circumstances. His Lordship concludes that authorisation was implied here because the parties lived in different towns and the offer was to remain open for several days. In other words, from that point onwards, it was too late for the offer to be revoked.

But it is contended on behalf of the Defendants that the acceptance was complete only when received by them and not on the letter being posted. It cannot, of course, be denied, after the decision in *Dunlop v Higgins* (2) in the House of Lords, that, where an offer has been made through the medium of the post, the contract is complete as soon as the acceptance of the offer is posted, but that decision is said to be inapplicable here, inasmuch as the letter containing the offer was not sent by post to Birkenhead, but handed to the Plaintiff in the Defendants' office at Liverpool. The question therefore arises in what circumstances the acceptance of an offer is to be regarded as complete as soon as it is posted. In the case of the *Household Fire and Carriage Accident Insurance Company v Grant* (3), Baggallay LJ said (4): "I think that the principle established in *Dunlop v Higgins* is limited in its application to cases in which by reason of general usage, or of the relations between the parties to any particular transactions, or of the terms in which the offer is made, the acceptance of such offer by a letter through the post is expressly or impliedly authorized." And in the same case Thesiger LJ based his judgment (5) on the defendant having made an application for shares under circumstances "from which it must be implied that he authorized the company, in the event of their allotting to him the shares applied for, to send the notice of allotment by post." The facts of that case were that the defendant had, in Swansea, where he resided, handed a letter of application to an agent of the company, their place of business being situate in London. It was from these circumstances that the Lords Justices implied an authority to the company to

(1) 5 CPD 344 (see above).
(2) 1 HLC 381 (see above).
(3) 4 ExD 216 (see above).
(4) *Ibid* 227.
(5) 4 ExD 218 (see above).

accept the defendant's offer to take shares through the medium of the post. Applying the law thus laid down by the Court of Appeal, I think in the present case an authority to accept by post must be implied. Although the Plaintiff received the offer at the Defendants' office in Liverpool, he resided in another town, and it must have been in contemplation that he would take the offer, which by its terms was to remain open for some days, with him to his place of residence, and those who made the offer must have known that it would be according to the ordinary usages of mankind that if he accepted it he should communicate his acceptance by means of the post.

> At this point Lord Herschell could have disposed of the case but chooses to make some additional comments about implied authorisation as the basis for acceptance of an offer by post. Since this discussion is not essential to the outcome of the case, it follows that they must be *obiter dicta*. (*Obiter dicta* are explained more fully at p. 94.)

I am not sure that I should myself have regarded the doctrine that an acceptance is complete as soon as the letter containing it is posted as resting upon an implied authority by the person making the offer to the person receiving it to accept by those means. It strikes me as somewhat artificial to speak of the person to whom the offer is made as having the implied authority of the other party to send his acceptance by post. He needs no authority to transmit the acceptance through any particular channel; he may select what means he pleases, the Post Office no less than any other. The only effect of the supposed authority is to make the acceptance complete so soon as it is posted, and authority will obviously be implied only when the tribunal considers that it is a case in which this result ought to be reached. I should prefer to state the rule thus: Where the circumstances are such that it must have been within the contemplation of the parties that, according to the ordinary usages of mankind, the post might be used as a means of communicating the acceptance of an offer, the acceptance is complete as soon as it is posted. It matters not in which way the proposition be stated, the present case is in either view within it. The learned Vice-Chancellor appears to have based his decision to some extent on the fact that before the acceptance was posted the Defendants had sold the property to another person. The case of *Dickinson v Dodds* (1) was relied upon in support of that defence. In that case, however, the plaintiff knew of the subsequent sale before he accepted the offer, which, in my judgment, distinguishes it entirely from the

(1) 2 ChD 463 (see above).

34   CHANCERY DIVISION   [1892]

present case. For the reasons I have given, I think the judgment must be reversed and the usual decree for specific performance made. The Respondents must pay the costs of the appeal and of the action.

> *Specific performance* is explained at p. 23.

Additional commentary on the report

Introduction
In addition to the commentary contained in the text boxes, a number of other points may usefully be made.

Material facts
We have already discussed the importance of deciding which facts are material (see p. 96). You will recall that a useful test of the materiality of a specific fact is to ask the question: 'If this fact had not been present, or had been different, would the outcome of the case still have been the same?' If the answer to this question is 'No', it follows that the fact is material.

In many cases, the materiality of one or more of the facts will often be the essential difference between the opposing advocates, as it is central to the technique of *distinguishing* other decisions (so that they are no longer binding on the court hearing the case). Applying this approach to the facts in *Henthorn v Fraser*, we can see that the fact that the property was in Flamank Street, Birkenhead, is immaterial. If the property had been in another street in Birkenhead, or for that matter in any other place in England or Wales, the outcome of the case would have been the same. Likewise, removing or varying the details of the postal transactions would not change the outcome of the case *unless* the changes of time were such that the building society had been able to communicate – and had in fact communicated – its revocation of its offer before Henthorn posted his acceptance. This would, of course, make the case significantly different *from a legal point of view* and therefore it helps us identify the materiality of the fact that the appellant had posted his acceptance of the offer before the respondent's revocation had reached him.

Ratio decidendi
The most difficult challenge when reading a law report is identifying the *ratio* of the case. The main reason for this difficulty is that when judges make statements of law in a judgment they are not expounding the law in general but are making qualified statements of law which are conditioned by the particular facts of the case. It follows that the descriptive *ratio* of a case will require both a consideration of the facts that the court determined material and any statements of law that the court articulated concerning these facts. Having completed both of these tasks in our analysis of Lord Herschell's judgment we can now turn to formulating the descriptive *ratio* of *Henthorn v Fraser* in the following paragraph.

Where a seller offers an option to purchase property at a fixed price, and agrees to keep the offer open for a specified time, the offer continues for the time specified or until any withdrawal is brought to the attention of the potential buyer. If, before it is revoked, the buyer accepts the offer using the post to communicate his acceptance, the contract is completed when the buyer places his acceptance in the post where (1) use of the post is impliedly authorised or (2) where the parties know, or ought to know, that post might ordinarily be used in such dealings.

This *ratio* is, of course, based only Lord Herschell's judgment, but since Lindley LJ explicitly concurs with Lord Herschell it represents the majority view in the case. On a cautionary note it is worth observing that identifying or formulating the *ratio* of a case is a matter of interpretation rather than a scientific task with a single correct answer. Much legal argument may turn on identifying the *ratio* of a particular case. At the same time, it cannot be denied, that the *ratios* of most leading cases are so well established that they are rarely questioned.

Obiter dicta
We have already noted (see p. 99) that *obiter dicta* (which are often called simply *dicta*) are never, strictly speaking, binding on later courts, but may be persuasive. However, as we also noted, it is seriously misleading to leave it at that. The truth of the matter is that *dicta* have widely varying degrees of weight, ranging from lightweight, mere throwaway, remarks at one end of the spectrum, to substantial and very strongly persuasive statements – so strongly persuasive, indeed, as to be practically binding – at the other end. In most cases, the weight of most *dicta* lies somewhere between these two poles, with the real weight of individual *dicta* not becoming apparent until they have been considered in later cases.

In *Henthorn v Fraser*, Lord Heschell's remarks on implied authorisation are clearly an attempt to clarify and develop the relevant law, and are a considered response to a point raised in argument by counsel for the appellants (p. 29 of the report), rather than being simply off the cuff. They can, therefore, reasonably be argued to be closer to – although by no means at – the 'practically binding' end of the spectrum of possible weights, rather than the mere 'lightweight throwaway' end.

Distinguishing
Lord Herschell concludes his judgment by *distinguishing* the case of *Dickinson v Dodds* (p. 33 of the report). When judges *distinguish* an earlier case they are simply saying that the case cited has no relevance to the

present case because its material facts were different. Lord Herschell had already indicated (p. 30 of the report) that he thought *Dickinson v Dodds* was distinguishable when he intervened in the respondent's arguments before the court. Closer consideration of both cases shows that two material facts in *Dickinson v Dodds* and *Henthorn v Fraser* were the same, because both cases involved a prospective buyer who was granted an option to purchase land and in both cases the owner of the land entered into a contract to sell the land to someone else before receiving the buyer's acceptance. However, the material fact which distinguishes *Dickinson v Dodds* from *Henthorn v Fraser* was that in *Dickinson v Dodds* (but not in *Henthorn v Fraser*) the prospective buyer knew about the contract to sell the land to the other person before he tried to accept the offer. It was this difference in the material facts which made the two cases essentially different, with the result that the earlier case was distinguishable (and was, therefore, not binding) in the later one. In fact, as Lord Herschell acknowledges (p. 30 of the report), even the judge at first instance could – and should – have distinguished *Dickinson v Dodds* on this basis.

Marginal markings and neutral citations
Some series of law reports use marginal markings, in order to make it easier to provide pinpoint citations, while others do not. The original report of *Henthorn v Fraser* contains no such markings, while the most common system in the 20th century was to provide marginal letters, evenly spaced down each page. The system of marginal letters worked reasonably well, but it was rather cumbersome for true pinpoint citations, which had to take a form such as 'page 234, letter D, line 3'. More importantly, this citation would vary from one set of law reports to another, according to the page numbering of the report in question.

The modern judicial practice (dating from 2001 and being an important part of the system of *neutral citation*, which is explained at pp. 82–83) is for official transcripts of judgments to number each paragraph. Since these numbers are part of the text, rather than depending on the page numbering of each series of reports, they can safely be relied upon, whichever series of law reports is being used. Unless judges use very long paragraphs, marginal markings are, therefore, superfluous in reports of modern cases.

Why not just read headnotes rather than full reports?
As we have just seen, a headnote contains formal details, such as the date or dates of the hearing and the names of the advocates, as well as the reporter's summary of the decision. One very good reason for reading the reporter's

summary is that it enables you to decide whether it is worth investing further time and energy in reading the decision itself. However, it is tempting to go beyond this, and simply read the summary as a substitute for reading the decision. The first of these reasons is perfectly respectable; the second is not.

Looking at the matter in more detail, there are two reasons why you should not rely unquestioningly on the summary part of a headnote as a substitute for reading the decision itself.

First, no matter how long and detailed it may appear to be, a headnote can only be a summary; and, therefore (although the standard of modern law reporting is almost uniformly very high), there is always the possibility that accuracy may have been sacrificed to brevity. (It is for this reason that some – but only a very few – purists insist on never reading the summary section of a headnote, preferring to decide for themselves exactly what a case is about and what it decides, rather than having their perception of these matters clouded by reading the reporter's version.)

Secondly, becoming a successful law student requires you to develop the skills of legal analysis and expression. One of the best ways of developing these skills is to undertake extensive reading of how the judges themselves analyse cases and express the results of their analyses, because this helps you to develop your sensitivity to the way in which judges function. Of course, having read a law report, it is only natural that you should write your own note, as an aid to remind you of what you have just learned, and this note will also be no more than a relatively brief summary. However, you will be using this note as a reminder of the understanding which you gained at the time, and you are very unlikely to have gained full understanding of a judgment which you have not read.

Nevertheless, it must be conceded that the advice given here is a counsel of perfection, and that many students do – at least from time to time – rely on headnotes. It must also be conceded that although using headnotes in this way – even in conjunction with your lecture notes and any other teaching materials you have been given – is bad practice, it is nevertheless preferable to never opening a law report at all. In short, therefore, it is up to you to decide whether you want to take the easy way out and, with luck, become a more or less adequate law student, or whether you want to become a good law student, in which case there is no alternative to doing things properly.

Returning specifically to *Henthorn v Fraser*, a minor inaccuracy may be found in the first line of the reporter's summary (p. 27), where reference is made to a 'land society'. Further study of the case shows that the body in question was, in fact, a 'building society'. While it seems that nothing turned on the precise nature of the prospective seller of the property in question, if you referred to a 'land society' when writing an essay, you would (without realising it) be betraying the very limited extent of your reading – which is not the best thing to communicate to anyone who is marking your work.

Conclusion

Having read the general discussion of the structure of a law report, together with both the excerpt from *Henthorn v Fraser* and the analysis of Lord Herschell's judgment, you should know how to identify the key elements in a report. Developing the skills of formulating the *ratio decidendi* of a case and assessing the weight of *obiter dicta* will not come quite so easily and will require perseverance and practice. Making your own notes on cases which you have read in full does, however, pay lasting dividends when it comes to preparing coursework and mooting, and – perhaps even more importantly – embarking on examination revision, because your notes will remind you of what *you* have read and know, rather than what someone else has said or written. More generally, reading law reports will also help you to develop your sensitivity to legal language and your skills of common law reasoning. The technique of answering problem questions (see Chapter 11) differs in degree rather than kind from the technique of judgment writing. Both involve identifying the material facts that give rise to the legal issues, selecting and applying the relevant law, and reaching a conclusion

Reading statutes

Introduction

We have chosen the Dealing in Cultural Objects (Offences) Act 2003 to illustrate many of the standard features of statutes because it is very short and does not require any prior knowledge of any other statutes.

The offences created by the Act have obvious similarities with the offence of dishonestly handling stolen property, knowing or believing it to be stolen, under the Theft Act 1968, but the new offence also applies to property which cannot be proved to have been stolen, as well as to events which occur abroad. It is relatively rare for an Act to have extra-territorial effect (or, in other words, to apply to events outside the United Kingdom). On the more restrictive side, when you read the Act you will see that it applies only to a relatively small class of objects.

The Dealing in Cultural Objects (Offences) Act 2003 and the boxed commentary
The presentation of the text of the Dealing in Cultural Objects (Offences) Act 2003 follows the same pattern as the presentation of the judgment in *Henthorn v Fraser* (pp. 110–119), with the text itself being punctuated with text boxes containing our commentary.

Dealing in Cultural Objects (Offences) Act 2003
2003 Chapter 27

CONTENTS

Section

An Act to provide for an offence of acquiring, disposing of, importing or exporting tainted cultural objects, or agreeing or arranging to do so; and for connected purposes.

This is the long title. It can be used to resolve ambiguities within the text of the Act. But if the meaning of the text of the Act is clear, that meaning must prevail over the long title: see *R v Galvin* [1987] 2 All ER 851.

[30th October 2003]

This is the date on which the Act received the Royal Assent, which means the date on which it was passed.

BE IT ENACTED by the Queen's most Excellent Majesty, by and with the advice and consent of the Lords Spiritual and Temporal, and Commons, in this present Parliament assembled, and by the authority of the same, as follows:-

> This is the standard enacting formula.

1 Offence of dealing in tainted cultural objects

(1) A person is guilty of an offence if he dishonestly deals in a cultural object that is tainted, knowing or believing that the object is tainted.

> The Act does not define *dishonesty* but the meaning of this word for the purposes of other offences involving dishonesty would probably be held to be so strongly persuasive as to be practically binding. The Act does, however, go on to define certain other key words.

(2) It is immaterial whether he knows or believes that the object is a cultural object.

(3) A person guilty of the offence is liable-
(a) on conviction on indictment, to imprisonment for a term not exceeding seven years or a fine (or both),
(b) on summary conviction, to imprisonment for a term not exceeding six months or a fine not exceeding the statutory maximum (or both).

> *Conviction on indictment* means conviction at the Crown Court. *Summary conviction* means conviction by a magistrates' court. The statutory maximum fine on summary conviction is £5000: see the Magistrates' Courts Act 1980.

2 Meaning of "tainted cultural object"

(1) "Cultural object" means an object of historical, architectural or archaeological interest.

Because the phrase *cultural object* and the word *tainted* have no obvious meanings, this section defines them for the purposes of this Act. As far as the words which are not defined are concerned, the court will have to fall back on the basic proposition that the meaning of an ordinary word of the English language is a question of fact: see *Brutus v Cozens* [1973] AC 854. The advocates may base their arguments on the meanings that certain words have in the context of other statutes, such as the meaning of *building* in the context of some environmental protection legislation. However, it is important never to lose sight of the proposition that the meaning of a word for the purpose of one statute will be no more than persuasive as to its meaning in the context of another statute: see *Carter v Bradbeer* [1975] 1 WLR 1204.

(2) A cultural object is tainted if, after the commencement of this Act-

The commencement of an Act is the date on which it comes into force. This may be – but hardly ever is – the date of the Royal Assent. For the commencement of this Act, see s. 6.

(a) a person removes the object in a case falling within subsection (4) or he excavates the object, and
(b) the removal or excavation constitutes an offence.
(3) It is immaterial whether-
(a) the removal or excavation was done in the United Kingdom or elsewhere,
(b) the offence is committed under the law of a part of the United Kingdom or under the law of any other country or territory.
(4) An object is removed in a case falling within this subsection if-
(a) it is removed from a building or structure of historical, architectural or archaeological interest where the object has at any time formed part of the building or structure, or
(b) it is removed from a monument of such interest.
(5) "Monument" means-
(a) any work, cave or excavation,
(b) any site comprising the remains of any building or structure or of any work, cave or excavation,

(c) any site comprising, or comprising the remains of, any vehicle, vessel, aircraft or other movable structure, or part of any such thing.

(6) "Remains" includes any trace or sign of the previous existence of the thing in question.

(7) It is immaterial whether-
(a) a building, structure or work is above or below the surface of the land,
(b) a site is above or below water.

(8) This section has effect for the purposes of section 1.

3 Meaning of "deals in"

(1) A person deals in an object if (and only if) he-

> In everyday English, the phrase *deals in* indicates commercial transactions. This section extends the meaning of the phrase beyond buying and selling, and (perhaps surprisingly) includes the giving and receiving of gifts.

(a) acquires, disposes of, imports or exports it,
(b) agrees with another to do an act mentioned in paragraph (a), or
(c) makes arrangements under which another person does such an act or under which another person agrees with a third person to do such an act.

(2) "Acquires" means buys, hires, borrows or accepts.

(3) "Disposes of" means sells, lets on hire, lends or gives.

(4) In relation to agreeing or arranging to do an act, it is immaterial whether the act is agreed or arranged to take place in the United Kingdom or elsewhere.

(5) This section has effect for the purposes of section 1.

4 Customs and Excise prosecutions

(1) Proceedings for an offence relating to the dealing in a tainted cultural object may be instituted by order of the Commissioners of Customs and Excise if it appears to them that the offence has involved the importation or exportation of such an object.

(2) An offence relates to the dealing in a tainted cultural object if it is-
(a) an offence under section 1, or
(b) an offence of inciting the commission of, or attempting or conspiring to commit, such an offence.

(3)   Proceedings for an offence which are instituted under subsection (1) are to be commenced in the name of an officer, but may be continued by another officer.

(4)   Where the Commissioners of Customs and Excise investigate, or propose to investigate, any matter with a view to determining-
(a) whether there are grounds for believing that a person has committed an offence which relates to the dealing in a tainted cultural object and which involves the importation or exportation of such an object, or
(b) whether a person should be prosecuted for such an offence,
the matter is to be treated as an assigned matter within the meaning of the Customs and Excise Management Act 1979 (c. 2).

(5)   Nothing in this section affects any powers of any person (including any officer) apart from this section.

(6)   "Officer" means a person commissioned by the Commissioners of Customs and Excise under section 6(3) of the Customs and Excise Management Act 1979.

After this Act was passed, the Commissioners for Revenue and Customs Act 2005 merged the functions of the *Commissioners of Customs and Excise* with those of the *Commissioners of Inland Revenue* to create the *Commissioners for Her Majesty's Revenue and Customs* (or *HMRC* as they are commonly known). The 2005 Act also created the office of the Director of Customs and Excise Prosecutions. Although the original text of the 2003 Act is reproduced here, Schedule 4 to the 2005 Act enacts a number of technical amendments to this text (along with the texts of many other statutes) to reflect the scheme which it introduces.

5 Offences by bodies corporate

(1)   If an offence under section 1 committed by a body corporate is proved-
(a) to have been committed with the consent or connivance of an officer, or
(b) to be attributable to any neglect on his part,
he (as well as the body corporate) is guilty of the offence and liable to be proceeded against and punished accordingly.

(2)   "Officer", in relation to a body corporate, means-
(a) a director, manager, secretary or other similar officer of the body,
(b) a person purporting to act in any such capacity.

(3) If the affairs of a body corporate are managed by its members, subsection (1) applies in relation to the acts and defaults of a member in connection with his functions of management as if he were a director of the body.

> Bodies corporate are organisations such as companies, local authorities, professional bodies and learned societies. Subsection (3) is most likely to be relevant to some learned societies.

6 Short title, commencement and extent

(1) This Act may be cited as the Dealing in Cultural Objects (Offences) Act 2003.
(2) This Act comes into force at the end of the period of two months beginning with the day on which it is passed.
(3) This Act does not extend to Scotland.

> The short title of an Act is a useful label by which it can be known. However, it should be regarded as no more than an approximate guide to the contents of the Act, because it may be too short to be entirely accurate: *Re Boaler* [1915] KB 21. Acts of Parliament may or may not become law in Scotland. This one does not extend to Scotland because its subject matter lies within the scope of the powers which have been devolved to the Scottish Parliament.

Additional commentary

Introduction
In addition to the comments contained in the text boxes, the following comments will help you when you start to read other statutes.

Interpreting the Act generally
Since the Act creates criminal offences, whenever there are two or more possible meanings, the defendant will seek to rely on the presumption of strict interpretation, in order to get the benefit of the meaning which is most favourable from his or her point of view. (See p. 101.)

When identifying the purpose of the Act, regard may be had to the Explanatory Notes which accompanied the Bill (which became the Act) during its progress through Parliament. Explanatory Notes are available at http://www.opsi.gov.uk/.

Headings and marginal notes
As you have seen in the Dealing in Cultural Objects (Offences) Act 2003, sections may appear under headings (which are sometimes known as cross-headings). In longer and more complicated statutes, these headings may introduce groups of sections rather than every individual section. Additionally, until 2001, the statutory text was accompanied by *marginal notes* (also known as *side-notes* or *shoulder notes*), which, obviously enough, appeared in the margin. Although the use of marginal notes has now been discontinued, you will, of course, still encounter them in pre-2001 statutes. The question, therefore, arises as to their status in the process of interpretation.

The most recent, and most authoritative, answer to this question was given, unanimously, by the House of Lords in *R v Montila* [2005] UKHL 50, [2005] 1 All ER 113:

> [34] ... Account must, of course, be taken of the fact that these components were included in the Bill not for debate but for ease of reference. This indicates that less weight can be attached to them than to the parts of the Act that are open for consideration and debate in Parliament .... One cannot ignore the fact that the headings and sidenotes are included on the face of the Bill throughout its passage through the legislature. They are there for guidance. They provide the context for an examination of those parts of the Bill that are open for debate. Subject, of course, to the fact that they are unamendable, they ought to be open to consideration as part of the enactment when it reaches the statute book.
> [35] ... It has become common practice for their Lordships to ask to be shown the explanatory notes when issues are raised about the meaning of words used in an enactment.
> [36] The headings and sidenotes are as much part of the contextual scene as these materials, and there is no logical reason why they should be treated differently.

Schedules
Many longer and more complicated statutes conclude with schedules. Whether there are schedules (and if there are, what goes into them) is a matter of style. However, in general terms, it can be said that schedules generally contain details that are unlikely to change very often. For example, a statute which creates a new public body may well state its function in the

main part of the text, with the detailed arrangements for the appointment and removal of members being put in a schedule. This arrangement makes the statute much easier to read, since the reader can grasp the overall scheme first, without having to wade through a mass of detail which can be read as and when it is necessary to do so. It follows, therefore, that schedules are integral parts of the statutes in which they appear, and must be interpreted as such. (*Attorney-General v Lamplough* (1878) 3 ExD 214.)

In passing, it may be worth mentioning that some other kinds of detail may well appear in delegated legislation (see p. 24), rather than in the statute itself. It is impossible to lay down hard and fast rules as to what sort of details should be left to delegated legislation. However, experience shows that details which are likely to change relatively frequently (such as fees payable to public bodies by users of their services) and details which can be finalised only after extensive consultation (such as the layout and precise contents of prescribed forms) are best enacted in this way. (The alternative would be to pass an amending statute every time a fee was increased to take account of inflation, or delaying the enactment of the statute until the last practical detail had been settled, or both.)

For a much more detailed treatment of the principles of statutory interpretation, see, for example, McLeod, *Legal Method*, 6th edn 2007, Palgrave Macmillan.

Conclusion

The skills involved in reading law reports and statutes need to be learned and practised. Both sets of skills require careful and analytical reading of the relevant texts, but both also involve a degree of creativity in developing arguments based on those texts.

When reading cases, it is always important to identify the material facts, so that you can analyse the judgments in terms of the concepts of *ratio decidendi* and *obiter dictum*. When reading statutes, the context within which the words are used is always of great importance.

9 Written English

All writing is an attempt to communicate something to the reader. If your writing is to be effective, you must make your meaning plain. Following the appropriate conventions of grammar, punctuation, spelling, and style, will all help improve the clarity of your writing. One important by-product of any improvement you achieve is that your marks will be better than they would otherwise be.

Introduction

Written English can be used in a wide variety of contexts, with equally widely varying degrees of formality. An example drawn from one end of the scale would be a simple note to remind yourself of something you need to do (in which more or less anything goes, including, for example, abbreviations which only you would understand, and from which grammar may be wholly absent). At the other end of the scale there are instruments such as wills and Acts of Parliament where a very high degree of formality is appropriate. Between the two extremes, there are of course many intermediate stages.

This chapter is about writing English in the relatively formal context of academic work. Many readers of this book will have highly developed skills in written English; but experience shows that there will be many others who lack the ability to express themselves clearly and accurately when writing formal English. Unfortunately, experience also shows that the latter category not infrequently includes students who embark on degree-level study with good A-level grades behind them, as well as students on postgraduate conversion courses whose degrees did not require much, if anything, in the way of essay writing in either coursework or examinations.

This chapter, therefore, provides a basic survival guide to the standard conventions of grammar, punctuation and spelling which will usually be expected when you are writing law essays and examination answers, together with some guidance as to the kind of style which will be appropriate. However, before turning to the substance of these topics, it must be conceded that those readers who have the greatest need to improve their written English are likely to find that a good deal of hard work is required. Nevertheless, these readers can be confidently assured of three things. First, the craft of good, formal writing can be learned by anyone who is prepared to work sufficiently hard at it. In the words of Alexander Pope, in his *Essay on Criticism*:

> True ease in writing comes from Art not Chance,
> As those move easiest who have learn'd to dance.

Secondly, once the craft has been learned, its practice becomes very largely automatic. Thirdly, the effort of learning how to write formal English well will not be wasted. As Dr Johnson put it, 'what is written without effort is in general read without pleasure'. From the student's perspective, of course, there is the additional – and not unimportant – point that material which is written in a way that pleases the examiner is likely to be rewarded with a higher mark than the less appropriately written offerings of other students.

Two problems face anyone who tries to teach people how to write formal English well. First, they lay themselves open to the charge of linguistic (and even cultural) fascism. After all, conventions of grammar, punctuation, spelling and style all change with the passing of time. Moreover, it is in the nature of things that most of those who teach and examine are likely to be older than most of those whom they are teaching and examining. Therefore, while it is reasonable to ask why the conventions which examiners absorbed – perhaps twenty, thirty or even forty years ago – should be regarded as being more appropriate than those absorbed much more recently by their students, the psychological fact of the matter is simply that many examiners do tend to see things this way. And wise students will accept this fact as being one which they cannot change. More particularly, as we have already said, pleasing the examiner is likely to pay dividends in terms of marks. Furthermore, as you move out of the world of education and into the world of employment, many of the people under whom you will be working will share the expectations which your examiners had.

Secondly, those who provide guidance as to what constitutes good, formal writing always put themselves at risk of being criticised for failing to follow their own prescriptions. In this case it is the teachers who are called upon to display wisdom by accepting that they are unlikely to maintain the highest standards all the time. However, few teachers should object to having their shortcomings drawn to their attention, since it is only capable students who will be able to do this; and there are few things more gratifying than teaching capable students.

Before we proceed to the substance of grammar, punctuation, spelling and style, it will be well worthwhile to introduce the *mongoose principle*, which will provide you with the solution to many of the problems you will encounter when writing formal English.

The mongoose principle

The mongoose principle takes its name from an old story about a customer who wrote to a pet shop:

Dear Sirs,

Please send me two mongooses.

Yours etc.,
A. Customer.

However, on reading the letter over, the writer felt that perhaps the plural of *mongoose* was not *mongooses*, and accordingly tore the letter up and wrote the following:

Dear Sirs,

Please send me two mongeese.

Yours etc.,
A. Customer.

After a few more moments of thought, the writer felt that perhaps this was not right either, and accordingly tore this letter up as well, before writing the following:

Dear Sirs,

Please send me one mongoose.

Yours etc.,
Customer.

PS: On second thoughts, make it two.

The *mongoose principle*, therefore, states: *if in difficulty or doubt, rewrite it.* The principle provides a simple solution to many problems and you ignore it at your peril.

Sentence structure

Simple sentences

Reduced to an absolute minimum, a sentence must have a *subject* and a *finite verb*. The subject is the person or thing who (or which) does something and the verb is what is being done. The basic form of a verb is the *infinitive*, which (as the word suggests) is *unfinished* or *open-ended*. In English, infinitives begin with *to* – for example, *to eat, to live, to sleep, to walk*. We will return to infinitives at p. 158, where the question will be whether they should or should not be split, but we are introducing them here in order to explain that, by way of contrast, the *finite* forms of a verb are no longer open-ended but have been *finished* in the sense that they show when something is (or was or will be) done. In other words the verb will have a *tense*, which will place the action in the present, the past or the future. Take the following example:

The boy rode.

Here the subject (the boy) did something (rode) in the past. If we had used the infinitive (to ride) we would have produced something which is unfinished to the point where it is nonsense:

The boy to ride.

On the other hand, we could have used the finite verb in other tenses and said, for example

The boy rides,

or

The boy will ride.

The first, third and fourth examples are very simple sentences, but we could make them more complicated by saying, for example

The boy rode a bicycle.

In this example, we have added an *object*. In grammatical terms, the word *object* simply signifies the person or thing to which the activity of the verb is done.

Another common form of sentence has no object but does have a *complement*. For example, in the following sentence *round the block* is the complement:

The boy rode round the block.

In English, unlike many other languages, the order of the words is crucial. The following two sentences use exactly the same words but mean fundamentally different things.

The boy killed the girl.
The girl killed the boy.

The basic principles to remember about simple sentences are:

- they begin with a capital letters (even when the first word is not the name of a person or a place);
- they have a finite verb;
- the order of the words determines the meaning of the sentence; and
- the subject and the verb must *agree as to number.*

Your response to these four points may be that you have no problem with the first three, but that you do not understand the fourth one. In fact, the fourth one has a very clear meaning: it is simply expressed in technical language. All it means is that if the subject is singular, the verb must also be singular; and if the subject is plural, the verb must also be in the plural. Most people find that, most of the time, they instinctively use language in such a way as to satisfy this need for agreement. So (leaving aside some dialect usages) most people would not have to think about any matters of grammar before saying

the boy was riding

rather than

the boy were riding;

or

the boys were riding

rather than

the boys was riding.

However, some words present a very common source of error in relation to agreement between subject and verb. Test yourself on the following two sentences:

There are a number of reasons why you should read this book.
There is a number of reasons why you should read this book.

Many people feel, intuitively, that the first version is correct on the basis that the plural *reasons* requires the plural verb *are*. As a matter of strict grammar, however, the second version is correct because it is the singular *number* which governs the verb, which is, therefore, also required to be in the singular. In fact, so many people would instinctively use the first version that you may wish to say that it constitutes an exception to the rule that a singular subject requires a singular verb. However, if you make this assertion implicitly by simply following this usage in your written work, you will be adopting a high-risk strategy. Some of your readers may have a stricter view of grammar that will lead them to conclude that you are writing ungrammatically as a result of ignorance. If you feel that the grammatically correct version sounds awkward, but you wish to avoid the grammatically incorrect version, the solution lies in the mongoose principle: rewrite your sentence. Nobody could object to

there are many reasons why you should read this book.

Therefore, rewriting it in this way will offend nobody, while avoiding a form of words which sounds awkward, and without having had to complicate your expression or compromise your meaning in any way.

A second trap for the unwary when making subjects agree with their verbs as to number is the apparently innocuous word *none*. Once again, test yourself on the following two sentences.

None of them were right.
None of them was right.

Many people would happily use the first version; and, if they heard it, would feel intuitively that it is grammatically correct. However, as with the previous example, this is an illusion. As a matter of strict grammar, the second example is preferable. The explanation is that, once again, people are misled by a grammatically irrelevant plural (in this case *them*), and have overlooked the fact that the grammatically relevant *none* originated as a shortened version of *not one* and is, therefore, singular. Of course, if you feel the grammatically correct version sounds awkward or pedantic, the answer is simple: remember the mongoose principle and write:

They were all wrong.

The final commonly encountered difficulty with singulars and plurals arises from *collective nouns*. These are singular in form but nevertheless refer to a number of people or things. Examples of collective nouns include *army*, *jury*, and *team* (each of which consists of a number of members), as well as companies and local authorities such as *Marks and Spencer* and *Camden London Borough Council* (which consist, respectively, of all the shareholders and all the councillors).

The basic principle is that either a singular or a plural verb may be used, provided internal consistency is maintained. So, for example, the following are both equally acceptable:

When the army comes home, it will be welcomed by the local community.

When the army come home, they will be welcomed by the local community.

However, it would be wrong (because it would be internally inconsistent) to say either of the following:

When the army comes home, they will be welcomed by the local community.

When the army come home, it will be welcomed by the local community.

This freedom of choice is limited in some cases, where the crucial issue is whether the collective noun is being used to identify a single entity, or as shorthand for all the members of the group. So, for example, the following are both wrong:

The family are an important social unit. (The *are* must be replaced by *is*.)

My family is the kindest people I know. (The *is* must be replaced by *are*.)

Finally, collective nouns which refer to inanimate objects (such as *cutlery*, *crockery* and *luggage*) are always singular. For example, it is correct to say:

the cutlery is in the drawer

and wrong to say

the cutlery are in the drawer.

Compound sentences

Simple sentences are all very well. They can convey meaning perfectly adequately. But they quickly become tedious to read. A succession of simple sentences will not please your examiners. Therefore you must be able to write compound sentences, consisting of two (or more) clauses, both (or all) of which could stand as simple sentences; or, in other words, both (or all) of which are main clauses. For example:

John rode his bicycle but Janet drove her car.

When writing compound sentences, you need to be careful with your use of the *joining* words (or *conjunctions*) which you use to link the two clauses. The most common are

- and;
- or;

and

- but.

The use of *however* presents a difficulty. Technically, it is an adverb and not a conjunction, although in *informal* communication this distinction is often lost and it tends to be used as a conjunction. For example, *I missed my train, however I still got home on time.* Clearly, in contexts such as this, *however* is being used interchangeably with *nevertheless*, and it is unlikely that anyone with any knowledge or intuition of grammatical convention would write *I missed my train, nevertheless I still got home on time*, without breaking it into two sentences. Bearing in mind, therefore, that this chapter is concerned with *formal* usage, our advice must be to avoid using *however* as a conjunction. This leaves you with a straightforward choice. The first possibility is to use a genuine conjunction:

I missed my train but I still got home on time.

Alternatively, you could retain *however* but use use two simple sentences

I missed my train. However, I still got home on time.

(The use of the comma after *however* in the second example is explained at p. 148.)

There is an old-fashioned 'rule' that *and* and *but* cannot properly be used to begin sentences, because (being conjunctions) their function is to join clauses together. Like many other 'rules', this one is based on a sound principle. However, also like many other 'rules', this one can be applied too strictly. The occasional use of *and* and *but* as opening words can be very striking. For example:

He was handsome. And I do mean handsome.

Similarly:

She had only one talent. But what a talent it was.

You will relatively seldom need such rhetorical devices in academic writing, but the possibility is worth noticing. In any event, of course, such usage may occasionally be justified on the ground of variation of sentence structure.

Just as *compound* sentences are one stage on from *simple* sentences, so *complex* sentences are one stage on from *compound* sentences. It is, therefore, to complex sentences that we now turn.

Complex sentences

Like *compound* sentences, *complex* sentences consist of at least two clauses. However, the distinction between the two categories lies in the fact that compound sentences contain two (or more) main clauses, while complex sentences contain a main clause and at least one *subordinate* clause. For example:

John rode the bicycle *that his parents had given him for his birthday*.

In this example, the words *his parents had given him for his birthday* could not stand as a sentence on their own and therefore they cannot be a main clause. To put it another way, they are dependent upon, or *subordinate to*, the main clause. At a functional level, they provide the reader with more information about the topic that is the subject of the main clause.

Subordinate clauses are introduced by a sub-group of words known – for obvious reasons – as *subordinating conjunctions*. The most common examples include:

after	once	until
although	since	when
as	than	where
because	that (*or* which)	whereas
if	unless	while

As a footnote to this list, it must be said that if you read more detailed discussions of grammar than we have space for here, you may well find extensive discussion of the uses of *that* and *which*. For our purposes, however, we need say no more than that, in practice, they are both widely used interchangeably as subordinating conjunctions. (Try seeing how the grammar-check on your word-processing programme treats these two words. You may well find that it wants you to use *that* much more often than *which*. There is nothing intrinsically wrong with this, but if writing is to be more than a mere mechanical exercise, and provided the basic conventions are respected, some scope for individuality is a good thing.)

Spelling

Introduction
It is widely believed that English spelling is an arbitrary mish-mash, devoid of principles. However, according to David Crystal, a leading academic authority on the English language, it has been estimated that

- only about 3% of commonly used English words have spellings which are so divorced from principle that they must simply be learned;
- the spellings of over 80% of words are regular (in the sense of conforming to established patterns); and

● whether the spelling of the remaining 15% or so of words can be said to be regular is open to discussion. (See *The Cambridge Encyclopaedia of the English Language*, Cambridge University Press, 2nd edn, 2003, p. 272.)

However, everyday users of language (as distinct from those skilled in the science of linguistics) may understandably remain unconvinced. Take, for example, what is probably the best known 'rule' of English spelling: *i before e except after c*. While this 'rule' undoubtedly helps you with the correct spelling of words like *believe, relieve, conceive, deceive,* and *receive,* it equally clearly has no application to words such as *ancient, conscience, efficient, science* and *society,* not to mention *eight, either, foreign* and *heir*. Of course, linguistics (like law) is a complex subject, and specialists in spelling will formulate and qualify their rules in such a way that they can identify regularity of spelling in many cases where it is not apparent to the untrained eye. All of which means that readers who find English spelling confusing are in a difficult position.

Two practical suggestions

Since this is not the place to launch forth upon a detailed discussion of the complex rules of spelling to which, according to Crystal, at least 80% of words conform, only two practical suggestions can be made.

First, the best way of learning how to spell is simply to read good writers carefully and learn from their example. Secondly, if this seems too haphazard, or your tastes are such that you seldom, if ever, read good writers, you may simply have to learn the correct spellings of a number of words which are commonly spelt incorrectly.

In terms of law, few things annoy examiners more than students who are unable to spell words which they should have read dozens, if not hundreds, of times. The following is a non-exhaustive list of common errors:

arguement (for *argument*),
contractural (for *contractual*),
defendent (for *defendant*),
enviroment (for *environment*),
goverment (for *government*),
interpretate (for *interpret*),
Parliment or *Parlament* (for *Parliament*),
perogative (for *prerogative*),
president (for *precedent*),

priveledge (or something similar) for *privilege*,
sovreign (for *sovereign*),
Westminister (for *Westminster*).

In more general terms, the following words are commonly misspelt in various ways:

accommodate;
committee;
definitely;
discipline;
embarrass;
exaggerate;
excellent;
except;
gauge;
guarantee;
guard;
harass;
necessary;
occasion;
opportunity;
recommend;
separate;
succeed.

In ordinary usage, *judgment* and *judgement* are normally regarded as being straightforward alternative spellings, with the only requirement being that you should be consistent as to which one you use within a single piece of work. However, in legal usage, *judgment* is always used when referring to a decision of a court and therefore there is much to be said for adopting this version as your standard usage in all cases.

Two pairs of words which are commonly confused are *principle/principal* and *practice/practise*.

Principle can only be a noun, as for example, in *the mongoose principle*. Principal can be either a noun or an adjective. For example, *The principal of the college*, and *the principal reason for buying this book is to improve your study skills in law* are both correct.

Practice is a noun; *practise* is a verb. For example, you would talk about *a solicitor's practice*, but you would say *I used to practise criminal law*.

This distinction between the noun form and the verb form also appears in a number of other words, including *advice/advise* and *licence/license*. For example, you give someone *advice* when you *advise* them; and when you have a *licence* to do something, you are *licensed* to do it.

Initial capitals

Few people have any difficulty with using initial capitals for the names of people (such as *John Smith*), places (such as *London*), and the days of the week and the months of the year (such as *Monday* and *August*). However, many people do find difficulty when the words in question are institutions or offices.

Traditionally, the basic rule has been perfectly clear and straightforward. The key distinction lies in writing about institutions or offices generally and writing about specific examples of institutions or offices. In the former context, no initial capitals are used, while in the latter context they are. Applying this in practice, you would write 'all governments tend to ...' but 'the Government lost a vote of confidence yesterday'. Or, 'most twentieth century *prime ministers* said ...' but 'the *Prime Minister* said ... '

Clear though this distinction is, there is no doubt that it is much less commonly observed now than it used to be, with the result that many people (including journalists writing for what have traditionally been called 'quality newspapers') will happily write, for example, *act of parliament*.

Punctuation

Introduction

Once we have made the elementary observation that a full stop must be used at the end of a sentence, it is difficult to know how much detail needs to be mastered before you can be considered competent at punctuation. For the present purposes, we will be satisfied with a few comments on commas, semi-colons and colons, together with an explanation of the correct use of quotation marks, parentheses (or round brackets) and brackets (or square brackets) and, finally, apostrophes. However, no matter how brief the discussion may be, the importance of punctuation cannot be emphasised too strongly. Punctuation can change the meaning of a sentence, and can even enable the reader to make sense of the apparently meaningless.

One frequently quoted example of the extent to which punctuation can create different meanings from the same words is:

Woman without her man is nothing.

Punctuation can make this mean two quite distinct things:

Woman: without her, man is nothing.
Woman, without her man, is nothing.

For further classic illustrations of punctuation as the linguistic equivalent of the philosopher's stone, consider the following two sentences.

The condemned man walked round the yard three minutes after he was hanged.

What this means is, of course:

The condemned man walked round the yard: three minutes after, he was hanged.

Yet another example of punctuation giving meaning to a statement which is apparently absurd, may be found in an old piece of doggerel, which is often quoted (in slightly varying forms) by writers on punctuation, and which was cited by Sir Robert Megarry V-C in *Marshall v Cottingham* [1982] Ch 82. With no more than a final full stop by way of punctuation, the piece reads:

Every lady in this land
Hath twenty nails upon each hand
Five and twenty on hands and feet
And this is true without deceit.

When punctuated – and minor differences are possible but the following suggestion is perhaps the clearest – it reads:

Every lady in this land
Hath twenty nails: upon each hand
Five, and twenty on hands and feet;
And this is true without deceit.

Punctuation may even bring meaning to a text which not only appears to be plainly wrong (as in the previous example), but also to one which is apparently meaningless. The classic example here is the truly mind boggling:

Janet where John had had had had had had had had had had had the examiners approval.

Once this is understood to be a comment on how an exercise in written English had been marked, it becomes relatively easy to punctuate the comment itself as follows:

Janet, where John had had 'had had', had had 'had': 'had had' had had the examiner's approval.

Three variations are possible. Taking them in the order in which they appear in the sentence, there is, first, the point that double quotation marks could have been used instead of single ones. Secondly, either a semi-colon or a full stop could have been used instead of a colon, although if a full stop had been used, a capital letter would be needed immediately after it, to start a new sentence. Thirdly, *examiners'* would be correct if there were two or more examiners. We will come to each of these points, albeit in a different order, shortly.

Commas, semi-colons and colons

Commas divide sentences into different types of component parts. Commas are generally used to separate grammatical units (words, phrases or clauses) from each other, as the following examples show:

By the great, grey, green, greasy Limpopo river.

On the other hand, when Sherlock Holmes considered the case ....

I came, I saw, I conquered.

If you read any or all of these examples aloud, you will immediately notice that, in addition to separating the grammatical elements from each other, the commas also indicate slight pauses. If a slightly stronger pause is needed, a semi-colon would be appropriate. Thus there is a more declamatory, perhaps even dramatic, tone to:

I came; I saw; I conquered.

There is significant variation of usage of commas where some single words are used to start sentences. For example, in

Originally, punctuation formed no part of written English ....

many highly literate writers would omit the comma after *originally*, and many commentators would regard both usages as being acceptable. Of course, the point is not limited to *originally*, but applies equally to all adverbs – such as *fortunately, eventually, slowly*, and so on – which are often used on their own to begin sentences. (Most English adverbs end in *ly*, although, as the next example will show, *however* is a very common exception.) On the other hand, there are *apparently* similar sentences where the use of a comma would be quite simply wrong by anyone's standards. For example,

However hard I try to lose weight ....

simply cannot take a comma after *however*. But the people who would regard it as optional in the previous example would also regard it as being optional in, for example

However, I found that taking more exercise helped me to lose weight.

Since the comma after *however* will sometimes be essential, sometimes optional and sometimes wrong (depending on the sentence in question), it follows that the interests of both consistency of style and immediate clarity of meaning, will be served by using it even where it is optional. If you follow this practice consistently, the reader will know that when you have omitted it, you have done so intentionally; and this will help to make your meaning clear in these cases without requiring too much re-reading.

The colon is the strongest pause short of a full stop, with which, in some situations at least, it is practically interchangeable. So, reverting to a previous example, it would be perfectly acceptable to write:

He was handsome: and I do mean handsome.

Indeed, by way of an aside, and as an indication of the incremental nature of these things, once you have seen this sentence written with a colon, you may realise that it could also be written with a semi-colon instead (we have already noted this possibility in the case of the *had had* example):

He was handsome; and I do mean handsome.

You could even use a comma, although this would lose a significant part of the emphasis which the other versions convey:

He was handsome, and I do mean handsome.

If you try reading all three versions aloud, varying the weight of the pause on an increasing scale of comma, semi-colon, colon, you will see clearly that, in examples such as these, the usage you choose is a question of the effect you wish to achieve, rather than of being right or wrong.

Returning to the potential interchangeability (at least in some situations), of colons and full stops, it is important to sound a note of caution. More particularly, you should not take this potential interchangeability as a licence to join long lists of clauses into very long sentences. As we shall say again in the context of style (see p. 154), there is a useful rule of thumb to the effect that any sentence of more than about 20 words should be scrutinised carefully, to see whether it could not, with benefit, be broken down into two or more sentences.

There are two final points to make about commas. First, they can be used in pairs to divide off a word, phrase or clause which could be removed without affecting the essential meaning of the sentence. Where this usage is employed, the commas function in much the same way as parentheses – see p. 151 – but without making the printed page look so cluttered. The following examples of a word, a phrase and a clause show this use.

The best writers, however, use punctuation very carefully.

The best writers, but not necessarily run-of-the-mill hacks, use punctuation very carefully.

The best writers, which is a category that unfortunately does not include all students, use punctuation very carefully.

In each case, the main point of the sentence is simply that the best writers use punctuation very carefully.

The third point to be made about commas is, in some ways, a variation on the second; but isolating it into a category of its own is a useful way of emphasising its importance. Consider the following sentence:

Essays which must be sent to the external examiner must be in a form suitable for photocopying.

This could bear either of two meanings. First, inserting two commas gives:

Essays, which must be sent to the external examiner, must be in a form suitable for photocopying.

In other words, all essays have to be sent to the external examiner *and* they all have to be in a form which is suitable for photocopying. If this is what is meant, it should be rewritten as:

Essays must be sent to the external examiner and must be in a form which is suitable for photocopying.

The second possibility is:

Essays which must be sent to the external examiner, must be in a form which is suitable for photocopying.

In this case, inserting a single comma has changed the meaning so that those essays which have to be sent to the external examiner are the only ones that have to be in a form which is suitable for photocopying.
If this is what is meant, it should be rewritten as:

If an essay must be sent to the external examiner, it must be in a form which is suitable for photocopying.

Quotation marks
Quotation marks (also known as *inverted commas*, *speech marks*, or simply *quotes*) are principally used to indicate *direct speech*. In other words, they are used round the actual words that someone has said or written, as in the following example:

In passing sentence the judge said to the defendant: 'You are a thoroughly evil man'.

On the other hand, they are never used to indicate *indirect* (or *reported*) speech. Assuming that the previous example is a true account of what the judge said, it would be incorrect to write:

In passing sentence, the judge said that 'the defendant was a thoroughly evil man'.

If this form of expression is preferred, no quotation marks are used, and you would simply write:

In passing sentence, the judge said that the defendant was a thoroughly evil man.

As well as being used in relation to direct speech, quotation marks are sometimes used round well-known phrases, almost as if the writer is apologising for the cliché. For example:

He was a 'Sunday afternoon' motorist.

It was an 'eleventh hour' plea for clemency.

In all the examples given here, the quotation marks are single, but they could just as well have been double. It is simply a matter of taste. However, it is important that you are consistent in your use of whichever form you choose, and that where you have a quote within a quote, you use the other form. Pursuing the second point, both the following are, therefore, correct:

She said, "Whenever I hear 'to be or not to be' I think of my school days".

She said, 'Whenever I hear "to be or not to be" I think of my school days'.

If you wish to use a quote within a quote within a quote (and so on), you should simply keep alternating between the two types of quotation marks. However, there is a danger that readers may soon lose track of your meaning. Therefore, once you are tempted to go beyond a quote within a quote, it will usually be a good idea to recall the mongoose principle and rewrite what you are trying to say.

Finally, as we will see in Chapter 10, it cannot be emphasised too strongly that scrupulous use of quotation marks, in conjunction with proper referencing, is the key to avoiding allegations of that form of cheating which is called plagiarism.

Round brackets (or *parentheses*)

Words which are enclosed in round brackets (which are technically known as *parentheses*) are an aside or explanation which can be omitted without affecting the gist what is being said. For example:

The temperature today is 68 °F (20 °C), but tomorrow will be cooler.

This is, of course, the general principle underlying the proposition (which we encountered at p. 84) that where the citation of a journal or a law report contains a date in round brackets, the date is an optional part of the citation.

Square brackets

Words in square brackets are essential to the meaning of what is being written (which, again, explains the point about square brackets in the citation of journals and law reports). One common use of square brackets is to make a quotation meaningful. For example, a judge who has heard a large number of witnesses, including the claimant's husband and son, may say, 'I did not believe either of the claimant's first two witnesses'. Unless you know who these witnesses were and their place in the succession of witnesses, this conveys practically nothing. Therefore, in writing, you would say:

> The judge said, 'I did not believe [the claimant's husband or son]'.

Apostrophes

Apostrophes have two uses. They can indicate that a word is a contraction of two other words; and they can indicate a relationship of belonging. The second use is known as *the possessive*.

The first use may be illustrated by what are essentially contractions of two words into one, such as *don't* (for *do not*); *I'm* (for *I am*); and *isn't* for *is not*). Such usages need no further discussion here, because they are generally considered to be inappropriate in formal writing. (It must, however, be conceded, that this consensus is weakening rapidly. Nevertheless, we suggest that you adhere to it, on the simple ground that this will annoy no-one, whereas breaching it will certainly annoy some people.) If you want to test your eye for detail, you might like to try to find the one point in this book – apart from examples of the use and misuse of apostrophes – where we have used such a contraction.

Turning to the possessive use of apostrophes, the basic rules are:

- adding *'s* to a singular noun creates the possessive form (so *the girl's bicycle* means *the bicycle belonging to the girl*); and
- where a plural ends in *s* (as most English plurals do), adding the apostrophe on its own creates the possessive form, without the need for a further *s* (so *the girls' bicycles* means *the bicycles belonging to the girls*).

Where a singular noun ends in *s* (which is most likely to be the case where names (such as *Jones*) are concerned, either *'s* or an apostrophe on its own is acceptable: *Tom Jones' bicycle* or *Tom Jones's bicycle*). However, where a word ends with *ss*, the possessive form does require *'s*, as in *the boss's bicycle*.

The only possessive forms which do not use apostrophes are possessive pronouns, such as *his*, *hers*, *theirs* and *its*. These forms require no apostrophe because the possessive is built into the word itself. So, to take a single example, you would write *the bicycle was hers*, rather than *the bicycle was her's*.

Unfortunately, one aspect of the use and non-use of apostrophes in the context of possessives causes persistent and serious difficulty for many people. These people are tempted to apply the basic rule of adding *'s* to *it* when they wish to create the possessive form. However, this overlooks the point that, as we have just seen, with possessive pronouns the possessive form is built into the word itself (so that no apostrophe is needed). Using an apostrophe in an attempt to mean *of it* is doubly unfortunate because *it's* is a perfectly legitimate word in the context of informal English, where it is an example of the other type of use of apostrophes (namely contractions) and where it means *it is*. So if you write *the dog was playing with it's bone*, what you are really saying is *the dog was playing with it is bone*. This cannot be what you really meant.

Fortunately, the correct use of *it's* presents no difficulty provided you follow the advice to avoid all such informal expressions in academic work. If you do try to follow this advice, but carelessness nevertheless leads you to write *it's* in a first draft, you will know that it must be corrected (either by removing the apostrophe or by writing *it is*, depending on what you meant).

Vocabulary and style

Introduction
As a student doing a piece of academic writing, you will be hoping to make a favourable impression on your examiners. This section of this chapter will, therefore, provide some advice on how to increase your chances of doing so.

The need for formal style
Academic writing requires a formal style of expression. One crucial aspect of this is that you should not use anything which might reasonably be considered to be slang. Thus, for example, you might say

> The defendant was clearly somewhat inexperienced in the ways of the world.

But, even though it may mean much the same thing, you would never say:

The defendant was clearly a bit of a wally.

Similarly, as we saw at p. 152, it is best to avoid contractions such as *don't*, *I'm* and *isn't*. Avoiding these forms will not only add to the formality of your style, but will also avoid the errors which flow from the common inability to distinguish between *its* and *it's*. (If you never use the latter form, the distinction will never trouble you.)

On the other hand, you should never use any form of words merely because you think it 'sounds good'. A very common error of this sort is to say *prior to* when you mean *before*.

Finally, you would be unwise if you allow the requirement of formality to act as a straitjacket. Even in formal writing, good style requires variation in sentence structure, so that, for example, you use a mixture of simple, compound and complex sentences (see pp. 136–142).

The importance of clarity

As with any other form of communication, if you are to be effective you must make your meaning plain. You could do a great deal worse that follow H. L. A. Hart (the leading English legal theorist of the 20th century), who almost said (and the following version is slightly edited in order to emphasise the point) 'Where I am clearly wrong, I hope that I may at least be wrong clearly'.

One important contribution to achieving clarity is to keep your sentences fairly short. As we have already said at p. 149, there is a useful rule of thumb to the effect that the clarity of a sentence which contains more than 20 words can often be improved by breaking the sentence down into two (or more) separate sentences.

The pursuit of clarity is hard work and requires a talent for self-criticism. It is alarmingly easy to say something which you did not quite mean, as evidenced by the old story of a judge who had to pass sentence on a man who had trussed up a teenage boy like a chicken before sexually molesting him. Clearly outraged by the defendant's conduct, the judge began passing sentence by saying 'I should very much like to give you a taste of your own medicine'. Of course, in oral communication what has been said cannot be unsaid, although instant feedback can result in equally prompt clarification or correction. In the case of written communication, you will, equally obviously, lack the benefit of instant feedback, but provided you develop the ability to be self-critical, this may be counterbalanced by the opportunity to read over what you have written and thus avoid putting the faulty version into circulation in the first place.

Some forms of words repeatedly cause difficulty and are, therefore, best avoided altogether unless you are absolutely confident that you have mastered them. Three examples will suffice.

First, suppose you are given a *Subject Handbook* at the beginning of your course, which tells you that the course is being delivered through a programme of lectures and tutorials. Basically, there is to be one lecture and one tutorial each week but, because of the difficulty of having a tutorial before (or very soon after) the first lecture, there is to be no tutorial in the first week. This is a common situation and one which can be easily explained with perfect clarity. Unfortunately, it can also be presented very ambiguously as the following form of words shows:

There will be a lecture every week. There will be no tutorial in the first week, but there will be one in the second week and every other week after that.

Bearing in mind that you know there is to be a weekly tutorial, you will understand this to mean that there will be a tutorial *in the second week and in every week thereafter*. However, unless you already knew what it meant, you could reasonably interpret it as meaning that there will be a tutorial *in the second week and in alternate weeks thereafter*.

A second example is illustrated by the following sentence.

Smith is the second greatest goalkeeper in the world after Brown.

Does this mean that Brown is number one and Smith is number two; or that Brown is number one, followed by someone else who is the greatest goalkeeper after him, with Smith tagging along in third place? Most people would probably assume the first meaning is the intended one; but if this really is the intended meaning, the word *second* is superfluous. In order to avoid the doubt, it would be useful to invoke the mongoose principle and rewrite the sentence. There are two obvious possibilities, one of which requires only additional punctuation rather than true rewriting. The punctuation possibility merely requires the use of parentheses, to produce

Smith is the second greatest goalkeeper in the world (after Brown).

The rewriting possibility requires an almost equally light touch, namely the omission of the word *second*, to produce

Smith is the greatest goalkeeper in the world after Brown.

The third and final example involves the use of the word *only*, which causes repeated difficulties, as the following sentences show.

Only she imagined the threat was real. (This suggests that nobody else took the threat seriously.)

She only imagined the threat was real. (This suggests that there was no evidence to support her view that the threat was real.)

She imagined only the threat was real. (This suggests that she had been on the receiving end of something else as well as the threat – such as a promise – but that it was only the threat which she had taken seriously.)

Using the active and passive forms of verbs

The active form of a verb deals with *doing something*, while the passive deals with *something being done*. For example, the first of the following two sentences contains an active verb, while the second contains a passive one.

Janet drove the car.

The car was driven by Janet.

The classic advice is to use the active and avoid the passive wherever possible, because the active is both shorter and more direct. Unfortunately, there is a very long tradition among lawyers of using the passive as their standard style, which means you will have to make a special effort not to find yourself slipping into the same bad practice. However, the effort is well worthwhile for two reasons. First, the active genuinely is a more direct – and, therefore, better – means of communication in most cases. Secondly, habitual use of the active means that, on those occasions when you feel the passive would make your point more clearly, it will stand out much more effectively. The following two sentences show how the emphasis of a sentence can depend on whether the verb is used actively or passively.

Janet drove the car, while John rode the bicycle.

The car was driven by Janet, while the bicycle was ridden by John.

The first sentence emphasises the identities of the people, while the second emphasises the means of transport.

Gender-neutral language

It is now well established that formal writing should be composed in gender-neutral terms.

One way of doing this is to use *he or she* (or *she or he*), coupled with *his or her* (or *her or his*) as appropriate. However, many people feel this is unduly cumbersome.

Another frequently encountered solution is to write *s/he* (coupled again with *her or his*), but this has at least three disadvantages compared with *he or she* and *she or he*:

- it has no obvious pronunciation except for *ess stroke he*, which not only betrays its origins as a non-word but also has the additional weakness of leaving the masculine form as the only one which is recognisable, which in turn means that this formula is not quite gender-neutral;
- it leaves no choice as to whether the masculine or the feminine is placed first;
- it has no associated forms corresponding to *his or her* (or *her or his*).

Some people might add a fourth objection, namely that it is grossly inelegant, but this would be nothing more than a matter of taste.

Fortunately, applying the mongoose principle provides a very simple formula that will almost always avoid the problem: *write in the plural*. Thus

a student will receive his or her marks within three weeks of the end of the examination period

becomes

students will receive their marks within three weeks of the end of the examination period.

The rewritten version is not only simpler and more elegant than the original, but it also has the advantage of containing nothing which could offend anyone.

Some people take a halfway house approach to the plural solution, which produces:

a student will receive their marks within three weeks of the end of the examination period.

While this usage has a pedigree stretching far beyond the origins of political correctness (with examples being found even in the works of Shakespeare), its mixture of singular and plural forms (*a student* and *their*) nevertheless grates on many an educated ear and has nothing to recommend it over the straightforward plural solution.

Splitting infinitives

The infinitive form of a verb begins with *to*. For example, *to stop*, *to go*, *to love* and *to hate* are all infinitives. This raises a question of where you should place an adverb. For example, should you say *suddenly to stop*, *to suddenly stop*, or *to stop suddenly*? The traditional view is that both the first and the third can be correct, but the second one is always wrong. Whether or not you subscribe to the traditional view, it is probably wise to pretend that you do and develop the habit of avoiding split infinitives. The reason is simple: split infinitives do (rightly or wrongly) annoy many people, and it is never a good idea to annoy people (such as examiners) when you want to make a favourable impression upon them.

Unfortunately, however, considerable care is needed when avoiding split infinitives, because the alternatives can give rise ambiguity. Does *he decided to stop suddenly* mean that it was the *decision* or the *stopping* which was sudden? Of course, the mongoose principle can, as always, provide a solution. You could say either *he made a sudden decision to stop*, or *he made a decision to stop suddenly*, depending on your meaning. If you still detect a hint of ambiguity in the latter version, you could be even more explicit and say *he decided that stopping suddenly was a good idea*.

Conclusion

It is important to write English which is sufficiently formal to be appropriate to academic work, without being pretentious. Essentially, this requires you to follow the conventions of grammar, punctuation, spelling and style, while ensuring that your vocabulary avoids anything that might reasonably be considered to be slang.

If you ever encounter difficulty or doubt when writing anything, remember the mongoose principle: *if in difficulty or doubt, rewrite it.*

10 Answering Essay Questions

Essay writing is a distinctive form of communication which requires you to interpret the instructions you are given, undertake the relevant research and structure your answer according to the demands of the particular question. The presentation should follow accepted conventions of foot-noting, referencing and legal citation to assist the reader and avoid allegations of plagiarism or cheating.

Introduction

Writing, like speech, is a form of communication, an attempt to convey meaning. To be an effective communicator you have to speak or write in a way that the people who hear or read your words will understand; and therefore you have to ask yourself, 'who is my audience?'.

Most of the time, when you speak or write you will naturally use language which is appropriate for your audience. If you are chatting informally with friends you do not speak in the same way as you would if you were presenting a seminar paper in class or presenting an argument to the court. If you are writing a letter of complaint to a business organisation, you approach it quite differently from the task of writing a brief note to a boyfriend or girlfriend.

Much of the written work you produce as a student will be assessed and the audience will be your lecturers and tutors. Your language and style must both be appropriate to this academic context. This means that your arguments must not only be logical, coherent and supported by authority, but also that you must present them in an *impersonal* way.

Expanding for a moment on the need for impersonal presentation, a lawyer addressing a court would never say, 'I believe my client should win this appeal', but would adopt the more impersonal style of 'I submit that the law in this appeal is all in favour of my client', before going on to cite the authorities which would enable the court to agree. And you should present your essays in the same style. So, for example, if you consider an outcome to be unfair, you must construct an argument to show why it is unfair, drawing on examples from sources such as dissenting judgments and academic criticism of the relevant law. What you should never do is simply say 'I think this outcome is unfair'.

Clarity and accuracy should be your aims in all your writing, but these are not always easy goals to reach. As we saw (in Chapter 7), much legal wrangling concerns the interpretation of words, but as we then went on to see (in Chapter 9), you can improve the clarity of your work by developing good habits of linguistic style and following the standard conventions of grammar, spelling and punctuation.

If you have not written in this way before, you may find it an uphill struggle in the early stages of your studies. However, it is a skill you need to master, since you will find that until you can write in a coherent, academic style, the real merit of your arguments will often go unappreciated. Crucially, this will be reflected in your marks, because examiners cannot know whether a muddled piece of work represents clear understanding that has been poorly presented, or poor understanding that has been clearly presented. From the point of view of assessment, however, this distinction is unimportant, because neither will be given a good mark.

As well as being clear, your writing should follow a consistent system of footnoting and referencing. Your lecturers and tutors will probably have a preferred system and you may be obliged to use that. You must be rigorous in citing your sources and providing references to all the materials you have used when preparing your work. This is not only good academic practice in its own right, but is also essential if you are to avoid allegations of *plagiarism*, or to put it another way, *academic dishonesty*, or – to put it even more bluntly – *cheating*.

Cheating

Plagiarism, which is the most common form of academic dishonesty or cheating, is essentially the act of taking the work of another and passing it off as your own. The work of others can include their thoughts and inventions, but by far the most common form of plagiarism is using the words and ideas of others without proper acknowledgement. Increasingly, with the advent of the World Wide Web and word processing, students claim that written work is their own when, in fact, the work includes the words and ideas of others which are not acknowledged. Clearly, therefore, plagiarism is a form of theft, because plagiarists are dishonestly taking the work of others and using is as if it were their own. This is a serious matter for any student because, quite apart from any penalty which may be imposed by your college or university, the fact that you have been found guilty of dishonest conduct is likely to be mentioned in any reference which your college or university provides in connection with any applications you may make for jobs or for postgraduate study. It is particularly serious for students who intend to enter the legal profession, because findings of dishonesty will also be reported to the legal professions' governing bodies.

While every college's or university's regulations will reflect what has been said so far, we now move on to matters where there may be differences of terminology. However, the important thing to grasp is that whatever terminology your college or university adopts, they will still be talking about *cheating*. Some institutions simply give an extended meaning to the word *plagiarism*, to include what others would call something like *academic dishonesty*. Whatever it is called, we are now dealing with matters such as:

- falsifying or inventing material (for example, inventing case names);
- providing false information about a source you have quoted (for example, claiming to have used a later edition of a book than that which you actually used);
- copying other people's work or allowing them to copy yours (both of which are forms of what is sometimes known as *collusion*);
- failing to put direct quotations in *quotation marks* (also known as *inverted commas* or *speech marks*); and
- making only minor changes to the writings of others and then failing to acknowledge the source.

Three matters are worth particular emphasis.

First, the fact that using quotation marks and citing your sources will protect you from allegations of plagiarism must not be taken as an invitation to produce work which is simply a string of quotations, such as: *Smith says [quotation]. But on the other hand, Brown says [quotation], while Jones says [quotation]*; and so on. Dictionaries of quotations are one thing; essays are another.

Secondly, you may feel that you cannot improve on the way the leading judges and commentators have expressed complex ideas, and that you would be foolish to try to do so. The answer to this is twofold.

- It is implicit in what we have already said that there will undoubtedly be situations in which it is acceptable – and indeed, desirable – that you should use someone else's actual words. (Of course, when you do so – and we make no apology for repeating the most basic point of all – you must use quotation marks and cite your source. But, provided you do this, you may be demonstrating that you have the ability to identify the very core of the point which is being made, and that you possess the discernment to be able to identify a telling turn of phrase.)

- In situations where direct quotation is not appropriate, you may experience difficulty in putting things into your own words. More particularly, you may find it difficult to get far enough away from the original form of words to avoid plagiarism, while still saying substantially the same thing. While conceding that this can be difficult, we must also point out that it is at least part of the essence of the exercise, because expressing things accurately in your own words is one way in which you demonstrate that you really understand them. Moving to a more practical response, one very useful technique for dealing with this problem is to take notes from (but do *not* simply copy out) the original text. Then, a few days later, return to your notes and rewrite them into proper, polished prose. This two-stage removal between the original text and your own version will usually be enough to ensure that you are producing your own work in your own words.

Thirdly, you need to take particular care if you set your written work out in such a way that lengthy quotations are indented as blocks of text (as they are in this book, as well as in many others). You might assume that the fact of indentation is sufficient to indicate that you are quoting someone else; and, for everyday purposes, this assumption may well be sound. Nevertheless, if you rely solely on the fact of indentation, without the addition of quotation marks (which, once again, is the style adopted in this book as well as in many others), you run the risk that a particularly strict marker may decide that you are guilty of plagiarism. While you may succeed on appeal (assuming – which will not always be the case – that the members of the appeal committee are less strict than your original marker), you will find the mere fact of being subjected to the allegation is stressful. Additionally, the timescales for processing appeals can extend to many months in some colleges and universities. Apart from prolonging the exposure to stress, such delays can have serious consequences in terms of progression to the next stage of your studies and even, at final year level, in terms of graduation. Fortunately, the solution is simple. Whatever the prevailing fashion in the typographical design of books may be, all you have to do, in order to put your academic integrity beyond doubt, is to add quotation marks at the beginning and end of your indented quotations.

Fourthly, a particular difficulty arises in the context of discussing assessed coursework with other people. More particularly, there is always the danger that, once you enter such discussions, you will cross the line which divides the offence of collusion from the kind of legitimate discussion which is a healthy part of belonging to any academic community. Where coursework requires you to collaborate with others (for example, in group presentations or any other form of teamwork) there will, of course, be no problem, provided you limit your discussions to other members of your own group or team. However, in the much more common case where coursework is required to be an individual effort (or, in the case of group or team work where you are tempted to discuss the work with people from outside your own group or team), you need to be very much more careful.

Ultimately, in many cases the distinction between collusion and discussion is a matter of degree, but in practical terms a disciplinary panel must draw a line and decide on which side of that line your conduct falls. A useful test is to ask yourself whether the discussion provides you (or others) with ideas that you (or they) would not otherwise have had. Giving yourself a scrupulously honest answer to this question should enable you to avoid straying into the forbidden territory of collusion.

The most important piece of advice is simply this: make sure you

- know,
- understand, and
- follow

your college's or university's regulations in relation to all forms of cheating, whatever terminology they may use.

Having emphasised the importance of acknowledging your sources, we must now turn to the nuts and bolts of how you do this, and discuss the techniques of *referencing* and *footnoting*.

Referencing and footnoting

Referencing and footnoting your work should, as we noted in the introduction to this chapter, follow whatever guidelines your college or university provides. If you are given a choice of systems to follow, it is important that you follow your chosen system consistently.

We dealt at length with the citation of cases and statutes in Chapter 6. Here we will look at referencing books, articles and Internet resources using both the Oxford Standard Citation of Legal Authorities (OSCOLA, available at `http://denning.law.ox.ac.uk/published/oscola.shtml`) and Harvard systems (which, as we shall see in a moment, has no definitive form). OSCOLA, as the name suggests, is a comprehensive guide to legal citation, providing extensive guidance on matters well beyond footnoting and referencing. Many institutions use variants on OSCOLA or the Harvard schemes. For example, some colleges and universities use a variant on Harvard citation, recommending the use of double rather than single quotation marks for the title of a journal article, whereas other institutions advise using single quotation marks. The examples below follow the OSCOLA system precisely (which is possible, since a definitive version is available), and (since no definitive version exists) the British Standards Institution interpretation of the Harvard scheme (BS 5605:1990 *Recommendations for citing and referencing published material*). The OSCOLA system uses numbered footnotes and the OSCOLA illustrations in the citations below would appear consecutively numbered throughout the essay at the bottom of the relevant page. The Harvard system uses brief citations within the body text and provides the full citation in a reference list at the end of the work. An example of a short paragraph, which includes a direct quotation from a book, illustrates the different approaches. Taking OSCOLA first:

> When speaking of the *ratio decidendi* of a case it is tempting to think in terms of a fixed and single entity with an objective and continuing existence, which merely needs to be located and identified, just as a treasure hunter may seek to locate and identify a sunken wreck within a given area of the seabed. As we shall see in the remainder of this chapter, however, this model is seriously misleading.[1]

The Harvard system, on the other hand would produce:

> When speaking of the *ratio decidendi* of a case it is tempting to think in terms of a fixed and single entity with an objective and continuing existence, which merely needs to be located and identified, just as a treasure hunter may seek to locate and identify a sunken wreck within a given area of the seabed. As we shall see in the remainder of this chapter, however, this model is seriously misleading. (McLeod 2007 p. 148).

Whichever system of citation you use, the same basic information must be included. When citing books you need to include the author's name (or authors' names), the title of the book (in *italics*), the edition, publisher, place and date of publication and, if quoting directly from the work or referring to a specific point, the relevant page number. The OSCOLA system discourages the use of full stops and commas in citations and includes the full reference in a numbered footnote at the bottom of the page. This would be footnote 1 from the example given above:

1 McLeod, *Legal Method* (6th edn Palgrave Basingstoke 2007) 148.

The same citation using the Harvard system would not include the page number, since this is cited in the short reference in the main body of the text. The full reference would be included in a reference list at the end of the work and could be cited thus:

McLeod, I., 2007. *Legal Method*. 6th ed. Basingstoke: Palgrave.

The basic information for journal articles is the author's name (or authors' names), the title of the article (in single quotation marks) and the year, volume and page reference of the article. Most law journals have preferred abbreviations of the journal title. The OSCOLA system encourages the use of the standard abbreviations where possible. An example of an OSCOLA journal article citation, from the *New Law Journal*, is:

JR Spencer, 'Retrial for reckless infection' (2004) 154 NLJ 762

The Harvard citation for this article could use either the accepted abbreviation, as in the OSCOLA form, or the full title of the journal, with the latter appearing thus:

Spencer J. R., 2004. 'Retrial for reckless infection'. *New Law Journal* vol. 154, p. 762.

Internet resources often provide very little citable information and frequently disappear into cyberspace as quickly as they appeared online. Include the author (if identified), the title of the article or the title of the page, the URL and the date the resource was accessed. In OSCOLA this would be:

Richard Garner, 'Electronic tags used to beat the A-level cheats' *The Independent* (London 11 May 2007) <http://education.independent. co.uk/news/article2530771.ece> accessed 14 May 2007

A Harvard style citation could be:

Garner, R. (2007, 11 May) 'Electronic tags used to beat the A-level cheats' (*The Independent*), Available: http://education.independent. co.uk/news/article2530771.ece (Accessed: 2007, 14 May).

Footnoting and referencing, like grammar that follows standard conventions, makes your work easier to read. Inconsistent footnoting and referencing in your work will undermine your attempts to create a well-presented composition and give the impression that your work is the product of an erratic and disorganised mind. Finally, it is worth repeating that full referencing and citation is also fundamental to avoiding allegations of plagiarism.

Writing good law essays

Introduction
The focus of this chapter is on how to write coursework essays, but most of the discussion is also relevant to examination essays. The only real difference (apart from length) between a coursework essay and one written under examination conditions is that you have time to research the coursework questions, while in the case of examinations your revision will be the equivalent of research.

The hallmarks of a good law essay
While most students will have written many essays before coming to the study of law, it is equally true that many law students experience difficulty in understanding exactly what they are being asked to do when they are required to write an essay. Perhaps the key difference between writing essays in law (and for the moment we include not only essays as such, but also case notes, dissertations and answers to problem questions) and writing in most other subjects within the general area of arts, humanities and social sciences, is the extent to which every proposition you make must be expressed with precision and supported by authority. We are well aware that, in saying this, we will annoy both teachers and students of other subjects, who will almost certainly feel that we are claiming law to be the only truly academically rigorous subject. Of course, we are not asserting that at all. We are merely recording the fact that many students, when coming to law for the first time, experience difficulty with the degree of precision and the extent of authority which is required. Furthermore, the fact that this

applies even to those doing postgraduate conversion courses would seem to suggest that success in degree-level study of other subjects does not necessarily ensure success in law. No doubt those who embark on the study of other subjects will have to learn the kind of academic rigour that those subjects require; but our concern is only with the law.

Law essays must not only be logically structured presentations of coherent arguments, but must also answer the question and be supported by authority. An essay should not simply be a series of paraphrases of the material you have been referred to, but a critical review of that material. Although your understanding of the relevant material is a prerequisite to success in essay writing, it will not, on its own, be enough. What you must do is *demonstrate* your understanding; and you will do this by

- interpreting the question,
- doing the relevant research, and
- writing a well-argued answer which demonstrates that you have interpreted the question perceptively and rigorously and done the relevant research thoroughly.

Before elaborating each of these points, it may be worth commenting briefly on two classically bad types of essay.

The more common type is known as the '£10 Note Answer', where the student summarises the whole of the law on the topic, rather than selecting and applying only the relevant parts. In other words, the student is effectively saying to the examiner 'take it out of that and keep the change'.

The other type, which while less common is still too common, is known as the 'Kings of Israel Answer', and takes the form of an answer to the question which the student wishes had been set, rather than the one which has actually been set. The name of this type of answer comes from the story of the divinity student who had calculated that an essay on the Kings of Israel was bound to come up in the examination. Unfortunately for the student, this turned out to be a miscalculation, but there was a question which required candidates to distinguish between the major and the minor prophets. Accordingly, our student began his (or was it her?) essay thus: 'Who am I to distinguish between the major and the minor prophets? However, the Kings of Israel are very interesting ... ' and then proceeded to reproduce the essay which he (or she) had meticulously prepared.

With these cautionary tales in mind, we can now return to the topic of how to write *good* essays.

Interpreting the question

Generally
Interpreting an essay question is the first step towards writing a good essay. In practice, what it means is that you must ask yourself these questions and sub-questions:

1. What is the question about?
   Sub-questions: Are there any presumptions, approaches or sub-issues implicit in the question?
2. What does the question ask me to do?
   Sub-questions: Are there any expansions or limitations in the question?

   Until you can identify the main ideas or key concepts in the question, *and* clearly understand what you are being asked to do, you risk falling into the trap of reciting all you know on a given subject and producing a £10 Note Answer. And you will never be asked to do this in a law essay.

   Identifying the key concepts tells you what the question is *about*, while the instructional words in the question tell you *what you are being asked to do*. Often the instructions will ask you to *evaluate* or *critically analyse* a particular topic. Alternatively, they may ask you to *discuss* or *explain* a specific issue. All these terms require you to do a great deal more than simply *describe* the relevant law and you must be clear from the outset about their meanings. (The most commonly used instructions are explained at the end of this section.) When thinking about the key concepts in the question, it is important to take into account whether you are being asked to look at the issues from a particular angle, and whether any statements in the question make presumptions or have implications that you need to address. When reflecting on what the question is asking you to do, you will find that identifying the scope of the question will also tell you what you are *not* being asked to do.

   Consider the following essay question which we will use as a working example throughout this chapter:

   'The Human Rights Act 1998 effectively gives the people of England and Wales a bill of rights... the Act is of enormous significance in that it has bestowed "higher law" status on most Convention rights.' Critically discuss.

   One way to begin interpreting the question is to highlight the text of the question, identifying the component parts as we have done below. We have done this for the present question as follows:

- the key concepts are in **bold** text,
- the approach which the question invites is in *bold italics*,
- the three sub-issues are in **bold** and each is asterisked*, while
- the instructional words are underlined, and
- a limitation on the scope of the essay is *italicised*.

'The **Human Rights Act 1998** *effectively gives* the people of *England and Wales* a **bill of rights***... the Act is of enormous significance in that it has bestowed **"higher law"*** **status** on most **Convention rights***.' Critically discuss.

Another way to interpret the question is to rewrite it in your own words. This is a little harder than highlighting the key terms in the title, but has the advantage of improving your analysis and understanding of the question. You might rewrite the question to read:

The way in which the Convention rights in the Human Rights Act 1998 are protected and elevated as 'higher law' means that to all intents and purposes the English and Welsh peoples have, in the Human Rights Act, a bill of rights.

By rewriting the question you have made explicit a link which is only implicit in the original question, namely that it is only because the Human Rights Act 1998 (HRA 1998) is a higher form of law that England and Wales now has something akin to a bill of rights.

An alternative to rewriting the question in your own words is to expand on the component parts of the question as a series of bullet points:

- What the statement says:
  - The Convention rights protected by the HRA 1998 have been given special status in English law, thus the HRA 1998 is to all intents and purposes a bill of rights.
- Approach:
  - The words 'effectively gives' make it clear that the HRA 1998 is not a bill of rights but indicate the angle the essay should take, i.e. an examination of whether:
    - The HRA 1998 protects the human rights of citizens in the same way as a bill of rights might.
    - The HRA 1998 is protected in the same way as a bill of rights would be protected or entrenched.
- What the question asks me to do:

- Explain the scheme of the HRA 1998 and 'Convention rights'.
- Explain what is meant by a bill of rights and whether the HRA fits that mould.
- Interpret the concept of 'higher law' and consider whether the HRA 1998 is such a 'higher law'.
- Limitations:
  - Discussion limited to England and Wales, i.e. English law.

This interpretation and analysis of the question produces something that has the beginnings of a plan, but in reality this is merely a sketch map for your research, rather than the plan you will use when you write your essay.

The instructional words ask for *critical discussion* of the statement, which calls for a consideration of a range of viewpoints, both for and against the statement, together with an assessment of the strengths and weaknesses of each of these perspectives. A lecturer or tutor setting this question would expect you to explain (among other things) what a bill of rights is. He or she would not be looking for a detailed description of a bill of rights, but would want to see whether you can identify the fundamental features of such basic constitutional documents, and then evaluate the HRA 1998 in order to detect whether it shared or lacked those necessary features. To reach such a judgment you will first need to have examined the views of authors and the courts. Having thus considered the strengths and weaknesses of each perspective, you will be able to make your own assessment. More particularly, it is not enough to present the arguments of authors who support the statement and those of authors who oppose the statement. *Critical discussion* requires the essay writer to express a judgment as to the merits of the arguments, together with a convincing argument in support of that judgment.

Before moving on to consider the topic of *researching the question*, it may be useful to consider, briefly, what is meant by a variety of other commonly used instructional words

Some commonly used instructional words
Unfortunately, many students never achieve their full potential in coursework and examination essays because they fail to understand what the question is asking them to do. This selection of commonly used instructional words should help you to interpret most of the essay questions you encounter. Learning to interpret instructional words when you have a term-time essay to complete will help you produce an answer appropriate to the question, but it will also prepare you for when the same instructions appear in examination questions.

Analyse: Analysis involves separating or breaking down something into its component parts *and* discussing the relationships between each of the parts.

Criticise: Criticising something involves coming to a judgement about a particular argument, point of view or theory, through a process of discussion in which you examine both the strengths and weaknesses of the particular argument *and* provide justification for your own assessment.

Discuss: The instruction to discuss something is often used interchangeably with the instruction to *critically discuss* something. Either instruction involves both description *and* interpretation. It requires you to explain the relevant ideas and arguments and examine them through reasoned argument, supported by authority, in order to reach a conclusion. A discussion should not be one-sided but a consideration of the arguments on *all* sides of the debate.

Distinguish: A question that asks you to distinguish one thing from another will usually focus on concepts that are commonly muddled. Distinguishing requires you to explain the *similarities and differences* between two or more things and provide illustrations wherever possible.

Evaluate: Evaluation involves reaching a *reasoned judgment* about the value or legitimacy of a particular argument, concept or theory. In doing this, you must scrutinise, with reference to appropriate evidence, the advantages, failings and limitations of the argument, concept, or theory.

Illustrate: Illustrating something involves giving concrete examples (such as decided cases) that support and help to explain your line of reasoning.

Justify: Justifying something involves providing and explaining relevant reasons to support your conclusions.

Researching the question

Once you know what the question is about, and what you are being asked to do, you can then begin to research the question. Just as the question is not an invitation to tell the reader all you know about the topic, so the research is not a quest to read everything in print, or on the Internet, about the topic. Researching the question is a search for *relevant* materials so, if you were answering the question on the HRA 1998, you would look for articles about the HRA 1998 and in particular at authors who suggest that the HRA 1998 has 'higher law' status, or shares the characteristics of a bill of rights or similar constitutional document, and authors who reject such views.

Essentially, the task at the research stage is to

- locate,
- read, and
- make notes on,

the materials that are relevant to your answer. Much of the material you need will be readily available, but there may well be many other students looking for the same information and working to the same deadline. You could, therefore, usefully photocopy journal articles as early as possible after receiving the question, and reserve books from the library as necessary.

Reading and making notes on the materials can be very time-consuming and to make the best use of the time available you will need to employ effective reading strategies while remaining focused on the question. To get a general impression of the issues you will first need to read broadly, though the extent of the overview reading you need to do will very much depend on the level of your existing knowledge of the essay topic. This general reading should help you discover the important themes around the key concepts of the essay and the range of possible answers to the question. When your understanding is such that you can take a stance on the answer you should then narrow the focus of your reading and concentrate in detail on the arguments that support your view. The detailed reading should, however, be a critical evaluation of the materials and you need to note the flaws as well as the strengths of the arguments you intend to rely on in your essay.

At this stage we can usefully return to the SQ3R technique which we first encountered at pp. 15–16. When using this technique to research an essay question, *surveying* and *questioning* the material are done at the same time by skim reading or quickly scanning the materials you think might be suitable for your essay, while always keeping the key concepts of the essay question at the forefront of your mind. To survey a book in this way, you would flick through the table of contents, and (if they are not included in the table of contents) the main headings and subheadings within each of the relevant chapters. You may also scan the most promising pages, looking for words and phrases which are relevant to your essay topic. When reading, you should ask yourself the following questions:

- is the material relevant to the key concepts of the essay?
- does the material support or contradict what I already know?

- is there anything new or interesting here that is worth pursuing further? (Remember that everything *must* be *relevant* to the question.)

You will then be in a position to progress to the *reading, recalling* and *reviewing* stages of the SQ3R process in the usual way.

Planning and writing the answer

Planning the answer
Planning your answer helps you create the direction and structure of your essay. Your efforts at this stage should focus on using the research materials to build a logical, coherent, well-structured essay. Remember, the essay is *your* work and *only you* can provide readers with the directions they need to find their way through your composition. A plan will help you to help them.

The form of your plan might be graphical, or it might simply use headings and subheadings. In practice it is helpful to use a piece of paper large enough to contain your complete plan so that you can both see the overall picture and ensure the component parts fit together. Here is part of a plan we will use at the writing stage. It includes the points we will discuss when creating a main body paragraph.

A. HRA 1998

  1. 'Convention rights'

    (a) From European Convention of Human Rights (ECHR)

      (i) Not all ECHR rights – arts 1 and 13 are excluded.

      (ii) Less far-reaching and more qualified than other bills of rights – e.g., German basic law – art 3 EHCR only absolute right.

    (b) ECHR not incorporated into English law but 'Convention rights' given special status by HRA 1998:

      (i) Courts cannot quash primary legislation – statutes declared incompatible with ECHR by courts still remain law – scheme retains legislative supremacy of Parliament. But

      (ii) Courts required – where possible – to interpret legislation (post and pre HRA 1998) compatibly with ECHR.

    (c) Not entrenched/protected in same way as constitutional documents:

      (i) Bill of Rights in United States Constitution – Congress and 75% of states must agree to amendments.

(ii)   German Basic Law – cannot be changed.

(d)   Does not bind Legislature

Other constitutional documents bind legislature executive and judiciary.

The level of detail you need in your plan will vary. At some points, short-hand terms that remind you of arguments you are familiar with will suffice; but where you are less sure, longer explanations will be necessary. What is important is that your plan must illustrate both the line and order of your argument(s) in a way that you understand and be sufficiently detailed to be genuinely useful when you write your essay. The plan is a tool to help you build an effective essay, just as an architect's plan directs the builder of a house. At first you might find it hard to construct and use the plan, but with increasing use you will learn how to customise the tool and make it work for you.

Writing the answer

Writing the answer is the place where many students start when tackling an essay question, and this is probably the most common reason for underperformance (and even failure) in assessment. Writing your essay will not always be easy, but it will be a great deal easier to write if you have prop-erly *interpreted* and *researched* the question, and equally carefully *planned* your answer.

The introduction should be short and simple. It needs to tell the readers what the essay is about and prepare them for the journey through your essay. What you are doing here is interpreting the question for your readers, and providing markers (or signposts) to give them an idea of the ground you are going to cover. This will enable them to build their own mental map of the territory they will be covering before they start on the journey itself. Here is an example of how the essay question we have considered throughout this chapter might be introduced:

The United Kingdom was, when it ratified the European Convention for the Protection of Human Rights and Fundamental Freedoms (ECHR), one of the first member states of the Council of Europe to do so. Those rights guaranteed in the ECHR which are now protected in English law by the Human Rights Act 1998 (HRA 1998) have been labelled by that Act as 'Convention rights'. This essay will discuss whether the HRA's approach to Convention rights can properly be described as giving those rights the status of 'higher law'; and whether, to all intents and purposes, this provides the citizens of

England and Wales with a constitutional document comparable to a bill of rights.

A consideration of the scheme of the HRA 1998 will show that the legislative supremacy of Parliament is left intact. An examination of the Bill of Rights in the Constitution of the United States of America and the fundamental law of Germany will reveal that the Act lacks the conventional protection of legal entrenchment usually seen in bills of rights. On the face of it, this would suggest that HRA 1998 does not have the 'enormous significance' the statement claims but an analysis of the impact and effect that the Act has had on English law reveals a new culture of human rights among citizens, an increased willingness on the part of the judiciary to protect human rights[1] and a sensitivity to human rights on the part of the government.[2]

[1] See the comments of Lord Hoffmann on the principle of 'legality' in *R v Secretary of State for the Home Department ex parte Simms* [1999] UKHL 33, [2000] 2 AC 115, 131-32.

[2] For example, the government's response to the decision in *R v Secretary of State for the Home Department (Respondent) ex parte Al-Hasan* [2005] UKHL 13, [2005] 1 WLR 688.

Having set the scene for the readers, you then need to write the main body of the essay, taking up each of your themes in linked paragraphs or sections. Treat each paragraph as a separate unit of thought or mini-essay, while ensuring that it is clearly related to the themes of your essay. Follow the order of your plan to move smoothly from one point to the next.

A tried and tested method for creating an effective paragraph is to begin with a *topic* sentence, followed by *supporting* sentences and then a *concluding* sentence. However, all good writing contains varying structures, so you should not treat this model as one to be followed on all occasions, although it will serve to sharpen your perception of what needs to be achieved in a paragraph. The topic sentence introduces the key idea you will discuss in the paragraph and helps connect the paragraph to the overall plan. Sometimes it may be preceded by a transitional clause or sentence, but the topic sentence should always appear early on in the paragraph. If you look back to the first sentence of this paragraph, you will see that we use a few transitional words (linking this paragraph to the preceding one), followed by a topic sentence which tells you that in this paragraph we are going to discuss writing the main body paragraphs of an essay.

The supporting sentences of a paragraph are where the critical discussion takes place. The topic is analysed and the evidence is critically examined to develop and advance the arguments of your essay. The concluding sentence of a paragraph does not require you to come to a conclusion, but it does require you to evaluate or indicate how the argument has moved on. This will keep your arguments alive and keep readers on track. If readers fail to follow your arguments, you will lose their attention; and in an assessed essay or an examination you will also lose marks. Where a point is developed over a series of paragraphs, the concluding sentence of each one will act as a bridge to the next, until your final paragraph contains a concluding evaluation. Here are two paragraphs based on our essay plan above:

The 'Convention rights' identified in the HRA 1998 are contained in Arts 2–12, and 14 ECHR, Arts 1–3 of the First Protocol and Arts 1 and 2 of Protocol 6. The HRA does not add to these Convention rights, which, after 50 years and the increasing remoteness of the specifically post-World War II perspective, might be criticised for having the limited aim of protecting the citizen from state interference. Many constitutional documents, such as the basic law of Germany, are more far reaching. German basic law includes a general right to equality[3] and a number of social rights such as the right of mothers to the 'protection and care of the community'[4]. Convention rights do not embrace social rights such as the right to a free education[5]; or minority rights like the right to be educated in one's own language[6]; nor does the HRA protect minority cultures[7]. Only one Convention right is absolute, namely Art. 3, the right not to be 'subjected to torture or to inhuman or degrading treatment or punishment', whereas a large part of Germany's basic law is 'inviolable'[8]. In enacting the HRA 1998 Parliament, it seems, did not intend to create a bill of rights along the typical lines of a constitutional document like Germany's basic law or Sweden's Instrument of Government. This is particularly apparent from the approach which is adopted towards Convention rights.

The scheme of the HRA which is often, albeit wrongly, described as 'incorporating' the ECHR into English law[9] preserves the legislative supremacy of Parliament and was designed, in the words of the Lord Chancellor of the day, 'to give the courts as much space as possible to protect human rights, short of the power to set aside or ignore Acts of Parliament'.[10] Ultimately, like every other statute, the Act could be repealed by the present or any future Parliament. However, unlike any other statute, it places an interpretative obligation upon the courts in relation to their interpretation of all other statutes, by requiring them to read all legislation, whenever passed, in such a way as to be compatible with Convention rights, wherever it is possible to do so. It may be objected that the HRA is not truly unique in this respect, since the Interpretation Act 1978 imposes a whole range of interpretative obligations in respect of all other statutes – except, in each case, 'where the context otherwise requires'. The answer to this objection is that the

Interpretation Act is limited to matters of technical convenience – such as the meaning of 'day' and 'month' and the presumption that the singular includes the plural and so on – whereas the HRA deals with a matter of constitutional principle. Thus this interpretative obligation, imposed by Parliament on the courts, is what gives the HRA its 'special status' in English law.

[3]Art. 3.

[4]Art. 6(4).

[5]Sweden: Instrument of Government, Chapter 2 Art. 21.

[6]Canadian Charter of Rights and Freedoms s. 23.

[7]Sweden: Instrument of Government Chapter 2 Art. 20.

[8]Arts 1, 4, 10, 13.

[9]Lord Clyde, *R v Lambert* [135].

[10]HL Debs, 3 November 1997, col. 1228.

In each of these paragraphs the topic is identified in the first sentence. Looking at the first paragraph, we see that it deals with Convention rights; the supporting sentences then analyse these rights and criticise them by a comparison to the rights protected in other constitutional documents. The evaluation in the concluding sentence is that Convention rights are not comprehensive and that Parliament did not intend to create a bill of basic rights in the HRA. The end of the last sentence in the first paragraph also acts as a transition clause, or bridge, between it and the next paragraph. This transition is maintained in the first sentence of the second paragraph, which then unfolds following a similar pattern to the first.

By the end of your essay your conclusions should be fairly easy to write. The key thing is that they must fit the preceding discussion. This has two main elements. First, do not introduce new material into the conclusion. Secondly, do not express opinions that are not substantiated by the evidence; and, in particular, do not come to a firm view unless it is very clearly supported by the evidence. Other ways of rounding an essay off include linking the conclusion to the introduction by picking up a phrase, quotation or anecdote again, or using a quotation from a primary source to amplify your point. Above all, remember that a conclusion does not need to tie together every strand of the essay into a neat bow. If the evidence is equivocal, or the arguments finely balanced, then you should present that to the readers and allow them to reach their own conclusions. For example:

The HRA is not so wide ranging in the kind of human rights it protects as many constitutional documents, and the Act lacks the legal
entrenchment usually found in such fundamental or basic laws. In a
strict legal sense, the HRA is not analogous to a bill of rights and Convention rights have not been given any 'higher status' than the provisions of any other Act of Parliament. Nevertheless, the HRA has
placed the protection of basic human rights firmly on the public
agenda and while Parliament may still 'as a matter of constitutional
legality ... be sovereign ... as a matter of constitutional practice [the
HRA] has transferred significant power to the judiciary'[11], a move
which Flinders[12] claims 'represents an unprecedented transfer of
political power from the executive and legislature to the judiciary'.
The enormity of the significance of the HRA is yet to unfold fully, and
it remains to be seen whether it turns out be such a major constitutional change. In the nature of the British constitution, the HRA may
evolve as a peculiarly British bill of rights, but only time will show
whether the HRA will be listed with the likes of 'Magna Carta... as a
"revolutionary" legal and historical document in the sense that it
changed man's and woman's thinking [turning] the UK's political and
legal culture upside down [and perhaps] the right way around'[13].

[11]KD Ewing, 'The Human Rights Act and Parliamentary Democracy' (1999) 62
MLR 79, 79.

[12]M Flinders, 'Mechanisms of judicial accountability in British central government' [2001] *Parl. Aff.* 54, 63.

[13]D McGoldrick, 'The United Kingdom's Human Rights Act 1998 in Theory and
Practice' (2001) 50 *ICLQ* 901, 953.

This conclusion returns to the themes identified in the introduction and, in
so far as is possible, it provides an answer to the question set. It also reminds
those readers who have to mark your work for assessment purposes that
you understand that the question is multi-layered and that the constitutional
implications of the HRA are still being worked out. The essay ends with a for-
ward-looking quotation, leaving the reader to continue thinking about the
question as the journey ends.

Editing the answer

The final stage in the journey of writing (rather than reading) is *editing* and
reviewing your answer. This is not an easy task. It is often far easier to spot
mistakes in the work of others than those in your own work. Ideally you
should put the essay aside for a day or two after writing it, before turning
your hand to the task of editing. There is a tendency when reading your own
work to read what you think you wrote rather than reading the words printed

on the page; and even if you do limit yourself to the words on the printed page, it is easy to assume that they mean what you intended them to mean, rather than meaning what they do actually say.

If you write your essay using word processing software, most obvious spelling errors will be identified by proprietary spell checks, although it is always a good idea to ensure that the spell check is set to British English. However, most standard word processing packages do not contain many legal terms or proper names, so you will still need to keep an eye out for spelling mistakes when reviewing your work.

When editing your work, look in particular at the

- structure,
- content,
- grammar, and
- style,

bearing in mind especially the need to ensure *coherence* while eliminating *inaccuracies* and *irrelevant material*. Additionally, you must always ensure that you have complied with any specific presentation instructions you have been given and that all your sources are properly referenced and acknowledged.

Conclusion

A good essay will be well written, well presented and contain only relevant material. And, above all, it will *answer the question*. Preparing your work thoroughly will help you to interpret the question, undertake appropriate research and formulate a plan. At the end of the planning stage, the content should have been adequately sifted so as to be *relevant* to the question and *directed* to an appropriate answer.

Writing your essay following the recognised conventions of grammar, spelling, punctuation and referencing will improve the style and presentation of your work. A careful final editing of the essay will pick up most of the errors that remain. This method of essay writing will not produce perfection and one or two errors will evade even the most meticulous editor. Nevertheless, if you plan and write essays following this approach you should begin to produce good law essays; and for your labours you should receive good marks.

11 Answering Problem Questions

Legal problem solving involves a number of distinct steps. First, you must identify both the legal and factual issues in a given situation. Secondly, you must select the relevant law from a wide range of cases and statutes. Thirdly, you must apply this law to the specific facts of the problem. Fourthly, you must conclude by either advising the parties of the probable outcome of the case, or summarising your discussion of the issue raised by the problem, depending on the instructions you have been given. As well as being an essential skill for students, problem solving is a skill used by professional lawyers on a daily basis. Ultimately, it is a skill best gained by practice.

Introduction

Although many people accept the truth of the saying that *knowledge is power*, the reality of the matter is a great deal less clear-cut. In fact, there is much to be said for the view that knowledge, like money, is intrinsically worthless. After all, taking the example of money, why should anyone want to accumulate mass-produced little metal discs carrying embossed images, words and figures, and mass-produced pieces of printed paper bearing one of a range of identical designs? The answer is obvious: *if the discs of metal and pieces of paper are coins and banknotes, you can spend them*; but if you were shipwrecked on a desert island, even the most immense fortune would be worthless *because you would not be able to use it*. Similarly, no matter how extensive your knowledge of law may be, it will be worthless *unless you can use it*. In this chapter we show you how to *use* your knowledge of the law to answer problem questions.

Law students are often given problem questions in the form of a factual scenario. They are then required to advise one or more of the parties, or to discuss the legal issues which arise. We will look at two problem questions shortly, but before doing so it is worth saying something about how you should approach them.

Planning and writing an answer

Introduction
The building blocks for answering a problem question are your *knowledge* and *understanding* of the relevant law. However, examiners do not want to see a pile of raw materials: they want to see the finished product. In this context, the finished product is the answer you have created using the building blocks of knowledge and understanding. The construction of a good answer, like the construction of a good building, requires careful planning and skilful execution. In the hands of the unskilled the best materials are not fully exploited. If you give an unskilled builder good bricks and mortar you will still end up with a badly constructed building, albeit one made of good materials. The four-stage process we outline below is a technique for developing the skills to construct a good answer to problem questions using your building blocks of knowledge and understanding. It is used first at the planning stage; it is then used again at the writing stage.

Identifying the issues
The first step in producing a good answer to a problem question is to *identify the issues*. This is a matter of identifying *what the question is about from a legal point of view*. At the *planning* stage, you will be reading through the question with a view to spotting and noting the issues. Identifying the issues is essentially a process of *analysis*, which in this context means separating the question into its distinct parts, recognising each fact and issue, and then ranking those facts and issues in terms of relevance and importance. At the *writing* stage you will write a short opening paragraph, setting out the issues you have identified and which you will then address in your answer.

The testing of skills begins with the reading of the problem question. First, you need to break down the problem and identify the *material facts*. Always read the question *questioningly*. If, in the facts of the problem question, you are told a child is seven years old ask, 'why have I been told this? What is the legal significance of this fact in the context of the question?' The only true exception to the proposition that all the facts are included for a reason (namely to be commented upon in answering the question) is that some facts are included simply to make the story more readable. The name of the café in the first example discussed below falls into this category. There is, however, also a quasi-exception, where facts are introduced by way of red herrings. Some students regard this as a form of cheating by the examiner, on the basis that such facts do not relate to the answer; but this is to misunderstand the point. Red herrings will only distract those who do not really understand the relevant law, and therefore their introduction is a perfectly legitimate way of testing the true extent of the students' understanding. In other words, and being perfectly consistent with the general principle that all facts are mentioned for a reason, red herrings are introduced so that you may comment on them, even though your only comment will be to identify their irrelevance.

Secondly, you need to identify the *legal issues* raised by the *facts*. It may be that you consider the facts to be too far-fetched to be taken seriously. Two points arise. First, the facts of some of the most important legal cases are themselves quite improbable, as the discussion of *Donoghue v Stevenson* (below) illustrates. Secondly, and perhaps more importantly, you must understand that the questions are constructed in order to bring out certain points which the examiner expects you to be able to identify and discuss. This may well result in an intrinsically improbable storyline; but problem questions never pretend to be essays in social realism anyway.

Finally, you need to identify any *legal claims* and *defences* that the parties may have. A party who has no recognisable legal claim, or a party who does have such a claim but who will be met with a cast-iron legal defence, will have no legal redress. Evaluating possible claims and defences at the planning stage will not only help you to identify the contentious legal issues raised by the problem, but will also enable you to dispose of any straightforward and uncontentious issues in a sentence or two.

Selecting the relevant law

At the planning stage, step two requires you to *select the law* which is relevant to the issues identified at stage one. At the writing stage, this is made explicit when you *state* the law you have selected to support the legal claims and defences you have identified. Selecting the relevant law is a filtering process where you sift out any irrelevant law and retain only the law which is pertinent to your answer.

The principal authorities in English law (and other common law jurisdictions) are statutes, delegated legislation, and case law, although in many subjects it will also be necessary to ask whether there are any relevant provisions of European Community law or of the European Convention on Human Rights as made relevant to the English legal system by the Human

Rights Act 1998. (The European Community dimension and the impact of the European Convention on Human Rights, together with the Human Rights Act, are discussed in Chapters 2 and 5, respectively.) It is important to bear in mind the weight of the various authorities (in terms of the level of court) when selecting the law to support your arguments. Remember that no court can quash primary legislation, and *persuasive authorities* (for example, cases decided by the Privy Council or the High Court of Australia) might influence a court to follow a particular line of reasoning but do not bind it to do so.

Applying the law

The third step in the problem-solving process requires you to *apply* the *relevant* law to the *material* facts. It is your ability to do this convincingly that demonstrates the true extent of your *understanding*. One type of classically bad answer simply reproduces, more or less accurately depending on the extent of your knowledge and understanding, *all* the law on the topic, with no attempt at selection or application. (In other words, it is a *£10 note answer*, of the kind we identified in the context of essay writing at p. 167.) In terms of professional practice, the equivalent would be simply to read aloud to the client the whole of the relevant chapter from a textbook and then claim that this amounts to giving the client legal advice.

Applying the law at the *planning* stage means considering how the law you have selected fits the material facts. Later, at the *writing* stage, you will apply the law to support your discussion, and thus demonstrate that you can construct a logical argument.

Concluding with advice

In most problem questions (as in the examples we shall be considering shortly) you will be asked either to advise one or more of the parties, or to discuss the legal issues which arise from the facts. If you are required to give advice, you may feel that once you have identified the issues, selected and applied the relevant law and produced a logical answer following the steps outlined above, it will be obvious to the examiner what your advice will be. Nevertheless, you should conclude your answer with a short paragraph containing your advice. Similarly, if the question requires you to *discuss the legal issues arising from the facts*, you should conclude with a short summary of the issues you have been discussing.

This four-fold approach to answering problems is not a quick fix solution. It does not help you avoid attending lectures and tutorials or seminars, nor does it exempt you from extending your knowledge of the law through appropriate library work. However, it does help you put your knowledge to good use.

Worked examples

Introduction

Having discussed the skills you will require when planning and writing answers to problem questions we will now look at some worked examples to illustrate the planning and writing process. We will do this by looking at two questions based on the type of work you will be doing in tutorials or seminars, for coursework and in examinations. In the first question we will establish the importance of planning if you are to construct a good answer to a problem question; in the second question we provide a step-by-step illustration of the planning and writing of an answer following our suggested four-fold approach. Of course, by the time you are answering actual questions, you will have studied a substantial body of law, and therefore those questions may be more complex than our examples. Nevertheless, our examples will provide a useful introduction to the skills you will need to master if you are to impress the examiners with the extent of your understanding of the law. Furthermore, since problem solving is a transferable skill, your study of our examples will also provide you with the basis for a structured approach to problem solving in other contexts, which will be invaluable to you in your future career, whether or not this lies within the legal profession.

Problem 1

Our first problem provides a relatively simple illustration of the points raised so far, but in order to understand it we must first consider the case of *Donoghue v Stevenson* [1932] AC 562.

The facts were that May Donoghue went with a friend to the Wellmeadow café in Paisley, Scotland, where her friend bought her an 'ice cream float'. This treat consisted of ice cream in a tumbler, into which ginger beer was poured. After Mrs Donoghue had consumed some of the drink, her friend topped up the tumbler with more ginger beer. This action revealed that the bottle, which was opaque, contained not only ginger beer but also the decomposed remains of a snail. (It is, of course, relevant that the bottle was opaque, because, if it had been clear, the remains of the snail would have been plainly visible.) Mrs Donoghue suffered prolonged and acute stomach pain, together with repeated vomiting and depression.

Since Mrs Donoghue had not bought the drink herself she could not sue in contract so she brought a claim in tort against the manufacturer. The basic elements of the tort of negligence were well known to the common law before *Donoghue v Stevenson*, and can be summarised thus:

- the defendant must owe the claimant a *duty of care*;
- this duty must have been *breached*;
- the breach must be the *cause* of the claimant's damage (or loss);
- the damage must *not* be too *remote*.

(Since *Donoghue v Stevenson* did not involve the question of *remoteness of damage*, we will not be exploring that idea here.)

The problem Mrs Donoghue faced was that the case law did not establish a general rule defining the relationships between parties that gave rise to a *duty of care*, but simply identified certain factual situations as creating duty relationships. For example, the cases established that dock-owners owed a duty of care to some (but not all) people using the gangways between docked ships. The cases also established that people who put into circulation 'articles dangerous in themselves' (like loaded firearms) owed a duty of care to people who might come within the vicinity of the dangerous articles. The decision of the House of Lords in *Donoghue v Stevenson* (which, incidentally, was in Mrs Donoghue's favour) led to the development of the modern tort of negligence, based on the *neighbour principle*. According to this principle, which is contained in the speech of Lord Atkin, you owe a duty of care to your neighbour. Crucially, this general formula goes on to define *neighbours* as *those people who are so closely and directly affected by your actions (or omissions) that, when you are considering your actions (or omissions), you would reasonably have these people in mind*.

Influential though Lord Atkin's *neighbour principle* has been in the subsequent development of the law, the actual *ratio* of *Donoghue v Stevenson* is somewhat narrower, and is neatly summed up in the headnote of the report.

> The manufacturer of an article of food, medicine or the like, sold by him to a distributor in circumstances which prevent the distributor or ultimate purchaser or consumer from discovering by inspection any defect, is under a legal duty to the ultimate purchaser or consumer to take reasonable care that the article is free from defect likely to cause injury to health.

For present purposes, this necessarily brief consideration of *Donoghue v Stevenson* will suffice and the first problem question can now be considered. In other words, having gained some useful legal *knowledge*, we are now in a position to *apply* it. Consider the following facts.

Adam buys a bottle of soda water from Cobra's café. Eve drinks some of the soda water. Later that day Adam discovers the decomposing remains of a slug in the bottle. Advise Eve of any claim(s) she may have in the tort of negligence.

A cursory reading of the problem might lead to an answer based simply on knowledge of *Donoghue v Stevenson*. Such an answer might read:

> *Donoghue v Stevenson* [1932] AC 562 establishes that the manufac-
> turer of a product owes a duty of care to the ultimate consumer.
> Where, through the carelessness of the manufacturer, a consumer is
> caused damage by a defect in a product (and the consumer had no
> opportunity to identify the defect) the manufacturer will be liable in
> the tort of negligence.

This is not a good answer. It makes no reference to the facts or the issues raised in the problem and simply repeats the material as originally presented. It demonstrates the ability to recall and reproduce information, but nothing more. A student who produced such an answer could be said to *know* about the law, but this is not enough: we need to get beyond this and show the examiner that we have *identified* the legal issues and *selected* the relevant law, and can *apply* it in the context of this particular factual situation. Consider this answer:

> Eve can sue Cobra's Café in the tort of negligence. The facts of this
> case are very similar to those in *Donoghue v Stevenson* [1932] AC 562;
> the slug in the soda water is as much a defect in the product as the
> snail was in the ginger beer. In *Donoghue* the court held that even
> though the claimant did not buy the product the manufacturer owed
> her a duty of care; thus even though Eve did not buy the soda water,
> the manufacturer will not escape liability.

A student who produced an answer like this is demonstrating some *understanding* of the law. One way of showing that you understand something is to rewrite it in your own words; this answer shows a familiarity with the case law and the capacity to reword and explain this comprehension to others. The issue (negligence) has been *identified*, the relevant case has been *selected* and there is some attempt to *apply* the law to a different set of circumstances. However, several criticisms may be made. First, in terms of *issue identification*, the answer does not set out the elements of the tort or identify the contentious issues in the problem. Secondly, in terms of style, it is much better to state the principle of law first and then apply this to the facts. Thirdly, and most importantly, the answer reveals that the student has not read the question with sufficient care.

You will recall that we said that, at the *planning* stage, *analysis* of the question requires a *careful* and *questioning* reading. Consider the problem and ask: do any facts that could have a bearing on your answer appear to have been omitted? Are there are any uncertainties in the facts we are given in the problem? An essential part of the planning stage is to break the problem apart so that we can identify the relationships between the parties and distinguish between relevant and irrelevant facts.

Careful analysis of the problem reveals three key issues:

- we are not told whether anyone has suffered any damage or sustained any losses;
- we do not know whether the bottle is clear or opaque or how Adam discovered the slug; and
- we do not know who the manufacturer is.

Since the facts of a problem question are to be taken as stated and cannot be investigated, it is a matter of judgment as to whether alternative analyses should be considered or whether to make a reasonable assumption on the facts. Consider this answer to the problem:

> The issue here is whether Eve (E) has a claim in the tort of negligence against the manufacturer of the soda water. To establish a claim, E will need to show that the defendant owed her a duty of care; that this duty was breached; that the breach caused her damage; and that this damage is not too remote. The main points here are whether E is owed a duty of care and if, as a matter of fact and of law, she suffered any damage.
>
> A manufacturer of a product owes a duty of care to the ultimate consumer of a product where through the manufacturer's negligence the consumer, who had no opportunity to inspect the product, suffers loss or damage (*Donoghue v Stevenson* [1932] AC 562).
>
> In *Donoghue v Stevenson*, the claimant could not see the decomposing snail in the opaque bottle; thus she was denied the opportunity to inspect the contents of the bottle before drinking the ginger beer. This was an important factor in the court's reasoning which led to the imposition of liability on the manufacturer. Although we know that Adam discovered the slug in the bottle of soda water, we do not know how he did this. If the soda water (a clear liquid) was in a transparent bottle the manufacturer may escape liability, since one of the central facts of this case would present an essential difference from the situation in *Donoghue v Stevenson*.
>
> We do not know from the facts whether E has suffered any damage. This is important because it is only if she has sustained

losses as a result of drinking the soda water that her claim in negligence will succeed.

E is, therefore, advised that unless (1) it is established that she could not inspect the contents of the soda water bottle and (2) that she suffered damage, she should not pursue a claim in the tort of negligence.

In this answer, the legal issues are clearly *identified* in the first paragraph and the elements of the tort are summarised. The most pertinent issues are highlighted and in three short sentences the scene is set. This can only be achieved by careful analysis at the *planning* stage. In the second paragraph the law which we *selected* (and which, of course, is somewhat limited in this example) is *stated* in so far as it is relevant to the facts. Note that there is no reference to the facts of *Donoghue v Stevenson*: only the applicable principle of law is stated. In the third paragraph the emphasis is on *application* of the law and building up an argument. At the *planning* stage, this involves asking how the facts of this problem differ from (or are similar to) the selected law. Here, at the writing stage, the material facts are evaluated against the law stated. The response concludes with advice to Eve. This is brief and not contrived: it simply answers the question posed.

The importance of understanding what you should be doing when answering a problem question is that, whenever you answer such a question, you can ask yourself: *have I demonstrated to the examiner that I know and understand the law and that I can employ the skills of analysis and evaluation in applying the relevant law to the problem*? Unless you can truthfully answer *yes* to this question, you should try again.

Problem 2

In Problem 1 we looked at some typical answers to a question on the basic elements of the tort of negligence and *Donoghue v Stevenson*. In Problem 2 we will look at a more complex factual scenario and work step-by-step through the four-fold approach to planning and writing in order to construct an answer to the problem. First, we will add to our knowledge of the tort of negligence by looking in more detail at the breach of duty point, and in particular at the standard of care owed by the drivers of motor vehicles.

We have already seen that in an action for negligence the first thing a successful claimant must establish is that the defendant owed him or her a duty of care. In many situations there will be no problem. For example, it is now well established that manufacturers owe a duty of care to the ultimate consumer of their products and that doctors owe a duty of care to their patients. Coming closer to the problem which we are about to consider, it is also well established that road users owe a duty of care to other road users. As Kennedy J stated, in *Dulieu v White* [1901] 2 KB 669, 671–672, a driver on a road owes a duty to use 'reasonable and proper care and skill so as not to injure either persons lawfully using the highway or property adjoining the highway, or persons ... occupying that property'.

Once the existence of a duty of care is established, the question of whether the defendant is in breach of that duty must be addressed. This is decided by judging the defendant's conduct against that of a hypothetical 'reasonable person'. This is primarily an *objective* test, because essentially the court asks, 'what would a reasonable person have done in these circumstances?' rather than seeking to enter the mind of the defendant in an attempt to identify what he or she was actually thinking. (There are many areas of law where the court will, indeed, seek to enter into the mind of a particular person: this is called applying a *subjective* test.) If the answer is that, on the particular facts of the case, the defendant's conduct fell below the standard of the 'reasonable person' then the defendant will be held to be in breach of the duty which he or she owed; and, if that breach of duty caused damage to the claimant, the defendant will usually be liable. With these points in mind, we will now look at two cases, in both of which the 'reasonable person' is the 'reasonable driver'.

In *Roberts v Ramsbottom* [1980] 1 WLR 823, the defendant suffered a stroke shortly before leaving his house to drive to work. Although the stroke had no obvious physical consequences, it did impair the functioning of his brain. The result was that Mr Ramsbottom drove off, without being conscious of the fact that he was ill. His journey lasted less than twenty minutes. In that time, he crashed into the back of a stationary van, narrowly missed running over two men working in the road, knocked a cyclist off his bicycle, and collided head-on with a parked car. The question for the High Court was whether the defendant could escape liability for the damage he had caused on the basis that his actions were completely beyond his control, or if he should be judged by the objective standard of care of an ordinary reasonable driver. Neill J, relying on a number of criminal cases, found that the courts had been reluctant to absolve drivers of liability where the disabling event was not sudden, and concluded, therefore (at p. 832), that 'nothing less than total loss of consciousness' would enable the defendant to avoid liability. Since Mr Ramsbottom's consciousness had only been impaired, rather than completely lost, he was held liable for the damage which he caused. Significantly, Mr Ramsbottom had got out of his car after crashing into the stationary van and had engaged in a brief discussion with the van's occupants before continuing his journey. The judge considered this would allow the claimants to succeed on a second ground, namely that the defendant had continued to drive not only when he was unfit to do so, but when he should have been aware of his unfitness.

The later case of *Mansfield v Weetabix* [1998] 1 WLR 1263, concerns a lorry driver who, unknowingly, suffered from a condition known as malignant insulinoma. As a consequence of this condition the driver's brain was starved of glucose, resulting in improper brain functions. The lorry's 40 mile journey ended when the driver approached a bend too quickly and crashed into the claimant's shop. The driver had been seen driving erratically at two earlier points in his journey, and had been stopped by the police after he collided with the rear of a trailer which he was following. The question for the Court of Appeal was whether the judge at first instance had correctly interpreted the law in applying *Roberts v Ramsbottom* to the case. Leggatt LJ, delivering the unanimous judgment of the court, said *Roberts* was wrongly decided on the first ground, preferring to say (at p. 1267) that, in civil cases, a driver could escape liability where 'the disabling event [was] gradual, provided that the driver [was] unaware of it'. The court went on to hold (at p. 1268) that although the driver suffered from only 'an impaired degree of consciousness' as a result of his malignant insulinoma, the fact that he was unaware that he suffered from the condition meant that he was not to be held liable for the damage that he had caused. The standard of care in the case was that of 'the reasonable competent driver [who is] unaware that he is or may be suffering from a condition that impairs his ability to drive'. (*Ibid.*)

Before reading the problem question that follows you might find it useful to check your knowledge of the law we have examined thus far. In particular, you will find it helpful to note the differences between *Roberts v Ramsbottom* and *Mansfield v Weetabix*.

Now, consider the following question.

Amber was diagnosed some years ago as being diabetic. She received a great deal of advice at that time, which placed particular emphasis on the importance of taking her medication conscientiously and eating regular meals, and how to identify the symptoms of hypoglycaemia (low blood sugar level), such as dizziness and blurred vision. One morning she oversleeps and in the rush to leave her house and get to work she gets into her car and drives off without eating any breakfast. On the way to work, Amber suffers from increasingly severe bouts of blurred vision and fails to stop at a red traffic signal. Amber narrowly avoids knocking Jade off her bicycle, but collides with Emerald's car.

Meanwhile, Beryl, having crashed her car into a lamppost, is stationary some 200 metres ahead of the traffic signal. Jade stops when she sees the accident and finds Beryl collapsed and unconscious in her seat. While Jade is calling the emergency services, Beryl regains consciousness and attempts to drive off, running over Jade's bicycle before bringing the car to a halt. Medical tests reveal that Beryl has suffered an epileptic seizure. Beryl has never had an epileptic seizure before and had no reason to believe she was susceptible to epilepsy.

Advise Amber and Beryl as to their liabilities in the tort of negligence.

To answer this question we first need to plan. *Identifying the issues means* re-reading the question, noting as we do so the *material facts* and the *legal issues* raised by those facts. Remember to read *questioningly*. For example, you might ask 'Is it significant that Amber did not eat breakfast?' The answer is 'Yes'. It is significant that Amber did not eat anything, because diabetics who skip meals increase their chances of hypoglycaemia. If you cannot answer all the questions you raise during re-reading the question, do what research you can in the circumstances. If you are in an examination, your general knowledge, your dictionary (if you are allowed to use one) and your wits may be your only resources. If you are answering the problem question as a piece of coursework, a quick search on the Internet will often provide the answer.

Returning to the question, and dealing first with Amber, we note:

- she knows that she suffers from diabetes and knows (or should know) that skipping meals might lead to hypoglycaemia;
- she knows (or should know) that blurred vision is a symptom of hypoglycaemia;
- she owes a duty of care to other road users;
- she might be in breach of that duty by failing to stop at the red traffic signal (with the key issue here being whether she should be judged by the objective standard of care of the reasonable driver and, if so, whether she fell below that standard of care);
- she caused damage to Emerald's car; and
- she might raise the defence that she had an impaired degree of consciousness.

Turning to Beryl, we note:

- she had a sudden epileptic seizure while driving her car and as a result of this has crashed into a lamppost;

- she had no knowledge of her condition;
- she owes a duty of care to other road users;
- she may be in breach of that duty by (i) crashing into a lamppost and (ii) driving over Jade's bicycle (with the main issue here being whether she fell below the standard of care of a reasonable driver suffering a sudden disability);
- she caused damage to the lamppost;
- she caused damage to Jade's bicycle;
- in respect of the damage to the lamppost (presumably owned by the Highway Authority), she could raise the defence that she suffered a sudden and total loss of consciousness and was not aware of the condition that caused her disability; and
- in respect of the damage to Jade's bicycle, she could raise the defence that through impaired consciousness she did not know she was unfit to drive.

Now that we have *identified* both the *material facts* and the *legal issues* arising from those facts, we need to *select* the relevant *law*. In our example this is straightforward, since we have only looked at relevant cases. In the problem questions you will answer during your studies there are three reasons why this process will not be so simple. First, you will have to select the relevant law from a much larger body of law drawn from both cases and statutes. Secondly, having selected the applicable cases and statutes, you will need to examine these materials in detail, and perhaps carry out further research to discover whether there are other cases or statutes which are relevant to the legal issues raised by the problem. (Clearly this point does not apply to examinations.) Thirdly, the level of the court that made the decision might be relevant to the arguments you intend to develop and therefore you should note this. For example, in the cases we have selected here, we note that *Roberts* is a first instance decision of the High Court and that *Mansfield* is a decision of the Court of Appeal.

The third step in the planning process to consider how to *apply the law to the facts* of the problem question. What we are doing here is seeing how the selected law fits (or does not fit) the facts. We have done this by constructing a simple table (see next page) that we can readily refer to when we come to the writing stage. In the left-hand column we note the law and in the right-hand column we consider how it applies to the facts of the problem.

In this question we have been asked to advise Amber and Beryl as to their liabilities in the tort of negligence. Our answer will *conclude* with advice drawing on our application of the law to the facts. Some points are uncontroversial and we effectively drew our conclusions on these points as we applied the law to the facts in the table. Other issues are less clear-cut and it is these points that we need to discuss in our answer if we are to gain high marks.

Dulieu v White (High Court) A driver owes a duty of care to other road users.	**Amber**	– Owes a duty of care to other road users.
	Beryl	– Owes a duty of care to other road users.
Roberts v Ramsbottom (High Court) (1) The standard of care is the ordinary 'reasonable driver' unless the driver suffers a sudden and total loss of consciousness.	**Amber**	– Suffers a gradual impairment of consciousness. – Liable under *Roberts*.
	Beryl	– Suffers a sudden and total loss of consciousness causing her to crash into a lamppost. – Not liable under *Roberts*.
(2) A driver who continues to drive when unfit to do so or when he should be aware of his unfitness to drive will not escape liability.	**Amber**	– Continues to drive when she experiences blurred vision. – Liable under *Roberts*.
	Beryl	– Drives over Jade's bicycle when she *might* have known she was unfit to drive. – Liable under *Roberts*?
Mansfield v Weetabix (Court of Appeal) The standard of care is the 'reasonable driver' who is unaware that he is suffering from a condition (that transpires gradually or suddenly) which impairs his ability to drive.	**Amber**	– Her condition gradually worsened but she knew she suffered from diabetes and knew/should have known that blurred vision is a symptom of hypoglycaemia. – Liable under *Mansfield*.
	Beryl	– Did not know that she had epilepsy; thus she could not anticipate an epileptic seizure. – Not liable to Highway Authority under *Mansfield*. – Not aware of the disabling condition which impaired her consciousness and her ability to drive. – Not liable to Jade under *Mansfield*.

The planning stage is now complete and we are now ready to write our answer. You might be wondering how you will ever manage to plan in this way under examination conditions. The simple answer is to practise throughout your course by using this method to prepare for seminars and tutorials and when doing coursework. You will also find that using this structure when planning answers to old examination questions will be a great help to you when revising for your examinations, because this will ensure that you revise actively, engaging with the kind of material you will encounter in the examination itself. You will also find that, if you plan effectively, you will spend less time writing; and, more importantly, you will answer the question in a structured fashion which will ensure that you keep the focus on the relevant issues. Here is our answer to the problem:

> The issue for Amber (A) in this scenario is whether she is liable to Emerald (E) for the damage she caused to E's car. Ultimately this will turn on whether A can successfully raise a defence, based on her impaired consciousness, in order to avoid liability in any negligence claim E might bring. Beryl (B) is likely to be sued by Jade (J) for the damage B caused to her bicycle; and by the owner of the lamppost, presumed to be the Highway Authority (HA). B will want to know whether she can resist these claims on the basis of her sudden and complete loss of consciousness and the fact that she was unaware of her unfitness to drive. To succeed in a claim in the tort of negligence, the claimants will need to show that the defendants owed them a duty of care; that this duty was breached; that the breach caused their damages; and that the damage was not too remote.
>
> In *Dulieu v White* [1901] 2 KB 669 it was held that road users owe a duty of care to other road users and to persons and property close to the highway. On this authority it is clear that A owes a duty of care to E and B owes a duty of care to HA and J. Having established that defendants owe the claimants a duty of care, the next issue to address is whether the defendants breached the duty of care owed. This is a key issue for both A and B and the court would determine the matter by measuring the defendants against the requisite standard of care. Two possible routes are open to the court. First it could judge the defendants against the objective standard of the ordinary 'reasonable driver'; secondly, it could use the more subjective test of the 'reasonable driver' who is unaware that she is suffering from a condition which impairs her ability to drive.
>
> Looking first at A, she has suffered a gradual impairment of consciousness due to a hypoglycaemic attack which is a classic symptom of diabetes. A knew that she was a diabetic and skipped eating breakfast, which is the probable cause of her hypoglycaemic attack.
>
> In *Roberts v Ramsbottom* [1980] 1 WLR 823 Neill J held that a defendant should be evaluated by the standard of care of the ordinary 'reasonable driver' unless the driver suffered a sudden and total loss of consciousness. Since A has suffered only a gradual and partial loss of

consciousness, she would be judged by the standard of the 'reasonable driver' under *Roberts*. The requirement for a sudden and total loss of consciousness was, however, overruled by the Court of Appeal in *Mansfield v Weetabix* [1998] 1 WLR 1263. The court applied the 'reasonable driver' test subjectively holding that the lorry driver in the case was to be judged by the standard of the 'reasonable driver' who is unaware that he is suffering from a condition, which transpires gradually or suddenly, that impairs his ability to drive. The difficulty A faces is that, although the law no longer requires the sudden and total loss of consciousness, the court in *Mansfield* limited the subjective test to drivers who are unaware of their condition. A is not unaware that she suffers from diabetes and should know that not eating her breakfast might lead to a hypoglycaemic episode. Further, applying the second element of the decision in *Roberts* (which was not overruled by the Court of Appeal in *Mansfield*), A could also incur liability for driving when she was unfit to do so, or when she should have been aware of her unfitness to drive. Applying this test, A ought to have stopped driving as soon as she realised that her vision was blurred.

Turning to B and considering first her potential liability to HA, B crashed into HA's property after a sudden epileptic seizure, causing complete loss of consciousness. This would satisfy the requirement for a sudden and total loss of consciousness under *Roberts* and the modified standard of care in *Mansfield*, making it highly probable that B would escape liability for the damage she caused to HA. This was B's first epileptic seizure and she did not know she was susceptible to epileptic seizures. She would be judged as the 'reasonable driver' who is unaware of a condition that impaired her ability to drive.

B was not, however, unconscious when she damaged J's bicycle, and the Court of Appeal did not criticise the second element of *Roberts* in *Mansfield* so it remains good law. If B were judged on this second part of *Roberts*, namely that she drove when unfit to do so or when she should have been aware that she was unfit to do so, the decision would turn on whether B was actually *aware* that she was unfit to drive. B is clearly unfit to drive, but given the seriousness of her condition it may well be that B was unaware of her unfitness to drive. The facts of the problem differ from those in *Roberts*, where the defendant never lost consciousness at any point and actually got out of his car and held a short conversation with the workmen whose van he crashed into before continuing his journey. Here, there is no evidence that B was ever roused to that level of consciousness and it may be that B was still very dazed and confused when she drove her car over J's bicycle. While the claimant might argue that B's ability to put the car into gear suggests some degree of consciousness, there is no indication that B's level of awareness is any higher (and some suggestion that it may well be lower) than that of the defendant in *Mansfield*. In that case, the defendant drove his lorry some 40 miles before crashing into the claimant's shop: here B has moved her car only a very short distance.

A is advised that she is likely to be held liable for the damage she caused to E's car, since she suffered no sudden and total loss of consciousness and either was aware or should have been aware that she was unfit to drive. B is advised that the sudden and total loss of consciousness will absolve her of fault and liability in respect of the damage to HA. B's liability to J is more problematic. However, it is submitted that she should not be held liable on the basis that she was not aware of her disabling condition and that her level of consciousness was seriously impaired to a degree at least equal to, and probably greater than, that of the defendant in *Mansfield*.

Conclusion

Having read this chapter you should have a satisfactory understanding of how to approach answering problem questions. If you want to move on from simply understanding *how* to answer problem questions and progress to actually *answering them well*, you will need to practise. Tutorials and seminars will provide ample opportunity for such practice. Practising the technique of answering questions will not only improve the structure and content of your work but will also help you to develop your written English skills (as discussed in Chapter 9) into an appropriate style of academic writing. A logical structure that draws on only relevant material is the key to a good answer, but to score high marks the structure and content need to be revealed through a written style which demonstrates your ability to use correct grammar, spelling and punctuation, as well as appropriate vocabulary.

12 Oral Skills

An effective oral presentation requires thorough preparation and real familiarity with the subject matter. A successful presentation will have explicit goals, be appropriately
structured for the needs of the audience and make creative
and sensitive use of visual, verbal and non-verbal communication. When approached in a careful way, delivering oral
presentations need not be as stressful an activity as many
students find it to be.

● Introduction

Your career as a student is likely to give you many opportunities for partici-
pating in oral presentations, some of which may well count for assessment.
The nature of these presentations, whether assessed or not, will vary quite
widely: some will involve working with other students and making joint or
group presentations, while others will be undertaken and presented alone.
Certain presentations will be quite informal and take place in small group
sessions, whereas others may require a more formal setting, such as a moot
court. Some contexts, such as mooting, require you to follow a particular
code of etiquette, but the basic skills and sensitivities required for fluent and
effective oral communication, which we discuss in this chapter, remain the
same whatever the situation.

   As with every skill, you will find that the best way to improve your mastery
of oral presentation skills is through practice. Every oral presentation you
make is an opportunity to develop your skills, refine your technique and
build up your self-confidence. Improving your oral skills will help you in your
academic studies and beyond. At the most obvious level, effective oral communication skills are essential to the advocacy work of many barristers and
solicitors. Additionally, however, these skills are increasingly tested and
valued by employers, which means you may well find that you are asked to
make oral presentations in a variety of job interviews, and not only in the
selection processes for aspiring trainee solicitors and pupil barristers.

Preparing the presentation

Identifying the purpose
The first thing you need to do is to identify the purpose of your presentation. This involves consideration of two questions:

- who is my audience? and
- what do I want to achieve?

In order to determine what you want to achieve, you will first need to clarify your goals and understand your role in the presentation. If, for example, you are asked to make an oral presentation, in a small group session, to other students, the purpose (in terms of what you want to achieve) might be to share your perspective on the topic. Your role in this case will be that of a teacher and will involve imparting information, explaining concepts or ideas and stimulating the group's understanding. If, however, your presentation requires you to participate in a debate, your role will be that of an advocate and you will concentrate on developing a compelling argument and persuading the audience to share your point of view. In each case you will want the audience:

- to understand what you are saying; and
- be interested in what you say.

Additionally, in some situations at least, you will want to

- convince your audience by the quality of your arguments.

You will, however, only achieve these goals if you take into account the expectations and needs of your audience.

People will listen to what you have to say when the subject matter is intrinsically interesting to them, or where you make it interesting to them by arousing their curiosity. Audiences will also listen to material that is likely to be useful to them. If you have a free choice of topic you might choose one that you think will interest the audience. If the topic is specified, you can still take a particular stance on the topic to engage the audience's attention. If your presentation requires expert knowledge of a subject, and the majority of your audience lack that expertise, pitch your presentation at a level that most people will understand. Keeping an eye on the audience's body language will often help you to keep track of whether they are following you, or whether you need to explain the technical aspects of the topic more clearly. Always bear in mind the simple fact that if you forget the needs of your audience, they will also forget you.

Sometimes your audience will be a mixed group in terms of ability and topic interest. When this happens, it is important to decide which groups in the audience are most valuable to you. Imagine, for example, that you are a student approaching graduation, who is appearing in the final of a prestigious mooting competition, and that the case concerns an issue of shipping law (which is an area of law in which you ultimately wish to specialise). The first, and most important, person to consider is the moot judge, even if you know that the audience also contains some first year students (who know nothing about shipping law), as well as a number of shipping law practitioners, who are your potential employers. Not surprisingly, most people, faced with such an audience, would focus on the judge, in the hope that this will deliver the double reward of winning the competition while also impressing the practitioners. (The topic of mooting is discussed in more detail at pp. 205–210.)

At a more mundane level, where a course is assessed by oral presentation, it is worth emphasising that a vital part of the purpose of your presentation will be to comply with the marking criteria and presentation rubric produced by your college or university. It is important to discover how your presentation will be evaluated, particularly in terms of the weighting between subject knowledge, analysis of the topic, and oral presentation skills.

Researching and planning

Once you have determined the purpose of your presentation, you can begin the research. You may find it helpful to formulate the purpose of your presentation as a question, or to draft a presentation title, to ensure that you know the boundaries of your research before you begin the process. The research method for an oral presentation is in some ways like that for an essay, in that it calls for active and selective reading (see the discussions of the SQ3R technique at pp. 15 and 172), where the emphasis is on identifying *only* that material which is relevant to your presentation. However, the processes also differ, since an oral presentation gives you the opportunity to use materials such as pictures, graphics, statistics and anecdotes. In particular, illustrations, whether graphic or anecdotal, are useful ways of varying the content of your presentation, since they provide your audience with breaks from the heavier material and thus increase your chances of keeping their attention.

Tailor your research to the length of the presentation: if your presentation is only seven or eight minutes long you will not be able to cover very much material and should not try to do so. Do not exceed the time limit for your presentation simply because you have too much material, nor for any other reason within your control. Audiences react badly to speakers who overrun their allotted time, and if the presentation is assessed you will lose marks.

Plan the presentation using the results of your research to build a logically ordered and coherent presentation. One commonly cited method for ordering material in an oral presentation is the 'three times rule' which says that when addressing your audience you should 'tell them what you are going to tell them; tell them; tell them what you have told them'. The introduction is the place to tell the listeners 'what you are going to tell them', the main body of the presentation is where you 'tell them' and the conclusion is where to 'tell them what you have told them'. In the conclusion you should take particular care to demonstrate that you have achieved all you promised in your introduction.

In one sense, there is nothing remarkable about the 'three times rule'. It simply reminds the speaker that a presentation must have a beginning, a middle and an end. However, it serves the additional, and very important, function of emphasising the need for *planned repetition* in public speaking. For this reason many people plan the main body of their presentation first. This reduces the risk of making claims in the introduction that cannot be achieved in the time available and also helps to ensure that only the aims that have been fulfilled in the presentation are featured in the conclusion.

Plan the main body of the presentation by listing the issues and sub-issues you need to cover, and then arrange them into some kind of order. Use headings and subheadings to represent each point and sub-point, and sketch out your plan on a single side of paper if at all possible. Ideally, you should provide yourself with an overview of what you are aiming to achieve. This will help you to identify not only any gaps in your material and flaws in your argument, but also any aspects of your material or argument that you can jettison because they do not contribute anything useful to the overall enterprise. Some topics work best if they are presented in a chronological order, while others lend themselves to a thematic, topic-based, structure. Where you need to develop an argument, your presentation should follow a logical order revealing each step of your line of reasoning. Above all, the content and structure of your presentation needs to be planned for delivery as speech, in a way that makes sense of the topic and in a manner which makes it as easy as possible for your listeners to follow what you are saying. Once the main body of the presentation is in order, create an outline of your introduction and conclusions, before starting to make notes for your presentation.

Using notes

One of the biggest temptations when preparing for oral presentations, especially for the inexperienced public speaker, is to produce a written text. This is not an appropriate or helpful way to prepare for oral presentations and should be avoided. The appeal of having a written text in front of you is easy to understand and is frequently justified by a comment like 'I just want it as a back-up in case I get lost or nervous'. Two problems usually emerge. First, when people get nervous during presentations and have the text to hand they cannot always quickly locate the information they want (since they have not actually been following the text word for word) which results in greater anxiety and, at times, complete panic. Secondly, once people turn to the text they never leave it; and, moreover, they begin to speak too quickly, their eyes remained glued to the script and all engagement with the audience is lost. Consequently, the oral presentation starts to sound like an essay being read aloud and the listeners are lost.

This does not mean that you should avoid using notes, but simply that they should be appropriate for the task. Most experienced public speakers use some kind of notes when speaking, if only to stay on track and maintain the balance of their presentation. One way of doing this is to use index cards of a size small enough to hold discreetly in your hand. Many Parliamentarians favour this system of notes; and, provided you do not cram the cards with text, you will readily be able to see, at a glance, the points you want to discuss, and the order in which you want to discuss them. An alternative method is simply to have a copy of your plan or extended outline of your presentation on a single piece of paper that you can glance at from time to time. Visual aids, such as overhead projector transparencies or slides produced in a presentation graphics program such as PowerPoint, can also be used as prompts. If you do use visual aids, however, you would do well also to print paper copies for yourself and keep them in front of you during the presentation. In most rooms and lecture theatres the projection screen is behind the speaker and you do not want to get into the habit of turning your back on your listeners and talking to the projection screen. It is poor style and does little to endear you to the audience.

Before you deliver your presentation, you should try to spend some time familiarising yourself with your notes. Ideally, your preparation schedule should allow enough time for you to put your notes aside for a few days, so that you can return to them with a relatively fresh mind. This will give you a more realistic idea of whether your notes are detailed enough to remind you of all you need to say, as well as giving you time to make any necessary changes. If you are making a presentation for the first time, you may find it helps if you practise by having a trial run in front of a friend. This should give you a fair idea of what the task entails, as well as, hopefully, providing you with some constructive feedback on the content and style of the presentation.

Delivering the presentation

First impressions

Whenever people meet other people for the first time, they make judgments about them very quickly. First impressions really do count, as people evaluate you by your dress, appearance and body language in a matter of minutes. As the saying known by all sales people goes: *you only get one chance to make a first impression.* If your oral presentation is made in a small group session your audience will, for better or worse, already have an impression of you and will not usually expect you to dress up for the occasion. If you are taking part in a moot, the audience may expect you to dress in formal attire, such as a dark suit; and even if they do not expect this, the judge will. The three key things are to:

- be sensitive to the occasion;
- dress appropriately; and, above all,
- remember that the audience begins evaluating you as soon as they see you.

An oral presentation involves direct face-to-face communication; your words are delivered in person, rather than through the medium of the written word. It is therefore an essential part of the exercise that you will be assessed (formally or informally) not only on *what* you say, but also on *how* you say it. Your audience will judge your delivery by the way you use your voice, maintain eye contact, and use body language such as posture and gestures. Behaviour such as standing with your hands in your pockets, or fiddling with jewellery, will project the wrong image.

Verbal communication

The first words you say will either confirm the audience's initial impression or give you at least some opportunity to alter it. Introduce yourself clearly and confidently, smile and make eye contact with the audience; and then tell them, quite briefly, the purpose of your presentation, before providing an outline of how you will proceed. Your voice is the principal tool through which you will communicate with your listeners and a number of factors need to be taken into account here, namely:

- volume;
- clarity;
- pace; and
- tone.

Your voice should be loud enough for people to hear without them having to struggle to listen. Straining to hear is very tiring and people will stop listening very quickly if they cannot easily hear what you are saying. If you are using a microphone to amplify your voice, or are speaking in unfamiliar surroundings, it is perfectly acceptable to ask the audience if they can hear you. Asking this question straight after you have introduced yourself is also a good way of engaging with the audience at an early stage of the presentation.

Your words will need to be more clearly enunciated when you speak in public than in your ordinary speech. Pronounce the syllables in words clearly and avoid dropping letters at the end of words and allowing words to merge together. A common difficulty is the letter 'g' at the end of words, thus 'going around' ends up sounding like 'goin-round'. Numbers can also be very difficult to hear unless they are clearly pronounced: for example, 'fifteen' and 'fifty' are readily confused.

As well as enunciation, the pace at which people speak affects the clarity of what they say. When addressing other people, even in a small group, you need to speak more slowly than you would in everyday conversation. This does not mean that you need to have long pauses and breaks in your delivery but it does mean that your delivery should be slow enough for your listeners to hear every word and at the same time should flow smoothly. Pauses should, of course, be inserted; both to give people time to consider points you have made, and for dramatic effect.

Finally, you need to vary the tone of your voice to emphasise important points and to keep the audience engaged. Speaking in a monotonous voice will send your audience to sleep and communicate a complete lack of interest in the subject on your part. Voice tone, pitch and pace can be used to deliver a number of signals to your listeners. For example, if you slow down or make a slight pause before increasing the volume of your voice slightly, the audience will realise that you are about to make an important point. Such implicit clues are much better than pausing and saying 'Now this point is very important, please listen carefully'. An audience will soon tire of such interventions.

Non-verbal communication

We have already noted that your dress and body language contribute to the first impression you make on first meetings. Body language is, however, culturally specific and what is acceptable behaviour in one country or society may be rude or offensive in another. It is important to recognise therefore, that our first impressions can also be the result of cultural misunderstandings, and that you may need to be sensitive to a variety of cultural norms if you have to address a multicultural audience.

Whatever the cultural setting, your gestures need to match your words; a wide grin will not usually help communicate the gravity of a serious point. You should use your hands, body posture and eye contact only to facilitate communication and you should avoid any gestures that positively distract or annoy your audience. Fiddling with pens, buttons or jewellery, and swaying to and fro at a lectern will undermine the effectiveness of your presentation, whereas a timely and appropriate hand gesture will reinforce your point. Avoid body language which communicates nervousness, such as covering part of your face with a hand or constantly clearing your throat, as well as anything that might suggest that you are untrustworthy, such as looking away from the audience when speaking. Above all, maintaining eye contact with the audience is vital for creating trust and sustaining engagement when addressing a Western European or North American audience.

Using visual aids and handouts

Visual aids can be very powerful presentation tools. They can help to reinforce ideas, compare information and to illustrate points that you make in your presentation. Any visual aids you use should match and enhance your words: an oral presentation should never be overshadowed by cutting edge graphics. PowerPoint slides should not be used as a shield to hide behind, and you should never simply read from the slides. Make sure the audience can read your slides by keeping colour combinations simple (light colours on dark backgrounds or dark colours on light backgrounds work best), and avoid red–green colour combinations since some 10% of the male population are red–green colour blind. The text should be large enough and the fonts clear enough for all the audience to see, and you should avoid cramming text onto slides, since white space on the screen makes the text easier to read. Always check in advance if you will be permitted to use visual aids for an assessed presentation; and, if so, what facilities are provided. There is no mileage in creating PowerPoint slides unless the room you will be speaking in has appropriate computer projection facilities. Finally, never be totally reliant on technology – it sometimes fails.

Handouts are a more difficult issue. A copy of your slides can save people writing notes and help them focus on what you are saying, but if you give the audience too much information in advance you run the risk that they will simply read the handout and not listen to what you have to say. Perhaps the best strategy is to distribute only outlines in advance and, where needed, provide fuller handouts at the end of the presentation.

Mooting

Introduction

A moot is a role-play exercise, in which two pairs of advocates (or sometimes two single advocates) conduct legal argument, based on an imaginary factual scenario, in front of a judge (or sometimes a bench of two or more judges). For the sake of simplicity, the rest of this section is written on the basis that there are two pairs of advocates and one judge, since this is by far the most common situation. At the end of a moot the judge will decide not only which side has won on the law, but also – and for the participants much more importantly – which side has won in terms of being the better mooters.

Most law schools offer at least some opportunity to moot, while many go further and incorporate mooting into your programme of assessment. In addition to any internal provision, there are also several inter-institutional mooting competitions. Either your law school or the promoters of inter-institutional mooting competitions will lay down the specific rules for the moots which they cover (for example, there will always be a time limit – typically 30 or 40 minutes for each side); but the advice contained in the rest of this section is offered by way of more general guidance to mooting.

Preparing for a moot

In academic terms, preparing for a moot is similar to preparing to write an answer to a problem question (see Chapter 11). This may sound odd, because in a problem question you have to discuss both the basis of any liability and the possibility of any defences which the facts may disclose, while in a moot you are required to argue only on one. In practice, however, this distinction between problem questions and mooting is more apparent than real, since each side in a moot must foresee – and be able to counter as best they can – the arguments which the other side will put forward.

Mooting problems are almost always couched in terms of appeals. This enables the person who sets the problem to identify the grounds of appeal.

You will be told which side of the case you have to argue and you will be given the name of your co-advocate. (You may or may not be told which of you is to be the leader and which the junior. If you are not told this, you will have to agree between yourselves.) The grounds of appeal you are given will, typically, contain two points of law, so that each advocate can argue one of them.

The person who is organising the moot (whose traditional title is Master – or Mistress – of Moots, but who will here, for the sake of simplicity, be called the organiser) may be a fellow student, a member of staff, or a fellow student with the support of a member of staff. After you have decided how you are going to argue your point of law, but before the moot itself, you must give both the organiser and your opponents a list of the authorities on which you will be relying. Naturally, your opponents must reciprocate.

Someone (it may be you, the organiser or someone who has been specifically allocated this task) must collect the authorities. Ideally, this will involve the law reports and the statutory material itself, but in some colleges and universities it will not be possible to take this material out of the library, so you will have to make do with photocopies or printed downloads. Even if you have the original source, you will still need a photocopy or a duplicate download as well, so that the judge can have one copy while you have another.

Advocacy for mooters

Introduction
Just as preparing for a moot has much in common with preparing to write an answer to a problem question, so performing as an advocate draws heavily on the advice given previously in this chapter in the context of oral skills generally. However, four points which are specifically relevant to mooting must be mentioned here, namely, addressing the judge, citing authority, using authority, and dealing with questions from the judge.

Addressing the judge
Moots are almost always located in either the Court of Appeal or the House of Lords. While there is no reason in principle why a moot should not be heard by a bench of three or five judges (depending on which court is involved), constraints of sheer practicality often mean that only a single judge will sit.

When addressing the judge, inexperienced advocates often have difficulty in handling the distinction between *My Lord* (or *My Lady*) and *Your Lordship* (or *Your Ladyship*). The easy way to work out the correct form is that, with one exception, *My Lord* (or *My Lady*) is appropriate only where you would use the name of the person you are addressing in a less formal relationship. So, for example, if a friend asks you how soon you will be ready to go out, you might say 'About another ten minutes, Mary'. Imagining this in the formal context of the High Court, the Court of Appeal or the House of Lords, with the judge asking you how much longer you need to complete the presentation of your case, you would say 'About another ten minutes, My Lord'. The exception is where you are addressing a bench consisting of two or more judges and you need to refer to one judge while speaking to another. Responding to the same question in this context, you would say, for example, 'I hope to be no more than another ten minutes, My Lord, but it may take me a little longer to provide a full response to the point which My Lord, Lord Justice Blank, raised a few moments ago'.

Turning to the correct use of 'Your Lordship' or 'Your Ladyship', the principle is, once again, clear. This usage is appropriate only where, in a less formal context, you would say 'you'. So, for example, if your housemate says 'shall we have pizza tonight?' you might reply 'if you like'. In the context of the courtroom, if the judge says 'I do not need to hear any further argument on this point', you would reply 'as Your Lordship (or Your Ladyship) pleases'.

When speaking about another judge at the level of the High Court or above who is not involved in the instant hearing, the correct usage is *His Lordship* (or *Her Ladyship*). So, for example, when citing an earlier case as an authority, you would say

> I refer Your Lordship to the speech of Baroness Hale of Richmond in the case of *R (Williamson) v Secretary of State for Education and Employment* in the second volume of the Appeal Cases reports for 2005, at paragraph [58], where Her Ladyship said '...'

Where the case dates from before the introduction of numbered paragraphs, the pinpoint citation would be to the page number and – where the series of law reports offers the opportunity – a marginal letter. In any case, an adjustment to *Lord* (or *Lady*) *Justice Blank* or *Mr* (or *Mrs*) *Justice Blank*, as appropriate, will be obvious.

When speaking of a circuit judge, you would say *His* (or *Her*) *Honour Judge Blank*, or, when speaking of the judge from whose court the instant appeal has come, you could simply say *the learned judge* or (if the judge was sitting at first instance) an alternative would be *the learned judge at first instance*, or even *the learned trial judge*.

Citing authority

Many students fall into the trap of thinking that textbooks and journal articles contain the law, even though it is clear (see p. 76) that they do not do so. All that any textbook or journal article can ever contain is what its author thinks the law is, with the law itself being contained in the relevant cases, statutes, treaties and so on. It follows, therefore, that when citing authority, you should cite an original source wherever possible, reserving the citation of textbooks and journal articles for those situations where the law is unclear, in which case the opinion of authors may well be useful as 'fertilisers of thought' (a phrase which comes from the judgment of Sir Robert Megarry in *Cordell v Second Clanfield Properties Ltd* [1969] 2 Ch 9). However, even when it is appropriate to cite textbooks and journal articles, it is important that you let the judge know that you understand the limited status of the material you are using.

Where a case is reported in The Law Reports you should cite that reference (see p. 82). When giving the reference orally, you should use the relevant words in full rather than articulating the established abbreviations. (The citation of *R (Williamson) v Secretary of State for Education and Employment* (above) shows how this is done.) When citing statutes, the short title is sufficient (see p. 86).

Using authority

Many students who study legal method (or whatever it may be called in their college or university) seem to regard it as an introductory chore which has been imposed upon them by the designers of their curriculum gratuitously, rather than as the foundation of their subsequent studies. If mooting achieves nothing else, it will at least dispel this misunderstanding, since a sound grasp of the principles of both binding precedent and legislative interpretation will prove indispensable when you are constructing and arguing your case – and perhaps even more so when you are trying to persuade the judge that your opponents' case is flawed. (Chapter 7 contains a useful overview of legal method, although by the time you are mooting you will be likely to have read a more substantial treatment of the subject, such as McLeod, *Legal Method*, 6th edn, 2007, Palgrave Macmillan.)

Dealing with questions from the judge

Every mooter must expect to be interrupted at least once by the judge. It is important to realise that this is not done out of spite or frustration, but because it is an essential part of the mooting exercise to find out how the advocates deal with questions. (As many an experienced mooter has discovered, preparing an address on the law is one thing: responding to questions may be quite another.) If you do not understand the question which is being asked, you should say so, although it is always good psychology to adopt a form of words which suggests that the lack of effective communication is your fault rather than the judge's. ('I am afraid I do not quite follow your Lordship's point' is likely to produce a much better response than 'If your Lordship could manage to express the question more clearly, I might be able to answer it'.)

The two-fold nature of the decision

The facts of life in relation to mooting are that, however hard the question setter has tried to be even-handed, one side will almost always have a stronger case than the other. It follows, that the odds of winning *on the law* are likely to be stacked in favour of one side rather than the other. However, while it is always pleasing to win on the law, what really matters in mooting is *who wins the moot.* In this connection – although it may seem perverse to say so – the side with the weaker case may even be in the stronger position in terms of mooting. After all, presenting a strong case well is likely to be less challenging (and, therefore, less impressive) than making the best of a bad job by putting up a creditable – even if ultimately unsuccessful – performance when presenting a weak one.

Once the judge has given his or her decision as to who wins the case, therefore, you will receive a distinct decision as to who has won the moot. This will normally follow on immediately from the decision on the case itself. Therefore, unless the rules under which you are operating make specific provision to the contrary, you can assume that you will not have to take part in the sort of wrangles which usually arise in reality, concerning matters such as applications for leave to appeal and for orders as to costs.

The difference between moots and mock trials

Although moots are sometimes referred to as *mock trials*, the two exercises are, in fact, quite distinct from each other.

More particularly, a mock trial is really a form of amateur dramatics which relies heavily on improvisation. Although mock trials will usually be staged in the context of the Crown Court, there is no reason why a scenario taken from civil law should not be used, with the trial being placed in a county court. However, the model of a criminal case in the Crown Court is so common that the remaining comments here will assume, for the sake of simplicity, that this is the kind of mock trial which is being staged. On this basis, therefore, the idea is that someone will be charged with an offence, for which he or she will then be tried.

Turning to the nuts-and-bolts of staging a mock trial, the offence itself may have been enacted, with potential witnesses being placed strategically so that they can give witness statements and – ultimately – evidence; or someone may simply write a set of witness statements, which are then treated as a script. As with mooting, there may be a pair of advocates for each of the prosecution and the defence, or there may be only one on each side. There will, of course, be a jury. Whoever conceives the mock trial (if the offence is enacted) or whoever writes the witness statements (where it is not) will take care to include at least one point of law which is capable of being argued either way. Whether the offence has been staged or merely scripted, much of the fun of a mock trial comes from the way in which the witnesses improvise answers to the questions put to them by the advocates in respect of matters which arise on an unforeseen basis as the trial unfolds.

The advantages of mock trials over moots is that they give far more students the opportunity to become involved, since witnesses, jurors and at least one defendant will be required, as well as the advocates. However, the disadvantages are substantial. First, a mock trial is much more complicated to set up (especially if the offence is enacted) and the actual performance takes much longer (it being difficult to get through any mock trial in less than two hours, with three being more realistic, in which time four or five moots could have been heard. Secondly, the advocates must have at least some knowledge of the law of evidence (and since this is typically taught at Level Three, the pool of students from which the advocates may be drawn is inevitably restricted). Thirdly, even where the offence has been enacted, it has clearly not been actually committed. (Even in the interests of artistic integrity, it would not be practicable to stage an actual murder or rape, for example; and if the offence is one of dishonesty there will equally clearly have been no actual dishonesty because the defendant would simply have been playing a part.) Finally, and leaving aside whether it is an advantage or a disadvantage, the practical difficulties in staging mock trials makes it impracticable to incorporate them into programmes of assessment.

Conclusion

Having read this chapter, you should realise that the key to successful oral presentations, is twofold:

- research and plan thoroughly; and
- remember that an oral presentation is not simply a written presentation read out loud.

Identifying the purpose of your presentation and considering the needs and expectations of your audience are paramount if you are to deliver effective presentations. Research and planning must focus on the fact that you are working towards an exercise in communication using the medium of speech, and the content must be simply and logically structured, using planned repetition where appropriate to reinforce your message. Delivering the presentation requires attention to style, acknowledging that appearance, body language and voice control will all contribute to the degree of success or failure of the presentation.

Appendix 1
Extracts From the European Convention on Human Rights and Fundamental Freedoms

Articles 2–12 and 14 of, and Articles 1–3 of the First Protocol, and Articles 1 & 2 of the Sixth Protocol to, the European Convention for the Protection of Human Rights and Fundamental Freedoms 1950

Section 1
Article 2

1. Everyone's right to life shall be protected by law. No one shall be deprived of his life intentionally save in the execution of a sentence of a court following his conviction of a crime for which this penalty is provided by law.

2. Deprivation of life shall not be regarded as inflicted in contravention of this Article when it results from the use of force which is no more than absolutely necessary:

   (a) in defence of any person from unlawful violence;

   (b) in order to effect a lawful arrest or to prevent the escape of a person lawfully detained;

   (c) in action lawfully taken for the purpose of quelling a riot or insurrection.

Article 3
No one shall be subjected to torture or to inhuman or degrading treatment or punishment.

Article 4

1. No one shall be held in slavery or servitude.

2. No one shall be required to perform forced or compulsory labour.

3. For the purpose of this Article the term 'forced or compulsory labour' shall not include:

(a) any work required to be done in the ordinary course of detention imposed according to the provisions of Article 5 of this Convention or during conditional release from such detention;

(b) any service of a military character or, in case of conscientious objectors in countries where they are recognized, service exacted instead of compulsory military service;

(c) any service exacted in case of an emergency or calamity threatening the life or well-being of the community;

(d) any work or service which forms part of normal civic obligations.

Article 5

1. Everyone has the right to liberty and security of person. No one shall be deprived of his liberty save in the following cases and in accordance with a procedure prescribed by law:

   (a) the lawful detention of a person after conviction by a competent court;

   (b) the lawful arrest or detention of a person for non-compliance with the lawful order of a court or in order to secure the fulfilment of any obligation prescribed by law;

   (c) the lawful arrest or detention of a person effected for the purpose of bringing him before the competent legal authority on reasonable suspicion of having committed an offence or when it is reasonably considered necessary to prevent his committing an offence or fleeing after having done so;

   (d) the detention of a minor by lawful order for the purpose of educational supervision or his lawful detention for the purpose of bringing him before the competent legal authority;

   (e) the lawful detention of persons for the prevention of the spreading of infectious diseases, of persons of unsound mind, alcoholics or drug addicts, or vagrants;

   (f) the lawful arrest or detention of a person to prevent his effecting an unauthorized entry into the country or of a person against whom action is being taken with a view to deportation or extradition.

2. Everyone who is arrested shall be informed promptly, in a language which he understands, of the reasons for his arrest and of any charge against him.

3. Everyone arrested or detained in accordance with the provisions of paragraph 1 (c) of this Article shall be brought promptly before a judge or other

officer authorized by law to exercise judicial power and shall be entitled to trial within a reasonable time or to release pending trial. Release may be conditioned by guarantees to appear for trial.

4. Everyone who is deprived of his liberty by arrest or detention shall be entitled to take proceedings by which the lawfulness of his detention shall be decided speedily by a court and his release ordered if the detention is not lawful.

5. Everyone who has been the victim of arrest or detention in contravention of the provisions of this Article shall have an enforceable right to compensation.

Article 6

1. In the determination of his civil rights and obligations or of any criminal charge against him, everyone is entitled to a fair and public hearing within a reasonable time by an independent and impartial tribunal established by law. Judgment shall be pronounced publicly but the press and public may be excluded from all or part of the trial in the interest of morals, public order or national security in a democratic society, where the interest of juveniles or the protection of the private life of the parties so require, or to the extent strictly necessary in the opinion of the court in special circumstances where publicity would prejudice the interests of justice.

2. Everyone charged with a criminal offence shall be presumed innocent until proved guilty according to law.

3. Everyone charged with a criminal offence has the following minimum rights:

    (a) to be informed promptly, in a language which he understands and in detail, of the nature and cause of the accusation against him;

    (b) to have adequate time and facilities for the preparation of his defence;

    (c) to defend himself in person or through legal assistance of his own choosing or, if he has not sufficient means to pay for legal assistance, to be given it free when the interests of justice so require;

    (d) to examine or have examined witnesses against him and to obtain the attendance and examination of witnesses on his behalf under the same conditions as witnesses against him;

    (e) to have the free assistance of an interpreter if he cannot understand or speak the language used in court.

Article 7

1. No one shall be held guilty of any criminal offence on account of any act or omission which did not constitute a criminal offence under national or international law at the time when it was committed. Nor shall a heavier penalty be imposed than the one that was applicable at the time the criminal offence was committed.

2. This Article shall not prejudice the trial and punishment of any person for any act or omission which, at the time when it was committed, was criminal according to the general principles of law recognized by civilized nations.

Article 8

1. Everyone has the right to respect for his private and family life, his home and his correspondence.

2. There shall be no interference by a public authority with the exercise of this right except such as is in accordance with the law and is necessary in a democratic society in the interests of national security, public safety or the economic well-being of the country, for the prevention of disorder or crime, for the protection of health or morals, or for the protection of the rights and freedoms of others.

Article 9

1. Everyone has the right to freedom of thought, conscience and religion; this right includes freedom to change his religion or belief, and freedom, either alone or in community with others and in public or private, to manifest his religion or belief, in worship, teaching, practice and observance.

2. Freedom to manifest one's religion or beliefs shall be subject only to such limitations as are prescribed by law and are necessary in a democratic society in the interests of public safety, for the protection of public order, health or morals, or for the protection of the rights and freedoms of others.

Article 10

1. Everyone has the right to freedom of expression. This right shall include freedom to hold opinions and to receive and impart information and ideas without interference by public authority and regardless of frontiers. This Article shall not prevent States from requiring the licensing of broadcasting, television or cinema enterprises.

2. The exercise of these freedoms, since it carries with it duties and responsibilities, may be subject to such formalities, conditions, restrictions or penalties as are prescribed by law and are necessary in a democratic society in the interests of national security, territorial integrity or public safety, for the prevention of disorder or crime, for the protection of health or morals, for the protection of the reputation or rights of others, for preventing the disclosure of information received in confidence, or for maintaining the authority and impartiality of the judiciary.

Article 11

1. Everyone has the right to freedom of peaceful assembly and to freedom of association with others, including the right to form and to join trade unions for the protection of his interests.

2. No restrictions shall be placed on the exercise of these rights other than such as are prescribed by law and are necessary in a democratic society in the interests of national security or public safety, for the prevention of disorder or crime, for the protection of health or morals or for the protection of the rights and freedoms of others. This Article shall not prevent the imposition of lawful restrictions on the exercise of these rights by members of the armed forces, of the police or of the administration of the State.

Article 12

Men and women of marriageable age have the right to marry and to found a family, according to the national laws governing the exercise of this right.

Article 14

The enjoyment of the rights and freedoms set forth in this Convention shall be secured without discrimination on any ground such as sex, race, colour, language, religion, political or other opinion, national or social origin, association with a national minority, property, birth or other status.

Articles 1–3 of Protocol 1 – Enforcement of Certain Rights and Freedoms not Included in Section 1 of the Convention

Article 1

Every natural or legal person is entitled to the peaceful enjoyment of his possessions. No one shall be deprived of his possessions except in the public interest and subject to the conditions provided for by law and by the general principles of international law.

The preceding provisions shall not, however, in any way impair the right of a State to enforce such laws as it deems necessary to control the use of property in accordance with the general interest or to secure the payment of taxes or other contributions or penalties.

Article 2

No person shall be denied the right to education. In the exercise of any functions which it assumes in relation to education and to teaching, the State shall respect the right of parents to ensure such education and teaching in conformity with their own religious and philosophical convictions.

Article 3

The High Contracting Parties undertake to hold free elections at reasonable intervals by secret ballot, under conditions which will ensure the free expression of the opinion of the people in the choice of the legislature.

Articles 1 and 2 of Protocol 6 – Concerning the Abolition of the Death Penalty

Article 1

The death penalty shall be abolished. No one shall be condemned to such penalty or executed.

Article 2

A state may make provision in its law for the death penalty in respect of acts committed in time of war or of imminent threat of war; such penalty shall be applied only in the instance laid down in the law and in accordance with its provisions. The State shall communicate to the Secretary General of the Council of Europe the relevant provisions of that law.

Note: Articles 16, 17 and 18 respectively provide that arts.10, 11 and 14 do not prohibit restrictions on the political activities of aliens; nothing in the Convention gives any right to do anything which would harm the rights which it protects; and the restrictions contained in the Convention may be applied only for the purposes for which they are prescribed.

Appendix 2
Law Reports and Journals (Some Useful References)

AC (formerly App Cas)	Appeal Cases (Law Reports)
Admin LR	Administrative Law Reports
All ER	All England Law Reports
All ER (EC)	All England Law Reports (European Cases)
Anglo-Am	Anglo-American Law Review
BLR	Building Law Reports
Bus LR	Business Law Reports
CJQ	Civil Justice Quarterly
CLY	Current Law Yearbook
CMLR	Common Market Law Reports
CMLRev.	Common Market Law Review
COD	Crown Office Digest
Ch (formerly ChD)	Chancery (Law Reports)
Co Law	Company Lawyer
Con LR	Construction Law Reports
Conv.(n.s.) (or Conv. or Conveyancer)	Conveyancer and Property Lawyer (New Series)
Cox CC	Cox's Criminal Cases
Cr App R (or CAR)	Criminal Appeal Reports
Cr App R (S) (or CAR(S))	Criminal Appeal Reports (Sentencing)
Crim LR	Criminal Law Review
DLR	Dominion Law Reports (a Canadian series)
EBLRev	European Business Law Review
ECR	European Court Reports
EG	Estates Gazette
EGLR	Estates Gazette Law Reports
EHRR	European Human Rights Reports
ELRev	European Law Review
ER	English Reports
FCR	Family Court Reporter
FLR	Family Law Reports

FSR	Fleet Street Reports
FTLR	Financial Times Law Reports
Fam	Family Division (Law Reports)
Fam Law	Family Law
Harv LR	Harvard Law Review
HLR	Housing Law Reports
ICLQ	International and Comparative Law Quarterly
ICR	Industrial Cases Reports
ILJ	Industrial Law Journal
Imm AR	Immigration Appeals Reports
IRLR	Industrial Relations Law Reports
ITR	Industrial Tribunal Reports
JBL	Journal of Business Law
JP	Justice of the Peace Reports
JPL	Journal of Planning and Environment Law (formerly Journal of Planning Law)
JPN	Justice of the Peace Journal (Abbreviating 'Journal' to 'N' may seem rather odd. The explanation is that this periodical was originally known as 'Justice of the Peace Newspaper', and the 'JPN' abbreviation has survived even though it is now commonly referred to as 'Justice of the Peace Journal' by way of contradistinction to 'Justice of the Peace Reports' – see 'JP')
JR	Juridical Review
JSPTL	Journal of the Society of Public Teachers of Law
JSWL	Journal of Social Welfare Law
KB	King's Bench (Law Reports)
KIR	Knight's Industrial Reports
LGR	Local Government Reports
LG Rev	Local Government Review (renamed as *Local Government Review Reports* in November 1993, and absorbed into the *Justice of the Peace* in 1996)
LJ	Law Journal
Ll L Rep	Lloyd's List Reports (1919-1950)
Lloyd's Rep	Lloyd's Reports (1951 onwards)
LQR	Law Quarterly Review
LS	Legal Studies
LS Gaz	Law Society's Gazette

LT	Law Times
MLR	Modern Law Review
Med LR	Medical Law Reports
NILQ	Northern Ireland Legal Quarterly
NZLR	New Zealand Law Reports
New LJ	New Law Journal
OJ	Official Journal of the European Communities
OJLS	Oxford Journal of Legal Studies
P (formerly PD)	Probate (Law Reports)
P & CR	Property and Compensation Reports (formerly Planning and Compensation Reports)
PL	Public Law QB (formerly QBD)
	Queen's Bench (Law Reports)
RPC	Reports of Patent, Design and Trade Mark Cases
RTR	Road Traffic Reports
SJ (sometimes given as Sol Jo)	Solicitors' Journal
SLT	Scots Law Times
STC	Simon's Tax Cases
Stat LR	Statute Law Review
TLR	Times Law Reports
US	United States Reports
WLR	Weekly Law Reports
Yale LJ	Yale Law Journal